Critical Race Feminism

Critical America

General Editors: RICHARD DELGADO and JEAN STEFANCIC

White by Law:
The Legal Construction of Race
Ian Haney López

Cultivating Intelligence:
Power, Law, and the Politics of Teaching
Louise Harmon and Deborah W. Post

Privilege Revealed:
How Invisible Preference Undermines America
Stephanie M. Wildman
with Margalynne Armstrong, Adrienne D. Davis, and Trina Grillo

Does the Law Morally Bind the Poor?
or What Good's the Constitution When You Can't Afford a Loaf of Bread?
R. George Wright

Hybrid:
Bisexuals, Multiracials, and Other Misfits under American Law
Ruth Colker

Critical Race Feminism:
A Reader
Edited by Adrien Katherine Wing

Immigrants Out!
The New Nativism and the Anti-Immigrant Impulse
in the United States
Edited by Juan F. Perea

CRITICAL RACE FEMINISM

A Reader

**Edited
by
Adrien
Katherine
Wing**

**Foreword
by
Derrick
Bell**

NEW YORK UNIVERSITY PRESS

New York and London

NEW YORK UNIVERSITY PRESS
New York and London

Copyright © 1997 by New York University

Library of Congress Cataloging-in-Publication Data
Critical race feminism : a reader / edited by Adrien Katherine Wing.
p. cm.—(Critical America)
Includes bibliographical references (p.   ) and index.
ISBN 0-8147-9293-6 (cloth: acid-free paper).—ISBN
0-8147-9309-6 (pbk. : acid-free paper)
1. Minority women—Social conditions. 2. Minority women—United
States—Social conditions. 3. Sex discrimination against women.
4. Sex discrimination against women—United States. 5. Race
discrimination. 6. Race discrimination—United States.
7. Feminism. 8. Feminist theory. I. Wing, Adrien Katherine.
II. Series.
HQ1154.C75 1996
305.8'0082—dc20   96-35675
                            CIP

New York University Press books are printed on acid-free paper,
and their binding materials are chosen for strength and durability.

Manufactured in the United States of America
10 9 8 7 6 5 4 3 2 1

Contents

	Acknowledgments	xi
	Foreword by Derrick Bell	xiii
	Introduction	1
PART 1	Essentialism and Anti-Essentialism: Ain't I a Woman?	7
1	Race and Essentialism in Feminist Legal Theory *Angela P. Harris*	11
2	Ain't I a Feminist? *Celina Romany*	19
3	Brief Reflections toward a Multiplicative Theory and Praxis of Being *Adrien Katherine Wing*	27
4	Racism, Civil Rights, and Feminism *Kathleen Neal Cleaver*	35
5	Obscuring the Importance of Race: The Implication of Making Comparisons between Racism and Sexism (or Other Isms) *Trina Grillo and Stephanie M. Wildman*	44
6	It Is Better to Speak *Angela D. Gilmore*	51

7 Máscaras, Trenzas, y Greñas: Un/masking the Self While Un/braiding Latina Stories and Legal Discourse
Margaret E. Montoya 57

Questions and Suggested Readings 65

PART 2 Outsiders in the Academy 69

8 Of Gentlemen and Role Models
Lani Guinier 73

9 On Being a Role Model
Anita L. Allen 81

10 Tokens, Role Models, and Pedagogical Politics: Lamentations of an African American Female Law Professor
Linda S. Greene 88

11 Two Life Stories: Reflections of One Black Woman Law Professor
Taunya Lovell Banks 96

12 Law Professors of Color and the Academy: Of Poets and Kings
Cheryl I. Harris 101

13 Meditations on Being Good
Margalynne J. Armstrong 107

14 On Being a Gorilla in Your Midst, or The Life of One Blackwoman in the Legal Academy
Jennifer M. Russell 110

15 Full Circle
Rachel F. Moran 113

16 A Tribute to Thurgood Marshall: A Man Who Broke with Tradition on Issues of Race and Gender
Anita F. Hill 118

Questions and Suggested Readings 123

PART 3   On Mothering or Not   125

17   Punishing Drug Addicts Who Have Babies: Women of
         Color, Equality, and the Right of Privacy
         Dorothy E. Roberts   127

18   Furthering the Inquiry: Race, Class, and Culture in the
         Forced Medical Treatment of Pregnant Women
         Lisa C. Ikemoto   136

19   Learnfare and Black Motherhood: The Social
         Construction of Deviance
         Nathalie A. Augustin   144

20   Spare Parts, Family Values, Old Children, Cheap
         Patricia J. Williams   151

21   A Story from Home: On Being a Black Lesbian Mother
         Isabelle R. Gunning   159

         Questions and Suggested Readings   163

PART 4   Sexual Harassment: After Anita   165

22   Race, Gender, and Social Class in the Thomas Sexual
         Harassment Hearings: The Hidden Fault Lines in
         Political Discourse
         Emma Coleman Jordan   169

23   The Legacy of Doubt: Treatment of Sex and Race in the
         Hill-Thomas Hearings
         Adrienne D. Davis and Stephanie M. Wildman   175

24   Invisible Woman: Reflections on the Clarence Thomas
         Confirmation Hearings
         Kim A. Taylor   183

25   Three Perspectives on Workplace Harassment of
         Women of Color
         Maria L. Ontiveros   188

26   The Harm That Has No Name: Street Harassment,
         Embodiment, and African American Women
         Deirdre E. Davis   192

27 Converging Stereotypes in Racialized Sexual
Harassment: Where the Model Minority
Meets Suzie Wong
Sumi K. Cho   203

Questions and Suggested Readings   221

PART 5 Criminality and Law Breaking   223

A. General Principles

28 Spirit-Murdering the Messenger: The Discourse of
Fingerpointing as the Law's Response to Racism
Patricia J. Williams   229

29 Black Women, Sisterhood, and the
Difference/Deviance Divide
Regina Austin   237

30 Sisters in the Hood: Beyond Bloods and Crips
Adrien Katherine Wing and Christine A. Willis   243

31 Scarlett's Code, Susan's Actions
Sherri L. Burr   255

32 Domestic Violence against Latinas by Latino Males:
An Analysis of Race, National Origin,
and Gender Differentials
Jenny Rivera   259

B. Variations on the Theme: The O. J. Simpson Case

33 Rosa Lopez, Christopher Darden, and Me: Issues of
Gender, Ethnicity, and Class in Evaluating
Witness Credibility
Maria L. Ontiveros   269

34 Orenthal James Simpson and Gender, Class, and Race:
In That Order
Crystal H. Weston   278

Questions and Suggested Readings   285

PART 6   On Working   287

35   Sapphire Bound!
         Regina Austin   289

36   A Hair Piece: Perspectives on the Intersection of Race
         and Gender
         Paulette M. Caldwell   297

37   Black Women and the Constitution: Finding Our Place,
         Asserting Our Rights
         Judy Scales-Trent   306

38   The Value of Black Mothers' Work
         Dorothy E. Roberts   312

39   Structures of Subordination: Women of Color at the
         Intersection of Title VII and the NLRA. Not!
         Elizabeth M. Iglesias   317

         Questions and Suggested Readings   333

PART 7   Beyond Our Borders: Global Issues   335

40   Motherhood and Work in Cultural Context:
         One Woman's Patriarchal Bargain
         Devon W. Carbado   339

41   Arrogant Perception, World Traveling, and Multicultural
         Feminism: The Case of Female Genital Surgeries
         Isabelle R. Gunning   352

42   Between *Irua* and "Female Genital Mutilation":
         Feminist Human Rights Discourse and the
         Cultural Divide
         Hope Lewis   361

43   Female Infanticide in China: The Human Rights Specter
         and Thoughts toward (An)other Vision
         Sharon K. Hom   372

44   Spouse-Based Immigration Laws:
         The Legacy of Coverture
         Janet M. Calvo   380

45 Black South African Women: Toward Equal Rights
Adrien Katherine Wing and Eunice P. de Carvalho 387

Questions and Suggested Readings 396

Bibliography 399
Contributors 411
Permissions 419
Index 425

Acknowledgments

I would first like to thank all the wonderful contributors for generously permitting me to gather their legal scholarship and share it with a wider audience. I deeply regret that one of the contributors, Tina Grillo, died before the publication of this volume. I am glad her voice will live on in these pages. I am grateful for the assistance of the coeditors of the Critical America series, Professor Richard Delgado and Jean Stefancic, of the University of Colorado Law School, who encouraged me and led me to New York University Press. The volume would not exist without the professional guidance, accessibility, and humble, down-to-earth inspiration I have received over many years from Professor Derrick Bell of New York University Law School and Professor Patricia Williams of Columbia Law School. I am deeply honored that Professor Bell made the time, despite his own busy schedule, to write the foreword to this volume. I would like to give a special thanks to my new colleague Devon Carbado, who went beyond the call of duty in assisting me with this project. I would also like to acknowledge the efforts of University of Iowa research assistants Christine Willis, Tina Bagby, Sonya Braunschweig, Jonathan Cardi, Daryl Davidson, Tashawn Eans, Lisa Frankel, Philip Harms, Fauzia Malik, Mark McPherson, Kevin Popp, Stuart Reid and Karen Tolbert, as well as my very able secretary, Bev Heitt. I am also very grateful for the unconditional support of Jim Brown, whose patience and strength has enhanced my ability to soar. Special thanks to my mother, Katherine Pruitt Wing, who gave me a love of learning that led me to join the family profession of teaching. Finally, I must acknowledge the joyous role that my very talented and patient sons Nolan, Ché, and Brooks play in enabling their mother to flourish wearing her multiple hats.

Foreword

Derrick Bell

When I accepted my good friend Adrien Wing's invitation to write the foreword for this anthology, I thought of the Benjamin E. Mays lecture I presented in the spring of 1995 at Morehouse College in Atlanta. My title, *Black Women: Secret Salvation of the Race,* reflects the essence of my talk to the impressive assembly of young black men. In order to point out the close connection between success and a strong relationship, I recalled that at a recent awards ceremony held at the college, each of the recipients took pains to say how valuable his wife had been to his career and his life. I did not claim that it is impossible for a man to succeed in life without marriage—or a successful marriage—noting simply that in the overwhelming majority of cases, male success and supportive relationships go together.

It is, I think, significant that the need or value of a strong relationship is not quite the sine qua non of success for women. Had Morehouse honored a half-dozen of our successful women, in all likelihood, many of them would have done what they accomplished on their own. It is true that the paucity of eligible men rather than lack of interest in marriage may have necessitated their solo accomplishments. But that is precisely my point. Women, no less than men, benefit from involvement in a strong and supportive relationship, but there is ample evidence all around us that many women seem able to move on to outstanding achievement without men and, I suspect, with that quality of prophetic insight alive and functioning—often on behalf of others.

Here, I suggested, may be the source of the dynamic energy black women have contributed to our history, going all the way back to slavery—usually behind the scenes. It causes one to wonder. Is there something more there than we (men or women) have been willing to acknowledge? Are we so committed to traditional gender roles and expectations that we are missing a potential resource for our race during a time when we are bearing the brunt of a conservative, retrograde tide that is eroding our hard-earned progress and threatening our expectations for the future as well as our children's survival? I would hope not, for we are already well into a dangerous period when we will need all our resources to survive a storm of economics-related racial hostility.

America is undergoing cataclysmic changes in our economy that are causing massive job losses and increasing disparities in wealth and opportunities. The hard reality that economists and politicians are reluctant to acknowledge is that manufacturing and much of the service sector are undergoing a transformation as profound as the one experienced by the agricultural sector at the beginning of the century, when machines boosted production, displacing millions of farmers. We are in the early stages of a long-term shift from "mass labor" to highly skilled "elite labor," accompanied by increasing automation in the production of goods and the delivery of services. Workerless factories and virtual companies loom on the horizon. Indeed, for steadily increasing numbers, this is becoming a third world country.

Government—influenced by monied interests—finds it easier to ignore the crisis, move to the political right, and take a self-righteous hard line against those who are the victims and not the cause of our economic convulsions. In such times, there is an automatic antipathy toward this society's traditional scapegoats: blacks and other people of color. In a "let's blame the minorities" climate, it is unlikely that our elected leaders will even try to address effectively the root causes of poverty, family disorganization, crime, homelessness, and substandard housing, the deplorable state of much public education, the inadequacy of health care, or the steady deterioration of the environment.

While people of color will feel a disproportional share of the loss in the economic turmoil, they are not alone. All Americans are at risk, but all too many are too easily convinced that the minorities are the source of their anxiety, the reason their futures are so uncertain. Rather than demand that leadership address unemployment levels, the gap in incomes and wealth, and the increasing power and influence of major corporations over every aspect of our lives, there is a fixation on crime, the death penalty, welfare, affirmative action, and immigration. Conservative politicians skillfully turn these serious problems into code words for racism.

Reviewing these dangers, I contend that black people must come to realize that our greatest strength, our salvation secret, if you will, is black women. At one level, we all acknowledge the characteristics that have kept our people alive, but out of an innate and—I fear—misplaced humility and the desire not to further burden our already heavily burdened men, our women have functioned without seeking the limelight or the leadership roles that, so often, they perform from self-imposed subordinate positions.

For our part, black men must surrender all misogynous practices, sexist assumptions, and patriarchal notions. Freed of beliefs and behaviors quite foreign to our African ancestors, whose societies functioned in what we would call a matriarchal model, black people would gain enormous strength and free energies and resources now consumed in bitter enmity and recriminations.

Black men must understand that black women know both what should be done and how best to do it in every aspect of our lives: business, educational, political, religious, economic, social, and personal. Just as we acknowledge women's power to give life, we must come to recognize their power to sustain us in life during the critical times to come. Black women have always been the salvation secret of our people. It is time for them to assume formally the positions they have always held—in fact.

A great many black men are definable by their absence or disruptive presence, particularly in lower economic classes. Even those who are skilled or educated are often dysfunctional when it comes to the commitments and sacrifices needed to save black people. This is not to deny the multitudes of black men who have and who are functioning to make a place for their families and to take on positions of importance in the world. But it is also true that for a generation now, a host of writers—many of them black women—have been telling the world about the inadequacy of black men. This often emotional testimony ranges from mournful frustration to flat-out rage. The revelations contain both deeply felt disappointment about what often is, as well as yearning hope about what might be. Again, while there are many, many black males who do not fit the woeful patterns, we know from statistics and personal experiences that the criticisms are far more real than mythical.

It is certainly true that many black women have been painfully scarred by racist oppression. And some, thwarted by the society, vent their frustrations and rage on their men. But rather than exhaust ourselves with recrimination, we need simply acknowledge the fact that this society has not much loved either black men or black women. Debate as to whether society's hostility or black male rage directed back on itself has done the most harm does not move us much toward the relief we both need. And much of that relief must come through building strength within ourselves and our communities.

In addition to rejecting the traditional, patriarchal notion that women must be protected and provided for by men, black men must stop trying to emulate the macho sexism of their white counterparts and work with women toward a more natural and healthy equality between the sexes. Indeed, false images of malehood may explain why struggle and racial adversity create strong black women and "weak and disempowered" black men. The African American female has fewer job opportunities and just as many stereotypes heaped on her as does the African American male. And yet, in a puzzling contradiction, many women of color derive strength from oppression, whereas many minority men use their oppression to justify unjustifiable behavior—often against women of color.

Contradictions abound. I write this in the wake of the Million Man March called by Nation of Islam minister Louis Farrakhan. In its concept, it appeared that a gathering that excluded women would serve all the sexist and patriarchal notions decried here and by many of the contributors to this book. Indeed, many of them opposed the march. In actuality, however, the largest gathering of black males in the nation's history served to advance the goal of black male responsibility, dignity, and gender equality. Because the racism and sexism that divide us are neither linear, nor logical, it may be that those actions that close divisions and strengthen allegiances may be better experienced than understood.

That is surely true of this compilation, written predominantly by women of color. These essays would not be less valid if they were interspersed with writings by men. But there is a focus, an emphasis, and a unique power in the present format that more than provides justification for this volume. Thus, I can recommend *Critical Race Feminism* to the students at Morehouse, to women and men of color everywhere, and to the rest of the American public.

Introduction

The idea for this project first germinated back in 1991, when the *Berkeley Women's Law Journal* devoted an entire issue to the views of black female law professors, the first time such words had been gathered together in a single place. The publication of the issue was especially timely since it coincided with the Clarence Thomas-Anita Hill hearings. Neither mammy, welfare queen, tragic mulatto, sex siren, athlete, or any other stereotype of a black woman, Anita Hill was the first black female law professor ever thrust into the national spotlight, and the American public, white and black, did not know what to make of her. There was no national precedent for dealing with or understanding the worldview of a black female law scholar and teacher. The intense denigration and vilification of her character wounded many of us deeply. We saw ourselves in her place, regarded as inherently unbelievable and untrustworthy despite years of hard-won educational and professional accomplishments. Lani Guinier suffered a similar fate a few years later, transmogrified by talking heads and spin doctors into a quota queen, her legal theories twisted beyond recognition.

These two events have resulted in the book you now hold in your hands, an attempt to bring together the legal writings of women of color so that they could speak for themselves. The views of these women are generally unknown to the American reading public since most of their work appears only in law journals not readily accessible to the nonlawyer. Ranging from the nationally known Anita Hill and Lani Guinier to women well known within legal academia, such as Anita L. Allen, Regina Austin, Linda S. Greene, Angela P. Harris, Emma Coleman Jordan, Dorothy E. Roberts, and Patricia J. Williams, *Critical Race Feminism* extends beyond the existing anthologies on race and gender, which have tended to feature a very small group of well-known women. In this book, you will also find the voices of lesser-known young stars, and thus a more complete account of the breadth and depth of our perspectives.

Nearly three hundred women of color teach in legal academia. In the last decade they have produced a substantial body of scholarship. A growing part of their work and that of others examines the intersection of race, gender, and sometimes class within a legal or multidisciplinary context. This volume makes available selected portions of this new legal genre—Critical Race Feminism—not only for the legal academy, but for the reading public at large.

Critical Race Feminism is not yet an organized or distinct movement, but part of an evolving tradition that originated with Critical Legal Studies (CLS), a radical movement of predominantly white male legal academics that sprang up in the 1970s. The premises embraced by CLS include postmodern critiques of individualism and hierarchy in modern Western society. A primary method of analysis for critical scholars is deconstruction, which entails analyzing supposedly neutral concepts to show the true nature of the contingent power relationships they mask and conceal.

People of color, white women, and others were attracted by CLS because it challenged orthodox ideas about the inviolability and objectivity of laws that oppressed minorities and white women for centuries. But some of these thinkers also felt that some of the CLS adherents, though well-meaning, often excluded the perspectives of people of color and white women and were not able to expand their analyses beyond the worldview of progressive white male elites.

These thinkers started the Critical Race Theory (CRT) genre. Although the intellectual underpinnings of the movement can be found in the work of Derrick Bell and others from the mid-1970s, CRT emerged as a self-conscious entity in 1989 and organized its first working session shortly thereafter. The genre developed because its scholars believed that the civil rights movement had stalled and the old approaches of amicus briefs, marches, and litigation were yielding smaller returns when confronting subtler manifestations of de facto discrimination. Additionally, while some CLS adherents seemed ready to disregard or deconstruct individual rights-based notions, some CRT followers called for an expansion of rights discourse to transcend its current limitations.

Today the relatively young CRT movement, of which Critical Race Feminism is also a part, has produced over three hundred articles and numerous books. Dynamic, eclectic, and growing, this group continues to challenge racial orthodoxy and shake up the legal academy. It challenges the ability of conventional legal strategies to deliver social and economic justice; it casts its net widely, covering a broad array of topics that include federal Indian law, hate speech, and affirmative action. A recent offshoot has, for instance, focused on whiteness (critical white studies), examining how whiteness functions as a social organizing principle.

One of the several organizing principles of CRT is that racism is an ordinary and fundamental part of American society, not an aberration that can be readily remedied by law. While some CRT theorists believe that racism's worst effects can be eliminated or substantially alleviated over time, others believe in the permanence of racism. Thus, formal equal opportunity laws may be able only to remedy the most egregious sorts of injustice, those that stand out from the ordinary racism that permeates society.

A second cornerstone is the belief that a culture constructs its own social reality in its own self-interest. CRT's critique of society thus often takes the form of storytelling and narrative analysis—to construct alternative social realities and protest against acquiescence to unfair arrangements designed for the benefits of others. These stories help expose the ordinariness of racism and validate that the experiences of people of color are important and critical bases for understanding an American legality that perpetuates their disenfranchisement.

Additionally, CRT holds that white elites will tolerate or encourage racial progress for minorities only if doing so also promotes white self-interest. Thus civil rights laws are a mechanism to permit racial progress *at a pace acceptable to broader society.*

Finally, CRT, skeptical of dominant legal theories supporting hierarchy, neutrality, objectivity, color blindness, meritocracy, ahistoricism, and single axis analyses, draws more from such intellectual traditions as liberalism, feminism, law and society, Marxism, postmodernism, pragmatism, and cultural nationalism.

Just as scholars of color felt excluded by well-meaning CLS adherents, women of color have at times felt somewhat excluded by well-meaning male CRT peers. Too often the perspectives presented assumed that women of color's experiences were the same as that of men. Additionally, these women observed that the various strands of traditional feminist jurisprudence, which had evolved during the same time period as CLS, were based almost entirely on the experiences of white middle- and upper-class women. If mentioned at all, the differing experiences of women of color were often relegated to footnotes. While mainstream feminism asserts that society is patriarchal, it does not "race" patriarchy; it overlooks the fact that this domination affects women and men of color differently than white women. Fundamental to Critical Race Feminism is the idea that women of color are not simply white women plus some ineffable and secondary characteristic, such as skin tone, added on. This anthology thus focuses on the lives of those who face multiple discrimination on the basis of race, gender and class, revealing how all these factors interact within a system of white male patriarchy and racist oppression.

Columbia law professor Kimberlé Crenshaw's *Demarginalizing the Intersection of Race and Sex: A Black Feminist Critique of Antidiscrimination Doctrine, Feminist Theory and Antiracist Politics,* U. Chicago Legal Forum 139 (1989) is an early critique of essentialism, which calls for embracing those individuals—women of color—who are currently marginalized by traditional legal, antiracist, and feminist analyses. Crenshaw argues that coupling theory with strategies to include the multiply discriminated against will ultimately benefit and transform the entire society. Georgetown law professor Mari Matsuda's *When the First Quail Calls: Multiple Consciousness as Jurisprudential Method,* 11 Women's Rts. L. Rptr. 7 (1989) is an equally compelling call for identifying the multileveled identities and multiple consciousness of women of color. Although these articles were not available, they are discussed by some of the authors featured in this and other units.

While full summaries can be found at the beginning of each part, a brief preview of each part, highlighting only a few of the articles, seems in order. The first part introduces the concept of essentialism, the idea that there is one authentic female or minority "voice." Much of feminist theory has presumed that white middle-class women's experiences can speak for all women. By the same token, much of the jurisprudence on race has unconsciously presumed that black males' experiences hold true for black women and all minorities. Critical race feminists are anti-essentialists who call for a deeper understanding of the lives of women of color based on the multiple nature of their identities. They emphasize conscious considerations of the intersection of race, class, and gender by placing them at the center of analysis.

Angela P. Harris's pathbreaking piece on race and essentialism in feminist legal theory begins part 1. Kathleen Neal Cleaver, a former Black Panther and the ex-wife of Panther leader Eldridge Cleaver, provides an original essay on the central roles of black women in the civil rights movement and the failure of white feminism to deal adequately with racism as it affects black women.

Part 2 explores the lives of the women of color who struggle and survive in a major social institution, higher education. Using the narrative technique of the CRT movement, the women discuss how they are viewed as outsiders, often sought out only for their potential as role models. Although they have achieved the rarified heights of the professorate, they are still viewed as undeserving and inferior by some colleagues and students.

Part 3 examines the interplay of race, class, and gender in the areas of pregnancy and motherhood. Dorothy E. Roberts, the foremost scholar in this area, reveals how black women are more aggressively prosecuted for using drugs while pregnant. Patricia J. Williams discusses the devaluation of black children in her critique of law and economics theorist Richard Posner. Isabelle R. Gunning adds sexual orientation to our understanding of multiple consciousness by analyzing her experiences as a black lesbian mother. To address the ongoing welfare debate, young lawyer Nathalie A. Augustin analyzes the concept of Learnfare and the awarding of welfare to black mothers.

Part 4 highlights sexual harassment, a legal and social phenomenon synonymous with the name of a black female legal academic, Anita Hill, and the man who harassed her, Supreme Court justice Clarence Thomas. Emma Coleman Jordan, Anita Hill's pro bono counsel during the confirmation hearings, addresses the race and gender issues that led to Hill's mistreatment in the Senate. Sumi K. Cho enriches our understanding of the sexual harassment of Asian women by focusing on the lawsuit brought by Dr. Jean Jew against the University of Iowa, in which a tenured Chinese American medical professor won a legal victory against both her employer and a colleague, after suffering more than a decade of harassing conduct.

Part 5 provides perspectives on criminality and law breaking. Patricia Williams contributes her foundational essay on the concept of spirit-murder, the psychological impact of racism and sexism. Sherri L. Burr's essay on the Susan Smith case explores Smith's role as a Southern belle, a modern-day Scarlett O'Hara, who thought she could get away with murder by accusing a black man of stealing her children. The part closes with two essays exploring the race, class, and gender aspects of the trial of the century, the O. J. Simpson case. Maria L. Ontiveros enhances our understanding of the testimony of Latina maid Rosa Lopez, and what role her ethnicity, class, and gender played in her testimony and representation by the media.

Part 6 discusses employment and discrimination, focusing on the failures of employment law to address the plight of women of color. Regina Austin's provocative article *Sapphire Bound,* unveils a black unwed mother's termination from a "role model" counselor position at a girls' club in Omaha. Dorothy Roberts' seminal piece concerning the value of black mothers' work returns to the welfare debate.

Finally, Part 7 presents Critical Race Feminism in a global context. Just as most collections on race or gender issues focus on the United States to the exclusion of the majority of the world's people of color, most volumes on international themes omit the concerns of women of color. The few international readers dealing with women's issues often omit legal perspectives. Part 7 fills this gap, exploring issues of international and comparative law affecting women of color. These articles address female genital mutilation in Africa, Chinese female infanticide, U. S. immigration law, and the status of black women in the new South Africa. Additionally, Devon Carbado of the University of Iowa uses the narrative technique of Critical Race Theory to augment our understanding of motherhood by drawing on what he refers to as unconscious patriarchy. He examines the sacrifices his Jamaican mother made raising nine children in Great Britain.

A variety of general questions are raised by the volume as a whole. I pose a few of them here.

First, critical race feminists are multidisciplinary in that they draw on the writings of women and men who are not legal scholars. What historical arguments are made to bolster the various authors' claims? What are the economic arguments? How often do nonlegal authors cite legal scholarship? What are the implications for scholarship generally if there is little cross-fertilization between legal and nonlegal disciplines?

Second, critical race feminists are concerned with both theory and practice, placing a heavy emphasis on the latter. As representatives of groups oppressed on the basis of both race and gender, they cannot afford to adopt the classic white male ivory tower approach of abstract theorizing, removed from the actual needs of their communities. Traditional scholarship has criticized feminist scholarship as insufficiently theoretical, with the implication that it is inferior. What then *are* the theoretical contributions of these authors? What are the practical aspects? What are the descriptive, analytical, and reformative notions? What are the interrelationships between all the concepts?

In part 2, Cheryl I. Harris discusses the need to construct a jurisprudence of *resistance.* What would be the theoretical components of a critical race feminist jurisprudence of resistance? What would be the practical applications? What kind of backlashes do women of color face from whites and men of color if and when the jurisprudence of resistance leads to legal or social advancement? How can women of color overcome the double bind they have historically faced as the needs of the entire ethnic group have taken precedence over female concerns?

Fourth, what role does the narrative or storytelling technique—an essential part of Critical Race Theory—play as method for critical race feminists? How would this notion be similar and different from feminist consciousness raising as method?

Most critical race theorists are not doctrinaire Marxists or socialists, but are concerned with the poor and oppressed. Do the authors sufficiently take into account class differences in their analyses? Are they guilty of essentializing the experiences of women of color and assuming that all the women are poor? Do they assume they are referring to all women of color when they may be only talking about elite women?

Randall Kennedy has raised the question of whether Critical Race Theory is distinctive or truly different from traditional legal scholarship. Is Critical Race Feminism truly distinctive? If so, in what ways? If not, why not? Does it differ from natural law, legal positivism, legal realism, postmodernism? How does it differ from Critical Legal Studies and even Critical Race Theory? How does it differ from the various strands of feminism: liberal, cultural, radical, postmodern? For instance, how does Critical Race Feminism view the notion of rights and how does it differ from all the other types of jurisprudence? Can men write critical race feminist scholarship? Can whites?

The bibliography includes many more entries with their full citations. Additionally, each part concludes with a number of suggested readings. The works included in the anthology have been edited for consistency and brevity: because of space limitations I have had to delete some passages and condense others. Many of the extensive footnotes that characterize law review articles have been omitted. Those readers whose appetites have been whetted by the morsels contained herein may consult the bibliography for the full citations of the previously published works.

Since the previously published readings come from a variety of sources with various citation styles, I have decided to standardize the citations to conform to *The Bluebook: A Uniform System of Citation* (15th ed. 1991). The *Bluebook* font styles are not followed.

It is my hope that this anthology will be the first of many volumes highlighting the evolving themes and contributions—past, present, and future—of Critical Race Feminism.

1

Essentialism and Anti-Essentialism: Ain't I a Woman?

Part 1 introduces the concept of essentialism, the idea that one authentic female or minority "voice" exists. Much of feminist legal theory presumes that white middle-class women's experiences can speak for all women. The subtitle of the unit, "Ain't I a Woman?" comes from the former slave, abolitionist, and feminist Sojourner Truth's mythical remarks to a women's rights convention in Akron, Ohio, in 1851. Legend has long held that Sojourner bared her sinewy arm and asked the question to highlight the fact that black women were women too, even though their concerns were not incorporated into the discussions of feminists or abolitionists. Modern-day women of color raise the same pertinent question, "aren't we women too?"

By the same token, much of the jurisprudence on race has unconsciously presumed that black males' experience holds true for black women and all minorities. Critical race feminists are anti-essentialists; they call for a deeper understanding of the lives of women of color based on the multiple nature of their identities. Using Critical Race Theory's storytelling method, these scholars emphasize theoretical and practical considerations of the intersection of race, class, and gender by placing these factors at the center of analysis.

Angela P. Harris's pathbreaking piece, *Race and Essentialism in Feminist Legal Theory,* criticizes prominent white feminist Catharine MacKinnon and other theorists for using white women as the epitome of all women. This process fragments black women's selves beyond recognition, often relegating them to footnotes if they are mentioned at all. Focusing on MacKinnon's color-blind analysis of rape, Harris illustrates the theory's failure as applied to the experiences of black women. For white women, rape may represent the subordination of all women to men. Black women are put in the ambivalent situation of balancing their victimization at the hands of black and white men against the acknowledgment of how the legal system

7

has historically been invoked discriminatorily against black men for the alleged rape of white women.

In *Ain't I a Feminist?* Celina Romany plays on Sojourner Truth's words in her title. She critiques feminist legal theory, legal liberalism, and postmodernist theory for their essentialist failure to take into account the experiences of women of color. She wants to be associated with a feminism with a capital *F* that aims at eradicating the various forms of oppressions that affect all women.

In *Brief Reflections Toward a Multiplicative Theory and Praxis of Being,* Adrien Katherine Wing interweaves poetry, narrative, theory, and praxis. She discusses how the many identities and discriminations that face women of color should be theoretically analyzed in terms of their multiplicative rather than additive nature. She is black x woman x mother x law professor, a holistic one person, and not black + female as characterized by white feminist theorists. Wing is not content to merely theorize, as more traditional scholarship, including some feminist theory, does. She also focuses on how the law can create multiplicative legal praxis to assist women of color in improving their lives.

In an original essay entitled *Racism, Civil Rights, and Feminism,* Kathleen Neal Cleaver's narrative highlights her own involvement in the 1960s Student Nonviolent Coordinating Committee (SNCC) and the Black Panther Party. She talks about the central role that black women played in the civil rights movement, and how they did not see the developing white feminist movement as relevant. Black women had to fight for liberation side by side with black men against the power of the state. Cleaver observes that while the courage of black people fighting against racism inspired white women to fight against sexism, white feminists have failed to deal adequately with racism. A feminism appropriate for black women would require a recognition of the racial dimension of gender subordination. Significantly, Cleaver also comments on the sexism in the black community, which, she maintains, is rarely condemned as strongly as it should be. Cleaver calls for black groups to take stronger antisexist positions and for an emphasis on the problems of black women, especially those women dealing with poverty, motherhood, domestic violence, and crime.

Trina Grillo and Stephanie M. Wildman focus on the dangers of analogizing sexism to racism in *Obscuring the Importance of Race: The Implication of Making Comparisons between Racism and Sexism (or Other Isms).* People who analogize sexism or other isms to racism essentialize and marginalize the experiences of people of color. The essay opens with the powerful story of Grillo's experience as a cancer patient, and how cancer became the filter through which she looked at the world. Wildman sympathized with Grillo's condition and thought she could understand how Grillo felt, since she also worried about getting cancer. Yet analogizers have the privilege of forgetting about the problem they do not experience, and Wildman's worry was not the same as Grillo's reality. Like cancer, racism/white supremacy is an illness; it is the filter through which its victims see the world. Whites can use analogies to give them greater comprehension about the illness of racism, but such analogies can create the danger of false understanding.

Angela D. Gilmore deepens our understanding of race, class, and gender by focusing on sexual orientation, a subject relatively ignored even within Critical Race Theory. Her essay, entitled *It Is Better to Speak,* is based on a poem written by the late black lesbian feminist Audre Lorde. Gilmore illustrates why it is important that she as a working-class, black, female, lesbian law professor be willing to speak out about her multiple identities. We cannot essentialize all women, all blacks, all black women as heterosexual, or we risk silencing gays and lesbians, even within communities of color.

Máscaras, Trenzas, y Greñas: Un/masking the Self While Un/braiding Latina Stories and Legal Discourse does a masterful job of braiding Spanish into English narratives in the life of Margaret E. Montoya. Masks or *máscaras* enable her to hide from or reveal herself to the gaze of the dominant culture, so as not to appear messy and uncombed—*greñuda.* The conceptual *trenzas,* or rebraided ideas of her multicultural life help validate interpretations of the *máscaras* she chooses to wear. Such masks can help women of color present themselves to a world that essentializes them as messy, dirty, uncombed "foreigners."

1 | Race and Essentialism in Feminist Legal Theory

Angela P. Harris

In feminist legal theory, the move away from univocal toward multivocal theories of women's experience and feminism has been slower than in other areas. In feminist legal theory, the pull of the second voice, the voice of abstract categorization, is still powerfully strong: "We the People" seems in danger of being replaced by "We the Women." And in feminist legal theory, as in the dominant culture, it is mostly white, straight, and socioeconomically privileged people who claim to speak for all of us.[1] Not surprisingly, the story they tell about "women," despite its claim to universality, seems to black women to be peculiar to women who are white, straight, and socioeconomically privileged—a phenomenon Adrienne Rich terms "white solipsism."[2]

In this essay I use the term "gender essentialism" to describe the notion that there is a monolithic "women's experience" that can be described independently of other facets of experience like race, class, and sexual orientation. A corollary to gender essentialism is "racial essentialism"—the belief that there is a monolithic "black experience" or "Chicano experience." The effect of gender and racial essentialism (and all other essentialisms, for the list of categories could be infinite) is to reduce the lives of people who experience multiple forms of oppression to addition problems: "racism + sexism = straight black women's experience," or "racism + sexism + homophobia = black lesbian experience." Thus, in an essentialist world, black women's experience will always be forcibly fragmented before being subjected to analysis, as those who are "only interested in race" and those who are "only interested in gender" take their separate slices of our lives.

Why, in the face of challenges from "different" women and from feminist method itself, is feminist essentialism so persistent and pervasive? I think the reasons are several. Essentialism is intellectually convenient, and to a certain extent cognitively ingrained. Essentialism also carries with it important emotional and political payoffs.

Finally, essentialism often appears (especially to white women) as the only alternative to chaos, mindless pluralism, and the end of the feminist movement. In my view, however, as long as feminists, like theorists in the dominant culture, continue to search for gender and racial essences, black women will never be anything more than a crossroads between two kinds of domination, or at the bottom of a hierarchy of oppression; we will always be required to choose pieces of ourselves to present as wholeness.

MODIFIED WOMEN AND UNMODIFIED FEMINISM: BLACK WOMEN IN DOMINANCE THEORY

Catharine MacKinnon[3] describes her "dominance theory," like the Marxism with which she likes to compare it, as "total": "[T]hey are both theories of the totality, of the whole thing, theories of a fundamental and critical underpinning of the whole they envision."[4] Both her dominance theory (which she identifies as simply "feminism") and Marxism "focus on that which is most one's own, that which most makes one the being the theory addresses, as that which is most taken away by what the theory criticizes. In each theory you are made who you are by that which is taken away from you by the social relations the theory criticizes."[5] In Marxism, the "that" is work, in feminism, it is sexuality.

MacKinnon defines sexuality as "that social process which creates, organizes, expresses, and directs desire, creating the social beings we know as women and men, as their relations create society."[6] Moreover, "the organized expropriation of the sexuality of some for the use of others defines the sex, woman. Heterosexuality is its structure, gender and family its congealed forms, sex roles its qualities generalized to social persona, reproduction a consequence, and control its issue."[7] Dominance theory, the analysis of this organized expropriation, is a theory of power and its unequal distribution.

In MacKinnon's view, "[t]he idea of gender difference helps keep the reality of male dominance in place."[8] That is, the concept of gender difference is an ideology that masks the fact that genders are socially constructed, not natural, and coercively enforced, not freely consented to. Moreover, "the social relation between the sexes is organized so that men may dominate and women must submit and this relation is sexual—in fact, is sex."[9]

For MacKinnon, male dominance is not only "perhaps the most pervasive and tenacious system of power in history, but . . . it is metaphysically nearly perfect."[10] The masculine point of view is point-of-viewlessness; the force of male dominance "is exercised as consent, its authority as participation, its supremacy as the paradigm of order, its control as the definition of legitimacy."[11] In such a world, the very existence of feminism is something of a paradox. "Feminism claims the voice of women's silence, the sexuality of our eroticized desexualization, the fullness of 'lack,' the centrality of our marginality and exclusion, the public nature of privacy, the presence of our absence."[12]

In MacKinnon's view, men have their foot on women's necks, regardless of race or class, or of mode of production: "Feminists do not argue that it means the same to women to be on the bottom in a feudal regime, a capitalist regime, and a socialist regime; the commonality argued is that, despite real changes, bottom is bottom." [13] As a political matter, moreover, MacKinnon is quick to insist that there is only one "true," "unmodified" feminism: that which analyzes women *as women,* not as subsets of some other group and not as gender-neutral beings.

Despite its power, MacKinnon's dominance theory is flawed by its essentialism. MacKinnon assumes, as does the dominant culture, that there is an essential "woman" beneath the realities of differences between women, that in the description of the experiences of "women," issues of race, class, and sexual orientation can therefore be safely ignored or relegated to footnotes. In her search for what is essential womanhood, however, MacKinnon rediscovers white womanhood and introduces it as universal truth. In dominance theory, black women are white women, only more so.

Essentialism in feminist theory has two characteristics that ensure that black women's voices will be ignored. First, in the pursuit of the essential feminine, Woman leached of all color and irrelevant social circumstance, issues of race are bracketed as belonging to a separate and distinct discourse—a process that leaves black women's selves fragmented beyond recognition. Second, feminist essentialists find that in removing issues of "race" they have actually only managed to remove black women—meaning that white women now stand as the epitome of Woman. Both processes can be seen at work in dominance theory.

DOMINANCE THEORY AND THE BRACKETING OF RACE

MacKinnon repeatedly seems to recognize the inadequacy of theories that deal with gender while ignoring race but having recognized the problem, she repeatedly shies away from its implications. Thus, she at times justifies her essentialism by pointing to the essentialism of the dominant discourse: "My suggestion is that what we have in common is not that our conditions have no particularity in ways that matter. But we are all measured by a male standard for women, a standard that is not ours." [14] At other times she deals with the challenge of black women by placing it in footnotes. For example, she places in a footnote without further comment the suggestive, if cryptic, observation that a definition of feminism "of coalesced interest and resistance" has tended both to exclude and to make invisible "the diverse ways that many women—notably Blacks and working-class women—have *moved* against their determinants." [15] In another footnote generally addressed to the problem of relating Marxism to issues of gender and race, she notes that "[a]ny relationship *between* sex and race tends to be left entirely out of account, since they are considered parallel 'strata,' " [16] but this thought simply trails off into a string of citations of black feminist and social feminist writings.

Finally, MacKinnon postpones the demands of black women until the arrival of a "general theory of social inequality"; recognizing that "gender in this country appears partly to comprise the meaning of, as well as bisect, race and class—even as race and class specificities make up, as well as cross-cut, gender." [17] She nevertheless is prepared to maintain her "color-blind" approach to women's experience until that general theory arrives (presumably that is someone else's work).

DOMINANCE THEORY AND WHITE WOMEN AS ALL WOMEN

The second consequence of feminist essentialism is that the racism that is acknowledged only in brackets quietly emerges in the feminist theory itself—both a cause and an effect of creating "Woman" from white woman. In MacKinnon's work, as I mentioned earlier, the result is that black women become white women, only more so.

In a 1982 article, MacKinnon borrows a quote from Toni Cade Bambara describing a black woman with too many children and no means with which to care for them as "grown ugly and dangerous from being nobody for so long," and then explains,

> By using her phrase in altered context, I do not want to distort her meaning but to extend it. Throughout this essay, I have tried to see if women's condition is shared, even when contexts or magnitudes differ. (Thus, it is very different to be "nobody" as a Black woman than as a white lady, but neither is "somebody" by male standards.) This is the approach to race and ethnicity attempted throughout. I aspire to include all women in the term "women" in some way, without violating the particularity of any woman's experience. Whenever this fails, the statement is simply wrong and will have to be qualified or the aspiration (or theory) abandoned. [18]

I call this the "nuance theory" approach to the problem of essentialism: by being sensitive to the notion that different women have different experiences, one can offer generalizations about "all women" while qualifying statements, often in footnotes, supplement the general account with the subtle nuances of experience that "different" women add to the mix. Nuance theory thus assumes the commonality of all women—differences are a matter of "context" or "magnitude," that is, nuance.

The problem with nuance theory is that if black women are defined as "different," white women quietly become the norm, or pure, essential Woman. Just as MacKinnon would argue that being female is more than a "context" or a "magnitude" of human experience, being black is more than a context or magnitude of all (white) women's experience. But not in dominance theory.

For instance, MacKinnon describes how a system of male supremacy has constructed "woman":

> Contemporary industrial society's version of her is docile, soft, passive, nurturant, vulnerable, weak, narcissistic, childlike, incompetent, masochistic, and domestic, made

for child care, home care, and husband care. . . . Women who resist or fail, including those who never did fit—for example, black and lower-class women who cannot survive if they are soft and weak and incompetent, assertively, self-respecting women, women with ambitions of male dimensions—are considered less female, lesser woman.[19]

In a peculiar symmetry with this ideology, in which black women are something less than women, in MacKinnon's work black women become something more than women. In MacKinnon's writing, the word "black," applied to women, is an intensifier. If things are bad for everybody (meaning white women), then they are even worse for black women. Silent and suffering, we are trotted onto the page (mostly in footnotes) as the ultimate example of how bad things are.

Thus, in speaking of the beauty standards set for (white) women, MacKinnon remarks, "Black women are further from being able concretely to achieve the standard that no woman can ever achieve, or it would lose its point."[20] The frustration of black women at being unable to look like an "all-American" woman is in this way just a more dramatic example of all (white) women's frustration and oppression. When a black woman speaks on this subject, however, it becomes clear that a black woman's pain at not being considered fully feminine is different qualitatively, not merely quantitatively, from the pain MacKinnon describes. It is qualitatively different because the ideology of beauty concerns not only gender but race.

MacKinnon's essentialist, "color-blind" approach also distorts the analysis of rape that constitutes the heart of her 1983 article on feminist jurisprudence. By ignoring the voices of black female theoreticians of rape, she produces an ahistorical account that fails to capture the experience of black women.

MacKinnon sees sexuality as "a social sphere of male power of which forced sex is paradigmatic."[21] As with beauty standards, black women are victimized by rape just like white women, only more so: "Racism in the United States, by singling out Black men for allegations of rape of white women, has helped obscure the fact that it is men who rape women, disproportionately women of color."[22] In this peculiar fashion MacKinnon simultaneously recognizes and shelves racism, finally reaffirming that the divide between men and women is more fundamental and that women of color are simply "women plus." MacKinnon goes on to develop a powerful analysis of rape as the subordination of women to men, with only one more mention of color: "[R]ape comes to mean a strange (read Black) man knowing a woman does not want sex and going ahead anyway."[23]

This analysis, though rhetorically powerful, is an analysis of what rape means to white women masquerading as a general account; it has nothing to do with the experience of black women. For black women, rape is a far more complex experience, and an experience as deeply rooted in color as in gender.

As a legal matter, the experience of rape did not even exist for black women. During slavery, the rape of a black woman by any man, white or black, was simply not a crime.[24] Even after the Civil War, rape laws were seldom used to protect black women against either white or black men, since black women were considered promiscuous by nature. In contrast to the partial or at least formal protection white women had against sexual brutalization, black women frequently had no legal protection whatsoever. "Rape," in this sense, was something that only happened to white women; what happened to black women was simply life.

Finally, for black people, male and female, "rape" signified the terrorism of black men by white men, aided and abetted, passively (by silence) or actively (by "crying rape"), by white women. Black women have recognized this aspect of rape since the nineteenth century. For example, social activist Ida B. Wells analyzed rape as an example of the inseparability of race and gender oppression in *Southern Horrors: Lynch Law in All Its Phases,* published in 1892. Wells saw that both rape law and Southern miscegenation laws were part of a patriarchal system through which white men maintained their control over the bodies of all black people: "[W]hite men used their ownership of the body of the white female as a terrain on which to lynch the black male."[25] Moreover, Wells argued, though many white women encouraged interracial sexual relationships, white women, protected by the patriarchal idealization of white womanhood, were able to remain silent, unhappily or not, as black men were murdered by mobs.

Nor has this aspect of rape become purely a historical curiosity. Susan Estrich reports that between 1930 and 1967, 89 percent of the men executed for rape in the United States were black;[26] a 1968 study of rape sentencing in Maryland showed that in all fifty-five cases where the death penalty was imposed, the victim had been white, and that between 1960 and 1967, 47 percent of all black men convicted of criminal assaults on black women were immediately released on probation.[27]

The experience of rape for black women includes not only a vulnerability to rape and a lack of legal protection radically different from that experienced by white women, but also a unique ambivalence. Black women have simultaneously acknowledged their own victimization and the victimization of black men by a system that has consistently ignored violence against women while perpetrating it against men. The complexity and depth of this experience is not captured, or even acknowledged, by MacKinnon's account.

MacKinnon's essentialist approach re-creates the paradigmatic woman in the image of the white woman, in the name of "unmodified feminism." As in the dominant discourse, black women are relegated to the margins, ignored, or extolled as "just like us, only more so." But "Black women are not white women with color."[28] Moreover, feminist essentialism represents not just an insult to black women, but a broken promise—the promise to listen to women's stories, the promise of feminist method.

NOTES

1. *See, e.g.,* Catharine A. MacKinnon, *On Collaboration, in* Feminism Unmodified 198, 204 (1987) ("I am here to speak for those, particularly women and children, upon whose silence the law, including the law of the First Amendment, has been built").

2. Rich defines white solipsism as the tendency to "think, imagine, and speak as if whiteness described the world." Adrienne Rich, *Disloyal to Civilization: Feminism, Racism, Gynephobia, in* On Lies, Secrets, and Silence 275, 299 (1979).

3. In my discussion I focus on Catharine A. MacKinnon, *Feminism, Marxism, Method, and the State: An Agenda for Theory,* 7 Signs 515 (1982) [hereinafter MacKinnon, *Agenda for Theory*]; and Catharine A. MacKinnon, *Feminism, Marxism, Method, and the State: Toward Feminist Jurisprudence,* 8 Signs 635 (1983) [hereinafter MacKinnon, *Feminist Jurisprudence*], but I make reference to the essays in Feminism Unmodified, *supra* note 1, as well.

4. Catharine A. MacKinnon, *Desire and Power, in* Feminism Unmodified, *supra* note 1, at 46, 49.

5. *Id.* at 48.

6. MacKinnon, *Agenda for Theory, supra* note 3, at 516.

7. *Id.*

8. MacKinnon, *supra* note 4, at 3.

9. *Id.*

10. MacKinnon, *Feminist Jurisprudence, supra* note 3, at 638.

11. *Id.* at 639.

12. *Id.*

13. MacKinnon, *Agenda for Theory, supra* note 3, at 523.

14. Catharine A. MacKinnon, *On Exceptionality: Women as Women in Law, in* Feminism Unmodified, *supra* note 1, at 70, 76.

15. MacKinnon, *Agenda for Theory, supra* note 3, at 518 & n.3.

16. *Id.* at 537 n.54.

17. MacKinnon, *supra* note 1, at 2–3.

18. MacKinnon, *Agenda for Theory, supra* note 3, at 520 n.7.

19. *Id.* at 530. Yet, having acknowledged that black women have never been "women," MacKinnon continues in the article to discuss "women," making it plain that the "women" she is discussing are white.

20. *Id.* at 540 n.59. Similarly, in *Feminism Unmodified*, MacKinnon reminds us that the risk of death and mutilation in the course of a botched abortion is disproportionately borne by women of color. Catharine A. MacKinnon, *Not by Law Alone: From a Debate with Phyllis Schlafly, in* Feminism Unmodified, *supra* note 1, at 21, 25, but only in the context of asserting that "[n]one of us can afford this risk." *Id.*

21. MacKinnon, *Feminist Jurisprudence, supra* note 3, at 646.

22. *Id.* at 646 n.22; *see also* Catharine A. MacKinnon, *A Rally against Rape, in* Feminism Unmodified, *supra* note 1, at 81, 82 (black women are raped four times as often as white women).

23. MacKinnon, *Feminist Jurisprudence, supra* note 3, at 653; *cf.* Susan Estrich, Real Rape 3 (1987) (remarking, while telling the story of her own rape, "His being black, I fear, probably made my account more believable to some people, as it certainly did with the police."). Indeed. Estrich hastens to assure us, however, that "the most important thing is that he was a stranger." *Id.*

24. *See* Jennifer Wriggins, *Rape, Racism, and the Law,* 6 Harv. Women's L.J. 103, 118 (1983).

25. Hazel V. Carby, *"On the Threshold of Woman's Era": Lynching, Empire, and Sexuality in Black Feminist Theory, in* "Race," Writing, and Difference 301, 309 (Henry L. Gates, Jr., ed., 1985).

26. Estrich, *supra* note 23, at 107 n.2.

27. Wriggins, *supra* note 24, at 121 n.113. According to the study, "the average sentence received by Black men, exclusive of cases involving life imprisonment or death, was 4.2 years if the victim was Black, 16.4 years if the victim was white." *Id.* I do not know whether a white man has ever been sentenced to death for the rape of a black woman, although I could make an educated guess as to the answer.

28. Barbara Omolade, *Black Women and Feminism, in* The Future of Difference 247, 248 (H. Eisenstein & A. Jardine eds., 1980).

2 | Ain't I a Feminist?

Celina Romany

I want to recover my faith in feminism during the 1990s. The feminism that gave me the strength to understand the story of a woman born and raised in a colony who migrates to the metropolis, feminism as a liberation project. The feminism that launches a multifaceted attack on legal institutions that perpetuate substantial inequities.

The current state of feminist legal theory makes me wonder whether I am still a feminist. The feminism I see myself associated with has a capital *F* and aims at eradicating the various forms of oppression that affect all women, a project overlooked by "small-town" feminism. I am willing to risk being outside current postmodern theoretical trends by supporting capital letters. My capital letters connote expansion, breadth, and inclusion. Far from claiming privileged access to truth with a capital *T,* feminism with a capital *F* thrives in a room with a great view of narratives about intersections.

Feminist legal theorists belong to a norm-forming group involved in what Robert Cover has described as the creation of new legal meanings.[1] As he suggested, we need to examine the juris-generative operation of such a group and how the process of creating new legal meanings depends on sustaining narratives, narratives that define both the vision of the juris-generative group and its location in making its work a viable alternative.

I would like to critique the feminist narratives that sustain the creation of feminist legal theory as new legal meaning. My principal claims are (1) that the feminist narrative deployed as a foundation with its monocausal emphasis on gender falls short of the liberation project feminism should be about: the emancipation of all women; (2) that feminism so defined cannot adequately address the shortcomings of liberal legalism; and (3) that postmodernism, although helpful in counteracting feminist essentialism by giving space and voice to a multiplicity of accounts, neverthe-

19

less lacks a material analysis of macrostructures of inequality and thus lacks translation potential for social change.

Feminist legal theory needs to allow room for the destabilization of gender as both a conceptual and practical tool of analysis. Feminist legal theory moves in the right direction when it pursues the humanist project of agency and subjectivity and attempts to redefine subjectivity to redress gross gender-related exclusions. Yet it needs to move beyond. The feminism with a capital *F* that I want to recover in the context of legal theory is that which redefines subjectivity in light of the key variables of subject formation: race, ethnicity, class, and gender. A feminist theory of subjectivity can adequately elaborate an alternative vision to the liberal self by showing the centrality of the political and cultural history in which the subject is born; a context of personal and social delegitimation. Through this route, the elaboration of feminist subjectivity can plausibly seize the deep meanings of difference, subordination, and oppression. By not filling this gap, we only catch a glimpse of meaning and experience exclusion. Universalist assumptions deny intersubjectivity any opportunity to liberate us from the appropriation and objectification of *others,* to pave the way for a real recognition of differences and commonalities and to serve as a reminder that "the *other* is just as entitled as I am to her/his humanity expressed in her/his cultural reality." [2]

What is the special claim of feminism in challenging core assumptions of liberalism? The emergence of what is currently characterized as many feminisms or post-feminism makes the project of identifying its unique contribution to the challenge of liberalism much more difficult. The liberal system, which is so fond of binary oppositions contained in the separate public/private arenas, is endorsed by the allegedly neutral, objective, and procedurally fair rule of law. In spite of the different twists and turns of feminism, we can recognize that both methodologically and substantively it has put on the table the subordination, oppression, and second-class citizenship brought about by the devaluation of the personal and the so-called domestic sphere. It gave personal experience epistemological standing, offering counternarratives that have served as critiques of the values and assumptions lying beneath our social and political organization, social contract included. It challenged male norms.

However, such material inscription of the ideological has insisted on the preeminence of gender subordination at the expense of other forms of oppression, missing a basic point. If feminism was to be about freedom for all women, it had to consequently address multiple experiences—not an easy task both for theoretical generalizations and for political strategy. There are historical and sociological explanations for the essentialism of the woman standpoint. First, there is the interplay of practice and theory: the cross-fertilization between the political practice generated by the feminist movement and its theoretical conceptualizations. bell hooks and other women of color have done excellent work in documenting the schism existing between women of color and white women in the context of the feminist movement, and the influence of color and class composition on these conceptualizations. [3] Second, there is a history of frustration brought about by the political left's inability to grasp the centrality of gender subordination, as shown by the many indictments against feminists' alleged misunderstanding of a class analysis.

Although solidarity, empathy, altruism, and collective attachments are dimensions increasingly explored through the acquisition of a feminist consciousness, the power dynamics generated by institutions creating and perpetuating the cultural and psychological manifestations of racism and classism are left intact. The elaboration of theoretical arguments exclusively resting upon gender sustains the narratives emerging from such feminist consciousness. Race, ethnicity, and class are viewed as diluting the thrust of gender oppression. The biggest irony is that just as gender is dismissed by reductionist Marxist critiques, race, ethnicity, and class are assigned by essentialist feminism to maximum security and solitary confinement. They are allowed to join the general prison population only for good behavior: when the race, ethnicity, and class categories learn to stay where they belong, when their subsidiary explanatory power is understood, when basic rules of grammar are comprehended and the auxiliary nature of the conjunction "and" is fully grasped. Bear in mind the by now familiar descriptions: gender *and* race, gender and class, gender and ethnicity.

I have critiqued elsewhere the essentialist and universalist character of feminist theorists who substitute the view from nowhere with the view from womanland.[4] I have specifically targeted the work of Carol Gilligan and her reliance on Nancy Chodorow's essentialist account of reproduction and motherhood. My critique has focused on those feminist legal theorists who have uncritically and enthusiastically adopted some of her limited findings as the basis of their work. Likewise I have critiqued radical feminists' reductionist accounts of sexual oppression.

For example, Catharine MacKinnon's critique of Gilligan adopts the essentialist standpoint of the silenced woman, without elaborating the multilayers of oppression vividly represented by women of color. For MacKinnon, there is no female subjectivity, as women are defined by men. In effect collapsing all forms of oppression, she views sexuality as a "pervasive dimension of social life, one that permeates the whole, . . . a dimension along which other social divisions, like race and class, partly play themselves out."[5] Her totalizing theory of social reality based on sexual oppression does not admit to a concept of identity, and therefore cannot account for the multilayered experience of women of color.[6] Symptomatically, even in her acknowledgment of the contribution of writings by women of color, in her most recent book, MacKinnon implies that these works lack a theoretical framework and, as such, others will have to build upon those writings in the coming years.[7] The experience of women of color seems to be viewed as the anecdotes that will unfold, with the passage of time, grand theoretical discoveries in sync with MacKinnon's overarching theory of sexual oppression.

Do feminist legal theory's sustaining narratives have the breadth required to challenge different strands of oppression within liberal legalism, as experienced by all women? Can this work, as Robert Cover suggested, offer a viable alternative? Think about the critique of rights, their affirmative and negative character, ascription of rights, the instrumental value of rights, the nature of adjudication, core principles such as property, the exchange of commodities (personal included), demarcations of the public and private, boundaries for state intervention and nonintervention, the discrimination principle, conflicts among different sources of discrimination, and reflect on the limited potential a gender-essentialist analysis has for a thorough analysis of these core institutions.

I am skeptical of the ability of a feminist legal theory based exclusively on gender narratives to deal with the overall challenge. Essentialist narratives overload feminism as a key tool in the critique of the liberal project and utterly fail to offer a comprehensive critical framework for liberal legal institutions. The paradigm selection process (the architectural design, selection of building materials, objectives, aesthetics) is informed by that limited experience. At their best, these narratives offer partial critiques with partial and insular results: small-town feminism generating small-town feminist theory and politics.

To the extent that a racial/ethnic/class "minority perspective" gets incorporated into the feminist redefinition of subjectivity, the latter's critique of rights and fairness also undergoes revision. The normative intuitions that are to guide such an analysis are "different." As the "minority" critique of Critical Legal Studies scholarship points out, the evaluation of rights stems neither from what a critical legal scholar would describe as an alienating experience originating from the fear of connection, nor from what a feminist legal scholar would characterize as a gender experience of connection that spells solidarity and responsibility to others in lieu of atomized individualism. The intersection of race and gender in the redefinition of subjectivity and intersubjectivity points to a different legal consciousness. Rights that "separate" individuals also trace boundaries of mutual respect in such separation and (no matter what amount of false consciousness is involved) can strengthen identities.

If feminism, and feminist legal theory in particular, is to remain a liberation project, it needs to come to grips with its cognitive distortions and self-idealized universal discoveries. Feminism needs to put forth sustaining narratives that capture the centrality of intersections in the intersubjective formation of identities. In the meantime, we could use a heavy dose of modesty, giving pretentiousness a deserved vacation and publicly announcing the incorporation of the project as "Feminism, Limited."

Postmodernism has been recruited in an effort to counter the essentialist dimension of the woman standpoint. Although I am sympathetic to the efforts of those (in particular the work of Nancy Fraser and Linda Nicholson)[8] who are trying to match feminism and postmodernism through the magic of supplementation (a match not necessarily made in heaven), I am highly skeptical of satisfactorily concrete outcomes. The postmodern fallibilistic and decentering approach moves away from a unitary concept of the woman standpoint and opens up the door for alternative accounts of difference. However, this new entrance leads us into a meeting of discourses rather than to an encounter of those differences at the very concrete level of power differentials and unequal distribution of privileges.

Discourse, the understudy for representation, supplants representation once it is discarded as an obsolete and decadent way of apprehending reality.[9] There is nothing outside the text in the realm of discourse; there is no point from which opposition forms. As Benita Parry accurately points out in her critique of Gayatri Spivak's work, the move is one to place "incendiary devices within the dominant structures of representation and not to confront these with another knowledge";[10] the subaltern voice is deemed irretrievable; counternarratives of resistance are labeled reverse discourse.

Linda Nicholson and Nancy Fraser talk about adopting a fallibilistic approach that would tailor its methods and categories to the specific task at hand, using multiple categories when appropriate and forswearing the metaphysical comfort of a single "feminist method" or "feminist epistemology."[11] Their approach would be more like a tapestry composed of threads of many different hues rather than one woven in a single color.[12] Not much is said, however, as to the relinquishment of privileges necessary for the multicolored, multiclass composition of the "weavers'" labor force.

When I attempt to figure out whether there is life after postmodernism, the recurrent image I have is one where I stand in the middle of a ballroom, paralyzed, surrounded by dancers experiencing the *jouissance* generated by dances of heterogeneous and fragmented accounts. Paralysis skyrockets my anxiety because I love to dance and thought I knew a lot about dancing.

Ain't I a feminist? I am a feminist with a broad and expansive liberation project. I advocate a broadening of horizons to show that the humanist project of subjectivity and agency need not be trashed but rather redefined. We have to expose those legal institutions that delay and obstruct the creation of conditions for strengthening identities, thereby enabling them to engage in dialogues that further refine our subjective perceptions and that serve as spaces for the creation of new narratives that are able to sustain the paradigm choices guiding the formation of new legal meanings.[13]

Autonomy and subjectivity have a lot of appeal to Third World women. Feminist scholars and feminist legal theories should pay more attention to the work of Third World cultural theorists, who expose the intimate connections between political and national history and the constitution of the subject, stress the importance of revealing marginality conditions that bring about nonidentity,[14] and grasp the meaning of the "border [that] houses the power of the outrageous, the imagination needed to turn the historical and cultural tables."[15] As the writings of Guillermo Gómez-Peña, George Yudice, and Juan Flores describe, "the view from the border enables us to apprehend the ultimate arbitrariness of the border itself, of forced separations and inferiorizations."[16]

POSTSCRIPT

Some time ago I presented a paper in which I attempted to describe what it meant to be the concrete embodiment of the abstract conversation of feminists at a feminist conference: my invisibility.

In my paper I described how I had looked around and saw that notwithstanding my unique location, the only Latina in the room, eye contact was avoided so as to reinforce my social invisibility. The experience is not exactly new. Yet, as at other times, I somehow nurtured hopes and expectations that my presence, or for that matter the presence of any other woman of color, could stir some interest in addressing the multifacetedness of oppression. While following and observing the dynamics in that room, I asked myself how many of those participants actually had a person of color as a good friend or lover. I knew that a high percentage of those who had children have at least had close contact with that woman of color who allowed them to pursue their professional careers and personal realization: the domestic servant. At a more distant level many had come into contact with them in the lower ladders of service. In fact, at that same conference we were served food by one of them.

Therefore my presence in that room served the dual purpose of reminding them of their previous limited contacts with women of color, evoking feelings of distance and separation, and generating a good deal of curiosity as to my presence in that group. As they talked of the need to find commonalities while asserting differences, I became the concrete embodiment of their abstract conversation. At one point an assertive student—why is it that students usually have the ability to generate honest confrontations?—directly gazed at me and asked the facilitators to discuss how those alluded differences were integrated into their feminist works. Loving and hating that student for her directness, which was an open invitation for my intervention, I realized that the secure yet uncomfortable position of *observadora* was coming to an end.

That student had spoiled my otherwise successful "observer approach" in American feminist conferences. Since the rage and indignation were, as usual, very much inside myself, it was easier than I thought to accept her invitation. My accent, my color, the Caribbean rhythm in my words felt "different." The established feminist authorities assented with their heads to my thoughts. Yet in their faces you could see their inability to grasp and apprehend my feelings and emotions. They were too distant; I was too "other." Their otherness as women allowed them to walk with me halfway. But only halfway.

Marisa, one of my students at CUNY, after having read that paper, wrote,

Dear Celina:

What was it like becoming the concrete embodiment of their abstract conversation? What was it like to become the personification of theory? Why were they too distant? Why were you too other? You wrote that "their otherness as women allowed them to walk with me halfway. But only halfway." Is there just one path? Many paths? A straight line, a direction? Is that direction involved with purpose? Or is it a continuum, reflecting each of our lives? I think you hedge on page 8 when you refer to your rage and indignation. Is it that this "genre" of writing does not allow for visceral truthfulness/primitive truthfulness? Level with me and talk about that rage and indignation.

What is it like being invisible? Being made invisible by the discourse, by deconstruction, by academia? Being invisible in a world you've chosen to be in; in a world you thrive in? Don't you see the paradox, the dichotomy, the schism? You passed the professional rituals—but still you are invisible. You seek to become truly visible in evaluating social structures based upon experiencing oppression as a way of being.

So why is this core forced into hiding? It is forced externally (I realize you talk about internalization and complicity yet I want to dwell in the external). The externality of tentacles and arms which have the ability to enter human flesh—which have the ability to penetrate and wound—the tension at the moment of penetration . . . once inside, the tentacles divide and turn themselves into open hands which reach out for and search for living essences, the heart, the brain—they reach and squeeze hard. The essences aren't destroyed, they merely escape and hide, hide behind the heart and mind and continue to exist within the grip of those tentacles, because the essences of life have gone into hiding so that the whole organism can survive. These essences live themselves in a shallow pool of water—crystal clear, walled in by purple flowers that are always in bloom, which grow to enormous heights as the grip becomes stronger.

What does your space look like? You see my space, I don't know if it is a space for feminist legal scholars, but it is mine. Where is yours?

I realized I was truly visible to Marisa.[17]

NOTES

1. Robert Cover, *Foreword: Nomos and Narrative,* 97 Harv. L. Rev. 4 (1983).

2. *See* Marnia Larzreg, *Feminism and Difference: The Perils of Writing as a Woman on Women in Algeria,* 14 Feminist Stud. 81, 98 (1988).

3. *See generally* bell hooks, Feminist Theory: From Margin to Center (1984); bell hooks, Talking Back: Thinking Feminist, Thinking Black (1989); bell hooks, Yearning: Race, Gender and Cultural Politics (1990); bell hooks, Ain't I a Woman? (1981, 1984).

4. Celina Romany, The Intersection of Race, Gender and Class in the Critique of the Liberal Self, Presentation at the Critical Legal Studies Conference (1988) (unpublished manuscript, on file with the *Yale Journal of Law and Feminism*).

5. Catharine MacKinnon, Toward a Feminist Theory of the State 130 (1989).

6. Marlee Kline's excellent critique of MacKinnon points out the tension in MacKinnon's work between her recognition of the multiplicity of race and class differences that exist among women and her emphasis on women's gender commonality. As Kline states, "[e]ven where MacKinnon provides an in-depth analysis of the particular experiences of women of color, she does not allow those experiences to challenge the premise of her theory. . . . Thus, it is not surprising that about half of MacKinnon's examples of the particular experiences of women of color in *Feminism Unmodified* refer to racism only in the context of pornography or rape. The other examples of the particular experiences of Black women and First Nations women are confined to brief comments or footnotes" (citations omitted). Marlee Kline, *Race, Racism and Feminist Legal Theory,* 12 Harv. Women's L.J. 115, 138–39 (1989). Kline further argues that MacKinnon's "construction of the feminist project [is] limited in its capacity to capture the complex impact of racism in the lives of women of color" and "neither the differences in interest and priority that exist between white women and women of color nor the unequal power relationship between the groups are confronted or dealt with in her work." *Id.* at 140–41.

7. MacKinnon, *supra* note 5.

8. Nancy Fraser & Linda Nicholson, *Social Criticism without Philosophy: An Encounter between Feminism and Postmodernism, in* Universal Abandon? The Politics of Post Modernism 83 (Andrew Ross ed., 1988).

9. Although postmodern feminists have attempted to move away from some of postmodernism's main tenets, the social critique of power differentials remains inadequate and the primacy of discourse remains significantly unaltered. *See* Feminism/Postmodernism (Linda J. Nicholson ed., 1990); Jean-Francois Lyotard, The Postmodern Condition (1984); Stephen A. Tyler, The Unspeakable: Discourse, Dialogue and Rhetoric in the Postmodern World (1988); F. Jameson, *Postmodernism or the Cultural Logic of Late Capitalism,* 146 New Left Rev. 53 (1984).

10. Benita Parry, *Problems in Current Theories of Colonial Discourse,* 9 Oxford Literary Rev. 27, 43 (1987).

11. Fraser & Nicholson, *supra* note 8, at 101.

12. *Id.* at 101–2.

13. Cover, *supra* note 1.

14. Abdul R. JanMohamed & David Lloyd, *Introduction: Minority Discourse—What Is to Be Done?,* 7 Cultural Critique 5, 16 (1987).

15. Juan Flores & George Yudice, *Living Borders/Buscando America: Languages of Latino Self-Formation,* 24 Soc. Text 57, 80 (1990).

16. *Id.*

17. Marisa Steffers.

Brief Reflections toward a Multiplicative Theory and Praxis of Being

Adrien Katherine Wing

we're anything brighter than even the sun
(we're everything greater/than books/might mean
we're everyanything more than believe
(with a spin/leap/
alive we're alive)
we're wonderful one times one

—e.e. cummings, *1 x 1*

SINCE FEELING IS FIRST

In an earlier stage of being, I used to be a poet. But studying the law killed my muse. At this point, it does not really matter, because another poet, e.e. cummings, has said it better anyway—one times one equals one.[1] The purpose of this reflection is to put forth the proposition that the experiences of black women, whether in legal academia or elsewhere, might reflect the basic mathematical equation that one times one truly does equal one. This reflection will then briefly propose how we might utilize this theoretical knowledge to construct a concrete legal program benefiting black women.

Several prominent female legal academics of color, such as Mari Matsuda, Kimberlé Crenshaw, Judy Scales-Trent, and Angela Harris, speak of multiple levels of consciousness to characterize our existence—shifting back and forth between our consciousness as persons of color and "the white consciousness required for survival in elite educational institutions."[2] The constant shifting between levels of consciousness "produces sometimes madness, sometimes genius, sometimes both."[3] This multiple consciousness can include "a sense of self-contradiction" or even a sense of "containing the oppressor within oneself."[4] It can produce a feeling of ambiguity and frustration as well. In my own case, these levels of consciousness combine to make me a young black, female, wife, mother, international lawyer, professor, and activist.

On a daily basis, I feel subjected to subtle or overt discrimination on one or more of these levels. An example is illustrative. Recently I passed through the San Francisco

Airport on my return home to Iowa after a hectic six-day trip. I had attended a Critical Race Theory conference in Madison, Wisconsin, and recruited prelaw students in Los Angeles, San Bernardino, and Berkeley.

I handed my return ticket to the reservation agent, a white woman in her forties, and waited to be upgraded to first class as a frequent flier Gold Privilege customer. After holding my ticket for what seemed like ages, she said, "May I see some picture ID, please?" Now, in the hundreds of thousands of miles I have traveled by air, I have never had an agent ask me for identification on the return portion of a domestic flight for a ticket that was already in my possession. Suddenly, all kinds of thoughts ran through my head. "Do I look like a scam artist or some kind of thief standing here at the TWA first class counter of San Francisco Airport?" As Patricia Williams put it, "[N]o matter what degree of professional or professor I became, people would greet and dismiss my black femaleness as unreliable, untrustworthy, hostile, angry, powerless, irrational and probably destitute." [5] I laid my Iowa picture ID driver's license, along with my faculty ID card, TWA Gold Privilege card, and gold American Express card on the ticket counter. After looking at the gold and silver plastic in front of her for a while, the agent finally returned my ticket and boarding pass.

Resentful but resigned, I queried, "Why did you ask for my picture ID? I've never had that happen before." Her words said it all: "Well, you just didn't look like you could be Professor A. Wing."

On the plane, I replayed the scene in my head. I realized that this experience could be interpreted in several different ways. What if I had not been black? Well, I was still a woman. What if I had not been young? Well, I was still black. Somehow I thought that one of my young white male colleagues would not have been challenged in the same way, even if he were in blue jeans.

To some people, such incidents of micro-discrimination may appear trivial and not worthy of discussion. After all, I should be thankful that I haven't been raped, beaten, or lynched as were countless numbers of my people. Yet the cumulative impact of hundreds or even thousands of such incidents has been devastating to my spirit.

SPIRIT INJURY

I have finally come to the realization that black women are lifelong victims of what Patricia Williams has so aptly called "spirit-murder." [6] To me, spirit-murder consists of hundreds, if not thousands, of spirit injuries and assaults—some major, some minor—the cumulative effect of which is the slow death of the psyche, the soul, and the persona. This spirit-murder affects all blacks and all black women, whether we are in the depths of poverty or in the heights of academe. The following examples are only a few of the numerous experiences that have occurred in my life.

The injury to my spirit was almost fatal when I was just nine and my beloved father—a brilliant, articulate medical doctor, the first black on the research staff of a major drug company, honor graduate of New York University Medical School, Phi

Beta Kappa graduate of the University of California at Los Angeles and the Bronx High School of Science, survivor of the Harlem streets, one of ten children—committed suicide. My interpretation of the death of this "model Negro" was that he had finally gotten sick and tired of being treated as a second-class citizen. After he was terminated from his job, his spirit withered and died. He fell into a profound depression and finally took his physical life.

Time passed; outwardly I flourished—honor roll, athlete, class president—in my predominantly white, all-girls prep school. Yet inside, the ongoing injury to my spirit was apparently so profound that I wrote a poem about nihility as a ninth-grader in 1970. By the end of high school, the nihilist had changed: the good Negro girl had become the militant Afro-American, wearing as much of an Afro as my long wavy hair would permit. I often ended up in discussions with darker-skinned blacks with "real afros" who would claim that no "high yellow girl" with "good hair" going to some fancy white private school wearing a uniform was really black.

Recently, I have discovered that my spirit injury reaches back down to the roots of my family's existence in America. In October 1990, I attended the National Conference of Black Lawyers Convention in New Orleans. It was my first trip to the City of Jazz, and I viewed it with some excitement because some of my ancestors hail from there. New Orleans is also the home of the historic landmark known as the Beauregard Mansion, named for the famous Confederate general who fired on Fort Sumter, Pierre Gustave Toutant Beauregard. My relatives had said I must see this famous tourist attraction.

I took the one-hour tour of the carefully preserved "city cottage" conducted by a woman in antebellum dress. She showed us what she had characterized as the "lovely" pictures of the general's "lovely" wife and his "lovely" daughters and the bedrooms where they all lived. As we walked out onto the back balcony, we gazed on an open courtyard fenced in by some buildings that looked like stables or storage space. As the only one of the small group asking questions, I said, "What are those small buildings?" The guide responded in her "lovely" Southern drawl, "Why, those were the slave quarters, of course. But we've renovated them and rented out the upstairs, so we won't be seeing inside them." I was riveted to the floor by the offhand manner in which she casually dismissed the bondage and confinement of human beings in such a small space, not historically worthy of the careful restoration and preservation of the main house. "And how many slaves lived there?" I queried, dreading the answer. "Well, we're not exactly sure, but the only census ever done indicates twenty-nine." I was dumbfounded. Twenty-nine black people cramped together to serve the needs of four white people living in a two thousand-square-foot "city cottage." "Of course, there were lots more living in the countryside plantation," the tour guide added.

At the end of the tour I purchased Beauregard's biography and paid a dollar extra for a sheet detailing his family tree. The tour guide said, "You certainly asked a lot of questions, young lady. Do you have a particular interest in our general?" I responded, "Not exactly. It's the general who has an interest in me—a property interest. General Beauregard was my great-great-grandfather." The intake of breath was audible. "Those pictures of his children on the wall, those were only his white children. The general had black children as well, including my maternal great-grandmother Susan," I said, repeating a fact that had been passed down in my family for generations. Our gracious guide did not even blink: "Well, we'd heard rumors that the general was like the other Southern gentlemen of his time. But we're not allowed to discuss it."

For the rest of the day an image continued to haunt me. It was of the long-dead general sneaking out of the main house, across the courtyard, to the slave quarters. Did he rape my great-great-grandmother Sally Hardin there?[7] Maybe it occurred on the plantation. Despite my extensive academic knowledge of slavery, actually seeing the *place* where my slave ancestors may have been raped, conceived, or born, the place where they may have loved, worked, or even died had a profound effect on me.

THE MULTIPLIER EFFECT

Constant overt and covert discrimination, both individual and institutional, augments the lifelong spirit injury of black women. "I find I am constantly being encouraged to pluck out some one aspect of myself and present this as the meaningful whole, eclipsing or denying the other parts of self."[8] I am also not the "essential" (white) woman discussed by many white feminists. I am not a white woman "leached of all color and irrelevant social circumstance—a process which leaves black women's selves fragmented beyond recognition."[9] My experience cannot be reduced to an addition problem: "racism + sexism = straight black woman's experience."[10] I am not a "white woman plus."[11] I am an *indivisible* black female with a *multiple* consciousness.

In this society, the law does not know how to characterize my experience as a black woman. For example, in *DeGraffenreid v. General Motors* a Maryland district court granted partial summary judgment in favor of the defendant in a suit brought by five black women challenging the seniority system.[12] The court stated that they were entitled to bring a suit for "race discrimination, sex discrimination, or alternatively either, but not a combination of both."[13] The court found that there was no case stating that "black women are a special class"[14] to be protected in and of themselves.

If black females do not constitute a class in and of themselves, then surely they should be allowed to represent classes containing all females or all blacks. Yet in another case, the court would not let a black female represent white females. In *Moore v. Hughes Helicopter,* the Ninth Circuit affirmed the district court's refusal to certify Moore, a black woman, as the class representative in the sex discrimination complaint on behalf of all women at Hughes.[15] "Moore had never claimed before the EEOC that she was discriminated against as a female, but only as a Black female. . . .[T]his raised serious doubts as to Moore's ability to adequately represent white female employees."[16] If black females cannot represent themselves or all women, then surely they should be able to represent all blacks. Yet in *Payne v. Travenol,* black women could not represent all blacks.[17] The Mississippi district court refused to let the black female plaintiffs represent black men in a suit alleging race discrimination at a pharmaceutical plant.

We, as black women, can no longer afford to think of ourselves or let the law think of us as merely the sum of separate parts that can be added together or subtracted from, until a white male or female stands before you. The actuality of our layered experience is *multiplicative*. Multiply each of my parts together, $1 \times 1 \times 1 \times 1 \times 1$, and you have *one* indivisible being. If you divide one of these parts from one you still have *one*.

NEGATIVITY/POSITIVITY DIALECTIC

Once the existence of this multiplicity affecting our being is acknowledged, another issue arises. What is the nature of this multiplicity? Is it negative or positive or both? I think it is becoming increasingly easy for at least certain sectors of society, including us ourselves, to see black women as victims subjected to multiple layers of oppression. A disproportionate number of black women are on welfare, in poverty, among the working poor, unemployed, underemployed, or underpaid. The majority of black families are now headed by women, predominantly single women. A disproportionate number of black men are dead, in jail, or unemployed.[18] It is estimated that less than 50 percent of all black men are actually in the workforce.[19] The life expectancy of black men is actually declining.[20] I realize how few black men I know are over the age of sixty.[21] The scourges of Drugs, Crime, AIDS, Homelessness, and Joblessness are wreaking havoc on our already weakened communities.

Yet I want to assert affirmatively to the legal academy, and to ourselves as well, that we black women are more than "multiply burdened"[22] entities subject to a multiplicity of oppression, discrimination, pain and depression. Our essence is also characterized by a multiplicity of *strength, love, joy* (with a spin/leap/alive we're alive), and *transcendence* that flourishes despite adversity.

Rather than let ourselves be defined by those who see the world in a unilinear fashion, we are beginning to celebrate our own multiplicative definition of self. Rather than seeing ourselves as distorted white males, we are beginning to see ourselves in our multiplicative, multilayered wholeness. We are beginning, "collectively and individually, to distinguish between mere speaking that is about self-aggrandizement, exploitation of the exotic 'other'; and that coming to voice which is a gesture of resistance, an affirmation of struggle."[23] Imagine a world where the richness of our experience and vision was the standard. Imagine God as a Black Woman.

TRANSLATING THEORY INTO PRAXIS

We must not only *talk* about our multiplicity, but *act* on it in ways that may not translate into entries on our résumés. On a micro level, black women law professors can transcend the negativity affecting our people. Whether married or not and whether we have children or not, we must mentor, inspire, nurture, and adopt, literally and figuratively, the black children and young people out there. We must regard *all* of them as our children and our responsibility. We can literally borrow other people's children for an afternoon or a week or a month. We can also fund prizes at local schools or our own alma maters to inspire students. We can do these things even though we may be in an environment where there are not many black children.

MULTIPLICATIVE LEGAL PRAXIS

On a macro level, we must use our legal skills to push toward forging social policy that allows black women to capitalize on their richness and strength by giving them the financial and educational tools to meet their true multiplicative potential. For instance, current poverty laws and programs (vastly underfunded as they are) "treat the nuclear family as the norm and other units as aberrant and unworthy of societal accommodation."[24] They are designed predominantly by white, male, elite, unilinear thinkers who have never personally experienced the problems that are the subject of the legislation they pass. If these men had to raise their children singlehandedly (without the support of housewives, spouses, or servants) plus work full-time, many would crack within a week.

A solution may be found in a comprehensive, multifaceted program that would link child care, health care, nutrition, education, job training, and positive emotional support together to enable women (and men) to leave poverty and contribute to society. The key elements of such a project are that it be (1) designed by the people affected, including women of color; (2) responsive to their multiple needs as defined by them; and (3) adequately funded.

It is my fervent hope that readers of this reflection will be motivated to care and to act because they are morally concerned about the plight of black women. But even if America is not intrinsically interested in saving black souls and bodies, according to Derrick Bell's self-interest paradigm,[25] it should nonetheless be interested in becoming globally competitive with Japan and united Europe in the 1990s. It ca not do that without the assistance of the 85 percent majority of the workforce who will be white women and people of color.[26] Thus, waging this war to save the souls and bodies of black women and the poor will result in saving America.

In conclusion, I am asserting that the experience of black women must be seen as a multiplicative, multilayered, indivisible whole, symbolized by the equation one times one, *not* one plus one. This experience is characterized not only by oppression, discrimination, and spirit-murder, but by strength and love and transcendence as well.

All of us with multiple consciousness must help society address the needs of those multiply burdened first. Restructuring and remaking the world, where necessary, will affect those who are singularly disadvantaged as well. By designing programs that operate on multiple levels of consciousness and address multiple levels of need, we will *all* be able to reach our true potential to the benefit of ourselves, our families, our profession, our country, and the world.

> For the blood of all people
> runs within me
> (Africa, Asia, Europe, Middle East and the Americas too)
> I respect them
> I embrace them
> I transcend with them
> For blood has only one color
> (can you tell black white brown yellow blood apart?)
> Red
> for Love.
> —The earth mother beckons
> Save the world!! she says.
> Love my children.

Well what do you know. My muse returns.

NOTES

1. The title of this section is from another cummings poem. e.e. cummings, *is 5* [originally published 1926], pt. 4, poem 7, *in* Complete Poems, 1913–1962, at 290 (1972): "since feeling is first / who pays any attention to the syntax of things / will never wholly kiss you."

2. Mari Matsuda, *When the First Quail Calls: Multiple Consciousness as Jurisprudential Method*, 11 Women's Rts. L. Rep. 7, 8 (1989).

3. *Id.*

4. Angela P. Harris, *Race and Essentialism in Feminist Legal Theory*, 42 Stan. L. Rev. 581, 608 (1990) (also chapter 1 in this volume). See Patricia Williams, *On Being the Object of Property*, 14 Signs 5 (1988), on coming to terms with the fact that her white slavemaster ancestor, Austin Miller, who raped her eleven-year-old great-great-grandmother, Sophie, was a lawyer. When Williams went to law school, her mother told her, "The Millers were lawyers, so you have it in your blood." *Id.* at 6.

5. Patricia Williams, *Alchemical Notes: Reconstructing Ideals from Deconstructed Rights*, 22 Harv. C.R.-C.L. L. Rev. 401, 407 (1987) (footnote omitted).

6. Patricia J. Williams, *Spirit-Murdering the Messenger: The Discourse of Fingerpointing as the Law's Response to Racism*, 42 U. Miami L. Rev. 127, 129 (1987) (also chapter 28 in this volume).

7. During slavery, the rape of a black woman by any man, white or black, was simply not a crime. Jennifer Wriggins, *Rape, Racism, and the Law*, 6 Harv. Women's L.J. 108, 118 (1983).

8. Audre Lorde, *Age, Race, Class, and Sex: Women Redefining Difference*, *in* Sister Outsider 114, 120 (1984).

9. Harris, *supra* note 4, at 592. This problem in feminist literature can be summed up by

Gloria T. Hull's book title, All the Women Are White, All the Blacks Are Men, but Some of Us Are Brave (Gloria T. Hull et al. eds., 1982).

10. Harris, *supra* note 4 at 588 (citing Deborah K. King, *Multiple Jeopardy, Multiple Consciousness: The Context of a Black Feminist Ideology,* 14 Signs 42, 51 (1988)). *See also* Elizabeth Spelman, Inessential Woman: Problems of Exclusion in Feminist Thought 114–32 (1988) (chapter on *Gender and Race: The Ampersand Problem in Feminist Thought*).

11. Harris, *supra* note 4, at 598.

12. 413 F.Supp. 142 (E.D. Md. 1976).

13. *Id.*

14. *Id.*

15. 708 F.2d 475 (9th Cir. 1983).

16. *Id.* at 480.

17. 416 F.Supp. 248 (N.D. Miss. 1976).

18. Eloise Salholz, *Short Lives, Bloody Deaths,* Newsweek, Dec. 17, 1990, at 33 (footnote omitted).

19. U.S. Department of Commerce, Bureau of Census, *Employment Status of the Civilian Population 16 Years and Over by Sex, by Race, and by Hispanic Origin: 1960–1988, in* Statistical Abstract of the U.S. 1990, table 628, at 380. *See also* The State of Black America, 1979, James D. Williams ed., at 26–27 (1979).

20. Philip J. Hilts, *Life Expectancy for Blacks in U.S. Shows Sharp Drop,* N.Y. Times, Nov. 29, 1990, at A1.

21. According to my informal survey, very few black children that I know, including my own, have any living grandfathers.

22. Kimberlé Crenshaw, *Demarginalizing the Intersection of Race and Sex: A Black Feminist Critique of Antidiscrimination Doctrine, Feminist Theory and Antiracist Politics,* 1989 U. Chi. Legal F. 139, 140.

23. bell hooks, Talking Back: Thinking Feminist, Thinking Black 18 (1989).

24. Crenshaw, *supra* note 22, at 165 n.72.

25. Derrick Bell, Race, Racism and American Law 7, 10, 25, 41 (2d ed. 1980).

26. U.S. Bureau of Labor Statistics, *Civilian Labor Force—Employment Status by Sex, Race, and Age: 1988: Employment and Earnings Monthly, in* Statistical Abstract of the U.S. 1990, table 618, at 386.

4 Racism, Civil Rights, and Feminism

Kathleen Neal Cleaver

The roots of the extraordinary protest movement culminating with the passage of the 1964 Civil Rights Act and the 1965 Voting Rights Act reach deep into the century-long struggle blacks waged to end slavery and secure full citizenship.[1] Feminists have drawn inspiration and legal ammunition[2] from those passionate struggles during both the nineteenth and twentieth centuries. Yet despite appropriating legal gains paid for in blood during the civil rights era, and benefiting in great numbers from legislation banning employment discrimination, white women who represent the dominant voice of American feminists seem nearly inaudible in their opposition to racism. The perceptions that motivated the radical feminists, Third World feminists, and progressive women devoted to ending racial oppression have become peripheral among leading feminist authors.

This silence, which seems especially paradoxical to me in light of the crucial role women played in the modern civil rights movement, demonstrates how profound efforts at collective transformation can remain trapped within deeply entrenched boundaries. For in many ways, the Southern-based struggle to end segregation during the 1950s and 1960s, which can be seen as a human rights movement, a struggle for community empowerment, or a collective effort to expand democracy, was a women's movement. If it were not for black women, there would have been no Montgomery Bus Boycott, few voting rights campaigns, far less marvelous educational impact—in short, the civil rights movement as we know it could not have occurred.

Black women supported the churches that sustained the movement; raised money for the National Association for the Advancement of Colored People (NAACP), the Southern Christian Leadership Conference (SCLC), and other groups; encouraged their children to become plaintiffs in desegregation suits, and fed and sheltered the young student activists who took the challenge against white supremacy to the countryside. Women sat in at lunch counters, boarded the buses that became Freedom Rides, walked in the boycott lines, marched in demonstrations, went to jail, and became civil rights leaders in their communities. The visual record always documents the presence of women, but in the printed texts of academic accounts women's participation tends to fade. Yet it was the women in the movement who insisted on the more radical approaches, showed the most determination, and kept the fires for radical change lit. And it was black women in the movement whose example transformed white women's understanding of what women could do.[3]

Ella Baker, whose lifelong civil rights career spanned the NAACP, the Urban League, the SCLC, and the Student Nonviolent Coordinating Committee, has stated that "the number of women who carried the movement is much larger than the number of men."[4] Baker, raised in North Carolina by grandparents who had been enslaved, continued that spirited resistance that animated the struggle against slavery in her lifework. And it was that concrete, real-time devotion to the destruction of oppression, which I think characterized the socialization of daughters in many Southern black families, that accounted for their deep attraction to the civil rights struggle. For the movement of that era was about *Freedom*—praying, singing, marching, planning, reaching, and organizing for freedom. And in Southern black communities it was patently obvious that freedom was not withheld simply because of gender, but denied to every man, woman, and child who was black.

What the women who financed, mobilized, and joined civil rights campaigns knew, what those whose community work empowered the charismatic leaders who rose to represent the civil rights cause knew was that the price of black women's freedom was freedom for the entire community. Historical accounts concentrate largely on national leadership figures, but most of the mass protests and insurgencies that exploded during the 1950s and 1960s were grassroots movements that emerged with little direction from national organizations or leaders.[5] And where there were grassroots, there were women, as Kay Mills wrote in her biography of Fannie Lou Hamer.[6] The intertwining of the concerns of women and the struggle to end black oppression have a long history. As far back as 1892, the African American feminist, scholar, and human rights activist Anna Julia Cooper wrote that "only the *Black Woman* can say 'when and where I enter, in the quiet, undisputed dignity of my womanhood, without violence and without suing or special patronage, then and there the whole Negro race enters with me.' "[7]

I was in high school when I first saw defiant young women engaged in civil rights protest. Those students who went to jail in Albany, Georgia, during the early voter registration campaigns impressed me immensely. The courage it took for them to challenge white racist laws and their determination not to let jail or mob violence turn them away were awe-inspiring. I learned what heroism and leadership meant from Diane Nash, who led student demonstrations in Nashville, Tennessee, and later organized Freedom Rides, from Gloria Richardson, who mobilized the black community to fight segregation in Cambridge, Maryland, and from Ruby Doris Robinson, who helped coordinate the 1964 Mississippi Summer Project. It never once entered my head that women could not be civil rights leaders or organizers.

Like hundreds of women of my generation, I was thrilled to get a chance to join the movement. Shortly after the Meredith March, which galvanized national attention on the cry of "Black Power" in the summer of 1966, I began working at the Student Nonviolent Coordinating Committee's office in New York. I moved on to the national office in Atlanta, where I helped organize a black student conference held at Fisk University. Eldridge Cleaver was invited to speak at the conference. We fell in love and were married at the end of 1967. I became the communications secretary of the Black Panther Party and devoted most of my effort to our campaign to prevent Huey Newton, the defense minister of the Black Panther Party, from going to the gas chamber on charges of murdering an Oakland policeman.

My involvement with the Black Panther Party began during a turbulent era marked by frequent urban rebellions, profound dissent over the Vietnam War, and extremist political violence. Leaders with progressive views—from the Democratic president Kennedy to the NAACP leader Medgar Evers to Malcolm X to Black Panther Fred Hampton—were all assassinated because their eloquent pleas for change inspired a generation. The Black Panthers were being subjected to constant police surveillance, harassment, and terrorism. By that I mean people were followed, our telephones were tapped, our mail was opened, our homes were raided, our offices were shot up, and our organization was infiltrated. Members were frequently arrested and jailed, our leaders were framed, and our organization was sabotaged by a secret counterintelligence program spearheaded by the director of the FBI.[8] The news media were enlisted to portray Black Panthers as dangerous criminals instead of young people engaged in a struggle for self-determination. We sought power for the people, and in return the power of the state came crashing down on our heads.

Such conditions made it obvious to women within the Black Panther Party that liberation was not something we could obtain separately, nor would consciousness-raising groups serve as an appropriate channel for our rage. Of course, as in the larger community, conflicts occurred between men and women, and sexism was an issue that Panthers struggled to confront. Yet we could see how these conflicts arising from sexism within our community were subordinate to the overwhelming violence of the domination imposed on our community by the armed representatives of the state.

The women's liberation movement was coalescing around this same time, but women in the Black Panther Party did not believe that the discussions white women were launching would derive solutions to the difficulties we faced. While white women were addressing the specific form of oppression they experienced within the dominant culture, we came to fight side by side with men for black liberation. In fact, the way we engaged the culture in our struggle against racism deeply encouraged white women to strike out against sexism.

As revolutionaries, we rejected the conventional definition of our economic, political, and social relationship to the dominant society as "second-class citizenship." That citizenship extended after the Civil War continued the subjugation historically enforced during slavery, and we analyzed the regime of segregation as a variant of colonialism. Instead of being separated by land, as was Angola from Portugal, for example, black colonies were dispersed throughout the American "mother country" in separate communities that police controlled like occupying armies. Under international human rights law, we saw blacks as colonial subjects just as entitled to fight for human rights and self-determination as Africans, Asians, and Latin Americans who were waging revolutionary wars against imperialist domination.

The first point in the Black Panther Party Ten Point Program stated, "We want power to determine the destiny of our own black community." Our colonized status was the basis on which we organized for liberation; therefore all members of the Black Panther Party were drawn from the colonized community. We worked with other peoples and groups on the principle of coalition, not combination within the same organization. We formed coalitions with the electoral Peace and Freedom Party, which was predominantly white, with the Chicano Brown Berets, with the Puerto Rican Young Lords, and with the Asian Red Guards. We challenged racism with solidarity, and violence with self-defense.

While the ultimate domination that we all struggled to destroy during that era may have been the same, that did not mean its distinct historical and social articulations were interchangeable. The ancient dynamic that elevated white men over white women was not rooted in the same historical economic processes that allowed them to extract forced labor from African slaves and their descendants in North America. Although both unequal power relationships were embedded within hierarchical structures of authority, the barbarism involved in constructing New World slave societies transcended the bounds of patriarchy and laid the foundation for imperialist domination of the world.[9] Nothing has so profoundly chiseled the contours of our national heritage as those formative centuries of American slavery. The central paradox of American history is that the rise of liberty and equality was accompanied by the rise of slavery.[10] And the stigma of that social death inherent in the slave condition has imprinted itself on the entire cultural fabric.[11]

When Supreme Court justice Roger Taney, a former slaveowner, refuted Dred Scott's claim to freedom in the middle of the nineteenth century, he wrote that blacks were "beings of an inferior order . . . altogether unfit to associate with the white race in either social or political relations."[12] Their social position was so degraded, Taney wrote, "that they had no rights which the white man was bound to respect."[13] He did not support his assertion with legal citations, but instead pointed to the fact that "the negro [was] justly and lawfully . . . reduced to slavery for his benefit. He was bought and sold and treated as an ordinary article of merchandise . . . whenever a profit could be made by it."[14]

In a society defined by its creation of a class of human property, gender has maintained the demarcation that race historically imposed between those who owned that property and those who became property. The alleged benefits of the cult of femininity did not accrue to the black woman, who was neither protected within the white patriarchal structure nor excluded from the market.[15] When the slave woman's children, her labor, and her person legally became a commodity, white women were both protected and subordinated by the authority, autonomy, and property of their fathers or husbands. An irony of the system that extracted the greatest labor benefits conceivable from its workers was that it released enslaved women from the conventions evoked by gender among the dominant group. But, as Angela Davis has cautioned, the onerous nature of this brutal equality with black men should never be overlooked.[16]

Eliminating gender discrimination in itself does not remove the contortion blighting the lives of women whose color, race, national origin, or economic marginalization causes them such pain. As a rule, the subtleties of entrenched racism are no better understood by whites, women or men, than sexual harassment is by men, whether they are black or white, rich or poor. Until white feminists discover how to see the insidious way that racism constricts the lives of millions of women, they cannot oppose it. Worse, they may blindly fail to perceive how their ancestry positions them to benefit passively from racism's perpetuation, and remain oblivious to the racialized nature of gender.[17] Cultural, political, and economic institutions that mask deeply entrenched patterns of thought and action sustain white superiority almost automatically, as they have sustained male power. This enables racism to function with very little conscious individual attention.

Educated, well-meaning whites will insist, "I am not a racist," which is quite true if one accepts their fragmentary definition of "racist."[18] But what is the source of those slights, remarks, insults, or overt behavior that blacks interacting with them interpret as revealing a belief in black inferiority? What explains the gross media stereotypes that pervert the image of blacks? Why are blacks singled out for suspicious or fearful treatment because of their appearance, even in the hallowed halls of the Ivy League? How did it happen that over 80 percent of white Americans live where they have no black neighbors?

Just like sexism, racist behaviors flourish unless conscious, systematic, organized opposition to their manifestation, including but not limited to administrative and legal regulation, is in place. Thirty years of civil rights law have not eliminated those social conditions molded by three centuries of black subjugation. Feminism does not inoculate women against racism, because gender for black women has represented a category differentiated from white women,[19] whose race reserved them a place within the dominant society from which black women were barred.[20] Not only did gender limit the earning power of black women pushed to the lowest rungs of the economic ladder, but it left them outside the realm of glorified white womanhood. Patriarchal norms, economic exploitation, and racial denigration give a polydimensional character to the sexism that oppresses black women, which one-dimensional feminism cannot combat. Instead, the feminism appropriate to African Americans requires a complex recognition of the gendered dimension of racial subjugation.

The social isolation, economic deprivation, and blatant terrorism meted out to blacks make it difficult for many to appreciate the subtler subordination and intimidation that women within the dominant community endure. Lacking an appreciation of these women's realities, many black people fail to recognize that women whom they perceive as privileged may in fact feel weak, and therefore they discredit the validity of the feminist movement. Further, the sexist attitudes that belittle and exclude women's contributions from major black institutions, including churches, colleges, and reform organizations, is rarely given the public acknowledgment and condemnation it deserves. The presence of a significant underclass, masses of solid working people, and an affluent middle class among blacks shows that we are neither liberated nor integrated, but have become a fragmented population, scattered through all levels of society from the Pentagon to the prison yard. To elevate awareness of feminist concerns within black communities requires facing hostile opposition and uncomprehending denial. Yet this work may become a new focus for black women's activism. Concern for gender equity knows no color line, and women of every community desperately need more respect.

Unless we intend to remain locked up in self-righteous boxes, it is time to replace cross-racial silence and hostility on gender with communication. But no one can speak truth to power until they find out what is true. The weaknesses, aspirations, and histories that divide as well as unite us need to be examined, understood, and demythologized. That may get us to the starting gate to look for the solution that seems to elude us. Those progressive organizations that advocate on behalf of black concerns must adopt stronger antisexist positions if they intend to mobilize their constituencies and retain their relevance. More attention must be devoted to problems facing black women, particularly those juggling poverty and motherhood, fending off domestic violence and community crime waves.

These changes may take place before mainstream feminists become motivated to develop antiracist positions, because whites have a stake in failing to examine the interplay of racism with their cultural identity. During the heyday of European imperialism, when race became elevated to the primary indicator of cultural achievement, the hierarchical theory of race placed whites at the pinnacle of historical development.[21] Masterfully fabricated justifications in science, religion, industry, politics, and art that entitled whites to live on the labor and property of the inferior colored peoples of the world distinguished the nineteenth century.[22] Everything great, everything fine, everything really successful in human culture was seen as white.[23] As that legacy has yet to be repudiated entirely, it abets American feminist scholarship in which race remains peculiarly invisible.

The analytical task is to include gender and race within the same critique instead of polarizing them. If these constructs are extracted separately from the cultural matrix that defines them both, each category loses layers of its coherence. As we look back on the twentieth century, we see that W. E. B. Du Bois was prophetic when he wrote in 1903 that the problem of the twentieth century was the problem of the color line.[24] Race, particularly in the United States, has come to serve as a "metalanguage" for the construction of social relations.[25] Not only is race manipulated to subsume gender and class, but it blurs, disguises, and suppresses their interplay, precluding unity within gender and permitting cross-class solidarity.[26] Without an understanding of the complex encoding that our mutual and interdependent identities acquire within racism's language, those women who seek to engage America in social reconstruction will be left whistling in the dark.

NOTES

1. *See* Vincent Harding, There Is a River: The Black Struggle for Freedom in America (1981).

2. Title VII of the Civil Rights Act of 1964 prohibited discrimination in employment on the basis of race, color, religion, sex, or national origin. 42 U.S.C. § 2000e-e17 (1990). The Equal Employment Opportunity Act of 1972 amended Title VII to extend its protection to employees of state, local, and federal governments and expanded its coverage to include businesses of more than fifteen employees. 42 U.S.C. §§ 2000e(b) and 2000e-16 (1990). Title IX of the Educational Amendments to the Civil Rights Act of 1964 prohibited sex discrimination in any educational program or activity that received federal financial assistance. 20 U.S.C. §§ 1681–1688 (1990). Under the Civil Rights Act of 1991, Title VII was amended along with numerous other statutes affecting employment discrimination to further enable victims of discrimination to obtain redress.

3. Feminist author Sara Evans wrote about this early change in consciousness in *Personal Politics*:

The daring of younger women, the strength and perseverance of "mamas" in local communities, the unwavering vision, energy, and resourcefulness of an Ella Baker, opened new possibilities in contrast to the tradition of the "southern lady." Having broken with traditional culture, young white women welcomed the alternative they represented. For them these black women became . . . new models of womanhood.

Sara Evans, Personal Politics 53 (1980).

4. Paula Giddings, When and Where I Enter: The Impact of Black Women on Sex and Race in America 284 (1984).

5. Carson, *African American Leadership and Mass Mobilization,* Black Scholar, Fall 1994, at 2.

6. Kay Mills, This Little Light of Mine 45 (1993).

7. Anna Julia Cooper, *A Voice from the South by a black Woman from the South* (1892), *in* The Schomburg Library of Nineteenth Century Black Women Writers 31 (1988).

8. In his book *Racial Matters: The FBI's Secret File on Black America, 1960–1972,* Kenneth O'Reilly describes the FBI activities against the Black Panthers as "outrageous." According to O'Reilly, "only the Martin Luther King case rivaled the Panther case in its ferocity with FBI officials pursuing the most prominent proponents of violent resistance to white racism with the same zeal that had characterized their pursuit of the most prominent proponent of nonviolence." Kenneth O'Reilly, Racial Matters 293 (1989).

9. *See, e.g.,* John Henrik Clarke, Notes for an African World Revolution 44 (1991). In the chapter *The Nineteenth Century Origins of the African and African American Freedom Struggle,* Clarke concluded that "the wealth obtained from African slave labor made the . . . Industrial Revolution possible and also created the basis for modern capitalism." In his study of the economic evolution of slavery predominantly in the West Indies, Eric Williams wrote that the discovery of America helped make international trade the central feature of the seventeenth and eighteenth centuries, and the slave trade was the parent of that prosperous triangular trade between Europe, Africa, and the Americas. "The profits obtained [in the triangular trade] provided one of the mainstreams of that accumulation of capital in England

which financed the Industrial Revolution." Eric Williams, Capitalism and Slavery 51–52 (1961).

10. Edmund Morgan, American Slavery, American Freedom 4 (1975).

11. *See* Orlando Patterson, Slavery and Social Death (1982), particularly chap. 2, *Authority, Alienation and Social Death,* at 35–76.

12. Scott v. Sanford, 60 U.S. 393, 407 (1856).

13. *Id.*

14. *Id.*

15. *See* Angela Davis, *Reflections on the Black Woman's Role in the Community of Slaves,* Black Scholar, Dec., 1971, at 3–15.

16. Davis examined what the "brutal status of equality" meant for a slave woman:

> she could work up a fresh content for that deformed equality by inspiring and participating in acts of resistance of every form and color. She could turn the weapon of equality in struggle against the avaricious slave system which had engendered the mere caricature of equality in oppression. The black woman's activities increased the total incidence of anti-slavery assaults. But most important, without consciously rebellious black women, the theme of resistance could not have become so thoroughly intertwined in the fabric of daily existence. The status of black women within the community of slaves was definitely a barometer indicating the overall potential for resistance.
>
> This process did not end with the formal dissolution of slavery. Under the impact of racism, the black woman has been continually constrained to inject herself into the desperate struggle for existence. She—like her man—has been compelled to work for wages, providing for her family as she was previously forced to provide for the slaveholding class. (*Id.* at 15)

17. The social dominance of whites allows them to relegate their racial distinctiveness to the realm of the subconscious, according to legal scholar Barbara Flagg. "Whiteness is the racial norm. . . . Once an individual is identified as white . . . his distinctive racial characteristics need no longer be conceptualized in racial terms; he becomes effectively raceless in the eyes of other whites." Barbara Flagg, *"Was Blind, But Now I See": White Race Consciousness and the Requirement of Discriminatory Intent,* 91 Mich. L. Rev. 953, 970–71 (1993).

18. White Americans prefer to think of a racist as an individual motivated by a virulent hatred toward an "outcast" group. It is rare to find acceptance of a broader definition that would account for more of the manifest social hierarchies that racism promotes. Such a definition of a racist would be a person who subscribed to any set of beliefs that attributed a socially relevant quality to real or imagined genetic characteristics that made the ranking and discrimination of groups defined by their race necessary. *See* Pierre L. Van Den Berghe, Race and Racism: A Comparative Perspective 11 (1978).

19. Historian Evelyn Brooks Higginbotham wrote in her seminal article, *African American Women and the Metalanguage of Race,* that "in a society where racial demarcation is endemic to [the] sociocultural fabric . . . to laws, . . . economy . . . and everyday customs . . . gender identity is inextricably linked to . . . racial identity." Evelyn Higginbotham, *African American 19. Historian Evelyn Brooks Higginbotham wrote in her seminal article, African American Women and the Metalanguage of Race, that "in a society where racial demarcation is endemic to [the] sociocultural fabric . . . to laws, . . . economy . . . and everyday customs . . . gender identity is inextricably linked to . . . racial identity." Evelyn Higginbotham, African American Women and the Metalanguage of Race,* 17 Signs 251, 254 (1992).

20. During the century of segregated public accommodations, separate toilet facilities were provided for "White Ladies" and "Colored Women."

21. In an early work elaborating the theory of race as the primary explanation of development, Robert Knox, M.D., asserted the rank inferiority of Negroes and darker peoples, who, he wrote, had been "slaves of their fairer brethren" since "the earliest of times." Robert Knox, The Races of Men 150 (1850).

22. *See* W. E. B. Du Bois, *The White Masters of the World, in* The World and Africa 16–43 (1969).

23. *Id.* at 20.

24. In his introduction to *The Souls of Black Folk,* W. E. B. Du Bois wrote that he intended to reveal the strange meaning of being black at the dawning of the twentieth century, which was important because "the problem of the twentieth century is the problem of the color line."

25. Higginbotham, *supra* note 19, at 255.

26. *Id.*

5 Obscuring the Importance of Race: The Implication of Making Comparisons between Racism and Sexism (or Other Isms)

Trina Grillo and Stephanie M. Wildman

While this chapter was being written, Trina Grillo, who is of Afro-Cuban and Italian descent, was diagnosed as having Hodgkin's disease (a form of cancer) and underwent several courses of radiation therapy. In talking about this experience, she said that "cancer has become the first filter through which I see the world. It used to be race, but now it is cancer. My neighbor just became pregnant, and all I could think was 'How could she get pregnant? What if she gets cancer?' "

Stephanie Wildman, her coauthor, who is Jewish and white, heard this remark and thought, "I understand how she feels; I worry about getting cancer too. I probably worry about it more than most people, because I am such a worrier."

But Stephanie's worry is not the same as Trina's. Someone with cancer can think of nothing else. She cannot watch the World Series without wondering which players have had cancer or who in the players' families might have the disease. Having this worldview with cancer as a filter is different from just thinking or even worrying often about cancer. The worrier has the privilege of forgetting the worry sometimes, even much of the time. The worry can be turned off. The cancer patient does not have the privilege of forgetting about her cancer; even when it is not at the forefront of her thoughts, it remains in the background, coloring her world.

This dialogue about cancer illustrates a principal problem with comparing one's situation to another's. The "analogizer" often believes that her situation is the same as another's. Nothing in the comparison process challenges this belief, and the analogizer may think she understands the other's situation fully. The analogy makes the analogizer forget the difference and allows her to stay focused on her own situation without grappling with the other person's reality.

Yet analogies are necessary tools to teach and to explain, so that we can better understand each other's experiences and realities. We have no other way to understand others' lives, except by making analogies to our own experience. Thus, the use of analogies provides both the key to greater comprehension and the danger of false understanding.

INTRODUCTION

Like cancer, racism/white supremacy is an illness. To people of color, who are the victims of racism/white supremacy, race is a filter through which they see the world. Whites do not look at the world through this filter of racial awareness, even though they also constitute a race. This privilege to ignore their race gives whites a societal advantage distinct from any received from the existence of discriminatory racism. Throughout this chapter we use the term "racism/white supremacy" to emphasize the link between discriminatory racism and the privilege held by whites to ignore their own race.

Author bell hooks describes her realization of the connection between these two concepts: "The word racism ceased to be the term which best expressed for me exploitation of black people and other people of color in this society and . . . I began to understand that the most useful term was white supremacy."[1] She recounts how liberal whites do not see themselves as prejudiced or interested in domination through coercion, yet "they cannot recognize the ways their actions support and affirm the very structure of racist domination and oppression that they profess to wish to see eradicated."[2] For these reasons, "white supremacy" is an important term, descriptive of American social reality.

This chapter originated when the authors noticed that several identifiable phenomena occurred without fail in any racially mixed group whenever sex discrimination was analogized (implicitly or explicitly) to race discrimination. Repeatedly, at the annual meeting of the Association of American Law Schools (AALS), at meetings of feminist legal scholars, in classes on Sex Discrimination and the Law, and in law school women's caucus meetings, the pattern was the same. In each setting, although the analogy was made for the purpose of illumination, to explain sexism and sex discrimination, another unintended result ensued—the perpetuation of racism/white supremacy.

When a speaker compared sexism and racism, the significance of race was marginalized and obscured, and the different role that race plays in the lives of people of color and of whites was overlooked. The concerns of whites became the focus of discussion, even when the conversation supposedly had been centered on race discrimination. Essentialist presumptions became implicit in the discussion: it would be assumed, for example, that all women are white and all African Americans are men. Finally, people with little experience in thinking about racism/white supremacy, but who had a hard-won understanding of the allegedly analogous oppression, assumed that they comprehended the experience of people of color and thus had standing to speak on their behalf.

No matter how carefully a setting was structured to address the question of racism/white supremacy, these problems always arose. Each of the authors has unwittingly participated in creating these problems on many occasions, yet when we have tried to avoid them, we have found ourselves accused of making others uncomfortable. Even after we had identified these patterns, we found ourselves watching in amazement as they appeared again and again, and we were unable to keep ourselves from contributing to them.

We began to question why this pattern persisted. We concluded that these phenomena have much to do with the dangers inherent in what had previously seemed to us to be a creative and solidarity-producing process—analogizing sex discrimination to race discrimination. These dangers were obscured by the promise that to discuss and compare oppressions might lead to coalition building and understanding. On an individual psychological level, the way we empathize with and understand others is by comparing their situations with some aspects of our own. Yet comparing sexism to racism perpetuates patterns of racial domination by marginalizing and obscuring the different roles that race plays in the lives of people of color and of whites. The comparison minimizes the impact of racism, rendering it an insignificant phenomenon—one of a laundry list of isms or oppressions that society must suffer. This marginalization and obfuscation are evident in three recognizable patterns: (1) the taking back of center stage from people of color, even in discussions of racism, so that white issues remain or become central to the dialogue; (2) the fostering of essentialism, so that women and people of color are implicitly viewed as belonging to mutually exclusive categories, rendering women of color invisible; and (3) the appropriation of pain or the rejection of its existence that results when whites who have compared other oppressions to race discrimination believe they understand the experience of racism.

TAKING BACK THE CENTER

White supremacy creates in whites the expectation that issues of concern to them will be central in every discourse. Analogies serve to perpetuate this expectation of centrality. The center stage problem occurs because dominant group members are already accustomed to being center stage. They have been treated that way by society; it feels natural, comfortable, and in the order of things.

The harms of discrimination include not only the easily identified disadvantages of the victims (such as exclusion from housing and jobs) and the stigma imposed by the dominant culture, but also the advantages given to those who are not its victims. The white male heterosexual societal norm is privileged in such a way that its privilege is rendered invisible.

Because whiteness is the norm, it is easy to forget that it is not the only perspective. Thus, members of dominant groups assume that their perceptions are the pertinent ones, that their problems are the ones that need to be addressed, and that in discourse they should be the speaker rather than the listener. Part of being a member of a privileged group is being the center and the subject of all inquiry in which people of color or other nonprivileged groups are the objects.

So strong is this expectation of holding center stage that even when a time and place are specifically designated for members of a nonprivileged group to be central, members of the dominant group will often attempt to take back the pivotal focus. They are stealing the center—often with a complete lack of self-consciousness.

One such theft occurred at the annual meeting of a legal society, where three scholars, all people of color, were invited to speak to the plenary session about how universities might become truly multicultural. Even before the dialogue began, the views of many members of the organization were apparent by their presence or absence at the session. The audience included nearly every person of color who was attending the meeting, yet many whites chose not to attend.

When people who are not regarded as entitled to the center move into it, however briefly, they are viewed as usurpers. One reaction of the group temporarily deprived of the center is to make sure that nothing remains for the perceived usurpers to be in the center of. Thus, the whites who did not attend the plenary session, but who would have attended had there been more traditional (i.e., white) speakers, did so in part because they were exercising their privilege not to think in terms of race, and in part because they resented the "out groups" having the center.

Another tactic used by the dominant group is to steal back the center, using guerrilla tactics where necessary. For example, during a talk devoted to the integration of multicultural materials into the core curriculum, a white man got up from the front row and walked noisily to the rear of the room. He then paced the room in a distracting fashion and finally returned to his seat. During the question period he was the first to rise, leaping to his feet to ask a lengthy, rambling question about how multicultural materials could be added to university curricula without disturbing the "canon"—the exact subject of the talk he had just, apparently, not listened to.

The speaker answered politely and explained how he had assigned a Navajo creation myth to accompany St. Augustine, which highlighted some similarities between Augustine's thought and pre-Christian belief systems and resulted in each reading enriching the other. He refrained, however, from calling attention to the questioner's rude behavior during the meeting, the fact that he was asking an already answered question, or his presumption that the material the questioner saw as most relevant to his own life was central and "canonized," while all other reading was peripheral and, hence, dispensable.

Analogies offer protection for the traditional center. At another gathering of law professors, issues of racism, sexism, and homophobia were the focus of the plenary session for the first time in the organization's history. Again at this session, far fewer white males were present than would ordinarily attend such a session. After moving presentations by an African American woman, a Latino man, and a gay white man who each opened their hearts on these subjects, a question and dialogue period began.

The first speaker to rise was a white woman who, after saying that she did not mean to change the topic, said that she wanted to discuss another sort of oppression—that of law professors in the less elite schools. As professors from what is perceived by some as a less-than-elite school, we agree that the topic is important and it would have interested us at another time. But this questioner had succeeded in depriving the other issues of time devoted (after much struggle) specifically to them, and turned the spotlight once again onto her own concerns. She did this, we believe, not out of malice, but because she too had become a victim of analogical thinking.

The problem of taking back the center exists apart from the issue of analogies; it will be with us as long as any group expects, and is led to expect, to be constantly the center of attention. But the use of analogies exacerbates this problem, for once an analogy is taken to heart it seems to the center-stealer that she is not stealing the center, but rather is continuing the discussion on the same topic, and one that she knows well.[3] So when the format of the program implicitly analogized gender and sexual preference to race, the center-stealer was encouraged to think, "Why not go further to another perceived oppression?"

When socially subordinated groups are lumped together, oppression begins to look like a uniform problem, and one may neglect the varying and complex contexts of the different groups being addressed. If oppression is all the same, then we are all equally able to discuss each oppression, and there is no felt need for us to listen to and learn from other socially subordinated groups.

FOSTERING ESSENTIALISM

Essentialism is implicit in analogies between sex and race. Angela Harris explains gender essentialism as "the notion that there is a monolithic 'women's experience' that can be described independently of other facets of experience like race, class, and sexual orientation."[4] She continues, "A corollary to gender essentialism is 'racial essentialism'—the belief that there is a monolithic 'black experience' or 'chicano experience.' "[5]

To analogize gender to race, one must assume that each is a distinct category, the impact of which can be neatly separated, one from the other.[6] The essentialist critique shows that this division is not possible. Whenever it is attempted, the experience of women of color, who are at the intersection of these categories and cannot divide themselves to compare their own experiences, is rendered invisible. Analogizing sex discrimination to race discrimination makes it seem that all the women are white and all the men African American. The experiential reality of women of color disappears.

THE APPROPRIATION OF PAIN OR THE REJECTION OF ITS EXISTENCE

Many whites think that people of color are obsessed with race and find it hard to understand the emotional and intellectual energy that people of color devote to the subject. But whites are privileged in that they do not have to think about race, even though they have one. White supremacy privileges whiteness as the normative model.

Being the norm allows whites to ignore race, except when they perceive race (usually someone else's) as intruding on their lives.

Whites need to reject this privilege and to recognize and speak about their role in the racial hierarchy. Yet whites cannot speak validly for people of color, but only about their own experiences as whites. Comparing other oppressions to racial oppression gives whites a false sense that they fully understand the experience of people of color. Sometimes the profession of understanding by members of a privileged group may even be a guise for a rejection of the existence of the pain of the unprivileged. For people of color, listening to whites who profess to represent the experience of racism feels like an appropriation of the pain of living in a world of racism/white supremacy.

The privileging of some groups in society over others is a fact of contemporary American life.[7] This privileging is identifiable in the ordering of societal power between whites and people of color; men and women; heterosexuals and gays and lesbians; and able-bodied and physically challenged people. This societal ordering is clear to children as early as kindergarten.[8]

Judy Scales-Trent has written about her own experience as an African American woman, of "being black and looking white," a woman who thereby inhabits both sides of the privilege dichotomy.[9] As one who was used to being on the unprivileged side of the race dichotomy in some aspects of her life, she discusses how the privilege of being able-bodied allowed her to ignore the pain of an unprivileged woman in a wheelchair, humiliated in seeking access to a meeting place. She realized that her role as the privileged one in that pairing likened her to whites in the racial pairing. The analogy helped her see the role of privilege and how it affects us, presenting another example of how comparisons are useful for promoting understanding. But this insight did not lead her to assume that she could speak for those who are physically challenged; rather, she realized that she needed to listen more carefully.

Not all people who learn about others' oppressions through analogy are blessed with an increased commitment to listening. White people who grasp an analogy between an oppression they have suffered and race discrimination may think they understand the phenomenon of racism/white supremacy in all its aspects. They may believe that their opinions and judgments about race are as fully informed and cogent as those of victims of racism. In this circumstance, something approximating a lack of standing to speak exists because the insight gained by personal experience cannot easily be duplicated, certainly not without careful study of the oppression under scrutiny. The power of comparisons undermines this lack of standing, because by emphasizing similarity and obscuring difference it permits the speaker implicitly to demonstrate authority about both forms of oppression. If we are members of the privileged halves of the social pairs, then what we say about the dichotomy will be listened to by the dominant culture. Thus, when we employ analogies to teach and to show oppression in a particular situation, we should be careful that in borrowing the acknowledged and clear oppression we do not neutralize it, or make it appear fungible with the oppression under discussion.

Given the problems that analogies create and perpetuate, should we ever use them? Analogies can be helpful. They are part of legal discourse as well as common conversation. Consciousness raising may be the beginning of knowledge. Starting with ourselves is important, and analogies may enable us to understand the oppression of another in a way we could not without making the comparison. It is important for whites to talk about white supremacy, rather than leaving all the work for people of color and without drawing false inferences of similarities from analogies. Questions remain regarding whether we can make analogies to race, particularly in legal argument, without reinforcing racism/white supremacy. There are no simple answers to this thorny problem. We will have to continue to struggle with it, and accept that our progress will be slow and tentative.

NOTES

This chapter reprinted from Stephanie M. Wildman, with contributions by Margalynne Armstrong, Adrienne D. Davis, and Trina Grillo, Privilege Revealed: How Invisible Preference Undermines America (1996); by permission.

1. bell hooks, *Overcoming White Supremacy: A Comment, in* Talking Back: Thinking Feminist, Thinking Black 112 (1989).

2. *Id.* at 113.

3. In one sex discrimination class, the assigned reading consisted of three articles by black women. In the discussion, many white women focused on sexism and how they understood the women of color by seeing the sexism in their own lives. The use of analogy allowed the white women to avoid the implications of white privilege and made the women of color feel that their distinct experience was rendered invisible.

Additionally, for the first time that semester, many members of the class had evidently not done the reading. Although the end of the semester was near, was this a guerrilla tactic to retake the center or simply a lack of interest by the dominant group in the perceptions of the nondominant group (another form of manifesting entitlement to centrality)?

4. Angela P. Harris, *Race and Essentialism in Feminist Legal Theory,* 42 Stan. L. Rev. 581 (1990) (also chapter 1 in this volume).

5. *Id.*

6. *See* Elizabeth V. Spelman, Inessential Woman (1988) (criticizing the way gender essentialism ignores or effaces the experiences of women perceived as different from the white norm).

7. *See, e.g.,* Stephanie Wildman, *Integration in the 1980s: The Dream of Diversity and the Cycle of Exclusion,* 64 Tul. L. Rev. 1625, 1629 (1990) (discussing the privileging of white males in the legal profession).

8. *See* F. Kendall, Diversity in the Classroom: A Multicultural Approach to the Education of Young Children 19–21 (1983) (describing the development of racial awareness and racial attitudes in young children).

9. Judy Scales-Trent, *Commonalities: On Being Black and White, Different and the Same,* 2 Yale J.L. & Feminism 305, 305 (1990).

6 | It Is Better to Speak

Angela D. Gilmore

In September 1990 I attended a lecture given by a noted feminist scholar. Her topic was women's bodies as portrayed by the fashion industry. I did not have the same reaction to pictures of thin, young, carefree models featured in fashion magazines as did the "universal woman." An audience member's question clarified my confusion: "What woman are you talking about?" When the lecturer admitted that she was talking about straight, white, middle-class women, I realized that it was no wonder that I, a Black lesbian from a working-class background, could not connect with the experiences of the lecturer's "universal woman."[1]

When I was a student in law school, I experienced this same sense of dissonance, of being an outsider, of not connecting. While I may have done well academically, overall my law school experience was not positive. Looking back, I realize that I viewed law school as a means to some vague and unclear end. I tolerated the journey in anticipation of the destination.

In class after class, a professor, almost always white, and almost always male, would spin hypothetical after hypothetical in which all the actors with any power at all would almost universally be identified as male. When students questioned this practice, the professor's justification would be that "he" or "man" was used in the generic sense, meaning, he said, that the gendered terms "he" and "man" encompassed all individuals. I did not believe this explanation, since the same professors would identify secretaries and victims and other less powerful individuals in the hypotheticals as females.

I often felt this same sense of dissonance and discomfort in law school when issues surrounding race were being considered. We were wary of having to defend race-conscious remedies or affirmative action plans; wary that our classmates would think that Blacks are unqualified on the merits and are accepted into graduate school or obtain jobs only because of race-conscious plans; wary that our classmates would think that we were sitting in class with them or working in law firms beside them as a result of race-conscious plans. As a result, the participants in the discussions surrounding these issues were often exclusively white.

I can recall only three classes in my entire law school career in which issues specifically related to lesbians or gay men were discussed. Thus, the only things I learned in law school that had to do with a sexual orientation other than heterosexuality were that, as a result of my sexuality, I would be denied the right to marry, my sexual activity could be criminalized, and employers could discriminate against me with impunity.[2]

This semester, Professor Jean Love is teaching a class at the University of Iowa College of Law entitled Anti-Discrimination Law: The Intersections of Race, Sex, and Sexual Orientation. The reading materials for a section of the class dealing with lesbian and gay issues included readings by Audre Lorde[3] and bell hooks,[4] Black female authors who write positively about lesbians and gay men. I think that if, along with reading cases about legalized discrimination against lesbians and gay men, I had also read articles that challenged homophobia, I would not have felt as invisible or legally insignificant.

As a person who is Black and female and lesbian all the time and all at the same time, I cannot always compartmentalize and distinguish either the oppression or the injury. When asked to do so I am reminded of what Audre Lorde has written: "As a Black lesbian feminist comfortable with the many different ingredients of my identity, and a woman committed to racial and sexual freedom from oppression, I find I am constantly being encouraged to pluck out some one aspect of myself and present this as the meaningful whole, eclipsing or denying the other parts of self."[5] Too many times, I have been confronted with racism at meetings of lesbians, and heterosexism at meetings of Blacks.[6] I was, however, profoundly aware of the intersection of the oppressions. I did not publicly identify myself as a lesbian when I was in law school. In fact, I worked very hard to establish an image that was heterosexual, but very progressive on issues of sexuality. At Black Law Students Association meetings I was sure that I was the only lesbian present, although then, and now, I have no idea whether that was true. At the two events of the gay rights organization that I attended under the guise of being intellectually interested in the subject matter, I knew that I was the only Black. I did not personally know any other Black lesbians, in law school or elsewhere.

The discomfort and dissonance did not disappear upon my graduation from law school. I practiced law with a 140-lawyer firm in Baltimore, Maryland, for approximately two years. During that time, the firm never had a Black partner, never had more than twelve female partners, and never had more than four Black associates. There were no identifiable gays or lesbians at the firm either. In fact, when I questioned one of the female partners about the firm's attitude toward gay and lesbian associates, I was told that it would be in my best interest to keep my personal life private. I was thus subject to a condition of employment that my heterosexual colleagues were not.

In the November-December 1990 issue of *Ms.* magazine, Barbara Smith relates a conversation she had with a Black woman graduate student as the student was driving her to the airport following a panel discussion at Yale University.[7] The student asked "how she might survive as an out [of the closet] black lesbian artist in the decades that lay before her."[8] Smith's response inspired me to write this reflection piece: "You don't have many role models, do you?"[9] In the article Smith explains, "Just saying the words made me furious because it struck me how the black women writers, academics, and politicos who protect their closets never think about people like [the student] or about how their silences contribute to the silencing of others."[10]

Last month I found my high school yearbooks. Two of my favorite inscriptions appeared next to one another. One read, "To Angela, a girl who always knows the right things to say." The second, obviously written by someone who knew me better, read: "To Angela, who may not always know the right things to say, but says something nonetheless." Somewhere along the way I stopped talking. I think that it happened in college. I left Chester, Pennsylvania, a city that is at least 80 percent African American, and traveled nearly 400 miles to Houghton College in Houghton, New York. The school had approximately twelve hundred students, less than 5 percent of whom were African American, and was situated in a rural western New York community, in which, as far as I could tell, no African Americans resided. My method of coping with the situation was to take many of my aspects of self—my laughter, my speech, my poetry—place them in a box, secure the lid, and store the box away.[11] It was not until after I completed college and law school and had practiced law for a while that I located my box of self. After I discovered a lesbian support group and an alliance of Black women attorneys, I was able to remove my box from its shelf, pry open the lid, put myself back together, and experience the joy of being all that I am. Having recently found my own voice, I do not want to contribute to the silencing of others.

Audre Lorde writes beautifully about the effects of silencing on the silenced in her essay *The Transformation of Silence Into Language and Action.*[12] She tells a story about a conversation she had with her daughter in which her daughter captured the essence of the spirit-murdering impact of silencing.[13] In response to Lorde's concerns over delivering a paper on the topic of transforming silence into action and language, her daughter said, "Tell them about how you're never really a whole person if you remain silent because there's always that one little piece inside you that wants to be spoken out, and if you keep ignoring it, it gets madder and madder and hotter and hotter, and if you don't speak it out one day it will just up and punch you in the mouth from the inside."[14] There are still times when I am silent, most often because I am afraid, sometimes justifiably, sometimes not. Yet usually I do not achieve anything as a result of my silence. Silence does not cause the fear to disappear. Silence does not make me feel more secure. Silence does not dispel ignorance.

Thinking about my experiences as a law student and lawyer and about breaking through my silence has led me to think about my role as a law professor. My limited experience in the legal academy has shown me that students respond to and respect professors who genuinely care about them as people and as students of the law. I do think that the experiences that I have had as a Black lesbian and the multiple consciousness[15] that I have developed make me an especially effective role model for Black women and for lesbians, two groups of women who have been without very many role models in law teaching for a long time.[16] One of the things that I hope I am able to do, as a professor of the law who is committed to ensuring that students do not feel invisible or legally insignificant in my classroom, is reduce the level of dissonance that students who may not be white, or may not be male, or may not be straight often feel in the classroom.

I wrote this essay not long after I entered law teaching and not long after I discovered the legal scholarship of women of color such as Regina Austin,[17] Kimberlé Crenshaw,[18] Angela Harris,[19] Mari Matsuda,[20] Judy Scales-Trent,[21] and Patricia Williams,[22] and of lesbians such as Patricia Cain[23] and Rhonda Rivera.[24] The writings of these women allowed me to see in a very tangible way that not only do women of color and lesbians belong in law schools and on law school faculties, but also that we need to be vocal about the ways the law and law schools silence us and students. The transformation of silence into language and action is an act of self-revelation, and is therefore dangerous;[25] however, the alternative, remaining silent, is more dangerous, and eventually on some level, deadly.[26]

Even as I was writing this essay I wondered whether the risks of having it published in a national law journal would outweigh any possible benefits the article might reap. I found myself unable to discuss the contents of this essay with colleagues because it is so personal. Recognizing the irony of the situation in light of the theme of my essay, I realized that if I did not submit this essay for publication I would once again be placing bits of myself in a box, on a shelf, perhaps never to be rediscovered.

NOTES

The title of this chapter comes from the poem *A Litany for Survival* by Audre Lorde. The poem reads in part, "and when we speak we are afraid / our words will not be heard / nor welcomed / but when we are silent / we are still afraid / So it is better to speak / remembering / we were never meant to survive." Audre Lorde, *A Litany for Survival, in* The Black Unicorn 31–32 (1978).

1. Angela Harris has labeled the lecturer's type of approach and perspective gender essentialism: "the notion that a unitary, 'essential' women's experience can be isolated and described independently of race, class, sexual orientation and other realities of experience." Angela P. Harris, *Race and Essentialism in Feminist Legal Theory,* 42 Stan. L. Rev. 581, 585 (1990) (also chapter 1 in this volume).

2. I do not think my law school experience was unusual. Conversations with friends who have studied and taught elsewhere lead me to believe that the curricula in most law schools do not adequately address and incorporate issues dealing with alternative sexualities.

3. Audre Lorde was a Black lesbian feminist writer and the author of many books, including Zami: A New Spelling of My Name (1982), her biomythography.

4. bell hooks is the author of Talking Back: Thinking Feminist, Thinking Black (1989). Chapter 17 of her book is entitled *Homophobia in Black Communities.*

5. Audre Lorde, *Age, Race, Class and Sex: Women Redefining Difference, in* Sister Outsider 114, 120 (1984).

6. Heterosexism can be defined as the system of beliefs that recognizes heterosexual roles and behaviors as the only acceptable ones. Heterosexism causes homophobia. Conversation with Papusa Molina, Workshop Leader, Women against Racism Committee, Iowa City, Iowa (Mar. 14, 1991).

7. Barbara Smith is a Black lesbian writer and activist. She is the editor of Home Girls: A Black Feminist Anthology (1983), and is a cofounder of Kitchen Table: Women of Color Press.

8. Barbara Smith, *The NEA Is the Least of It,* Ms., Nov.-Dec. 1990, at 65, 67.

9. *Id.*

10. *Id.*

11. Charles Lawrence, at the 1991 annual meeting of the Association of American Law Schools, told of a similar experience his sister had upon matriculating at Swarthmore College. Statement to the Society of American Law Teachers Robert Cover Memorial Study Group (Jan. 3, 1991).

12. Audre Lorde, *The Transformation of Silence into Language and Action, in* Sister Outsider, *supra* note 5, at 40.

13. Patricia Williams, in her article *Spirit-Murdering the Messenger: The Discourse of Fingerpointing as the Law's Response to Racism,* describes spirit-murder as "disregard for others whose lives qualitatively depend on our regard. . . . [I]ts product is a system of formalized distortions of thought. It produces social structures centered around fear and hate; it provides a tumorous outlet for feelings elsewhere unexpressed." 42 U. Miami L. Rev. 27, 151–52 (1987) (also chapter 28 in this volume).

14. Lorde, *supra* note 12, at 42.

15. Mari Matsuda, *When the First Quail Calls: Multiple Consciousness as Jurisprudential Method,* 11 Women's Rts. L. Rep. 7 (1989). Matsuda explains multiple consciousness as "not a random ability to see all points of view, but a deliberate choice to see the world from the standpoint of the oppressed." *Id.* at 9.

16. I have not had any Black female teachers since nursery school. I did, however, work as a research assistant for Anita Allen at the University of Pittsburgh School of Law. I am not saying that I did not have any role models until that time, since that is not true. However, I can still remember the pride and excitement I felt when Allen was introduced to the class on orientation day, and my immediate adoption of her as a mentor and role model.

17. Regina Austin is the author of *Sapphire Bound!,* 1989 Wis. L. Rev. 539 (also chapter 35 in this volume). Every time I read this article I am inspired by her declaration that "I simply refuse to be doubly or triply bound in the negative sense of the term by a racist, sexist, and class-stratified society without its hearing from me." *Id.* at 549. I would add heterosexism to her list of oppressions operating in society.

18. Kimberlé Crenshaw is the author of *Demarginalizing the Intersection of Race and Sex: A Black Feminist Critique of Antidiscrimination Doctrine, Feminist Theory and Antiracist Policies,* 1989 U. Chi. Legal F. 139. I met Crenshaw at the Critical Race Theory Conference in Madison, Wisconsin, in November 1990. She is one of the first people who encouraged me to consider writing about the intersection of race, gender and sexuality.

19. *See supra* note 1.

20. *See supra* note 15.

21. Judy Scales-Trent is the author of *Commonalities: On Being Black and White, Different and the Same,* 2 Yale J.L. & Feminism 305 (1990). Scales-Trent, a Black woman who appears white, writes about the intersection of race and color as well as about the intersection of gender and sexuality. She writes that just as she becomes more clear about who she is by "coming out" to people as a Black woman, her lesbian sisters "come out" as lesbians so that they can be honest with themselves and with other people. *Id.* at 321–22. I feel that when I am silent about my sexuality, in situations where speaking out is called for (for instance, I am ashamed to number the conversations in which I have been a participant where anti-lesbian jokes and statements were made and I did not protest), I internalize and perpetuate the fallacy that silence is a suitable response.

22. *See supra* note 13.

23. Patricia Cain is the author of *Feminist Jurisprudence: Grounding the Theories,* 4 Berkeley Women's L.J. 191 (1989–90).

24. Rhonda Rivera is the author of *Queen Law: Sexual Orientation Law in the Mid-Eighties,* pts. 1 and 2, 10 Dayton L. Rev. 459 (1985) and 11 Dayton L. Rev. 275 (1986).

25. Lorde, *supra* note 12, at 42.

26. ACT UP, the AIDS Coalition to Unleash Power, has shown the world in a powerful way through the slogan "Silence = Death" that this failure to transform silence into language and action, in this case to transform silence into research for a cure for AIDS, quite literally leads to death. The slogan is frequently printed in white, underneath a pink triangle on a black background. The pink triangle is the symbol used in Nazi concentration camps to identify gays. The emblem declares that "in the time of AIDS the death camps are not forgotten." Christopher Knight, *Art Review,* L.A. Times, July 18, 1990, at F1.

7 | Máscaras, Trenzas, y Greñas: Un/masking the Self While Un/braiding Latina Stories and Legal Discourse

Margaret E. Montoya

MÁSCARAS: UN/MASKING THE SELF

> I put on my masks, my
> costumes and posed for each
> occasion. I conducted myself
> well, I think, but
> an emptiness
> grew
> that no thing
> could fill. I think
> I hungered for myself.[1]

MY STORY

One of the earliest memories from my school years is of my mother braiding my hair, making my *trenzas*.[2] In 1955, I was seven years old. I was in second grade at the Immaculate Conception School in Las Vegas, New Mexico. Our family home with its outdoor toilet was on an unpaved street, one house from the railroad track. I remember falling asleep to the subterranean rumble of the trains.

That year was an important one in my development, in my understanding of myself in relation to Anglo society.[3] I remember 1955 as the year I began to think about myself in relation to my classmates and their families. I began to feel different and to adjust my behavior accordingly.

We dressed in front of the space heater in the bedroom we shared with my older brother. Catholic school girls wore uniforms. We wore blue jumpers and white blouses. I remember my mother braiding my hair and my sister's. I can still feel the part she would draw with the point of the comb. She would begin at the top of my head, pressing down as she drew the comb down to the nape of my neck. "Don't move," she would say as she held the two hanks of hair, checking to make sure that the part was straight. Only then would she begin, braiding as tightly as our squirming would allow, so the braids could withstand our running, jumping, and hanging from the monkey bars at recess. "I don't want you to look *greñudas* [uncombed]," my mother would say.

My mother's use of both English and Spanish gave emphasis to what she was saying. She used Spanish to talk about what was really important: her feelings, her doubts, her worries.[4] She also talked to us in Spanish about gringos, Mexicanos, and the relations between them. Her stories were sometimes about being treated outrageously by gringos, her anger controlled and her bitterness implicit. She also told stories about Anglos she admired—those who were egalitarian, smart, well-spoken, and well-mannered.

Sometimes she spoke Spanish so as not to be understood by Them. Usually, however, Spanish and English were woven together.[5] *Greñuda* was one of many words encoded with familial and cultural meaning. My mother used the word to admonish us, but she was not warning us about name-calling: *greñuda* was not an epithet our schoolmates were likely to use. Instead, I heard my mother saying something that went beyond well-groomed hair and being judged by our appearance—she could offer strategies for passing *that* scrutiny. She used the Spanish word partly because there is no precise English equivalent, but also because she was interpreting the world for us.

The real message of *greñudas* was conveyed through the use of the Spanish word—it was unspoken and subtextual. She was teaching us that our world was divided, that They-Who-Don't-Speak-Spanish would see us as different, would judge us, would find us lacking. Her lessons about combing, washing, and doing homework frequently relayed a deeper message: be prepared, because you will be judged by your skin color, your names,[6] your accents. They will see you as ugly, lazy, dumb, and dirty.

As I put on my uniform and as my mother braided my hair, I changed; I became my public self. My *trenzas* announced that I was clean and well cared for at home. My *trenzas* and school uniform blurred the differences between my family's economic and cultural circumstances and those of the more economically comfortable Anglo students. I welcomed the braids and uniform as a disguise that concealed my minimal wardrobe and the relative poverty in which my family lived.

As we walked to school, away from home, away from the unpaved streets, away from the "Spanish" to the "Anglo" part of town, I felt both drawn to and repelled by my strange surroundings. I wondered what Anglos were like in their big houses.[7] What did they eat?[8] How did they furnish their homes? How did they pass the time? Did my English sound like theirs? Surely their closets were filled with dresses, sweaters and shoes, *apenas estrenados*.[9]

I remember being called on one afternoon in second grade to describe what we had eaten for lunch. Rather than admit to eating *caldito* (soup) *y tortillas*,[10] partly because I had no English words for those foods, I regaled the class with a story about what I assumed an "American" family would eat at lunch: pork chops, mashed potatoes, green salad, sliced bread, and apple pie. The nun reported to my mother that I had lied. Afraid of being mocked, I unsuccessfully masked the truth, and consequently revealed more about myself than I concealed.

In those days, before the ecumenical reforms, Catholicism still professed great concern about sinning. Although elementary school children were too young to commit most sins, lying was a real spiritual danger. Paradoxically, we were surrounded by Truth disguised in myriad ways. Religious language was oblique and filled with multiple meanings: Virgin Mother, Risen Son, bread that was the Body and wine that was the Blood. Our teachers, the Nuns, were completely hidden— women without surnames, families, friends, or homes of their own. They embodied the collapsing of the private into the public. Their black and white habits hid their breasts, waists, legs, hair color, and hair texture.

Our school was well integrated with "Spanish" students because it was located in a town with a predominantly Latino population.[11] The culture of the school, however, was overwhelmingly Anglo and middle-class. The use of Spanish was frowned on and occasionally punished.[12] If a child had any trace of an accent when speaking English, the accent would be pointed out and sarcastically mocked.[13] This mocking persisted even though, and maybe because, some of the nuns were also "Spanish."[14]

I remember being assigned to tutor another second-grader in reading. He wore denim overalls, had his hair shaved for some medical procedure, and spoke mostly Spanish. I think of him now, and perhaps thought of him then, as being exposed— exposed by not being able to read, exposed by not having a uniform, exposed by not having hair, exposed by not knowing English. From my perspective as a child, it all seemed connected somehow—Spanishness, sickness, poverty, and ignorance.

By the age of seven, I was keenly aware that I lived in a society that had little room for those who were poor, brown, or female. I was all three. I moved between dualized worlds: private/public, Catholic/secular, poverty/privilege, Latina/Anglo.[15] I moved between these worlds. My *trenzas* and school uniform were a cultural disguise. They were also a precursor for the more elaborate mask I would later develop.

Presenting an acceptable face, speaking without a Spanish accent, hiding what we really felt—masking our inner selves—were defenses against racism passed on to us by our parents to help us get along in school and in society. We learned that it was safer to be inscrutable. We absorbed the necessity of constructing and maintaining a disguise for use in public. We struggled to be seen as Mexican but also wanted acceptance as Americans at a time when the mental image conjured up by that word included only Anglos.

OUTSIDER MASKS

Being masked may be a universal condition, in that all of us control how we present ourselves to others.[16] There is, however, a fundamental difference when one feels masked because one is a member of one or more oppressed groups within the society. When members of the dominant culture mask themselves to control the impressions they make, such behavior is not inherently self-loathing. But when we attempt to mask immutable characteristics of skin color, eye shape, or hair texture because they historically have been loathsome to the dominant culture, then the masks of acculturation can be experienced as self-hate. Moreover, unmasking for members of the dominant culture does not involve the fear or depth of humiliation that it does for the subordinated, for whom the unmasking is often involuntary and unexpected.

For Outsiders, unmasking is a holistic experience: I do not have separate masks for my femaleness and Latina-ness. The construction of my public persona involves all that I am. My public face is an adjustment to the present and a response to the past. Any unmasking resonates through the pathways of my memory. For Outsiders, the necessity of unmasking has been historical. Strategies are passed on from one generation to another to accommodate, to resist, to subvert oppressive forces. Involuntary unmasking is painful; it evokes echoes of past hurts, hurts one has suffered, and hurts one has heard stories about.

Outsiders are also faced with the gnawing suspicion that the public identities available to them are limited to those reflecting the values, norms, and behavior of the dominant ideology. Through my cultural disguise, I sought to mirror the behavior of those who mattered more than I. As a child, I altered or denied my language, my clothes, my foods. My *trenzas* helped me fit in, get by, move up. As an adult, I still alter or deny my self/selves, both consciously and unconsciously.

A significant aspect of subordination is the persistence with which we mimic the styles, preferences, and mannerisms of those who dominate us, even when we have become aware of the mimicry. Lost to the Outsider are those identities that would have developed but for our real and perceived needs to camouflage ourselves in the masks of the Master. Lost to all are the variety of choices, the multiplicity of identities that would be available if we were not trapped by the dynamics of subordination, of privilege.

For stigmatized groups[17] such as persons of color, the poor, women, and gays and lesbians, assuming a mask is comparable to being "on stage." Being "on stage" is frequently experienced as being acutely aware of one's words, affect, tone of voice, movements, and gestures because they seem out of sync with what one is feeling and thinking.[18] At unexpected moments, we fear that we will be discovered to be someone or something other than who or what we pretend to be. Lurking just behind our carefully constructed disguises and lodged within us is the child whom no one would have mistaken for being anything other than what she was. Her masking was yet imperfect, still in rehearsal, and at times unnecessary.

New discursive formats, including the use of Latina autobiography in legal scholarship, enable us to reinvent ourselves. We can reject the dualistic patriarchal masks that we shrank behind and seize instead our multiple, contradictory, and ambiguous identities. As we reinvent ourselves we import words and concepts into English and into academic discourse from formerly prohibited languages and taboo knowledge. The disruption of hegemonic tranquility, the ambiguity of discursive variability, the cacophony of polyglot voices, the chaos of radical pluralism are the desired by-products of transculturation, of *mestizaje*.[19] The pursuit of *mestizaje*, with its emphasis on our histories, our ancestries, and our past experiences, can give us renewed appreciation for who we are as well as a clearer sense of who we can become.

Our conceptual *trenzas*, our rebraided ideas, even though they may appear unneat or *greñudas* to others, suggest new opportunities for unmasking the subordinating effects of legal discourse. Our rebraided ideas, the *trenzas* of our multicultural lives, offer personally validating interpretations for the *máscaras* we choose to wear. My masks are what they are, in Santayana's words, merely "arrested expressions and echoes of feelings," the cuticles that protect my heart.[20]

NOTES

Máscaras, Trenzas, y Greñas: masks, braids, and uncombed, messy hair.

1. Alma Villanueva, *Mother, May I?, in* Contemporary Chicana Poetry 303, 324 (Marta Ester Sánchez ed., 1985).

2. Other women of color have used hair metaphors in discussing the quotidian experience of subordination. *See, e.g.,* Paulette M. Caldwell, *A Hair Piece: Perspectives on the Intersection of Race and Gender,* 1991 Duke L.J. 365, 381–83 (also chapter 36 of this volume). Analyzing Renee Rogers v. American Airlines, 527 F. Supp. 229 (S.D.N.Y. 1981) (allowing employer to prohibit braided hairstyles), Caldwell writes, "Hair seems to be such a little thing. Yet it is the little things, the small everyday realities of life, that reveal the deepest meanings and values of a culture, give legal theory its grounding, and test its legitimacy." Caldwell, *supra,* at 370.

3. "Anglo" and "gringo" are regionalisms used in the Southwest to name and describe the dominant culture and ideology. This article also uses the designation of "Latina/o" to identify U.S. residents of Mexican, South and Central American, Puerto Rican, or Cuban descent. Occasionally the word is used to make connections to the subordinated peoples of this continent. In some instances, however, I have used alternate designations, such as "Mexican-American," "Chicana," or "Spanish," to remain faithful to the literature being discussed or because the terms have particular meaning.

4. My mother, like most bilingual Latinas or Latinos, moved between English and Spanish in the same sentence. This type of language mixing has been dismissed as Tex-Mex or Spanglish. Analyses of this code switching have revealed that it is linguistically competent. *See* Rodolfo Jacobson, *The Social Implications of Intra-Sentential Code-Switching, in* New Directions in Chicano Scholarship 227, 240–41 (Richard Romo & Raymond Paredes eds., 1978) (observing that such code mixing is linked to psychological and sociological cues; for

instance, some speakers switch to the stronger language when the topic relates to emotional issues and back to the other language when the conversation returns to general topics).

5. At various points throughout this article, I use the passive voice when I am making a connection to what I believe are collective experiences. While this construction is disfavored in legal writing, the purposely vague subject is meant to suggest an inclusiveness to the idea or the experience being described.

6. Names and surnames always have been cultural markers among Latinas/os. Many of us suffered an early trauma when our names were anglicized as we began school. I did not have that experience. I was named Margaret Elizabeth for my maternal grandmother, who was half Irish. Her name was Margaret Wallace. My brother was named Richard David; he goes by Ricardo. My sister was named Maria Elena; she goes by Mary Ellen.

7. For empirical information on various aspects of Chicano family life, demonstrating the differences between Chicano and Anglo kinship structures, see Oscar Ramírez & Carlos H. Arce, *The Contemporary Chicano Family: An Empirically Based Review, in* Explorations in Chicano Psychology 3 (Augustine Barón, Jr., ed., 1981).

8. Food habits can identify a particular ethnic group or nationality in a pejorative manner. For example, a common racial slur used for Latinos is "beaners." *See* Paul Fieldhouse, Food and Nutrition: Customs and Culture 82–83 (1986). Studies have shown that immigrants more rapidly change their style of clothing than their food preferences. Mexican-Americans have been shown to retain beans, rice, and tortillas in the diet even as the family income allows for convenience foods. Laurie Carter, Attitudes of Mexican-American Mothers about Food and Nutrition (1981) (unpublished M.A. thesis, California State University (Long Beach)).

9. *Apenas estrenados* is a Spanish concept that has no English equivalent. *Apenas* translates as "hardly," "barely." *Estrenar* connotes wearing something for the first time and conveys the special privilege that attaches to the first wearing. We had few opportunities to *estrenar* new clothes.

10. George Sanchez, "Go after the Women": Americanization and the Mexican Immigrant Woman, 1915–1929 (1984) (unpublished manuscript, SCCR Working Paper no. 6, on file with the Stanford Center for Chicano Research), describes programs aimed at Mexican women established during the period 1915–29 for the purpose of changing the cultural values of immigrant families. Two particular areas of focus were diet and health.

In the eyes of reformers, the typical noon lunch of the Mexican child, thought to consist of a "folded tortilla with no filling," became the first step in a life of crime. With "no milk or fruit to whet the appetite," the child would become lazy and subsequently "take food from the lunch boxes of more fortunate children" in order to appease his/her hunger. "Thus," reformers alleged, "the initial step in a life of thieving is taken." Teaching immigrant women proper food values would keep the head of the family out of jail, keep the rest of the family off the charity lists, and save the taxpayers a great amount of money. *Id.* at 17 (quoting Pearl Idelia Ellis, Americanization Through Homemaking 19–29 (1929)).

11. Attendance at highly integrated schools is an important factor in the academic success of professionally educated Latinas. *See* Patricia Gándara, *Passing through the Eye of the Needle: High-Achieving Chicanas*, 4 Hispanic J. Behav. Sci. 167, 167 (1982).

12. *See, e.g.,* Renato Rosaldo, Culture and Truth: The Remaking of Social Analysis 149 (1989):

> For Chicanos, "our" felt oppression derives as much from cultural domination as from the brute facts of poverty. During my junior high school days in Tucson, Arizona, for example, Chicano students could be obliged to bend over and grab their ankles so that teachers could

give them "swats" with a board. This punishment somehow fit the "crime" of speaking Spanish in school. . . . In "our" everyday lives, cultural domination surfaces as myriad mundane sites of cultural repression and personal humiliation.

13. *See* Mari J. Matsuda, *Voices of America: Accent, Antidiscrimination Law, and a Jurisprudence for the Last Reconstruction*, 100 Yale L.J. 1329, 1391–92 (1991) (asserting that accent resides in one of those "sacred places of the self" and arguing for an extension of Title VII to outlaw accent discrimination). Accents have complex intragroup aspects.

14. For analyses of the internalization of colonization, see, e.g., Frantz Fanon, Black Skin, White Masks (1967); Antonio Gramsci, Letters from Prison, vols. 1–2 (Frank Rosengarten ed. & Raymond Rosenthal trans., 1994); Albert Memmi, The Colonizer and the Colonized (1965).

15. *Cf.* Francoise Lionnet, Autobiographical Voices: Race, Gender, Self-Portraiture 18 (1989):

[T]o internalize patriarchal law is to create mutually exclusive categories of "reality" (male/female; white/black; primitive/civilized; autobiographical/fictional; etc.) and to forget that the production of discourses can function according to Darwinian divergence: that a given space (text) will support more life (generate more meanings) if occupied by diverse forms of life (languages). . . . [S]ubvert[ing] all binary modes of thought . . . privileg[es] (more or less explicitly) the intermediary spaces where boundaries become effaced and Manichean categories collapse into each other.

16. *See* Erving Goffman, The Presentation of the Self in Everyday Life 9–10 (1959).

17. Although I emphasize group status by relying on categorical discourse, my purpose is not to essentialize disparate experiences. I seek to identify the subordinating effects of the masking process and the manner in which masking can reinforce the meanings of the categories. *See generally* Angela Harris, *Categorical Discourse and Dominance Theory,* 5 Berkeley Women's L.J. 181 (1990) (discussing categorical discourse and essentialism).

18. Andrew J. Weigert et al., Society and Identity 58–60 (1986):

Problematic situations are characterized by a sense of being personally "on stage." When an individual feels "on," the taken-for-granted and undoubted self-consciousness of one's presented identity is lost, and a dramaturgical consciousness emerges. . . .

Stigmatized persons necessarily learn to develop skill in handling problematic situations. . . . [M]ental patients, closet homosexuals, ethnics who pass, transsexuals who emerge . . . constitute a constituency highly skilled in the universal tasks of dramaturgical effectiveness. Those type of persons are explicitly skilled at what we all learn to do more or less well and without forethought: present, negotiate, and control multiple identities in a reasonable, organized hierarchy.

19. Angela Harris has used Gloria Anzaldúa's *mestiza* representation to write about the "personal i, not the universal unmarked I." In concluding a narrative that I, as a Latina, found particularly moving and evocative, she writes,

Quietly my students and colleagues claim their invisibility. They resent a world that gives them gender, race, class, sexuality. They wish to be talking heads. They wish we could all just be individuals.

La mestiza dances at the funeral of the individual in a red dress.

What is la mestiza's distinctive contribution to her students, colleagues, and institutions? Restlessness, ambiguity, disruption. Creative chaos. And also, maybe most important: Her refusal to be either innocent or invisible.

Angela Harris, *Women of Color in Legal Education: Representing La Mestiza*, 6 Berkeley Women's L.J. 107, 112 (1991).

20. Santayana writes,

[M]asks are arrested expressions and admirable echoes of feeling, at once faithful, discreet, and superlative. Living things in contact with the air must acquire a cuticle, and it is not urged against cuticles that they are not hearts; yet some philosophers seem to be angry with images for not being things, and with words for not being feelings. Words and images are like shells, not less integral parts of nature than are the substances they cover, but better addressed to the eye and more open to observation.

George Santayana, Soliloquies in England and Later Soliloquies 131–32 (1924).

Questions and Suggested Readings for Part 1

1. Angela Harris critiques Catharine MacKinnon for essentializing women's experiences. Is it possible to formulate a political or social theory without engaging in some form of essentialism? In our efforts to ameliorate racial subordination, isn't it sometimes necessary to speak about discrimination against blacks as a group, without further particularity? Why, then, is it problematic to speak about discrimination against women as women?

2. Angela Gilmore argues that "it is better to speak" about one's sexual identity than to be silent. Does this approach always work or make sense? Is it clear that the psychological and emotional costs associated with "silence" (i.e., not coming out of the closet) outweigh the physical, economic, and social cost associated with "speaking" (i.e., living openly as a homosexual)?

3. Several of the authors in part 1 invoke some notion of multiple consciousness as a basis for constructing a feminist agenda. But is it possible for a feminist agenda to negotiate equitably various levels of consciousness? In other words, black women's multiple consciousness will necessarily be different from white women's multiple consciousness; which will necessarily be different from Asian American women's multiple consciousness. Is it possible for a single feminist agenda to incorporate all the differences? Or does feminism necessarily involve exclusion?

4. Adrien Wing and Angela Gilmore discuss aspects of the spirit injury/spirit murder concept that was originated by Patricia Williams. (Her article on this topic can be found in part 5.) How does the race-sex analogy described by Grillo and Wildman contribute to the spirit injury of women of color? How does invisibility add to the spirit injury? How could we create a legal remedy for spirit murder? Does

the tort (personal injury) remedy for intentional infliction of emotional distress hold some possibilities?

5. Trina Grillo and Stephanie Wildman distinguish between white supremacy and racism. Isn't this distinction more semantical than substantive? Grillo and Wildman further argue that there are dangers involved in analogizing sex discrimination to race discrimination. Do the benefits of such analogies subvert the costs?

For further reading, see Kimberlé Crenshaw, *A Black Feminist Critique of Anti-Discrimination Law and Politics, in* The Politics of Law (D. Kairys ed., 1990); Richard Delgado, The Rodrigo Chronicles: Conversations about Race in America 106 (1995) (Rodrigo's Sixth Chronicle: Intersections, Essences, and the Dilemma of Social Reform); Marlee Kline, *Race, Racism, and Feminist Legal Theory,* 12 Harv. Women's L.J. 115 (1989); Mari Matsuda, *When the First Quail Calls: Multiple Consciousness as Jurisprudential Method,* 14 Women's Rts. L. Rep. 297 (1992); Pam Smith, *We Are Not Sisters: African-American Women and the Freedom to Associate and Disassociate,* 66 Tul. L. Rev. 1467 (1992); Richard Wasserstrom, *Racism, Sexism, and Preferential Treatment: An Approach to the Topics,* 24 UCLA L. Rev. 581 (1977); Joan Williams, *Dissolving the Sameness/Difference Debate: A Modern Path beyond Essentialism in Feminist and Critical Race Theory,* 1991 Duke L.J. 296.

For sources on Critical Legal Studies, see Critical Legal Studies (James Boyle ed., 1992); Richard Delgado, *Critical Legal Studies and the Reality of Race: Does the Fundamental Contradiction Have a Corollary?,* 23 Harv. C.R.-C.L. L. Rev. 133 (1989); Richard Delgado, *The Ethereal Scholar: Does Critical Legal Studies Have What Minorities Want?,* 22 Harv. C.R.-C.L. L. Rev. 301 (1987); Critical Legal Studies (Peter Fitzpatrick & Alan Hunt eds., 1987); Critical Legal Studies (Allan C. Hutchinson ed., 1989); Mark Kelman, A Guide to Critical Legal Studies (1987); Matthew Kramer, Critical Legal Theory and the Challenge of Feminism: A Philosophical Reconception (1995).

For sources on Critical Race Theory, see Roy Brooks and Mary Jo Newborn, *Critical Race Theory and Classical-Liberal Civil Rights Scholarship: A Distinction without a Difference?,* 82 Cal. L. Rev. 787 (1994); Critical Race Theory: The Key Writings That Formed the Movement (Kimberlé Crenshaw et al. eds., 1996); Critical Race Theory: The Cutting Edge (Richard Delgado ed., 1995); Alan D. Freeman, *Racism, Rights, and the Quest for Equality of Opportunity: A Critical Legal Essay,* 23 Harv. C.R.-C.L. L. Rev. 295 (1988); Mari Matsuda et al., Words That Wound: Critical Race Theory, Assaultive Speech, and the First Amendment (1993) (containing a summary of CRT at 6); Gerald Torres, *Critical Race Theory: The Decline of the Universalist Ideal and the Hope of Plural Justice: Some Observations and Questions of an Emerging Phenomenon,* 75 Minn. L. Rev. 993 (1991); Robert Williams, *Taking Rights Aggressively: The Perils and Promise of Critical Legal Studies for People of Color,* 5 Law & Ineq. J. 103 (1987).

For general works on feminism and sex discrimination law, see Katherine Bartlett, Gender and Law: Theory, Doctrine, Commentary (1995); Feminist Legal Theory:

Readings in Law and Gender (Katherine P. Bartlett & Rosanne Kennedy eds., 1991); Mary Becker et al., Feminist Jurisprudence: Taking Women Seriously (1994); Pat Cain, *Feminist Jurisprudence: Grounding the Theories,* 4 Berkeley Women's L.J. 199 (1989); J. Donovan, Feminist Theory: The Intellectual Traditions of American Feminism (1990); Feminist Theory, Conflicts in Feminism (M. Hirsch & E. Keller eds., 1990); M. Humm, The Dictionary of Feminist Theory (1990); Sex-Based Discrimination: Text, Cases and Materials (Herma Hill Kay ed., 3rd ed. 1988); Catharine MacKinnon, Feminism Unmodified: Discourses on Life and Law (1987); Carrie Menkel-Meadow, *Feminist Legal Theory, Critical Legal Studies, and Legal Education, or The Fem-Crits Go to Law School,* 38 J. Legal Educ. 61 (1988); Martha Minow, Making All the Difference: Inclusion, Exclusion and American Law (1990); Feminism/Postmodernism (L. Nicholson ed., 1990); Joan Nordquist, Feminist Theory: A Bibliography (1992); Feminist Legal Theory (Frances E. Olsen ed., 1994); Deborah Rhode, Justice and Gender (1992); Deborah Rhode, *Feminist Critical Theories,* 42 Stan. L. Rev. 617 (1990); Elizabeth Spelman, Inessential Woman: Problems of Exclusion in Feminist Thought (1988); Feminist Legal Theory: Applications (D. Kelly Weisberg ed., 1995); Feminist Legal Theory: Foundations (D. Kelly Weisberg ed., 1993); Robin West, *Deconstructing the CLS-Fem Split,* 2 Wis. Women's L.J. 85 (1986).

For nonlegal works on women of color and feminism, see Patricia Hill Collins, Black Feminist Thought: Knowledge, Consciousness, and the Politics of Empowerment (1991); Angela Davis, Women, Race, and Class (1981); Paula Giddings, When and Where I Enter: The Impact of Black Women on Race and Sex in America (1984); bell hooks, Ain't I a Woman? (1981); bell hooks, Feminist Theory: From Margin to Center (1984); bell hooks, Killing Rage: Ending Racism (1995); bell hooks, Talking Back: Thinking Feminist, Thinking Black (1989); bell hooks, Yearning: Race, Gender and Cultural Politics (1990); All the Women Are White, All the Men are Black, but Some of Us Are Brave (Gloria Hull et al. eds., 1982); Theorizing Black Feminisms: The Visionary Pragmatism of Black Women (Stanlie James & Albina Busia eds., 1993); Kumari Jayawardena, Feminism and Nationalism in the Third World (1986); Deborah King, *Multiple Jeopardy, Multiple Consciousness: The Context of a Black Feminist Ideology,* 14 Signs 42 (1988); Black Women in White America (Gerda Lerner ed., 1972); Audre Lorde, Sister Outsider (1984); Afrekete: An Anthology of Black Lesbian Writing (Catherine McKinley & L. Joyce Delaney eds., 1995); Third World Women and the Politics of Feminism (Chandra Mohanty et al. eds., 1991); This Bridge Called My Back: Writings by Radical Women of Color (Cherríe Moraga and Gloria Anzaldúa eds., 1981); Home Girls: A Black Feminist Anthology (Barbara Smith ed., 1983).

2 | Outsiders in the Academy

Part 2 explores the lives of the women of color who now struggle and survive in higher education. The unit must be read in the context of Derrick Bell's spring 1990 decision to leave his tenured full professorship at Harvard Law School because of its failure to hire and tenure any women of color. His boycott made national headlines and evoked responses such as "The Harvard Law School is not a southern lunch counter." One of the arguments raised by Bell and others was the need for women of color to serve as role models. Regina Austin of the University of Pennsylvania Law School was a visiting professor at Harvard at the time, and she was immediately followed by Anita Allen of Georgetown Law School. Neither woman subsequently received a permanent job offer from the Harvard law faculty. As of the writing of this volume, there are still no women of color or any Asian, Latino, or Native American males on the Harvard law faculty.

Bell, who wrote the foreword to this volume, refused to return to Harvard after his two-year leave period expired, and the university subsequently terminated him. (He currently teaches at the New York University Law School, which has two tenured women of color, former judge Peggy Davis and Paulette Caldwell, whose work is featured in part 6. See the bibliography for citations to Davis's work. Bell's views on his boycott can be found in *Confronting Authority: Reflections of an Ardent Protester* [1994]. This book has been reviewed by the editor in the *Harvard BlackLetter Journal* [1995].)

Using the narrative technique of the CRT movement, the authors discuss how they are viewed as outsiders, often sought out only for their role model potential. Although they have achieved the rarified heights of the professorate, they are still viewed as undeserving and inferior by some of their colleagues and their students. While these women all happen to be affiliated with the legal academy, their experiences will resonate with many women who work in corporations, government, and the not-for-profit sector as well. Additionally, students of color and white women in university settings may also relate to the token situation.

Lani Guinier, one of the two black women law professors generally known by the American public, provides a piece written well before she was nominated by President Clinton for a Justice Department position. In *Of Gentlemen and Role Models*, she discusses the value of role models who become true mentors to all their students. She reflects on the alienation that women of color face in universities because they do not conform to the faculty notion of what an educated gentleman should be.

In *On Being a Role Model*, Anita L. Allen discusses Derrick Bell's protest as it took place right after she had accepted a visiting offer from Harvard. She analyzes the power and the limitations of relying primarily on black women's value as role models as a justification for hiring them. She distinguishes between three kinds of role models—ethical templates, symbols, and nurturers—and points out that black women cannot be hired solely to be role models. They must be great scholars, teachers, and service providers as well.

Linda S. Greene started teaching in 1978, when there may have been only a dozen women of color teaching in the legal academy. She adds to the theme of part 2 in *Tokens, Role Models, and Pedagogical Politics: Lamentations of an African American Female Law Professor*. Greene points out the political nature of tokenism and discusses three perceptual tendencies of a token: visibility, contrast, and assimilation. These tendencies imply that women of color are inferior, unsuitable, and inappropriate to profess. Yet paradoxically, tokenism admits the possibility of individual success without questioning the concept of group inferiority.

Taunya Lovell Banks, a third-generation college teacher, delves into the difference between role models and mentors in *Two Life Stories: Reflections of One Black Woman Law Professor*. The term "mentor" has a scholarly connotation that the role model concept does not. Utilizing the storytelling technique of CRT, Banks focuses on how the life experiences of women of color can enrich the academy. Her story involves a group of well-dressed black female law professors who were feared by white women in a high-rise luxury apartment building. The white women would not get on the elevator with the black women. Banks then focuses on how her gender and class status did not shield her from the generalized fear of black people as criminal.

In *Law Professors of Color and the Academy: Of Poets and Kings*, Cheryl I. Harris mentions how her own attainment of a position as the first black tenure-track professor at the Chicago-Kent Law School, despite a nonconventional career path, was linked with Derrick Bell's Harvard protest. She utilizes the work of Nigerian novelist and poet Chinua Achebe to comment on the responsibilities of people of color in the academy. Achebe calls for the poet to be in trouble with the king, if she is to be true to her own work. Similarly, professors of color, as outsiders in the academy, need to be able to confront power and create a jurisprudence of resistance by telling different stories and making the lives of the invisible visible. Harris has taken her own advice and subsequently published a pathbreaking work entitled *Whiteness as Property* in the *Harvard Law Review* (1993).

Margalynne J. Armstrong focuses on a student's comment in *Meditations on Being Good*. She deconstructs the possible meanings of a black female student's comment to her as the first black female professor, "Girl, you'd better be good." By interpreting the comment as advice, warning, plea, cheer, and challenge, Armstrong highlights the burdens that women of color may feel in any environment where they are tokens.

Jennifer M. Russell, the first black female law professor at Case Western Reserve University, provides her reaction to a *National Geographic* magazine cover of a gorilla placed in her mailbox in *On Being a Gorilla in Your Midst, or The Life of One Blackwoman in the Legal Academy*. To her, the message was clear. Women of color in the academy are not even human. They are hired for "diversity" reasons that assume their inferiority, as juxtaposed to the "merit" reason that is used to hire white males. The discussion then focuses on whether merit can be sacrificed for diversity.

Rachel F. Moran of the University of California at Berkeley is the first Latina to teach at an American law school outside Puerto Rico. In *Full Circle,* she discusses both the individual commitments and the societal transformations that have constituted her archipelago of upward mobility. Moran discusses how it feels to be asked to implement the University of California Board of Regents decision to end affirmative action.

Finally, Anita F. Hill, the first black tenured professor at the University of Oklahoma Law School, focuses on the case of Ada Lois Sipuel Fisher, the first black woman law student at the law school. In *A Tribute to Thurgood Marshall: A Man Who Broke with Tradition on Issues of Race and Gender,* Hill addresses the little-known fact that *Gaines ex rel. Canada v. Missouri* and *Sweatt v. Painter* were not the only pre-*Brown v. Board of Education* cases that attacked segregation in law schools. Thurgood Marshall, as an attorney for the NAACP, challenged notions held by the black and white community about gender and race when he chose to represent a black woman in her ultimately successful quest to attend the University of Oklahoma. Hill acknowledges that she could not be where she is today as a tenured professor if it were not for Marshall's efforts. Moreover, she would not be able to continue to believe in the ability of the legal system to right injustice if it were not for Thurgood Marshall. Despite the system's failure to treat her appropriately in the Clarence Thomas confirmation hearings, Hill's continued faith speaks for all those who have suffered.

8 Of Gentlemen and Role Models

Lani Guinier

In 1984 I returned to Yale Law School to participate on a panel of mainly black alumni reminiscing about the thirty years since *Brown v. Board of Education*. It was a symposium sponsored by the current black students, who were eager to hear the voices of those who came before them. Each of us spoke for ten minutes in a room adorned by the traditional portraits of larger-than-life white men. It was the same classroom in which, ten years earlier, I had sat for Business Units (corporations) with a white male professor who addressed all of us, male and female, as *gentlemen*. Every morning, at ten minutes after the hour, he would enter the classroom and greet the upturned faces: "Good morning, *gentlemen*." He explained this ritual the first day. He had been teaching for many years; he was a creature of habit. He readily acknowledged the presence of the few "ladies" by then in attendance, but admonished those of us born into that other gender not to feel excluded by his greeting. We, too, in his mind, were simply *gentlemen*.

In his view, *gentlemen* was an asexual term, one reserved for reference to those who shared a certain civilized view of the world and who exhibited a similarly civilized demeanor. If we were not already, law school would certainly teach us how to be *gentlemen*. *Gentlemen* of the bar maintain distance from their clients, are capable of arguing both sides of any issue, and, while situated in a white male perspective, are ignorant of differences of culture, gender, and race.[1] That lesson was at the heart of becoming a professional. By his lights, the greeting was a form of honorific. It evoked the traditional values of legal education to train detached, neutral problem solvers. It anticipated the perception, if not the reality, of all of us becoming *gentlemen*.

It took many intervening years for me to gain the confidence to question directly this term that symbolically stripped me of my race, my gender, and my voice.[2] Now, seated at the podium in the familiar classroom preparing to address a race- and gender-mixed audience, I felt the weight of the presence of those stern, larger-than-life *gentlemen* portraits. For me, this was still not a safe place.[3]

Yet all the men on the panel reminded us how they felt to return "home," with fondly revealed stories about their three years in law school. The three black men may not have felt safe either, but they each introduced their talks with brief yet loving recollections of their law school experiences.

It was my turn. No empowering memories stirred my voice. I had no personal anecdotes for the profound senses of alienation and isolation caught in my throat every time I opened my mouth. Nothing resonated there in that room for a black woman, even after my ten years as an impassioned civil rights attorney. Instead I promptly began my formal remarks, trying as hard as I could to find my voice in a room in which those portraits spoke louder than I ever could. I spoke slowly and carefully, never once admitting, except by my presence on the podium, that I had ever been a student at that school or in that room before. I summoned as much authority as I could to be heard over the sounds of silence erupting from those giant images of *gentlemen* hanging on the wall, and from my own ever-present memory of slowly *disappearing* each morning and becoming a *gentleman* of Business Units I.

Immediately after my presentation, the other black woman on the panel rose to speak. She too did not introduce herself with personal experiences or warm reminiscences about her past association with the law school, but, like me, remained upright and dignified. Afterwards, she and I huddled together to talk about how different the law school we had experienced was from the one recollected by our male colleagues.

We were the *disappeareds,* she and I. The alienation stirred by our return to the place where we first became *gentlemen* was too profound and silencing to share except between ourselves. Continuously scrutinized by those larger-than-life portraits, our humanity, culture, frames of reference, and identity as women of color were dislocated by those memories of our law school experience.[4] We were the minority within a minority whose existence, even physical presence, had been swallowed up within "neutral" terms and other marginalizing traditions associated with educating *gentlemen.* Except at private intersections of blackness and womanhood, our voices had been silenced.[5]

Four years later, at the first Women of Color and the Law Conference, I again returned to Yale Law School. I was invited to speak at a panel entitled "Roots in Our Communities: What Roles for Lawyers and Professionals?" This time I was invited by young female students of color who asked me to speak explicitly about the personal choices and conflicts I had experienced in my career as a black female civil rights attorney. At the conference, I tried to overcome my training as a surrogate *gentleman* who distances her personal self from her professional self. I also tried to overcome the self-protective silence that earlier helped me survive as a *gentleman* in Business Units I. This time I found my voice.

I revealed myself in context, talking about my family, my colleagues, my adversaries, and my clients. In all my professional roles, I experienced what Mari Matsuda calls "multiple consciousness," meaning the bifurcated thinking that allows one to shift back and forth between one's personal consciousness and the white male perspective that dominates the legal profession.[6] Multiple consciousness allows us to operate within mainstream discourse and "within the details of our own special knowledge,"[7] producing both madness and genius.

Multiple consciousness provides intellectual camouflage and emotional support for the outsider who always feels the threeness[8] of race, gender, and marginality. It engenders the spirit of W. E. B. Du Bois's idea of double-consciousness, two warring selves within one black body, living within the "veil" yet gifted with "second-sight."[9] Even while performing insider roles, many of us still function as outsiders. As a black woman civil rights attorney with insider privileges and outsider consciousness, I moved along the perimeter of cultural norms (roots, community, race, and gender) and cultivated status (mainstream professional role) as an explorer and translator of these different identities.

For outsiders, who do not experience the world through color blindness or gender neutrality, multiple consciousness is a cultural norm. Those with outsider conscious-ness live with the peculiar sensation of always looking at one's self through the eyes of others. We are self-conscious precisely because of, not in spite of, our race and gender. In our insider roles, we are still outsiders. As a result, we experience color blindness, gender neutrality, and individual perspective as unfamiliar, mainstream, existential luxuries. "Neutrality" feels very different from the perspective of an outsider.[10] A race-neutral, gender-neutered perspective is apparently enjoyed, to the extent it exists at all, by *gentlemen*: those with a white male perspective, those in the majority, and those *gentlemen* surrogates to whom the majority grants insider privi-leges. For self-conscious, second-sighted outsiders, multiple consciousness centers marginality and names reality.[11]

I recounted to the students at the conference how multiple consciousness often became a burden in my professional relationships with male lawyers and colleagues. I was never certain when to situate myself outside a white male perspective or with whom to disengage from value-neutral problem solving. Even my mother complained that sometimes I "cross-examined" her.

As a law professor, I now take the podium daily under the watchful eyes of those ever-dominant portraits of *gentlemen* that still guard the periphery. I am at the podium; but for women and people of color like myself, this is not yet a safe place. Legal education still teaches value-neutral detachment. As legal educators we still distance our personal selves from our professional selves. Our race and our gender and those of the litigants in our casebooks are still, for the most part, an unspoken subtext.

Nevertheless, recent events remind me that my presence in legal education offers some students refuge. Renewed calls have been made for more black women law professors to be "role models" for black female students.[12] In the conventional sense of the term, I function not only as a teacher but as a symbol for certain student voices and aspirations.[13]

Repercussions from these public calls for more black women role models prompt me to explore further the uneasiness I have with the role model rationale for hiring black women law professors. I do not object to being a role model—even if I had a choice about the matter, which I probably do not. Indeed, I do feel special respon-sibilities as a black woman law professor. But in my eyes I am a mentor more than a role model. As such, I rely on a *communicative* discourse,[14] actively and construc-tively listening to empower my students' own voices. As a teacher I act as a mentor who takes from the margin[15] to facilitate student reflection, insight, and professional responsibility.

I prefer the term "mentor" to "role model" in part because I worry about the way the role model argument is often used to diminish the role outsiders play, a role that benefits insiders as well as other outsiders. I question the way the role model argument measures successful outsiders by an insider yardstick. In addition, I take issue with the representational justification currently in vogue. Role models may grant a passport to power or status to people who then take no account of how they arrived at their destination.

The first problem with the role model argument is that it trivializes the important contribution that outsiders make in diversifying a faculty. Presenting black women law professors primarily as role models ignores their roles as scholars and intellectual leaders whose presence on a faculty might alter the institution's character, introduc-ing a different prism and perspective.[16] Black women legal scholars may challenge their white male colleagues to perform their own roles better.

Using her outsider perspective, a black woman law professor may take "informa-tion from the margin to transform how we think about the whole."[17] She contributes to legal education not merely through her physical presence but by pulling from the richness and rootedness of her experience, by continuously reaching for the transformative possibilities of her role.[18]

But the term "role model" is often used insidiously to refer only to a faculty "mascot" who counsels and keeps students in line, a pacifier of the status quo who won't bite the hand that uplifted her.[19] As prototypes of achievement, role models illustrate, through example, the possibility of success for their constituency. In fact, black role models may become powerful symbolic reference points serving as camou-flage for the continued legacy of past discrimination.[20] Institutionally acceptable role models may simply convey the message "we have overcome" in language calculated to exact admiration from, but not necessarily to inspire, those not yet overcoming.

Black women role models are also defended as group spokespersons or "spokes-models."[21] For example, some blacks claim that as teachers they have "a clear, racial representational function," meaning that they both "comprehend" and "represent" the needs and interests of all black students. Thus, some argue that black women role models *represent* aspiring young black women's needs and affirm the status of black women as law school citizens who can participate in the process of making policy decisions that affect their lives in law school and beyond.

The representational view posits an inspirational figure based disproportionately on mere physical attributes, potentially institutionalizing acceptable or assimilated "*gentlemen* of color" to serve as group representatives to the outside world. By their presence, such role models presumably articulate black interests and act as living symbols of the equal opportunity process.

But these aspects of the role model as spokesperson overemphasize the representational value of passive, individual success unconnected to a dynamic, rooted concept of socially responsible, emotionally engaged leadership. Without an introspective or reflective understanding of their own experience, and an open ear listening and responding to the voices of group and nongroup members, the role model as respectable insider simply presents success as an illusion of privilege. The possibilities for social change become the possibilities for individual advancement.

To realize their value as catalysts for meaningful group "upward mobility" (meaning mobility beyond their own individual advantage), role models need ties to their community: heeding their own accounts of their experience and internalizing reference points of what is or should be responsible and responsive behavior. For me, role models should be more than mere "*gentlemen* of color"—detached, neutral, wooden images for emulation or admiration.

Role models have responsibilities, not just privileges. To be effective group representatives rather than institutionally acceptable achievers, role models must reflect the values of the group whose aspirations they symbolize. Role models should be people with whom members of the out-group identify and should be held accountable to other outsider aspirants. Especially to the extent they are seen as agents for others, role models need to nurture their roots, not just model their roles.

This rootedness needs to be incorporated more directly into the definition of the term "role model." As a self-referential term, "role model" fits only to the extent that my own polar experiences-as a marginalized student and as an empowered and empowering civil rights attorney-root me in the sturdy soil and rocky terrain of multiple consciousness. Rooted in community, a law professor can be "an organic intellectual with affiliations not restricted to the walls of the academic institution."[22] She can produce legal scholarship and engage in educational instruction, not in isolation, but in solidarity with other like-minded scholars. Authenticity and faithfulness to her own voice connect her to "the richness of [her] own experience" and empower her to overcome silencing even by well-intentioned white male colleagues.[23] Her stories help construct a shared reality as a means of "psychic self-preservation" and of "lessening [her] own subordination."[24]

Students—those to whom a teacher should be accountable—often find her stories empowering. In this sense, an effective teacher is less a role model than a mentor, an educator who empowers through feedback, guidance, and sharing rather than one who commands through example, visibility, or physical stature. I find meaning in this alternative, mentoring view of the so-called role model relationship.

Mentors see learning as an active process that builds on students' emotional engagement and emphasizes the mutuality of their role in the educational conversation. Second-sighted within the "veil," a mentor may draw on the outsider consciousness of a minority group advocate and member. From this vantage point, she may see that women and students of color, already silenced by their status and their low numbers, respond less enthusiastically to learning by intimidation than to teaching techniques that foster security and respect for multiple viewpoints.

I do not aspire to be a cultural icon in the conventional or group representative sense. I value my role as a translator and facilitator, a beneficiary of and contributor to a transformed and transformative educational conversation with black women, people of color, and minority viewpoints of all colors. But I play this role not just for black women, or even for people of color. Despite special concerns and responsibilities to engage particular students, I take information from the margin to transform the educational dialogue for *all* my students. I play the role of teacher, mentor, counselor, and educational facilitator for white male students too.[25] As if peeling an onion, I unlayer these preliminary, still tentative thoughts on our continuing negotiation over shared cultural space. I puzzle over demystifying the traditional image of legal educators and lawyers as detached, problem-solving, neutral *gentlemen*. The nature of my own education and of the schools with which I have associated makes it difficult either to reject the opportunities afforded passive symbols of achievement or to transcend traditional, established ways of viewing the world.

Nevertheless, through the process of careful listening and mutual discovery, I join other black women in telling our stories. Collective action engages our personal selves with our professional roles, asserts the value of our lived experiences, takes account of the way others perceive our contribution, and attempts to empower and build community. A rooted, communicative discourse emboldens us to explore the unclaimed territory of our experience on the margins of legal education.

Many more law professors of color, including black women, should be hired, but not simply to "unbecome" *gentlemen* or to become role models instead. Indeed, to the extent that we are role models, it is not because we become *gentlemen* with race and gender added. To be a role model is not just a privilege, but a responsibility to those who come after us and to those whom we follow.

Thus, I write this essay to collaborate with other black women law professors, to find our voices, and to help other people find theirs. And if we find in our voices a race, a gender, and an outsider perspective with roots deep in the rocky terrain and sturdy soil of multiple consciousness, we also may finally dislodge from our throats the alienation and isolation begotten by *gentlemen* orthodoxies, including those ever-present *gentlemen* portraits that still guard the citadel.[26]

NOTES

1. For the purpose of this essay, the term "gentlemen" describes the lawyers' role as that of being neutral, dispassionate, unemotional but courteous advocates for a client's interest. While "gentlemen" primarily refers to males, and in particular to those of good breeding, it assumes men who possess neither a race nor a gender. *Compare* Peggy McIntosh, *White Privilege and Male Privilege: A Personal/Account (Coming to See Correspondences through Work in Women's Studies* (1990) (Working Paper no. 189, Wellesley College Center for Research on Women) (for white men, their race and gender are an "invisible package of unearned assets").

2. In law school I resisted through silence. Only later did I learn to question out loud how much of a gentleman I ever was, or even how much of a lady I ever could be.

3. In some ways, the gigantic male portraits symbolized my alienation as a student from

class, race, and gender privilege. Yet, because I had attended an Ivy League college, perhaps it is surprising that I continued to find the *gentlemen's* portraits so alienating. My intuition is that law school, as a professional school, was simply more homogeneous, with even more explicitly homogenizing institutional norms (such as value-neutral detachment), than I had either expected or previously experienced.

4. *See* Suzanne Homer & Lois Schwartz, *Admitted but Not Accepted: Outsiders Take an Inside Look at Law School*, 5 Berkeley Women's L.J. 1, 37–38, 43–44 (1989–90) ("marginalized persons" develop a counter-code of silence in response to an interrogation technique and an educational atmosphere that are perceived as assaulting their privacy and dignity; "women and persons of color experience frustration instead of growth" when forced to develop an identity within an academic institution dominated by a white male perspective).

5. Indeed, our sense of disassociation appears consistent with the contemporary school experience of other black women and black girls. *See* Suzanne Daley, *Little Girls Lost Their Self-Esteem on Way to Adolescence, Study Finds*, N.Y. Times, Jan. 9, 1991, at B9 (survey of three thousand adolescents concluded that black girls in high school draw apparent self-confidence "from their families and communities rather than the school system"; in order to maintain their self-esteem, black girls must disassociate themselves from school experience). Although admittedly neither as intense or painful, my invisibility also revived memories of my father's experience a generation earlier as the only black student entering Harvard College in 1929. *See* C. Gerald Fraser, *Ewart Guinier, 79, Who Headed Afro-American Studies at Harvard*, N.Y. Times, Feb. 7, 1990, at B7 ("Because of his color, Mr. Guinier said, he was barred from the dormitories, was denied financial aid because he had failed to send his picture with his application, and was spoken to inside and outside of class by only one person").

6. Mari J. Matsuda, *When the First Quail Calls: Multiple Consciousness as Jurisprudential Method*, 11 Women's Rts. L. Rep. 1 (1989).

7. *Id.*

8. *See* W. E. B. Du Bois, The Souls of Black Folk 16–17 (A.C. McClurg, 1903).

9. *Id.*

10. Richard Delgado, *Storytelling for Oppositionists and Others; A Plea for Narrative*, 87 Mich. L. Rev. 2411, 2425 (1989). As a black woman who has experienced minority status and stigma associated with my race and/or gender, I am self-conscious about both race and gender.

11. *See* Kimberlé Williams Crenshaw, *Race, Reform, and Retrenchment: Transformation and Legitimation in Antidiscrimination Law*, 101 Harv. L. Rev. 1331, 1336 (1988) (describing blacks' greatest political resource as the ability to speak and share a collective identity based on experiences of racism and to "name [their] political reality").

12. Indeed, my decision to join this anthology of self-reflective essays was precipitated by the role model characterizations that abounded during Derrick Bell's protest in the spring of 1990. Claiming he could not function as a "role model" for women students, Bell refused to accept his Harvard Law School salary until a woman of color was hired as a professor. *See* Fox Butterfield, *Harvard Law School Torn by Race Issue*, N.Y. Times, Apr. 26, 1990, at A20 ("As a male," Bell said, he "could not serve as a role model for female black students").

13. A role model may be nurturing mentor, symbol of achievement, or template for how this particular role might be performed. See the chapter by Anita L. Allen, *On Being a Role Model*, in this volume (the conspicuous presence of role models as symbolic achievers may rebut assumptions of group inferiority that undermine student confidence and performance).

14. Iris M. Young, Justice, Democracy and Group Difference 9–15 (Sept. 1, 1990) (unpublished paper prepared for presentation to the American Political Science Association, on file

with the *Berkeley Women's Law Journal*) (describing a communicative model of democracy that rejects a disciplined, unemotional style of expression, which often operates to exclude, silence, and disadvantage members of some groups; communicative style does not require emotional detachment or rigid argumentation but employs a broader conception of permissible forms of discourse, including personal narrative).

15. Harlon L. Dalton, *The Clouded Prism,* 22 Harv. C.R.-C.L. L. Rev. 435, 444 (1987) (quoting bell hooks: "With creativity and an open mind, 'we can use information from the margin to transform how we think about the whole.' ").

16. Delgado, *supra* note 10, at 2421.

17. *See* Dalton, *supra* note 15, at 444.

18. Richard Delgado, *When A Story Is Just a Story: Does Voice Really Matter?,* 76 Va. L. Rev. 95, 99 (1990) (describing outsiders' accessibility to and stake in disseminating information that persons without their experiences may not have).

19. Delgado, *supra* note 10, at 2423–27 (describing conventional faculty concern that black professor who causes trouble by stirring up students "wouldn't be a good role model even for the minorities," at 2426 n.45).

20. Regina Austin, *Sapphire Bound!,* 1989 Wis. L. Rev. 539, 575 (also chapter 35 in this volume) (role models who offer "pride" and "positive identities" are not substitutes for effective, committed teachers and leaders).

21. *See* Lani Guinier, *The Triumph of Tokenism: The Voting Rights Act and the Theory of Black Electoral Success,* 89 Mich. L. Rev. (1991) (spokesmodels are attractive group spokespersons with no accountability to group goals; the term "spokesmodel" derives from the television program *Star Search,* in which young women are scouted for their poise, looks and articulation).

22. Kendall Thomas, Remarks at the AALS Annual Meeting, Law and Interpretation Section, Washington, D.C. (Jan. 4, 1991).

23. *See* Dalton, *supra* note 15, at 441.

24. Delgado, *supra* note 10, at 2436.

25. Although the law school admits a class of almost one-half women, and for the first time in 1990, one-third nonwhite persons, my upper-level courses have always consisted primarily of white men. This is not surprising, considering the small absolute number of African American, Asian American, and Latin American students, and the relatively small percentage of these students admitted prior to 1990.

26. And we may eventually help the *gentlemen* change the pictures. In 1990, a student group organized by women and people of color at the University of Pennsylvania raised enough money, with the active support of the dean, to commission the first "official" portrait of a black woman law school graduate, Sadie T. M. Alexander. In the course of writing this essay I learned to my great surprise that at Yale Law School a seminar room display of graduates practicing public interest law now also includes the photograph of at least one black woman—me.

9 | On Being
a Role Model

Anita L. Allen

THE JOURNALIST'S QUESTION

In the spring of 1990, Harvard Law School students demanding faculty diversity took over the dean's office.[1] Derrick Bell, Harvard's first and most senior black law professor, announced that he would sacrifice his $120,000 annual salary until the Law School tenured a black woman.[2] Bell's action soon became a mass media event, and my telephone began to ring.

Most callers were friends who knew that a month before the students' protests and Bell's announcement, I had accepted Dean Robert Clark's offer to teach at Harvard as a visiting professor of law. Clark's offer had been flexible; I would be welcome any time within the next few years. A variety of personal and professional considerations had seemed to point toward visiting sooner rather than later. Therefore, in consultation with the husband I would have to leave behind and my Georgetown dean, I had made arrangements to teach at Harvard during the 1990–91 academic year. Now friends wondered whether I regretted my plans. They inquired whether, as a black woman, I viewed the unresolved, nationally publicized diversity drama as a reason to renege on my agreement to begin at Harvard in September 1990.

One memorable caller was not a friend, but a savvy newspaper reporter. She phoned to ask what I thought of the "role model argument" Bell purportedly used in urging his school to hire black women. The journalist explained that, according to the role model argument, the primary justification for adding black females to a law faculty that may already include black males and white females is that black female law students need black female role models.[3] The reporter's pointed question caught me off guard. I resorted to equivocation, mouthing something mildly approving of the role model argument, followed by something mildly critical of it.

After the call, I began to think seriously about the case for black female role models in American law schools. I pondered a stance that at first seemed ambivalent, then inconsistent, and finally correct. Black women law teachers have unique contributions to make as role models for black female law students. Yet incautious, isolated appeals to role modeling capacities are potentially risky. They can obscure the wider range of good reasons institutions have for recruiting black women to their faculties. They also can obscure the fact that some very accomplished black women may fit no one's ideal description of the "positive" minority role model.

I believe there are good reasons for hiring black women that have little or nothing to do with role modeling. It is abundantly evident that black women can teach, write, and do committee work as well as anyone else. Individual black women, in fact, often excel at one or more of these tasks. To be sure, individual black women also often excel as role models. It is nonetheless misleading to single out role modeling and purport to rank it as the "primary" or "only" reason schools have for appointing black women to their faculties.

The significance to black women of black women teachers must be more widely understood if there is to be serious public discussion of the role model argument for faculty diversity. In this essay I will share what my personal experiences suggest to me about the value of black women teachers and role models to black women students. I will also elaborate my sense of the adverse implications of premising the recruitment of black women law teachers solely or primarily on their role modeling potential. The fate of women of color in higher education depends on a recognition of the power and the limitations of the role model argument.

THE CASE FOR BLACK WOMEN ROLE MODELS

It will sound self-serving to insist on this point, but black women teachers have something special to offer students. Some of what black women law teachers do, say, and write is indistinguishable from the contributions of their black, white, brown, or other male colleagues. It does not follow, however, that black women law teachers are superfluous.

Black female students deserve teachers who will assume their competence. They deserve teachers who will motivate them to do their best work, listen with understanding, and validate their life experiences. Black female students deserve teachers who will sponsor special events and provide insight into how to deal professionally and sanely with the problems women of color inevitably face in legal practice and the academy. Many black women teachers are interested in helping black female students in just these ways.

Racial insensitivity, prejudice, and racism are facts of life. For women of color, sexism and sexual harassment magnify race-related burdens. Black female students have much to learn from black female teachers. We know what it is to experience insecurity about the stereotypes of black women as fit only for sex and servitude, or as having faces that belong on cookie jars or syrup bottles rather than on the pages of bar journals.

Black women may be better able to take themselves seriously as intellectuals knowing that others like them are concerned professors, deans, provosts, and university presidents. Black female law students benefit from opportunities in law school to relate precisely as black women to some of their teachers.

AGAINST THE ROLE MODEL ARGUMENT

ATTENUATED SUPPORT FOR AFFIRMATIVE ACTION

Against the background of the compelling case for black women role models, the role model argument for hiring black women teachers has a certain appeal. In the age of racially integrated higher education, the role model argument acknowledges that black women are indispensable. The argument provides a pragmatic link for affirmative action proponents between the case for affirmative action in student admissions, on the one hand, and the case for affirmative action in faculty hiring, on the other. According to the role model argument heard today, white institutions that now admit significant numbers of black females need energetic black women to teach, counsel, mentor, and inspire.

But the relationship between the case for affirmative action and the case for black role models is not as close as one might suppose. Logically speaking, the soundness of the role model argument does not entail or presuppose the soundness of the argument for affirmative action. A stern opponent of affirmative action could favor hiring black female role models to improve the educational experiences of students "wrongly" admitted on an affirmative action basis.

Black teachers, like black students, may be fitting beneficiaries of affirmative action. But the role model argument defends employing black women on utilitarian grounds referring to student and institutional need, rather than on grounds referring to compensatory justice or to our own remedial desert.[4]

Affirmative action arguments are sometimes premised on the perceived importance of empowering blacks economically, politically, and socially. Empowerment presupposes education. Black female role models are potential power enhancers. Black female educators can help black citizens manage autonomous communities, share power with other groups, and give voice to blacks' concerns. Black women's presence in higher education promises to help lift the political and economic status of blacks. The presence of black women professors is also evidence of our actual power as minority group members situated to help set educational and scholarly priorities.

However, the romantic image of black women as inherent power-enhancers is misleading. If, as sometimes happens, black women professors are either disaffected or marginalized by colleagues and scholarly associates, then our presence does not truly indicate that blacks are sharing or will someday significantly share power with other groups. Keeping black women out of academia surely thwarts black empowerment. But regrettably, letting us in does not guarantee it.

AMBIGUITY: TEMPLATES, SYMBOLS, AND NURTURERS

The role model argument loses additional appeal when we consider the ambiguity it tolerates. In some senses of the popular term, being a black woman is neither a necessary nor a sufficient condition for being a role model for black women students.

All teachers are role models. But not every teacher is a role model in every sense. All teachers are role models in one familiar sense. They "model" their roles as teachers. They are what I will call "ethical templates," men and women whose conduct sets standards for the exercise of responsibilities. Only some teachers are role models in the stronger, equally familiar senses I will label "symbols" of special achievement and "nurturers" of students' special needs.

The roles of template, symbol, and nurturer are often conflated in role model arguments for including black women in higher education. As a practical matter, it is not always important to distinguish between the template, the symbol, and the nurturer. As templates, our mere presence can reshape conceptions of who can teach law and what law teachers appropriately do and say. Moreover, many black women teachers serve willingly and well, both as symbols and as nurturers.

However, some black women "symbols" do not give a "nurturer's" priority to the advancement of the interests of black students and wider black communities. And a few nonsymbol white males do. In arguments for academic role models for black women, the tasks one expects the role model to perform must be clearly specified. Not every black woman will be willing or able to perform every task.

WHISPERS OF INFERIORITY

Whether premised on the template, the symbol, or the nurturer conception, the role model argument for recruiting black women faculty has serious limitations. One problem with the role model argument is that while it trumpets our necessity, it whispers our inferiority. Black women, like black men, often are presumed to be at the bottom of the intellectual heap. Employing us is perceived as stepping over the deserving in favor of the least able. Unlike arguments that aggressively contest mainstream notions of merit, qualification, and competence, the role model argument gives white males a reason for hiring minority women that is perfectly consistent with traditional assumptions of white male intellectual superiority.

Unassisted by other arguments, the role model argument leaves intact the presumption that black women have third-rate intellects. The argument makes it possible to assume that black women can be more competent than whites only insofar as they are better role models. The inability of many academics to communicate with blacks and women is indeed an incompetence, but not one of which society teaches anyone who is not black or female to be especially ashamed. If schools are encouraged to premise hiring black women primarily or solely on the ground that we are better than others at guiding our kind, faculties may avoid confronting the truth that black women think, research, and write as well as whites.

FRAUDULENT UNDERVALUATION

Understandably, some black female academics resent the role model argument. We resent it the way we resent all faint praise. It undervalues. Black women may want badly to help educate and inspire black students. But we know we are smarter and more valuable even than our status as role models implies. Black women are valuable to students of all races and to our institutions generally. We teach classes, write, and serve on committees just as our colleagues do. At some institutions we publish more and get better teaching evaluations than do our average white colleagues, many of whom were hired when standards were lower than they are now.

Abstracted from the full spectrum of our capacities and contributions, the role model argument is thus a damning understatement. Our utility includes our contribution to black students, but is greater still. Moreover, the role model argument is a kind of "bait and switch." We are hired ostensibly to be templates, symbols, and nurturers. Then we are expected to do scholarship and much more for which we are seldom separately recognized or separately compensated.

PSYCHOLOGICAL BURDENS

In candid conversation with black women teachers, one learns that the "role model" label, even willingly embraced, can be a special psychological burden. It makes those of us who take it seriously worry that we have to be perfect—perfectly black, not just black; perfectly female, not just female. Since we are told that our reason for being is that we are role models, we attach undue weight to everything we do.

WHITE MEN OFF THE HOOK

A final problem with the role model argument is that it signals to faculty members who are not black females that they may abandon efforts to serve as positive role models for black women. The logic of the role model argument is such that it lets most faculty off the hook when it comes to educating black women. The argument implies that some blacks are simply unreachable—unteachable by nonblacks. While it may be viewed as responsibly recognizing the reality of racial and gender differences, the role model argument must also be seen as providing teachers who are not black women with a convenient excuse to remain inept at dealing with black women in their classrooms. The role model argument justifies hiring black female teachers, but it also condones a degree of indifference toward black female students. Black women have much to learn from white faculty who care to extend themselves. Thus, trying to hire black females solely as role models looks disturbingly close to something privileged Americans have always done: hire black women to perform the tiresome, unappealing tasks.

HONEST RHETORIC

In the final analysis, it is plain that we should applaud black female role models, but reject the journalist's version of the role model argument—that the principal reason for adding black women to a faculty that may already include white women and black men is that they are role models. We should not pretend that we can rank-order the many good reasons for hiring black women any more than we should pretend that we can rank-order the many good reasons for hiring other categories of teachers. We should also reject any version of the role model argument that portrays role modeling capacities as the only reason to hire black women. It is futile scholasticism to speculate about whether role modeling capacities could be a sufficient reason for hiring a black woman since they, in fact, never would be.

Rejecting exclusive use of role model arguments to persuade schools to hire black women is consistent with the reality that all teachers, black women included, are role models in the "ethical template" sense. It also is consistent with the moral expectation that blacks will take responsibility, as symbols and nurturers, for educating blacks. Concern for black students is paramount among reasons for rejecting exclusive reliance on role model arguments. Black students must understand the full range of demands that black teachers face and that they, too, will someday face should they assume comparable roles.

The point of raising and clarifying concerns about the role model argument is neither to cripple activism on behalf of diversity nor to silence progressive voices fighting for the inclusion of black women. What I am after is something I believe students and faculty concerned about diversity are also after, namely, supporting minority communities through fairness and honesty in the reasons institutions give for hiring black women. If progressives' arsenal of political rhetoric is to include role model arguments, the limitations of those arguments must be well understood.

NOTES

1. *See* Fox Butterfield, *Harvard Law Professor Quits until Black Woman Is Named,* N. Y. Times, Apr. 24, 1990, at 1. The students' rallies and "sit-ins" pressed law school administrators for a commitment to a "diverse" faculty broadly conceived. However, media reports often focused on the question of a permanent tenured appointment for a particular black woman, Regina Austin, a visiting professor at Harvard during the 1989–90 academic year. See *id.* (quoting discordant students perspectives on Austin's teaching).

Critical of the tenor of the *New York Times* coverage, a group of prominent black women law teachers wrote a letter to the editor stressing that by appointing Austin, Harvard "would [not] depart from its usual standards of quality." *See* Paulette M. Caldwell et al., *Law School Standards: The Old and the New: "A Superb Scholar,"* N. Y. Times, May 11, 1990, at 34. Austin returned home to the University of Pennsylvania Law School without an offer to join the Harvard faculty.

2. Butterfield, *supra* note 1.

3. When this article was written, there had never been a tenured or tenure-track black woman on the Harvard Law School faculty. At the time of the student protests and lawsuit in 1990, Derrick Bell was one of three tenured black men on the faculty. (The other two were Christopher Edley, Jr., and Randall Kennedy.) The faculty also included five tenured white women and two untenured black men. (David Wilkins and Charles Ogletree were the black men; Martha Field, Elizabeth Bartholet, Mary Ann Glendon, Martha Minow, and Kathleen Sullivan, the white women.) Another black man, Scott Brewer, had accepted a tenure-track faculty position that he is expected to assume after judicial clerkship. The tenured and tenure-track faculty included a Brazilian citizen, Roberto Unger, but no Hispanic Americans, Asian Americans, or open gays or lesbians. Subsequently, Harvard Law School extended invitations to visit to two black women—Kimberlé Williams Crenshaw and Lani Guinier, neither of whom accepted.

4. This is not to say that there are only utilitarian arguments for hiring role models or for affirmative action. See, by analogy, Ronald Dworkin, Taking Rights Seriously 232 (1977) (discussing Sweatt v. Painter, 339 U.S. 629 (1945) and DeFunis v. Odegaard, 416 U.S. 312 (1974)) (in some cases a discriminatory policy that puts some individuals at a disadvantage may be justified because the average welfare of the community improved or because the community was rendered more just or ideal).

10 Tokens, Role Models, and Pedagogical Politics: Lamentations of an African American Female Law Professor

Linda S. Greene

Professor: a person who professes something; . . . one who openly declares *his* sentiments

—*Oxford English Dictionary*

In a world undivided along racial and gender lines, we would not have the occasion to ponder the relevance of race and gender to our role as *professors* of law. Instead, we might be freer to choose among a variety of responsibilities that ordinarily accompany our official titles without regard to the impact of our race/gender on our status. In an ideal world, a world untainted by slavery and subordination, we might take the podium without threatening the legitimacy of an academic world in which males—primarily white males—are hegemonic. But we live in a country that only recently repudiated our own *Plessy*-driven apartheid, a world that clings stubbornly to comfortable notions of intellect, notions that seem inextricably, if unconsciously, bound to color and gender.

Against the background of this history, it is impossible for us to expect that our participation in the transmission and critique of legal culture will be apolitical. To the contrary, our participation is profoundly political and disturbing to many. Our scattered presence draws the attention of students and faculty alike to a past in which we were completely absent and to a present in which we are virtually absent. Our limited presence visually politicizes the past and present by reminding students, faculty, alumni, and others of the rationales for our historical and current exclusion. Our demand *to profess,* to authoritatively declare and critique society's norms, is at odds with our historical roles and status. Until the moment of our appointment, faculty members wring their hands and commiserate (for attribution) about the "difficulties of the search process," the "lack of qualified applicants," and the "limited pool." Immediately after our appointments, and often in press releases, faculties publicly announce our appointments and remind each other "how lucky we are to have her." The ubiquitous white male law professor arouses no curiosity or attention based solely on his presence. Yet we are the object of curiosity and scrutiny whenever we are present, and the subject of rationalizing explanations when we are not. In this context, the occasional African American female law professor becomes less an individual and more a symbol or a sign with ambiguous meaning. As a result, it is impossible to have any meaningful discussion of our roles and role choices without a careful analysis of the context in which we teach.

One of the most important factors in our professional lives is tokenism. Tokenism masks racism and sexism by admitting a small number of previously excluded individuals to institutions. At the same time, a system of tokenism maintains barriers of entry to others. Tokenism is therefore a symbolic equality. Our own role options are limited by the high visibility and symbolic significance of our token presence. These conditions make it difficult, if not impossible, for African American women to enjoy significant control over the roles we play in law teaching and a significant measure of professional privacy. The only way we can effectively reduce the impact of tokenism is to collectively repudiate it and to demand that our law schools do the same. It is only through these efforts that we can move beyond tokenism's sham equality to a meaningful equality in which we truly have a choice of roles.

LAMENTATIONS OF A TOKEN AND SOME REFLECTIONS ON THE SYSTEM OF TOKENISM

After teaching law for a few years, I realized that the hostility and bitterness that I and other African American female law teachers experienced might be related to the scarcity of our numbers and the ambiguity surrounding the legitimacy of our presence. The year was 1983; I had been teaching since 1978, and by this time I had had numerous conversations with the small number of African American women teaching law. Many reported experiences in the classroom and with colleagues that resembled verbal lynching and rapes. More than one of my African American female colleagues reported being shouted down in the classroom by white males, being shunned by colleagues, having her teaching qualifications openly challenged in the classroom, receiving anonymous and detailed hate notes critical of her teaching style, syntax, and appearance, and learning of colleagues who had encouraged students to act disrespectfully toward her.

My early experiences were an intellectual version of a nighttime ride through the countryside in the deep South: I had a constant awareness of racist and sexist danger, both real and imagined. I never knew when a student's seemingly innocuous response to my questions would slide into a challenge to my right *to profess*. I came to fear this almost daily assault on my psyche. Had I not received significant support and encouragement from several other African American professors, I would not be teaching today.[1]

I was not prepared to relive Jackie Robinson's 1947 experiences thirty years later. Little did I know about the phenomenon—and the politics—of tokenism. Little did I know that I was one of about a dozen African American women law professors in the United States, a fact that obscured my individuality and made my teaching controversial. My opportunity to be heard, understood, and accepted was severely limited by this statistical fact. I was a smart, savvy, hardworking, articulate woman. Or so I thought. My self-doubt grew with my negative experiences. The indulgent reactions of faculty "colleagues" to the virulent criticism of students, the readiness of students to judge and dismiss my decisions in the classroom, the insistence of alumnae that I must be a student after I had been introduced as "Professor," as well as hundreds of other experiences, suggested to me that my modest aspiration to teach law threatened deeply held notions about who ought to exercise this authority.

Though these experiences were painful ones, I continued to search for some framework or perspective that might give them meaning and coherence. The fact that so many of us told each other similar stories suggested to me that our individual characteristics did not necessarily create the faculty and student responses we endured. I speculated that the skepticism, hostility, and isolation directed toward us were less a matter of our own characteristics than a concomitant of the context in which we taught. I concluded that context was tokenism—a regime in which the number of African American women teaching is extremely limited. This limitation occurs against a background of historical exclusion based on arguments of inferiority and unsuitability.

Limited inclusion of persons visibly different from the dominant group is the essence of tokenism. In the regime of tokenism, "the continuation of segregation . . . occurs against an ideological background of equality fostered both by legal changes as well as by the cultural unacceptability of overt racism and sexism. . . . Total exclusion . . . give[s] way to token inclusion."[2]

The work of Rosabeth Moss Kanter and others confirms that the effect of tokenism is to distort the manner in which members of the dominant group perceive the "token" individual.[3] In an institutional culture, changes result that profoundly affect the conditions under which tokens live and work.[4]

Rosabeth Moss Kanter argues that tokens and tokenism are prevalent in "skewed groups"—groups that are dominated by one type of individual.[5] These groups control the institutions' culture. Those outside the dominant groups are "tokens."

Three perceptional tendencies reinforce tokenism: visibility, contrast, and assimilation.

> The visibility phenomenon is self-explanatory—tokens are highly visible because their physical features set them apart from the dominants. Contrast, the second perceptional tendency, results when dominant group members exaggerate the differences between themselves and the token as a defensive measure to maintain and guarantee their commonalities. Assimilation is the increased use by the dominant group of generalizations with respect to the token individual. In effect, the dominant group distorts its perception of the token individual in order to maintain the stereotypical generalizations it holds as to the token group. The assimilation phenomenon insures that the token's "true characteristics" are dominated—and overshadowed—by those stereotypes which are believed to identify the group to which the token belongs.[6]

The result of these phenomena is that the token is highly visible, yet not perceived as an individual. The dominant group merges her true individual characteristics with the stereotypes it applies to her group. Because the token is highly visible, she bears more performance pressure than members of the dominant group.[7]

The dynamics created by a skewed group context are exacerbated in the case of the African American female law professor. There are probably fewer than a hundred tenure-track African American female law professors in the entire United States. There are few institutions that have more than one African American female law professor, if they have one teaching at all.[8] These stark numbers cry out for explanation and tar those of us in teaching with implicit and explicit questions about the legitimacy of our presence.

The short explanation is that the scarcity of African American female law professors is the product of both our past exclusion from certain prestigious law schools that have traditionally supplied law professors as well as historically held pre- and post-*Brown* assumptions about the suitability of certain groups for certain roles. Though this history is as recent as the late 1960s, many deny its current relevance and urge new reasons and rationales for our absence. Notwithstanding this "plausible deniability" approach to past racism, the fact that there are so many "first" African American female law professors at law schools brings to the fore both the past and present exclusion. In the past, the dominant group rationalized exclusion based on a belief in its intellectual superiority and a belief in the intellectual inferiority of people of color. After the passage of civil rights legislation forbidding racial discrimination in institutions receiving federal financial assistance, our law schools formally embraced new norms to govern inclusion and exclusion. In spite of this normative flexibility—in spite of the admission of African American law students—faculty ranks remain virtually devoid of African American female professors.[9] The recent segregative past and the current scarcity of African American female professors cause others to perceive our presence as an unusual event—an occurrence, a symbol, a sign.

The *Oxford English Dictionary* gives several meanings for the word "token": "something that serves to indicate a fact, an event, an object; a token is a sign or symbol."[10] "In token of" means "as a sign, as a symbol or evidence of."[11] What does our limited presence as professors indicate? One inference is that our limited presence indicates the overall inferiority of our group in general. Another inference that may be drawn from our limited presence is that our group is not suited to teach: it is inappropriate for us to *profess*. Our limited presence also permits inferences about the overall superiority of the dominant group.

Our limited number also encourages others to draw negative inferences about the qualifications of individual members of our group. The dominant group historically justified our exclusion based on our "inferiority" as a group.[12] These justifications, when coupled with our limited presence, invite a searching scrutiny designed to answer the question whether a particular African American woman ought to occupy the role of law professor. Can the performance of a particular woman rebut all the presumptions of inferiority attributed to our group? No. The paradox of tokenism is that it admits the possibility of individual success without giving ground on the question of group inferiority. Thus, even if one African American female succeeds in rebutting the presumptions of group inferiority, or successfully bears the burden of historically ascribed inferiority, other African American women do not necessarily benefit. Rather, as an individual, she has simply demonstrated that she does not possess the characteristics attributed to the group. There is no group victory in the achievement of one, no triumph over this permutation of racism-sexism that relegates us to the margins of intellectual authority while our token presence serves to shield law schools against accusations of racism-sexism.[13]

In a regime of tokenism, there can be no group victory if one accepts, as certain of our colleagues do both openly and silently, the proposition that the remainder of our African American sisters are simply unqualified to *profess*. Our presence as token individuals masks racism and sexism. This presence serves two inconsistent purposes: it "proves our law schools' commitment" to equality while illustrating the overall inferiority of our group.

PEDAGOGICAL POLITICS AND PROFESSIONAL PRIVACY

So far I have suggested that historical circumstances and perceptional distortion limit our choices of roles. A related issue is whether we have a legitimate expectation of some measure of professional privacy in the vortex of the largely male and white legal academy. Ordinarily the intellectual professor has the option of a high- or low-profile existence. The white male intellectual's mere presence engenders no curiosity. Instead, he is the beneficiary of an assumption that his presence is ordinary—even comforting. He may choose to be a notorious celebrity by representing unusual and controversial clients or by engaging in prolific, unintelligible, or provocative scholarship. But there is no controversy or excitement generated as a result of his mere presence. In contrast, our presence as African American women law *professors* is inextricably bound up in the race and gender power politics of legal intellectual authority.

While it is legitimate to expect a measure of personal privacy during the performance of our roles, it is unreasonable for African American women law professors to rely on this expectation of personal privacy, because the assumptions surrounding our presence are entirely different.

Because there are so few African American women law professors, the presence of one does not escape notice.

"Why her?"

"Why now?"

"Was this special treatment?"

"Wasn't there a white woman or white male *more qualified?*"

"Can she teach?"

"Will she write?"

"Is she *too black?*"

"Is she *black enough?*"

"We don't want to make a mistake! It wouldn't be fair to her or to the others."

And so on.

Our presence creates two perceptional effects that flow from the inclusion-exclusion dialectic of tokenism. On the one hand, our presence suggests the repudiation of the presumption against intellectual authority roles for African American women in historically white institutions. This presumption is especially strong in law schools, where the role of professor permits one to participate in the reproduction of legal culture and in a dialogue about the very allocation of private and public authority. On the other hand, our token presence continues to affirm the presumption against our participation in this process.

We have a legitimate longing for professional privacy and for freedom from the dialectic of tokenism. But we will not escape the effects of this new Jim Crow regime without exposing its essence and eliminating its epiphytic hold on our lives.

Though our efforts to strip away tokenism's equality mask are essential to our future enjoyment of some measure of professional privacy, we may be reluctant to take drastic actions for many reasons. It is exceedingly difficult to address the elimination of racism-sexism, which manifests itself in invisible, structural terms. Indeed, exploring the manner in which new forms of racism and sexism manifest themselves is the key challenge of the post-civil rights era. A decision to work toward eliminating tokenism in law schools is a decision to undermine foundational assumptions about "merit" and the legitimacy of our "meritocracy." It might also be a decision to reject the personal benefits of a tokenism regime. But it is not the sort of decision that will make one popular in the halls of important legal education institutions. There are indeed risks.

While tokenism continues, this generation of African American female law professors will probably not have the option of professional privacy. It is unlikely that in our lifetime our biological and color characteristics will be ignored as unrelated to the legitimacy of our presence and the legitimacy of the ideas we *profess.*[14] The presence—and absence—of African American females symbolized by tokenism speaks volumes in a modernized whispering anthology of racism and sexism. If we remain silent about the equality sham of tokenism, we remain complicit in tokenism's assertion that we should not teach law. On the other hand, if we decide to speak out against the sham of tokenism—and to work toward ending it—we take an important step in affirming our group consciousness and political consciousness. Such a decision would reflect our increasing sophistication and our understanding of the relationship between tokenism and the politics of intellectual authority.

NOTES

1. The late Professor Denise Carty-Bennia of Northeastern Law School was one of the people who supported me during these dark times. She was always there to say something

clear about the racism and sexism manifested in these experiences and to encourage me to keep teaching.

I wrote about these experiences contemporaneously. I did not share them then, nor did I share my conceptualization of the problem of tokenism because I believed the incorporation of my personal experiences into my analysis of racism-sexism would have been scorned. But for the path my colleague Patricia Williams broke by writing in her own voice (rather than in a "neutral" voice), we might have reserved these words for the most private of conversations among sisters and dared not write them down, even to each other.

2. Linda Greene, *Equal Employment Opportunity Law Twenty Years after the Civil Rights Act of 1964: Prospects for the Realization of Equality in Employment,* 18 Suffolk U. L. Rev. 593, 608 (1984).

3. Rosabeth Moss Kanter, Men and Women of the Corporation 209–42, 274–76 (1977) (There is "extensive evidence that intergroup perception and judgment are often irrationally distorted."). Other sources that address the stereotyping and cognitive changes that can result from tokenism include Gordon Willard Allport, The Nature of Prejudice (1954); Henri Tajfel, Human Groups and Social Categories (1981); David L. Hamilton, *Illusory Correlation as a Basis for Stereotyping, in* Cognitive Processes in Stereotyping and Intergroup Behavior 115 (L. Erlbaum Assoc., 1981); David A. Wilder, *Perceiving Persons as a Group: Categorization and Intergroup Relations, in supra,* at 213.

4. Linda Greene, *Twenty Years of Civil Rights: How Firm a Foundation?,* 37 Rutgers L. Rev. 707, 722 n.lo5 (1984) ("Group domination speaks a powerful, self-perpetuating message of prestige and superiority for one group, and of weakness and inferiority for others." *Id.* at 752). *See also* Greene, *supra* note 2, at 602 ("Sociological and psychological research reveals that group membership affects the perception, cognition, and judgment process, often unconsciously. More important, however, is the suggestion of a prominent social psychologist that perceptional and judgmental distortion serve to cognitively and practically preserve a social world consistent with the power held by dominant groups in the society" (footnote omitted)).

See also id. at 611 ("[P]erception research suggests that group membership has an important influence on judgments, and that skewed groups generate perceptional dynamics that render fair perception—and equal opportunity—less likely, if not impossible.").

5. Kanter, *supra* note 3, at 209–10.

6. Greene, *supra* note 2, at 607.

7. *Id.*

8. These include the University of Wisconsin, with Patricia Williams, Beverly Moran (fall 1991), and me; Georgetown University Law Center, with Patricia King, Emma Jordan, Anita Allen, and Elizabeth Patterson; Tulane University, with Wendy Brown and Sabrina McCarthy; Temple University, with Phoebe Northcross and Joan Epps; and New York University Law School, with Paulette Caldwell and Peggy Cooper Davis.

9. According to a Society of American Law Teachers (SALT) survey, the percentage of African American law professors in white-run institutions rose from 2.8 percent in 1980–81 to 3.7 percent in 1986–87. *See* Richard H. Chused, *The Hiring and Retention of Minorities and Women on American Law School Faculties,* 137 U. Pa. L. Rev. 537, 538 (1988). In 1986–87, one-third of these law schools had no African American faculty members, one-third had one, and less than a tenth had more than three. *Id.* at 539.

According to the American Association of Law Schools, there are 6,162 people teaching in the AALS- and ABA-accredited law schools. Of these, 1,347 are women, and 122 are African

American women. American Association of Law Schools Statistical Profile of All Female Full-Time Law Teachers for 1990–91 (on file with the *Berkeley Women's Law Journal*).

10. 18 Oxford English Dictionary, 196 (Clarendon, 2d ed. 1989).

11. *Id.*

12. We are, of course, disproportionately represented in certain occupations, but the nature of those occupations still confirms the primary proposition of presumptive inferiority. Those occupations are always low-status, low-paying, low-power occupations. Our disproportionate inclusion in these groups also implicitly asserts our inferiority and creates conscious and unconscious presumptions against our suitability for different roles.

13. Each group and subgroup on a law school faculty is affected differently by tokenism. White males, who are the predominant members of law school faculties, are the beneficiaries of a culture in which it is presumed that their exercise of intellectual authority is legitimate. African American males have told us their own stories of humiliation; they too have suffered from tokenism's paradox of inclusion and exclusion. But some African American males have different experiences than we have because they *are* males. Students and faculty can more easily imagine them in the dominating, if often caricaturist, roles male law professors often play. Some of this imagining likely has its source in popular sports images that reinforce traditional and often negative notions about African American male intellect and African American male physicality. My point is that, while African American males have been the victims of tokenism, they also may be the beneficiaries of a shared male culture in which assumptions about male authority and the appropriateness of aggressive behavior may benefit them in the law school culture—especially in the classroom.

White women also have experienced tokenism; but their experiences are different from ours in kind and degree. They have not suffered the stereotype that they are intellectually unfit, but rather that it is somehow inappropriate for them to exercise a "male" role. Also, they have benefited from the decision of law faculties to admit large numbers of white female law students. Thus, the presence of a white female is not necessarily an occasion for notice. In addition, a white female is now less likely to be the only white female on a faculty or the first white woman to teach at a particular law school. Nonetheless, white female law professors do suffer burdens as a result of tokenism, but they are different in kind and degree from those we experience.

14. More caveats. I decided to focus on issues that go to the very legitimacy of our presence as *professors* in law schools rather than focus on our many contributions to the law school. These issues transcend any discussion of what we might "profess" if we had the opportunity to do so, free of the perceptional constraints that accompany the state of tokenism.

I also want to say, very tentatively, that we should be careful not to rest the entire argument for our presence on the special content of our ideas or our commitment to convey to students the African American women's perspective on law. It would be another form of discrimination to require that each African American female be capable of untangling the strangling threads of racism and sexism from the fabric of her life and the law; we should not all be required to be African American legal feminists.

11 | Two Life Stories: Reflections of One Black Woman Law Professor

Taunya Lovell Banks

The dispute at Harvard Law School over the absence of Black women from the faculty is disturbing. Particularly distressing is the use of the term "role model" as the articulated rationale for hiring a Black woman law professor.[1] The term "role model" seems soft, unlike the word "mentor." A role model is a person whose "behavior in a particular role is imitated by others."[2] Most often a "role model" is passive, an image to be emulated. On the other hand, a mentor is more aggressively involved with her protégé. The word "mentor" has an intellectual connotation that the term "role model" generally lacks. Because mentors provide some intellectual guidance, they also must be respected intellectually.

Good law teachers are intellectually challenging and aggressively involved with students. Thus the need for Black women mentors/intellectuals is a better justification for hiring Black women as law teachers than is the need for role models. Law faculties may not take this argument seriously because of the societal bias against all women (and Black men) as intellectuals and leaders. Today there still are teachers at prominent colleges and universities who openly espouse the intellectual inferiority of Blacks and all women.[3] My argument for the inclusion of more Black women law teachers to serve as mentors/intellectuals goes beyond role modeling arguments to the very nature of the scholarly dialogue. In arguing for the inclusion of Black women on law faculties, I cannot pretend that there is a single set of common experiences that defines all Black people or Black women. Nor do I contend that any single Black woman can capture the complexities, varied lifestyles, and ways of approaching legal issues of concern to all Black women. However, our varied life experiences of being Black and female in a White male dominated society affect our individual perspectives. Thus, the absence of Black women from the legal landscape—especially as legal academics—impoverishes the imagination of law students and other legal academics.

96

There is, however, an important but subtle difference between opening the legal landscape to Black women and attempting to discover, prove, and legitimate their intellectual worth.[4] If the legal landscape is opened to Black women, generally perceived as being at the bottom of the American hierarchy, it is possible to open the legal landscape to all members of American society. However, any attempt to justify the inclusion of Black women law professors based on some assertion of a special perspective of all Blacks, or all Black women, may be both difficult to make and politically risky—although ultimately right. If not carefully crafted, these arguments can be distorted by opponents simply to legitimate further charges of our intellectual inferiority.

As it is, Black women academics/intellectuals already occupy a precarious position in legal education. We are misfits, not fully accepted by the Black or White community, and as women, we still are not full members of the feminist community. We are, as Harold Cruse characterized Black intellectuals almost thirty years ago, a "rootless class of displaced persons"—outsiders even within our own communities.[5] Thus, my struggle as an academic is to teach and write, truthfully and accurately, despite the feeling that I fit into no world.

Truth telling for me is easier for some issues, notably race, than others, especially class. I still have some discomfort with my own class background. Only lately have I come to accept that I am a third-generation college teacher. All my grandparents attended college and both my parents have doctoral degrees. This part of my background is unusual, even among most of my White colleagues. Although not wealthy, I grew up middle-class in Black Washington, D.C., a community infamous for its class and color (literally, shades of skin color) consciousness. In these respects, my background is different from many other Black women law teachers.

As with all people, there are degrees of difference among Black women academics. We are part of multiple cultures based on gender, race, class, region, and for some, ethnicity and sexuality. Unfortunately, the nature of traditional legal dialogue within law schools and legal education devalues life experiences. Instead it favors the notion that bland, so-called objectively reasoned arguments, often devoid of any humanistic concern, are the only way to convey important legal ideas. This is a one-dimensional scholarly dialogue, a cerebral discussion of law. The body of legal scholarship should be more diverse, since the law, at the very least, is two-dimensional.

This second dimension, the inclusion of multiple life experiences, is missing from the legal scholarly dialogue. These excluded or devalued life experiences raise legal, social, and moral issues that are worthy of discussion and should be addressed by legal scholars because they reflect law as it operates. This second dimension is missing from classroom discussions as well. For example, my presence in the classroom and the academic community creates a potentially richer learning experience because I bring a whole segment of life experiences related to law that is missing from the legal landscape. Law teachers, like scholars, tend to ignore or minimize these experiences because they are unaware of the negative consequences of exclusion. They are unaware because law faculties are so homogenized, especially as to race and gender.[6]

I will use a story to illustrate how my life experiences affect my point of view. The story looks at my perceived position in American society and relates an experience common to almost all Black people. It illustrates how Black people who are unknown to Whites are categorized by them, only by color.

THE ELEVATOR

One Saturday afternoon I entered an elevator in a luxury condominium in downtown Philadelphia with four other Black women law professors. We were leaving the apartment of another Black woman law professor. The elevator was large and spacious. A few floors later, the door opened and a White woman in her late fifties peered in, let out a muffled cry of surprise, stepped back, and let the door close without getting on. Several floors later the elevator stopped again, and the doors opened to reveal yet another White middle-aged woman, who also decided not to get on.

Following the first incident we looked at each other, somewhat puzzled. After the second incident we laughed in disbelief, belatedly realizing that the two women seemed afraid to get on an elevator in a luxury condominium with five well-dressed Black women in their thirties and forties.[7] Our laughter, the nervous laugh Blacks often express when faced with the blatant or unconscious racism of White America, masked our shock and hurt.

The elevator incident is yet another reminder that no matter how well-educated, well-dressed, or financially secure, we are Black first and thus still undesirable "others" to too many White Americans. It reminds me that no matter what my accomplishments, I am still perceived as less than equal—and even dangerous!

The elevator incident is a painful reminder that White attitudes about race have not changed and that too often we "assimilated" Blacks buy into these White attitudes. I used to think that Whites were afraid only of Black men, and I felt safe from that form of racism due to my gender. Now, I realize any Black person is threatening. Groups of Black women are very threatening even to their White "sisters." We are threatening even when encountered during the day in a security building complete with doorman.

We should not have been surprised by the White women's fear because of the dominance of fear in women's lives generally. As women we fear rape, assault, and harassment in the street or workplace. Feminist writers point out that the dominance of fear as a part of women's life experience is one way our experiences differ from men's, at least White men's.[8]

On the other hand, we tend to think that only Black men's lives are dominated by the experience of "being feared." But in this instance, by virtue of color alone, we too were feared. Thus being feared is not simply a Black male experience, it is part of the Black experience.[9]

However, I think some of us were surprised that we were not insulated by gender (and perhaps class) from the fear Whites have of Blacks. We were instantly categorized, stripped of our individuality, before those women waiting for the elevator had a chance to know us. We were deprived of our community of gender (and perhaps class) simply because we were classified Black at birth. It is an experience that can happen to any Black woman; in this way Black women's experiences are not simply sometimes Black and sometimes female. Our experiences as Black women fit neither paradigm. In the elevator we were feared, but not because of being Black and male.

Nevertheless, as a Black academic woman in America, I am constantly asked to fit within only one paradigm at a time. I am categorized as being part of a Black world, or a White world, or a female world, or a world of poverty and cultural deprivation. Being so variously categorized often causes me to think about all these worlds collectively when viewing common life experiences. It is this frame of reference I bring into my classroom. My life stories influence my perspective, a perspective unable to function within a single paradigm because I am too many things at one time. My perspective often transcends race and gender and is sometimes fully or partially conscious of the complexities and intersection of race, gender, and class. It is a multiple perspective not represented in our casebooks or legal literature.

NOTES

1. In April 1990, Harvard law professor Derrick Bell, a Black man, announced that he was taking a leave of absence without pay until the law school appointed a tenured Black woman to its faculty. Bell said that he could not in "good conscience" continue to serve as a "role model" for both Black men and Black women. Not only did Bell use the term "role model," but the *New York Times* quoted one Black first-year woman student as saying, "we need black women role models." Fox Butterfield, *Harvard Law School Torn by Race Issue*, N.Y. Times, Apr. 26, 1990, at A20.

2. A Supplement to the Oxford English Dictionary 1021 (Clarendon, 1982).

3. *See, e.g., Campus Is Split over Statement by a Professor,* N.Y. Times, Dec. 23, 1990, at 28 (tenured University of California anthropology professor makes statements that suggest that women have smaller brains than men and that race makes a difference in academic ability).

4. Hazel Carby faults Black feminist criticism, along with the women's and Black studies movements, for accepting in large part the prevailing paradigms of academic scholarship. Hazel Carby, Reconstructing Womanhood: The Emergence of the Afro-American Woman Novelist 15–16 (1987).

5. Harold Cruse, The Crisis of the Negro Intellectual 454 (1967).

6. Richard Chused's 1987 study of law faculties found that women occupy 15.9 percent and Blacks 3.7 percent of all tenured or tenure-track positions at the American Association of Law School member institutions participating in the survey. Richard H. Chused, *The Hiring and Retention of Minorities and Women on American Law Faculties,* 137 U. Pa. L. Rev. 537, 540 n.19, 548 (1988).

7. In all fairness, I later learned that the first woman refuses to get on an elevator with anyone, but that still does not adequately resolve my feelings about the second incident.

8. For example, Robin West points out that patriarchy as experienced by modern women is profoundly negative and pervasively violent. Robin West, *Feminism, Critical Social Theory and Law,* U. Chi. Legal F. 59, 61 (1989) (citations omitted). She notes that fear, specifically of

sexual violence, is a defining role in women's lives. *Id.* at 62–63. *See also* Christine Littleton, *Equality and Feminist Legal Theory,* 48 U. Pitt. L. Rev. 1043, 1043–44 (1987); Kristin Bumiller, *Rape as a Legal Symbol: An Essay on Sexual Violence and Racism,* 42 U. Miami L. Rev. 75, 76, 91 (1987).

9. Robin West uses the term "ethical fear" to describe "a fear so pervasive that it forces [those who have it] to adapt continually to its pressures and begins actually to determine their personality and character." Robin West, *The Supreme Court 1989 Term: Foreword: Taking Freedom Seriously,* 104 Harv. L. Rev. 43, 91 (1990). West takes the term "ethical fear" from Czechoslovak President Vaclav Havel, but uses it in a different context. Havel uses the term to describe "the pervasive threat of official violence engendered by a police state." *Id.* at 91–92 n.209 (citing V. Havel, *Letter to Gustáv Husák, in* Vaclav Havel, or Living in Truth 3, 5 (J. Vladislava ed., 1986). But West uses the term to describe the consequences of living with the threat of violence from other citizens, a fear she characterizes as common to both women (fear of rape) and residents of crime-ridden neighborhoods (fear of violent crime). *Id.* However, the Black experience in America includes both Havel's and West's "ethical fear." We have adapted to the threat of official violence and we adapted to the threat of random violence (lynching). Starting with the slave experience, Black women have adapted to the fear of sexual violence. But in addition, Black men *and* women are forced to adapt to another "ethical fear," the fear of being feared and the dangers implicit in generating this fear.

12 Law Professors of Color and the Academy: Of Poets and Kings

Cheryl I. Harris

Throughout the body of his work, Chinua Achebe, premier novelist and poet of Nigeria, has drawn infinitely poignant and ever more illuminating pictures of the African struggle to emerge from colonialism and to forge a new society. In *Anthills of the Savannah*, he gives full vent to an oppositional voice—a poetic voice that tells the stories of aspiration, disappointment, triumph, and failure of a struggling people and so situates the poet in opposition to the dominant regime.[1] The vehicle of Achebe's critique is Ikem Osodi, a central character in the novel and (like Achebe) a leading journalist and poet. Ikem is finally fired as chief editor of the national newspaper of Kangan, a fictional African country, for his continuous stream of editorials critical of "His Excellency's" increasingly compromised political positions. In commenting on Ikem's fate, Achebe has argued that Ikem as poet is bound to "stay in trouble with the king." Indeed, says Achebe, "if poets are not in trouble with the King [because of their stories], then they are in trouble with their work."[2]

By this metaphor I take Achebe to underscore the inherent risks in confronting power, and the necessity of assuming those risks in embracing the central task of social transformation, which is the work of the artist, the poet, and the scholar in any imperfect, unjust society. While I acknowledge the thousands of miles and years that separate the experience of Achebe in contemporary Africa and my own as a Blackwoman[3] in the United States, Achebe's work presupposes and evokes images I find extremely resonant. To a woman of color in the legal academy, the paradigm of the poet in an unjust society is one that I suggest has much to offer.

The challenge for scholars of color in the academy, like the challenge to the poet in the unjust society, is to render the invisible visible and tangible, to move what is in the background to the foreground; to tell a different story that is neither known or familiar and indeed may be disturbing, annoying, and frightening. Because the past is with us in the present, because subordination existed and exists, the work of the scholar of color involves the task of exposing the jurisprudence that oppresses in order to work toward articulating a jurisprudence that resists subordination and empowers. As the scholar of color discovers the transformative power of the law, a necessary tension is implied in her relationship to the academy, so that in performing her task, like the poet, she must not only survive, but tell a story that is both hers and is larger than hers—a story that undermines the prevailing order—thereby risking "trouble with the king."

The purpose of this essay is not to prescribe how each person should deal with this challenge. Rather, I presume to tell a tale—my own tale—about my entry into the legal academy and some of what I have encountered during my sojourn here. As is true of all people, my experience and perspective have been shaped and filtered by race, gender, and class. But if I begin with who I am—a Blackwoman whose particular experience is located within and at the borders of prevailing and inter-secting hierarchies of race, gender, and class—then I am more likely to get it right and, for the purposes of this piece, move from the task of self-conscious reflection, which is intimately tied with any role that we assume, toward more general and, hopefully, useful observations.

In many respects, mine is not a unique story. So much here is not. In some respects, what I relate is not my story alone, but is entwined with the stories of many I have encountered as well. That is, even my experiences of isolation are not isolated from the experiences of others who, like myself, in some ways are outside the traditional venue of the academy. My path—my story—is interwoven with the paths and stories of others. As I do not own their stories, my story is not owned solely by me. For in the sharing of stories, the line between what is my story and what is another's story is not experienced as a closely guarded boundary. My sense of who I am is made stronger by the sharing of these stories. That sharing has become a crucial tonic for my own healing and a necessary weapon in the fight to subvert the crushing weight of the prevailing story—the story that says that existing norms and modes of behavior and assessment of value, worth, and contribution are natural, inevitable, fair, and neutral. So it is in this context that I chart my journey.

Neither my route to law teaching nor my experience as a lawyer has followed conventional paths. After ten years of practicing law in areas that ranged from criminal trial work to landmark regulation, from a community-based law practice to working in local government for the city's first Black mayor, in early 1990 I found myself once again confronting the ambiguity I experienced in law school, the same compelling question about whether "being a lawyer" was something I really wanted. My constant search both during and after school had been to find more socially flexible and creative avenues of personal expression and development that I had found lacking in the law. My own personal reexamination of options caused me to again consider law teaching, as I had been encouraged to do some five years before. Instead I thought that I would first spend some time abroad in London working on a degree in an international relations program.

Then came the unexpected in two forms. The first was a phone call from a friend and colleague with whom I have done movement work, who informed me that

Chicago-Kent Law School was seeking to fill a full-time, tenure-track position and, further, that the school was interested in qualified minority candidates. The second thing that happened was that the national press reported that Derrick Bell announced he was taking an unpaid leave of absence from Harvard Law School until such time as the school hired a woman of color in a tenured or tenure-track position.[4] His decision was accompanied by student protests at the school in support of his stance and in vocal opposition to Harvard's claim that it had found no qualified candidates. All of this caused me to reflect on my experiences in law school and marvel at the fact that in the ten years that I had been away from the academy, the more things changed—the increase in the number of people of color in the legal profession—the more things stayed the same—the lack of people of color in law teaching. Apparently, change is still provoked only by crisis. Consequently, when I received the offer to enter the academy here at Chicago-Kent (following the process of interviews and a presentation to the faculty), I accepted with great anticipation, but not without some degree of hesitancy and awareness that all of this was occurring in a context of power relationships that had not been reordered by the passage of time.

In 1990, I became the only person of color on Chicago-Kent's full-time tenure-track faculty. I do not know whether history would support my bearing the dubious honor of being the "first" as well as the "one and only."[5] I do know that I was the first woman of color ever. (I should mention not so parenthetically that I was pleased to relinquish the position of being "the only" and was joined this fall by another person of color on the tenure-track faculty.)

There was certainly no reason to believe that in this respect this institution was vastly different from many American law schools. There was no evidence of venal intent, no hooded sheets in the closet, not even a set of subtly coded standards that were facially neutral but embodied hidden discriminatory intent. In fact, many colleagues greeted my arrival with almost visible relief that at least in 1990 they would not have to raise the same concern about the total lack of faculty diversity. What was in evidence here is what is in evidence in many places of power and influence: the same inexorable institutional logic that operates to exclude those who are always excluded; a vision constricted to the narrow confines of what is close and familiar, making invisible that which is tangible but not present; a deafness to voices speaking unfamiliar stories.

My entry as a Blackwoman into a previously unaccessed place has caused me to become ever more attuned to the dual consciousness so eloquently described by W. E. B. Du Bois.[6] Du Bois's notion is that, by reason of the history of being violently rent from Africa and the past and present experience of being violently excluded from official American identity, Blacks in the United States have a sense of double-consciousness, of "two-ness" that both filters and permeates our experience. It is a dialectic of being both within and without, of being without a self-defined and safe place.

Even in the academy, a place of privilege and power, by experience, history, and memory I remain connected still to those without and thus acquire the curious and layered perspective of an outsider's inside view. I do not seek either to romanticize nor overdraw the image of an outsider. Yet, though I am inside the academy, I am "without" in the sense that this is not a place in which either by experience or tradition the world that I know is considered, contemplated, validated, or seen as a fit subject of scholarly legal inquiry.

As an outsider then, I have faced unique challenges, demands, and occasional rewards. Many of these experiences are familiar ground shared by many people of color in the profession, although they are by no means universal and I do not intend to write consensus history here. But perhaps most well documented is the sense of tangible and intangible burdens that specifically derive from being a member of "a society of one."[7]

Such burdens also took the form of nonspecific, nonparticularized visits from students who were not in any of my classes but who came to inquire whether or not things that I was reported to be saying in my class were possibly true—such as, was it really true that I had said that race was less a scientific or genetic construct than a social one, defined to provide the basis of domination and subordination?[8] How could I be believed since I was not objective, not a dispassionate observer, but a Blackwoman with a particular view of things?

At the personal level, students have assumed and asserted that neither my intellectual qualifications nor my teaching abilities could match those of my white male counterparts. Early in my third semester of teaching, a Black student appeared in my office visibly distraught following a "conversation" with one of her fellow classmates. The Black student reported that while sitting in the library, a fellow white classmate, a student in my class, had approached and asked the Black student's view about the professor teaching the other section of the course I was teaching. The Black student responded that the professor was OK. In turn the Black student asked what opinion the white student held of me, since I was teaching the same course. The white student responded that "Professor Harris is pretty good," but that this was unexpected since, as a Blackwoman, "she probably wasn't qualified." The Black student was stunned and vigorously argued that this was a gross assumption. The white student went on to charge that affirmative action was unfair and an unwarranted derogation from merit standards. As the argument continued, the white student suggested that perhaps one of the reasons for Black underachievement was the high birth rate of Blackwomen on welfare. It was clear that the white student did not see any of this discussion as infected by racism or, in fact, as an aggressive attack on the competency or well-being of the Black student. To the white student, these were simply neutral facts and opinions about which reasonable people differ.

None of these experiences is unique; indeed, all of them have analogs in many of the experiences of scholars of color who have preceded me. Traversing this ground, however, does force me to confront the fundamental question of why I should be a law professor, apart from the reasonable level of material comfort it affords. What should I be doing here? In searching for some answers, I find guidance from those men and women who have preceded me in confronting the same questions. In their history, their scholarship, their struggles, their stories, I find the ongoing challenge to the dominant presumptions of neutrality, inevitability, and formality that undergird and have built a jurisprudence that has oppressed. The work of Charles Hamilton Houston, Thurgood Marshall, Vine de Loria, Derrick Bell, Haywood Burns, Kimberlé Williams Crenshaw, Mari Matsuda, Patricia Williams, and many others begins the task of documenting the lies, subverting the false assumptions, and reconstructing options in furtherance of the task of social transformation.

This is the foundation of a jurisprudence of resistance. Obviously, we—people of color—cannot singlehandedly transform the academy. It is far too entrenched, too complex, too deep-rooted in the sustenance of power and privilege to be overturned by the efforts, however heroic, of one, two, five, or ten minority faculty and their nonminority allies. But the lives of our people are in fact the bridge that we crossed over to enter the academy, and our organic connection to that reality cannot be allowed to fall by the wayside.

The other source in which I find guidance on this question is poetry and literature—the stories and myths forged out of reality. Achebe has suggested that in the context of social tasks it is the obligation of the poet to stay in trouble with the king. It is the task of the artist to take risks, point out contradictions, raise consciousness, and develop an oppositional role—not for its own sake, but for the sake of those of us who remain under the burden of inequities and injustice in the social order.

If the task beyond survival is social transformation, then this too requires of us—all of us—a critical insurgent stance that relentlessly challenges the lies that kill. There is much room for debate as to how we achieve this—what are the strategies and tactics. And, of course, it is always crucial that we analyze our failures. Our task cannot merely be to accommodate ourselves to the demands of the academy, although first we must survive. But we will not survive on our own any more than our predecessors did. We can choose to make use of our positions as intellectuals of color in the legal academy to agitate and at the concrete level to open the theories we develop to the check and test of reality. We can learn to survive and to stay in trouble with the king. Only in doing both will we discharge our duty and aid the birth of freedom for which we all long.

NOTES

1. Chinua Achebe, Anthills of the Savannah 117–18 (1988).

2. Chinua Achebe, Informal Address following the Publication of *Anthills of the Savannah,* Delivered at Guild Books, Chicago, Illinois (1987).

3. I use the word "Blackwoman" to describe myself to emphasize the unity of my identity as Black and woman, with neither unit primary or subordinate to the other. This is part of my refusal to accede to society's inability to conceive of the social constructs of race and gender as joined and intersecting, and to resist the constant pressure on Blackwomen to disaggregate themselves into categories defined as "women" or "Black" when they speak or otherwise assert concerns or demands.

4. The Bell incident is discussed in more detail in the chapters by Anita Allen and Lani Guinier in this volume.

5. Based on my informal survey and discussions with faculty members, there were other

Black professors at Chicago-Kent before me, but none were either tenured or in tenure-track positions in the J.D. program.

6. William E. B. Du Bois, *The Souls of Black Folk, in* Three Negro Classics 214–15 (1965).

7. This phrase is borrowed and used in the sense employed by Rachel Moran in her eloquent essay on minorities in the legal academy. Rachel F. Moran, *Commentary: The Implications of Being a Society of One,* 20 U.S.F. L. Rev. 503 (1986).

8. I do not take the view that racial distinctiveness or racial characteristics are matters of fiction. Noting and respecting differences among peoples is not racist, but to be either determinist or dismissive about race is to only perpetuate domination. Thus I argue that, given the course of human history, those who would describe or define race cannot claim a state of innocence. Because definition is a central part of domination and redefinition a critical part of liberation, the issues as they pertain to defining race are not principally biological or genetic, but social and political: who is defining, how are they defining, and why are they defining?

13 | Meditations on Being Good

Margalynne J. Armstrong

When I reflect on my experiences as a Black woman professor of law, I find myself thinking more about the students than about any other aspect of my work. Students are the reason that I am teaching law, perhaps more so for me than for other professors. This is so even though I know that being student-oriented is not the traditional path to success in this profession. My thoughts about students are not always positive; I am often frustrated with or exasperated by them. Nevertheless, I confess I sometimes identify with the students more than with other faculty. After all, when I was a law student I never encountered a professor of my race and gender. During my first two years of teaching there were students, but no faculty, who looked like me. Because I feel so connected to them, what I might mean to students and what I believe I should be to students are the focus of this meditation. One sentence, spoken to me by a student, is the springboard from which I dive into these reflections.

During my first week as a law professor, two Black women students dropped by my office to introduce themselves and welcome me. Toward the end of the visit one of the women finally blurted out the message she had come to relay to me, a Black woman new to this law school. She said, "Girl, you'd better be good." I still deliberate about these words and the various meanings they carry. These were words of advice and warning (how ominous they sounded); they were a plea, a cheer, and a challenge.

The advice contained in the admonition to be good would be useful to any new law professor without regard to the novice's race or gender. After all, doesn't every new teacher have to be good? At least these days, new law professors must be outstanding teachers, scholars, and community servants. There are so many excellent candidates competing for the privilege of teaching law that a poor teacher can easily be replaced by someone better.

Was the warning to be good a way of communicating the danger I faced as a Black woman in a world that has so many preconceptions about minority women, few of which relate to the image of a law professor?

It is possible that the ominous tone I heard in her words was merely a projection of the fear I felt as I began teaching. I feared the students, their judgment of me, and their power over me. Their assessment of my performance would determine my future as a law professor. Although I am sure that all new teachers are frightened of students at first, I felt my fears were enhanced because I was so noticeably different from most of my audience. I feared that students would not respect me because of my differences, despite my achievements, qualifications, and experience. I doubt that I will ever completely dispel my fear of discrimination because my fears are confirmed time and time again, particularly when I let down my guard.[1]

When I think of the plea in "Girl, you'd better be good," I consider the significance of the fact that this student felt that she could or should speak to me so. The student spoke as one Black woman speaks to another at home or at the beauty parlor, somewhere comfortable, but certainly not at a law school. At law school, if women of color speak at all,[2] we tend to conform our speech to the environment. Many minorities must be bicultural and bilingual in order to succeed in our society. People of color often leave behind the language and culture of home when we go off to work or to the university. The separate world of home is unrecognized and irrelevant at the law school.

But this student, who had made it through two years of law school and knew its language and forms, spoke to me as if she were at home. I was not her superior, the professor. I was "Girl" the same way she was Girl and the student who came with her was Girl. Girl could be an equal or a coconspirator or an ignoramus who had better listen because she could learn a thing or two from the speaker.

It must have felt good to use a voice that she had learned to subordinate in her professional life. To use the home voice in law school is an affirmation of the self that Black women professionals often must leave behind. Our home voices are wise and helping voices, nurturing voices, voices accorded much respect at home but valued little in the outside world. That student's home voice had knowledge to share. Her voice had insight and experience that could help me find my way around this new place. The suppression of our home voices in the academic and working world is a loss, both for Black women and for all others. If only our worlds were not so disjointed!

This student also spoke because she had some investment in me. I think she felt that Black law students stood to lose if I were not good. They would be identified with me because of our shared race. If I failed, *they* would somehow be undermined by my disgrace. The plea within her words was to "refrain from doing anything to set us back." Although this is the negative side of her identification with me, I also see positive aspects. I feel the student wanted me to do well. She was rooting for me the same way I root for the Black quarterback or the Black actor playing Macbeth, those who are doing what "They" said we could never do.

I finally come to the challenge in "Girl, you'd better be good." The challenge to be good is what sticks with me, what I hope I will always remember. I am overwhelmed by the many meanings of being good and by the difficulty of being good. Being good means doing good, doing the right thing (I struggle with even knowing what the right thing is, much less doing it). Being good means being a good teacher, somehow helping students become good and just lawyers. I usually find that I do not need to teach students to be good people; they already are. If I am to be good, I need to help students see that their goodness applies to the study and practice of law. A good part of being a good law teacher is imparting the relevance of our individual goodness to the law.

When I reflect on the student who came to tell me I'd better be good, I think of how I must strive to recognize and sustain the voices that students bring to law school. These are the voices of real life, and they are often suppressed by traditional legal education. I will succeed as a Black woman law professor if I help students preserve their home voices even as they succeed in law school. I will be a good teacher if I enable them to cherish their voices as important resources in the practice of law. I will be good if I teach my students to make their home voices a part of the legal world, a part that contributes generously to the formation of the law of the future.

NOTES

1. For example, I was on vacation in Portland, Oregon, a few summers ago and was denied a motel room because of my race. Had I anticipated discrimination, I certainly would have avoided the establishment, as the experience was quite upsetting. I eventually received a settlement after filing an administrative complaint.

2. Women law students report voluntary class participation less often than men, and their voluntary participation decreases over time. Taunya Lovell Banks, *Gender Bias in the Classroom,* 38 J. Legal Educ. 137, 141–42 (1988). The rates of women of color at predominantly white law schools who never volunteer are slightly higher than the rates of white women. Taunya Lovell Banks, Minority Women and Law School: Testimony Prepared for the ABA Minority Women Lawyers Subcommittee Roundtable 4 (Oct. 18. 1989).

14 On Being a Gorilla in Your Midst, or The Life of One Blackwoman in the Legal Academy

Jennifer M. Russell

Somewhere out there in the wilderness is a dispossessed white male whose privation was caused by my appointment to the law faculty. Chances are, he is the same white male from whom I earlier misappropriated an entitlement when New Jersey's third largest law firm hired me as an associate attorney, when the U.S. Securities and Exchange Commission hired me as a staff attorney, and when New York University Law School accepted me as a member of the class of 1984. My undergraduate enrollment at Queens College of the City University of New York probably did not disinherit this white male, since even in its heyday Queens College never stood among that group of elite institutions to which the white male seeks a coveted admission. Queens College notwithstanding, my achievements, academic and professional, will forever enjoy only a presumption of theft. That perceived rapaciousness is just one of the many dilemmas I confront as a gorilla in your midst.

I had never equated maternity with a loss or diminution of self. But as our society at large persisted in its demand for my exclusive mothering of my newborn son, I felt a great urgency to preserve and reclaim the prematernal selves I had come to know and value greatly—my scholarly self, my teacher self, my student self, my lawyer self, my career self, and so on. Faced with the possible extinction of my many nonmothering selves, within weeks of my son's birth I unofficially returned to my office (officially, I was still on maternity leave) eager to function as colleague, teacher, and legal scholar. There, in my office at the law school, I could strut my stuff on familiar, safe territory.

So I thought, until one morning a nostril-flaring beast with bloodshot eyes, menacing canines, and mauler hands ambushed me as I negotiated my way through the law school. It was a gorilla whose hairy bulk occupied the cover of the *National Geographic* magazine that had been placed anonymously in my mailbox. I stopped dead in my tracks. My heart raced and sank in one simultaneous beat. I harbored no doubts about the loud, unambiguous message conveyed: "Claim no membership in the human race. You are not even a subspecies. You are of a different species altogether. A brute. Animal, not human." It was a time-worn message communicated to persons who are not white. Similarly degrading messages have been sent to those who are not male. How ironic that it would be delivered to me at a time when I most needed all the complexities of my humanity embraced.

I reached for the magazine, picked it up, removed my other mail, and replaced the magazine in my mailbox. Those flaming eyes separated by those flaring nostrils steadily gazed at me. I was overtaken by a wave of empathy. How did such a gentle, now endangered creature become a signifier for crass, cruel messages? My empathy lasted a fleeting moment. I wiped the hand that had touched the magazine on my clothing; at least, I thought, I should not be defiled physically. For the remainder of the day, I sought refuge behind the closed door of my office.

For several days the gorilla peered out at me, watching my comings and goings from the vantage point of my mailbox, which I purposely avoided. Finally, my secretary, upon returning to the office after an extended absence, quietly disposed of the magazine. Her actions indicated to me that she too understood its message. Unaware that I had been in and out of the law school building during her absence, she assumed her interception of the message had been successful and said nothing to me about the magazine. She comforted me in a way that was calculated not to alert me to the offense, and for her tact I am grateful.

I was hurt and enraged by the gorilla message. But my token status as the first blackwoman law professor at the university counseled against any public expression of my pain and anger. I am to look on the bright side and accept the gorilla message as one more opportunity for character building and fortification (that never-ending task). Only through silent introspection am I to affirm my worth and self-esteem.

Given the demands of a professional career as a teacher and a legal scholar, it is almost inevitable that the law school becomes an important venue for the pursuit of meaningful associations that are both ego-nurturing and identity-affirming. It has never been my understanding, however, that a healthy self-esteem could flourish in environments punctuated by acts of hostility, including those of an anonymous nature.

In fairness, I must acknowledge the one-time appearance of the gorilla messenger. But even in the absence of other similarly crude emissaries, the reality is that black-women can expect to have only dysfunctional relationships in the legal academy.

The presence of the blackwoman faculty member is a daily reminder that the law school as an institution has been adjudicated a practitioner of racial and gender discrimination, an immoral act of rank order. Her presence symbolizes the institution's contrition. Her presence also evokes an ugly history of subordination from which white males (and females), directly and indirectly, purposely and fortuitously, benefited. Presented daily with such a burdensome history, many colleagues of the blackwoman faculty member are awash in guilt and shame. The need for self-preservation causes some to resort to discrete, unwitnessed acts of animosity. Others, obviously conflicted, inconsistently grant and deny her their friendship. Most have to consciously remind themselves that she is their equal. Otherwise, the tendency is to assume her inferiority, to believe that her appointment was unmerited, and was thus nothing more than a grant of their grace.

There are consequences flowing from a clemency appointment. In the parlance of the appointments process, the blackwoman is a "diversity candidate" to be contrasted against the "stellar candidate." It means that after her appointment she will be treated like an intellectual waif. She cannot legitimately claim any special competence or expertise in any subject or field. Her considered judgments regarding course coverage, teaching methodology, examinations, and grading can be challenged with impunity. Brave colleagues can query of her, "So, how does it feel not knowing whether you were appointed to our faculty because of affirmative action or because of your qualifications?"

Through it all, the blackwoman scholar must appear neither hypersensitive nor paranoid. Her white male and female colleagues will quickly note the occurrence of superficially similar events involving themselves to discredit what she knows to be the truth. The blackwoman scholar must be mindful, too, that oftentimes the touted congeniality of the faculty in actuality amounts to little more than cold civility among colleagues. How then can she—a gorilla in their midst—expect more?

The academy speaks of "diversity" because it worries about its ability to recognize the stellar candidate who appears in the guise of a blackwoman. The academy's history justifies that worry, although some believe that any invocation of the incongruities in generations past (and present) is nothing more than a cheap claim to a so-called victim status. Yet life for the blackwoman ain't never been no set of crystal stairs. So, just as the academy is about to slip into a habitual state of collective amnesia, the language of "diversity" awakens it (most times reluctantly) to face up to the haunting reality of blackness and femaleness and to its exclusionary practices premised on those attributes. The language of "diversity" forces the academy to make an accounting of its racist and sexist proclivities.

The problem is that the language of "diversity" is not sufficient to move the academy beyond mere recognition that something regrettable occurred (or is occurring). Confronting past horrors is psychologically and fiscally exhausting; it leaves the academy feeling that whatever happened, no matter how unfortunate, the egregious happening is nonetheless irremediable or politically uncorrectable. This false sense of helplessness produces a linguistic as well as a cognitive shift. Rather than speak of "diversity," the academy talks about "merit" as if the two are bipolar considerations. The discourse then maunders over whether the academy can afford to sacrifice "merit" for the sake of "diversity."

As if to substantiate the academy's misgivings about "diversity," out in the wilderness of the nonacademic world roams a white male with all his star qualities, but allegedly without his due. He is a caricature with whom many sympathize; he is accorded most-favored-person status. Deep in the wilderness of the academy there is an exceptional blackwoman; however, her just deserts remain contested. She is constructed as a gorilla. Does anyone in the academy care that she might be in harm's way?

15 | Full Circle

Rachel F. Moran

When I was invited to give the talk on which this essay is based, I must confess that I had some mixed feelings. First, I kept thinking that I was too young to start telling autobiographical stories, but I suppose this is a reminder of how recently people of color have entered the legal academy. As it happens, though still in my thirties, I am one of the senior faculty among Latinos in law teaching. Second, I am a very private person. I recall Philip Roth's observation that he could be more honest in his fiction than his autobiography.[1] By this, I think he meant that when we try to speak directly about ourselves, we can not. We can speak only through the layers of denial, fear, hope, self-doubt, self-love, and self-protection we carry with us as our armor against a frightening and uncertain world. Still, I am going to tell these stories as best and as honestly as I can, and if they resonate with you, perhaps they have some authenticity.

When I was a child, my family moved to an all-white suburb in the Midwest. Our arrival was a subject of concern among some of our neighbors because although my father was Irish, my mother is Mexican. Several families gave us a friendly reception, but others kept a chilly social distance. Yet everyone observed the basic rules of civility until the day an unidentified man appeared in the afternoon to confront us and tell us that we did not belong in the neighborhood and should get out. My father was at work, and my mother shepherded my baby brother and me to the middle of a large room, out of the range of any windows. We huddled quietly on the floor as this man peered into our home and shouted for us to come out and get what we deserved. Eventually, he must have concluded that no one was at home, gave up, and went away. At first, I felt nothing but relief, though I also regretted that the police had not shown up quickly enough to catch this intruder. After another twenty minutes had gone by, however, I realized that the police were not coming, presumably because no one had called them. I knew that some of our neighbors were at home, and I was sure that at least one or two of them had observed this man's theatrics. The realization that not one person had cared enough to contact the police on my family's behalf made me feel lonelier than any isolated act of individual hatred. In my own childish way, I vowed to do better. I promised myself that if I ever got anywhere, I would not stand by silently as people were victimized; I would speak out.

Of course, there was the little problem of getting there. I have certainly faced obstacles along the way, but I also have been very fortunate that at critical stages in my life, people reached out to me to help me along. I call these individuals my archipelago of upward mobility. They are people who despite their own burdens, limitations, and vulnerabilities took the time and effort to show me life's promise. When I was nominated last year for a distinguished teaching award at the University of California at Berkeley, I was asked to write an essay on my teaching philosophy. In contrast to other candidates, who talked about their experiences in higher education or how their teaching and research relate to each other, I singled out my second-grade teacher, the person who introduced me to the tradition of teaching as an act of nurturance, a gift passed down from one generation to the next. For me, she epitomized the archipelago of upward mobility and made my very presence at Berkeley possible.

At the time that I entered the second grade, my family was still living in the all-white Midwestern suburb I have described. Our neighbors by and large had made a fragile peace with us, but this delicate truce was broken when I was placed in a class for gifted children based on my IQ score. I knew that parents had called the school to complain; they felt that there must be something wrong with the intelligence test if "the Mexican kid," as they called me, had been put in the gifted program and their children had not. Some of my peers even complained to me directly, advising me that "My parents told me that it's not fair that you're in and I'm not." As I wrote in my essay for the distinguished teaching award:

> On the first day of second grade, I arrived at class feeling both excited and apprehensive, curious and wary. I knew that a number of people felt that I didn't belong there, and I wasn't sure what my reception would be. Imagine my delight, then, when I discovered that my teacher, Mrs. Lola Cleavenger, liked me. She smiled at me, encouraged me, and believed in me. She seemed to see all the potential in me that others had denied, and I thrived under her tutelage. During difficult times that followed, Mrs. Cleavenger's legacy of goodwill remained with me. . . .

> Approximately thirty years after I entered my second-grade classroom with a mixture of hesitation and hope, I like to think that I have been nominated for this teaching award because I have never forgotten what it is like to be a student. Though there are times when I am tired and when I fail, during my best moments of teaching I know that I reach out to the lonely, frightened child in each of us still searching for Mrs. Cleavenger.[2]

I believe that people like Mrs. Cleavenger made a huge difference in my life, but I do not think individual acts of kindness alone account for my success in reaching the upper echelons of legal academia. At about the time that I was in Mrs. Cleavenger's class, I remember walking through the halls of my elementary school and overhearing another teacher remark, "What a shame! Such a bright girl, but there's no future for her." Just as she was bemoaning my lack of opportunity, a technological innovation called television was bringing images of social transformation into my home. I could watch people linking arms, chanting, and being confronted by the police. I saw lines of protesters being held back and being broken. At the time, I did not really understand what was happening, because in the wonderful world of television, these figures were in some ways as unreal to me as my childhood hero, Whizzo the Clown, who had his very own show. Later, however, I realized that all of that chanting and confrontation had been moving social boundaries, and someday I would navigate through a new space of educational and economic opportunity opened up to me through that struggle. The elementary school teacher, commenting on my limited possibilities, could not foresee these changes. She just did not know that the world would be transformed, and I would slip through to a new life.

I have worked hard to make it in the legal profession, but I also have been extraordinarily lucky both in having an archipelago of upward mobility and in traversing it at a time when it could extend further than ever before. In fact, these combined strokes of good fortune are precisely what enabled me to survive and thrive in the legal academy. When I arrived at the law school in Berkeley, I was the first entry-level faculty member of color ever hired there. Shortly before I started teaching, a Latino colleague at another institution called me to say, "Rachel, I want you to know that it's not going to be easy. It's a tough crowd at Berkeley, but you should also know that there are many people there who want you to succeed. Lean on those people." I took his wise counsel; I leaned on my allies, and they supported me, making it possible to endure in the sometimes difficult role of trailblazer. Just like Mrs. Cleavenger, these individuals have been critical to my personal success, but I believe that I gained access to Berkeley because of structural changes in the definition of who belongs in the academy. My law school dean has been conducting a study of "firsts" for women in law; one day, she informed me that so far as she could tell from her research, I was the first Latina appointed to an American law school outside Puerto Rico. Realizing that I had been appointed in the 1980s, I told her, "That's terrible," for change had been so long in coming. She responded, "No, that's wonderful," because after all, change had finally arrived. It is always flattering to be a "first," but in my heart, I know that I am not the first woman of Latino origin gifted enough to belong on the faculty of an American law school. Rather, I am simply the first one in the right place at the right time to be admitted to the ranks of legal academia. My life has been one long, sweet song of serendipity, and I have savored every note.

As a law teacher, I have known both the pain and the pleasure of identity politics. At times, the focus on personal characteristics can be terribly frustrating. For example, students regularly ask me about my background, sometimes because I challenge their stereotypes. While I was on an academic visit, one member of my class advised me that "There's a rumor going around that you're Latina. But a lot of people don't believe it because your class isn't Mickey Mouse enough." In response, I provided a quick overview of my genealogy and told the student to feel free to tell others so that everyone would know exactly who I am. I am still not sure that this was the right response; it seems singularly awkward to have to reveal my personal history for the unquestioned privilege of teaching torts. On another occasion, a female student came to complain that women in my class were not speaking as much as men. She accused me of silencing women because of unconscious sexism; somehow, in making it to the top of the legal profession, I had become an honorary male. This time, I advised her that I made it a point to call on people who had not previously spoken in class, but my task would be much easier if women students volunteered more often. Our conversation had a happy ending; afterwards, women did raise their hands with greater frequency, perhaps as an act of feminism. However, I must confess that the whole exchange left me feeling a bit exasperated, and I complained to a colleague: "First, the question is, 'Am I really a Latina?' Now, it's, 'Am I really a woman?' What's next?"

Although identity politics can be burdensome at times, my distinctive background also has been a definite asset. Some new faculty flail around trying to find a topic that they care enough to work on for years at a time, but I knew from the minute I was appointed at Berkeley that I wanted to study an issue of importance to the Latino community, bilingual education. I have written extensively on this subject, and I am now working on a book on interracial intimacy. As an academic, I have been able to undertake this study not only as an inquiry into important social questions but also as a project of self-exploration. Through my scholarly work, I confront issues of identity and belonging that I have perhaps hidden even from myself. Moreover, I have enjoyed opportunities early in my career that I otherwise might not have had or that might have come much later. For example, for the last two and a half years, I have chaired the Chicano/Latino Policy Project at the Institute for the Study of Social Change. In this position, I have had the chance to meet scholars from a range of disciplines who are working on Latino-related policy issues. My own perspective on Latino concerns has been enriched and expanded, and I am still young enough to apply the lessons I have learned to scholarly projects in the prime of my academic career. Through this work as an academic, I believe that I have kept the promise made so long ago in that Midwestern suburb to speak up if I ever had the chance.

Still, just when I think I have found my equilibrium, the ground shifts under me. As a professor in the University of California system, I am affected by a recent vote of the regents that eliminates all racial or ethnic preferences in hiring, contracting, and admissions.[3] I have felt very torn by what has happened. I have always been deeply committed to the concept of an open and accessible public university that offers the highest quality of education. After the regents' vote, I was asked to serve on a law school committee and campus task force that would shape implementation of the regents' resolutions. As I proceed with this work, I often wonder whether I am preserving what can be salvaged of my vision or dismantling structures that I struggled years to defend and legitimate. In the midst of this quandary, I also find myself contemplating my future at Berkeley in the wake of the regents' decision. After the vote, a white male colleague of mine stopped by to sympathize and say that he knew how I felt. He was well meaning, but I had to insist that he did not know how I felt. I told him that he might feel bad, but I was pretty sure that I felt worse. After all, he does not have to look forward to a time of racial and ethnic isolation on the campus. He does not have to worry about populist rhetoric about racial and ethnic conflict; he does not have to read hate mail and racist tracts that paint him as inferior and undeserving; and he does not have to fear rumors of racial McCarthyism.

I am grieving at this moment for the losses sustained at Berkeley and throughout the University of California system, but as I struggle to figure out my new persona in this strange world of identity politics, I am comforted by the knowledge that people wiser than I have struggled too. In particular, I remember a story by Jorge Luis Borges in which in his old age, he confronts himself as a young man.[4] The elder Borges is amazed at the youthful Borges, who is so confident of all his answers. The mature Borges marvels at this assurance born of inexperience and energy born of naïveté. Nevertheless, the older Borges is not bitter, nor does he wish to be young again. He believes that what he has traded for his youth has been worth the cost. He realizes that with the loss of innocence has come wisdom, and he knows that faith, no matter how battered, is a surer and more constant companion than naive optimism.

NOTES

This talk is based on remarks I made as part of a panel on "The Lives of Faculty of Color: Teacher, Scholar, Activist" at the Association of American Law Schools Workshop for Law Teachers of Color, Washington, D.C., October 6, 1995.

1. Philip Roth, The Facts: A Novelist's Autobiography (1988).

2. Rachel F. Moran, Statement of Teaching Philosophy, Distinguished Teaching Award (1995).

3. Regents of the University of California, Resolution: Ensuring Equal Treatment—Admissions (SP-1, July 20, 1995); Regents of the University of California, Resolution: Ensuring Equal Treatment—Employment and Contracting (SP-2, July 20, 1995).

4. Jorge Luis Borges, *El Otro,* in El libro de arena (1975).

16 | A Tribute to Thurgood Marshall: A Man Who Broke with Tradition on Issues of Race and Gender

Anita F. Hill

This chapter gives me an opportunity to express my own feelings of respect and appreciation for the contributions to principles of equality made by Thurgood Marshall as a judge and, prior to his appointment to the Supreme Court, as an attorney. My tribute to Marshall attempts to put his work within the framework of the institutions and the lives he impacted, directly and indirectly—within the framework of the vast majority of black Americans—and in particular within the framework of the experiences of African American women.

This tribute comments on his commitment, as a lawyer and judge, in his life and in his jurisprudence, to gender equality. I bring to this writing my own distinctive perspective. As an African American woman, I am a member of two categories of persons who have been historically and presently victimized by the discrimination Marshall fought against. In addition, as a law professor whose respect for the law increases with my study of it, I am deeply indebted to Thurgood Marshall. Many of his contributions to the quality of my life and to my career were made before I was born and certainly before I was old enough to recognize them. Yet, particularly in these days when some of the legal advances he made have been seemingly reversed, and when others are threatened, it is critical that we pay tribute to what he so ably accomplished over the course of his career. By doing so we can only hope to encourage others to believe in and continue his struggle.

Of particular significance to those of us associated with the University of Oklahoma is Thurgood Marshall's representation of Ada Lois Sipuel Fisher in her suit, initiated in 1946, against the board of regents of the university for admission into our law school.[1] Integration gave Sipuel and other black students the opportunity to attend law school in her home state.[2] In addition, integration improved the educational opportunities for all the students who attended the school.[3] The atmosphere of the College of Law, the entire university, and the society in which it operates were forever changed by the *Sipuel* case. As a native Oklahoman, a female, and the first African American to hold a tenured faculty position at the university's College of Law, I am keenly aware of those changes. Having been called by the highest court in the country to account for the injustice of the rules that prevented admission of blacks to the state's "flagship" institution, and having been challenged to narrow the gap between the reality and the rhetoric of "equal protection under the law," the College of Law is a better institution, a better law school.

The role the *Sipuel* case was to play in the dismantling of the "separate but equal" doctrine has been the subject of commentary on the strategy of Thurgood Marshall and the civil rights agenda of the NAACP.[4] One commentator has suggested that the timing of *Sipuel,* immediately following the decision in *Gaines ex rel. Canada v. Missouri,*[5] and on the heels of *Sweatt v. Painter,*[6] indicates that the NAACP Legal Defense Fund perhaps saw *Sipuel* as the final challenge to the "separate but equal" doctrine established in *Plessy v. Ferguson,* the case that would result in the overturning of legalized segregation.[7]

What became more evident during the litigation of the *Sipuel* case was that Ada Lois Sipuel undoubtedly suffered from the contemporary legal and social biases against all black people. Nevertheless, little comment has been made about the fact that Marshall chose to pursue the dismantling of *Plessy* through the representation of a black female plaintiff. The choice of a female plaintiff was significant and, I believe, indicative of Marshall's commitment to racial and gender equality for African Americans, a commitment further exemplified during his time as a judge.

Ada Lois Sipuel was a nineteen-year-old honors student and junior at the State College for Negroes in Langston, Oklahoma, when she decided to apply for admission to law school. Based on her qualifications she would have easily been accepted for admission into the law school at the University of Oklahoma. Nevertheless, her race precluded her admission to the only public law school in Oklahoma. According to Census Bureau statistics, of the 3,243 lawyers in the state in 1940, only twenty-five were black males and fifty were white females.[8] In 1946, Sipuel's gender, alone, would have prevented her from admission to many outstanding law schools, among them Harvard Law School.[9] In 1950, only 3 percent of the lawyers and judges in the United States were women and 0.04 percent of the lawyers and judges were African American women. The plaintiffs in all other landmark higher education desegregation cases had been black males.[10] Plaintiffs in the higher education desegregation suits pursued by the NAACP were carefully selected for their likelihood of success in the programs for which they sought entrance.[11] Ada Lois Sipuel was no different. Nevertheless, Marshall was indeed challenging a double barrier of cultural perceptions in his representation of Sipuel—a barrier bolstered not only by the *Dred Scott* and *Plessy* opinions but by the *Bradwell* opinion as well.[12] As one commentator recently noted, "For a black woman in those days . . . to be in the vanguard of the struggle for the liberation of black people—male and female—required a rare brand of courage."[13] Sipuel, at nineteen, exemplified that courage when she decided to seek the assistance of the NAACP after a 1945 state NAACP meeting produced a memorandum announcing that the state would be sued because of its failure to provide an education for blacks who wanted to study the law.

Sipuel and Roscoe Dunjee, a lawyer and publisher in the Oklahoma City area, met with then University of Oklahoma president George Lynn Cross, who informed her that she would be denied admission on the basis of her race. The basis for his refusal to enroll her was a state provision that prohibited the education of black and white students in the same institution and provided penalties for individuals who violated the prohibition.

In April 1946, the case was filed in state court and, after the usual delays, her claim was heard. Eventually, the state supreme court denied Sipuel's request for admission on the ground that she could not use a writ of mandamus to challenge the constitutionality of the state provision. Marshall's appeal to the U.S. Supreme Court was granted. In the brief filed in the *Sipuel* case, Marshall directly challenged the "separate but equal" doctrine of *Plessy*.[14] Though the Supreme Court issued its decision in the *Sipuel* case in a "move of startling suddenness," four days after hearing the oral argument, it did not seize the opportunity to overturn *Plessy*.[15] Instead, rather than ordering Sipuel's admission into the law school, the Court gave the state of Oklahoma the alternative of providing a separate school for blacks within the state. A redeeming point of the decision was that it mandated that the opportunity for education must be provided for Sipuel and other black students "as soon as it [was] for applicants of any other group."[16] The state supreme court responded by ordering the establishment of a law school for blacks. The order came on January 17, 1948, only five days after the U.S. Supreme Court's decision, and had to be implemented by January 29, 1948, the scheduled date for registration of white students at the existing law school. Further litigation ensued in state court to determine whether the newly established school was equal to the law school at the University of Oklahoma. Eventually the state abandoned this pursuit. The Jim Crow school, established to avoid granting Sipuel admission to the existing law school, was closed, and she entered the University of Oklahoma, graduating with her law degree in 1950. Because the Supreme Court refused to address the challenge to *Plessy* as presented to it on *Sipuel,* the doctrine of "separate but equal" was changed very little by Sipuel's admission into the law school at the University of Oklahoma.[17]

Though Sipuel's qualifications were beyond questioning, her role as a plaintiff must have been the subject of some discussion by the legal team of the NAACP. Yet Marshall's willingness to pursue the case and represent Sipuel before the U.S. Supreme Court speaks to his real commitment to equality even beyond that of many of his contemporaries. By representing Sipuel in her pursuit of a law degree, Marshall challenged notions held by the larger community about race and gender as well as notions held by the black community about gender.

Today's national statistics on women studying to become lawyers are very different from what they were in 1948. Currently women make up between 40 percent and 50 percent of the incoming law school classes.[18] With regard to both race and gender, the state of Oklahoma has changed. The University of Oklahoma College of Law has graduated ninety black lawyers; fifty-two of those graduates are women. Currently, according to the Oklahoma Bar Association, of the approximately 13,000 members of the Oklahoma bar who reside in the state, 2,738 are women.[19] No information is available from the bar association on the race of bar members.

In 1992 Ada Lois Sipuel was inducted into the Order of the Coif at the College of Law. The following year she received an honorary doctorate of law degree and took her seat on the University of Oklahoma Board of Regents, the very entity that had sought to exclude her nearly forty years earlier. She was the second African American and second African American woman to sit on the board. In the interim years Sipuel was a college professor at Langston University, her undergraduate alma mater, and a practicing attorney.

Karen Hastie Williams,[20] a former law clerk to Justice Marshall, gave a moving tribute to him in August 1992 at the American Bar Association annual meeting, part of which I will never forget. Had it not been for Marshall, she said, there would not have been a Karen Hastie Williams, or a Stephen Carter,[21] or, she went on, an Anita Hill. Williams made it clear to me that were it not for Marshall, perhaps, I would never have been educated at Oklahoma State University, attended Yale Law School, or been tenured at the University of Oklahoma College of Law. Without Marshall, I certainly would not continue to believe in the ability of the legal system to right wrongs, cure injustices, and positively impact the lives of people far removed from the court's decisions. We must continue in our own ways to pay tribute by telling the story.

NOTES

1. *See* Fisher v. Hurst, 333 U.S. 147 (1948); Sipuel v. Board of Regents of the Univ. of Oklahoma, 332 U.S. 631 (1948).

2. At the time of the lawsuit, the University of Oklahoma College of Law was the only public law school in the state. It remains so today.

Though she was married, Ada Lois Sipuel Fisher used her maiden name, Sipuel, in the litigation. This was an unusual practice for the time and was the subject of discussion by the NAACP team. The explanation given was that she used her maiden name to keep her application in conformance with her undergraduate record. *See* Mark V. Tushnet, The NAACP'S Legal Strategy against Segregated Education, 1925-1950, at 192 (1987).

3. A contemporaneous editorial in the student newspaper at the university, the *Oklahoma Daily,* argued, "Separate school systems are impractical, undesirable and unnecessary." Tushnet, *supra* note 2, at 121.

4. *See* Richard Kluger, Simple Justice: The History of Brown v. Board of Education and Black America's Struggle for Equality 258–60 (1975).

5. 305 U.S. 337 (1938).

6. 339 U.S. 629 (1950).

7. *See* Tushnet, *supra* note 3, at 120.

8. *See* J. Clay Smith, Jr., Emancipation: The Making of the Black Lawyer, 1844–1944, at tbl. 13 (1993).

9. Women were admitted to Harvard Law School for the first time in 1949, the same year Sipuel was admitted to the University of Oklahoma Law School. Karen B. Morello, The Invisible Bar: The Woman Lawyer in America, 1638 to the Present 101 (1986).

10. Lloyd Gaines, the plaintiff in *Gaines ex rel. Canada v. Missouri,* was a twenty-five-year-old graduate of Lincoln University in Missouri. Lincoln University was the state of Missouri's public institution for black students. Kluger, *supra* note 4, at 200. Herman Sweatt, the plaintiff in *Sweatt v. Painter,* was a black mailman. *Id.* at 260.

11. *See* Tushnet, *supra* note 3.

12. Bradwell v. Illinois, 83 U.S. (16 Wall.) 130 (1872) (upholding the right of a state to bar women from the practice of law).

13. Nathaniel R. Jones, *In Memoriam: Juanita Jackson Mitchell,* 52 Md. L. Rev. 503, 503 (1993).

14. Brief for Petitioner, Sipuel v. Board of Regents of the Univ. of Oklahoma, 332 U.S. 631 (1948) (No. 363).

15. Tushnet, *supra* note 3, at 121.

16. *Sipuel,* 332 U.S. at 633.

17. *See* Jack Greenburg, Crusaders in the Courts: How a Dedicated Band of Lawyers Fought for the Civil Rights Revolution 65 (1994).

18. Telephone Interview with Sue Velie, Career Advisor, University of Oklahoma College of Law (Jan. 11, 1995).

19. Telephone Interview with Chery Steele, Computer Operator, Oklahoma Bar Association (Jan. 11, 1995).

20. Williams clerked for Marshall during the 1974–75 term. She is now a lawyer with the firm of Crowell and Moring. For her moving tribute, see Karen H. Williams, Eulogy Delivered at the Funeral of the Honorable Thurgood Marshall (Jan. 28, 1993), *in* Debra L. W. Cohn, Foreword, *Thurgood Marshall and His Legacy: A Tribute,* 2 Temple Pol. & Civ. Rts. L. Rev. 155, 159 (1993).

21. Carter is the author of a number of works and is writing a history of Thurgood Marshall based on interviews with Marshall conducted in 1992 and 1993. *See* Tony Mauro, *Thankfully, Marshall's Stories Can Be Told,* Legal Times, Feb. 1, 1993, at 8.

Questions and Suggested Readings for Part 2

1. All of the articles in part 2 address the extent to which women of color perceive themselves to be outsiders in the academy. Why should we be concerned about the mistreatment of a few "privileged" women when many more women are on welfare, are homeless, or are otherwise materially disadvantaged? Does this entire part obscure the more fundamental aspects of gender discrimination?

2. Anita Allen contends that the role model argument creates a "whisper of inferiority." Is this necessarily the case? Many white people talk about the need for positive role models. Are such individuals deemed to be inferior or just the opposite?

3. How are the "disappeared" discussed by Lani Guinier similar to the "invisible" discussed by Celina Romany in part 1? Should some women be labeled as honorary males if they have "bought" into the system? What does buying into the system actually mean?

4. In her first week of teaching law, a black woman law student told Margalynne Armstrong, "Girl, you'd better be good." How are the issues of tokenism and affirmative action reflected in this student's statement? Contrast the interpretations of the comment as advice, warning, plea, cheer, and challenge. Compare Armstrong's concern about being "good" to Linda Greene's concern about not wanting to be a token. How important is it that Armstrong was inspired to meditate on being good by a law student? An African American student?

5. What did the gorilla message represent to Jennifer Russell? Are there alternate interpretations? Does she attach too much significance to this single incident? Compare her use of gorilla to Guinier's use of the term "gentlemen." How do such

messages constitute spirit injury as discussed by Wing in part 1 and spirit murder as discussed by Williams in part 5? Why is calling for "diversity" not sufficient to remedy the exclusionary practices within the legal academy?

For further reading, see entire issue of 6 Berkeley Women's L.J. (1990–91), entitled Black Women Law Professors: Building a Community at the Intersection of Race and Gender; Frontiers of Legal Thought: Gender, Race, and Culture in the Law, 1991 Duke L.J. 271–412; Taunya Lovell Banks, *Gender Bias in the Classroom,* 38 J. Legal Educ. 137 (1988); Robin Barnes, *Black Women Law Professors and Critical Self-Consciousness: A Tribute to Professor Denise Carty-Bennia,* 6 Berkeley Women's L.J. 57 (1990–91); Derrick Bell, Confronting Authority: Reflections of an Ardent Protestor (1994); Alice Bullock, *A Dean's Role in Supporting Recruitment of Minority Faculty,* 10 St. Louis U. Pub. L. Rev. 347 (1991); Linda Crane, *Colorizing the Law School Experience,* 1991 Wis. L. Rev. 1427; Okainer Dark, *Cosmic Consciousness: Teaching on the Frontiers,* 38 Loy. L. Rev. 101 (1992); Linda Greene, *Serving the Community: Aspiration and Abyss for the Law Professor of Color,* 10 St. Louis U. Pub. L. Rev. 297 (1991); Lani Guinier, *Becoming Gentlemen: Women's Experiences at One Ivy League Law School,* 143 U. Pa. L. Rev. 1 (1994); Angela Harris, *Women of Color in Legal Education: Representing La Mestiza,* 6 Berkeley Women's L.J. 107 (1990–91); Beverly Moran, *Quantum Leap: A Black Woman Uses Legal Education to Obtain Her Honorary White Pass,* 6 Berkeley Women's L.J. 118 (1990–91); Denise Morgan, *Role Models: Who Needs Them Anyway,* 6 Berkeley Women's L.J. 122 (1990–91); Odeana Neal, *The Making of a Law Teacher,* 6 Berkeley Women's L.J. 128 (1990–91); Wilma Pinder, *When Will Black Women Lawyers Slay the Two Headed Dragon: Racism and Gender Bias?,* 20 Pepp. Law Rev. 1053 (1993).

See generally Milner Ball, *The Legal Academy and Minority Scholars,* 103 Harv. L. Rev. 1855 (1990); Richard H. Chused, *The Hiring and Retention of Minorities and Women on American Law School Faculties,* 137 U. Pa. L. Rev. 537 (1988); Richard Delgado, *Minority Law Professors' Lives: The Bell-Delgado Survey,* 24 Harv. C.R.-C.L. L. Rev. 349 (1989); Leslie Espinoza, *Masks and Other Disguises: Exposing Legal Academia,* 103 Harv. L. Rev. 1878 (1990); Andrew Haines, *Minority Law Professors and the Myth of Sisyphus: Consciousness and Praxis within the Special Teaching Challenges in American Law Schools,* 10 Nat'l Black L.J. 247 (1988); Alex Johnson, *The New Voice of Color,* 100 Yale L.J. 2007 (1991); Alex Johnson, *Racial Critiques of Legal Academia: A Reply in Favor of Context,* 43 Stan. L. Rev. 137 (1990); Duncan Kennedy, *A Cultural Pluralist Case for Affirmative Action in Legal Academia,* 1990 Duke L.J. 705; Gary Peller, *Race Consciousness,* 1990 Duke L.J. 758.

3 | On Mothering or Not

Part 3 examines the interplay of race, class, and gender in the areas of pregnancy and motherhood. Dorothy E. Roberts's provocative analysis, entitled *Punishing Drug Addicts Who Have Babies: Women of Color, Equality, and the Right of Privacy*, discusses how poor black women are disproportionately prosecuted for using drugs while pregnant. Such prosecutions deter women from seeking prenatal care and constitute a continuation of the historic devaluing of black motherhood. If the state's concern was with the health of the baby, Roberts asks, why does the state not pursue the far more common instances of affluent white users of alcohol, prescription medication, or even marijuana? The constitutional right at issue is not the right to use cocaine, but the right to decide to have a baby, even though one is a drug addict.

In *Furthering the Inquiry: Race, Class, and Culture in the Forced Medical Treatment of Pregnant Women*, Lisa C. Ikemoto finds that almost all the women subjected to forced medical treatment in a 1987 survey were poor women of color. Her analysis, like that of Roberts, indicates that these women are regarded by the predominantly white male medical community and courts as bad mothers, not fit for motherhood. Yet, in many instances, the mother's refusal to submit to treatment may be based on a correct sense of self-awareness and of class and cultural realities. She calls for coalition building that leads to more choice for the "have-nots."

To address the ongoing welfare debate, young lawyer Nathalie A. Augustin analyzes the concept of Learnfare and the awarding of welfare in *Learnfare and Black Motherhood: The Social Construction of Deviance*. Stereotypes about the welfare mother as a lazy black unfit single mother undergird Wisconsin's Learnfare program, which ties AFDC welfare payments to attendance of teenagers in school. Involving three interrelated systems of oppression—racism, classism, and patriarchy, such programs place the blame for the child's truancy solely on the welfare mother and do not consider the societal factors of poverty, crime, joblessness, and illiteracy that contribute to the problem.

Critical Race Feminist foremother Patricia J. Williams discusses her experience as an adoptive single black mother in *Spare Parts, Family Values, Old Children, Cheap*. She critiques the degree to which society devalues black children as unwanted surplus and notes that they can be "bought" for half the price of white babies from adoption agencies. This market valuation of babies embodies what is wrong with community and family life in America. Her analysis attacks a well-known article by Judge Richard Posner and his colleague Elisabeth Landes for its Law and Economics approach to the valuation of children, according to which desired white babies are in high demand, while surplus black babies are unwanted and should be discouraged.

Finally, Isabelle R. Gunning adds sexual orientation to our understanding of multiple consciousness by discussing her experiences as a black lesbian mother in *A Story from Home: On Being a Black Lesbian Mother*. She details how she and her partner deal with homophobia and the coming out process as lesbian parents within the larger black community at the black school their adoptive daughter attends.

17 Punishing Drug Addicts Who Have Babies: Women of Color, Equality, and the Right of Privacy

Dorothy E. Roberts

In July 1989, Jennifer Clarise Johnson, a twenty-three-year-old crack addict, became the first woman in the United States to be criminally convicted for exposing her baby to drugs while pregnant.[1] Florida law enforcement officials charged Johnson with two counts of delivering a controlled substance to a minor after her two children tested positive for cocaine at birth. Because the relevant Florida drug law did not apply to fetuses, the prosecution invented a novel interpretation of the statute. The prosecution obtained Johnson's conviction for passing a cocaine metabolite from her body to her newborn infants during the sixty-second period after birth and before the umbilical cord was cut.

A growing number of women across the country have been charged with criminal offenses after giving birth to babies who test positive for drugs. The majority of these women, like Jennifer Johnson, are poor and Black.[2] Most are addicted to crack cocaine. The prosecution of drug-addicted mothers is part of an alarming trend toward greater state intervention into the lives of pregnant women under the rationale of protecting the fetus from harm. Such government intrusion is particularly harsh for poor women of color. They are the least likely to obtain adequate prenatal care, the most vulnerable to government monitoring, and the least able to conform to the white middle-class standard of motherhood. They are therefore the primary targets of government control.

The prosecution of drug-addicted mothers implicates two fundamental tensions. First, punishing a woman for using drugs during pregnancy pits the state's interest in protecting the future health of a child against the mother's interest in autonomy over her reproductive life—interests that until recently had not been thought to be in conflict. Second, such prosecutions represent one of two possible responses to the problem of drug-exposed babies. The government may choose either to help women have healthy pregnancies or to punish women for their prenatal conduct. Although it might seem that the state could pursue both of these avenues at once, the two responses are ultimately irreconcilable. Far from deterring injurious drug use, prosecution of drug-addicted mothers in fact deters pregnant women from using available health and counseling services because it causes women to fear that, if they seek help, they could be reported to government authorities and charged with a crime. Moreover, prosecution blinds the public to the possibility of nonpunitive solutions and to the inadequacy of the nonpunitive solutions that are currently available.

The debate between those who favor protecting the rights of the fetus and those who favor protecting the rights of the mother has been extensively waged in the literature.[3] This chapter seeks to illuminate the current debate by examining the experiences of the class of women who are primarily affected—poor Black women.

Providing the perspective of poor Black women offers two advantages. First, examining legal issues from the viewpoint of those they affect most helps to uncover the real reasons for state action and to explain the real harms it causes. It exposes the way the prosecutions deny poor Black women a facet of their humanity by punishing their reproductive choices. The government's choice of a punitive response perpetuates the historical devaluation of Black women as mothers. Viewing the legal issues from the experiential standpoint of the defendants enhances our understanding of the constitutional dimensions of the state's conduct.

Second, examining the constraints on poor Black women's reproductive choices expands our understanding of reproductive freedom in particular and the right of privacy in general. Much of the literature discussing reproductive freedom has adopted a white middle-class perspective, which focuses narrowly on abortion rights. The feminist critique of privacy doctrine has also neglected many of the concerns of poor women of color.

My analysis presumes that Black women experience various forms of oppression simultaneously, as a complex interaction of race, gender, and class that is more than the sum of its parts. It is impossible to isolate any one of the components of this oppression or to separate the experiences that are attributable to one component from experiences attributable to the others. The prosecution of drug-addicted mothers cannot be explained as simply an issue of gender inequality. Poor Black women have been selected for punishment as a result of an inseparable combination of their gender, race, and economic status. Their devaluation as mothers, which underlies the prosecutions, has its roots in the unique experience of slavery and has been perpetuated by complex social forces.

This chapter advances an account of the constitutionality of prosecutions of drug-addicted mothers that explicitly considers the experiences of poor Black women. The constitutional arguments are based on theories of both racial equality and the right of privacy. I argue that punishing drug addicts who choose to carry their pregnancies to term unconstitutionally burdens the right to autonomy over reproductive decisions. Violation of poor Black women's reproductive rights helps perpetuate a racist hierarchy in our society. The prosecutions thus impose a standard of motherhood that is offensive to principles of both equality and privacy.

Although women accused of prenatal crimes can present their defenses only in court, judges are not the only government officials charged with a duty to uphold the Constitution. Given the Supreme Court's current hostility to claims of substantive equality and reproductive rights, my arguments might be directed more fruitfully to legislatures than to the courts.

BACKGROUND: THE STATE'S PUNITIVE RESPONSE TO DRUG-ADDICTED MOTHERS

THE CRACK EPIDEMIC AND THE STATE'S RESPONSE

Crack cocaine appeared in America in the early 1980s, and its abuse has grown to epidemic proportions. Crack is especially popular among inner-city women.[4] Most crack-addicted women are of childbearing age, and many are pregnant.[5] This phenomenon has contributed to an explosion in the number of newborns affected by maternal drug use. Some experts estimate that as many as 375,000 drug-exposed infants are born every year.[6]

Babies born to drug-addicted mothers may suffer a variety of medical, developmental, and behavioral problems, depending on the nature of their mother's substance abuse. Data on the extent and potential severity of the adverse effects of maternal cocaine use are controversial.[7] The interpretation of studies of cocaine-exposed infants is often clouded by the presence of other fetal risk factors, such as the mother's use of additional drugs, cigarettes, and alcohol and her socioeconomic status.

The response of state prosecutors, legislators, and judges to the problem of drug-exposed babies has been punitive. They have punished women who use drugs during pregnancy by depriving these mothers of custody of their children, by jailing them during their pregnancy, and by prosecuting them after their babies are born.

THE DISPROPORTIONATE IMPACT ON POOR BLACK WOMEN

Poor Black women bear the brunt of prosecutors' punitive approach. These women are the primary targets of prosecutors, not because they are more likely to be guilty of fetal abuse, but because they are Black and poor. Poor women, who are disproportionately Black,[8] are in closer contact with government agencies, and their drug use is therefore more likely to be detected. Black women are also more likely to be reported to government authorities, in part because of the racist attitudes of health care professionals. Finally, their failure to meet society's image of the ideal mother makes their prosecution more acceptable.

It is also significant that, out of the universe of maternal conduct that can injure a fetus, prosecutors have focused on crack use. The selection of crack addiction for punishment can be justified neither by the number of addicts nor the extent of the harm to the fetus. Excessive alcohol consumption during pregnancy, for example, can cause severe fetal injury, and marijuana use may also adversely affect the unborn.[9] The incidence of both these types of substance abuse is high as well. In addition, prosecutors do not always base their claims on actual harm to the child, but on the mere delivery of crack by the mother.

Focusing on Black crack addicts rather than on other perpetrators of fetal harms serves two broader social purposes. First, prosecution of these pregnant women serves to degrade women whom society views as undeserving to be mothers and to discourage them from having children. If prosecutors had instead chosen to prosecute affluent women addicted to alcohol or prescription medication, the policy of criminalizing prenatal conduct very likely would have suffered a hasty demise. Society is much more willing to condone the punishment of poor women of color who fail to meet the middle-class ideal of motherhood.

In addition to legitimizing fetal rights enforcement, the prosecution of crack-addicted mothers diverts public attention from social ills such as poverty, racism, and a misguided national health policy and implies instead that shamefully high Black infant death rates [10] are caused by the bad acts of individual mothers. Poor Black mothers thus become the scapegoats for the causes of the Black community's ill health.

PUNISHING BLACK MOTHERS AND THE PERPETUATION OF RACIAL HIERARCHY

The legal analysis of the prosecutions implicates two constitutional protections: the equal protection clause of the Fourteenth Amendment and the right of privacy. These two constitutional challenges appeal to different but related values. A basic premise of equality doctrine is that certain fundamental aspects of the human personality, including decisional autonomy, must be respected in all persons. Theories of racial equality and privacy can be used as related means to achieve a common end of eliminating the legacy of racial discrimination that has devalued Black motherhood. Both aim to create a society in which Black women's reproductive choices, including the decision to bear children, are given full respect and protection.

The equal protection clause [11] embodies the Constitution's ideal of racial equality. State action that violates this ideal by creating classifications based on race must be subjected to strict judicial scrutiny. The equal protection clause, however, does not explicitly define the meaning of equality or delineate the nature of prohibited government conduct. As a result, equal protection analyses generally have divided into two visions of equality: one that is informed by an antidiscrimination principle, the other by an antisubordination principle. [12]

The antidiscrimination approach identifies the primary threat to equality as the government's "failure to treat Black people as individuals without regard to race." [13] The goal of the antidiscrimination principle is to ensure that all members of society are treated in a color-blind or race-neutral fashion. The Supreme Court's current understanding of the equal protection clause is based on a narrow interpretation of the antidiscrimination principle. [14] The Court has confined discrimination prohibited by the Constitution to state conduct performed with a discriminatory intent. State conduct that disproportionately affects Blacks violates the Constitution only if it is accompanied by a purposeful desire to produce this outcome.

Black women prosecuted for drug use during pregnancy may be able to make out a prima facie case of discriminatory purpose.[15] The Court has recognized that a selection process characterized by broad government discretion that produces unexplained racial disparities may support the presumption of discriminatory purpose.[16]

A Black mother arrested in Pinellas County, Florida, could make out a prima facie case of unconstitutional racial discrimination by showing that a disproportionate number of those chosen for prosecution for exposing newborns to drugs are Black. In particular, she could point out the disparity between the percentage of defendants who are Black and the percentage of pregnant substance abusers who are Black. A *New England Journal of Medicine* study of pregnant women in Pinellas County found that only about 26 percent of those who used drugs were Black.[17] Yet over 90 percent of Florida prosecutions for drug abuse during pregnancy have been brought against Black women. The defendant could buttress her case with the study's finding that, despite similar rates of substance abuse, Black women were ten times more likely than white women to be reported to public health authorities for substance abuse during pregnancy. In addition, the defendant could show that both health care professionals and prosecutors wield a great deal of discretion in selecting women to be subjected to the criminal justice system. The burden would then shift to the state "to dispel the inference of intentional discrimination" by justifying the racial discrepancy in its prosecutions.

The antisubordination approach to equality would not require Black defendants to prove that the prosecutions are motivated by racial bias. Rather than requiring victims to prove distinct instances of discriminating behavior in the administrative process, the antisubordination approach considers the concrete effects of government policy on the substantive condition of the disadvantaged. Under this conception of equality, the function of the equal protection clause is to dismantle racial hierarchy by eliminating state action or inaction that effectively preserves Black subordination.

The prosecution of drug-addicted mothers demonstrates the inadequacy of antidiscrimination analysis and the superiority of the antisubordination approach. First, the antidiscrimination approach may not adequately protect Black women from prosecutions' infringement of equality, because it is difficult to identify individual guilty actors. Who are the government officials motivated by racial bias to punish Black women? The hospital staff who test and report mothers to child welfare agencies? The prosecutors who develop and implement policies to charge women who use drugs during pregnancy? Legislators who enact laws protecting the unborn?

It is unlikely that any of these individual actors intentionally singled out Black women for punishment based on a conscious devaluation of their motherhood. The disproportionate impact of the prosecutions on poor Black women does not result from such isolated, individualized decisions. Rather, it is a result of two centuries of systematic exclusion of Black women from tangible and intangible benefits enjoyed by white society. Their exclusion is reflected in Black women's reliance on public hospitals and public drug treatment centers, in their failure to obtain adequate prenatal care, in the more frequent reporting of Black drug users by health care professionals, and in society's acquiescence in the government's punitive response to the problem of crack-addicted babies.

In contrast to the antidiscrimination approach, antisubordination theory mandates that equal protection law concern itself with the concrete ways government policy perpetuates the inferior status of Black women. From this perspective, the prosecutions of crack-addicted mothers are unconstitutional because they reinforce the myth of the undeserving Black mother by singling out—whether intentionally or not—Black women for punishment. The government's punitive policy reflects a long history of denigration of Black mothers dating back to slavery, and it serves to perpetuate that legacy of unequal respect. The prosecutions should therefore be upheld only if the state can demonstrate that they serve a compelling interest that could not be achieved through less discriminatory means. A public commitment to providing adequate prenatal care for poor women and drug treatment programs that meet the needs of pregnant addicts would be a more effective means for the state to address the problem of drug-exposed babies.

CLAIMING THE RIGHT OF PRIVACY FOR WOMEN OF COLOR

IDENTIFYING THE CONSTITUTIONAL ISSUE

In deciding which of the competing interests involved in the prosecution of drug-addicted mothers prevails—the state's interest in protecting the health of the fetus or the woman's interest in preventing state intervention—we must identify the precise nature of the woman's constitutional right at stake. In the *Johnson* case, the prosecutor framed the constitutional issue as follows: "What constitutionally protected freedom did Jennifer engage in when she smoked cocaine?" That was the wrong question. Johnson was not convicted of using drugs. Her "constitutional right" to smoke cocaine was never at issue. Johnson was prosecuted because she chose to carry her pregnancy to term while she was addicted to crack. Had she smoked cocaine during her pregnancy and then had an abortion, she would not have been charged with such a serious crime. The proper question, then, is "What constitutionally protected freedom did Jennifer engage in when she decided to have a baby, even though she was a drug addict?"

Understanding the prosecution of drug-addicted mothers as punishment for having babies clarifies the constitutional right at stake. The woman's right at issue is not the right to abuse drugs or to cause the fetus to be born with defects. It is the right to choose to be a mother that is burdened by the criminalization of conduct during pregnancy. This view of the constitutional issue reveals the relevance of race to the resolution of the competing interests. Race has historically determined the value society places on an individual's right to choose motherhood. Because of the devaluation of Black motherhood, protecting the right of Black women to choose to bear a child has unique significance.

OVERVIEW OF PRIVACY ARGUMENTS

Prosecutions of drug-addicted mothers infringe on two aspects of the right to individual choice in reproductive decision making. First, they infringe on the freedom to continue a pregnancy that is essential to an individual's personhood and autonomy. This freedom implies that state control of the decision to carry a pregnancy to term can be as pernicious as state control of the decision to terminate a pregnancy. Second, the prosecutions infringe on choice by imposing an invidious government standard for the entitlement to procreate. Such imposition of a government standard for childbearing is one way society denies the humanity of those who are different. The first approach emphasizes a woman's right to autonomy over her reproductive life; the second highlights a woman's right to be valued equally as a human being.

TOWARD A NEW PRIVACY JURISPRUDENCE

In this section, I will suggest two approaches that I believe are necessary in order for privacy theory to contribute to the eradication of racial hierarchy. First, we need to develop a positive view of the right of privacy. Second, the law must recognize the connection between the right of privacy and racial equality.

The definition of privacy as a purely negative right serves to exempt the state from any obligation to ensure the social conditions and resources necessary for self-determination and autonomous decision making. Based on this narrow view of liberty, the Supreme Court has denied a variety of claims to government aid.[18] Laurence Tribe has suggested an alternative view of the relationship between the government's negative and affirmative responsibilities in guaranteeing the rights of personhood: "Ultimately, the affirmative duties of government cannot be severed from its obligations to refrain from certain forms of control; both must respond to a substantive vision of the needs of human personality."[19]

Thus, the reason legislatures should reject laws that punish Black women's reproductive choices is not an absolute and isolated notion of individual autonomy. Rather, legislatures should reject these laws as a critical step toward eradicating a racial hierarchy that has historically demeaned Black motherhood. Respecting Black women's decision to bear children is a necessary ingredient of a community that affirms the personhood of all its members.

Our understanding of the prosecutions of drug-addicted mothers must include the perspective of the women who are most directly affected. The prosecutions arise in a particular historical and political context that has constrained reproductive choice for poor women of color. The state's decision to punish drug-addicted mothers rather than help them stems from the poverty and race of the defendants and society's denial of their full dignity as human beings.

A policy that attempts to protect fetuses by denying the humanity of their mothers will inevitably fail. The tragedy of crack babies is initially a tragedy of crack-addicted mothers. Both are part of a larger tragedy of a community that is suffering a host of indignities, including, significantly, the denial of equal respect for its women's reproductive decisions.

It is only by affirming the personhood and equality of poor women of color that we will ensure the survival of their future generation. The first principle of the government's response to the crisis of drug-exposed babies should be the recognition of their mothers' worth and entitlement to autonomy over their reproductive lives. A commitment to guaranteeing these fundamental rights of poor women of color, rather than punishing them, is the true solution to the problem of unhealthy babies.

NOTES

1. See State v. Johnson, No. E89–890-CFA, slip op. at 1 (Fla. Cir. Ct. July 13, 1989), aff'd, 578 So. 2d 419 (Fla. Dist. Ct. App. 1991), rev'd, 602 So. 2d 1288 (Fla. 1992).

2. According to a memorandum prepared by the ACLU Reproductive Freedom Project, of the fifty-two defendants, thirty-five are African American, fourteen are white, two are Latina, and one is Native American. See Lynn Paltrow and Suzanne Shende, State by State Case Summary of Criminal Prosecutions against Pregnant Women (Oct. 29, 1990). In Florida, where two women have been convicted for distributing drugs to a minor, ten out of eleven criminal cases were brought against Black women. Id. at 3–5.

3. For arguments supporting the mother's right to autonomy, see, e.g., Goldberg, Medical Choices during Pregnancy: Whose Decision Is It Anyway?, 41 Rutgers L. Rev. 591 (1989). For arguments advocating protection of the fetus, see, e.g., Walker and Puzder, State Protection of the Unborn after Roe v. Wade: A Legislative Proposal, 13 Stetson L. Rev. 237, 253–63 (1984).

4. Approximately half of the nation's crack addicts are women. See Alters, Women and Crack: Equal Addiction, Unequal Care, Boston Globe, Nov. 1, 1989, at 1. The highest concentrations of crack addicts are found in inner-city neighborhoods. See Malcolm, Crack, Bane of Inner City, Is Now Gripping Suburbs, N.Y. Times, Oct. 1, 1989, at 1.

5. Many crack-addicted women become pregnant as a result of trading sex for crack or turning to prostitution to support their habit. See Alters, supra note 4, at 1.

6. See Besharov, Crack Babies: The Worst Threat Is Mom Herself, Wash. Post, Aug. 6, 1989, at B1.

7. See Koren et al., Bias against the Null Hypothesis: The Reproductive Hazards of Cocaine, Lancet, Dec. 16, 1989, at 1440, 1440.

8. Black women are five times more likely to live in poverty, five times more likely to be on welfare, and three times more likely to be unemployed than are white women. See United States Comm'n on Civil Rights, The Economic Status of Black Women 1 (1990).

9. See, e.g., Fried et al., Marijuana Use during Pregnancy and Decreased Length of Gestation, 150 Am. J. Obstetrics & Gyn. 23 (1984).

10. In 1987, the mortality rate for Black infants was 17.9 deaths per 1,000, compared to a rate of 8.6 deaths per 1,000 for white infants. See U.S. Dep't of Commerce, Bureau of Census, Statistical Abstract of the United States 77 (table 110) (1990).

11. The Fourteenth Amendment provides, in relevant part, that "[n]o State shall make or

enforce any law which shall . . . deny to any person within its jurisdiction the equal protection of the laws." U.S. Const. amend. XIV, § 1.

12. These competing views of equal protection law have been variously characterized by commentators. *See, e.g.,* L. Tribe, American Constitutional Law §§ 16–21, at 1514–21 (2d ed. 1988).

13. Dimond, *The Anti-Caste Principle: Toward a Constitutional Standard for Review of Race Cases,* 30 Wayne L. Rev. 1, 1 (1983).

14. *See* Strauss, *Discriminatory Intent and the Taming of Brown,* 56 U. Chi. L. Rev. 935, 953–54 (1989).

15. For a discussion of equal protection challenges to racially selective prosecutions, see *Developments in the Law: Race and the Criminal Process,* 101 Harv. L. Rev. 1472, 1532–49 (1988).

16. *See* Kennedy, McCleskey v. Kemp: *Race, Capital Punishment and the Supreme Court,* 101 Harv. L. Rev. 1388, 1425–27 (1988).

17. *See* Chasnoff et al., *The Prevalence of Illicit Drug or Alcohol Use during Pregnancy and Discrepancies in Mandatory Reporting in Pinellas County, Florida,* 322 New Eng. J. Med. 1202, 1204 (table 2) (1990).

18. *See, e.g.,* DeShaney v. Winnebago County Dep't of Social Servs., 489 U.S. 189, 196 (1989) ("[O]ur cases have recognized that the Due Process Clauses generally confer no affirmative right to governmental aid, even where such aid may be necessary to secure life, liberty, or property interests of which the government itself may not deprive the individual.").

19. Tribe, *supra* note 12, § 15–2, at 1305.

18 Furthering the Inquiry: Race, Class, and Culture in the Forced Medical Treatment of Pregnant Women

Lisa C. Ikemoto

When the state restricts reproductive choice, it takes control of women's bodies and women's lives. By focusing the power of the state on women with regard to their biological capacity to bear children, the law devalues women as persons and describes women as "vessels," "mother machines," or "incubators." In this article I hope to illustrate how describing and addressing the issues surrounding reproductive choice as a gendered issue without regard to race and class precludes a full understanding of the nature of patriarchy and, in fact, perpetuates it. As a context for an inquiry beyond gender, I look to cases in which doctors and hospitals have petitioned courts to order the forced medical treatment of pregnant women. Before I proceed, two points must be made here. First, the standard legal story about forced medical treatment opens the door for a discussion of biologically based gender and justifies such distinctions. By responding only to the standard story, we let it dominate the discourse. Elaborating on gender as a socially constructed, historically rooted category is one way of "seizing the discourse."[1] Second, the standard legal story does not expressly speak to race and class. By failing to look to the experience of women who have been raced and impoverished, we let the standard story blind and silence us. The de facto standard then used to identify, prioritize, and address subordination is the experience of white middle class women. This excludes and diminishes women of color, particularly those who live in poverty.

In this article I set forth the standard formulae that are used to justify forced medical treatment of pregnant women, and I question some of its basic premises. I inquire into the social construction of gender and look beyond the legal and moral formulae to subordination perpetuated on the "local" or social level; I postulate one feminist response and argue that this response, too, perpetuates patriarchy. Continuing the inquiry into race, class, and culture, I explore the silence as well as the words that reveal a mother model premised on negative and positive stereotypes and two claims to cultural superiority. I also suggest a possibility for building choice from coalition.

THE STANDARD STORIES

Within the past ten years there have been a number of cases in which doctors and hospital administrators have petitioned for and received court orders for the medical treatment of pregnant women without their consent. A 1987 national survey of obstetricians published in the *New England Journal of Medicine* revealed that twenty-one court orders had been sought.[2] The courts issued orders in eighteen of the cases. Most cases simply go unreported. But according to cases described in other medical articles and law reporters, the trend of performing cesarean surgeries, blood transfusions, and other therapies against the woman's will continues.

The legal formulae tell the standard story of court-ordered medical intervention. They speak of rights and interest balancing. The moral formulae tell the same story but speak of social utility and preventing harms. The storytellers, the judge, and those who concur with the idea of forced intervention purport to tell a gender-neutral tale. Critics of the standard story look to the effects of the standard story, indicated by the national survey, and question the claim that these decisions reflect a gender-neutral perspective. They retell the story in ways calculated to reveal that it is in fact gender-biased and explore the implications for all women.

In nearly all the cases reported in medical and legal journals, it was the doctors and/or hospital who petitioned the court. The outcome, as the 1987 survey indicates, strongly favors the medical factors over the woman's personal decision. Curiously, the standard story begins inappositely, by recognizing the individual's interests. It then progresses to a balancing of interests. This formulaic approach, according to traditional legal assumptions, prescribes consistent, evenhanded, and neutral decision making. The standard story's integrity stands, if one does not question these conclusions. Gendered questioning, however, reveals that the story really begins by devaluing the woman's interests; it then progresses to a weighted balancing premised on a concept of social good and ordered liberty that excludes women.

THE SOCIAL CONSTRUCTION OF GENDER IN THE MATERNAL-FETAL CONFLICT

The standard story about pregnant women describes women as childbearers. It focuses on the biological capacity to reproduce. From that, it extracts a moral duty to make decisions on behalf of the fetus without regard to self but perhaps with regard to a greater or higher good. When that greater good becomes synonymous with state interest, it can be enforced at law. A critique of the standard story rejects the notion that women can be regulated as childbearers. It criticizes the reduction of women to biological vessels whose interests can be justifiably subordinated. It reclaims or redefines rights and depicts a liberalism that is not gender-biased.

The response to the standard story, however, is premature. One cannot call for an end to gender bias without understanding how gender is constructed. Further inquiry is necessary. The cases must be questioned again. We must look beyond the standard legal story to the descriptions of pregnant women, mothers, and doctors. We must look to the gaps between the standard story and the social, political, and economic reality in which women live.

STORIES ABOUT PREGNANT WOMEN

Looking beyond the formulae means looking to a time before the invocation of rights and the balancing of interests. It means looking beyond the law, to the way that social reality constructs the conflict. The apparent conflict that takes place between the woman and the doctor provides a starting point.

The contents of judicial opinions reflect the relative significance accorded to doctors' and women's views. These opinions may illustrate that socially constructed biases are at work—judges listen to doctors because they are usually also male professionals and therefore presumptively rational; judges listen to doctors because medicine is regarded as a source of authority whereas individual women are regarded as a source of trouble. In other words, the outcome of these cases may be partially explained by the fact that stereotypes about men, doctors, women, and pregnant women inform the law.

STORIES ABOUT DOCTORS AND MEN

Doctors and other medical staff are presumptively rational, steady, and well motivated. It is recognized that by having two patients—mother and fetus—doctors have a difficult task. And it is assumed that they are motivated primarily by their ethical duty to care for both patients. The point of view from which these cases are discussed strikingly illustrates the presumption in favor of doctors.

It is as if the woman is the only person who lacks standing in these cases. More accurately, the social devoicing of women both precedes and controls application of the legal formulae, making her legal standing irrelevant. The formal legal analysis begins by presuming an autonomous, independent individual. This presumption would bestow an equal range of choices for men and women. But the fact of social hierarchy deprives women of choice before it is offered. And when choice is formally offered, it occurs as a weighing of preconstructed interests by a judge living within a reality where the privileging of men and doctors and the devoicing of women is no longer obvious. The standard story only expresses preexisting social conclusions. And a response tailored to (and by) the legal formula only perpetuates the denial of status that occurs within our private political lives.

THE LIMITS OF A GENDER-ONLY INQUIRY

In looking beyond the standard story and examining the social construction of gender, we enrich our understanding of patriarchy. This furthered inquiry, however, seems to assume that subordination has conferred a universalizing experience on all women. "Inequality on the basis of sex, women share. It is women's collective condition."[3] The assumption of universality is appealing. It expresses a sense of community, perhaps to galvanize its members to unite in participation in transformative politics. It suggests, however, that the universal experience should define the agenda. It also indicates that elaborating gender on a social level completes the inquiry.

Using "women's collective condition" to define the agenda ignores real and lived distinctions drawn on lines of race, class, and culture. The forms of subordination that will rise to the top will be those experienced or understood by white middle-class women. In other words, race, class, and culture will continue to deprioritize issues. The antisubordination principle will be implemented only against forms of oppression recognized by the dominant class of the subordinated collectivity.

If the inquiry does not progress beyond gender, then we will learn of and understand only gender-based patriarchy. We will address subordination only on a limited basis. The standard story may also dictate this result. Two aspects of the standard story are in evidence here. One is the gender-only inquiry itself. The standard story does speak to gender. It does so by essentializing women, by describing them with regard to the biological capacity to bear children. It uses physical difference to justify social stratification. But none of the reported cases mention race, class, or culture. The furthered inquiry fails in the same way, perhaps blinded by the standard story. The second aspect of the standard story also used by those who tell of socially constructed gender is the notion of universality and collectivity. The standard story assumes only one concept of the social good; it assumes the truth of stereotypes of pregnant women, well-motivated doctors, and rational, competent decision makers; and it assumes that only rights against the state need be defined. And the assumption of universality within the standard story has the same effect as that within the furthered inquiry—more patriarchy.

In theory, a gender-only inquiry could at least eliminate one tier of the hierarchy. But even the most generous interpretation assumes that the subordination experienced by women of color and nonmajority culture can be parceled. That is, the gender-only inquiry seems to consider gender bias separable from other biases, such as those based on race, class, and culture. The experience of women of color does differ from that of white women, but it is also similar. And it is not separable. A woman of color is not subordinated partly as a woman and partly as a person of color. The intersection between gender and race is more subtle and complex than that. To say that women of color have a particular place in the hierarchy only begins to describe the intersection.

CONTINUING THE INQUIRY INTO RACE, CLASS, AND CULTURE

In this section, we must look hard into the silence. The cases at hand do not expressly speak of race, class, or culture. They can address gender directly, even while excluding women's interests and women's voices from the discussion. But the law purports to be blind to color, class, and culture. How is it then that the 1987 survey of obstetricians revealed that of the twenty-one petitions for court-ordered medical treatment, seventeen of the orders were sought against Black, Asian, or Hispanic women?[4] And all the orders were sought against women being treated at public hospitals or receiving public assistance.[5] The furthered inquiry must ask why pregnant women who are not white and who live in poverty are at a significantly greater risk of forced medical treatment. These women are being measured and found wanting according to nonobvious standards. We must look for those standards and reveal them.

STORIES ABOUT MOTHERS

The gender-only inquiry does suggest that a standard for good motherhood is being used. The point has already been made that the standard story regulates women as childbearers. These cases express norms of proper pregnancy behavior. When a court orders the forced medical treatment of a woman for the sake of fetal interests, it deems that woman a bad mother. So, at the least, these cases tell us that a good mother would consent.

We can infer additional details of the model mother by looking to expressions of disappointment within the case reports. The good mother is self-sacrificing and nurturing. The good mother is also white and middle-class. The silence within the case reports and the loudness of the results indicate that race and class add dimension to the model of motherhood. Within that gap, one can sense negative stereotypes forming a picture of the bad mother.

She has little education. Perhaps she does not understand the nature of her refusal to consent. She is unsophisticated, easily influenced by simple religious dogma. She is pregnant because of promiscuity and irresponsibility. She is hostile to authority even though the state has good intentions. She is unreliable. She is ignorant and foreign. She does not know what is best. The cases ascribe these characteristics to the bad mother; this is the subtext, the things that can nearly be said. They make it easier to assume that the woman's will should be overridden. They also offer moral grounds for intervention. The expressions of anger, frustration, and righteousness in the case reports and opinions strongly evoke the things that can nearly be said. Not stated is that these assumed characteristics are particular to stereotypes of poor women of color. So, what goes unsaid is that she is Black; she is Hispanic; she is Asian; and she is poor.

The act of subordinating occurs first in the mind of those with authority. It is the implicit assumption that women of color, particularly those who live in poverty, are not fit for motherhood. This assumption is rooted in the experience of domination and in the construction of stories—negative stereotypes—about the "others" to justify the resulting privileged status. Those who call to rights and the feminist critical theorists respond to the good mother model and to the things that can nearly be said. But they overlook the catalyst for subordination in these cases—the mindset of domination with respect to race, class, and culture, the set of assumptions that includes an expectation of conformity, and in the absence of such, an expectation of unfitness.

THE CULTURE CLASH

A dominant culture of pregnancy and childbirth attaches to the good mother model and effects subordination on race, class, and cultural lines. The forced medical treatment cases illustrate a revealing tension between the dominant culture and the individual women, which reflects a parallel conflict generated by the broader dominant culture. The dominant culture, constituted largely of institutions, is largely authoritarian. Deference to authority, institutional or other, is expected. It has become a cultural practice.

The authoritarian nature of the dominant culture yields two corollaries. One is that privileging institutional knowledge precludes self-knowledge. It disallows women to make self-diagnoses based on their own body-awareness, experience, and beliefs. Most of these cases arise from a woman's refusal to consent to cesarean surgery. Both doctors and women offer a number of reasons for the increase in the percentage of cesarean births. But all these reasons express a greater concern for physician control than for patient determination. It also indicates that many interventions are medically unnecessary and that the women who felt that labor was progressing normally were right.[6]

The other corollary is that privileging norms of exclusive institutions devalues nonmainstream culture. It prefers the strongly risk-averse medical culture of pregnancy and childbirth to the woman-culture developed by the lived experience of women. Pregnancy is now most often described as a medical event. This can prevent a woman from making a decision based not only on her self-diagnosis but also on facts of life outside the hospital walls.

Janet Gallagher reported the case of a Nigerian woman, pregnant with triplets.[7] The medical norm prescribes cesarean delivery for multiple births. The Nigerian woman and her husband refused, in part because the woman was healthy and in part because they planned to return to a region of Nigeria where lack of medical facilities would make future cesareans inaccessible. She understood pregnancy and childbirth in the context of her future. The court, however, focused solely on the medical assessment and issued the order without the woman's knowledge. The medical staff had to tie her down in order to perform the surgery. The effects of this decision include not only three healthy babies but also the physical violation of this woman and the forcible recharacterization of her understanding of pregnancy—a personal experience implicating health and future—to that of the medical profession—a pathology meriting physician control.

BUILDING CHOICE FROM COALITION

We gain a more replete understanding of patriarchy by continuing the inquiry. The first lesson was that patriarchy, expressed as the standard story, not only blinds and silences us, it also separates us. If we respond only to the formulae or to gender subordination, we can agree to reclaim rights or we can agree to reformulate the concepts of rights and equality in ways that speak of women's reality. But we cannot agree, without excluding women by race, class, and culture, on priorities and strategies that will affect the lives of each woman. At the most, we can create a thin sense of likeness.

The furthered inquiry does not necessarily reveal a deeper, truer pool of commonality. Even the deeper understanding of patriarchy we gain will not provide a shared experience. Our understandings will differ. But we begin the process of consciousness raising,[8] and we learn to reject rather than accept justifications for domination. Perhaps we also learn to think of ourselves as a source of promising variety.

We may open doors, through which we may gain insights and form commitments, or whatever is needed to value difference and locate relationships. We may create coalitions and from those, we may build choice. Opening another door, then, is always the next step. We have looked beyond gender, but we still have not looked to the experience of each subordinated person. The persons most likely to suffer a subtraction of their reproductive rights include not only women of color and culture but also lesbians, gays, and persons institutionalized by criminal conviction or civil commitment. Locating other "have-nots" of reproductive choice can help us learn about both patriarchy and possibilities.

By continuing the inquiry beyond the standard story and beyond gender, we break the silence and we learn to listen. We learn to understand refusals of consent as moments of dissonance that offer lessons. A woman who refuses consent to cesarean surgery out of fear may have reason to fear. She may know that she cannot provide for the child because she lacks the necessary financial and social support. Thus, we can see these refusals as moments of integrity, not to glorify, but to respect, and to use to identify real problems—poverty, overuse of medical intervention—not bad mothers.

NOTES

1. Linda Greene, Conference on Race Consciousness and Legal Scholarship, Affirmative Action Panel, University of Illinois College of Law (Feb. 22, 1992).

2. Veronika E. B. Kolder et al., *Court-Ordered Obstetrical Interventions,* 316 New Eng. J. Med. 1192, 1192 (1987).

3. Catharine A. MacKinnon, Toward a Feminist Theory of the State 241 (1989).

4. Kolder et al., *supra* note 2, at 1193.

5. *Id.*

6. The 1987 national survey of obstetricians revealed that of fourteen infants delivered by court-ordered cesarean, "[o]nly 2 of 14 infants (14 percent) had important morbidity. . . . No fetal deaths occurred." *See id.* at 1193. The authors concluded that "court-ordered interventions may ultimately cause more problems than they solve. They rest on dubious legal grounds, may expand rather than limit physicians' liability, and could adversely affect maternal and infant health." *Id.* at 1194.

7. Janet Gallagher, *Prenatal Invasions and Interventions: What's Wrong with Fetal Rights,* 10 Harv. Women's L.J. 9 (1987).

8. I use "consciousness raising" the way Matsuda has defined it: a "collective practice of searching for self-knowledge through close examination of our own circumstances, in conjunction with organized movements to end existing conditions of domination." Mari Matsuda, *Pragmatism Modified and the False Consciousness Problem,* 63 S. Cal. L. Rev. 1763, 1779 (1990).

19 | Learnfare and Black Motherhood: The Social Construction of Deviance

Nathalie A. Augustin

The "welfare mother" is a deviant social creature. She is able-bodied, but unwilling to work at any of the thousands of jobs available to her; she is fundamentally lazy and civically irresponsible; she spends her days doing nothing but sponging off the government's largesse. Despite the societal pressure to be gainfully employed, she enjoys her status as a "dependent" on the state and seeks at all costs to prolong her dependency. Promiscuous and shortsighted, she is a woman who defiantly has children out of wedlock. Without morals of her own, she is unlikely to transmit good family values to her children. She lacks the educational skills to get ahead and the motivation to acquire them. Thus, she is the root of her own family's intergenerational poverty and related social ills. She is her own worse enemy. And she is Black.

The image of the welfare mother painted above represents the prevailing consensus among the majority of Democrats and Republicans in this country about who receives Aid to Families with Dependent Children (AFDC) payments from the government and what her most salient behavioral and psychological characteristics are. This image also forms the bedrock on which current welfare "reform" policy is based. In this essay, I explore some of the faulty and demeaning assumptions about AFDC recipients in the context of Learnfare, or the conditioning of AFDC payments on school attendance records. I focus in particular on how Learnfare rigidifies, rather than challenges, the extant conception of welfare motherhood. I expose Learnfare's role in the ideological devaluation of Black motherhood by situating Learnfare at the intersection of three interrelated systems of domination: racism, classism, and patriarchy. First I will briefly outline the mechanics of Learnfare, exposing the program in its most sympathetic light. I will then discuss why Learnfare is ill suited to curb truancy and the "welfare problem."[1] I argue that what informs this type of program has nothing to do with "helping" AFDC recipients and their children stay

in school and has everything to do with penalizing a fungible group of outcasts—
Black mothers.

THE RHETORIC OF LEARNFARE AND THE VENEER OF LEGITIMACY:
HOW LEARNFARE IS SUPPOSED TO WORK

Initiated in Wisconsin in 1988, the Learnfare program was the legislative response to alarmingly high truancy and dropout rates among students in general, basic skills deficits among many AFDC recipients, and the specter of long-term welfare dependency for the poorly educated. The Wisconsin legislators recognized certain facts: (1) excessive absenteeism is a predictable indicator of eventual academic failure; (2) poor youths are four times as likely to have substandard basic skills as youths from families living above the poverty line; and (3) students with poor basic skills, which are defined as testing in the bottom 20 percent of students in the relevant age group on a standard basic literacy exam—such as the Armed Forces Qualifying Test—are nine times as likely to drop out of school as are students with average basic skills.[2] In light of these facts, Wisconsin legislators saw education as the antidote to economic hardship and AFDC grant reductions for truancy as the proper mechanism for improving the educational outcomes of the AFDC population.

The Learnfare program is applicable to all AFDC teens between the ages of thirteen and nineteen who have not graduated from high school and who are physically able to attend school. When a family is applying for AFDC or when a family's eligibility is periodically redetermined, an AFDC caseworker reviews any teenage family member's school attendance records from the most recently completed semester. If the teenager has had more than ten unexcused absences during that time, he or she will be required to meet a monthly attendance requirement for his or her family to continue to qualify for the full AFDC amount.

To meet the attendance requirement, a student can have no more than two full days of unexcused absences in a calendar month. What constitutes an unexcused absence is left to the local school district to determine. Failure of the teenage family member to meet these enrollment and attendance requirements will result in the loss to his or her family of the teenager's share of the AFDC grant.[3] If the teenager is the only minor in the home, his or her disqualification for assistance renders the mother or caretaker categorically ineligible for AFDC, since there is no longer an "eligible" needy and dependent child in the home.

Once a teenager has been identified as obligated to meet the monthly attendance requirement, his or her school will regularly forward the student's attendance data to the local social services agency. If the data reveal more than two unexcused absences, the AFDC household will be notified in writing of the attendance violation and of the amount of aid to be withheld from the next grant payment.[4] The grant reduction remains in effect for one month for each month the student fails to meet the attendance requirement. Sanctions average $100 for families with more than one child and $220 for teenage parents living alone with a child.[5] If the student is sanctioned for dropping out, the reduction remains in effect until the student produces verification that he or she has reenrolled in school and met the attendance requirement for at least one month.[6]

Sanctions are not imposed, and a student is not subject to attendance reporting, under several circumstances, including (1) the student is the caretaker of a child less than ninety days old; and (2) the minor parent is unable to obtain child care from a licensed or certified provider or from a school-based program, because such care is unavailable, inaccessible, or available only at a cost that exceeds the maximum authorized county reimbursement rate.[7]

THE IDEOLOGY OF LEARNFARE AND THE REALITY OF POOR, SINGLE BLACK MOTHERS: WHY LEARNFARE DOES NOT WORK

Perhaps the most fundamental conceptual flaw of Learnfare is its assumption that the problem of social deviancy is endemic to a child's family, rather than a function of external sources. More specifically, Learnfare locates the causes of truancy and other forms of deviancy in the individual mother rather than on the societal forces with which poor single mothers are faced. The individual mother is, in the political and cultural imagery of Learnfare, the single Black mother in the ghetto[8]—the "welfare queen"—who, but for the punitive, patriarchal intervention of the state, cannot be a good, productive citizen or mother.

Learnfare has two official objectives: (1) to encourage teenagers in AFDC households to complete high school or its equivalent, thereby acquiring the minimum level of education to become "productive" citizens; and (2) to establish a relationship of mutual responsibility between the state and AFDC recipients.[9] Thus, Learnfare explicitly defines the AFDC recipient (the mother) as the architect of her predicament and that of her family. It is predicated on the appealing assumption that the teenager can transcend her socioeconomic reality if only she has the motivation to complete high school and if only she and her mother are "responsible" vis à vis the state.

The benevolent pretensions of Learnfare notwithstanding, the social problems Learnfare purports to address—the truancy and the (putative) social irresponsibility of individuals in an AFDC household—cannot be alleviated by the punitive intervention of the state through an AFDC check. An AFDC payment is a government transfer to individuals who would otherwise lack the financial resources to eat and to provide clothing, housing, and other necessities for family members. Thus, it represents the government's attempt to relieve some of the misery poor children experience. What Learnfare's advocates have failed to articulate is (1) the nexus between relieving misery and curbing truancy or encouraging social responsibility; and (2) the reasons the former should be conditioned on the latter.

Moreover, Learnfare's focus on the individual welfare mother is informed by three mutually reinforcing paradigms that operate to entrench this individual's status in society: racism, classism, and patriarchy. Perhaps the ideology with the less obvious presence in Learnfare is patriarchy, which Martha Fineman defines as a dominant ideology that "has as one of its organizing premises the belief that the primary affiliation in society is the sexual bond" realized through marriage.[10] By rejecting the traditional familial structure, the welfare mother is culturally defined to exist at the margins of a good, virtuous society. The Learnfare sanction is a way of reaffirming the values of mainstream society and confirming status. Dignity and virtue are reserved for those who work (outside the home) and for those who do not have children out of wedlock.[11] Under Learnfare's patriarchal ideology, AFDC recipients have responded to their subjugation in a way that violates the norms of family decency.[12] Thus, they are rebels against society and worthy of punishment.

Indeed, Learnfare is the product of a patriarchal and classist vision of how the state should intervene to "help" people in need. By reducing the amount of an AFDC payment because a child skips school, the Learnfare sanction punishes AFDC mothers who do not comport with the white middle-class majoritarian ideal of mother.[13] That ideal is a married white woman who has the financial and social resources to care for and "control" her children. She is someone who is concerned about her children's educational progress and sends her children to the best schools in her suburban area. The middle-class ideal mother can also afford (without government transfers) child care, adequate health care, and therapy and counseling services for her children.

Juxtaposed to this ideal, and through Learnfare's distorted lens, the welfare mother should never have become a mother in the first place. Her single, unwed and poor status necessarily prevents her from being a "good" mother because these characteristics derive inevitably from her deviancy. If she would get married like the rest of us, she would have a male breadwinner in the family to cure her financial woes. If she were motivated enough, she would surmount the educational obstacles before her. If she looked hard enough, she could find a job. And if she were not "unfit" to care for her children, she would not have a problem with truancy in her household.[14] Because the operation of Learnfare depends on this imagery of who the AFDC recipient is and the extent to which she controls her destiny, Learnfare reproduces a certain racialized, patriarchal, and class-based hierarchy between "good" mothers and "bad" mothers. Only married, middle-class white women can be the former; the welfare mother is inescapably the latter.[15]

Thus, the racist and classist ideology underlying Learnfare is in part the assumption that women receiving AFDC benefits have unbridled choices regarding their educational achievement and their employment. Learnfare ignores the fact that the choices of these women are circumscribed by poverty. The opportunity to get a good education is more often than not unavailable to them. They do not have the option of moving to a less drug-infested area. They cannot send their children to better or safer schools, nor can they afford therapy or special services for their children. They cannot afford child care or counseling services for their children without the financial support of the state. Upward job mobility is not available to them. In short, women receiving AFDC cannot insulate themselves from the violence of poverty and inner-city life. Yet all these factors directly impact the extent to which teenagers living below or near the poverty line are truant, and the extent to which mothers can provide financially for their children.[16]

Instead of probing the complex causes and effects of the education crisis in poor communities, Learnfare simply ignores the existing disadvantages that AFDC recipients confront. For students who are already years behind in educational achievement, who receive no social services counseling or advice, and who are denied access to alternative or bilingual education programs (e.g., vocational education and GED programs), completing high school with basic skills proficiency is an unlikely result, Learnfare notwithstanding.[17] Indeed, without challenging the factors that engender truancy and dropping out, Learnfare sanctions may actually aggravate the stresses that inhere in poverty.[18]

Finally, to the extent that Learnfare makes the individual the cause of and solution to her own socioeconomic predicament, Learnfare denies the role of the state and private actors in circumscribing the economic mobility of poor people generally, and people of color specifically. The focus on the individual mother morally absolves public and private actors from their obligations to play a role in transforming the conditions of subjugation under which AFDC recipients live.

Despite its intuitive appeal, Learnfare disparages Black motherhood because it constructs "welfare motherhood" as Black and pathological. It buys into the societal (mis)perception that there is something inherent in poverty that makes AFDC recipients particularly "unfit" to care for their children. It endorses, rather than challenges, the myth that the "aberrant" behavior of those who "depend" on subsistence benefits can be changed through the punitive intervention of the state.[19] By ignoring the existing disadvantages AFDC recipients face, Learnfare perpetuates the disadvantages and rigidifies the negative societal perception of who the AFDC recipient is and what her behavioral characteristics are. Thus, it is part and parcel of a new right agenda of "family values," one that has manipulated public opinion by highlighting racial and gender biases.

NOTES

1. This essay is part of a larger work in progress. It is not within the scope of this essay to examine the ways Learnfare does violence to children in AFDC households or to highlight the empirical inaccuracies of its assumptions. Rather, the focus of this essay is the extent to which Learnfare reinforces the existing negative stereotypes regarding Black women as mothers and the extent to which Learnfare ignores the complex causes of truancy.

2. Josie Foehrenbach, *Preparing for Learnfare: Setting the Conditions for a Questionable Experiment,* Clearing House Review, Feb. 1989 (citing Children's Defense Fund, Preventing Adolescent Pregnancy: What Schools Can Do 5 (Sept. 1986)).

3. Wisconsin Department of Health and Social Services, Wisconsin Welfare Reform Package, Section 1115(a) Waiver Application to U.S. Department of Health and Human Services (May 1, 1987) [hereinafter 1987 Wisconsin Waiver Application].

4. The sanction notice also advises the family of its right to contest the reduction at a hearing. *Id.*

5. Lois M. Quinn et al., *Employment Training Institute, Division of Outreach and Continuing Education Extension, University of Wisconsin-Milwaukee, in* Report on the Learnfare Evaluation 4 (1988).

6. 1987 Wisconsin Waiver Application, *supra* note 3.

7. 1987 Wisc. Laws 27.

8. This stereotype persists notwithstanding the fact that only 8.9 percent of the total poor live in "ghettos," that is, metropolitan census tracts having poverty rates above 40 percent. Under any of the prevailing definitions, the urban "underclass" is but a small percentage of the AFDC population, and African Americans constitute less than 40 percent of the AFDC population. Even among poor African Americans, fewer than 20 percent live in large cities in ghettos. *See, e.g.,* David T. Ellwood, Poor Support: Poverty in the American Family 190–95 (1988); The Urban Underclass 251 (Christopher Jencks & Paul E. Peterson eds., 1991).

9. 1987 Wisconsin Waiver Application, *supra* note 3.

10. Martha L. Fineman, *Images of Mothers in Poverty Discourses,* 1991 Duke L.J. 274, 290 (addressing the role of patriarchal ideology in the construction of "mother" in poverty discourses).

11. Joel F. Handler & Yeheskel Hasenfeld, The Moral Construction of Poverty 19 (1991) ("Because the failure to earn one's living was considered an individual moral failure, and because this failure would lead to other, even more serious forms of deviant behavior, welfare policy had to be extremely careful not to encourage dependency."); *see also* M. Katz, In the Shadow of the Poorhouse 40 (1986).

12. *See* Regina Austin, *Sapphire Bound!,* 1989 Wis. L. Rev. 539, 555 (also chapter 35 in this volume) (discussing the "possibility that young, single, sexually active, fertile, and nurturing black women are being viewed ominously because they have the temerity to attempt to break out of the rigid economic, social, and political categories that a racist, sexist, and class-stratified society would impose upon them"). *See also* Dorothy E. Roberts, *Racism and Patriarchy in the Meaning of Motherhood,* 1 Am. U. J. Gender & L. 1, 27–28 (1993) (exploring the notion of single Black motherhood as an example of resistance against patriarchy).

13. I note here that Learnfare is degrading to AFDC recipients whether or not sanctions are actually imposed, not only because of the assumptions it makes about mothers receiving AFDC, but because it puts AFDC recipients on "welfare probation." Unless they comply with the school attendance rules, "Big Father" cuts their payments. Whether or not they comply, however, they are "watched" Orwellian-style by school and social welfare officials who are waiting to impose sanctions against those who misbehave.

14. *See* Lucy A. Williams, *The Ideology of Division: Behavior Modification Welfare Reform Proposals,* 102 Yale L.J. 719, 728 (1992) (discussing Learnfare's assumption that AFDC parents are "unparentlike").

15. Married middle-class Black women are not "ideal mothers" because the ideal is racialized. *See* Roberts, *supra* note 12, at 15–16. To the extent that Black middle-class women comport with the "ideal mother," such women are exceptionalized in political and social discourses. That is to say, they are constructed as different from "them"—the pathological Black mothers.

16. Williams, *supra* note 14, at 729.

17. *See, e.g.,* Handler & Hasenfeld, *supra* note 11, at 224–28 (arguing that since AFDC

children are educationally disadvantaged, the current education reforms, including Learnfare, "could very well make matters worse for AFDC families"); H. Levin, Educational Reform for Disadvantaged Students: An Emerging Crisis (1986) (arguing that a major shortcoming of the proposed reforms is that they have little to offer to those with low academic achievement and high dropout rates).

18. Learnfare also compounds the educational disadvantages of the AFDC population by focusing on an inadequate barometer of educational achievement—school attendance. This singular focus on school attendance as a proxy for educational achievement detracts attention from the low rate of functional literacy among high school graduates and the extent to which graduates continue to receive AFDC payments.

19. My argument in this essay is not that skipping school, as a general matter, should be encouraged. But one of the cultural myths around welfare is that the AFDC recipient is somehow more deviant than the non-AFDC recipient, that she has less morality than her non-AFDC counterpart. This myth coexists with the reality that AFDC recipients are asymmetrically situated (economically and socially) vis-à-vis middle-class and upper-middle-class whites in this country—that the burdens of poverty, class bigotry, gender, and race often intersect to subordinate AFDC recipients in ways that middle-class whites cannot experience.

20 | Spare Parts, Family Values, Old Children, Cheap

Patricia J. Williams

Last week I was reading an article by that great literary mogul of the University of Chicago's School of Law and Economics, Judge Richard Posner, and his associate Elisabeth Landes. In their short opus, *The Economics of the Baby Shortage,* newborn human beings are divided up into white and black and then taken for a spin around a monopoly board theme park where the white babies are put on demand curves and the black babies are dropped off the edge of supply sides.[1] "Were baby prices quoted as prices of soybean futures are quoted," they say, "a racial ranking of these prices would be evident, with white baby prices higher than nonwhite baby prices."[2] The trail of the demand curve leads straight into the arms of the highest bidder; the chasm of oversupply has a heap of surplus at the bottom of its pit.[3] In this house of horrors, the surplus (or "second quality") black babies will continue to replicate themselves like mushrooms, unless the wise, invisible, strong arm of the market intervenes to allow the wisdom of pure purchasing power to effect some clearing away of the underbrush. In a passage that some have insisted is all about maximizing the kindness of strangers, Landes and Posner argue that "[b]y obtaining exclusive control over the supply of both 'first quality' adoptive children and 'second quality' children residing in foster care but available for adoption, agencies are able to internalize the substitution possibilities between them. Agencies can charge a higher price for the children they place for adoption, thus increasing not only their revenues from adoptions but also the demand for children who would otherwise be placed or remain in foster care at the agency's expense. Conversely, if agency revenues derive primarily from foster care, the agencies can manipulate the relative price of adopting 'first-quality' children over 'second quality' children to reduce the net flow of children out of foster care."[4] The conclusion that these authors make, in a not surprising rhetorical turn, is that the current "black market" for adoptive children must be replaced with what they call a "free baby market."

When this article first appeared almost twenty years ago, it created a storm of controversy. Since Judge Posner has reaffirmed its premises many times, most recently in his book *Sex and Reason,* the article has remained a major bone of contention in his constellation of publications.[5] My purpose in resurrecting this piece as a reference for this essay is to examine (1) the degree to which it is a reflection of what goes on in the world of not just adoption but reproduction in general; (2) the degree to which market valuation of bodies, even when for ostensibly noble purposes, embodies what is most wrong with community as well as family in America; and (3) the possibility that a shift in focus could help us imagine a more stable, less demeaning, and more inclusive sense of community.

When I decided to adopt a child, I was unprepared for the reality that adoption is already a pretty straightforward market. I was unprepared for the "choices" with which I was presented, as to age, race, color, and health of prospective children. I was unprepared for the fact that I too would be shopped for, by birth mothers as well as social workers, looked over for my age, marital and economic status, and race. All that was missing was to have my tires kicked.

"Describe yourself," said the application form. Oh lord, I remember thinking, this is worse than a dating service. What's appealing about me, and to whom? Responsible nonsmoker omnivore seeks . . . what? Little person for lifetime of bicycle rides, good education, and peanut butter sandwiches? Forty and fading fast so I thought I'd better get a move on? "You can't tell them you're forty," advised a friend of mine. "No one will ever pick you." OK, I sighed. "Very well rounded," I wrote.

"Describe where you live." At the time, I was still at the University of Wisconsin, even though I was visiting at Columbia, and traveling almost every week to places like Indiana and Georgia in a frenzied ritual of academic legitimation. I struggled, as I straddled worlds, with which side I should present my "dear birth mother" letter. Chic New York apartment with expansive square footage, north-south exposure, and a refrigerator stocked with the leftovers of fifteen different types of ethnic take-out food? Your child will grow up riding the subways and knowing the finer shades of the chardonnay and caviar lifestyle of the middlebrow and not-so-famous? Or should I just offer a well-childproofed home in that friendly dairy production center of the universe, Wisconsin, land o' butter, cream, and lakes? "Your child will taste the world," I wrote.

"What age, what sex," asked the social worker. "Doesn't matter," I said, "though I'd like to miss out on as little as possible."

"If you're willing to take a boy, you'll get younger," she replied. "There's a run on girls."

"What races would you accept?" asked the adoption agency. "And what racial combinations?" There followed a whole menu of evocative options, like Afro-Javanese, Sino-Germanic, and just plain "white." I assume that this list, so suggestive of the multiple combinations of meat offered at, say, Kentucky Fried Chicken, would make Elisabeth Landes and Richard Posner very happy indeed. They advise that "The genetic characteristics of natural children are highly correlated with their parents' genetic characteristics, and this correlation could conceivably increase harmony within the family compared to what it would be with an adopted child. Nevertheless, there is considerable suitability between natural and adopted children and it might be much greater if better genetic matching of adopted children with their adoptive parents were feasible—as might occur, as we shall see, under free market conditions." [6]

"Any," I wrote, knowing that harmony genes abound in my ancestral bloodlines— yet wondering whether the agency really meant to address that question to black parents. Would they truly consider placing "any" child with me if this agency happened to have a "surplus" of white babies? Would I get a Korean baby if I asked? And for all the advertised difficulties, what does it mean that it is so relatively easy for white American families to not just adopt black children but also choose from a range of colors, nationalities, and configurations from around the world? (And I do mean relatively easy—for all the publicity about the "impossibility" of white people adopting black American children, doing so is still in most instances far easier than going to Romania or China, for example. While there are well-publicized instances of white families who are barred by local social service office policies, in most states a waiting period of about six months is the biggest institutional hurdle they will face. In addition, there are a good number of reputable private adoption agencies that facilitate and even specialize in "interracial" adoptions.)

What does it reveal, moreover, about the social backdrop of such transactions that if I "chose" a "white" child, it might reveal something quite alarming about my own self-esteem? What does it mean that if a white parent chose a black child, I daresay most people would attribute it to an idealistic selflessness that—however some blacks might feel is misguided and threatening to cultural integrity—is not generally perceived as necessarily proceeding from a sense of diminishment? Is race-neutral adoption the answer—even to the extent of barring "mild-preferences for same-race placements," as Elizabeth Bartholet has suggested? While I very much agree with the impulse behind that solution, does the social reality of unbalanced race relations and racial power not suggest some constraints on complete color blindness?

While there are apparently a number of studies that claim to show that black children fare just fine when adopted into white families—and I have no doubt that this is true on any number of levels—I am at times troubled by some of the conclusions drawn from such representations: the claims that such children have "unique" abilities to deal with white people, or that they are "more tolerant." I always want to ask, more tolerant of what, of whom? More tolerant than other blacks? Or than whites? More tolerant of whites? Or of other blacks? I am particu- larly troubled by the notion that black children in white families are better off simply because they may have access to a broader range of material advantages by having white parents and living in a largely white and relatively privileged world. Such an argument should not, I think, be used to justify the redistribution of children in our society, but rather to bolster a redistribution of resources such that blacks can afford to raise children too. Moreover, assertions that black children actually do better in white homes play dangerously against a social backdrop in which slavery's history of paternalistic white protectionism still demands black loyalty to white people and their lifestyle as a powerful symbolic precedent for deeming black social organization "successful." Such assertions do not take into account the imbalanced intervention of state agencies in the lives of poor women and women of color—particularly in view of the disproportionate rate at which children of color are removed from their homes and put into foster care or up for adoption, with little thought for the possibility of the kinds of facilitative family counseling that are available at the higher ends of the socioeconomic ladder.

In any event, I wonder how many social science studies there are about how white children fare in black homes.

"What color?" asked the form. You've got to be kidding. I looked quizzically at the social worker. "Some families like to match," she said. You mean, like color-coordinated? You mean like the Louisiana codes? Like ebony, sepia, quadroon, mahogany? Like matching the color of a brown paper bag? Like red, like Indian, like exotic, like straight-haired, like light-skinned? Like 1840, is that what this means? Like 1940, sighed my mother, when I mentioned this to her. (And is this what the next generation will be sighing about, so sadly like that, in 2040?)

"I don't care," I wrote.

And with that magical stroke of the pen, the door to a whole world of plentiful, newborn, brown-skinned little boys with little brown toes and big brown eyes and round brown noses and fat brown cheeks opened up to me from behind the curtain marked "Doesn't Care."

My son, because he is a stylish little character, arrived at my home in a limousine. (Credit for this must also be shared with the social worker, who was a pretty jazzy sort herself.) I had a big party and a naming ceremony and invited everyone I knew. I was so happy that I guess I missed that price tag hanging from his little blue-knit beanie. A few weeks later I got a call from the agency: "Which fee schedule are you going to choose?"

"What's this?" I asked the adoption agent, flipping madly through Landes and Posner for guidance: "Prospective adoptive parents would presumably be willing to pay more for a child whose health and genealogy were warranted in a legally enforceable instrument than they are willing to pay under the present system where the entire risk of any deviation from expected quality falls on them."[7]

"Are you going with the standard or the special?" came the reply. There followed a description of a system in which adoptive parents paid a certain percentage of their salaries to the agency, which fee went to administrative costs, hospital expenses for the birth mother, and counseling. Inasmuch as it was tied exclusively to income, in a graduated scale, it clearly met the definition of a fee for services rendered. This, it was explained to me, was the standard price list.

"And the special?" I asked. After an embarrassed pause, she told me that that referred to "older, black, and other handicapped children," and that those fees were exactly half of those on the standard scale. Suddenly, what had been a price system based on services rendered became clearly, sickeningly, irretrievably, a price system for "goods," a sale for chattel, linked not to services but to the imagined quality of the "things" exchanged. Although it is true that, as the agency asserted, this system was devised to provide "economic incentives" for the adoption of "less requested" children, it is perhaps more than true, in our shopping mall world, that it had all the earmarks of a two-for-one sale.

I was left with a set of texts resounding in my brain, rattling with the persistence of their contradiction. One text is Frederick Douglass's description of his own escape from slavery as a "theft" of "this head" and "these arms" and "these legs." He employed the master's language of property to create the unforgettable paradox of the "owned" erupting into the category of a speaking subject whose "freedom" simultaneously and inextricably marked him as a "thief." That this disruption of the bounds of normative imagining is variously perceived as dangerous as well as liberatory is a tension that has distinguished racial politics in America from its inception to this day.

The contrasting stories are a medley of voices like descriptions of Americans adopting children in Latin America and of having to hide them for fear of kidnapping until they were back on the plane to the United States because "desirable" children were worth a great deal of money on the open adoption block; or like the *New York Times Magazine* cover story of a white American couple who adopted a little girl from China: when the couple finally returned from Wuhan to New York City with the child, they felt as though they "had walked off with something of incalculable value—a baby—with the approval of everyone involved. What a coup, what a blessing—what a relief!"[8]

What links these sets of narratives for me is the description of a powerful emotional state that styles itself as theft, as a coup, a walking off with something right under the disapproving noses of everyone: "Sara and I regarded each other with a deep sense of disbelief."[9] I am troubled; the theft of one's own body is a kind of trickster's inversion of one's life reduced to a chattel status. But the acquisition of another for a sum considered as either a "deal" or a "steal," if not outright slavery, resembles nothing less than bounty hunting.

(A friend of mine who has given birth to two children assures me that biological parents who have not paid out any money feel exactly the same way—exhilarated, disbelieving, unworthy of the life with which they are suddenly charged. I am sure that it is true—I too feel great amazement at my own motherhood. But my point is that the ideology of the marketplace devalues such emotions, either by identifying them as externalities in and of themselves, or by using them to infuse, even impassion, certain price structures, uncritically crystallizing into a dollars and cents equivalent what we might be better off trying to understand as "priceless" relation.)

How will my son's price at birth relate to what value doctors put on his various parts if he ever has an accident and shows up at a hospital? Will he be valued more as a series of parts in the marketplace of bodies or more as a whole, as a precious social being with not just a will but a soul? Will his fate be decided by a fellow human being who cares for him or will his "outcome" be negotiated by some formulaic economic tracking policy based on his having health insurance or a job? Will his idiosyncratic, nonmarket value be visible in the subconscious, well-intentioned decisions of a nice suburban doctor who has never known, spoken, lived, or worked with a black person in a status position of anything close to equality? Will "ethics" be able to consider this complicated stuff or will we decide the whole topic is too risky, too angrifying, so that forced neutrality and pretend-we-don't-see-ness will rule the day? How will our children, figured as the tidy "consumption preferences" of unsocial actors, be able to value themselves?

I was unable to choose a fee schedule. I was unable to conspire in putting a price on my child's head.

One feature of the market as politics is that where consumer demand is supposedly high, market actors are rationalized by succumbing to the pressure to produce more; where, on the other hand, the soy surplus is great, growers stop growing. It is no wonder that as long as one's head is locked within the box of this paradigm, a deference like Judge Richard Posner's to the fundamentally absurd notion of a purely private preference for white babies might not reveal itself immediately as insidiously eugenic. The language of the market is so clean and impersonal after all—it hardly hurts a bit when Landes and Posner slip into thinking up incentives to actually produce more white babies, not merely to provide incentives to white women to "give up" more of their babies for adoption. Giving things up and other artifacts of a gift economy, after all, have little place in the logical order of a productive market economy. Most alarming of all, the troublesomely excessive supply of black and other socially discarded categories of babies—the babies for whom there is this relatively low "demand"—inspires Landes and Posner not only to try to create a set of incentives to "consume" or "take" them. Rather, they actively pursue ways of creating disincentives from producing at all.

THE INVISIBLE BODY SNATCHERS

Not long ago, some law students at New York Law School told me of an experience they had while teaching a so-called street law class in a New York City public high school. They asked a class of twelfth-graders to break up into small groups and envision that they had to send an expedition of people to populate a new planet. They were to describe the six new architects of the brand-new world, giving their race or ethnicity and their professions. In every group, Hispanics, if they were included, were car mechanics ("They're good at stripping cars" was the explanation some students gave); Asians were included in every group and were always scientists ("They're smart"); whites (including ethnics such as "French," "Italian," "Russian," as well as just "white") had the greatest numerical presence and variety of profession. No blacks were included in the new world (the one student who listed a Nigerian doctor thought Nigeria was in Asia). The kicker is that this school was 53 percent black and 45 percent Hispanic—a milieu, and I'm guessing here, in which most whites might be surprised to find themselves the object of such double-edged veneration. Moreover, when the law students attempted to discuss the significance of such an impressive skewing, the students—sounding for all the world like the *National*

Review—uniformly protested that race had nothing to do with it, and why did the law students (who, by the way, were white) have to "racialize" everything?

This image of a planet with a handpicked nonblack, non-Hispanic population is what *Brown v. Board of Education*[10] and the entire civil rights movement were supposed to prevent. But the tragic persistence of de facto segregation in the United States has resulted in this recurring reconstruction of an ideal world, this dream of elimination, this assemblage of parts into an imaginary whole, this habit of shopping among the surplus of the living for the luxury of self-effacement. It has resulted in a massively expensive web of idealized sensation and deep resentment.

What are the limits of this attribution to "choice" to eliminate oneself just before the emptiness swallows one up? At least some public urgency about such matters came to the fore in the recent media brouhaha in Great Britain about a black woman, married to an Italian white man, who gave birth to a "healthy boy with fair hair and blue eyes."[11] The mother had been implanted with a white woman's egg to ensure that their offspring would be "spared the misery of racism."[12] I remember when I first heard about the "Baby M" case (the first case of surrogate motherhood to receive widespread national and international attention), I had a dream that I was in one of those gigantic silos in which chickens are mass-produced. As I looked up into the dizzying height of the vast industrial space, all I could see were black women, like brood hens, sitting on thousands of little nests, a little white egg nestled beneath each one of them.

What I did not anticipate at that time was that black women would emerge as not only the vehicles through which more efficient white baby production would be fostered, but that black women would be out there busying *themselves* with the acquisition of more profitable racial properties. "Uh-oh, I'll bet that's really got them scared," chuckled a friend of mine in response to the British case. "Us really *having* 'their' children." She was laughing, I think, at the strange juxtaposition of both mammy imagery and a kind of devilishly clever and efficient breach of the supposed bounds of "white race." But she paused, grew serious, and then said, "Uh-oh. This is really *scary.*" This scenario, after all, is enabled by nothing less than the transformation of the social difficulty of being black into an actual birth defect, an undesirable trait that technology can help eliminate.

Such complicated imagery of desire for survival, of wanting continuity even in disguise, of wanting to pass into new life even where a part of one has already died.

"In a regime of free baby production and sale," write Landes and Posner, "there might be efforts to breed children having desirable characteristics and, more broadly, to breed children with a known set of characteristics that could be matched up with those desired by prospective adoptive parents. Indeed, one can imagine, though with some difficulty, a growing separation between the production and rearing of children. No longer would a woman who wanted a child but who had a genetic trait that might jeopardize the child's health have to take her chances on a natural birth. She could find a very close genetic match-up to her and her husband's (healthy) genetic endowment in the baby market. However, so long as the market for eugenically bred babies did not extend beyond infertile couples and those with serious genetic disorders, the impact of a free baby market on the genetic composition and distribution of the human race at large would be small." [13]

Sometimes I feel as though we are living in a time of invisible body snatchers—as though some evil force had entered the hearts and minds of an entire nation and convinced them that they should shed their skin, cut off their noses, fly out of their bodies, and leave behind their genetic structure as they climb the DNA ladder to an imagined freedom. It is as though some invisible hand were nudging us toward a nice obliging mass suicide, disguised as a fear of looking into one another's faces without masks, disguised as fear not of difference but of being not enough "the same as . . ." The body has become a receptacle for the tracks of a cruel iconography. We risk a high-tech internalized fascism, where it is difficult to live in a world without a conformed exterior and a submissive will.

NOTES

1. Elisabeth M. Landes & Richard A. Posner, *The Economics of the Baby Shortage*, 7 J. Legal Stud. 323 (1978).

2. *Id.* at 344.

3. *Id.* at 327. "The thousands of children in foster care . . . are comparable to an unsold inventory stored in a warehouse." *Id.*

4. *Id.* at 323, 347. *See also* Ronald A. Cass, *Coping with Life, Law, and Markets: A Comment on Posner and the Law-and-Economics Debate*, 67 B.U. L. Rev. 73 (1987).

5. Richard A. Posner, Sex and Reason 409–17 (1992).

6. Landes & Posner, *supra* note 1, at 336.

7. *Id.* at 341.

8. Bruce Porter, *I Met My Daughter at the Wuhan Foundling Hospital*, N.Y. Times, Apr. 11, 1993, Magazine, at 46.

9. *Id.*

10. 374 U.S. 483 (1954).

11. Ronald Singleton, *A Child to Order: Black Mother Chooses White Test-Tube Baby So He Won't Suffer from Racism*, Daily Mail, Dec. 31, 1993, at 3.

12. *Id.*

13. Landes & Posner, *supra* note 1, at 345.

21 A Story from Home: On Being a Black Lesbian Mother

Isabelle R. Gunning

When I talk about racism in the larger lesbian community I end up talking about the need to form coalition, to network, to interconnect. Different peoples struggling to come together. When I talk about homophobia in the Black community I often feel I am talking about a painful dysfunctional family fight. Most families, whatever their race, do have some "dysfunction." And they do fight. And it hurts more than if a stranger did exactly the same thing.

While the Black community is not more homophobic than the white community, *some* parts of the Black community are indeed homophobic.[1] In some respects the reasons are very similar to why the white community is homophobic in parts. Black males may not have a lot of patriarchal power as compared to white males, but the little they do have, many are unwilling to lose. Accepting and understanding lesbianism and gayness demand a rethinking of male-female relationships.[2]

Unfortunately, homosexuality is taboo in some segments of the Black community just as it is taboo in some segments of the white community. Some of our progressive African American intellectuals, the feminists in particular, are talking about the need to be antihomophobic.[3] But in popular culture it is still too rare.[4] I do need to flag, though, a bright light on, of all things, television. *Roc,* a favorite show of mine—which of course has been canceled—actually did deal with these issues on one occasion. The show centered around the life of a working-class Black family. Roc was a garbageman, his wife was a nurse, and they lived with Roc's father and brother. The particular episode to which I am referring involved Roc's uncle, his dad's brother—who was played by Richard Roundtree, the actor who portrayed one of the more famous macho Blaxploitation heroes, Shaft—coming out as a gay man with a white lover.

There was a moment in the show when Roc's dad is in a bar agonizing because he cannot determine whether he is more upset that his brother is gay or that his brother's lover is white. To the show's credit, the gay issues were not a lightning rod for homophobic cracks as they often are in *In Living Color.* Rather, the jokes revolved around the absurdity of homophobia in the face of a family's love. The show ends with the wedding of the two gay men in the family home.

I have certainly felt the absurdity of homophobia in the face of family love. I consider the Black community a mother, and I have been afraid of becoming motherless. It has been easier for me to be "in your face" about my lesbianism to white folk than to Black. Still, my mate and I live in a section of Los Angeles that is considered a Black middle-class area of town. And recently we have found ourselves quite "out" in the Black community. We have become mothers to a gorgeous and delightful seven-year-old girl we recently adopted. Perhaps it is ironic that motherhood has so outed us. Some lesbian writers have suggested that motherhood for lesbians may be almost politically reactionary; it is just a way to appear normal.[5] For us it has meant that we must move beyond our circle of Black lesbian/gay or progressive Black community member friends. Maybe the fact that family and children are such core themes for the Black community[6] accounts for our largely positive interactions so far.

Our first "moment" came three days after we met our daughter. We met her, things clicked, and eventually she moved in with us. Then came the project of us— two Black lesbian mommies—taking her to school.

Our first day at school we met one of the two teacher's aides for the kindergarten class, who is a Black woman probably in her late fifties. "Hi, we are Jolanda's new adoptive parents." She didn't miss a beat. "How wonderful!" So far so good. We get to J.J.'s classroom and meet her teacher, who is a young Black woman probably in her late twenties. Same introduction. She literally steps back away from us. She gets it. She knows what we are. And I say that because in subsequent "moments" we have seen many people struggle to make sense of it. They decide that Pam, my mate, is my mother—she is ten years older than I and does not look it. We are cousins, we are sisters, something. Teacher got it. She now has to make a choice: What is more important here, the myths she has heard or the people she is meeting? And as she and I talked about my daughter and her schoolwork and her strengths, I guess I transformed from bulldagger to Black mother. And it was over. The awkwardness passed and this woman continued to be a positive support in our lives for our daughter.

We have had to repeat this coming out process. Her summer school was in another public school that was entirely Black and brown. The day care program that we put her in the half days of summer when summer school was out is in our neighborhood and virtually all-Black and run by a Black woman. After a bitter struggle with our school district (which had nothing to do with our being lesbian and everything to do with our being Black), we decided to put her in a private, independent Black school, run by a Black woman and her husband. To be sure, Dr. Wilkerson, the private school's founder and principal, was trying to figure what was what when we first approached her—two women, were there two children involved? No. We are both her mothers and she has a hyphenated last name, our names. So far—knock on wood—it has been fine.

Do we think there are some parents who are not happy? Yes. We have been snubbed occasionally. But we have our allies too. Indeed, our first real indication that some parents might not be happy came because one of the chairwomen of the PTA called us about doing something for our hot lunch program and went on and on about how pleased everyone was with Jolanda and her being a part of the school. It sounded like excessive pleasure even for a child as delightful as our own. We suspected that she was trying to let us know that we had a supporter. And we have. As I was writing this I was reminded that at the last parents' meeting—the first one that Pam had to attend alone—Gwen, the chairwoman of the PTA who called us, approached Pam to tell her to tell me that I had been missed at the meeting and that she hoped I would make it the next time. The other chair is a friend of ours who introduced us to the school. The principal and her husband, who is the vice principal, seem to have adjusted just fine. Early in the school year they kept labeling everything Jolanda Snowden instead of Gunning-Snowden. We would try, via our daughter, to correct that, and one morning Mr. Wilkerson flagged me down and said, "Now, what is her last name?" I assumed I would get some subtle but surely negative reaction as I responded, "Gunning hyphen Snowden." His response was to sigh with relief, "Oh good. She uses both names. I thought I would have to remember which one."

NOTES

1. bell hooks, *Homophobia in Black Communities, in* Talking Back: Thinking Feminist, Thinking Black 122–23 (1989).

2. Gloria I. Joseph, *Styling, Profiling and Pretending, in* Common Differences: Conflicts in Black and White Feminist Perspectives 192 (Gloria I. Joseph & Jill Lewis, 1981).

3. *See, e.g.,* Audre Lorde, Sister Outsider (1984); Audre Lorde, Zami: A New Spelling of My Name (1982); Audre Lorde, A Burst of Light (1988); Cohambee River Collective, *A Black Feminist Statement, in* This Bridge Called My Back: Writings by Radical Women of Color 210 (Cherríe Moraga & Gloria Anzaldúa eds., 1983); Cheryl Clarke, *Lesbianism: An Act of Resistance, in* This Bridge Called My Back, *supra* at 128; Cheryl Clarke, *The Failure to Transform Homophobia in the Black Community, in* Home Girls: A Black Feminist Anthology 197 (Barbara Smith ed., 1983); John O. Calmore, *Critical Race Theory, Archie Shepp and Fire Music: Securing an Authentic Intellectual Life in a Multicultural World,* 65 S. Cal. L. Rev. 2129, 2191–93 (1992); Jackie Goldsby, *Queen for 307 Days: Looking B[l]ack at Vanessa Williams and the Sex Wars, in* Afrekete: An Anthology of Black Lesbian Writing 165 (Catherine McKinley & L. Joyce Delaney eds., 1995); Linda Villarosa, *Revelations, in* Afrekete, *supra* at 214; hooks, *supra* note 1; Joseph, *supra* note 2.

I do not mean to suggest that this list is complete, and I realize that I have, perhaps not appropriately, privileged those intellectuals who write nonfiction prose over those who have explored and exposed the issue through poetry, biography, and fiction.

4. *But see, e.g.,* Nadine Smith, *Back Talk: Homophobia: Will It Divide Us?,* Essence, June 1994, at 128.

5. Nancy Pollkoff, *Lesbians Choosing Children: The Personal Is Political Revisited, in* Politics of the Heart: A Lesbian Parenting Anthology 51–53 (Sandra Pollack & Jeanne Vaughn eds., 1987).

6. Jewelle Gomez, *Repeat After Me: We Are Different, We Are the Same,* 14 N.Y.U. Rev. L. & Soc. Change 939 (1986).

Questions and Suggested Readings for Part 3

1. How are all the mothers portrayed in this part "bad" mothers? Is it possible for them to become "good" mothers? Is it desirable? What kinds of programs can be devised to help all the mothers discussed. (See Wing's essay in part 1.)

2. Nathalie Augustin argues that women's welfare benefits should not be conditioned on the truancy of their children. Why not? Shouldn't incentive be created for women to be more responsible mothers? Isn't this what Learnfare was designed to do?

3. Why was Learnfare expected to combat the problems of dropout and truancy rates among students in general? How does Learnfare define the AFDC mother as the "architect of her predicament"?

4. What is wrong with punishing women who use drugs while they are pregnant? Dorothy Roberts suggests that part of the problem is that women of color are more vulnerable to prosecution because they are more likely to be poor. Does this mean that such women should not be punished, or does it mean that we should find ways to punish women who use drugs while pregnant? Is Roberts's argument that black women should not be locked up because the criminal justice system is racist? Is this argument compelling?

5. How might women of color's sexuality be treated as property in the realm of reproduction? Do you agree with Patricia Williams that at some future point poor women of color will be employed as surrogates for the white majority? Should women be allowed to make that choice? Wouldn't this be a way for poor women to achieve financial stability?

For further reading, see Anita Allen, *The Black Surrogate Mother*, 8 Harv. BlackLetter J. 17 (1991); Anita Allen, *Surrogacy, Slavery and the Ownership of Life*, 13 Harv. J.L. & Pub. Pol'y 139 (1990); Laura Gomez, Misconceiving Mothers: Lawmakers, Prosecutors and the Politics of Prenatal Drug Exposure (1996); Barbara Omolade, *The Unbroken Circle: A Historical and Contemporary Study of Black Single Mothers and Their Families*, 3 Wis. Women's L.J. 239 (1989); Dorothy Roberts, *Racism and Patriarchy in the Meaning of Motherhood, in* Feminist Legal Theory (Frances E. Olsen ed., 1994); Dorothy Roberts, *The Future of Reproductive Choice for Poor Women and Women of Color*, 12 Women's Rts. L. Rep. 59 (1990); Patricia Williams, *Fetal Fictions: An Exploration of Property Archetypes in Racial and Gendered Contexts*, 42 U. Fla. L. Rev. 81 (1990).

4 Sexual Harassment: After Anita

Part 4 highlights sexual harassment, a legal and social phenomenon synonymous with the name of a black female legal academic, Anita Hill, and the man who harassed her, Supreme Court justice Clarence Thomas. Although polls indicated that she was initially not believed by a majority of black and white Americans, her saga has led to a revolutionary change in our understanding of the phenomenon. The issue of sexual harassment has now penetrated the private sector workforce, the armed forces, government, universities, and even the U.S. Senate. Many publications have appeared about the Clarence Thomas Supreme Court confirmation hearings; for example, Hill has collaborated as coeditor with Emma Coleman Jordan of Georgetown Law Center to produce *Race, Gender and Power in America: The Legacy of the Hill-Thomas Hearings* (1995). Toni Morrison earlier edited *Race-ing Justice, En-gendering Power: Essays on Anita Hill, Clarence Thomas, and the Construction of Social Reality* (1992).

In this unit, Emma Coleman Jordan, cocounsel for Anita Hill's pro bono legal team during the Supreme Court hearings, leads off with *Race, Gender, and Social Class in the Thomas Sexual Harassment Hearings: The Hidden Fault Lines in Political Discourse.* She points out the dilemma that black women face when there are conflicts with black men. Racism trumps sexism, and therefore black women's needs and concerns go unaddressed. Stereotypes about women as delusional and untrustworthy, coupled with the view of black women as a Sapphire, a "gonad-grinding woman" out of control, combined to make Anita Hill initially unbelievable to a majority of Americans.

Adrienne D. Davis and Stephanie M. Wildman joined forces to write *The Legacy of Doubt: Treatment of Sex and Race in the Hill-Thomas Hearings.* They focus on the high-tech lynching metaphor that Clarence Thomas raised, to show how Anita Hill was de-raced and thus partially erased. Black men have historically been lynched by white men, not by black women. The image of a predominantly white male Senate that did not understand sex discrimination and harassment is emphasized by the authors. Extrapolating from this article, one may note that the spectacle led to the election of several more female senators in the 1992 elections, including the first African American female, Carol Moseley Braun. It probably also played a role in forcing the resignation of Senator Bob Packwood amid sexual harassment allegations in 1995.

In *Invisible Woman: Reflections on the Clarence Thomas Confirmation Hearings*, Kim A. Taylor-Thompson plays upon the title of Ralph Ellison's famous novel *Invisible Man*. Anita Hill was like the invisible (wo)man, who is rendered invisible because everyone refuses to see her. Taylor-Thompson speculates that the confirmation process failed because the senators were blinded by their positions of privilege. She raises the possibility of a different outcome if Hill had been white, which might have forced some of the senators to rise in defense of one of "their" women. Taylor-Thompson notes that white feminists also misunderstood Hill's complexity and attempted to make her into a race-less woman. They could not relate to the problems she faced within the black community for "daring to air the dirty laundry." Polls taken a year later indicate that public opinion had shifted in Hill's favor. Perhaps people were more able to see her as made of "flesh and bone," like Ellison's invisible man.

The last three chapters in part 4 take us beyond the Supreme Court confirmation hearings to other issues of harassment. These contexts have now become visible after Anita Hill. Maria L. Ontiveros focuses on the job site in *Three Perspectives on Workplace Harassment of Women of Color*. One of the questions asked of Anita Hill was why she did not leave her job if she was harassed. Ontiveros addresses this question by looking at the perspectives of the harasser, the victim, and the judicial system. Harassers of color are most likely to harass women of color, because of the disproportionate reaction they would face if they harassed white women. In the excerpt, the viewpoint of a Latina is emphasized; Ontiveros shows that these women, because of language, immigration status, class, and culture, are highly unlikely to sue the harasser. They need their jobs. Since the legal system disbelieves these women, Ontiveros calls for a modification of the rules surrounding sexual harassment or the creation of a new cause of action prohibiting discrimination against women of color.

Deirdre E. Davis delves into another heretofore invisible area in *The Harm That Has No Name: Street Harassment, Embodiment, and African American Women*. Defining the harm of street harassment and naming it help society see it as a form of gender subordination. Studying its racialized impact on black women highlights the ability of both white and black men to participate in the subordination of black women. Such harassment constitutes a form of what Patricia Williams has called spirit-murder, the psychological effect of racism.

Finally, law professor and political scientist Sumi K. Cho enriches our understanding of the sexual harassment of Asian women in *Converging Stereotypes in Racialized Sexual Harassment: Where the Model Minority Meets Suzie Wong*. She illustrates how the model minority stereotype is used to objectify and denigrate Asian American women. The stereotype of the female who slept her way to the top is paired with stereotypes of Asian women as the "Singapore Girl," passive and compliant, lacking professional merit. Cho uses two case studies to illustrate how these two images converge and affect how Asian American women experience sexual harassment.

22

Race, Gender, and Social Class in the Thomas Sexual Harassment Hearings: The Hidden Fault Lines in Political Discourse

Emma Coleman Jordan

To understand the public perception and interpretation of the Anita Hill/Clarence Thomas hearing requires consideration of the presumptions based on, among other things, race and gender. The cues to race, gender, and social class were oddly distorted in that superheated weekend under the intensity of the klieg lights. Many preexisting racial and sexual stereotypes undercut Anita Hill's credibility: a man does not commit sexual harassment unless the woman encouraged his sexual interests in some way; a charge of sexual harassment made against a man of high status by a woman of lesser status is to be viewed with suspicion because the woman has something to gain from publicity, no matter how unflattering; sexual harassment charges are frequently concocted and therefore there must be independent corroboration of the events alleged; black women are unchaste; black women who report sexual misconduct by black men are traitors to the race and do not deserve community support. Anita Hill found herself burdened by all these stereotypes.

RECKONING WITH THE RACIAL REALITIES

In the Hill-Thomas dispute, the fact that the central figures of this high-stakes dispute are both black was at once supremely important and of no particular importance. For Clarence Thomas, the process by which he had risen in the ranks of black conservatives required him to carve a deep ravine between his own views and the social and political preferences of a majority of black citizens.

Thomas was introduced to the American public by a president who was willing to assert boldly that Thomas's race had nothing to do with his selection.[1] Two profoundly contradictory messages soon became apparent. On the one hand he was a black man from Pin Point, Georgia, whose dramatic rise from poverty and the crushing limitations of racial segregation made him an icon of neoconservatism, whose success could be cited as proof of the viability of self-help economics and the racial fairness of white conservatives who supported him. On the other hand, it was argued that because Thomas's successes were achieved despite traumatic incidents of racism, he would bring a deep personal sensitivity to the resolution of the racial conflicts that often form the basis of Supreme Court litigation.[2]

Anita Hill's racial identity also rested on a foundation of ambiguous characterization. Thomas and his supporters sought to portray her as a "white" feminist who happened to be black, a tool of abortion rights supporters who sought to bring down Thomas with a last-minute claim of sexual harassment.

This characterization was plausible because of the inflexibility of our models for race and gender debates. In the shorthand of public policy discourse about gender conflicts, we assume that all women are white[3] and that all blacks are men. When a black woman appears to speak for herself, these unspoken assumptions force her to shed one identity or the other. Moreover, when there are conflicts between a black man and a black woman, racism "trumps" sexism. The hierarchy of interests within the black community assigns a priority to protecting the entire community against the assaultive forces of racism. This conceptualization of the relationship between the entire community and the interests of its female members creates a powerful dynamic in which black women must subordinate matters of vital concern in order to continue to participate in community life. Women who break the expectation of silence may be made to feel disloyal, shunned, or vilified.[4]

A new organization of black women, African American Women in Defense of Ourselves, has sought to project a zone of political and cultural self-defense for black women by refusing to honor the expectation of silence regarding black male sexual misconduct. They note that "[m]any have erroneously portrayed [the hearings] as [addressing] an issue of either gender or race. As women of African descent, we understand sexual harassment as both. . . . This country has never taken the sexual abuse of Black women seriously. Black women have been sexually stereotyped as immoral, insatiable, [and] perverse."[5]

Complex racial and cultural arguments are now being developed, in a series of highly publicized controversies, in defense of black men who use obscene, often violent language and imagery in communicating with and about black women. One such argument is that obscenity is part of the black vernacular and should be understood by both black men and women as harmless, situationally appropriate repartee between the sexes.

An important recent contributor to this postmodern cultural defense of language that enshrines a culture of degradation and violence against black women is Henry Louis Gates, Jr., chairman of the Afro-American Studies Department at Harvard University. Gates offered a cultural defense to the obscenity charges brought against the 2-Live Crew rap group.[6] Although the First Amendment is certainly broad enough to protect even the blackwoman-hating lyrics of 2-Live Crew, the cultural acceptability of such language is a distinct question that cannot be answered solely with reference to black male subcultures.[7]

Harvard sociologist Orlando Patterson extends Gates's argument, dismissing Hill's claim of sexual harassment as oversensitivity to a black male's "down-home style of courting."[8] Patterson thus joins the debate with the implausible assertion that the pornographic descriptions attributed to Thomas were within the cultural tradition of conversation between black men and women, and therefore "immediately recognizable to Professor Hill and most women of Southern working-class backgrounds, white or black, especially the latter."[9]

Patterson's relativistic approach is also misguided. Cultural relativism in the workplace will quickly become a slippery slope if workers are permitted to carve cultural exemptions to Title VII. Moreover, even if one might want to take cultural factors into account, surely neither Thomas nor Patterson on his behalf would want to argue that the early childhood conventions of Pin Point and Savannah, Georgia should be the standards by which then EEOC chairman Thomas's conduct should be measured.

THE LYNCHING METAPHOR

In his opening statement to the Senate, Thomas charged the Senate Judiciary Committee with conducting a "high-tech lynching."[10] He went on to say that "I wasn't harmed by the Klan. I wasn't harmed by the Knights of Camellia. I wasn't harmed by the Ar[y]an race. I wasn't harmed by a racist group. I was harmed by this process."[11]

Because no one on the committee responded to his lynching charge, the country was left with a distorted image of a racial victim. No one pointed out that it was a black woman who claimed he had victimized her. No one pointed out the terrible harms and stereotypes to which black women have been subjected. Although the sexual stereotypes of all black people are damaging, "[t]he institutionalized rape of black women has never been as powerful a symbol of black oppression [within the black community] as the spectacle of lynching."[12]

HISTORICAL RESISTANCE TO SEXUAL PREDATION

The history of the struggle of black women has always contained an element of resistance to sexual predation. The most vivid illustrations of such self-defense are those of slave women who forcefully resisted the rape of masters.

The story of Celia, a young slave woman who murdered her master, is one example.[13] John Newsom purchased Celia at age fourteen and raped her repeatedly. She had two children by him, but subsequently developed a stable relationship with a fellow slave named George. Celia then attempted, unsuccessfully, to terminate the abusive relationship with Newsom. She warned her master not to come to her private cabin, and when he disregarded her wishes, she struck him with a club, killing him. Celia was tried for murder. However, she was not permitted to testify on her own behalf, because a slave could not legally testify against a white person. Nor did the law recognize the crime of rape against a slave. However, a statute did make it a crime "to take any woman against her will."[14] Celia's lawyer introduced evidence of the ongoing rapes and made the innovative argument that "even a slave woman could resist sexual advances with deadly force."[15] Although the statute applied to "any woman," the court rejected the argument that it included slave women.[16] Today, black women seek to claim that vital core of individual dignity, the right to determine one's sexual interactions. These efforts present complex challenges to the definitions of acceptable interaction between the genders. The slave legacy stands as a reminder that black women can successfully resist sexual imposition despite disabling legal doctrine.

THE POWER OF RACIAL MEMORY

Clarence Thomas's use of powerful racial imagery transformed him from sexual harasser to racial victim, perhaps the single most important element leading to his confirmation. His use of race worked to his advantage because "the critical segment of public opinion was the opinion of black voters in the black belt of the South. Thomas reminded black people that he was a black man who was in danger of being oppressed for being uppity, by going beyond his assigned station in life."[17]

This perception tapped the widely shared belief among large segments of the black community that black politicians and other prominent leaders are subject to a double standard of morality.[18] Thomas, like former Washington, D.C., mayor Marion Barry, was able to tap a deep and "well-founded skepticism about the effort of the white power structure to embarrass prominent black men."[19]

A GENDERED UNDERSTANDING

Those who sought to discredit Anita Hill made use of a treacherous combination of stereotypes and myths about black and white women. The Freudian notion of women's hysterical fabrication of claims of sexual abuse[20] merged with the politico-psychiatric diagnosis of erotomania[21] to provide a formidable tool with which to shape public opinion and diminish Hill's powerful presentation. This senatorial diagnosis of a hysterical, delusional female was then buttressed by the testimony of John Doggett, a witness who made the term "erotomania" come alive.

Because Hill is a black woman, she was portrayed not only as delusional, but also as Sapphire: the black, gonad-grinding woman "out of control."[22] The Sapphire image, with all its connotations of black male emasculation, resonated within the black community. Hill's status as a black woman multiplied the possible lines of attack by making available additional stereotypes that could be used against her. Hill's credibility was also challenged by the fact that she only revealed specific details of Thomas's pornographic references gradually. That such gradual revelation is the norm for women who have undergone traumatic experiences was a fact lost on both the senators and the public.[23]

A PERSONAL EPILOGUE

The Thomas-Hill sexual harassment hearings left me drained but energized. Like Anita Hill, I too came to a moment of awakening when I realized that African American women face a formidable challenge within our communities. The challenge is to speak without anger, to teach, and to discover the path to restructure our community values in order to embrace black women as full citizens. If my two daughters find the world a better place because of our efforts, I will know that the discomfort we experienced was worth it. I remain committed to the goal, and optimistic that it will draw nearer to complete achievement each day that we are "willing to speak truth to power." [24]

NOTES

1. *See* Terry Atlas, *Bush Chooses Conservative for Supreme Court: Judge's Views on Abortion May Hold Key*, Chi. Trib., July 2, 1991, at 1.

2. *Cf.* Thomas's dissent from the 7–2 majority in *Hudson v. McMillian*, 503 U.S. 1 (1992). The majority held that the Eighth Amendment's cruel and unusual punishment clause protected prisoners from being beaten while incarcerated, even if the beatings did not cause serious injury.

3. Some view the women's liberation movement as a dispute between white women and white men. *See* Paula Giddings, When and Where I Enter: The Impact of Black Women on Race and Sex in America, 309 (1984). This is especially true when racial tensions are high. At such times "black women's feminist reactions tend to be muted." *Id.* at 311.

4. *See, e.g.,* Rosemary Bray, *Taking Sides against Ourselves*, N.Y. Times, Nov. 17, 1991, Magazine, at 56 ("Anita Hill put her private business in the street and she downgraded a black man to a room filled with white men who might alter his fate—surely a large enough betrayal for her to be read out of the race.").

5. *African American Women in Defense of Ourselves*, N.Y. Times, Nov. 17, 1991, Campus Life, at 53.

6. *See* Sara Riemer, *Rap Band Found Not Guilty in Obscenity Trial*, N.Y. Times, Oct. 21, 1991, at 1. Gates testified that 2-Live Crew were "literary geniuses." Drawing on his research into black folklore, he concluded that the often violent, misogynistic lyrics were within the tradition of parody in the black community. *Id.*

7. Critiques of the cultural acceptability defense have come from men as well as women. *See, e.g.,* Michael Wilbon, *Entitled to Everything He Got*, Wash. Post, Feb. 12, 1992, at B1 ("I'm sickened by the open-season-on-women atmosphere that would allow Tyson to fondle and grab and offend and frighten [women] for years").

8. Orlando Patterson, *Race, Gender and Liberal Fallacies*, N.Y. Times, Oct. 20, 1991, § 4, at 15.

This defense was also evident in the rape trial of former heavyweight boxing champion Mike Tyson. During the trial, Tyson's attorneys sought to portray him as a crude, unrefined "street dude" who courted women on the first meeting by asking them if they wanted to "f——." *See* William Raspberry, *The Real Victim in Indianapolis,* Wash. Post, Feb. 14, 1992, at A25.

9. Patterson, *supra* note 8. *But see* Telephone Interview with Professor Roy Brooks, Univ. Of San Diego (Oct. 24, 1991) (this argument "is alien to the black culture that I know. This is a bold and ridiculous assertion. It degrades black women to suggest that this is acceptable courting conversation.").

10. *Hearing of the Senate Judiciary Committee,* Fed. News Serv., Oct. 12, 1991.

11. *See supra* note 5 and accompanying text.

12. Hazel V. Carby, Reconstructing Womanhood: The Emergence of the Afro-American Woman Novelist 39 (1987).

13. Melton A. McLaurin, Celia: A Slave (1991).

14. *Id.* at 91.

15. *Id.*

16. *Id.* at 90–91.

17. Interview with Professor Patricia King, Georgetown University Law Center, in Washington, D.C. (Oct. 24, 1991).

18. *See* Alison Muscatine, *Answering Credibility Question: Accuser's Testimony Proof Enough; Tyson Caught by Words, Image,* Wash. Post, Feb. 12, 1992, at B3.

19. Telephone Interview with Professor Lani Guinier (a black Yale Law School classmate of Clarence Thomas), Univ. of Pennsylvania Law School (Oct. 23, 1991).

20. *See* Sigmund Freud, Collected Papers 32–33 (Ernest Jones ed., 1959).

21. *See* American Psychiatric Association, Work Group to Revise D.S.M. III, D.S.M. III-R in development, 2d Draft (Aug. 1, 1986) (defining erotomania as "a delusional disorder in which the predominant theme of the delusion(s) is that another person of higher status is in love with him or her").

22. Bray, *supra* note 4, at 94–95.

23. Clients in sexual harassment cases rarely tell every detail the first time. Telephone Interview with Vickie Golden, Employment Discrimination Lawyer (Oct. 25, 1991).

24. This phrase, often repeated by Quakers during confrontations with official authority, reflects the spirit of moral commitment to change. *See, e.g.,* Robert Myers, *Hans J. Morgenthau: On Speaking Truth to Power,* Society, Jan.-Feb. 1992, at 65.

23

The Legacy of Doubt: Treatment of Sex and Race in the Hill-Thomas Hearings

Adrienne D. Davis and Stephanie M. Wildman

Clarence Thomas has been sworn in as the 106th Supreme Court justice. He is the second African American justice. After weeks of televised confirmation hearings, extensive public debate among citizens and in the media, and the final Senate vote, questions still remain whether justice has been served. There has been massive broadcast and print coverage of these events, which captured the country's attention. Television added a different dimension to the process, which became a human drama when Anita Hill's sexual harassment claim and Thomas's denial were aired. The nation watched mesmerized, waiting for a Perry Mason to rise and announce who lied, but no Perry appeared. We have only ourselves to assess credibility and to record history.

GENDERING THE SYMBOL "RACE" AND THE INVISIBILITY OF RACISM

A series of symbols mediated the public collective understanding of the Thomas confirmation hearings. In modern society, symbols increasingly mediate relationships in a variety of ways, from how people learn history to how they purchase commodities. Symbols provide indicators for historians of the "essence" of historical eras, the main images of words, pictures, and sounds that people welcomed (or rejected) in their lives.[1] Symbols represent efforts to render understandable a complex world and to synthesize variant ideas and metaphors operating at multiple levels into a single, graspable entity.

To the extent that symbols filter understanding of events and in particular affect the way history will record them, the ability to share in their creation and presentation is paramount to constructing reality.[2] When Clarence Thomas was first nominated, race became a prime symbol that served as a synthesis of questions over President

Bush's motivations in nominating Thomas, his qualifications, his background, and affirmative action.

Race as a symbol appeared in fora as diverse as popular comedy shows, political cartoons, news coverage, and intellectual debate. From the beginning, Thomas controlled this symbol of race. He was the object, the referent of the symbol "Black." But unlike most objects, Thomas enjoyed an advantage: the press and the Bush administration gave him substantial power to define himself and the symbolic value of his signifier. The manipulation of the symbol was amazing: it was formally discounted, and yet the continued references to its absence made attention focus on it all the more. Race as constructed by Thomas became a symbol of making it on one's own; of searing poverty turned to economic privilege; of self-reliance over handouts. He attempted to depict as minimal any benefits of racial preferences he had received.[3]

The symbolic value of race was temporarily replaced with that of gender when Anita Hill alleged she had been sexually harassed while on Thomas's staff. Women rallied to Hill's support because of the powerful symbol of sexual abuse, familiar to many women. At this point, those seeking to discredit Hill transformed the image of gender oppression by sexual abuse into one of unrestrained sexuality.[4] These two images, gender oppression and sexuality, were vying for primacy when Thomas reintroduced the symbol of race, which then became the axis around which all subsequent discourse revolved.

Clarence Thomas, a firm disbeliever in the use of race as an excuse for one's behavior or as a reason for acting affirmatively to increase representation of underrepresented groups,[5] invoked race with a vengeance against the Senate Judiciary Committee. In claiming he was the victim of a high-tech lynching, Thomas claimed he was being accused because he was African American.

Consider the many valid reasons for which the senators should have called Thomas to account for his conduct: Anita Hill's charges were supported by four different witnesses; the charges she brought would have exposed not only his character (as if that would not be enough), but also his lack of respect for the rule of law;[6] and if true the charges would have demonstrated that he had perjured himself. Thomas's invocation of race at this point in the confirmation process was truly ironic. His use of race in these hearings rested on the implicit assertion that he was called to answer Hill's charges by virtue of the fact that he was an African American. Thomas seemed to believe and to make others believe that he was called to answer only because of his race. Yet his accuser was also African American. The inconsistent treatment of the symbol "Black" as applied to Hill and Thomas revealed that the symbol was gendered. In this struggle, the symbol "Black" equaled "male."[7]

By saying he was being lynched, Thomas implicitly claimed he would have been treated differently (better?) if he had been white. Yet senators treated him quite well, deferring to his demands and tirades. No one suggested he was misusing race. No one pointed out that to do as he had suggested, let the whole matter go, would fit an equally heinous and embarrassing racial paradigm, that of ignoring the claims of sexual abuse brought by African American women. Instead, Thomas declared that suddenly his Senate friends were out to get him and that the white people he had claimed would respect hard work and self-reliance were treating him as if he were—Black?

Thus, in Clarence Thomas's manipulation of the symbol of race, Anita Hill became somehow "de-raced" and partially erased. For Thomas to have confronted the fact that his accuser was Black would have confused the racial point he was trying to make. Instead, in a stunning sleight of hand, he managed to convince all involved, including the Senate, that white racism, rather than a Black woman, had accused him of harassment. Thus, race became something Hill did not have. In an ironic twist of fate she became "Yale-educated female law professor" to Thomas's "lynched Black man." She became a part of the white racist conspiracy that Thomas asserted was after him. He had gained exclusive control over the content of the symbol "race," giving it a gender that allowed Hill no place within it, rendering her race invisible.

Patricia Williams has commented on this modern inclination to present issues of race as invisible. She told the story of her late godmother's bedroom, which she had cleared of furniture in order to paint. Even empty, the memories in the room had come flooding back to her; "the shape of the emptiness" confronted her each time she was about to enter:

> The power of that room, I have thought since, is very like the power of racism as status quo: it is deep, angry, eradicated from view, but strong enough to make everyone who enters the room walk around the bed that isn't there, avoiding the phantom as they did the substance, for fear of bodily harm. They do not even know they are avoiding; they defer to the unseen shapes of things with subtle responsiveness, guided by an impulsive awareness of nothingness, and the deep knowledge and denial of witchcraft at work.[8]

Williams's powerful description of racism as the phantom affecting everyone in society explains much about the Thomas hearing dynamic. The rendering invisible of Anita Hill's race, its exclusion from a discussion of her sexual harassment charge, meant that racism/white supremacy[9] was not discussed except on Clarence Thomas's terms. Hill made her charge as an African American woman in a society dominated by white male values. The erasure of her race allowed racism to act as a phantom once again.

The senators tried to avoid looking racist by refusing to ask Thomas any hard questions, and in doing so deferred to the "unseen shape" of racism. Yet by deferring, they fostered racism and its companion in America, white supremacy. bell hooks has explained that liberal whites do not see themselves as prejudiced or interested in domination through coercion, yet "they cannot recognize the ways their actions support and affirm the very structure of racist domination and oppression that they profess to wish to see eradicated."[10] The avoidance of race, the failure to talk about it or acknowledge its role in history, maintains and perpetuates racism/white supremacy. By avoiding race, we never have to confront the implications of change, and we default to the status quo, which makes white the hidden referent to race.

Failing to talk about race forces racism off limits, but it does not make either be gone. Like people avoiding the phantom furniture in Williams's godmother's bedroom, we tiptoe around the dynamic of racism, keeping it intact.

Williams reported a chilling example of this denial of race in her own experience. She, a Black woman, was barred from admittance to Benetton's at Christmastime by a white clerk who refused to activate the buzzer that admitted shoppers. When she described this outrageous example of racism in a law review article, the editors edited out all reference to her race. When she retold this tale of law school editing, as showing the need to talk about race and to engage in affirmative action, her speech was reported as being against affirmative action. And finally, when another law professor discussed these events in class, a rumor started that Williams had made up the story about her exclusion from Benetton's.[11]

Thus, her complaint about racism, exclusion from the store, was first distorted and then relegated by the white audience to the realm of fantasy, the ultimate denial of the presence of racism. The senators accused Anita Hill of fantasy, denoting a similar attempt to deny the possible existence of discriminatory behavior.[12] Is the fate of Black women like Williams and Hill, who tell stories of racism and sexism, that they will not be believed?

THE LEGACY OF DOUBT

After watching the televised Senate hearings, each member of society should be extremely frightened about the Senate's insensitivity to the needs and lives of the majority of its constituency, women. This concern should also prompt examination of the Senate's record on broader gender and racial issues. Can the powerless in this country truly have a represented voice when all the authority to which the Senate defers is male, white, heterosexual, and economically privileged?

After the allegations brought by Anita Hill became public, many watched in disbelief, realizing that our representative institution was in fact filled with people who did not or would not comprehend the substance and standards of sex discrimination law. As they proved in their comments to the press and in their questioning of Hill, few, if any, members of the Senate Judiciary Committee know what constitutes sexual harassment. Senator Alan Simpson distinguished sexual harassment from "real harassment."[13] Senator Arlen Specter was unsure whether speech without physical contact was included in its ambit.[14] The most elite electoral institution found itself floundering hopelessly when attempting to face the issue of sexism, a problem that plagues more than half the country's citizens. Consequently, because the senators could not fathom the issue of sexism, they certainly could not understand the intersection of sexism with racism.

More than 50 percent of the people in this country are females of all races. This fact is cited every time feminists (men and women) attempt to suggest that political representation is uneven, insensitive, and arguably nonexistent for this special interest, which happens to be a majority. In a nation where institutions overwhelmingly cater to the interests of power and money (if these things are separable), both of which are controlled by males, it is not surprising that more women's voices are not heard. Patriarchal structures govern access to advertising, the media, banks, and most jobs. Even when women are present, such as Senator Nancy Kassebaum, it is often because they have met and adopted male standards. Thus, Senator Kassebaum was able logically to say that she resented being forced to choose between being a senator and being a woman: "[T]hroughout my years here I have taken pride in the fact that I am a U.S. Senator, not a woman Senator." [15] She unwittingly pointed out that a hidden referent in "senator" is male.

Media and money are all-important to politicians as they seek "image" and financing in their quest for constituents and power bases. Neither the media nor the economic institutions of the country have tended to value women for much other than as commodities used to sell most everything from beer to cars. Struggles for true valuation in areas such as comparable worth and child care and in corporate positions have proved elusive.

Thus, to say the Senate is male means not only that 98 percent of its members are men, but also that its values and abstractions derive from male perspectives which influence its definitions of power and empowerment and, ultimately, freedom. This should make women and feminist men across the country nervous as civil rights advocates reluctantly turn away from the federal courts and toward the legislatures for protection of the wavering right to reproductive freedom, the formulation of a national child care policy, and a forum to address issues of battery and rape within and without the home, as well as sexual harassment. Why are these policies and laws, which are crucial to women's lives, given such short shrift in legislative forums?

Clarence Thomas joins a Supreme Court that is often described as "conservative." Yet it has acted as a very radical body, overturning precedent without compunction.[16] Thomas's confirmation has not eased doubts, about him, about the Senate, or ultimately about the system of justice. Is there a person in this nation who believes that Clarence Thomas never discussed *Roe v. Wade* with anyone?[17] Is there a person in this nation who believed President Bush when he said that Clarence Thomas was the best-qualified person for the job and that race had nothing to do with his nomination?[18] As Thomas played the race card, a card he had proclaimed was not in his deck, he raised more questions: How could he have been treated better? Should the claims of African American women be ignored when they are brought against African American men (as they frequently are)? Most important, how can society prevent the misuse of race? As we sift among the symbols, how many more doubts do we have?

NOTES

1. *See* Michel Foucault, The Archeology of Knowledge 7 (1971) (discussing the changing role of "documents" in historical study). In reflecting on historical periods, people sometimes are in danger of seizing on leftover symbols without sufficiently probing what they represented or, more importantly, how they were constructed.

2. Terence Hawkes, Structuralism and Semiotics 13–15 (1977).

3. Charley Roberts & Richard C. Reuben, *Anti-Bias Plans Aided Thomas during Career: Affirmative Action Boosted Nominee at Critical Points: Hypocrisy Is Charged,* L.A. Daily J., July 16, 1991, at 1 (detailing preferential treatment that Thomas had been a beneficiary of, including a race-based scholarship to attend college, affirmative action acceptance to Yale Law School, employment by the Missouri attorney general, presidential appointments to two civil rights posts, nomination to the federal appeals court, and, most recently, nomination to the Supreme Court).

4. *See, e.g.,* William Safire, *Myths of the Confirmation,* N.Y. Times, Oct. 17, 1991, at A27 (calling Hill's allegations "unsubstantiated sex charges"). *But see* Ellen Goodman, *Honk If You Believe Anita,* Boston Globe, Oct. 17, 1991, at 17 ("To accept Anita Hill's story, you had to believe only that Clarence Thomas would lie to salvage his honor in front of the country and his family. To accept Thomas's denial, you had to believe that Hill was a psychopath.").

5. "I firmly insist that the Constitution be interpreted in a colorblind fashion. It is futile to talk of a colorblind society unless this constitutional principle is first established. Hence, I emphasize black self-help, as opposed to racial quotas and other race-conscious legal devices that only further and deepen the original problem." *The Supreme Court: Clarence Thomas in His Own Words,* N.Y. Times, July 2, 1991, at A14.

After an interview with Thomas, Paul Weyrich wrote, "Mr. Thomas personally disapproves of affirmative-action programs and the use of goals and timetables to remedy employment discrimination, but he insists that he enforced such measures during his tenure at EEOC." Weyrich notes that a number of civil rights advocates who worked with the EEOC under Thomas disagree. Paul Weyrich, *Clarence Thomas: Here Comes the Judge,* Wash. Times, Mar. 1, 1990, at E1.

6. As chair of the EEOC, Thomas was responsible for enforcing Title VII as well as the EEOC guidelines prohibiting sexual harassment. Guidelines on Discrimination Because of Sex, 29 C.F.R. § 1604.11 (1990) (originally enacted on Nov. 10, 1980 (45 Fed. Reg. 74,677 (1980)) ("Harassment on the basis of sex is a violation of § 703 of Title VII.").

7. *See* All the Women Are White, All the Blacks Are Men, but Some of Us Are Brave (Gloria T. Hull et al. eds., 1982) (landmark Black women's studies text).

8. Patricia J. Williams, The Alchemy of Race and Rights 49 (1991).

9. bell hooks has explained her realization that racism and white supremacy were connected: "The word racism ceased to be the term which best expressed for me exploitation of black people and other people of color in this society and . . . I began to understand that the most useful term was white supremacy." bell hooks, *Overcoming White Supremacy: A Comment, in* Talking Back: Thinking Feminist, Thinking Black 112 (1989).

10. *Id.* at 113.

11. Williams, *supra* note 8, at 242–43 n.5.

12. Senator Strom Thurmond said, "I have been contacted by several psychiatrists, suggesting that it is entirely possible that she is suffering from delusions. Perhaps she is living in a fantasy world." Nomination of Clarence Thomas, of Georgia, to be an Associate Justice of the Supreme Court of the United States, 137 Cong. Rec. S14,649 (daily ed. Oct. 15, 1991) (statement of Sen. Thurmond). A lengthy discussion in the hearing between Senators DeConcini and Specter with John Doggett and Dean Charles Kothe also repeatedly raised the issue of whether Hill suffered from delusions. *Id.* Finally, Senator Kennedy rebuked his fellow politicians: "[S]hame on anyone who suggests that [fantasy] is what happened." *Id.* at S14,641.

13. "So I think it's a cruel thing we're witnessing. It's a harsh thing, a very sad and harsh

thing, and Anita Hill will be sucked right into the . . . very thing she wanted to avoid most. She will be injured and destroyed and belittled and hounded and harassed, real harassment, different than the sexual kind." *Quoted in Comments by Senators on Thomas Nomination,* N.Y. Times, Oct. 10, 1991, at B14. Senator Simpson evidently did not regard sexual harassment as injurious, destructive, or belittling.

14. Senator Arlen Specter said one reason he had not planned to change his vote despite knowledge of the harassment charge was that, "in light of the lateness of the allegation, the absence of any touching or intimidation, and the fact that she moved with him from one agency to another, [he] felt [he] had done [his] duty." *Quoted in* Derrick Z. Jackson, *Sexual Harassment, According to Teens,* Boston Globe, Oct. 13, 1991, at B3. Specter later said he did not mean it. *Id.*

15. Senator Kassebaum continued, "When some of my male colleagues have suggested that I know nothing about national defense issues because I am a woman, I have been offended. In the same vein, I have to assume that many of my male colleagues are offended by the notion that they cannot begin to understand the seriousness of sexual harassment or the anguish of its victims. On the question before us, some women suggest that I should judge this nomination not as a Senator but as a woman, one of only two women in the Senate. I reject that suggestion." Nomination of Clarence Thomas, of Georgia, to be an Associate Justice of the Supreme Court of the United States, 137 Cong. Rec. S14,661 (daily ed. Oct. 15, 1991).

16. *Compare* Wards Cove Packing Co. v. Atonio, 490 U.S. 642, 651, 653–61 (1989) (reinterpreting *Griggs v. Duke Power* to find heightened requirements constituting prima facie disparate impact case under Title VII) *with* Griggs v. Duke Power Co., 401 U.S. 424, 431 (1971) (initially articulating standards for prima facie case); Richmond v. J. A. Croson Co., 488 U.S. 469, 498–506 (1989) (awarding of minority business set-asides in subcontracting industry amounted to discrimination under Fourteenth Amendment despite city's finding of and articulated attempt to remedy prior discrimination) *with* Fullilove v. Klutznick, 448 U.S. 448, 476–78, 482–84 (1980) (rejecting constitutional challenge to minority set-aside of federal monies in subcontracting industry); Webster v. Reprod. Health Servs., 492 U.S. 490, 514–16 (1989) (state may define time at which its interest in fetal life becomes compelling) *with* Roe v. Wade, 410 U.S. 113, 163–65 (1973) (state's compelling interest in protecting fetal life does not begin until end of the first trimester); Patterson v. McLean Credit Union, 491 U.S. 164, 176–78 (1989) (§ 1981 applies only to initial formation of contract, and employment relationship under contract is not covered) *with* Runyon v. McCrary, 427 U.S. 160 (1976) (applying § 1981 to making and enforcing of contracts in private, nonsectarian school that discriminated on the basis of race).

Justice Rehnquist wrote, "*Stare decisis* is a cornerstone of our legal system, but it has less power in constitutional cases, where, save for constitutional amendments, this Court is the only body able to make changes." *Webster,* 492 U.S. at 518; see also *Patterson* at 172 (Justice Kennedy expresses same sentiment). At least one reporter believes statements by Rehnquist during oral argument may suggest he would overturn Miranda v. Arizona, 396 U.S. 868 (1969), as well as diminish the separation of church and state. *See* David G. Savage, *The Rehnquist Court,* L.A. Times, Sept. 29, 1991, at 12. For scholarly views on the subject, see for example, John Denvir, *Justice Rehnquist and Constitutional Interpretation,* 34 Hastings L.J. 1011 (1983) (orthodox theory of constitutional interpretation fails to explain Rehnquist's judicial philosophy).

17. Ruth Marcus, *Thomas Refuses to State View on Abortion Issue: Nominee Steadfast Amid Senators' Questions,* Wash. Post, Sept. 12, 1991, at A1 ("Clarence Thomas yesterday

said he had no opinion on whether the Constitution protects the right to abortion and had not discussed the issue, even in a private setting, in the 18 years since the court decided it.").

18. John E. Yang & Sharon LaFraniere, *Bush Picks Thomas for Supreme Court,* Wash. Post, July 2, 1991, at A1 ("President Bush yesterday chose Clarence Thomas, a conservative black federal appeals court judge, to replace Thurgood Marshall on the Supreme Court, saying he is 'the best person at the right time.' "); Derrick Bell, *Choice of Thomas Insults Blacks,* Newsday, July 10, 1991, at 85 (It was "typically disingenuous" for Bush to nominate Thomas and call him the best-qualified candidate when "there are at least a half-dozen other black judges whose accomplishments, both on the bench and before becoming federal judges, put those of Thomas to shame.").

24 | Invisible Woman: Reflections on the Clarence Thomas Confirmation Hearings

Kim A. Taylor

I am an invisible [wo]man. No I am not a spook like those who haunted Edgar Allan Poe; nor am I one of your Hollywood-movie ectoplasms. I am a [wo]man of substance, of flesh and bone, fiber and liquids-and I might even be said to possess a mind. I am invisible, understand, simply because people refuse to see me. Like the bodiless heads you see sometimes in circus sideshows, it is as though I have been surrounded by mirrors of hard, distorting glass. When they approach me they see only my surroundings, themselves, or figments of their imagination-indeed, everything and anything except me.

—Ralph Ellison, *Invisible Man*

As I sat behind Anita Hill during the second round of hearings for the confirmation of Clarence Thomas to the Supreme Court, I felt as if I had stepped into a carnival fun house, where the world simultaneously becomes larger than life and fundamentally warped. Here were members of the U.S. Senate Judiciary Committee, despite promises to engage in a genuine fact-finding hearing into the allegations of sexual harassment raised by Hill, distorting the hearing process with the verbal equivalent of mirrors and lights. Even on the occasion of recommending a nominee for a lifetime appointment to this nation's highest court, U.S. senators appeared incapable of rising above their large egos and petty politics to take their investigatory task seriously. Because they could appreciate the complexity of neither the issue of sexual harassment nor the person who sat before them, they failed to establish a process that might have begun to unearth the truth about what had transpired between Clarence Thomas and Anita Hill. Instead, they allowed the hearing to degenerate into a circus sideshow.

WHY THE PROCESS FAILED

The stark image of a young African American woman seated alone at a table facing a panel of fourteen white male senators remains vivid. Even more striking than the visual image of Anita Hill testifying before the Judiciary Committee is the realization that the men entrusted with the task of evaluating the evidence presented during the hearings were limited and, ultimately, blinded by their positions of privilege. Perhaps these men, who had rarely, if ever, been forced to see folks who resembled Hill as their equals, had become all too accustomed to ignoring their concerns. Dismissing such voices had become so commonplace in our nation's capital, that even when Hill was brought center stage by the media, these men seemed unable, or at least unwilling, to see the woman of color who sat before them answering questions for seven hours. The senators failed to appreciate the significance of Hill's experience as a woman in the workplace, and they were completely ignorant of her life struggles as an African American. The real Anita Faye Hill remained invisible to them.

It is now painfully apparent that the failure of the process was emblematic of society's inability to recognize and appreciate the double oppression of race and gender. Perhaps, as some have suggested, had this complaint been lodged by a white female law professor, the outcome would have been different. Southern Republican senators, such as Strom Thurmond and Jesse Helms, might not have embraced Clarence Thomas so readily because personal and cultural politics might have shifted their sympathies away from the "carousing" African American man to one of "their" women. Had she been white, the argument continues, the Judiciary Committee would have conducted a closed inquiry, away from the cameras, to determine the truth of the allegations. In my view, had she been a different woman of color, one who fit societal presumptions about politics and place, reactions by the Senate and the American public at the time of the hearing might have been dramatically different. Instead, in very complicated ways, Anita Hill challenged many of the myths and presumptions about people of color and, more specifically, about women of color. When the Senate and the public were asked to evaluate Hill and her message, her differences made the task more difficult.

At the time of the hearing, not only the Senate but also the American public (at least those segments that were polled) failed to see and appreciate Anita Hill and the complexity of her situation. Even those groups that might have been expected to rally to her side seemed to see only those aspects of her that served their purposes. Perhaps this failure to understand Hill was due in part to the fact that she did not fit into the tidy categories that we as a society use to define individuals. She appeared to be politically conservative, yet she was delivering testimony that could have derailed the nomination of a conservative judge to the Supreme Court. She poignantly discussed Clarence Thomas's conduct, but seemed reluctant either to characterize the conduct as sexual harassment, or to use her testimony as a platform to raise the American consciousness about sexual harassment in the workplace. She appeared to be the product of a traditional African American family, yet she seemed to be breaking ranks with African Americans by openly attacking an African American man. In another setting, Hill's complexities might have widened her appeal; during the hearing, those complexities only alienated her from much of the American public.

The Senate's failure to appreciate Anita Hill's complexity was highlighted by Senator Arlen Specter's cross-examination of her. Each time Specter expressed his incredulity that a Yale Law School graduate could not simply have quit her job and accepted one of the supposedly endless opportunities awaiting her, I found myself thinking, not for the first time, "he just doesn't get it." Perhaps Specter based his conclusions about options available to a Yale Law School graduate on the experience of white male graduates. Or maybe his comments grew out of an exaggerated view of the "benefits" of affirmative action. Whatever the reason, Specter's comments demonstrated precisely how little he knew about Hill's reality: Doors that may have been open to her white male counterparts would not have been open to her. He simply refused to acknowledge that the double burden of race and gender might restrict the choices and opportunities facing a woman of color working in a profession dominated by white males.

Arlen Specter seemed to forget that at the time Clarence Thomas began subjecting Anita Hill to the harassment she described, she had not yet become the composed, tenured law professor who appeared before the senators. She was twenty-four years old and in only her second year of law practice. She had already resigned from a law firm and had assumed a position at the Department of Education. Anyone familiar with the legal profession would acknowledge that when a person seeks employment in the more conventional segments of the profession, two moves in as many years would not have been viewed favorably by most employers. Specter once again displayed his ignorance when he contended that Hill could have made a third move, after the harassment began, without consequence. As Hill knew even from her limited experience in the workforce, she could not afford to leave her job no matter how much she longed to do so.

The interplay of race and gender that defined and delineated Anita Hill's dilemma was missed not just by the Senate, but by some white feminists as well. In their efforts to tout her as spokesperson for all women who had been victims of sexual harassment, some feminists attempted to distill her voice into simply that of a woman and, as a result, denied her complexity. Many who acknowledged the difficulty of finding the courage to speak as a victim of sexual harassment overlooked the additional measure of strength that Hill needed to summon in order to speak those words against an African American man. Having been raised in a tradition that taught her not to "air our dirty laundry in public," Hill did not violate that directive lightly. Yet many white feminists seemed, at best, unaware of or, worse, insensitive to the painful reality that speaking out could alienate Hill from her African American community.

Indeed, at the time of the hearing, the loyalties of African American communities were divided. During those three days in October, the silence of my community was almost deafening. Although there were notable exceptions, which did not garner the type of media attention paid to those people of color who opposed Anita Hill,[1] the second round of the confirmation process saw notably few African American activists raise their voices in support of Hill. Voices from the NAACP and National Urban

League, for example, were not even raised in condemnation of sexual harassment as it peculiarly affects African American women. Suddenly, those prominent African American leaders who had spoken so eloquently in opposition to Clarence Thomas in the first set of hearings seemed to have lost their voices. Instead of embracing Hill's testimony as further evidence of Clarence Thomas's incompetence to serve, these "leaders" said nothing. And I wondered why.

Could these organizations have swallowed the Republican line that Anita Hill was acting on a personal vendetta? Or in the vernacular of my community, could they have believed that she was simply interested in "bringing a brother down"? Perhaps at a time when attacks on the African American man have increased in number and intensity, the airing of Hill's complaint on prime-time television was destined to be viewed as the latest in a wave of attacks. However, in their rush to define her testimony as an effort to malign an African American man, these designated spokespersons for the African American community inadvertently missed or, worse, consciously discounted her victimization. While the African American community and our national organizations remained attuned to racial subordination and outraged over its impact, many within my community failed to recognize and acknowledge the devastating impact of gender subordination.

"Why didn't she quit if this really happened?" was a question that emerged not just from Arlen Specter but from my community as well. Interestingly, African Americans who had been subjected to racist remarks in the workplace knew all too well that they had often tolerated such abuse and then swallowed their anger to maintain their jobs. Now these same individuals were suggesting that Anita Hill's experience was somehow different and less important; they were suggesting that she should be held to a different standard than the one they applied to their own behavior. The message behind these attitudes, which registered painfully in my head and heart, was that issues facing African American women should be sacrificed in our efforts to close ranks around an African American man. Our "leaders" and segments of my community quite simply chose to embrace a man (who had only recently discovered his own heritage in the first set of hearings) and elected to abandon this African American woman.

Anita Hill stood alone, invisible to those entrusted with the task of seeing her and evaluating her words, and at best an enigma to the communities that should have understood and supported her most. Yet while some at the time may have discounted and misunderstood Hill's testimony, the events that took place in October 1991 continue to provoke national debate over sexual harassment, the politics of power, and sexual and racial stereotypes. As I reflect on this process and attempt to make some sense of the experience, I am encouraged that the passage of time has allowed the American public to revisit the issues Hill attempted to raise. Although the Senate failed to provide a meaningful process by which Hill's allegations could be considered, and polls taken at the time of the hearing revealed that much of the American public did not believe her allegations, Anita Hill may have finally become visible. Polls conducted one year after the hearing demonstrate that at least now the public recognizes that Hill does indeed consist of "flesh and bone, fiber and liquids," and, what is more important, a voice that spoke for countless others who could not find their own.

NOTE

1. For example, a coalition of African American professors of law and social science issued a press release supporting Hill and opposing the Thomas confirmation. The statement received little coverage in the national media.

25 | Three Perspectives on Workplace Harassment of Women of Color

Maria L. Ontiveros

In this chapter, I suggest a framework for understanding how issues of race and culture play a pivotal role in what we have thought of as "sexual harassment."[1] This framework views an incident of workplace harassment from the perspectives of the three key players: the harasser, the victim, and the judicial system.

PERSPECTIVE 1: THE HARASSER

Since workplace harassment is a power dynamic, women of color serve as likely targets because they are the least powerful participants in the workplace. Unlike white women, they are not privileged by their race. Unlike men of color, they are not privileged by their gender. Although a white man might harass any woman, a man of color is not likely to feel that he has the prerogative to harass a white woman. He may feel that he is not able to harass her because of his lack of racial status or because he knows he could be subject to a disproportionate reaction stemming from society's deep-seated, historical fears of attacks on white women by nonwhite men. If the harasser is a man of color, then, the victim is likely to be a woman of color. Harassers may also prefer those women of color, such as Latinas and Asian American women, whom they view as more passive and less likely to complain.

Additionally, racism and sexism can blend together in the mind of the harasser and be displayed as an inseparable whole. The types of statements used and actions taken incorporate the unique characteristics of women of color, subjecting each race and ethnicity to its own cruel stereotype of sexuality.

Society considers Latinas (like African American women and Asian American women) naturally sexual, evoking the image of the "hot-blooded" Latin.[2] In addition, Latinas are often perceived as readily available and accessible for sexual use, and there are few recriminations to be faced for abusing them.[3] Sonoma County district attorney Gene Tunney has seen this perception become reality. In commenting on one case that typifies this situation, he stated, "we've become aware of people who have imported Mexican women, usually from rural villages in the middle of nowhere, and brought them here for sexual reasons. My suspicion is there is a lot of it going on."[4] Thus, race plays a critical role in workplace harassment of women of color because of the perspective of the harasser. In addition, the perspectives of at least two other key players affect the outcome of a harassment episode.

PERSPECTIVE 2: WOMEN OF COLOR AS MEMBERS OF THE MINORITY COMMUNITY

The community in which a woman lives and the culture in which she was raised influence her reaction to workplace harassment. For example, some women of color have been raised to be more passive, defer to men, and not bring attention to themselves. Barriers may face Latinas growing up in a "macho" culture. For these women to resist an act aggressively or to pursue a legal remedy, they must first confront these cultural issues.

Additionally, many women wrestle with feelings that they will be blamed for the harassment. One Mexican immigrant victim of harassment, when asked why she did not report the harassment earlier, told a rape counselor that "a woman who is raped in Mexico is the one at fault, maybe because her parents didn't watch her."[5] Upon learning of the harassment, her husband denounced her as a permanent shame to her family.[6]

Immigrant or illegal status and a lack of understanding of their legal rights further handicap women of color. Marie DeSantis, a community advocate for Sonoma County Women against Rape, notes that immigrant women are often victims of what she terms "rape by duress."[7] They do not report such crimes because they are too intimidated by their fear of deportation, their ignorance of their legal rights, and the presumed power of their employers. In the situation of the Mexican housekeeper, she stated that because she was here illegally and was paid by her employer, she had no place else to go. She worried that "He could have cut me up in a million pieces, and no one would have known."[8]

Finally, victims recognize that accusations of workplace harassment will negatively implicate their cultures and likely bring adverse community response. For example, one Latina community worker was urged by two female coworkers (who had also been harassed and remained silent) to not report an incident of harassment "for fear that exposing the perpetrators would undermine their movement and embarrass the Latino community."[9] This adverse community response may be especially painful for women of color, to whom community is particularly important.

PERSPECTIVE 3: THE LEGAL SYSTEM

Once an incident of workplace harassment becomes a lawsuit, the legal system provides the final construct of the event. The legal system's perception of women of color affects cases of workplace harassment brought by these women in at least three ways: judges and juries tend to disbelieve what they say; the dominant culture's construct of their sexuality influences the cases' outcomes; and the entire justice system misperceives relationships between men and women of color, thereby excusing discriminatory acts by men of color.

The story of the Mexican immigrant woman evidences the credibility problem. She told the Sonoma district attorney that she believed her employer was "a doctor . . . and that is a title of some esteem and high position in Mexico. . . . If you're a peasant girl, and it's your word against his, you don't have a chance." [10]

Penalties are affected because women of color are believed to have been "asking for it," to not be greatly affected by the abuse, or simply to not be worthy of the same legal protection given to the rest of society. One study concluded that defendants who assault African American women are less likely to receive jail time than those who assaulted white women. [11] Another study found that assailants of African American women receive an average sentence of two years, compared to an average sentence of ten years for defendants who assault white women. [12] One juror, sitting in the case of a rape of a black preteen, stated that "being from that neighborhood she probably wasn't a virgin anyway." [13]

A final problem occurs when the legal system misinterprets relationships between men and women of color. The so-called cultural defense has been used by people of color to explain why their action is understandable and even excusable in their culture, even when it offends American values. [14]

Courts, in attempting to accommodate different cultures, seem to privilege the race of the defendant while simultaneously divesting the victim of her gender. This misunderstanding of the relationships between people of color serves to excuse actions taken against women of color. Thus, like the credibility problems and stereotypes of sexuality, it causes the legal system to discount workplace harassment of women of color.

We need to reconstruct our perception of "sexual harassment" to face the issue of workplace harassment of women of color. This transformation must take place because the elements of a sexual harassment case are different and more onerous than those in a racial harassment case. [15] Treating these cases as "sexual harassment," then, not only misstates the dynamic but also further disadvantages these women. Such a solution could be reached either by modifying the rules governing "sexual harassment" or by creating a new cause of action prohibiting discrimination against women of color as women of color.

This reform would address some of the problems discussed here, but true solutions are not so simple because the problems and interrelationships are so complex. Deeply held notions of race, gender, identity, sexuality, and power must be examined and reevaluated. Furthermore, this discovery must take place both within and across cultural and class boundaries. Only in this way will we be able to answer the challenges raised by the Hill-Thomas hearings and no longer pretend that racism and sexism are not inseparable issues in all of our lives.

NOTES

1. I prefer to use the term "workplace harassment of women of color." The use of "sexual harassment" or "racial harassment" fails to capture the complexity of the experience. For an early article on the issue, see Judy Trent Ellis, *Sexual Harassment and Race: A Legal Analysis of Discrimination*, 8 J. Legis. 30, 41–42 (1981).

2. To defend himself from accusations that he had repeatedly sexually harassed and abused the Mexican woman in his employ, one man argued that she had been the sexual aggressor, saying. "she is a lady with quite a high sexual drive." Carla Marinucci, *Despair Drove Her to Come Forward*, S.F. Examiner, Jan. 10, 1993, at A11.

3. The treatment of this victim, whose story is referred to throughout this article, is typical of many immigrants, according to the results of a four-month investigation conducted by a Northern California newspaper. The investigation included interviews with immigrants, community leaders, and government officials, as well as examination of documents from courts, labor agencies, and the Immigration and Naturalization Service. *Id.* at A10 (insert entitled *The Series,* explaining methodology for the article). She left her family in Mexico to become a housekeeper in the United States. Upon her arrival, her employer immediately began to sexually abuse and harass her. She did not immediately report the harassment because she was afraid of the man, feared deportation, and felt she would not be believed. *Id. See also* Suzanne Espinosa, *Female Immigrants Tell of Abuse*, S.F. Chron., Mar. 9, 1993, at A11.

4. *Id.*

5. Marinucci, *supra* note 2.

6. *Id.*

7. *Id.*

8. *Id.*

9. Kimberlé Crenshaw, *Race, Gender, and Sexual Harassment*, 65 S. Cal. L. Rev. 1467, 1474 (1992).

10. Marinucci, *supra* note 2.

11. Crenshaw, *supra* note 9, at 1470.

12. *Id.*

13. *Id.*

14. *See, e.g.,* Melissa Spatz, *A "Lesser" Crime: A Comparative Study of Legal Defenses for Men Who Kill Their Wives*, 24 Colum. J.L. & Soc. Probs. 597 (1991).

15. *See, e.g.,* Davis v. Monsanto Chemical Co., 858 F.2d 345, 348 (6th Cir. 1988) (different standard for showing "sufficiently severe conduct" in the two types of cases). Sexual harassment plaintiffs must show that the conduct was "unwelcome." Meritor Savings Bank v. Vinson, 477 U.S. 57, 68 (1986). A racial harassment plaintiff does not have to prove that the harassment was "unwelcome."

26 | The Harm That Has No Name: Street Harassment, Embodiment, and African American Women

Deirdre E. Davis

In her article *Street Harassment and the Informal Ghettoization of Women,* law professor Cynthia Grant Bowman explores street harassment as a harm and the necessity of legally recognizing street harassment's oppressive effects.[1] This chapter explores the idea that "[w]e cannot hope to understand the meaning of a person's experiences, including her experiences of oppression, without first thinking of her as embodied, and second thinking about the particular meanings assigned to that embodiment"[2] in the context of street harassment and African American women. Street harassment silences women. Similarly, racism has silenced and continues to silence African American women. Writing about street harassment and African American women legitimizes and recognizes the existence and importance of both.

THE MECHANICS OF STREET HARASSMENT

There are three ways to define and understand street harassment. Specifically, particular acts constitute street harassment. Normatively, the following characteristics identify particular acts of street harassment: the locale; the gender of and the relationship between the harasser and the target; the unacceptability of "thank you" as a response; and the reference to body parts. Systematically, street harassment can be understood as an element of a larger system of sexual terrorism.

SPECIFIC ACTS OF STREET HARASSMENT

Cheris Kramarae, professor of speech communication and sociology, and Elizabeth Kissling describe street harassment as "verbal and nonverbal markers ... wolf-whistles, leers, winks, grabs, pinches, catcalls and street remarks."[3] Specific remarks commonly include "Hey, pretty," "Hey, whore," "What ya doin' tonight?" "Look at them legs," "Wanna fuck?" "Are you working?" "Great legs," "Hey, cunt," "Smile," "Smile for me, baby," "Smile, bitch," "Come here, girl," and "I'll be back when you get a little older, baby." When these acts occur on a public street, street harassment takes place.[4]

STREET HARASSMENT'S ROLE IN SEXUAL TERRORISM

Recognizing street harassment's role in sexual terrorism is crucial to understanding its potential to harm. Carole Sheffield defines sexual terrorism as men's systematic control and domination of women through actual and implied violence.[5] She views sexual terrorism as both the objective condition of women's existence and the theoretical framework that creates and maintains social orders.[6] Sexual terrorism and violence play crucial roles in the ongoing process of female subordination.[7] Violence is not one particular act, nor is it static; rather, it is a continuum of behavior in which street harassment must be placed if we are to understand the depth and pervasiveness of sexual terrorism.[8]

Street harassment "frightens women and reinforces fears of rape and other acts of terrorism."[9] Rape is generally viewed as a violent act of power occurring in a context limited to particular individuals or situations. However, rape may begin with an act of street harassment. Potential rapists can test the accessibility of a victim by making derogatory sexual comments to determine whether she can be intimidated.[10] As a result, street harassment plays a definite role in the objective condition of women fearing bodily harm on a day-to-day basis.

Women also experience the connection between rape and street harassment on a subjective level. Regardless of whether there is the possibility of actual rape, when women endure street harassment, they fear the possibility of rape.[11] That one of every eight adult women has been raped makes rape a constant possibility on a subjective level.[12] The sexual content of street harassment "reminds women of their vulnerability to violent attack in American urban centers, and to sexual violence in general" and intensifies the fear of the possibility of rape.[13] As a precursor to rape and an escalator of the fear of rape, street harassment entraps women in a sexually terroristic environment.

Within the framework of sexual terrorism, the specific acts and normative characteristics of street harassment identify the range of behavior that constitutes street harassment. Once it is realized that "street harassment is not a product of a sexually terroristic culture, but an active factor in creating such a culture," then the ability of an act of street harassment to cause harm becomes clearer.[14]

GENDERIZATION OF THE STREET: THE EFFECTS AND CONTEXT OF STREET HARASSMENT

Street harassment genderizes the street by distributing power in such a way that perpetuates male supremacy and female subordination.[15] Consequently, street harassment transforms the street into yet another forum that perpetuates and reinforces the gender hierarchy.

In order for the social effects of street harassment to occur, a preexisting context must exist that enables street harassment. Psychological oppression serves as the context that allows street harassment to genderize the street.

Despite street harassment's clear socially and psychologically oppressive effects, street harassment remains invisible as a harm. Because men do not suffer street harassment to the extent women do, street harassment is characterized as something other than harassment. Acts that are legally cognizable harms gain recognition "as an injury of the systematic abuse of power in hierarchies [when it is an exercise of] power men recognize."[16] Men view street harassment as innocuous, trivial, "boys will be boys" type of behavior and blame women for attaching negative meanings to their acts. Street harassment remains invisible because it is not a harm men suffer, and therefore it is not a harm men, or society as a whole, recognize.

While some women view street harassment as a trivial part of their everyday lives, they can still suffer extreme consequences. First, because street harassment has been trivialized, women do not talk about it and are thus silenced. This reinforces the invisibility of street harassment and its effects. Moreover, when a woman thinks about ending the silence, she may have a lot of doubt, given that street harassment— a pervasive part of everyday life—is so trivialized. Ignoring street harassment causes women to become complicit supporters of a system of sexual terrorism.[17] Finally, the failure to perceive street harassment as a harm causes women to "transform the pain into something else, such as, for example, punishment, or flattery, or transcendence, or unconscious pleasure."[18]

Giving a harm a name is the first step in making the harm visible. Given that "an injury uniquely sustained by a disempowered group will *lack a name,* a history, and in general *a linguistic reality,*" it is crucial for the targets of street harassment to name the harm.[19] Naming is not a random or neutral process, but is biased. One need only look at workplace sexual harassment, date rape, domestic violence, and marital rape to understand the importance of naming a harm. While these harms have been a part of society for a long time, once they had a name, their visibility, both as acts and as harms, increased and led to the possibility of redress.

It is important for women to name the harms they suffer, because "[b]y taking the power of naming for themselves [and gaining cultural autonomy], women can determine with what bias street harassment will be encoded."[20] Discussing and naming street harassment are crucial steps toward erasing a constant source of women's pain and making street harassment visible as a harm.

INCLUDING AFRICAN AMERICAN WOMEN IN THE DISCOURSE ON STREET HARASSMENT: GENDERIZATION AND RACIALIZATION OF THE STREET

AFRICAN AMERICAN WOMEN AND STREET HARASSMENT: RECURRING IMAGES OF SLAVERY

By refusing to acknowledge difference, street harassment discourse has excluded African American women's experiences. Many have argued that street harassment just "is," and that race, class, and sexual orientation are irrelevant: "In fact, women will sometimes comment that they think that women of all races, classes, and ages are subject to attacks from men—of all races, classes, and ages."[21] This statement relies on the idea that street harassment is primarily based on gender domination. Consequently, this statement implies that, because all women experience street harassment, it has no significance beyond its gender meaning: "[T]he women who do find street remarks disturbing, disgusting, or dangerous evidently hear them as more sexist than racist or classist."[22] The race of the harassers has also been disregarded: "You can say what you like about class and race. Those differences are real. But in this everyday scenario, any man on earth, no matter what his color or class is, has the power to make any woman who is exposed to him hate herself and her body."[23] This nuanced treatment of race ignores the relevant inquiry: the issue is not the act's independence from these differences, but the fact that the act occurs in spite of the differences. Abstracting the categories of identity limits understanding of the dynamics of street harassment.

All women are subjected to street harassment and, consequently, street harassment is a form of gender subordination. However, when African American women are subjected to street harassment, street harassment is, at the very least, genderized and racialized. This is not to say that street harassment has one meaning for African American women and a different meaning for all other women. Given the various histories of women of differing races and ethnicities, including white women, street harassment is both genderized and racialized for every woman; but the racial aspect is set in the particular historical context to which the particular woman belongs.

During and as a result of slavery, African American women have experienced the preexisting context that enables street harassment to be a factor in our sexually terroristic environment. Consequently, the psychological oppression of street harassment has a different—not a double—impact on African American women given their embodiment as indivisible beings. Street harassment forces African American women to realize that the ideologies of slavery still exist.

Although slavery has been legally eradicated, the racist ideology perpetuated during the slave era still exists with a different face. While the "formal barriers and symbolic manifestations of subordination"[24] have disappeared, "[t]he white norm . . . has not disappeared; it has only been submerged in popular consciousness."[25] White men struggle to maintain their hierarchical position in a social structure that is constantly being challenged, questioned, and chiseled away.

Street harassment is a forum that allows white men, in the absence of slavery, to maintain the boundaries of their relationship with black women and to perpetuate the image of African American women as "blackwomen." The legal and cultural invisibility of street harassment gives white men a way of oppressing African American women that replaces the historical slave/master structure.

The Cult of True Womanhood: The White Woman as Paradigm

Street harassment oppresses women because it denies women an authentic choice of self and mandates conformance to gender stereotypes. Such oppression also formed the basis of the slave era's dominant gender ideology. In her work *Reconstructing Womanhood,* English and African American studies professor Hazel Carby explores women slaves' relationship to the predominant ideology of the "cult of true [white] womanhood."[26] Based on notions of motherhood and womanhood, the cardinal tenets of piety, purity (sexual and nonsexual), submissiveness, and domesticity characterized the cult of true womanhood.[27]

The ideology had two cultural effects: "[I]t was dominant, in the sense of being the most subscribed to convention governing female behavior, but it was also clearly recognizable as a dominating image, describing the parameters within which women were measured and declared to be, or not to be, women."[28] White men used the cult of true womanhood to establish the normative ideal for white women and to establish the boundaries outside of which slave women were placed.[29] Despite the opposing definitions of motherhood and womanhood for white women and slave women, the definitions were dependent on one another.[30]

The cult of true womanhood also illustrates how stereotypes obscure women's reality by focusing on men's interpretations. During slavery, slave owners and buyers perceived some characteristics as negative in white women, yet as positive, economic assets in slave women. For example, "[s]trength and ability to bear fatigue, argued to be so distasteful a presence in a white woman, were positive features to be emphasized in the promotion and selling of a black female field hand at a slave auction."[31]

African American slave women internalized the underlying ideological beliefs; "[b]y completely accepting the female role as defined by patriarchy, enslaved black women embraced and upheld an oppressive sexist social order and became (along with their white sisters) both accomplices in the crimes perpetuated against women and the victims of those crimes."[32] Consequently, cultural domination has led African American women to believe that street harassment is an acceptable, natural part of everyday life, given the slave culture.

The Controlling Image of Jezebel: African American Woman as (White) Man's Temptress

During slavery, white men developed a racist ideology particular to slave women, which consisted of four "interrelated, socially constructed controlling images."[33] Created by white men to justify, maintain, and perpetuate the subordination of

African American women, the most powerful of these controlling images is that of the female slave as a Jezebel. The Jezebel image—the slave woman as "whore, sexually aggressive wet nurse," and "sexual temptress"—served two functions. First, it justified white men's sexual abuse of slave women. Second, it justified the inapplicability of the cult of true womanhood to slave women—if a slave woman was seen as a sexual animal, then she was not a real woman. The hypersexual Jezebel image dehumanized black women and justified their exploitation in the fields. White men used the controlling image of Jezebel, in conjunction with other images, to create and maintain the existing slave/master social and economic structure.

Multiple Subordination: The Intersection of White Men's and African American Men's Objectification of African American Women While "[r]acism has always been a divisive force separating black men and white men, [it has been] sexism [that] has been a force that unites the two groups." [34] Like white men, African American men have been socialized to exercise their male status to oppress women: "As Americans, they [African American men] had not been taught to really believe that social equality was an inherent right all people possess, but they had been socialized to believe that it is the nature of males to desire and have access to power and privilege." [35] One of the entitlements of being a member of the male gender is the ability to exercise dominance over women. During the slavery era, the African American man, "though obviously deprived of the social status that would enable him to protect and provide for himself and others, had a higher status than the black female slave based solely on his being male." [36] Again, the binary framework of racism and sexism ignores the fact that "[r]acism does not prevent black men from absorbing the same sexist socialization white men are inundated with." [37] As a result of the intersection of race and gender, while racism "cause[s] white men to make black women targets," [38] "sexism . . . causes all men to think they can verbally or physically assault women sexually with impunity." [39]

When African American Men Seek a Position of Whiteness: The Experience of Intraracial Harassment Given the pervasiveness of the controlling images of African American womanhood created and perpetuated by white men, African American men also view African American women "as nothing more than mammies, matriarchs, or Jezebels." As bell hooks points out, "[a]s sexist ideology has been accepted by black people, these negative myths and stereotypes have effectively transcended class and race boundaries and affected the way black women [are] perceived by members of their own race." [40]

African American men exercise the power implicit in sexism from a "position of whiteness." A position of whiteness consists of the "historically derived constellation of privileges associated with white [male] racial domination." [41] A person acting from a position of whiteness creates a racial hierarchy and produces and reinforces stereotypical images. This position of whiteness is not limited to white men, but can be seen as a position of authority attended by the privileges associated with authority.

Whereas white men assign and invoke the Jezebel image of African American women in order to maintain dominance, African American men use the same image in order to try to obtain that which white men have—the power to define the position of whiteness. As bell hooks has noted, "[t]heir [black men's] expressions of rage and anger are less a critique of the white male patriarchal social order and more a reaction against the fact that *they have not been allowed full participation in the power game.*"[42] Engaging in any form of oppression when you are a member of a marginalized group may make a person feel more powerful and less oppressed. Nevertheless, the established social order, though possibly capable of change, is still relative. Consequently, "men of color are not able to reap the material and social rewards for their participation in patriarchy. In fact they often suffer from blindly and passively acting out a myth of masculinity that is life-threatening. Sexist thinking blinds them to this reality. They become victims of the patriarchy."[43]

Some have argued that street harassment does not harm African American women because "[i]n many African American communities, men and women engage in sexually oriented banter in public."[44] Even if this rapping does exist between African American men and women, the speech rights are asymmetrical because "although many African American women respond assertively to rapping, they typically do not initiate it."[45] Furthermore, the fact that some African American women may engage in rapping does not negate the fact that

[b]lack leaders, male and female, have been unwilling to acknowledge black male sexist oppression of black women because they do not want to acknowledge that racism is not the only oppressive force in our lives. *Nor do they wish to complicate efforts to resist racism by acknowledging that black men can be victimized by racism but at the same time act as sexist oppressors of black women.*[46]

Finally, characterizing street harassment as an African American cultural phenomenon ignores the intersection of race and gender by "overlook[ing] the way in which this sexual discourse reflects a differential power relationship between men and women."[47] This characterization also allows society to avoid examining "the different means by which these [African American cultural] practices are maintained and legitimated," thereby perpetuating the subordination of African American women.[48]

MULTIPLE CONSCIOUSNESS AND STREET HARASSMENT: INCORPORATING AFRICAN AMERICAN WOMEN'S EXPERIENCE

Including African American women's experiences in the street harassment discourse enlightens women to their multiple consciousness and provides all women with a tool that enables them to cope with the social and psychological oppressive effects of street harassment. By embracing the multiplicitous self, African American women, as the descendants of slaves, have learned how to handle the multiple forms of oppression, including gender and racial oppression. Recognizing a multiple consciousness helps women deconstruct and accept their experiences with street harassment. By embracing the multiple parts of self and moving away from a binary construction of "self," we also recognize the possibility for internal contradiction.

African American women have historically and consistently existed in a zone of dissonance. African American women, as society's "other," are disenfranchised and excluded from society in many ways. At the same time, African American women are "essential for [society's] survival because those individuals who stand at the margins of society clarify its boundaries. African American women, by not belonging, emphasize the significance of belonging."[49]

The multiple consciousness is yet another site of identity, where both the subjective self and the objective self coexist. Recognizing this site of identity will allow women to shift their energies from deconstructing and understanding women's response to street harassment, to eradicating street harassment.

A NEW DEFINITION FOR THE EFFECTS OF STREET HARASSMENT: SPIRIT-MURDER

Including African American women's experiences in street harassment discourse provides a fuller understanding of how all women may experience street harassment. This inclusion also provides access to a broader term that may more fully reflect street harassment's invidious role in terrorizing all women. Law professor Patricia Williams states that "[a] fundamental part of ourselves and of our dignity is dependent upon the uncontrollable, powerful, external observers who constitute society."[50] Engaging in racist behavior, which is the overt expression of the internalized "system of formalized distortions of thought,"[51] leads to the "disregard for others whose lives qualitatively depend on our regard."[52] Williams terms this disregard "spirit-murder," a phenomenon that creates and perpetuates social structures that are defined by hate and fear, and give unexpressed feeling an outlet. While Williams's discussion of spirit-murder encompasses only race, Adrien Wing incorporates sexism into the concept of spirit-murder.[53] While spirit-murder is the cumulative effect, it is made up of micro aggressions, "[h]undreds, if not thousands of spirit injuries and assaults—some major, some minor—the cumulative effect of which is the slow death of the psyche, the soul and the persona."[54] In the context of street harassment, it is easy to understand spirit murder as being subjected to many incidences of street harassment each day. To gain a fuller understanding of street harassment and its impact on African American women, it is necessary to place street harassment in the continuum of behavior that includes spirit-murder. Using these terms, one can understand the full extent to which all women are terrorized.

Redefining street harassment as spirit murder benefits not only African American women, but all women. It allows for recognition of the "other" harms that women suffer, which may or may not be due to their gender. Furthermore, defining street harassment as "spirit-murder" both helps to give street harassment a name and identifies the harasser's wrong instead of focusing on the target. An objective definition of street harassment focuses on the harasser's actions as a form of intrusion instead of "looking to" or blaming the female target. When African American women's experiences are incorporated into the street harassment discourse, women are empowered with a terminology that fully portrays the depth of women's experiences with street harassment.

The first step in recognizing an act as a harm is the accurate construction of that act. Once street harassment is constructed and understood to be a harm that plays a role in the sexual terrorism that governs women's lives by genderizing the street in order to perpetuate female subordination, street harassment becomes visible as a harm. In order to address, deconstruct, and eradicate a harm, we must give the harm a name. Employing the term "street harassment" to describe the type of behavior is one step toward breaking the silence and misconceptions that surround street harassment.

Including African American women's experiences within street harassment and recognizing the different ways African American women experience street harassment due to their experiences with slavery broaden street harassment discourse. This inclusion provides both access to a term, multiple consciousness, that defines the site in which the harm occurs, and a broader meaning of the effects of street harassment, spirit-murder. These terms give women a fuller understanding of the harm street harassment causes.

Naming the harm gives all women the tools with which street harassment can be dismantled and gives them the strength to speak out, up, and loud in response to street harassment.

NOTES

1. Cynthia G. Bowman, *Street Harassment and the Informal Ghettoization of Women,* 106 Harv. L. Rev. 517 (1993).

2. Elizabeth V. Spelman, Inessential Woman: Problems of Exclusion in Feminist Thought 129–30 (1988).

3. Elizabeth A. Kissling & Cheris Kramarae, *Stranger Compliments: The Interpretation of Street Remarks,* 14 Women's Stud. Comm. 75, 75–76 (1991) (reporting results from a computer notes file discussion on street harassment).

4. I focus on the street/sidewalk as the situs. I exclude places like buses, bus stations, taxis, stores, and other public accommodations to highlight the arbitrariness of street harassment. Although I choose to focus on the street, harassment can and does occur in other places.

5. Carole J. Sheffield, *Sexual Terrorism: The Social Control of Women, in* Analyzing Gender 171, 171 (Beth B. Hess & Myra Marx Ferree eds., 1987).

6. *Id.* at 172. The manifestations of sexual terrorism include wife-battering, sexual harassment in the workplace, incest, sexual slavery, prostitution, and rape. *Id.* at 171.

7. *Id.* at 172.

8. There is an "unstated relationship [between] compliments, verbal hostility and physical attack." Kissling & Kramarae, *supra* note 3, at 78; *see also* Cristina Del Sesto, *Our Mean Streets: D.C.'s Women Walk through Verbal Combat Zones,* Wash. Post, Mar. 18, 1990, at B1 ("I'm afraid everyday that a verbal assault is going to turn into a physical one.").

9. Elizabeth A. Kissling, *Street Harassment: The Language of Sexual Terrorism*, 2 Discourse & Soc'y 451, 456 (1991).

10. *See* Bowman, *supra* note 1, at 536.

11. Kissling & Kramarae, *supra* note 3, at 84–85.

12. Bowman, *supra* note 1, at 536 n.86 (quoting *Study: Rapes Far Underestimated*, Chi. Trib., Apr. 24, 1992, § 1, at 3).

13. Kissling & Kramarae, *supra* note 3, at 76.

14. *See* Kissling, *supra* note 9, at 456.

15. *See* Catharine A. MacKinnon, *Difference and Dominance: On Discrimination, in* Feminism Unmodified: Discourses on Life and Law 32, 40 (1987).

16. Catharine A. MacKinnon, *Sexual Harassment: Its First Decade in Court, in* Feminism Unmodified, *supra* note 15, at 103, 107.

17. Kissling, *supra* note 9, at 456.

18. Robin West, *The Difference in Women's Hedonic Lives: A Phenomenological Critique of Feminist Legal Theory*, 3 Wis. Women's L.J. 81, 85 (1987). This is also something the street harasser does.

19. *Id.* (emphasis added).

20. *See* Kissling, *supra* note 9, at 457.

21. Kissling & Kramarae, *supra* note 3, at 90.

22. *Id.* It would be helpful to know the race, sexual orientation, and economic status of the women commentators.

23. Meredith Tax, *Woman and Her Mind: The Story of Everyday Life, in* Radical Feminism 23, 28 (Anne Koedt et al. eds., 1973). While this may be true, there is still a power differential among men based on race.

24. Kimberlé W. Crenshaw, *Race, Reform, and Retrenchment: Transformation and Legitimation in Antidiscrimination Law*, 101 Harv. L. Rev. 1331, 1378 (1988).

25. *Id.* at 1379.

26. Hazel V. Carby, Reconstructing Womanhood: The Emergence of the Afro-American Woman Novelist 23 (1987).

27. *Id.* at 20–39.

28. *Id.*

29. Hazel V. Carby, Lecture in Class on Black Women Writers at Wesleyan University (Sept. 9, 1987).

30. For example, although all women "had" to reproduce, white women were responsible for producing heirs and slave women were responsible for producing property for the heirs to inherit. Carby, *supra* note 29.

31. Carby, *supra* note 26, at 25.

32. bell hooks, Ain't I a Woman? Black Women and Feminism 49 (1981).

33. Patricia Hill Collins, Black Feminist Thought: Knowledge, Consciousness, and the Politics of Empowerment 71 (1991). The other controlling images of African American womanhood are the "mammy," the "matriarch," and the "welfare mother." *See Id.* at 71–77.

34. bell hooks, Feminist Theory: From Margin to Center 99 (1984).

35. *Id.* at 98.

36. *Id.* at 88–89.

37. *Id.* at 101–02.

38. *Id.* at 68.

39. *Id.* at 68–69 (emphasis added).

40. hooks, *supra* note 32, at 70.

41. Neil Gotanda, "Race-ing" Racial Non-Recognition, and Racial Stratification: Re-Reading Judge Joyce Karlin's Sentencing Colloquy in *People v. Soon Ja Du* 23 (Mar. 12, 1993) (unpublished manuscript).

42. hooks, *supra* note 32, at 94 (emphasis added).

43. bell hooks, *Reflections on Race and Sex, in* Yearning: Race, Gender and Cultural Politics 57, 63 (1990).

44. Bowman, *supra* note 1, at 532. This type of banter has been referred to as "rapping."

45. *Id.* at 532.

46. hooks, *supra* note 32, at 88 (emphasis added).

47. Kimberlé W. Crenshaw, *Whose Story Is It Anyway? Feminist and Antiracist Appropriations of Anita Hill, in* Race-ing Justice, Engendering Power: Essays on Anita Hill, Clarence Thomas, and the Construction of Social Reality 402, 429 (Toni Morrison ed., 1992).

48. *Id.* at 431.

49. Collins, *supra* note 33, at 68.

50. Patricia J. Williams, *Spirit-Murdering the Messenger: The Discourse of Fingerpointing as the Law's Response to Racism,* 42 U. Miami L. Rev. 127, 151 (1987) (also chapter 28 in this volume).

51. *Id.*

52. *Id.*

53. Adrien K. Wing, *Brief Reflections toward a Multiplicative Theory and Praxis of Being,* 6 Berkeley Women's L.J. 181, 186 (1990–91) (also chapter 3 in this volume).

54. *Id.*

27 Converging Stereotypes in Racialized Sexual Harassment: Where the Model Minority Meets Suzie Wong

Sumi K. Cho

I'll get right to the point, since the objective is to give you, in writing, a clear description of what I desire. . . . Shave between your legs, with an electric razor, and then a hand razor to ensure it is very smooth. . . .

I want to take you out to an underground nightclub . . . like this, to enjoy your presence, envious eyes, to touch you in public. . . . You will obey me and refuse me nothing. . . .

I believe these games are dangerous because they bring us closer together, yet at the same time I am going to be more honest about the past and present relationships I have. I don't want you to get any idea that I am devoting myself only to you—I want my freedom here. . . . The only positive thing I can say about this is I was dreaming of your possible Tokyo persona since I met you. I hope I can experience it now, the beauty and eroticism.[1]

The above passage comes from a letter written by a white male professor to a Japanese female student at a major university. The more unsavory details referring to physical specifications and particularly demeaning and sadistic demands by the professor have been edited. In her complaint against him, the student stated that the faculty member "sought out Japanese women in particular" and "uses his position as a university professor to impress and seduce Japanese women." The professor had a history of targeting Japanese women because "he believes they are submissive and will obey any parameters he sets for the relationship," according to the student's complaint. "He said that he wants sex slaves, that he considers and treats women as disposable. . . . He rarely takes precautions in a sexual relationship."[2]

Another Japanese female student and former officer of a campus Japanese student organization submitted testimony in support of the student's complaint. She recalled that the same professor had approached her outside of a 7-11 store near the campus and asked for her phone number, stating that he was interested in meeting Japanese females. "I gave him my number because I was the vice-president [of the Japanese student organization] and felt I should be gracious." Through the course of their conversations, the professor told the woman that he "hangs around campus looking for Japanese girls" and asked "where [he] could meet them." By his own admission, "[he] stated that he was not popular in high school and college." However, "when he went to Japan he found out that he was popular" and was now "making up for lost time." The professor told the student that "[h]e liked Japanese females because they were easy to have sex with and because they were submissive."[3]

I have long been haunted by the unsuccessful resolution to this case due to the effective intimidation of the courageous student and those who sought redress.[4] Victims of sexual harassment often fear coming forward because of precisely the type of administrative, legal, and community discouragement or intimidation that constituted the "secondary injury" in this case. Here, the secondary injury was inflicted by the university's affirmative action office that claimed to find no evidence of an actionable claim worth investigating,[5] the self-proclaimed "feminist law firm" in town that defended the predator-professor,[6] and the university counsel that bolstered the intimidatory tactics of the professor's lawyer.[7] The perverse racial and sexual stereotypes at work in such cases, the university's support for the accused faculty member, and the widening racial chasm among feminists are all too familiar to me. My own informed suspicion is that this case, rather than being an aberration, merely represents the tip of the iceberg. At almost every campus I have been on both as a student and faculty member I have encountered appalling cases of sexual harassment against Asian Pacific and Asian Pacific American women.[8]

What I hope to reveal in this article is how converging racial and gender stereotypes of Asian Pacific American women help constitute what I will refer to as "racialized sexual harassment." Racialized sexual harassment denotes a particular set of injuries resulting from the unique complex of power relations facing Asian Pacific American women and other women of color in the workplace. More specifically, this article explores how race and gender combine to alter conceptions of both the "primary injury" (the offending conduct legally recognized as sexual harassment) and the "secondary injury" (the actions of employers and institutions that ally with the harasser). In two cases that I discuss, stereotypes of Asian Pacific American female plaintiffs and the racial and gender politics of the plaintiffs' work environment are determining factors in the harms suffered and systemic responses thereto. The law's refusal to recognize and address the compoundedness of racialized sexual harassment lets flourish converging stereotypes and the oppressive structures that give rise to such injuries.

CONVERGING STEREOTYPES: THE MODEL MINORITY MEETS SUZIE WONG

Asian Pacific American women are at particular risk of being racially and sexually harassed because of the synergism that results when sexualized racial stereotypes combine with racialized gender stereotypes. The "model minority myth," a much criticized racial stereotype of Asian Pacific Americans, has been shown to paint a misleading portrait of groupwide economic, educational, and professional super-success. In addition, the mythical model minority is further overdetermined by associated images of political passivity and submissiveness to authority. But despite the many critical articles written by Asian Pacific Americans on the model minority stereotype, few have theorized specifically how it relates to Asian Pacific American women.[9] Model minority traits of passivity and submissiveness are intensified and gendered through the stock portrayal of obedient and servile Asian Pacific women in popular culture.[10] The repeated projection of a compliant and catering Asian feminine nature feeds harassers' belief that Asian Pacific American women will be receptive objects of their advances, make good victims, and will not fight back.

Similarly, the process of objectification that affects women in general takes on a particular virulence with the overlay of race upon gender stereotypes. Generally, objectification diminishes the contributions of women, reducing their worth to male perceptions of female sexuality.[11] In the workplace, objectification comes to mean that the material valuation of women's contributions will be based not on their professional accomplishments or work performance but on men's perceptions of their potential to be harassed.[12] Asian Pacific women suffer greater harassment exposure due to racialized ascriptions (exotic, hyper-eroticized, masochistic, desirous of sexual domination) that set them up as ideal-typical gratifiers of western neocolonial libidinal formations. In a 1990 *Gentleman's Quarterly* article entitled, "Oriental Girls," Tony Rivers rehearsed the racialized particulars of the "great western male fantasy":

Her face—round like a child's, . . . eyes almond-shaped for mystery, black for suffering, wide-spaced for innocence, high cheekbones swelling like bruises, cherry lips. . . .

When you come home from another hard day on the planet, she comes into existence, removes your clothes, bathes you and walks naked on your back to relax you. . . . She's fun you see, and so uncomplicated. She doesn't go to assertiveness-training classes, insist on being treated like a person, fret about career moves, wield her orgasm as a non-negotiable demand. . . .

She's there when you need shore leave from those angry feminist seas. She's a handy victim of love or a symbol of the rape of third world nations, a real trouper.[13]

As the passage reveals, colonial and military domination are interwoven with sexual domination to provide the "ultimate western male fantasy."[14] Asian Pacific women are particularly valued in a sexist society because they provide the antidote to visions of liberated career women who challenge the objectification of women.[15] In this sense, the objectified gender stereotype also assumes a model minority function as Asian Pacific women are deployed to "discipline" white women, just as Asian Pacific Americans in general are used against their "non-model" counterparts, African Americans.

The "ultimate western male fantasy," part of colonial sexual mythology based on western perceptions of women in Asia, is applied to Asian Pacific American women in an international transfer of stereotypes through mass media and popular culture. Military involvement in Asia, colonial and neocolonial history, and the derivative Asian Pacific sex tourism industry establish power relations between Asia and the West which in turn shape stereotypes of Asian Pacific women that apply to those in and outside of Asia.[16] As his article continues, Rivers suggests that the celluloid prototype of the "Hong Kong hooker with a heart of gold" (from the 1960 film, *The World of Suzie Wong*) may be available in one's own hometown: "Suzie Wong was the originator of the modern fantasy.... Perhaps even now, ... on the edge of a small town, Suzie awaits a call."[17] Internationalized stereotypes and the inability of U.S. Americans to discern between Asian Pacific foreigners and Asian Pacific Americans combine to form a globalized dimension in the social construction of Asian Pacific American women.

Given this cultural backdrop of converging racial and gender stereotypes in which the model minority meets Suzie Wong so to speak, Asian Pacific American women are especially susceptible to racialized sexual harassment. The university, despite its well-cultivated image as an enlightened, genteel environment of egalitarianism, unfortunately does not distinguish itself from other hostile work environments facing Asian Pacific American women. I now turn to two cases in which Asian Pacific American women faculty were subjected to *quid pro quo* and hostile environment forms of harassment.[18] Although racialized sexual harassment experienced by professionals should not be assumed identical to that facing women of color employed in blue- and pink-collar jobs, the social construction of the victims across settings may represent an overarching commonality that allows for broadened theoretical linkages.

QUID PRO QUO: THE ROSALIE TUNG CASE

Rosalie Tung joined the University of Pennsylvania Wharton School of Business (hereinafter, "Business School") in 1981 as an associate professor of management. In her early years at the Business School, she garnered praise for her performance.[19] In the summer of 1983 a change in leadership brought a new dean and new department chair to the School. According to Tung, "shortly after taking office, the chairman of the management department began to make sexual advances toward me."[20] In June 1984 the chair awarded Professor Tung a 20 percent increase in salary and offered high praise for her achievements in the areas of research, teaching, and community service.

However, when Tung came up for tenure[21] review in the fall of 1984, her chair's evaluation of her performance changed dramatically. "After I made it clear to the chairman that I wanted our relationship kept on a professional basis," she stated in her charge, "he embarked on a ferocious campaign to destroy and defame me. He solicited more than 30 letters of recommendation from external and internal reviewers when the usual practice was for five or six letters."[22] Although a majority of her department faculty recommended tenure, the personnel committee denied Professor Tung's promotion. Contrary to the rules, the department chair deliberately withheld news of the decision for one week to deliver it to Tung on Chinese New Year's Day. He offered no reason for her tenure denial. Tung later learned through a respected and well-placed member of the faculty that the justification given by the decision makers was that "the Wharton School is not interested in China-related research."[23] Tung understood this to mean that the Business School "did not want a Chinese American, an Oriental [on their faculty]." Of over sixty faculty in the management department, there were no tenured professors of color and only one tenured woman. At the entire Business School with over three hundred faculty, there were only two tenured people of color, both male.

Tung filed a complaint with the Equal Employment Opportunity Commission (EEOC) in Philadelphia alleging race, sex, and national origin discrimination. She also filed a complaint with the university grievance commission. Tung's file and those of thirteen faculty previously granted tenure in a recent five-year period were turned over to the grievance commission. During this process, the peer review files revealed that out of multiple batches of mailings the department chair had arranged specifically to solicit negative letters, only three such letters were in her file—two of which had been written by the chair himself! One of the chair's negative letters was written only six months after his rave review in June 1984. Professor Tung's file constituted an impressive list of achievements with over thirty letters consistently praising her as one of the best and brightest young scholars in her field, including one from a Nobel Prize laureate. Her contributions had been acknowledged by her peers through election to the board of governors of the Academy of Management, a professional association of over seven thousand management faculty. Tung was the first person of color ever elected to the board. Following forty hours of hearings, the university grievance commission found that the university had discriminated against Tung. Despite a university administrative decision in her favor, the provost overseeing the matter chose to do nothing. Professor Tung suspects that race and gender stereotypes played a role in shaping the provost's inaction:

> [T]he provost, along with others in the university administration, felt that I being
> an Asian, would be less likely to challenge the establishment, because Asians have tradi-
> tionally not fought back. In other words, it was okay to discriminate against Asians,
> because they are passive; they take things quietly, and they will not fight back.[24]

Tung also noted the comments of one of her colleagues, describing her in a newspaper article as "elegant, timid, and not one of those loud-mouthed women on campus." Her colleague continued, "[i]n other words, [Professor Tung was] the least likely person to kick over the tenure-review apple cart."[25]

In light of the university's non-response to its own internal committee's findings, Rosalie Tung pursued her EEOC claim. In order to investigate, the EEOC subpoenaed her personnel file along with those of five male faculty members who had been granted tenure around the same time she had been denied. The University of Pennsylvania refused to turn over the files, and the case, known as *University of Pennsylvania v. EEOC*, eventually reached the Supreme Court.

Among its claims, the university asserted a First Amendment privilege of "academic freedom" to fight the subpoena. It argued that one of the essential First Amendment freedoms that a university enjoys is the right to "determine for itself on academic grounds who may teach."[26] Insofar as the tenure system determines "who may teach," university attorneys argued that disclosing the personnel files and peer review evaluations would create a "chilling effect" on candid evaluations and result in the impairment of "the free interchange of ideas that is a hallmark of academic freedom."[27]

Rejecting the university's claims, the Court took very lightly the university's assertion that compliance with the subpoena violated its First Amendment rights.

> [T]he infringement the university complains of is extremely attenuated. To repeat, it argues that the First Amendment is infringed by disclosure of peer review materials because disclosure undermines the confidentiality which is central to the peer review process, and this in turn is central to the tenure process, which in turn is the means by which petitioner seeks to exercise its asserted academic freedom right of choosing who will teach. To verbalize the claim is to recognize how distant the burden is from the asserted right.[28]

The unanimous decision in favor of Tung's EEOC investigation by a conservative Rehnquist Court set an important precedent in establishing baseline procedures for Title VII claims in academic employment. *University of Pennsylvania v. EEOC* represents the Court's willingness to alter, at least slightly, its long-standing tradition of absolute deference to higher education's decision-making process in the face of egregious discrimination and harassment. The Tung case exposed and rejected the "academic freedom trumps harassment and discrimination" rationale that served to hide the evidence of wrongdoing in tenure denials.[29]

HOSTILE ENVIRONMENT: THE JEAN JEW CASE

Dr. Jean Jew arrived at the University of Iowa in 1973 from Tulane University along with another physician and her mentor who had just been appointed chair of the anatomy department in the college of medicine. Almost immediately, rumors circulated about her alleged sexual relationship with her mentor. These rumors persisted for the next thirteen years. Despite the increased number of incidents of harassment and vilification Jew experienced after joining the anatomy department, she was recommended by the department for promotion to tenure in December 1978. Her promotion, however, did not quiet her detractors. In a drunken outburst in 1979, a senior member of the anatomy department referred to Jew as a "stupid slut," a "dumb bitch," and a "whore."[30] Jew and three other professors complained separately to the dean about the slurs.

Jean Jew's tenure promotion not only failed to quiet her critics, it apparently further fueled the rumor mill and provided colleagues with an opportunity to air personal grievances and exploit departmental politics. Jean Jew was the only woman in the anatomy department and one of a few Asian Pacific American women among the University of Iowa faculty. In this homogenous setting, stereotypes flourished to such an extent that the faculty did not even recognize the difference between jokes and racial slurs. One faculty member who referred to Dr. Jew as a "chink" contended that he was merely "using the word in a frivolous situation" and repeating a joke.[31] The model minority stereotype of competence and achievement fed existing insecurities and jealousies in a department that was already deeply polarized.[32] In responding to these insecurities, a traditional gender stereotype informed by racialized ascriptions acted to rebalance the power relations. Gender stereotypes with racial overtones painted Jew as an undeserving Asian Pacific American woman who traded on her sexuality to get to the top. To Jew, this stereotyping and her refusal to accede to it played a large role in the "no-win" configuration of departmental power relations:

> If we act like the [passive] Singapore Girl, in the case of some professors, then they feel "she is [unequal to me]." If we don't act like the Singapore Girl,[33] then [our] accomplishments must have derived from "a relationship with the chair." There were quite a few people that felt that way to begin with. They thought because I was working with the chair, I was his handmaiden. Many faculty testified that in inter-collaborative work, I was doing work that led to publication but that he was the intellectual, with Jean Jew as his lackey. The term used was that I was the collaborative force, but not independent.[34]

This construction of Dr. Jew is perhaps most evident in the continued attack on her credentials. One of her primary harassers, whose advanced degrees were not in anatomy but in physical education, may have felt the need to attack Jew's professional standing and personal character out of his own academic insecurities. Among the many incidents, this faculty member intimated to a lab technician that Dr. Jew held a favored status in the department which he attributed to her willingness to engage in a sexual relationship with the chair in exchange for economic and professional gain. For example, he commented to the technician that, "obviously [other faculty and staff] are not going to get a big raise because [they] can't do for Dr. Williams what Jean can do for Dr. Williams."[35] Overall, this faculty member made more than thirty-three demeaning and harassing statements about Jean Jew in an attempt to discredit her professional and personal reputation.[36]

Other colleagues also denigrated Jew. After he was denied tenure in 1991, one doctor filed a grievance with the university stating that his qualifications were better than those of Jew who had been tenured. To support his case, the doctor submitted an anonymous letter to the dean, indicating that Jew's promotion was due to her sexual relationship with the chair. The letter stated, in fortune-cookie style, "[b]asic science chairman cannot use state money to . . . pay for Chinese pussy."[37] Another doctor who held administrative responsibilities in the department frequently posted outside his office where students congregated obscene *Playboy* magazine-type line drawings depicting a naked copulating couple with handwritten comments referring to Jew and the department chair.[38] On the very day that the senior departmental faculty were to evaluate Jew for promotion to full professor, the following off-color limerick appeared on the faculty men's restroom wall:

> There was a professor of anatomy
> Whose colleagues all thought he had a lobotomy
> Apartments he had to rent
> And his semen was all spent
> On a colleague who did his microtomy.[39]

The faculty voted three in favor, five against Jean Jew's promotion, and she was denied full professorship.

Following her denial, Jew registered a complaint of sexual harassment with the university affirmative action office, the anatomy review and search committee, and the university's academic affairs vice-president. No action was taken on her complaint. In January of 1984, her attorney, Carolyn Chalmers, submitted a formal written complaint alleging sexual harassment to the vice-president. In response to the written complaint from legal counsel, a panel was appointed to investigate Jew's charges. On November 27, 1984, the panel made four findings: (1) a pattern and practice of harassment; (2) defamatory statements by two members of the anatomy faculty; (3) inaction by the administration; and (4) resulting destructive effects on Jew's professional and personal reputation locally and nationally. The panel recommended that the administration take immediate action to inform the department of their findings and that a "public statement [be] made on behalf of the University of Iowa." The university took no meaningful action. In utter frustration at the university's unwillingness to correct the hostile work environment, Jew and Chalmers took the case to court.

Jean Jew's first suit in federal district court alleged that the University of Iowa failed to correct the hostile work environment from which she suffered. After fourteen days of testimony, the judge issued a ruling, finding *inter alia* that the University of Iowa had failed to respond to Jew's complaints. According to the judge, the faculty in the anatomy department displayed "a pattern of verbal conduct which sexually denigrated Dr. Jew . . . in a concerted and purposeful manner."[40] He reasoned that "Dr. Jew has conducted herself throughout her employment at the university as a serious and committed teacher, scholar and member of the academic community."[41]

The judge also found that sexual bias played a significant role in her denial of promotion to full professor in 1983. He found that four of the five professors who voted negatively on her promotion had displayed sexual bias. Judge Vietor ordered the university to promote Jew to full professor and awarded over $50,000 in back pay and benefits dating back to 1984, a rare remedy given the federal courts' historic deference to university academic personnel decisions.

Jew also filed a defamation suit in state court in October 1985. The suit alleged that she was sexually harassed by another member of her department. The six-woman, one-man jury unanimously found for Jew and awarded five thousand dollars in actual damages and thirty thousand dollars in punitive damages. Jew had won her second legal battle, but her adversarial relationship with the University of Iowa was not over.

One of the most disturbing aspects of the university's behavior in the *Jew* case is how the defense of academic freedom was employed to shield from legal liability slanderous faculty comments and university inaction. The university attempted to dismiss Jew's complaint on the basis that the statements later found to amount to sex discrimination and sexual harassment were merely legitimate criticism and "speech protected from regulation by the First Amendment." [42] As such, the university argued that it was under no obligation to regulate speech privileged by the First Amendment's implied recognition of academic freedom. Of course, university lawyers had to downplay the fact that the statements in question were not made in conjunction with any formal proceedings about the candidate's performance.

The federal judge rejected out of hand the university's academic freedom argument. "There is no merit in defendants' contention that they cannot be held liable because [defendants'] comments were constitutionally protected free speech," Judge Vietor wrote. "Rights of free speech and academic freedom do not immunize professors from liability for slander or their universities from Title VII liability for a hostile work environment generated by sexual-based slander." [43] Despite the unsuccessful attempt to sanitize the harmful speech as academic freedom, the university stated that it would appeal the judge's decision on First Amendment grounds in October 1990. The Iowa Board of Regents governing the university provided the public rationale for the appeal, stating that Vietor's decision made the university responsible "for policing the statements and behavior of faculty members in ways that appear inconsistent with academic life and constitutional protections." [44] "In an academic community this is extremely disturbing," the statement continued. "The effect of chilling speech in a community dedicated to the free exchange of ideas and views— even unpleasant ones—requires that the board and the university pursue the matter further." [45] Jew's attorney Carolyn Chalmers interpreted the board's comments as a defense of the university's freedom to promote faculty members without judicial intervention even when it engages in sexual discrimination. As for the free speech claim, Chalmers observed that "[w]hat they're arguing is that academic freedom protects gutter talk." [46]

Only when considerable community criticism surfaced did the university decide to cut its losses and accept the validity of the verdict. In an editorial criticizing the university's strategy for appeal, Professor Peter Shane of the University of Iowa College of Law wrote:

> No proper concept of academic freedom . . . could immunize the public denigration of Dr. Jew as a "slut," a "chink," a "bitch" and a "whore"—all this by people actually permitted to vote on her qualifications for promotion! Neither should academic privilege protect the circulation of unfounded rumors about any person. . . . The only connection between academic freedom and Dr. Jew's experience is that university offi-

cials essentially ostracized her for insisting that promotions be evaluated in a way that does not disadvantage women. That ostracism and the consequent chill on her sympathizers' expression surely did compromise academic freedom.[47]

Similarly, a local editor asserted that "academic freedom is better served by a compassionate environment than a continuing lawsuit."[48] Faculty and staff supporting the federal judge's finding of sexual harassment brought added pressure against the university appeal effort by forming the Jean Jew Justice Committee and distributing the judge's order and findings of fact to the campus community.[49]

The university's unwillingness to accept responsibility for the racialized sexual harassment of Jean Jew extends beyond the attempt to appeal the decision. That the University of Iowa paid for the legal expenses to defend the offending professor's defamation suit for over five years as well as the thirty-five-thousand-dollar judgment entered by the court in his guilty verdict, reveals the depth of complicity between the university and the adjudged harasser. Clearly, the administration sided with the wrongdoer after its own internal investigative panel supported Dr. Jew's claims and even after a verdict was returned against him. The university's adversarial treatment of Jew, its inaction following the internal committee's findings, its futile appeal attempt, and its shouldering of the harasser's individual civil liability reflect a disturbing pattern whereby academic institutions circle the wagons to protect the harasser against the harassed. One wonders to what extent the university's persistent litigiousness in the face of adverse administrative and legal findings reflects the prevalence of racial and sexual stereotypes that led it to side with the harasser and formulate an aggressive legal strategy to "bully" a plaintiff perceived to be politically weak and passive. As Professor Martha Chamallas, former University of Iowa law professor and founding member of the Jean Jew Justice Committee, observed:

> the rumor campaign against Jew was successful and persistent because it drew upon deep-seated and harmful stereotypes about professional women and about Asian academics in American universities. In contrast to the official fact-finders who were constrained to base their judgment solely on the evidence presented, many within the University community making less considered judgments may have allowed stereotypes to influence their views.[50]

In light of the prevalent and converging racial and gender stereotypes of Asian Pacific American women as politically passive and sexually exotic and compliant, serious attention must be given to the problem of racialized sexual harassment revealed by the two cases discussed. On a theoretical level, new frameworks that integrate race and gender should be developed to take account of the multidimensional character of racialized sexual harassment that occurs and is challenged across races, social classes, and borders.[51] The law's current dichotomous categorization of racial discrimination and sexual harassment as separate spheres of injury is inadequate to respond to racialized sexual harassment. On a doctrinal level, critical race feminists should be particularly concerned about the way in which "academic freedom" as a

First Amendment defense is selectively deployed by universities and faculty organizations as a legal strategy to sanitize discriminatory acts and the circulation of stereotypes.[52] On an advocacy level, women's and Asian Pacific American organizations should affirmatively address racialized sexual harassment and seek ways to counter the compounded vulnerability[53] that Asian Pacific and Asian Pacific American women face in confronting both the primary and secondary injuries. Finally, on an international level, insofar as the problem of racialized sexual harassment of Asian Pacific American women—even in elite employment sectors such as institutions of higher education—derives in part from internationalized stereotypes that feed upon unequal power relations, military history, and uneven economic development between Asia (especially in the Philippines and Thailand) and the United States, it is important for critical race feminists to commit to eradicating the sources of racialized sexual harassment not only in the United States, but also in the lives of sister counterparts overseas.

NOTES

This chapter is dedicated to the spirit of resistance displayed by Professor Rosalie Tung, Dr. Jean Jew, attorney Carolyn Chalmers, and the students at the unnamed university who organized for justice for Asian Pacific women fighting racialized sexual harassment. My dissertation advisor, Ronald Takaki, and graduate mentors in Ethnic Studies at U.C. Berkeley, Elaine Kim, Ling-chi Wang, and Michael Omi, provided invaluable training and support for this interdisciplinary research and writing. I am particularly indebted to Adrien Wing for editing this volume and chapter, Devon Carbado for his editorial assistance, and Beverly Heitt for her attention to detail in processing various revisions. I would like to thank the Asian Pacific American Law Students Association at the University of Michigan for inviting me to present this article in April 1996. I also benefited from generous comments by Harlon Dalton and Eric Yamamoto on an early version of this chapter. Finally, I would like to acknowledge Michelle Oberman, Morrison Torrey, Steve Landsman, Keith Aoki, Patty Gerstenblith, Alicia Alvarez, Judith Reed, and Bruce Ottley for their encouragement and constructive comments on more recent drafts. This research was also funded in part by a grant for a larger project on Asian Pacific American women in academia from the Center for the Study of Women in Society in Eugene, Oregon, with special thanks to Diana Sheridan and Ruth Johanna.

1. Letter from white male professor to Japanese female student. This letter and other materials cited for this case are on file with author. I am not at liberty to disclose publicly the sources related to this case.

2. Formal complaint of Japanese female student to university Affirmative Action Office, at 2 (on file with author) (hereinafter "formal complaint").

3. Transcript of conversation with former vice-president of Japanese student organization (on file with author).

4. As in many such cases involving abuse of power in sexual relationships, the woman was reluctant to come forward to file a complaint. When she learned that the professor had initiated and ended relationships with at least two other Japanese students, she decided to report him to campus officials so that other women could be warned of his pattern of racial

stalking. Her requests were modest and would have preserved his anonymity. She merely suggested that the professor undergo counseling so that he no longer "acts in a predatory manner toward Japanese women, and no longer needs to subordinate women sexually." She also recommended that he undergo HIV counseling. Formal complaint, *supra* note 2, at 2.

5. The administrative body in charge of reviewing such complaints decided not to pursue the claim. In a letter to the complainant, the affirmative action officer concluded that the professor was not acting as an "agent" of the university and that such actions fell within the sphere of "private" behavior outside the reach of the university's administrative regulations. This defensive, liability-conscious response for pursuing an investigation as an internal administrative remedy reflects the unnecessarily legalistic interpretation of standards that must be met simply to investigate a complaint of wrongdoing. The denial of university liability as a basis for dismissing the complaint reflects the general conflict of interest of internal university administrative offices ostensibly created to hear such discrimination or harassment complaints but whose staff are paid by the university. This central conflict of interest poses a Catch-22 for a complainant: If a complaint establishes an agency relationship and resulting injury, then the office assumes an adversarial position against the grievant and is naturally unhelpful in providing a remedy. If a complaint cannot articulate the imposed nexus between the offender and the university, then no liability or responsibility to address the complaint exists. In this case, the conflict of interest between the purpose of the affirmative action office and the university's interest is further implicated through the removal of two previous African American officers for doing their job too effectively. Following the departure of the second African American, the current officer (who rejected the student's complaint) was hired for the job through an internal promotion, absent a search, itself a violation of the university's affirmative action policy that he was hired to safeguard. The current officer is white. Letter from affirmative action officer (on file with author).

6. Following the affirmative action office's decision not to investigate, frustrated and concerned Asian Pacific American and Japanese student organizations attempted to warn incoming students of the possible targeting of Japanese women by the professor. Even this small, cautionary effort would not be allowed. An attorney retained by the professor wrote the student organizations threatening them with legal action for defamation and invasion of privacy. The attorney claimed the relationship was consensual and that because the student was not in the faculty member's class, there was no harassment. The lawyer did not deny the relationship. "[Y]ou can be held liable for dissemination of 'true' facts as well as false ones in some instances." The irony of the legal intimidation is that the lawyer defending the sexual predator had recently formed a "feminist" law firm to address issues of discrimination against women. The lawyer closed her letter to the students advising them "to seek legal counsel immediately." "I expect a written apology, if appropriate," she continued, "and written confirmation of your intention to abide by the requirements of the law within ten days of the date of this letter." Letter from feminist lawyer (on file with author).

7. Within days of the attorney's letter, the university counsel also emphasized the "possible legal liability for invasion of privacy or defamation" should the organization alert their members. "Your own endeavors, if more narrowly focused, should have the benefit of careful legal review for your own protection." Letter from university counsel (on file with author).

8. While this chapter addresses U.S.-based racialized sexual harassment against "Asian Pacific American" women as a point of departure, stereotypes of Asian Pacific American women involve an international transfer of stereotypes and the conflation of Asian Pacific women in Asia and in the United States. *See infra* note 17 and accompanying text. Because of

this fluidity of stereotypes that affect Asian Pacific women across borders, this chapter consciously refers at times to Asian Pacific and/or Asian Pacific American women, though not interchangeably, to acknowledge the linked social construction.

9. Colleen Fong provides a notable exception to this usual blindspot in model minority literature. In her dissertation on model minority images of Chinese in popular magazines, she focuses specifically on Chinese women. Colleen Valerie Jin Fong, Tracing the Origins of a "Model Minority": A Study of the Depictions of Chinese Americans in Popular Magazines 16–18 (1989) (unpublished Ph.D. dissertation, University of Oregon).

10. I refer to this popular servile depiction of Asian Pacific women as the "Mrs. Livingston syndrome" after the loyal, soft-spoken maid attending to the needs of the bachelor father and son in *The Courtship of Eddie's Father,* a television sitcom that ran from 1969–72. Mrs. Livingston, a likely war bride, never complained, and never appeared to have any social life or concerns other than dutifully and contentedly providing for her boss's needs. The actress portraying Mrs. Livingston, Miyoshi Umeki, epitomized the stereotypical passive, traditional Asian woman in major Hollywood films such as *Sayonara* (1957) and *Flower Drum Song* (1961). *See* Darrell Hamamoto, Monitored Peril 11–12 (1994); *see also* Gina Marchetti, Romance and the "Yellow Peril" 126 (1993).

11. Catharine MacKinnon discussed the psychological function of sexual harassment:

> How many men find it unbearable that a woman out-qualifies them in an even competition? Perhaps they assuage their egos by propagating rumors that the woman used her sexuality—something presumptively unavailable to men—to outdistance them. These stories may exemplify a well-documented inability of both sexes to see women in anything but sexual terms. Willingness to believe the stories may illustrate the pervasive assumption that, since a career is so intrinsically inappropriate for a woman, her sexuality must define her role in this context, as well as in all others.

Catharine MacKinnon, Sexual Harassment of Working Women 39 (1979). *See also* Morrison Torrey, *We Get the Message: Pornography in the Workplace,* 22 S.W. U.L. Rev. 53, 75–77 (1992) (discussing how competent, attractive women, in contrast to competent, attractive men, are disliked by coworkers and "are often believed to have exploited reasons other than skill and talent to achieve their position").

12. *Id.* at 44 (discussing sexual harassment as a condition of work for which there is an economic connection between harassment "compliance" and material job benefits).

13. Tony Rivers, *Oriental Girls: Tony Rivers Examines the Enduring Appeal of the Great Western Male Fantasy,* Gentleman's Quarterly (British ed.), Oct. 1990, at 161, 163. I thank Margaret Lin for bringing this article to my attention and for her activism organizing protest against the article. *See* Letter from The Coalition Against Negative Media Portrayal of Women to Condé Nast Publications Re: "Oriental Girls: The Ultimate Accessory" (undated, on file with author).

There is a booming sub-genre in pornography of Asian Pacific women, but I was unable to stomach this research after one attempt to document some of the offerings. The sub-genre is replete with the submissive stereotype and frequently uses Asian Pacific women in particularly masochistic and demeaning forms of pornography. Researchers who have investigated this sub-genre report titles of videos such as *Asian Anal Girls, Asian Ass, Asian Slut, Asian Suck Mistress, Banzai Ass, China deSade, Oriental Encounters, Oriental Sexpress, Oriental Lust, Oriental Callgirls, Oriental Sexpot, Oriental Squeeze, Oriental Taboo, and Oriental Techniques of Pain and Pleasure. Final Report of the Attorney General's Commission on Pornogra-*

phy, 388–433 (1986), *cited in* James Moy, Marginal Sights: Staging the Chinese in America 136–37 (1993). *See also* Diana Russell, Against Pornography 53–55, 61–62, 64, 65, 102–5 (1993) (observing that pornographic portrayals of Asian Pacific women reveal "common racist stereotypes about Asian women as extremely submissive and knowledgeable about how to serve and 'please a man' " and documenting the considerable reliance upon bondage and torture in this sub-genre that caters to male arousal through the domination) Michael Stein, The Ethnography of an Adult Bookstore: Private Scenes, Public Spaces 60–61 (1990), *cited in* Eddy Meng, Note, *Mail Order Brides: Gilded Prostitution and the Legal Response*, 28 U. Mich. J.L. Ref. 197 n. 204. (1994) (citing magazines such as Oriental Pussy and Hong Kong Hookers, in addition to pornographic video titles). Meng also uncovered an internet service entitled "Oriental Fetish" that encourages users to "[l]earn the secrets of Oriental Sexuality." *Id.* at 230n. 206.

In addition to the seamy industry of pornography, there are semi-pornographic portrayals of Asian Pacific women in other more "respectable" outlets. Sweeps week often features sensational "exposés" of sex tourism industries in Bangkok, Thailand, or in the Philippines for talk shows and local news stations. Teaser ads for such "news" segments typically expose as much skin of young Asian Pacific girls as is allowed on television. The advertising industry has bestowed its highest Clio award on the Singapore Girl commercials whose soft-focus, smiling flight attendants in traditional dress comprised the entire campaign along with the tag line, "Singapore Girl, You're a great way to fly." A recent CD cover for New York recording artist John Zorn displays sadomasochistic images of Japanese women "bound and suspended by ropes taken from Japanese pornographic films." Elisa Lee, *Uprooting the Garden of Torture,* Third Force November/December 1994, at 18. Mail-order bride industries posing as match-making businesses with names such as "Cherry Blossoms" or "Lotus Blossoms" also exploit stereotypical images of willing, pliant, and impoverished Asian Pacific sex partners for middle-aged American males disenchanted by "liberated" American women. *See* Venny Villapando, *The Business of Selling Mail-Order Brides,* Making Waves 318, 320 (Asian Women United of California, ed., 1989).

14. As the article continues, "The stereotype of the Oriental girl is the greatest sexual shared fantasy among western men, and like all the best fantasies it is based on virtual ignorance and uncorrupted by actuality." Rivers, *supra* note 13, at 163. Post-World War II Hollywood churned out a number of films that chronicled the interracial sexual relationships between white American military men and Japanese women as a metaphor for U.S. military victory and dominance over Japan. Gina Marchetti analyzes the Geisha genre—including films such as *Teahouse of the August Moon* (1956), *The Barbarian and the Geisha* (1958), *Cry for Happy* (1961) and *My Geisha* (1961)—as metaphorically representing "a bellicose Japan, through the figure of the geisha," as a "yielding and dependent nation." Marchetti, *supra* note 10, at 179. Marchetti analyzes postwar Hollywood films set in Hong Kong such as *Love Is a Many Splendored Thing* (1955) and *The World of Suzie Wong* (1960) as cold war narratives that allow "America to assert and legitimize its presence in Asia as an 'enlightened' Western power opposed to British colonialism and promising a neocolonial prosperity in the face of socialist leveling." *Id.* at 110.

15. *See, e.g.,* Michael Small, *For Men Who Want an Old-Fashioned Girl, The Latest Wedding March Is Here Comes the Asian Mail-Order Bride,* People, Sept. 16, 1985, at 127–29; *see also* Marchetti, *supra* note 10, at 158 (stating that Hollywood films in the 1950s and early 1960s such as *Three Stripes in the Sun, Teahouse of the August Moon, Sayonara, The*

Barbarian and the Geisha, The Crimson Kimono, and *Cry for Happy,* among others, portrayed interracial love affairs between Japanese and Americans by using the "myth of the subservient Japanese woman to shore up a threatened masculinity in light of American women's growing independence during World War II").

16. For more information on these interconnected power relationships and their impact on the international transfer of stereotypes, *see* Eddy Meng, *supra* note 13, at 200–209 ("Gender and ethnic stereotypes of Asian Pacific women as submissive, exotic, and erotic run rampant in marketing materials which hawk Asian Pacific brides as sex partners who double as domestic servants."); Elaine Kim, *Sex Tourism in Asia,* 2 Critical Perspectives of Third World America 214 (1984) (volume on file at the Asian American Studies Library at U.C. Berkeley) (analyzing the links between colonial domination, U.S. military presence, and sex tourism in Asia); Elisa Lee, *Ordering Women,* Third Force, July/Aug. 1995, at 22 (Lee notes the link between the stereotype of Asian Pacific women as "submissive sexpots" and the history of U.S. militarization in Asian countries. "The Philippines and Thailand were often considered prime 'R & R' stops for American military men, and the prostitution industries that serviced the U.S. military exploded there during the Vietnam and Korean wars."). *See generally* Thanh-Dam Truong, Sex, Money and Morality: Prostitution and Tourism in Southeast Asia (1990) (exploring the vast sex tourism industry in Thailand); Elizabeth Uy Eviota, The Political Economy of Gender: Women and the Sexual Division of Labour in the Philippines (1992) (discussing the lucrative sex tourism industry in the Philippines); Saundra Pollock Sturdevant and Brenda Stolzfus, Let the Good Times Roll: Prostitution and the U.S. Military in Asia (1992) (examining the connection between U.S. military presence in Asia and the development of sex tourism industries).

17. Rivers, *supra* note 13, at 163. Suzie Wong is the Hollywood prototype of the masochistic eroticism of Asian Pacific American women. In *The World of Suzie Wong,* a classic for such stereotypes, Nancy Kwan portrays "Suzie Wong," a prostitute who falls in love with a struggling American artist self-exiled in Hong Kong, played by William Holden. The Hong Kong hooker invites Holden to beat her so she can show her injuries to her Chinese girlfriends as a measure of his affection. In the final "love scene," Suzie pledges to stay with her American man until he says, "Suzie, go away." *The World of Suzie Wong* (1960).

18. There are two legally recognized forms of sexual harassment. *Quid pro quo* involves harassment that is implicitly or explicitly linked to the conferral or denial of economic benefits as a condition of employment. *See* Meritor Sav. Bank, FSB v. Vinson, 477 U.S. 57 (1986); 29 C.F.R. § 1604.11(a) (1), (2) (1993). *Hostile environment* consists of harassment that is so intimidating or offensive that it unreasonably interferes with one's work performance. *See* Harris v. Forklift Systems, 114 S. Ct. 369 (1993); 29 C.F.R. § 1604.11(a)(3) (1993). *See generally* MacKinnon, *supra* note 11.

19. Out of three hundred faculty, for example, she was selected by her dean to represent the school at Harvard Business School's 75th anniversary in 1983. Speech by Rosalie Tung, "Asian Americans Fighting Back," University of California, Berkeley, California, April 1990 [hereinafter, "Tung Speech"], Reprinted in *Rosalie Tung Case Pries Open Secret Tenure Review,* The Berkeley Graduate, April 1991, at 12–13, 30–31 (copy and videotape of speech on file with author).

20. *Id.*

21. Tenure is the grant of lifetime employment for faculty at institutions of higher education. Once tenure is granted, one can be fired only for cause, financial crisis, or programmatic,

institutional changes. Historically, tenure was offered to guarantee one's academic freedom to express even unpopular ideas without threat of dismissal. See B. N. Shaw, Academic Tenure in Higher Education (1971).

22. According to Tung, the thirty letters were collected in batches. After an initial attempt to procure negative letters in the first set of letters, he mailed a second set, and then a third. Tung Speech, *supra* note 19.

23. University of Pennsylvania v. Equal Employment Opportunity Commission, 493 U.S. 182, 185 (1990). Tung's research focused on bilateral U.S.-China and Pacific Rim trade relations.

24. Tung Speech, *supra* note 19. *See also* Maria Ontiveros, *Three Perspectives on Workplace Harassment of Women of Color,* 23 Golden Gate U. L. Rev. 817, 818 (1993) (observing that some women of color, particularly Asian Pacific American women and Latinas, are perceived to be "less powerful, less likely to complain, and the embodiment of particular notions of sexuality").

25. *Id.* (citing comments quoted in January 26, 1990, issue of *Newsday*).

26. University of Pennsylvania, 493 U.S. 182 (1990).

27. *Id.* at 182.

28. *Id.* at 199–200.

29. At the same time, the Court suggested two loopholes for violators to exploit: the elimination of "smoking gun" evidence and the redaction of tenure files. "Although it is possible that some evaluators may become less candid as the possibility of disclosure increases, others may simply ground their evaluations in specific examples and illustrations in order to deflect potential claims of bias or unfairness." University of Pennsylvania, 493 at 200–201. Writing for the unanimous Court, Blackmun further emphasized that "[n]othing we say today should be understood as a retreat from [the Court's] principle of respect for legitimate academic decision making." *Id.* at 199. These passages can be interpreted as a telegraphing of a legally permissible way to discriminate. Gil Gott, *Court Limits Tenure Review Secrecy,* The Berkeley Graduate, Feb. 1990, at 5, (commenting that faculty may interpret the opinion to mean they can continue to discriminate as long as they "beef up their 'academic' arguments to better conceal their real motivations in order 'to deflect potential claims of bias or unfairness' "). The Court failed to discuss the issue of redaction, a process that removes attributions of comments from evaluations to preserve anonymity. Redactions can create a jigsaw puzzle that subverts the purpose of gaining access to peer review files in order to root out discrimination. *See generally* Tim Yeung, Comment, *Discovery of Confidential Peer Review Materials in Title VII Actions for Unlawful Denial of Tenure: A Case Against Redaction,* 29 U.C. Davis L. Rev. 167 (1995).

30. Plaintiff's Memorandum in Opposition to Defendant's Motion for Summary Judgment, at 20, Jew v. University of Iowa et. al., 749 F.Supp. 946 (1990) (No. 86–169-D-2) (hereinafter, Plaintiff's Memo) (on file with author).

31. Jew v. University of Iowa, 749 F.Supp. 946, 949 (S.D. Iowa 1990).

32. The federal trial record reveals the depth of this academic jealousy toward Jew. During her promotion deliberations, one faculty member voting against Dr. Jew commented that "women and blacks have it made." Another "no" vote stated that Dr. Jew had received many more advantages than he had received. Soon after deliberations, another opponent asserted that "women and blacks don't have any trouble getting jobs." *Id.* at 953.

33. According to Jew:

The image white men still have of Asian women is the Singapore Girl. In *[Traveler]* magazine, the top twenty travel items are listed. Singapore Airlines is again the number one airline. The most cited reason is the Singapore Girl. Despite the strides we've made in overcoming sex stereotypes, even the most enlightened of travelers admit they enjoy this very much.

Interview with Dr. Jean Jew, in Berkeley, Calif. (Oct. 15, 1991), *cited in* Sumi Cho, "The Struggle for Asian American Civil Rights," at 41 (1992) (unpublished dissertation, University of California, Berkeley). The article Dr. Jew is referring to appeared in the October 1991 issue of Condé Nast's *Traveler* magazine reporting the Readers' Choice Awards for the one hundred top travel experiences. Under "Top 10 Airlines," Singapore Airlines finished first under the article headline, *The Singapore Girls Aim to Please—and Always Do*. The article recognized the calming and contradictory nature of the stereotype of the Asian Pacific female stereotype for allegedly "enlightened" U.S. travelers: "Yet how curious that the American traveler, having absorbed two decades of feminism, feels so sanguine about an airline that trades without hesitation on the image and allure of the 'Singapore Girl.' This young and lissome creature, a vision of Asian beauty, attentiveness, and grace in a sarong kebaya . . . earn[s] just $1,200 a month and can't do more than fifteen years of basic cabin service. But this clearly bothers their passengers not at all." *The Singapore Girls Aim to Please—and Always Do,* Traveler Oct. 1991. at 223.

34. Interview with Dr. Jean Jew, *supra* note 33. *See also* Martha Chamallas, *Jean Jew's Case: Resisting Sexual Harassment in the Academy,* 6 Yale J.L. and Feminism 71, 84 (1994). Chamallas agrees that stereotypes played a key role in shaping the primary injury:

The false narrative constructed about Jew was believable in part because of its familiarity. Jew was portrayed as a cold, conniving woman whose success was due to her sexual relationship with a man in power rather than her achievements as a teacher and researcher. The narrative drew on both sexual and racial stereotypes. It supported the stereotype that women sleep their way to the top; that women are not really good at science and if they achieve in that area, it must be due to the talent of men; that women of color are promiscuous; and that Asians overachieve in their jobs, but are not truly talented or creative.

35. Plaintiff's Memo, *supra* note 30, at 5 of Timeline addendum.

36. *Id.* at 19.

37. *Id.* at 19, 6 of Timeline addendum.

38. Jew, 749 F.Supp. at 949.

39. Plaintiff's Memo, *supra* note 30, at 7 of Timeline addendum.

40. Chris Osher, *U of I to Promote Professor in Bias Case,* Des Moines Register, Aug. 29, 1990.

41. Andy Brownstein and Diana Wallace, UI, *Regents Liable in Sexual Harassment Case,* The Daily Iowan, Aug. 29, 1990.

42. Jew, 749 F.Supp at 946 (citing Defendants' Memorandum for Summary Judgment at 21).

43. *Id.* at 961.

44. Linda Hartmann, *UI Faculty Say Appeal Sends Bad Message,* Iowa City Press-Citizen, Oct. 13, 1990.

45. Andy Brownstein, *Regents: First Amendment Behind Appeal,* The Daily Iowan, Oct. 15, 1990.

46. *Id.*

47. Peter Shane, *Harassment Is Not Privileged Speech*, The Daily Iowan, Sept. 28, 1990, at 8A.

48. David Crawford, *Harmful Appeal*, The Daily Iowan, Aug. 31, 1990. *See also* Charles Bullard, *U of I Urged Not to Appeal Bias Ruling*, Des Moines Register, Sept. 15, 1990.

49. Chamallas, *supra* note 34, at 81–90 (providing a detailed description of the Jean Jew Justice Committee's successful organizing efforts to convince the university not to appeal the case to the Eighth Circuit Court of Appeals).

50. *Id.* at 84.

51. Catharine MacKinnon laid the groundwork for a legal definition and theory of sexual harassment. Critical race feminists must continue to build upon this work to theorize more comprehensively the racial, ethnic, and class dimensions of sexual harassment. *See, e.g.,* Elvia Arriola, *"What's the Big Deal?" Women in the New York City Construction Industry and Sexual Harassment Law, 1970–1985*, 22 Col. Hum. Rts. L. Rev. 21, 59–60 (1991) (contending that the "swift merging of racial and sexual harassment" is a functional aspect of defending traditional working conditions and exclusionary practices that perpetuate the dominant white male [power] structure); Maria Ontiveros, *supra* note 24, at 818 (suggesting a complex understanding of the interwoven racial and sexual harassment injuries in the workplace as well as a method for analyzing differential risk that subgroups of women of color encounter in experiencing and redressing what she refers to as "workplace harassment"); Kimberlé Crenshaw, *Race, Gender, and Sexual Harassment*, 65 S. Cal. L. Rev. 1467, 1473 (1992) (arguing that the organized women's movement must "go beyond the usual practice of incorporating only those aspects of women's lives that appear to be familiar as 'gender' while marginalizing those issues that seem to relate solely to class or to race").

52. The critique of "free speech" and First Amendment to sanction discrimination has been initiated by critical scholars analyzing law. *See generally* Words That Wound (Mari Matsuda et. al., eds., 1993) and The Price We Pay (Laura Lederer and Richard Delgado, eds., 1995).

53. For a related concept, see Kimberlé Crenshaw, *supra* note 51, at 1467–68 (referring to the dynamics of racism and sexism in the workplace as the "dual vulnerability" confronting women of color).

Questions and Suggested Readings
for Part 4

1. None of the authors in this part seriously consider the possibility that Anita Hill was being "used" by white feminists. What do you think about this argument? Could this explain why some members of the black community considered Hill the villain and Thomas the victim?

2. Why is sexual harassment a common abuse of power by men? What purpose does it serve? Can a woman harass a man? In what contexts? Is it possible for a man of lower status in the workplace to harass his female boss? What about a female subordinate harassing her male boss? How does switching the races of the individuals involved affect your answers?

3. Do you agree with Emma Jordan that in conflicts involving black men, black women, and the white power structure "racism trumps sexism"? Can this concept be applied to the conviction of black boxer Mike Tyson for raping eighteen-year-old beauty contestant Desiree Washington? What about the conviction of Washington, D.C., mayor Marion Barry, for cocaine use after being videotaped with his black mistress? What about the resignation of NAACP leader Reverend Ben Chavis over the use of organization money to pay off a sexual harassment allegation raised by a black female? What other principles may be at work in these cases? What should be the position of black feminists with respect to the prosecution of sexist rap groups? (*See* Kimberlé Williams Crenshaw, *Beyond Racism and Misogyny: Black Feminism and 2 Live Crew, in* Mari J. Matsuda et al., Words That Wound: Critical Race Theory, Assaultive Speech, and the First Amendment 111 (1993)).

4. How can we link the 1995 downfall of Senator Bob Packwood on sexual harassment allegations and the 1992 election of six female senators, including the

first black female, to the Anita Hill episode? What about the increase in sexual harassment complaints and sexual harassment codes in the workplace? How can we link the Tailhook and other military scandals? Does all this mean that Anita Hill actually won? What kind of societal backlashes are we seeing? See Susan Faludi, Backlash (1991).

5. It is clear from reading Sumi Cho's essay that Asian American women experience different racial and gender stereotypes than, for example, black women. Is this difference significant? How is this difference manifested in the nature of sexual harassment toward black and Asian American women?

For further reading on the hearings, see Race, Gender, and Power in America: The Legacy of the Hill-Thomas Hearings (Anita Hill & Emma Coleman Jordan eds., 1995) and articles therein. *See* Kimberlé Crenshaw, *Whose Story Is It Anyway? Feminist and Antiracist Appropriations of Anita Hill,* and other articles *in* Race-ing Justice, En-gendering Power: Essays on Anita Hill, Clarence Thomas, and the Construction of Social Reality 402 (Toni Morrison ed., 1992); *Gender, Race, and the Politics of Supreme Court Appointments: The Import of the Anita Hill/Clarence Thomas Hearings,* 65 S. Cal. L. Rev. 1279 (1992), entire issue, including Kimberlé Crenshaw, *Race, Gender, and Sexual Harassment,* 65 S. Cal. L. Rev. 1467 (1992); Estelle Freedman, *The Manipulation of History at the Clarence Thomas Hearings,* 65 S. Cal. L. Rev. 1361 (1992); Anita Hill, *Sexual Harassment: The Nature of the Beast,* 65 S. Cal. L. Rev. 1445 (1992). *See generally* Judy Trent Ellis, *Sexual Harassment and Race: A Legal Analysis of Discrimination,* 8 J. Legis. 30 (1981).

5 | Criminality and Law Breaking

Part 5 provides perspectives on criminality and law breaking. Patricia J. Williams opens part 5 with *Spirit-Murdering the Messenger: The Discourse of Fingerpointing as the Law's Response to Racism,* calling for recognition of the crime of spirit-murder, an acknowledgment that racism is as devastating as robbery or assault. Tying together narratives involving her own denial of entry into a Benetton's store with the New York police shooting of black elder Eleanor Bumpers, she makes the case for a crime similar to rape, in which the victim is placed on trial. This concept of spirit-murder has been further developed by other critical race feminists featured in this anthology.

Regina Austin discusses African American women who are prostitutes in *Black Women, Sisterhood, and the Difference/Deviance Divide.* The focal point for the chapter is the defamation suit of *Ruby Clark v. ABC,* in which an ABC broadcast left the ambiguous impression that Clark might be a prostitute. Austin calls for a true black sisterhood in which those women who are not deviant should try to understand, support, and perhaps even embrace those who are deviant. While this process is risky, and may result in everyone being labeled deviant, at times it is truly difficult to tell "us" from "them."

Expanding our understanding of black female deviance, Adrien Katherine Wing and Christine A. Willis collaborate in an original essay entitled *Sisters in the Hood: Beyond Bloods and Crips.* This chapter is based on research that Wing has conducted with the Los Angeles-based black gangs known as the Bloods and Crips. Most sociological juvenile delinquent research has been male-centered, and the topic has been ignored so far in the law reviews. The authors define six particular ways that black women relate to gang members and call for a critical race feminist theory of deviance. They call for pragmatic solutions to gang violence that involve moving black women from the margins to the center of theoretical and programmatic options.

In *Scarlett's Code, Susan's Actions,* Sherri L. Burr uses literary analogy to make legal points. Her narrative begins with her visiting teaching assignment at a Southern university. One student's yearning to live in the time of *Gone with the Wind* provides the context for an analysis of the Susan Smith case. The student's desire to live in a time when white women had it easy is a jumping-off point to explore Smith's role as a Southern belle, a modern-day Scarlett O'Hara, who thought she could lie and get away with murder. Just as Scarlett lied and cheated in an attempt to woo the man she wanted, Ashley Wilkes, Smith thought her machinations would result in Tom Findlay marrying her. The interweaving of the Southern theme of the evil black man who did the crime, fortunately, did not result in any modern-day lynchings, although five hundred were detained. Burr speculates that a black defendant would not have received the lenient life sentence that Smith did for the crime of double infanticide.

The O. J. Simpson case has made domestic violence a household word in the same way that Anita Hill now symbolizes the issue of sexual harassment. Jenny Rivera focuses on the abuse syndrome in the Latino community in *Domestic Violence against Latinas by Latino Males: An Analysis of Race, National Origin, and Gender Differentials.* She provides concrete suggestions for reform as she examines the multiple barriers Latinas face because of their race, national origin, language, and gender. The stereotypes about Latinas as either the good, innocent virgin or the sexy siren confront the images of Latino males as macho. Even where domestic abuse statutes exist, they may not be enforced in the Latino context because of these stereotypes. There has been a failure within the battered women's movement to address the concerns of Latinas. Many shelters will not accept Spanish speakers or women with children. Additionally there has been a failure in the Latino community to aggressively address the problem of domestic abuse because of patriarchal structures. Latinas are in the same double bind as black women who must decide if their own empowerment will come at the price of the disempowerment of their own men at the hands of a state that respects neither gender.

The part closes with two essays exploring the race, class, and gender aspects of the trial of the century, the O. J. Simpson case. First, Maria L. Ontiveros enhances our understanding of the videotaped deposition testimony of the Latina housekeeper in *Rosa Lopez, Christopher Darden, and Me: Issues of Gender, Ethnicity, and Class in Evaluating Witness Credibility.* The author provides an alternate interpretation of the media's disparaging depiction of Lopez. The author highlights the translation difficulties involved in Spanish to English, and even the original use of a Mexican translator instead of a Salvadoran one. For example, *no me recuerdo,* which translates literally into "I don't remember," may have constituted an indirect, less confrontational way to say no to the powerful prosecutor. Ontiveros also points out the differential approach to time and the use of maternal and paternal surnames as well as the deference to authority that constitute the parameters of Lopez's existence. One of the interesting anomalies in this case, not explored by the author, is the fact that the authority in this case was an African American male prosecutor, whose own conflicts with white male authority nonetheless provided him with no context to understand Lopez's life as a Latina maid.

Finally, Crystal H. Weston contributes *Orenthal James Simpson and Gender, Class, and Race: In That Order.* Her provocative analysis of the variables that this anthology focuses on would privilege gender before race and require a reading of the O. J. Simpson case as misogyny teaming up with white supremacy to acquit a wealthy, good-looking hero. O. J. Simpson had successfully surpassed his "niggerdom." She calls for an end to nationalist arguments within the black community that continue to subsume women's subjugation beneath the call for unity around the "brother."

General Principles

Spirit-Murdering the Messenger: The Discourse of Fingerpointing as the Law's Response to Racism

Patricia J. Williams

WINDOWS AND MIRRORS

Buzzers are big in New York City, favored particularly by smaller stores and boutiques. Merchants throughout the city have installed them as screening devices to reduce the incidence of robbery. When the buzzer sounds, if the face at the door looks "desirable," the door is unlocked. If the face is that of an "undesirable," the door stays locked. Predictably, the issue of undesirability has revealed itself to be primarily a racial determination. Although the buzzer system was controversial at first, even civil rights organizations have backed down in the face of arguments that the system is a "necessary evil,"[1] that it is a "mere inconvenience" compared to the risks of being murdered,[2] that discrimination is not as bad as assault,[3] and that in any event, it is not all blacks who are barred, just "17-year-old black males wearing running shoes and hooded sweatshirts."[4]

Two Saturdays before Christmas, I saw a sweater I wanted to purchase for my mother. I pressed my brown face to the store window and my finger to the buzzer, seeking admittance. A narrow-eyed white youth who looked barely seventeen, wearing tennis sneakers and feasting on bubble gum, glared at me, evaluating me for signs that would pit me against the limits of his social understanding. After about five seconds, he mouthed, "We're closed," and blew pink rubber at me. It was one o'clock in the afternoon. There were several white people in the store who appeared to be shopping for things for their mothers.

I was enraged. At that moment I literally wanted to break all the windows in the store and take lots of sweaters for my mother. In the flicker of his judgmental grey eyes, that saleschild had reduced my brightly sentimental, joy-to-the-world, pre-Christmas spree to a shambles. He had snuffed my sense of humanitarian catholicity, and there was nothing I could do to snuff his, without simply making a spectacle of myself.

I am still struck by the structure of power that drove me into such a blizzard of rage. There was almost nothing I could do, short of physically intruding on him, that would humiliate him the way he humiliated me. His refusal to let me into the store was an outward manifestation of his never having let someone like me into the realm of his reality. He saw me only as one who would take his money and therefore could not conceive that I was there to give him money.

In this weird ontological imbalance, I realized that buying something in that store was like bestowing a gift: the gift of my commerce. In the wake of my outrage, I wanted to take back the gift of my appreciation, which my peering in the window must have appeared to be. I wanted to take it back in the form of unappreciation, disrespect, and defilement. I wanted to work so hard at wishing he could feel what I felt that he would never again mistake my hatred for some sort of plaintive wish to be included. I was quite willing to disenfranchise myself in the heat of my need to revoke the flattery of my purchasing power. I was willing to boycott this particular store, random white-owned businesses, and anyone who blew bubble gum in my face again.

The violence of my desire to have burst into that store is probably quite apparent to the reader. I wonder whether the violence and the exclusionary hatred are equally apparent in the repeated public urging that blacks put themselves in the shoes of white store owners[5] and that, in effect, blacks look into the mirror of frightened white faces to the reality of their undesirability; then blacks would "just as surely conclude that [they] would not let [themselves] in under similar circumstances."[6]

This essay will consider how the rhetoric of increased privatization, in response to racial issues, functions as the rationalizing agent of public unaccountability and, ultimately, irresponsibility. I will analyze the language of lawmakers, officials, and the public in order to present racial discrimination—so pervasive yet so hard to prosecute, so active yet so unactionable—in a new light. To this end, I will examine the death of Eleanor Bumpurs, an elderly black woman shot by police in the Bronx.

The second purpose of this essay is to examine racism as a crime, an offense so deeply painful and assaultive as to constitute something I call "spirit-murder." Society is only beginning to recognize that racism is as devastating, as costly, and as psychically obliterating as robbery or assault; indeed, they are often the same. It can be as difficult to prove as child abuse or rape, where the victim is forced to convince others that he or she was not at fault, or that the perpetrator was not just "playing around." As in rape cases, victims of racism must prove that they did not distort the circumstances, misunderstand the intent, or even enjoy it.

CRIMES WITHOUT PASSION

ELEANOR BUMPURS AND THE LANGUAGE OF LAWMAKERS

On October 29, 1984, Eleanor Bumpurs, a 270-pound, arthritic, sixty-seven-year-old woman, was shot to death while resisting eviction from her apartment in the Bronx. She was $98.85, or one month, behind in her rent. New York City mayor Ed Koch and police commissioner Benjamin Ward described the struggle preceding her demise as involving two officers with plastic shields, one officer with a restraining hook, another officer with a shotgun, and at least one supervising officer. All the officers also carried service revolvers. According to Commissioner Ward, during the course of the attempted eviction Eleanor Bumpurs escaped from the restraining hook twice and wielded a knife that Commissioner Ward says was "bent" on one of the plastic shields. At some point, Officer Stephen Sullivan, the officer positioned farthest away from her, aimed and fired his shotgun. It is alleged that the blast removed half of her hand, so that, according to the Bronx district attorney's office, "it was anatomically impossible for her to hold the knife."[7] The officer pumped his gun and shot again, making his mark completely the second time around.[8]

Since 1984, Mayor Koch, Commissioner Ward, and a host of other city officials repeatedly have described the shooting of Eleanor Bumpurs as completely legal.[9] At the same time, Ward has admitted publicly that Bumpurs should not have died. Koch admitted that her death was the result of "a chain of mistakes and circumstances" that came together in the worst possible way, with the worst possible consequences.[10] Ward admitted that the officers could have waited for Bumpurs to calm down, and that they could have used tear gas or mace instead of gunfire. According to Ward, however, these observations are made with hindsight. As to whether this shooting of a black woman by a white police officer had racial overtones, he stated that he had "no evidence of racism."[11] Ward pointed out that he is sworn to uphold the law, which is "inconsistent with treating blacks differently,"[12] and that the shooting was legal because it was within the code of police ethics.[13] Finally, city officials have resisted criticism of the police department's handling of the incident by remarking that "outsiders" do not know all the facts and do not understand the pressure under which officers labor.

The root of the word "legal" is the Latin word *lex,* which means law in a fairly concrete sense—law as we understand it when we refer to written law, codes, and systems of obedience.[14] The word *lex* does not include the more abstract, ethical dimension of law that contemplates the purposes of rules and their effective implementation. This latter meaning is contained in the Latin word *jus,* from which we derive the word "justice."[15] This semantic distinction is not insignificant. The law, whether statutory or judicial, is a subcategory of the underlying social motives and beliefs from which it is born. It is the technical embodiment of attempts to order society according to a consensus of ideals.

Cultural needs and ideals change with the momentum of time; redefining our laws in keeping with the spirit of cultural flux keeps society alive and humane. In the

Bumpurs case, the words of the law called for nonlethal alternatives first, but allowed some officer discretion in determining which situations are so immediately life endangering as to require the use of deadly force.[16] This discretionary area was presumably the basis for the claim that Officer Sullivan acted legally. The law as written permitted shooting in general, and therefore, by extension of the city's interpretation of this law, it would be impossible for a police officer ever to shoot someone in a specifically objectionable way.

If our laws are thus piano-wired on the exclusive validity of literalism, if they are picked clean of their spirit, then society risks heightened irresponsibility for the consequences of abominable actions. We also risk subjecting ourselves to such absurdly empty rhetoric as Benjamin Ward's comments to the effect that both Eleanor Bumpurs's death and racism were unfortunate, while stating, "but the law says . . ."[17] The law thus becomes a shield behind which to avoid responsibility for the human repercussions of both governmental and publicly harmful private activity.

A related issue is the degree to which much of the criticism of the police department's handling of this case was devalued as "noisy" or excessively emotional. It is as though passionate protest were a separate crime, a rudeness of such dimension as to defeat altogether any legitimacy of content.

But undue literalism is only one type of sleight of tongue in the attainment of meaningless dialogue. Mayor Koch, Commissioner Ward, and Officer Sullivan's defense attorneys have used overgeneralization as an effective rhetorical complement to their avoidance of the issues. For example, allegations that the killing was illegal and unnecessary, and should therefore be prosecuted, were met with responses such as "The laws permit police officers to shoot people."[18] "As long as police officers have guns, there will be unfortunate deaths."[19] "The conviction rate in cases like this is very low." The observation that tear gas would have been an effective alternative to shooting Eleanor Bumpurs drew the dismissive reply that "there were lots of things they could have done."[20]

"DISCRIMINATION DOESN'T HURT AS MUCH AS BEING ASSAULTED," OR "A PREJUDICED SOCIETY IS BETTER THAN A VIOLENT SOCIETY"

The attempt to split bias from violence has been this society's most enduring and fatal rationalization. Prejudice does hurt, however, just as the absence of prejudice can nourish and shelter. Discrimination can repel and vilify, ostracize and alienate. White people who do not believe this should try telling everyone they meet that one of their ancestors was black. I had a friend in college who, having lived her life as a blonde, grey-eyed white person, discovered that she was one-sixteenth black. She began to externalize all the unconscious baggage that "black" bore for her: the self-hatred that is racism. She did not think of herself as a racist (nor had I), but she literally wanted to jump out of her skin, shed her flesh, and start life over again. She confided in me that she felt "fouled" and "betrayed." She also asked me whether I had ever felt this way. Her question dredged from some deep corner of my suppressed memory the recollection of feeling precisely that, when at the age of three or so, some white playmates explained to me that God had mixed mud with the pure clay of life in order to make me.

In the Vietnamese language, "the word 'I' (toi) . . . means 'your servant'; there is no 'I' as such. When you talk to someone, you establish a relationship."[21] Such a concept of "self" is a way of experiencing the other, ritualistically sharing the other's essence, and cherishing it. In our culture, seeing and feeling the dimension of harm that results from separating self from "other" require more work.[22] Very little in our language or our culture encourages or reinforces any attempt to look at others as part of ourselves. With the imperviously divided symmetry of the marketplace, social costs to blacks are simply not seen as costs to whites,[23] just as blacks do not share in the advances whites may enjoy.

This structure of thought is complicated by the fact that the distancing does not stop with the separation of the white self from the black other. In addition, the cultural domination of blacks by whites means that the black self is placed at a distance even from itself, as in the example of blacks being asked to put themselves in the position of the white shopkeepers who view them.[24] So blacks are conditioned from infancy to see in themselves only what others who despise them see.[25]

It is true that conforming to what others see in us is every child's way of becoming socialized.[26] It is what makes children in our society seem so gullible, so impressionable, so "impolitely" honest, so blindly loyal, and so charming to the ones they imitate. Yet this conformity also describes a way of being that relinquishes the power of independent ethical choice. Although such a relinquishment can have quite desirable social consequences, it also presumes a fairly homogeneous social context in which values are shared and enforced collectively. Thus, it is no wonder that Western anthropologists and ethnographers, for whom adulthood is manifested by the exercise of independent ethical judgment, so frequently denounce tribal cultures or other collectivist ethics as "childlike."

By contrast, our culture constructs some, but not all, selves to be the servants of others. Thus, some "I's" are defined as "your servant," some as "your master." The struggle for the self becomes not a true mirroring of self-in-other, but rather a hierarchically inspired series of distortions, in which some serve without ever being served, some master without ever being mastered, and almost everyone hides from this vernacular domination by clinging to the legally official definition of "I" as meaning "your equal."

In such an environment, relinquishing the power of individual ethical judgment to a collective ideal risks psychic violence, an obliteration of the self through domination by an all-powerful other. In such an environment, it is essential at some stage that the self be permitted to retreat into itself and make its own decisions with self-love and self-confidence. What links child abuse, the mistreatment of women, and racism is the massive external intrusion into psyche that dominating powers impose to keep the self from ever fully seeing itself.[27] Because the self's power resides in another, little faith is placed in the true self, that is, in one's own experiential knowledge. Consequently, the power of children, women, and blacks is actually reduced to the "intuitive" rather than the real; social life is necessarily based primarily on the imaginary. Furthermore, because it is difficult to affirm constantly with the other the congruence of the self's imagining what the other is really thinking of the self, and because even that correlative effort is usually kept within very limited family, neighborhood, religious, or racial boundaries, encounters cease to be social and become presumptuous, random, and disconnected.

THE GIFT OF INTELLIGENT RAGE

OWNING THE SELF IN A DISOWNED WORLD

While I was in grammar school in the 1960s, a white man acting out of racial motives killed a black man who was working for some civil rights organization or cause. The man was stabbed thirty-nine times, a number that prompted a radio commentator to observe that the point was not just murder, but something beyond.

Taking the example of the man who was stabbed thirty-nine times out of the context of our compartmentalized legal system, and considering it in the hypothetical framework of a legal system that encompasses and recognizes morality, religion, and psychology, I am moved to see this act as not merely body murder but spirit-murder as well. I see it as spirit-murder, only one of whose manifestations is racism; cultural obliteration, prostitution, abandonment of the elderly and the homeless, and genocide are some of its other guises. I see spirit-murder as no less than the equivalent of body murder.

One of the reasons that I fear what I call spirit-murder, or disregard for others whose lives qualitatively depend on our regard, is that its product is a system of formalized distortions of thought. It produces social structures centered around fear and hate; it provides a tumorous outlet for feelings elsewhere unexpressed. I think we need to elevate what I call spirit-murder to the conceptual, if not punitive level of a capital moral offense.[28] We need to see it as a cultural cancer; we need to open our eyes to the spiritual genocide it is wreaking on blacks, whites, and the abandoned and abused of all races and ages. We need to eradicate its numbing pathology before it wipes out what precious little humanity we have left.

MIRRORS AND WINDOWS

My life experiences had prepared me better to comprehend and sympathize with the animating force behind the outraged, dispossessed knife wielding of Eleanor Bumpurs. What I found more difficult to focus on was the "why," the animus that inspired such fear, and such impatient contempt in a police officer that the presence of six other heavily armed men could not allay his need to kill a sick old lady fighting off hallucinations with a knife. It seemed to me a fear embellished by something beyond Bumpurs herself; something about her enlarged to fill the void between her physical, limited presence and the "immediate threat and endangerment to life" that filled the beholding eyes of the officer. Why was the sight of a knife-wielding woman so fearfully offensive to a shotgun-wielding policeman that he felt that blowing her to pieces was the only recourse, the only way to preserve his physical integrity? What offensive spirit of his past experience raised her presence to the level of a physical menace beyond real dimensions? What spirit of prejudgment and prejudice provided him with such a powerful hallucinogen?

However slippery these questions may be on a legal or conscious level, unresponsiveness to them does not make these issues go away. Failure to resolve the dilemma of racial violence merely displaces its power. The legacy of killing finds its way into cultural expectations, archetypes, and "isms." The echoes of both dead and deadly others acquire a hallucinatory quality; their voices speak of an unwanted past, but also reflect for us images of the future. Today's world condemns those voices as superstitious and paranoid. Neglected, they speak from the shadows of such inattention, in garbles and growls, in the tongues of the damned and the insane. The superstitious listen, and perhaps in the silence of their attention, they hear and understand. So-called enlightened others who fail to listen to the voices of demonic selves, made invisibly uncivilized, simply make them larger, more barbarously enraged, until the nearsightedness of looking glass existence is smashed in upon by the terrible dispossession of dreams too long deferred.

NOTES

1. Gross, *When 'By Appointment' Means Keep Out*, N.Y. Times, Dec. 17, 1986, at B1.

2. *Id.*

3. Michael Levin & Marguerita Levin, letter to the editor, N.Y. Times, Jan. 11, 1987, at E32.

4. *Id.*

5. Gross, *supra* note 1.

6. Levin & Levin, *supra* note 3. The fact that some blacks might agree with the store owners shows that some of us have learned too well the lessons of privatized self-hatred and rationalized away the fullness of our public, participatory selves.

7. N.Y. Times, Jan. 12, 1987, at B2.

8. N.Y. Times, Feb. 27, 1987, at B1.

9. Benjamin Ward (Police Commissioner of New York City), Remarks at City University of New York (CUNY) Law School (Nov. 1985) (audiotape on file at CUNY).

10. N.Y. Times, Nov. 21, 1984, at B3.

11. *Id.*

12. Ward, *supra* note 9.

13. Raab, *Ward Defends Police Actions in Bronx Death*, N.Y. Times, Nov. 3, 1984, § 1, at 27.

14. *Webster's Ninth Collegiate Dictionary* 682 (1983).

15. *Id.* at 655.

16. Laws requiring police officers to use nonlethal alternatives are prevalent in this country.

[N]ationwide, a majority of the states have specific provisions governing the use of deadly force.

As a general proposition, efforts to control the use of deadly force have not fared too well over time. For example, the Missouri legislature rejected the suggestion of its advisory committee to limit the use of deadly force when he or she "reasonably believes" such force is necessary. Of the states evaluated, over half dealt with the issue of the use of force, but few adhered to the standard of the Model Penal Code concerning the police decision to use force. The approach of the legislatures evaluated has to be described as one of maintaining extensive discretion in the use of force—not of limiting it.

Williams, *The Politics of Police Discretion, in* Discretion, Justice, and Democracy 23 (C. Pinkele & W. Louthan eds., 1985).

17. Ward, *supra* note 9.

18. Raab, *supra* note 13.

19. *Id.;* Ward, *supra* note 9.

20. Ward, *supra* note 9; *see also* N.Y. Times, Nov. 21, 1984, at B3 (Mayor Koch's description of the Bumpurs incident).

21. D. Berrigan & T. Nhat Hanh, The Raft Is Not the Shore 38 (1975).

22. *See generally* J. Lacan, *Aggressivity in Psychoanalysis, in* Ecrits: A selection 23–24 (1977) (challenging the tendency of our language to equate "I" with the subject).

23. The starkest recent example of this has been the disastrous delay in the response to the AIDS epidemic; as long as AIDS was seen as an affliction affecting Haitians, Hispanics, Africans, and other marginalized groups such as intravenous drug users and homosexuals, its long-term implications were ignored. *Health Experts Fault U.S. on Response to AIDS,* N.Y. Times, Aug. 12, 1987, at A20, col. 1.

24. *See* Levin & Levin, *supra* note 3.

25. *See generally* K. Clark, Dark Ghetto (1965); K. Clark, Prejudice and Your Child (1955); J. Comer & A. Poussaint, Black Child Care (1975); W. Grier & P. Cobbs, Black Rage (1968).

26. *See generally* Selznick, *Law, Society and Moral Evolution, in* Readings in Jurisprudence and Legal Philosophy 931, 947–49 (P. Shuchman ed., 1979).

27. *See generally* A. Miller, The Drama of the Gifted Child (1984).

28. *See, e.g.,* Delgado, *Words That Wound: A Tort Action for Racial Insults, Epithets and Name-Calling,* 17 Harv. C.R.-C.L. L. Rev. 133 (1982).

29 Black Women, Sisterhood, and the Difference/Deviance Divide

Regina Austin

SHADES OF DIFFERENCE AND DEVIANCE

"Sameness" and "difference" do not neatly encompass all the categories into which deserving black women might be placed or might place themselves. To be sure, "sameness" and "difference," vis-à-vis whites of course, have been useful rhetorical devices by which blacks have launched assaults at the border between liberation and oppression and captured new ground. Yet there is a third, unspecified category beyond and implicit in "difference" of which black women must be especially mindful; that category is "deviance." Given the number and prevalence of stereotypes that exist concerning black women, we cannot afford to ignore how the dominant, white male-controlled society goes about labeling us deviant. We must hold ourselves open to the possibility that deviance includes attitudes and behaviors we ought to defend.

Because blacks have somewhat disparate interests at stake at home and abroad, our responses to conduct the dominant society labels "deviant" are numerous and complex. Some of those who are considered deviant by whites are excluded from good standing within "the community" because they undermine our claims to greater respect and a larger share of the nation's bounty. In other instances, "the community" responds in a less harsh and more sympathetic manner to those adjudged deviant by the rest of the society. Attributing deviance to systemic sources like racism and material deprivation, "the community" champions the cause of lawbreakers and thereby champions the cause of us all.

In general, gender makes a difference in the evaluation of deviant behavior. If the assessment is positive when the lawbreaker or norm violator is a male, it is likely to be less so or quite the reverse if the lawbreaker or norm violator is a female. If the assessment is negative when the wrongdoer is a male, it is likely to be more so if the wrongdoer is a female. As is true in other aspects of American social life, black women who break the rules are judged in accordance with the biases of both white supremacy and male domination. Black female offenders accordingly receive harsher treatment at the hands of the law than do female lawbreakers of other races and ethnicities.[1]

But black women have reason to challenge the appraisals of black female deviants, whether they are based on the standards of the dominant society or those prevailing in the black community. In the name of a "black sisterhood," a "community" within "the community," we might respond to female deviance with understanding, support, or praise based on the distinctive social, material, and political interests of black women. In doing so, however, we risk being labeled deviant ourselves. For this and other reasons, we tend to differentiate ourselves from those whose conduct falls within traditional definitions of deviance when we advance our claims for greater esteem and resources. The implications of this approach for the existence and maintenance of a true dynamic black sisterhood are best illustrated with a concrete case.

RUBY CLARK V. ABC

Ruby Clark, a black woman, sued the American Broadcasting Company (ABC) for defamation after her photograph appeared on the screen during a 1977 *ABC News Closeup* program on commercialized sex.[2] The particular segment that gave rise to her complaints focused on the impact of street prostitution on a Detroit neighborhood. The plaintiff was among three women pictured as they walked in public. Just before their appearance, a neighborhood woman was shown saying, "Whether you're fifteen or forty-five, constantly being approached—it's degrading—feels terrible." Another followed with the statement "[y]ou want to . . . just kill 'em . . . 'cause it makes you so angry to be placed down to a hooker's level." There followed in sequence three women walking in public. Ruby Clark was the last of the trio featured. The opinion describes the visual image and the verbal accompaniment as follows:

> The plaintiff appeared to be in her early to mid-twenties. She was attractive, slim, and stylishly dressed. Apparently, Plaintiff was unaware that she was being photographed. As Plaintiff appeared, the narrator made the following remarks: "But for black women whose homes were there, the cruising white customers were an especially humiliating experience."

Sheri Madison, a black female resident of the neighborhood plagued by prostitution, appeared on the screen seconds after Clark. She stated, "Almost any woman who was black and on the street was considered to be a prostitute herself. And was treated like a prostitute."

Ruby Clark, who viewed the program with her husband and young son, was shocked by its portrayal of her. A number of persons—friends, relatives, acquaintances, fellow church members, and prospective employers—thought the program presented her as being a prostitute, and some even concluded that she actually was one.

The district court awarded ABC summary judgment on the ground that Clark had not been libeled because "nothing in Plaintiff's appearance suggested that her activity paralleled that of a street prostitute." On appeal, this ruling was reversed. A majority of the Sixth Circuit panel concluded that the portrayal of the plaintiff was "reasonably capable of two meanings, one defamatory and the other non-defamatory." The issue was accordingly one for the jury.

Clark was definitely not a prostitute; she was not even a resident of the affected neighborhood. Thus, it clearly would have been libelous for ABC to depict her as a prostitute, and ABC contended that it did not do so.

Yet, in context, the plaintiff's status was equivocal. The subject was street prostitution, and the prostitutes were said to be black. Clark was clearly distinguishable from the two women whose features preceded her own. They were portly matrons, one white, the other black and bespectacled, both carrying bags, while she was young, slim, attractive, and black. The court stated, "[w]hen her appearance is juxtaposed with that of the two matrons, it is not clear whether she is a resident of this middle class neighborhood or one of the street prostitutes who plagued this community." Although the commentary that accompanied her picture suggested that she was one of "the black women who resided in the neighborhood" for whom "the presence of the cruising white customers was a humiliating experience," the interview footage that followed restored the ambiguity about Clark's status by referring to the frequency with which black women on the street were considered to be and treated like prostitutes. Thus, it was up to the jury to decide whether ABC presented the plaintiff as being "one of those middle class women erroneously considered to be a prostitute or . . . in fact, a prostitute."

ABC, in essence, permitted its viewers to do to Clark the very thing that the women complained of in the program. In reporting what was happening on the streets, ABC invited those watching the broadcast to engage in the johns' speculation—is she or isn't she? ABC bore some of the risk that its viewers were no more discriminating than the men cruising the affected neighborhood in search of prostitutes and might therefore exercise the same sort of erroneous judgment.

The court might have gone further and concluded that it was even defamatory to present Clark as the type of black woman who gets mistaken for a prostitute. Such a portrayal of Clark would have been neither flattering nor likely to enhance her reputation among her friends and associates. If the segment involving Clark was as ambiguous as the court suggests, it is not clear that a jury was capable of definitively assessing its meaning.

Ruby Clark's libel action challenged not only her own possible wrongful inclusion in the category of prostitutes, but also the general stereotyping that associates black women with street prostitution. Before and since slavery, black women's supposed sexual promiscuity and licentiousness have been relied on to justify the sexual exploitation of black women by white males intent on rape, cheap sex, harassment on the job, or torment on the street.[3] Since emancipation, combating our sexual denigration and establishing our entitlement to the same respect accorded white "ladies" have been significant components of black women's organized politics.[4] Clark's lawsuit was in keeping with this well-developed strand of black women's quest for freedom from white men's sexual domination.

Despite the breadth of her claim, Clark was still required to distinguish herself from and participate in the broader societal put-down of other black women. She succeeded in proving that the program possibly portrayed her as a prostitute by emphasizing the stark contrast between herself and the two other women, "the bag ladies" as it were, with whom she appeared. She accomplished this at the cost of perpetuating notions about the sexual undesirability of females who are no longer young, no longer svelte, and no longer (if they ever were) carefree. For a black woman to be required to join in this sort of disparagement of other black women is a very serious matter.

The impact of the attack on the femininity and sexuality of low-status black female workers is quite broad. Black women who try to distance themselves from the black drone role via simplistic negation and antithetical behavior do not thereby free themselves from the hold of a racist patriarchy; they merely give themselves over to it. In any event, such an approach is a futile one for many poor and working-class black females because their diets, jobs, limited expendable income, and restricted leisure time interfere with their ability to satisfy white, bourgeois, heterosexual norms of sexual attractiveness. Of course, many black women dismiss and defy the dominant standards by adopting distinctively black styles of dress and adornment. They pay for their resistance, however.

The other black females from whom the plaintiff had to distinguish herself were black prostitutes. The opinion in *Clark* suggests that black prostitutes represented a direct threat to the social standing, dignity, and well-being of upstanding black women. "Prostitutes are considered immoral and socially undesirable." Their presence in the Detroit neighborhood was shown to produce "devastating social problems," including an increase in robberies, assaults, and drug trafficking. The fact that some black women were actually prostitutes increased the chances that those who were not would be subjected to street harassment.

To make out a claim, Ruby Clark had to ignore any clichés that pertain to black prostitutes and middle-class women alike and accept the misconceptions that apply to black prostitutes while disputing their application to upstanding black women like herself. Clark's right to recover was dependent on her articulating her complaints within the confines of mainstream sexual morality, however racist, sexist, homophobic, or bourgeois it might be. The two groups of black women from whom the plaintiff had to distinguish herself, the matrons and the prostitutes, represent the Scylla and Charybdis of the narrow strait in which bourgeois black women are supposed to channel their sexuality. On one side are the "desexed," "de-hetero-sexed," and androgynous females who are lumped in with the self-declared lesbians; on the other side are the wild, wicked women who are written off as whores. If Clark veered too far in either direction, she risked censure, a decline in her reputation, and increased exploitation. If she succeeded in keeping to the straight and narrow, she got rewarded with a recovery.

While law and convention work to drive wedges between black women who express their sexuality in different ways, their actual impact could be quite the reverse. A common oppression and a common quest for liberation provide some basis for solidarity among black females. All the black females shown in the program shared white society's devaluation of black women's sexuality, although it affected them differently. It compelled the black prostitutes to stroll the streets in search of customers, subjected those who were not prostitutes to unwelcome public overtures, and rendered the portly matron (and her white counterpart) a neuter object, respectable but out of the game. They all have an interest in opposing the full range of negative categorizations of black women's sexuality. They all would have gained from an attack on the attempts of white men (including the cruising johns and ABC) to restrict black women's sexual expression and to label it in ways dictated by the white men's purposes. Naturally, defamation law does not allow such broad claims.

DEFYING THE DIVISIVENESS OF DEVIANCE

Contrariness is not a suitable basis for a vibrant and affirmative community. Black women must do more to build and sustain a sisterhood than unite against a common enemy and combat him on his own terms. Distinctions still have to be drawn. The difference/deviance divide cannot be avoided. Prostitutes present an especially hard case. If black women united to dispute the unwarranted denigration of black street-walkers, it might be assumed that we also mean to suggest that black females should be more attractive prospects for commercial intercourse than they presently are. Moreover, it remains true that black prostitutes bring traffic and confusion in their wake and their presence is more than morally problematic for the black folks who live in their environs. There comes a point at which blacks will or must adjudge the activities of these women to be "deviant" and condemn them as being on the wrong side of the difference/deviance divide.

To affix the label and forget it or to write off the women so tagged as being beyond redemption would not be sisterly. Black women who consider themselves virtuous cannot be part of an effective community with black sex workers if the former have no respect for the sex workers beyond that dictated by maternalism and assume that the sex workers can teach them nothing. Finding something positive in the practices and concerns of women in street life may not be easy, but it should not be impossible. For example, prostitutes might teach straight women a thing or two about identifying and dealing with pimps. We will not know the extent to which vice has its virtues until we come to know street women better. No external source of morals and values can supply the norms and values by which black women interact with each other. We certainly cannot expect the law to provide us with a cause of action that redresses the harm Ruby Clark suffered in a way that acknowledges how problematic the behavior of the prostitutes can be, yet does not put them down, and even concedes (without romanticization) the appeal of some of the values that are meaningful to them . . . until we can take such a position ourselves.

A genuine sisterhood would be a modern moral community, one in which political positions and ethical stances are constructed by the sisters as a matter of "common sense, ordinary emotions, and everyday life." [5] It may be time to recognize that the only true communities of black females are voluntary associations of women who are bound by shared economic, political, and social constraints and find strength, economic support, and moral guidance through effective, face-to-face engagement with each other. Such an admission would interfere with our nostalgic longing for a not-too-distant past when national success obviated the need to come together locally, as well as highlight our reluctance to analyze the contemporary material landscape and the full extent of the class cleavages that separate black women. The enormous comfort that comes from being able to think, talk, and act in terms of being a "black community" or a "black sisterhood" would be threatened if we called core assumptions into question. Dare we?

The social and economic liberation of black female deviants and nondeviants alike would proceed faster if we acknowledged that sometimes it is indeed difficult to tell "us" from "them." We must work to turn the boundary between difference and deviance into free space, a time and place in which racial, sexual, and economic emancipation can be imagined, experimented with, and even enjoyed. In collectively working the line between street and straight, straddling it, and pushing it, we can increase and intensify those moments in which we control our own sexuality and economic destiny. Only we can deliver ourselves into freedom,[6] and dancing on the difference/deviance divide may be one way to do that.

NOTES

1. *See generally* Vernetta D. Young, *Gender Expectations and Their Impact on Black Female Offenders and Victims,* 3 Just. Q. 305, 310–18 (1986).

2. Clark v. American Broadcasting Co., 684 F.2d 1208, 1210–11 (6th Cir. 1982), *cert. denied,* 460 U.S. 1040 (1983). Quotes that follow in the text are from this case.

3. *See generally* bell hooks, Ain't I a Woman? 51–67 (1981).

4. *See generally* Paula Giddings, When and Where I Enter: The Impact of Black Women on Race and Sex in America 31, 85–94 (1984).

5. Alan Wolfe, Whose Keeper?: Social Science and Moral Obligation 211 (1989).

6. The metaphor comes from a Nadine Gordimer short story. Nadine Gordimer, *A Lion on the Freeway, in* A Soldier's Embrace 23, 27 (1980).

30 | Sisters in the Hood: Beyond Bloods and Crips

Adrien Katherine Wing and Christine A. Willis

Gang violence plagues many of our inner cities and has spread into the American heartland. Law enforcement and governmental agencies are overwhelmed. Parents are emotionally distraught. Educators are frustrated and businesses are fleeing the urban centers. But the gang phenomenon is not a new problem. Historically, gangs have flourished in the United States since the early part of this century, and they were usually based on ethnicity: Irish, Jewish, and Italian. Today, gangs are not merely based on ethnicity but rather on race, culture, geography, political beliefs, or criminal activity.[1] For many Americans, however, gangsterism in the 1990s is synonymous with black male criminality. Groups like the Los Angeles-based Bloods and Crips are publicized and glamorized in pop culture, rap music, books,[2] movies,[3] and television. Potential solutions to the "gang problem" emphasize the punishment of black males. Yet despite an increase in black male incarceration rates,[4] the gang problem continues to escalate. Preventive and rehabilitative programs are de-emphasized and remain underfunded,[5] and the criminal justice system is left with inadequate alternatives to deal with gang-affected youths.

Perhaps what is more troublesome than the focus on black male criminality as the solution to the gang problem is the extent to which the debate ignores the roles of black women in gang life. The title of the well-known black feminist book, *All the Men Are Black, All the Women Are White, but Some of Us Are Brave,* describes black women's forgotten and endangered lives.[6] This essay attempts to demarginalize black women;[7] to bring to the fore their association with gangs not only as full-fledged gang members, but also as the mothers, sisters, daughters, wives, girlfriends, and comrades to male and female gang members. These women have the capacity to affect gang members on profoundly intimate levels. Therefore, black women must play a vital role in providing solutions to the gang problem. Not until we make a "deliberate choice to see the world from the standpoint of the oppressed"[8] can we

243

craft solutions to the "gang problem" that will impact on the entire community and thus have greater likelihood of success. After identifying the various roles that women play, this essay will suggest several comprehensive strategies for dealing with the dilemma.

FEMALES AND GANGS

There are at least six different ways to conceptualize black women's involvement with gangs.[9] First, black women belong to female gangs with their own set of rules and customs. Second, black women serve as female auxiliaries to male gangs. Third, black women are often female gangsters in coed gangs. Fourth, black women are often the girlfriends and occasionally the wives of gang members. Fifth, black women are often the mothers of a gang member's child or children. Finally, black women are the female blood relatives of gang members—mothers, sisters, and daughters. These roles frequently overlap or occur simultaneously, and represent the multiple identities of black women.[10]

FEMALE GANGS

Although there is insufficient data, it is estimated that 10 percent to 30 percent of the entire gang population is female.[11] Some of these women are members of all-female gangs, which are found in nearly every large city. Female gangs tend to be smaller and more dispersed than male gangs.[12] Like the male gangs, the female gangs claim their territory, wear colors and insignias, and fight with rival gangs.[13] Female gangs—although they commit less violent offenses than their male counterparts[14]— are increasingly involved in criminal activities, such as theft, narcotics sales, and prostitution.[15] Female gang members are as violent as males in their physical confrontations and turf wars. For example, a black female gang in Philadelphia, the Holy Whores, reportedly knifed and kicked pregnant women and also mutilated and scarred "cute" girls.[16]

Many social science researchers have attempted to identify the reasons children join gangs. Knowledge of these reasons helps policy makers and social service providers develop programs that are targeted at young people's needs. The classical theoretical explanations of juvenile gang involvement have focused primarily on males of various ethnicities, while feminist theories of female juvenile delinquency have focused primarily on white females. In this brief essay we cannot present a comprehensive explanation of black female gang participation. Since a theory of black female delinquency may involve aspects of classical, feminist, and Afrocentric approaches, a few of the most prominent theories will be discussed to promote an interest in developing a critical race feminist construct to deal with this issue.[17]

The 1936 classic study by Frederick Thrasher found that "the presence of adult crime influences gang behavior because many of the adults who have high status in the community are adult criminals."[18] This is especially true in today's inner-city communities, where the lack of resources and opportunities results in drug dealers and criminals who are idolized by some as role models because of their wealth and power.[19] Black girls also may perceive these men as potential protectors, father figures, and boyfriends.

Robert Merton's strain theory posits that a person's desire for status, money, possessions, and power pressures the individual to pursue these goals by any means possible. Those individuals lacking the skills and resources needed to attain these goals by legitimate means will turn to crime and delinquency to acquire them.[20] Under this theory, black youths—male and female—engage in gang behavior to attain wealth, power, and success.

Walter B. Miller's study found that gangs reflect lower-class subcultures and thus are not affected by traditional societal values. This subculture provides a basis for the gang's criminal behavior. Gang membership satisfies what Miller calls lower-class norms, which involve trouble, toughness, smartness, excitement, fate, and autonomy.[21] Thus, gang behavior is not deviant behavior, but is a norm of the particular subculture. The black gang subculture is exhibited in gangsta rap music by artists like Snoop Doggy Dog, Niggas with Attitude, and Tupac Shakur. The female role models are female gangsta rappers like Bitches with Problems, Ho's with Attitudes, and BOSS. This gang subculture is also reflected in the misogynist song by the rapper Apache, "I Want a Gangsta Bitch."

Albert Cohen's theory suggests that gangs give working-class youths a coping mechanism to deal with their "humiliation, frustration, anxiety, hostility, and bitterness toward the middle class."[22] Gangs express resentment and hostility by attacking middle-class values, such as the concept of private property, through graffiti, vandalism, and theft.[23] Under this theory, black gangsters, who commit criminal offenses and generate violence, are reacting to their subordinate position within American society. Black females, despite their predominance as the heads of households, remain at the bottom of employment and economic hierarchies, which only intensify their subordination. Thus, some black females may be acting out profound "spiritual injuries" when they join gangs.[24]

R. R. Kornhauser's disorganization theory posits that familial and community disarray contributes to gang violence. It is the gang that provides social relations and social structure.[25] As a result of the breakdown in inner-city communities, black juveniles may be attracted to gang life for its rules and structures. Gangs supply the family-like relationships, emotional support, and social controls that are lacking in many poverty-stricken urban communities.

Black researcher Useni Perkins placed African American youth at the center of his analysis. He argues that five factors make gangs appealing to black youths: sense of identity, sense of belonging, sense of power, sense of security, and sense of discipline.[26] When one or more of these elements is unattainable through traditional channels, some black youths feel compelled to seek them out through gang affiliation.

Feminist theories of female delinquency have developed to counter the male-centered theories. However, the feminist theories have analyzed delinquency from the white female perspective. Liberal feminists hypothesize that young women imitate male gang members in their desire to achieve the same goals pursued by males, that is, money, power, and status. The merger of gender roles has thus resulted in more female violent crime.[27] Radical feminists postulate that a girl's involvement in crime may be linked to the girl's undocumented status as a victim of physical and sexual abuse.[28] Further empirical research is needed for an exploration of how these and other feminist theories may have relevance for black female gang members.

FEMALE AUXILIARIES

Female gangs also form as adjuncts to male gangs. These female gangs are not independent, but are affiliated with and usually take their names from an established male group. The Crips in Los Angeles have female auxiliaries such as the Crippettes and Hooverettes. These auxiliary groups were thought to be the most common type of female gang.[29] In 1975, it was reported that half of the gangs in New York had female branches.[30]

While the female groups may not participate in all the activities of the male gang, their actions are influenced by the men.[31] Anne Campbell found that it is the "male gang that paves the way for the female affiliate and opens the door into many illegitimate opportunities."[32] The auxiliaries are a principal source of violence within the community because of their close affiliation with the male gangs. They are also responsible for hostile activities independent of the dominant group, including criminal behavior, turf wars, and group fights.

Many gangs consider black female gang members the "property" of the gang.[33] Patriarchal notions about "women's" roles and women's "proper place" are evident within the gang structure. Black male gang members, who are not able to exercise the traditional roles as head of household, breadwinner, or captain of industry, exert their unsatisfied sexual, financial, and emotional desires for control on the women in their lives, including female auxiliary members. The female auxiliary members often have to be sexually active with male members of the gang to prove their worthiness. These women are subjected to rape, gang bangs, and other group sexual activities. The female's status in the auxiliary group often depends on her ability to attract a high ranking male: an O.G.'s[34] woman has a higher status than a female only good for "running a train."[35]

COED GANGS

Black females also participate in sexually integrated gangs, usually in a subordinated role consistent with their perceived status as property.[36] These coed gangs function in the same manner as traditional gangs, allowing female participation in most of the gang's affairs. Yet the females are often excluded from the decision-making and planning aspects of gang activity.[37] Sometimes the female's function is purely sexual, servicing the needs of the male gang members.[38] Their initiations into the gang often require having sex with male gang members.[39] Female gang members frequently use sex to obtain gifts, money, and status in the gang hierarchy.[40]

GIRLFRIENDS AND WIVES

Girlfriends and wives are extremely influential women in male gang member's lives.[41] It is said that they are both the cause and the cure of much of the gang violence. These women, who may or may not be gang or auxiliary members, are often the source of provocation between gangs and the source of jealous rivalries within the gang. The women constitute the "prize" that men may be willing to die to secure.[42] Girlfriends and wives are also regarded as the male's property and may be subject to the same sort of sexual activity as female gang members and auxiliaries. A female's status within the gang world and broader community may be linked to the stature of her boyfriend or husband within the gang and whether he can protect her, provide for her, or keep her for himself. Girlfriends also actively or passively participate in the gang's criminal activities. These women have been known to hold drugs, guns, or money for gang members and also to have driven the "getaway" car during crimes and drive-by shootings.

Because of the high incarceration and mortality rates of black males and the breakdown of traditional family structures, there is an incredible shortage of black males in many urban centers.[43] Males have access to multiple females, with whom they can have varying levels of relationships. These relationships include one-night stands, occasional sexual encounters, nonexclusive dating, monogamous dating, and occasionally marriages.

These black women can have a positive influence on the gang member. Some black women have refused to date or marry a gang member, thereby forcing him to leave the gang if he wants to continue the relationship. Women also have persuaded their men to settle down in traditional, noncriminal lifestyles.[44] These women play a key role in convincing male gang members to avoid or cut down gang violence. One ex-gang member, who was married while still a member, said, "If it wasn't for her . . . , I'd be dead or in the penitentiary, or a whole lot of other people would be dead."[45] Moreover, having a wife and sometimes children fulfills the need that gang members have for a family, and the gang is no longer needed as a substitute.

MOTHERS OF GANG MEMBERS' CHILDREN

Females, whether they be wives, girlfriends, or one-night stands, are also the mothers of gang members' children. These gang members may have multiple children, either from the same woman or several different women. Many of these gang fathers see procreation as a powerful indicator of masculinity, and are proud of the number of children they have by different women. It is not uncommon to find that most black male gang members have at least one child by the age of twenty. A twenty-five-year-old father with seven children by seven different women asked Adrien Wing whether he should "give" his current girlfriend the baby she wanted.[46]

The women often raise the children alone with little or no contact and support from the father, who may be unknown, uninterested, incarcerated, unemployed, or deceased. If the father is relatively uninvolved, it may be because his pride in procreation does not extend to supporting the children he has sired. In many cases, the gang father has difficulty fulfilling this role as he has never been fathered himself.[47] Because of the precarious financial situation of most gang members, who may have poor educational skills and criminal records that render them unemployable, the gang member father cannot consistently provide financial support. For example, one father told Wing he was proud he had provided diapers that week for one of his five children. Welfare policies, which provide benefits and food stamps only to single mothers and children, provide an economic base, however inadequate, that the gang member cannot consistently replicate. In many instances, the gang member father has a nomadic lifestyle, and resides with various girlfriends, mothers of his children, and female relatives.[48] He may not fulfill his duties as a father because the mother does not inform him that he is a father.[49]

Some mothers of gang members' children are gang or auxiliary members themselves. The rapper Ice-T describes his daughter's mother as a "Criplette" who was "down" with the Hoover Crips when he got involved with her.[50] Many of these children will be prone to becoming gang members and criminals themselves. The absence or lack of contact with their own fathers, along with role models who are adult male criminals in ravaged ghetto communities, contributes to this condition.

Some gang members leave the gang life because of their concerns for their children. "Monster" Kody Scott, a former Crip, stated in his autobiography, "To continue banging would be a betrayal first of my children, who now depend on me for guidance, morals and strength."[51] Black mothers of gang members' children often do have a positive influence by encouraging gang members to take responsibility for their actions and be fathers to their sons and daughters.

RELATIVES: MOTHERS, SISTERS, AND DAUGHTERS

Black women are also the mothers, sisters, and daughters of gang members. Mothers potentially play the most important role in a gang member's life, since they are the ones primarily responsible for the transmission of morals and values. They are the ones responsible for supervising and educating these children, especially because there is a shortage of fathers. Often these women are the only individuals who have some influence over their gang member children. Tough gangsters who kill at the slightest provocation may allow their mothers to hit or berate them for misbehaving. More often than not, these women are single parents struggling at the poverty level and in violent surroundings.[52] These mothers simply cannot lavish emotional, financial, and spiritual attention on their children to the extent they wish, as their basic physical survival is at stake. They may be overburdened with working a job to support their children and working within the home to care for the children; and they simply cannot keep track of the children's activities outside the home. Others are doing everything they can for their children and are then shocked, appalled, and finally resigned when street life claims him or her.[53] Sometimes the child is already too involved with the gang and thus may ignore, attack, or even kill his or her mother if she attempts to exert some influence. Some mothers are involved in criminal behavior such as drug use, drug sales, or prostitution, and they are too overwhelmed by their own personal situations to deal with their children.[54]

Some researchers have stated that parents of gang members probably will not be part of the solution.[55] It seems intuitive to us, however, that these women must be included in strategies to end gangs. They can play a positive role by preventing or discouraging their children from joining gangs. One gang member encouraged mothers to exert control over their children who are gang members: "You have weight with your children, you just don't know it."[56]

The sisters and daughters of gang members can be influential in persuading the gang member to avoid violence and to leave the gang. By giving the gang member a sense of family, the sisters and daughters will be helping to diminish dependency on gang association. All these females can contribute to the solution of the gang problem by helping to keep their children, siblings, and parents out of gangs. Because of the difficult conditions they live under, mothers cannot be expected to exhort their gang-affected children in a vacuum. Their efforts must be tied to practical and effective programs providing solutions to the gang problem.

SOLUTIONS: IT TAKES A VILLAGE

There is an African proverb, "It takes a whole village to raise one child." Solutions to the gang problem will have to involve the entire American village. Only well-funded, highly coordinated, multidimensional, and community-based approaches will limit and prevent gang violence.[57] Black women must be involved as organizers, administrators, and participants in these programs. Two possible directions that these programs could take are to focus on the gang-affiliated female or to focus on the general conditions within the community and the various roles of females.

First, programs must be implemented that target gang members and at-risk youths. This type of strategy must take into account the economic, social, and cultural contexts of the gang-affected youth. One such program is a preventive and rehabilitative program known as Amer-I-Can. It is a life skills management curriculum that was founded in 1988 by football Hall of Famer, actor, and activist Jim Brown.

Currently operating in a dozen states, Amer-I-Can is suitable for all types of people, but it works particularly well with gang members, juvenile offenders, at-risk youth, and adult prisoners. Females have been involved not only as participants but also as teachers, consultants, and as the executive director.[58] The Amer-I-Can program is designed to assist in the development of personal skills in eight critical areas: motivation and attitudes, goal setting, problem solving and decision making, emotional control, family relationships, financial stability, effective communication, and employment search and retention. The training methods are based on peer group relationships and lesson repetition. By introducing self-determination techniques, by motivating people to have attainable goals, and by showing them how to achieve success and financial stability, this type of program has proven extremely effective.

Another program, the federally funded Youth Gang Drug Prevention Program, has targeted females at risk. Several cities' programs have focused on black females.[59] Preventive programs such as this, which specifically address the roles of female offenders, are examples of a multidimensional approach that is needed to resolve the gang problem.

Second, comprehensive, multifaceted programs must be targeted at improving the status of black women in all their roles. Young women must be given educational and employment opportunities to lower the risk that they will become involved with criminal gang activity. Mothers must be given adequate resources so that they will be better able to raise their children in a caring and supportive environment, eliminating or at least lessening the need for gang involvement. Linking child care, health care, education, job training, and positive emotional support will make a difference. An example of this type of approach was passed in New Jersey as the Hispanic Women's Demonstration Resource Centers Act.[60] Some of the services provided at the centers are English language skills; bicultural resources; assertiveness, survival, and coping skills; tax, insurance, and business assistance; legal assistance for domestic violence; and family planning.[61] Unfortunately, the New Jersey program received only $400,000. If such programs were fully funded, they could make an immense impact on the lives of women who interact with gang members.

Effective solutions to gang violence involve placing black women at the center rather than at the margins of the analysis. As we have discussed, these women have multiple identities and play many roles, inextricably linking them to the problems and also to the solutions of gang violence and crime. Through programs that are targeted at the black woman as gang member, mate, and family member, we can provide these women with the resources they need to improve their lives and the lives of their children. In this way, we can improve the quality of life in the American village and help raise our children free from the violence and crime that plague us.

NOTES

This chapter is based on research Adrien Wing has completed that will be incorporated into a book, Jim Brown and Adrien K. Wing, Gangs: Beyond Bloods and Crips (working title).

1. For a general discussion of gangs, see Martin Sanchez Jankowski, Islands in the Street: Gangs and American Urban Society (1991). For a discussion of Asian gangs, see Ko-Lin Chin, *Chinese Gangs and Extortion, in* Gangs in America 129 (C. Ronald Huff ed., 1990); Betty Lee Sung, Gangs in New York's Chinatown (1977); James Diego Vigil & Steven Chong Yun, *Vietnamese Youth Gangs in Southern California, in* Gangs in America, *supra,* at 146. For a general discussion of black gangs, see Leon Bing, Do or Die (1991); Claude Brown, Manchild in the Promised Land (1965); John Hagedorn, People and Folks: Gangs, Crime, and the

Underclass in a Rustbelt City (1988); R. Lincoln Keiser, The Vice Lords: Warriors of the Streets (1969); Useni Eugene Perkins, Explosion of Chicago's Black Street Gangs: 1900 to Present (1987); Carl Taylor, Dangerous Society (1990). For a general discussion of Latino gangs, see Joan W. Moore, Going Down to the Barrio: Homeboys and Homegirls in Change (1991); Felix Padilla, The Gang as an American Enterprise (1992); James Vigil, Barrio Gangs: Street Life and Identity in Southern California (1988).

2. *See* Sanyika Shakur, Monster: The Autobiography of an L.A. Gang Member (1993); Bing, *supra* note 1; Yusuf Jah & Sister Shah'Keyah, Uprising: Crips and Bloods Tell the Story of America's Youth in the Crossfire (1995).

3. *Colors* is one of the movies that focuses on Bloods and Crips.

4. A study released on October 5, 1995 by the Justice Department showed that one-third of black men aged twenty to twenty-nine are incarcerated or court supervised. Fox Butterfield, *More Blacks in Their 20's Have Trouble with the Law,* N.Y. Times, Oct. 5, 1995, at A5. Only five years ago the corresponding figure was a slightly less startling one-fourth of young black men. Bill McAllister, *Study: 1 in 4 Young Black Men Is in Jail or Court Supervised: Author Warns of Risk of Losing Entire Generation,* Wash. Post, Feb. 27, 1990, at A3.

5. Kenneth Cooper, *GOP's Beef with Beleaguered Crime Bill Shifts to "Pork,"* Wash. Post, Aug. 14, 1994, at A17. The 1994 Crime Bill provided for a total of $30.2 billion to be spent; only $7 billion will be spent on prevention programs. Many legislators thought this was too much and called it "pork" spending.

6. All the Men Are Black, All the Women Are White, but Some of Us Are Brave (Gloria Hull et al. eds., 1982).

7. Kimberlé Crenshaw has developed the notion of demarginalizing the experiences of women of color. Kimberlé Williams Crenshaw, *Demarginalizing the Intersection of Race and Sex: A Black Feminist Critique of Antidiscrimination Doctrine,* Feminist Theory and Antiracist Politics, 1989 U. Chi. Legal F. 139.

8. Mari Matsuda, *When the First Quail Calls: Multiple Consciousness as Jurisprudential Method,* 11 Women's Rts. L. Rep. 7, 9 (1989).

9. We leave to others to characterize how these roles may apply to other ethnic groups. For more information on females in gangs, see Anne Campbell, The Girls in the Gang (1984); Mary Harris, Cholas: Latino Girls and Gangs (1988); K. Hansen, Rebels in the Streets: The Story of New York Girl Gangs (1964); Moore, *supra* note 1; John Quicker, Homegirls: Characterizing Chicana Gangs (1983).

10. Mari Matsuda speaks of multiple consciousness that women of color often possess. Matsuda, *supra* note 8. The constant shifting back and forth between levels of consciousness "produces sometimes madness, sometimes genius, sometimes both." *Id.* at 8.

11. Irving Spergel, The Youth Gang Problem: A Community Approach 57 (1995).

12. *Id.* at 101; *see also* Waln K. Brown, *Black Female Gangs in Philadelphia,* 21 Int'l J. Offender Therapy & Comp. Criminology 221 (1978); Campbell, *supra* note 9.

13. Jack E. Bynum & William E. Thompson, Juvenile Delinquency: A Sociological Approach 295 (1989). In one 1992 study there were ninety-nine independent female gangs found in thirty-five different jurisdictions. G. David Curry et al., Gang Crime and Law Enforcement Recordkeeping (1994).

14. Spergel, *supra* note 11, at 57.

15. *See* Campbell, *supra* note 9; Carl Taylor, Girls, Gangs, Women and Drugs (1993); and Harris, *supra* note 9. For more on black female criminality, see Regina Austin, *"The Black*

Community," Its Lawbreakers, and a Politics of Identification, 65 S. Cal. L. Rev. 1769, 1791 (1992).

16. Brown, *supra* note 12, at 223.

17. The authors plan to develop an Afrofeminist theory in a future law review article.

18. Frederick Thrasher, The Gang (1936).

19. Taylor, *supra* note 15, at 9.

20. Robert Merton, *Social Structure and Anomie,* 3 Am. Soc. Rev. 5 (1938).

21. Walter B. Miller, *Lower Class Culture as a Generating Milieu of Gang Delinquency,* 14 J. Soc. Issues 5 (1958). Miller's concept fits in with the "culture of poverty" theories that were the center of debates on the status of blacks in the 1960s. *See, e.g.,* Daniel Patrick Moynihan, The Negro Family: The Case for National Action (1965). It is expressed today in "cultural deficiency" models. *See, e.g.,* Maxine Baca Zinn, *Family, Race and Poverty in the Eighties,* 14 Signs 856 (1989). To contest these theories, the structural-behavioral theorists posit unemployment, poverty, and perhaps gender and race oppression as the causes of problems confronting the black community. *See, e.g.,* William Julius Wilson, The Truly Disadvantaged (1987). Some of these theorists then posit that structural oppression has led to the emergence of a deviant culture, which some say may have some positive, rational, and dynamic qualities. *See, e.g.,* Richard Majors & Janet Mancini Billson, Cool Pose: The Dilemmas of Black Manhood in America (1992).

22. A. K. Cohen, Delinquent Boys: The Culture of the Gang (1955).

23. *Id.*

24. Patricia Williams of Columbia Law School developed the concept of spirit-murder to refer to racism's psychological effects. Patricia Williams, *Spirit-Murdering the Messenger: The Discourse of Fingerpointing as the Law's Response to Racism,* 42 U. Miami L. Rev. 127, 129 (1987) (also chapter 28 in this volume). Wing took the concept a step further to characterize the combined psychological impact of racism/sexism as a series of spirit injuries. Adrien Katherine Wing, *Brief Reflections toward a Multiplicative Theory and Praxis of Being,* 6 Berkeley Women's L.J. 181, 186 (1990–91) (also chapter 3 in this volume).

25. R. R. Kornhauser, Social Sources of Delinquency (1978); Irving A. Spergel, *Violent Gangs in Chicago: In Search of Social Policy,* 60 Soc. Service Rev. 94 (1984).

26. Perkins, *supra* note 1.

27. Freda Adler, Sisters in Crime (1975).

28. Meda Chesney-Lind, Girls' Crime and Women's Place: Toward a Feminist Model of Female Delinquency, Paper Presented at the Annual Meeting of the American Society of Criminology (Nov. 10–14, 1987), *in* Clemens Bartollas, Juvenile Delinquency 248 (3d ed. 1993).

29. Campbell, *supra* note 9, at 23.

30. *Id.*

31. Carl Taylor, *Youth Gangs Organize for Power, Money, in* School Safety (1988).

32. Campbell, *supra* note 9, at 32.

33. Jankowski, *supra* note 1, at 146; Austin, *supra* note 15, at 1785 ("In the mythology of black banditry, women—like cars, clothing and jewelry—are prized possessions.").

34. Original Gangster, term for a senior gang member.

35. This means a woman who is only good for gangbanging or casual sex.

36. Campbell, *supra* note 9.

37. Lee Bowker & Malcolm Klein, *Female Participation in Delinquent Gang Motivation, in*

Adolescence 15 (1980). Females are seen as secondary within the gang by the gang members themselves and also by most researchers. This marginalizing of the female role is sometimes attributed to the cultural bias of the predominantly male researchers. Campbell, *supra* note 9, at 27.

38. Frederick Thrasher, The Gang: A Study of 1,313 Gangs in Chicago (1927).

39. William Gale, The Compound (1977).

40. Daniel J. Monti, Wannabe: Gangs in Suburbs and Schools 77 (1994).

41. In the black urban centers, marriage is rare, and most families consist of women with children, from one or more fathers. From 1959 to 1987, the proportion of black families headed by women rose from 46 percent to 74 percent. Audrey Rowe, *The Feminization of Poverty: An Issue for the 90's,* 4 Yale J.L. & Feminism 73, 74 (1991). *See also* Barbara Omolade, *The Unbroken Circle: A Historical and Contemporary Study of Black Single Mothers and Their Families,* 3 Wis. Women's L.J. 239 (1987).

42. Campbell, *supra* note 9, at 31.

43. Jonathan Kozol, Savage Inequalities 15 (1991) (describing East St. Louis, Missouri, where the decimation of the men is nearly total).

44. Spergel, *supra* note 11, at 109. Lee Bowker et al., *Female Participation in Delinquent Gang Activity, in* Adolescence, *supra* note 37, at 509. Shakur, *supra* note 2; Sanyika Shakur, a.k.a. Monster, credits his wife with helping him turn his life around.

45. Jah & Shah'Keyah, *supra* note 2, at 139, interview with General Robert Lee (ex-gang member) and his wife of twenty-one years, Shelia.

46. Adrien Wing, Interview with Gang Member, in Los Angeles (June 1994).

47. Adrien Wing, Interview with Rudolf "Rockhead" Johnson, in Los Angeles (June 1994). Johnson, a former Compton Crip, was one of eight children by seven fathers. He has never met his father.

48. *See* Campbell, *supra* note 9, at 242.

49. One ex-gang member found out just recently that he is the father of a seventeen year old son. Jah & Shah'Keyah, *supra* note 2, at 155, interview with Godfather Jimel Barnes.

50. *Id.* at 9, foreword by Ice-T.

51. Shakur, *supra* note 2, at 357.

52. Dorothy E. Roberts, *The Value of Black Mother's Work,* 26 Conn. L. Rev. 871 (1994) (also chapter 38 in this volume) (discussing the stereotype of welfare dependent mothers and their contributions to society as caregivers).

53. See Bing, *supra* note 1, at 183, for description of Mrs. Lunceford, who became resigned to her son G-Roc's personal choice to be a gang member.

54. One of Carl Taylor's case studies, Erica, demonstrates this phenomenon. Erica is a twenty-three-year-old mother of five who is living with her boyfriend, selling drugs out of the house. Taylor, *supra* note 15, at 59.

55. Catherine Conley, Street Gangs: What They Are and What Is Done about Them 54 (1991) (draft).

56. Jah & Shah'Keyah, *supra* note 2, at 62, interview with OG "Red".

57. Bartollas, *supra* note 28, at 350.

58. Wing is a consultant for Amer-I-Can. Other successful gang-oriented programs include Mad Dads of Omaha, Nebraska, the Chicago Intervention Network, and the Alternatives to Gang Membership Program of Paramount, California. For a description of the latter two programs, see Bartollas, *supra* note 28, at 350.

59. G. David Curry, *Gang Related Violence,* Clearinghouse Rev. 443, 447 (Special Issue 1994).

60. See Gloria Bonilla-Santiago, *Legislating Progress for Hispanic Women in New Jersey,* Social Work, May 1989, at 270, for discussion of the process of enacting this legislation (Pub. L. No. 87–378 (1988)). Wing refers to programs such as this as examples of multiplicative legal praxis. Wing, *supra* note 24, at 198.

61. Bonilla-Santiago, *supra* note 60. The centers also provide job training, educational evaluations, career information, legal assistance, health care information concerning substance abuse, nutrition, and mental health, and child care information.

31 | Scarlett's Code, Susan's Actions

Sherri L. Burr

I first read *Gone with the Wind* in my senior year in high school. I became fascinated by Margaret Mitchell's description of an era long since passed and her characterization of a woman with grit and determination who conquered the ruins of her shattered life to avoid starvation. When I saw the movie later that year, I told my Advanced Placement English teacher that I thought Clark Gable as Rhett Butler was cute. "Cute! Cute!" she exclaimed in horror upon hearing such a mundane word applied to the dashing Gable.

Seventeen years later, I found myself teaching in the South and similarly horrified upon hearing certain words from my students and from a young woman named Susan Smith who invaded my life through a television screen. During the first days of a new semester, I learn the names of my students by asking them a few questions about themselves. I asked second- and third-year law students at the University of Tennessee College of Law what was their favorite book and movie, and if they could have lived at any other time in history when would it have been.

Grisham's several works topped the author and movie charts, followed by Margaret Mitchell's *Gone with the Wind*. Most white students said they would have liked to have lived in the 1950s, a time of relative peace and prosperity. Most black students said they would have preferred the 1960s, a time of revolution and change. One white man said he wanted to have lived in the 1800s as an Indian fighter. And one white woman, whose favorite book and movie was *Gone with the Wind,* said she would have wanted to live in the "pre-Civil War South on a plantation when life was easy."

I thanked the students for their honesty, though their comments stung. As the great-great-granddaughter of a Cherokee woman, I associate the 1800s with the pain that my ancestors endured as they were removed from an area where Georgia borders with Tennessee. For me, their misery has no Custer-related romance. Additionally, my paternal great-grandfather was a black man born in the South in 1863. His life and that of his parents were far from easy. While I was immensely entertained by *Gone with the Wind,* I never considered Scarlett's life either before, during, or following the Civil War as one to be imitated, for the "easy" part of that life was obtained at the expense of a difficult existence for many blacks.

Conceivably, this Tennessee student associated Scarlett's life in the pre-Civil War South with a time when life for white women was easy. In the first hundred pages or so of Margaret Mitchell's mammoth novel, Scarlett dances and flirts, pouts and whines, eats abundantly, and dresses divinely. Indeed, in those early days, Scarlett "never raised her hand even to pick up her discarded stockings from the floor or to tie the laces of her slippers." [1]

But the zenith of plantation society lasted approximately forty years and thus, as a historical time frame, was almost as short as the pages devoted to it in Mitchell's novel. I thought Scarlett as a fictional character was a marvelous creation because she was so flawed. When Civil War life became difficult, Scarlett astonished me when she declared, "If I have to lie, steal, cheat, or kill—as God is my witness—I'll never be hungry again." [2] True to her word, she lies to steal her sister's beau, Mr. Kennedy, cheats customers, and kills a Yankee cavalryman who she thinks is going to steal her food.

Scarlett felt protected by custom to lie. Mitchell writes, "She knew she was perfectly safe in lying. . . . Southern chivalry protected her. A lady could lie about a gentlemen but a Southern gentleman could not lie about a lady or, worse still, call the lady a liar." [3]

Perhaps Susan Smith believed that the same Southern chivalry would shield her from the consequences of her actions. Like many Americans in late October 1994, I watched television in fascination and puzzlement as Susan Smith cried and begged a generic black carjacker to return her two sons. Occasionally, she spoke to her sons, always looking at the ground instead of at the camera "Y'all be good now. Your mama loves you."

I wondered why Susan Smith's body language was so curious—usually mothers in her situation look directly into the television camera. Nine days after she had initially reported her car and sons missing, I knew the answer. Susan Smith's sons were dead, victims of her own hands.

Susan Smith obviously did not expect reporters and law enforcement officials to investigate her story. After Scarlett lied again and again, with only her slave mammy's occasional looks as a warning, why shouldn't Susan?

Eventually, Scarlett and Susan became outcasts for doing things that Southern women were not supposed to do. Atlantans gossiped about Scarlett for having "unsexed" herself by running a store and a mill, and bargaining with the best of the men. If Scarlett had run the mill into the ground, her social peers might have forgiven her ungenderlike behavior. But Scarlett succeeded, running her business better than most men ran theirs.

Even before Susan Smith became a national figure, she was described as "someone who was more or less a hunk of hell." [4] Her ex-husband David wrote that when they worked at Winn-Dixie supermarket, "[e]veryone talked about Susan at the store, the stack boys and baggers and clerks. . . . Susan was a 'slut' or a 'whore,' dating a married man who was old enough to be her father, and sneaking around behind his back with someone else."[5] Her flirtations ended when both men were transferred to other stores and Susan attempted suicide by swallowing a nonlethal dose of Anacin.

South Carolinians were willing to support Susan when they believed her time of terror was wrought by a black man who she said had stolen her car and kidnapped her children. Across the country, approximately five hundred black men were detained on suspicion of carjacking and kidnapping, though fortunately none were left swinging from trees.

The South Carolinians who supported Susan were shocked when she confessed to having pushed her burgundy Mazda with her kids strapped into their car seats into John D. Long Lake, and they subsequently denounced her. For Susan Smith brought shame upon their Southern town; women are not supposed to kill their kids.

Scarlett and Susan ultimately succumbed to their web of deceit spun in their efforts to capture men who could not fully return their love. Scarlett lost Rhett, whom she really loved, because she deceived herself as to her desire for Ashley Wilkes. By killing her sons, Susan sought the freedom to marry Tom Findlay, the son of a wealthy merchant who had told her that he was not ready to become a father. When Susan's race fabrications could no longer shield her from the consequences of her horrifying actions, she lost her freedom and almost lost her life.

Susan Smith enhanced a visit to the South that taught me much about race relations. Susan carried her culture's tolerance of lies about black men to its logical extreme and proved the pervasiveness of stereotypes associated with black males.

Would Susan have received the national and international media attention if she had said that a white male stole her children? I think not, as evidenced by the few reporters who covered her trial compared to the huge number who covered her initial pitiful wails for the return of her children. Without a black perpetrator, Susan joined other nameless women who have committed infanticide.

After finding Susan guilty of committing two murders, a jury of her peers voted to sentence her to life in prison. I wondered whether that Southern jury would have been so generous if the facts had been as she said; if, for example, a black man had kidnapped her children and they were eventually found at the bottom of a lake. Would that black man have received life in prison? Our culture is not race-blind.

Perhaps in another era, the 1950s to which my white Tennessee students so long to return, Susan Smith would have been spared the consequences of her actions. A Mark Fuhrman-type police officer would have rounded up a usual suspect and forced a confession, which an all-white male jury would have used to convict. The hapless black male would have gone to jail, if he were lucky, a victim of his race and gender.

My white Tennessee students' sentiments notwithstanding, I am thankful that the 1950s and the pre-Civil War South are no more.

Even Scarlett's second most memorable line, "I'll think of it all tomorrow. . . . After all, tomorrow is another day,"[6] is appropriate for Susan. Her life spared, Susan will have many tomorrows to ponder her crime and suffer the consequences. From her jail cell, she told her visiting ex-husband, "David, when I get out . . . *if* I get out of here, I hope that maybe we can get back together and have more kids."[7]

NOTES

1. Margaret Mitchell, Gone with the Wind 421 (1936).

2. This is the line Scarlett spoke in the movie version. In the book, Scarlett said, "If I have to steal or kill—as God is my witness, I'm never going to be hungry again." *Id.* at 421.

3. *Id.* at 654.

4. David Smith & Carol Calef, Beyond All Reason: My Life with Susan Smith 34 (1995).

5. *Id.* at 35.

6. Mitchell, *supra* note 1, at 1024.

7. Smith & Calef, *supra* note 4, at 244.

32

Domestic Violence against Latinas by Latino Males: An Analysis of Race, National Origin, and Gender Differentials

Jenny Rivera

Although the general issue of domestic violence has received tremendous attention, the specific issue of violence inflicted on Latinas by their spouses and male partners has not been comprehensively examined and discussed within the mainstream battered women's movement or in literature on domestic violence. This specific issue deserves consideration because differences of gender, race, and national origin shape Latinas' experiences with domestic violence.

This chapter represents an effort to shed light on domestic violence in the lives of Latinas within the Latino community. It examines the various factors unique to the political, social, and economic status of Latinas and includes a critique of the most significant current efforts currently within the legal and social service sectors to assist survivors of domestic violence. In addition, this chapter explores the role of culture, community, and language, as points of departure for recognizing the experiences of Latinas.

BACKGROUND

SELECTED DEMOGRAPHIC AND STATISTICAL DATA

Without an understanding of the economic, social, and political factors that impact on Latinas' lives, an analysis of domestic violence against Latinas would be incomplete. The data reveal that the Latino community is in a precarious economic position. Moreover, statistics specific to Latinas indicate that, as a class, they are particularly susceptible to external economic fluctuations and occupy a marginal financial existence within the market economy structure. Latinas have lower earning potential and power compared to all men, regardless of race or national origin. Latinas are in an acutely tenuous position because of their low rates of educational attainment and their high rates of sole stewardship of families. Moreover, Latinas are not merely unemployed and underemployed, but also unemployable at higher rates.[1]

This economic gap is not a unilateral problem of patriarchal market structures; Latinas also have a lower earning status among women. Thus, the interplay and intersection of race and gender issues act dynamically on Latinas, greatly influencing their experiences and forging their marginalized economic, political, and social status.

STEREOTYPES BASED ON RACE AND NATIONAL ORIGIN: "EL MACHO" AND THE SEXY LATINA

Historically, Latinos have been stereotyped as violent and alien. This caricature of the Latino has developed during the past century, and non-Latino society today continues to express and exploit inaccurate images of Latinos and Latino family life.

Popular myth has become accepted as truth; Latino males are believed to be irrational and reactive. The standard description of Latino males as hot-blooded, passionate, and prone to emotional outbursts is legendary. "Macho" is the accepted—and expected—single-word description synonymous with Latino men and male culture.

The outer boundaries of stereotypes and expectations of Latinas are emphasized when the image of the Latina is juxtaposed against this stereotype or "profile" of the Latino male. Latinas are presented as both innocent virgins and sexy vixens.[2] The Latina is regarded as accepting of the patriarchal structure within her community.[3] Accustomed to a male-centered community, the Latina is constructed as docile and domestic.[4] In order to satisfy her hot-blooded, passionate partner, however, the Latina must also be sensual and sexually responsive.

The intersection of gender, national origin, and race denies Latinas a self-defined, experientially based feminist portrait. Those within the Latino community expect Latinas to be traditional, and to exist solely within the Latino family structure. A Latina must serve as a daughter, a wife, and a parent, and must prioritize the needs of family members above her own. She is the foundation of the family unit. She is treasured as a self-sacrificing woman who will always look to the needs of others before her own. The influence of Catholicism throughout Latin America solidifies this image within the community, where Latinas are expected to follow dogma and to be religious, conservative, and traditional in their beliefs.[5]

The proliferation of stereotypes, which are integral to institutionalized racism, obstructs the progress and mobility of Latinas. Assumptions about Latinas' intellectual abilities and competence are formed on the basis of stereotypes and justified by reference to poor educational attainment statistics. Unless these myths and misconceptions are revealed and dispelled, the reality of Latinas as targets of Latino violence will remain unexplored, and Latinas' critical problems will remain unsolved.

STRATEGIES IN RESPONSE TO VIOLENCE AGAINST WOMEN

LEGAL INITIATIVES IN RESPONSE TO VIOLENCE AGAINST WOMEN

Legislation and Law Enforcement

To evaluate the effectiveness of state and local legislation, we must consider the numerous obstacles Latinas must surmount in order to exercise their rights to security and protection. First, state law enforcement officers and judicial personnel continue to reflect the Anglo male society.[6] Latinos and bilingual personnel are rarely found within the legal system, and women continue to represent only a small percentage of the police force.

Second, the protection or sanctions set forth in state laws notwithstanding, domestic violence legislation remains susceptible to poor enforcement by police and judicial personnel. Indeed, one study in Milwaukee revealed that 95 percent of domestic violence cases were not prosecuted. Thus, even in states with a legal basis for prosecuting batterers, it remains incumbent on women's advocates to monitor the utilization and enforcement of these hard-won legal rights.

Law enforcement officials' failure to respond appropriately to violence against women has received harsh criticism, as it negatively impacts on women and on efforts geared toward ending domestic violence.[7] The general discourse surrounding appropriate techniques and mechanisms for ensuring women's protection have failed to address Latinas as a specific group.

Various reforms have been suggested and implemented to ensure that police officers adequately respond to violence against women. Reforms are guided by the social construct of law enforcement officials' roles as peacemakers and protectors of the common good. The idealized image of the police officer as a kind governmental guardian, however, is not a common experience among ethnic groups or whites in this country.

Latinos in the United States have had a long, acrimonious history of interaction with local police and federal law enforcement agencies.[8] The history of racism and current racial tensions affect the success of any domestic violence enforcement strategy. For example, Latinas are suspicious of police, who have acted in a violent and repressive manner toward the community at large. In addition, a Latina must decide whether to invoke assistance from an outsider who may not look like her, sound like her, speak her language, or share any of her cultural values.

The limitations of domestic violence enforcement strategies—which justify Latinas' suspicions, hesitance, and concerns—can be addressed through comprehensive, intensive education of both enforcement personnel and the Latino community about domestic violence and arrest policies. Officials must develop such education strategies with input from community-based organizations and Latino advocates. Otherwise, education programs will reflect ingrained stereotypes and replicate the same problems that the programs are designed to address. To be successful, community education projects must be founded and located within the target communities. Advocates and members of community-based organizations should set the pace and the tone of these projects. These leaders should ensure that the projects are culturally specific and reflect the community's level of knowledge and sensitivity about domestic violence. Latina advocates must be at the forefront of these efforts to ensure that patriarchal structures are not integrated into the dialogue.

A second factor affecting current enforcement strategies is the failure of activists to consider the impact of racist attitudes on police behavior. Officers often fail to make an arrest, minimize the seriousness of the situation, or treat the woman as if she were responsible for the violence. Battered women's advocates have criticized male police officers for their sympathetic attitudes toward batterers. This criticism, however, reveals a major flaw in the approach of the activists: such an approach does not consider the race of the batterer, which is a relevant factor in the police response to a domestic violence situation. The history of aggression toward Latino males by police officers cannot be ignored, nor can the police's collegial mentality of "them against us" be denied in an assessment of institutional enforcement. There may be a sense among police officers that violent behavior is commonplace and acceptable within the Latino community, and that both men and women expect Latinos to react physically in situations of domestic conflict.

Arguably, a mandatory arrest policy represents one solution to this problem. Restricting a police officer's discretion by requiring an arrest in all cases where probable cause exists would minimize the disparate treatment Latinos receive. Under such a policy, Latinas would receive fairer treatment in response to their requests for assistance. By focusing on the ultimate arrest of the batterer, however, a mandatory arrest policy ignores the dynamics among police officials, Latinas, and batterers.

The history of police abuse toward the Latino community makes the content of the interaction a relevant issue. If a Latina or her male partner is physically or verbally abused during the arrest, or if she is not given any further information concerning her rights or available support services, a Latina gains only a temporary benefit. Nevertheless, some activists argue that a mandatory arrest policy can empower women by providing them with some control over their situation.

Several aspects of the Latinas' status, however, diminish the possible empowering effects of a mandatory arrest policy. First, Latinas face the precarious, often untenable situation of the "double bind"—empowerment through the disempowerment of a male member of the community. The internal conflict and external pressure to cast police officials as outsiders, hostile to the community, frustrates the development of Latinas' empowerment. Second, when the officer does not speak Spanish and the woman speaks little or no English, the empowerment potential again is diminished. Third, evidence suggests that some police officers react to such arrest policies through retaliatory conduct by arresting both the man and the woman—so-called dual arrests.[9] Empowerment is unlikely when women are treated as if they have acted illegally, are as culpable as their batterers, or cannot be believed. Finally, subsequent official responses, as well as resources available to the woman, determine her ability to end the violence and take control of her situation.[10] Latinas have neither access to, nor the benefit of, extensive resources to ensure their safety.[11]

If a Latina decides to go beyond the perimeters of her community and seek assistance from outsiders—persons already considered representatives of institutional oppression—the community may view her acts as a betrayal. A Latina, therefore, may tolerate abuse rather than call for outside help. This hesitance to seek assistance provides the community with an excuse for ignoring or denying violence against Latinas, as well as for trivializing and resisting Latina activists' efforts to create a community strategy to end the violence.

The Criminal Justice System

Many of the same concerns and issues, manifested in the development of policies designed to ensure proper police enforcement, also exist with respect to the role of the prosecutor's office and the judiciary. The Latino community's long-standing fear that, in general, Latinos are prosecuted more frequently and more vigorously than whites mitigates perceptions that Latinos will be treated less harshly because the crime involves domestic violence. In order for Latinas to feel that they have been treated justly—and to give them actual just treatment—reforms must address traditional institutional racist structures.

There are numerous obstacles, based on language and culture, that must be removed in order for a Latina to use the criminal justice system effectively and ensure a criminal prosecution against her batterer. First, the shortage of bilingual and bicultural personnel—prosecutors, judges, clerks, and psychologists, all of whom are crucial and can influence the ultimate outcome of a Latina's case—creates a system unprepared for and unwilling to address claims by Latinas. Second, Latinas have limited resources to fill the gaps in available support services to assist them.

Third, Latinas face racial and ethnic barriers. Latinas receive different treatment because of stereotypes and myths about Latinas and about Latinos generally. Latinas are devalued and dehumanized in this process, having no connection to those who have been assigned to prosecute and adjudicate their complaints.

Fourth, the "cultural defense" raised by men in response to prosecution for killing their wives represents another barrier to Latinas.[12] The defendant's theory in each of these cases is that violence against women, or the particular violent act at issue, is sanctioned by the culture and may, in fact, be a recognized cultural norm. Although this defense seeks to mitigate the punishment of the defendant, it serves only to promote violence within the community.

The cultural defense tactic's fundamental premise—that a particular norm or set of norms is culturally inherent to an identifiable group of persons—is problematic, because defining and identifying culture, or specific aspects of culture, is difficult. A survivor's response that the conduct is certainly not "cultural" is equally credible.

Furthermore, even if violent actions against women are inherent to a particular culture in certain situations, such conduct or norms are often based on patriarchal structures. Legitimizing violent actions as cultural norms only reinforces patriarchy, and would only lead to further abuse of women. The actions must also be rejected because they run counter to a legal system allegedly founded on the equality of all individuals.

SOCIAL SERVICES

Any legal initiatives designed to address domestic violence must be complemented by social services and programs devised to address the economic, social, psychological, and emotional needs of women seeking to escape or reduce the violence in their lives. These services include counseling, assistance in securing entitlements and health coverage, and temporary or permanent housing for women who leave their homes.[13] Because of linguistic, cultural, and institutional barriers, Latinas have limited access to such services. These social services are especially critical for Latinas, whose access to and utilization of judicial and law enforcement remedies are also limited.

In general, there are not enough battered women's shelters. For every woman who seeks shelter, five are turned away, and 95 percent of shelters do not accept women with children.[14] Moreover, some Latinas have been turned away from shelters because they speak little or no English. Indeed, the lack of bilingual and bicultural personnel among these service providers represents a major barrier to Latinas' access to programs and shelters.

Shelters without bilingual and bicultural personnel claim that they would do a disservice to Latinas by accepting them, because the language barrier would prevent personnel from providing Latinas with adequate services. Latinas are therefore denied access to shelters on the basis of national origin. Unfortunately, the shelter is often the only resource available to Latinas, thus compounding the negative impact of this exclusionary practice.

When they are accepted into a shelter, Latinas find themselves in foreign and unfamiliar surroundings, because a shelter rarely reflects a Latina's culture and language. For purposes of safety, women are often placed in shelters outside their community, which contributes to Latinas' sense of loneliness and isolation. Without bilingual and bicultural personnel and a familiar community environment, these shelters can provide only the barest services and temporary shelter. Insensitivity based on racism or on a lack of knowledge about or exposure to other cultures, by both shelter personnel and other residents, further isolates Latinas and escalates their sense of alienation from the shelter, personnel, and residents.

Nor do shelters facilitate the Latina's return to her own community. Due to insufficient numbers of Spanish-speaking personnel, Latinas cannot develop the skills and strengths necessary to escape the violence permanently and establish a new, independent life. These shelters currently provide only temporary, short-term services; Latinas cannot hope to become empowered when they are placed in such a disempowering, dependent position.

RESPONSES

Latina antiviolence activists have effectively provided services for the Latina survivors of violence whom they could reach. Nevertheless, the Latino community has not yet developed a comprehensive strategy to end violence within the community. This failure reflects more than mere oversight. Historically, activists and leaders within the community have confronted racism and national origin discrimination with clear, focused strategies.[15] Moreover, Latinos have vehemently opposed the characterization of those in their community as violent and uneducated. This commitment to equality and civil rights stops short, however, of addressing issues such as "women's rights" that are of specific importance to Latinas. Struggles within the Latino community to recognize the pervasiveness of domestic violence and its impact on the lives of women and their families must continue. Unfortunately, demands for a community response to the violence have been met with claims that such issues are private matters that cause division within the community, and consequently impact negatively on the larger struggle for equality. These references to solidarity obfuscate the real issue: Latinas are physically, emotionally, and psychologically abused on a daily basis by the men who are closest to them.

Latina advocates continue to work within the community through existing institutions[16] and media to educate one another on the nature of domestic violence. They also work within the battered women's movement to educate other activists on the unique needs of Latinas, and to demand that the larger movement be responsive to these needs. Their efforts to politicize what is often considered a "private" issue will help ensure that the concerns of Latinas are factored into the equation of feminist reform of domestic violence discourse.

The development of strategies to address domestic violence must be grounded in the reality and experiences of all women; we must recognize that there may be tensions and conflicts associated with developing reforms. It must be accepted that Latinas face multiple barriers because of their race, national origin, language dominance, and gender; that this multiple discrimination factors into how Latinas experience and respond to domestic violence; and that institutional racism and patriarchal structures are interrelated in the experience of Latinas. A reform movement that recognizes these realities and experiences will acknowledge the need to work in unison, but only from a strong base. Latino community-based organizations must be strengthened and provided with the financial and political flexibility to develop and establish domestic violence shelters and services. The Latino community must prioritize domestic violence initiatives. The lives of women and the well-being of an entire community depend on it.

NOTES

1. *See* Denise Segura, *Labor Market Stratification: The Chicana Experience*, Berkeley J. Sociology 57 (discussion of Chicanas' economic and employment status, which applies an intersectional analysis).

2. These images are infamous. For example, Maria in *West Side Story* can only be described as sweet, innocent, God-fearing, and virginal. Anita, the gang leader's girlfriend, on the other hand, was the sexy, loud, and promiscuous Puerto Rican seamstress. West Side Story (Mirisch Corp. 1961).

3. Yvonne Pacheco Tevis, *Feminism and the Mexican American Woman,* 28 U.C. Mexus News 1 (1991).

4. *Id.*

5. *Id.*

6. Carolyne R. Hathaway, Case Comment, *Gender Based Discrimination in Police Reluctance to Respond to Domestic Assault Complaints,* 75 Geo. L.J. 667, 673–75 (1986).

7. *See generally* Symposium, *The Influence of Criminology on Criminal Law: Evaluating Arrest for Misdemeanor Domestic Violence,* 83 J. Crim. L. & Criminology 1 (1992).

8. People from Latin America share a common regional heritage marked by abuse inflicted at the hands of governmental officials, the military, and local law enforcement officers. Immigrants often come to the United States to escape police and military physical abuse. Because the use of force has often been condoned by repressive governments in the immigrants' native countries, these immigrants possess negative memories and suspicions about the assistance available from law enforcement agencies.

9. Sara Mausolff Buel, *Mandatory Arrest for Domestic Violence,* 11 Harv. Women's L.J. 213, 225–26 (1988) (citing Epstein, The Problem of Dual Arrest in Family Violence Cases 2–6 (discussion paper), reprinted in Connecticut Coalition Against Domestic Violence, From All Sides: An Examination of Connecticut's Family Violence Prevention and Response Act, § 3, at 3 (1987)).

10. *See* Merle H. Weiner, *From Dollars to Sense: A Critique of Government Funding for the Battered Women's Shelter Movement,* 9 Law & Ineq. J. 185, 212–26 (1991).

11. *See* Edward W. Gondolf et al., *Racial Differences among Shelter Residents: A Comparison of Anglo, Black, and Hispanic Battered,* 3 J. Fam. Violence 39, 48–49 (1988).

12. *See* Pat Eng, *Asians, Domestic Violence, and Criminal Justice,* Asian Times, Sept. 1989, at 1; Note, *The Cultural Defense in the Criminal Law,* 99 Harv. L. Rev. 1293 (1986).

13. For a description of services recognized by Congress, see Family Violence Prevention and Services Act, 42 U.S.C. § 10408(5) (Supp. 1993).

14. Jane E. Brody, *Personal Health,* N.Y. Times, Mar. 18, 1992, at C12.

15. For example, the Latino community successfully fought for equal opportunity in education, and secured bilingual education services for Latino students with limited English proficiency. *See* Aspira of New York v. Board of Educ. of City of New York, 423 F. Supp. 647 (1976).

16. Community-based shelter and service programs, such as New York City's Violence Intervention Program and the District of Columbia's Hermanas Unidas, are examples of Latina-run services specifically designed to address Latinas' needs. They are bilingual and bicultural, and are effectively run by Latinas who are sensitive to issues unique to individual Latinas and the Latino community.

Variations on the Theme:
The O. J. Simpson Case

33 | Rosa Lopez, Christopher Darden, and Me: Issues of Gender, Ethnicity, and Class in Evaluating Witness Credibility

Maria L. Ontiveros

As a Latina who grew up in Los Angeles, I felt kinship with the Salvadoran house-keeper who worked next door to O. J. Simpson. Odd, I thought, that I would feel such empathy with this woman. What did we have in common? She, a Salvadoran with a fourth-grade education; I, a third-generation Mexican American with three graduate degrees. I grew up in a comfortable, secure home to become a lawyer and law professor. She grew up as a field worker and housekeeper in war-torn El Salvador, losing three children during childbirth and two to the war. Yet, across the borders of class and cultural differences, enough similarities of gender and culture survived. I felt I knew and understood her.

This essay revisits the ordeal of Rosa Lopez to examine her testimony and test its credibility. I will summarize Rosa Lopez's testimony before the court and present an alternative view of her testimony that takes into account issues of culture, class, and gender. I will conclude with some observations on her credibility and the importance of viewing all witness credibility through the lens of culture, class, and gender.

ROSA LOPEZ AND HER TESTIMONY

ROSA LOPEZ'S BACKGROUND

Born in El Salvador, Rosa Lopez grew up as one of ten children. After she left school at the age of ten, when her parents could no longer afford pencils and paper, she went to work in the fields with her parents. As an adult, she gave birth to seven children, but three did not survive infancy. Of her four remaining children, one son became a helicopter pilot and was killed in El Salvador's civil war. Her fifteen-year-old daughter disappeared during the war and is presumed dead. She came to the United States twenty-seven years ago, but she returns to El Salvador once or twice a year and still considers it her home. She became enmeshed with the O. J. Simpson case while working as housekeeper for Simpson's neighbor.

TESTIMONY AT THE HEARING ON THE RISK OF FLIGHT

In her direct examination, Rosa Lopez established two things. First, O. J. Simpson's Ford Bronco was parked in front of his house sometime after 10:00 P.M.—the alleged time of the murder.[1] She said she saw the car when she took her employer's dog outside to relieve itself. Second, she planned to leave the United States and not return. She gave several reasons for planning to leave, including her fear that she would be physically harmed if she remained in the United States.

On cross-examination, Christopher Darden attacked her credibility in several ways. He argued that Lopez had previously given incomplete or different reasons for why she wanted to leave and that her action in filing for unemployment was inconsistent with her statement of intent to leave. He also argued that Rosa Lopez had no reasonable fear for her physical safety. Finally, he established that she had not in fact purchased tickets or made reservations to leave the country.[2]

VIDEOTAPED TESTIMONY

Rosa Lopez's direct testimony followed the lines of her testimony at the prior hearing. She testified to seeing the Bronco, hearing voices, and subsequently talking with Detective Fuhrman. As in the earlier hearing, her testimony was given with the aid of an interpreter. The attorney's questions to her were translated from English to Spanish.

Christopher Darden's cross-examination was broad-ranging. He attacked the substantive alibi evidence, suggesting that Lopez had poor eyesight, did not go out at ten, and could not have seen the Bronco from her alleged position in the front yard. Most important, his questions argued that she either manufactured the sighting or changed its time at the suggestion of the defense.

He spent even more time attacking Rosa Lopez's credibility on collateral issues. Among other things, he revived the inconsistencies from the earlier hearing in her statements about airline reservations. He found inconsistencies in her answers about filing a claim for unemployment. He challenged her on providing conflicting names, birthdates, and addresses on official documents that had been completed under the penalty of perjury. He argued that Lopez was biased against Nicole Brown Simpson because the latter had slapped a housekeeper and, further, that Lopez had been bribed by the defense.

Evaluators of Rosa Lopez's credibility found her demeanor just as important as the actual answers in cross-examination. She often (fifty to one hundred times) said that she "did not remember" having seen something or said something.[3] She often appeared to be agreeing with Darden's questions, answering, "if you say so, sir." She appeared to concede or change her answers. She appeared hesitant and unsure. Sometimes her answers were nonresponsive or did not seem to make sense.

Two exchanges capture the flavor of the cross-examination. First, with regard to the time of the sighting and the influence of the prosecution in the guise of Bill Pavelic:

DARDEN: Well, did Mr. Pavelic tell you or mention to you first that you saw the Bronco at 10:15 or 10:20?
LOPEZ: All I said was that it was after 10:00.
DARDEN: So you don't know how long after 10:00, correct? . . .
LOPEZ: No, sir.
DARDEN: Okay. Mr. Pavelic is the one that first suggested 10:15 or 10:20, correct? . . .
LOPEZ: If that is what he is saying, that is fine. . . .
DARDEN: During the conversation you had with Mr. Pavelic you would give times and he would give other times, correct? . . .
LOPEZ: If you say so, sir.[4]

The cross-examination on filing for unemployment application reads as follows.

DARDEN: Okay. When you told us last Friday that you hadn't filled out your unemployment forms, that wasn't true, was it? . . . That was a lie, correct?
LOPEZ: No.
DARDEN: You had filled out your unemployment forms, hadn't you?
LOPEZ: I was referring to the application that is—that one is given for one to take it back.
DARDEN: Okay. You never applied for unemployment?
LOPEZ: Yes.
DARDEN: Okay. You told us last week that you weren't turning in your forms for unemployment because you were leaving the country, correct?
LOPEZ: Yes.
DARDEN: But in fact you had turned in your forms, correct? . . .
LOPEZ: No, I didn't understand you. . . .
DARDEN: Have you filed for unemployment?
LOPEZ: Yes, sir.
DARDEN: And you filed for unemployment on what, February 15th, correct?
LOPEZ: Yes.
DARDEN: You filed for unemployment knowing that you were going to leave the country for several months, correct?
LOPEZ: If I was given unemployment, sir, there was no reason for me to leave the country. . . .
DARDEN: So if I understand you correctly then, if you get unemployment insurance you won't leave the country; is that right? . . .
LOPEZ: I have thought of leaving right away when I am out of here, you know.[5]

CREDIBILITY VIEWED THROUGH THE LENS OF CULTURE, CLASS, AND GENDER

I would not be writing this essay if I agreed with the vast majority of U.S. media, if I did not find their evaluation of Rosa Lopez's credibility shallow and troublesome. During her testimony, many things occurred that made Lopez look less credible to commentators than to me. She appeared to change her answers, especially when challenged; she talked in generalities; she responded, "I don't remember"; and some of her answers seemed nonsensical. The perception that these things destroy credibility lacks any understanding of how Lopez's culture, gender, and class affected her testimony.

LANGUAGE DIFFERENCES AND TRANSLATORS

The impact of language differences occurs at many levels.[6] At the most obvious level, the use of two different languages provides an opportunity for misunderstanding and confusion. This is perhaps why Judge Ito replaced one Mexican-born interpreter with a Salvadoran interpreter after his court received several calls that the Mexican-born translator was not sufficiently familiar with Salvadoran dialects and idioms.[7]

But replacing one interpreter with another does not completely solve the problems presented by language differences. Although transcripts of the Simpson trial are readily available, no service could provide the actual Spanish words used by Rosa Lopez in her testimony. Part of the problem is that court reporters do not record the non-English testimony, only the translation.[8] Appeals based on faulty translation therefore become extremely difficult because there is no record to refer to.[9]

A more subtle and important problem occurs when the meaning of a certain phrase varies according to the culture, gender, and class of the witness. For example, all interpreters and court watchers agree that when Rosa Lopez said, *"No me recuerdo, señor,"* she was saying, "I don't remember, sir." However, the message she sought to convey by saying "I don't remember" is not clear. She may have indeed remembered but felt unable to repeat herself again. As a Latina, she may not have wanted to continue to disagree and confront the prosecution, and so she used the phrase as an alternative, more subtle, indirect, and less confrontational way to say no. Similarly, when she replied, "If you say so, sir," to Christopher Darden, she may not have intended to communicate agreement, but rather deference.[10]

Linguist Vincent C. Gilliam sent a letter to the court summarizing these issues:

> First, a point that may easily be lost to Americans is the difference in cultures being manifested by Miss Lopez' responses. Not only does she display a tendency to defer somewhat meekly to people in authority (Mr. Darden) by saying, quote, "if you say so, sir," as one might suspect from someone from a humble background and from El Salvador at that, but Spanish-speaking cultures are much more subtle than one such as the U.S. Thus, when Miss Lopez says, "no," and then "no, I don't remember having said that, sir," with further prodding, it is not an equivocal response, nor is it prevari-

cating that she change her response. It is simply that [she] comes from a more indirect and less confrontational type of culture. And more importantly, quote, "no I don't remember having said that," end quote, does not mean, "possibly yes" as Mr. Darden was attempting to make it mean.[11]

On redirect examination, Rosa Lopez confirmed that her use of the phrase *"no me recuerdo"* meant "no," and that this was a common usage of the phrase in El Salvador.[12]

THE SUBSTANTIVE ALIBI

Rosa Lopez provided one key piece of testimony for the defense: an alibi. Her credibility appeared damaged in this area because she could not give what the prosecutors and commentators, and maybe even the interpreter, considered a "specific time" for seeing his Bronco. She could only say it was "after ten." When cultural differences in perceptions of time and the importance of specific, rather than general, information are taken into account, her answer becomes much less equivocal.

Many Western cultures, including the United States, consider time to be objective—something true and mathematical that can and must be precisely measured.[13] Other cultures approach time differently—they see it as a general reference for coordinating activity, not a set schedule.[14] These cultures, which include Latinos, have been characterized as "polychronic," as opposed to the "monochronic" United States.[15] In polychronic cultures, set time schedules are not as important as forming and nurturing human relationships, even if that requires "taking" more time or being "late." Thus, many Latinos naturally view information about time more generally and simply cannot see the judicial system's need for specificity and exactitude.[16]

COLLATERAL IMPEACHMENT

Much of the prosecution's attack on Rosa Lopez's credibility dealt with collateral matters. On these issues, the prosecution's lack of cultural, gender, and class awareness became most apparent. For example, Christopher Darden sought to attack Lopez's general credibility by pointing out that she used several different addresses.[17] Harriet Murphy, a Texas newspaper reader, commented in a roundtable discussion, "Darden shows little understanding of low-income people without a permanent address. It is common to give one's relative's address as a residence for mail while living with another relative or friend and not be lying."[18]

Darden asked several questions regarding the fact that Lopez never mentioned the events to her employers, even though she saw them every day in the morning and the evening.[19] His implication that she must not have seen anything because she obviously would have said something ignores the class differences. Lopez was not likely to have intimate conversations with them while she was serving them their meals.[20] Even the commentators on Court TV recognized that this might not be a very convincing line of impeachment because of the class relationship between the players.[21]

Other differences in perspective caused by class differences echoed throughout the cross-examination. When trying to insinuate that Rosa Lopez lied about taking her employer's dog out at ten o'clock, Christopher Darden challenged, "Well, why would you take the dog out a second time if you had already taken it out once?" Rosa Lopez responded, "Sir, because I don't want the dog to urinate inside the house, sir." When he snidely asked, "So you knew the dog was about to urinate inside the house?" she answered from her own experience, an experience obviously far from his, "Well, I don't know, but I have to take her out because I don't want to mop the dog's pee the next day, sir."[22] Similarly, Darden challenged Lopez to explain why Lopez disliked Nicole Brown Simpson when Simpson had slapped her housekeeper, not Lopez. Lopez responded in a way that showed her class consciousness: "But we are friends. We are both housekeepers and we earn our living with the sweat of our brow."[23] Her actions in both contexts suddenly seemed quite credible, given the reality of her life.

In addition to issues of class difference, many of Darden's attacks in cross-examination ring hollow when the listener understands the cultural differences. For example, in the hearing on whether Rosa Lopez was a flight risk, Darden questioned her assertion that she feared for her personal safety if she stayed in the United States. He asked, "No one has threatened to beat you up, correct?" and "But no one has threatened you with physical harm, correct?"[24] She answered, "Not me," and "But many of my friends tell me to be very careful because this case is very difficult and that I could even be killed," and then, when pressed, "no," no one had threatened her with physical harm.[25]

Although he implied with these arguments that Rosa Lopez was not really afraid, he ignored several realities in her life. First, in El Salvador, thousands of people, *including her own fifteen-year-old daughter,* "disappeared" during the war.[26] Most were taken and killed by the government, even though they were never first "threatened with physical harm." Additionally, Rosa Lopez had already heard about the arrest of another defense witness, Mary Ann Gerchas, whom the prosecution pursued on forgery charges.[27] Later on, the prosecution justified Lopez's fears of arrest when they considered the possibility of prosecuting her for address and name discrepancies on official forms.[28] Since being "arrested" in El Salvador could be life-threatening, Rosa Lopez's fears become much more believable.

In the main hearing, Darden suggested that the witness was dishonest because she had used several different last names. Lopez tried her best to answer his questions, but she did not see a problem with the usage.[29] In response to the question, "What is your true and correct name?" the transcript reads,

LOPEZ: Rose Maria Lopez.
DARDEN: Have you ever gone by the name of Maria Reyes?
LOPEZ: I—that way in my birth certificate, but they tell me here that those be two last names.
DARDEN: So you're also known as Maria Reyes then?
LOPEZ: Yes. Yes, sir. I've already said so.

DARDEN: Okay. Are you known by any other name?

LOPEZ: Not that I know.

DARDEN: How about Martinez?

LOPEZ: Martinez because of my father.

DARDEN: And Lopez because of what?

LOPEZ: For my mother.

DARDEN: Okay. And Reyes because of what?

LOPEZ: Because that's the name, sir.

DARDEN: Did you pick that name, Maria Reyes?

LOPEZ: Sir, how could I choose that name if when I was born I couldn't talk?

DARDEN: Okay. Did you choose Martinez and Lopez?

LOPEZ: I would have to ask my father.

The difference in perception stems from Darden's ignorance of Latino naming conventions. In traditional Latino culture, people use the last names of both their mother and father, with their father's name appearing first.[30] I should be Maria Linda Ontiveros Luna, and neither Ontiveros nor Luna (or both) would be my "last name." Because of this difference in appellations, U.S. officials routinely make mistakes on official forms.[31] Finally, the court interpreters in the Simpson case explained that Reyes could easily be a religious name, given because Rosa Lopez was born on January 6—the feast of the three kings.[32] Again, the information that Darden tried to portray as lies simply displayed his own lack of cultural knowledge.

I do not find Rosa Lopez to be the clear-cut liar depicted by the prosecution and ridiculed in the press. On the other hand, I did not find her totally believable. I think she probably saw the Bronco late in the evening while walking the dog. I doubt, however, that she knows what time she saw it. But even if I cannot reach a conclusion myself about Rosa Lopez, her ordeal provides me an important lesson to pass on to my evidence students: when a witness's credibility is being evaluated, issues of class, culture, and gender must be taken into account.

NOTES

1. People v. Simpson, No. BA097211, 1995 WL 77473, *30–33 (Cal. Super. Ct. proceedings of Feb. 27, 1995).

2. People v. Simpson, No. BA097211, 1995 WL 77464, *14–15, 19 (Cal. Super. Ct. proceedings of Feb. 24, 1995).

3. Jim Newton & Andrea Ford, *Key Simpson Witness Admits Contradictions*, L.A. Times, Mar. 3, 1995, at A1 (Lopez answered, "I don't remember, sir" about fifty times). Phil Reeves, *Black Week for OJ As Memory of His Alibi Witness Fades*, Independent, Mar. 4, 1995, International Section, at 9 (Lopez replied, *"no me recuerdo"* no fewer than eighty-nine times).

4. People v. Simpson, No. BA097211, 1995 WL 85407, *14–15 (Cal. Super. Ct. proceedings of Mar. 2, 1995).

5. *Id.,* *6–7.

6. *See, e.g.,* Margaret E. Montoya, *Máscaras, Trenzas, y Greñas: Un/masking the Self While*

Un/braiding Latina Stories and Legal Discourse, 17 Harv. Women's L.J. 185 (1994) (also chapter 7 in this volume).

7. Stephanie Simon, *Translations Can Complicate Trials,* L.A. Times, Feb. 28, 1995, at A13.

8. Mark Caro, *Interpreters Speak Volumes about Linguistic Confusion,* Chi. Trib., Sept. 26, 1994, at N7.

9. Susan Freinkel, *Language Problems,* Recorder, Feb. 4, 1991, at 1.

10. Her constant use of the word "sir" stems from both her class consciousness and her gender.

11. People v. Simpson, No. BA097211, 1995 WL 88128, *1 (Cal. Super. Ct. proceedings of Mar. 3, 1995). *See also Linguists' Views on Rosa Lopez,* S.F. Chron., Mar. 4, 1995, at A9.

12. People v. Simpson, No. BA097211, 1995 WL 88129, *4 (Cal. Super. Ct. proceedings of Mar. 3, 1995).

13. Don Oldenburg, *You It's about Time,* Wash. Post, Apr. 26, 1985, at F4. This and the following notes draw heavily from work done by the anthropologist Edward T. Hall and his works The Dance of Life: The Other Dimensions of Time (1985) and The Hidden Dimension (1966), which deal with cultural perceptions of time and cultural differences in styles of communication.

14. Don Oldenburg, *Fast Forward: Living in Artificial Time,* Health, Sept. 1988, at 52.

15. Gary Blonston, *The Cultural Barriers to Communication,* Chi. Trib., July 28, 1985, at Tempo 1.

16. This may also explain why we are always late.

17. People v. Simpson, No. BA097211, 1995 WL 85407, *9 (Cal. Super. Ct. Proceedings of March 2, 1995).

18. *Trial Watchers,* Austin American-Statesman, Mar. 3, 1995, at 11.

19. People v. Simpson, No. BA097211, 1995 WL 85408, *12 (Cal. Super. Ct. proceedings of Mar. 2, 1995).

20. *Id.* Darden also tried to impeach her with what she had told her former employer Sylvianne Walker. When Darden tried to characterize Walker as a "friend" of Lopez, Rosa Lopez responded, "She's not my friend, sir. She's my boss. She is too rich to be my friend." *Id.* at *22.

21. *Live Trial Coverage: CA. v. Simpson—Day 25—Part 15* (Courtroom Television Network, Mar. 2, 1995), available in LEXIS, NEWS Library, CURNWS File.

22. People v. Simpson, No. BA097211, 1995 WL 88128, *4 (Cal. Super. Ct. proceedings of Mar. 3, 1995).

23. People v. Simpson, No. BA 097211, 1995 WL 85408, *28 (Cal. Super. Ct. transcript of Mar. 2, 1995).

24. People v. Simpson, No. BA097211, (Cal. Sup. Ct. proceedings of Feb. 24, 1995 (LEXIS, Cal Library, OJTRAN).

25. *Id.*

26. *See* U.S. Dep't of State Dispatch, U.S. Dep't of State 1990 Human Rights Report: El Salvador (Feb. 1, 1991) (Section B *Disappearance,* discusses a number of abductions and personal stories).

27. Commentary, *Live Trial Coverage: CA v. Simpson—Day 26—Part 1* (Courtroom Television Network, Mar. 3, 1995), available in LEXIS, NEWS Library, CURNWS File.

28. People v. Simpson, No. BA 097211, 1995 WL 85408, *34 (Cal. Super. Ct. proceedings of Mar. 2, 1995) (Judge Ito points out that answers to questions regarding name discrepancies could provide proof of a crime, even though "it's not something we normally prosecute a

whole lot of people for"); and People v. Simpson, No. BA097211, 1995 WL 88129, *2 (Cal. Super. Ct. proceedings of Mar. 3, 1995) (Darden says he is "not about to grant Miss Lopez immunity" on the issue).

29. People v. Simpson, No. BA097211, 1995 WL 85408, *33 (Cal. Super. Ct. proceedings of Mar. 2, 1995).

30. Marge Landrau, *How Metropolitan Life Direct Markets to Hispanic-Americans*, DM News, Aug. 1, 1989, at 38. To further complicate things, married women may insert "de" into their name, leading to misfiling. *Id.* Additionally, many married women do not take their husbands' last name. Shelly Emling, *Undertaking Understanding: From Lawsuits to Birth Announcements, New Hispanic Project Is Bridging a Gap*, Atlanta J. & Constitution, Oct. 1, 1992, at G2.

31. *See, e.g.*, Emling, *supra* note 30 (birth certificates); and Bob Rowland, *Poway Rape Case Figure Held by INS*, San Diego Union-Tribune, July 8, 1988, at B2 (arrest records and Border Patrol files).

32. People v. Simpson, No. BA097211, 1995 WL 85408, *33 (Cal. Super. Ct. proceedings of Mar. 2, 1995).

34 | Orenthal James Simpson and Gender, Class, and Race: In That Order

Crystal H. Weston

The O. J. Simpson trial was fascinating. I watched it every chance I got. I watched it because it was entertaining: court is theater. I watched it because it was educational: court is a procedural and evidentiary lesson. And I watched it because I wanted to see how onlookers, as well as the legal system, would treat a wealthy, handsome, African male woman-beater who was on trial for murder.

Yes, the trial—or should I say the O. J. Simpson Show—was multiply appealing. But after digesting the entertainment, we are left with an unpleasant aftertaste. We are forced to contend with the sociological, economic, and political issues that have created a climate in which a Nicole Brown Simpson could be repeatedly beaten by one of the most famous and well-liked persons in the world and then murdered.

These are more commonly known as gender, class, and race issues. Gender is the social construction of what is "feminine" and "masculine," that is, what the culture defines as male and female. In this article I use the word "gender" instead of the word "sex" to refer, primarily, to women and women-related issues. Like gender, race is a social construction. Like gender, it is a convenient categorization based on physical and biological differences between groups of people. Class is also socially constructed: it hails from the distribution of wealth based on a constructed economic system, in this case, capitalism. "Class" is used in this essay to refer to wealth-based societal positioning.

The media pundits and the general observing population infused race as a major issue since O. J.'s first contact with the police. Many observers believed that O. J. Simpson, as a Black person, would not receive a fair trail for the murder of two White people in a climate of American racism. As a result, too much attention was being paid to race. This essay will examine why gender should have led the analysis of the O. J. Simpson trial, how class was the major costar, and why race should have been the supporting actor—at least until the discovery of the Fuhrman tapes.

GENDER AND MISOGYNIST VIOLENCE

I believe that gender was the controlling factor in the Simpson case because, regardless of who actually carved the life out of Nicole, she was a casualty of misogynist violence. Seventeen of her thirty-five years were spent with someone who repeatedly pummelled, belittled, and mistreated her, to the point where she became more and more vulnerable to just the sort of violent and abrupt demise she experienced. Thus, in the context of the battering that preceded Nicole's death, race should have been removed from its most-favored-issue status and misogyny and patriarchy should have been placed at the helm of the analysis, where they rightfully belong.

Nicole's death took place in the context of what is commonly called "domestic violence." The original use of the phrase "domestic violence" probably served as a way to indicate the locale of the violence, in the home or related to the home. And politically, the term has been used to historically privatize this sort of violence that is perpetrated—overwhelmingly by men—against women.

I shun the term "domestic violence" because it is an oxymoron, a misnomer, and a euphemism.

"Domestic violence" is an oxymoron because the word "domestic" suggests sanctity, peace, and safety. It suggests a happy chorus singing in your ear, "Be it eeever so huuumble, there's nooo place like hooome . . ." Conversely, *Webster's Dictionary* defines "violence" as an "exertion of physical force so as to injure or abuse." This word obviously suggests a *lack* of safety or sanctity. The words "domestic" and "violence" actually cancel each other out.

"Domestic violence" is a dangerous misnomer because this sort of violence happens everywhere and anywhere, including outside the home. We know that the home is only *one* of the many locales in which it occurs. So-called domestic violence extends far beyond a one-on-one confrontation in one's abode with the curtains pulled. This abuse includes harassing and stalking women, isolating women, and verbally abusing women.

"Domestic violence" is a problematic term also because it too easily lends itself to other terms that water down the "violence" component of the issue. For example, Johnnie Cochran regularly used the term "domestic discord." This phrase removed violence from the phenomenon entirely!

I submit that there is no such thing as domestic violence and that the term is a euphemism for what is actually a form of misogynist violence. I submit that we cease to reference partner abuse or abuse that stems from an intimate relationship as "domestic violence" so that we are better able to place it in the context of the everyday violence that women experience, such as the male gaze, sexually suggestive comments, unsolicited touches from absolute strangers, and outright physical and verbal threats.

If trends continue, however, women are looking into a future that is effectively as bleak as our past. The statistics are startling: a woman is beaten every fifteen seconds; one in four women is beaten by a male partner every year; antiwoman violence that stems from an intimate relationship is the leading cause of injury to women between the ages of fifteen and forty-four, injuring more women than car accidents, muggings, and rapes combined; each month fifty thousand women seek restraining or protection orders; and women who leave their batterers are at a 75 percent greater risk of being killed by the batterers than those who stay.

It is this last statistic that is particularly jolting to me. It is this last statistic that makes it very easy and natural for me to believe that O. J. Simpson murdered Nicole Brown Simpson. This last statistic makes the odds that he did it extremely high; theirs was a textbook relationship of a battered woman who separated, divorced, regularly broke up with and went back and forth with her abuser, and throughout the relationship blamed herself for her own beatings.

Nicole Brown Simpson's death must remind us all that misogynist violence is pervasive. Although many women do physically survive it, as Tina Turner did, most will not have their accuser's trial broadcast on CNN, nor will their stories be told on film and shown in movie houses throughout the country. Most batterees will continue to suffer in fear, shame, and silence, until feminists and progressive men have taught their regressive counterparts that women are not property and that we are equal to men.

CLASS PRIVILEGES: WEALTH, MALENESS, FAME, AND BEAUTY

The money factor is the current on which both O. J.'s Blackness and his maleness ride. He may be Black, a least-favored status in this nation, but he is also rich and he is a man: *two* most-favored statuses from which he benefits greatly. Some would argue that the combination of his maleness and Blackness actually places him in the least-favored category, but let us consider the many privileges his wealth and accompanying fame have allowed him to enjoy—both before and after the murders.

The first privilege we witnessed was the very gentle wealth-based treatment of O. J. by the police after the bodies of Nicole Brown Simpson and Ronald Goldman were found. Because he is rich, O. J. was seldom handcuffed when the police were questioning him or while he attended Nicole's funeral, held immediately after the murders. It is because he is a rich man that he was given the option to turn himself in, instead of the police going to his estate to collect him like any other suspect. This you-may-turn-yourself-in option that O. J.'s fame and money bought him is what gave him the opportunity to escape, and so began the famous Ford Bronco slow-speed freeway "chase," or more accurately, a stately escort through southern California. But for his privilege, O. J. would not have been given an option to turn himself in. Because he is rich, O. J. was not charged with resisting arrest when he was finally caught. And, arguably, because he is rich, famous, and handsome, the prosecution did not pursue the death penalty.

Next, consider the male-based privileges he was afforded throughout his dealings with the judicial system as they pertain to his relationship with Nicole. Consider, for example, O. J.'s sentence for the 1989 New Year's Day beating he inflicted on Nicole.

As he did after the murders, O. J. fled from the police after the 1989 attack. He eventually pleaded no contest to a charge of misdemeanor spousal battery, but was not even required to appear at his own sentencing! As punishment, O. J. was sentenced to two years probation, was required to undergo mandatory psychological counseling via telephone, was required to perform 120 hours of community service, was forced to make a five hundred dollar donation to a battered women's organization, and was fined two hundred dollars.

To the disbelief of most people, O. J.'s sentence for the 1989 beating is *typical* for male batterers! He was not afforded any special treatment because he is O. J. Simpson; he received the very common, and yet very special treatment that male batterers receive as a benefit of being a man in a male-dominated criminal justice system. This male privilege allowed him to be treated most gently in a case where had Nicole been anyone other than a family member and a woman, he would have surely been jailed for assault. Instead, O. J. beat Nicole in 1989 with virtual impunity.

O. J. is also privileged because he is an athlete. And Americans have a warped definition of "hero." Thus they are willing to give him the benefit of the doubt, and not necessarily because the prosecution has not proven its case, but because they do not want to believe that this rags-to-riches, athletic, crossover marketing device known as O. J. Simpson could possibly take the life of someone he had been pounding on for over a decade and a half.

O. J. also benefited from his handsome face. Historically and in modern times, physically attractive defendants receive less harsh sentences than unattractive defendants. When this benefit of "good looks" is combined with the fact that O. J. is wealthy, famous, male, and an athlete, there is no denying that he has successfully surpassed his niggerdom.

RACE AND NATIONALISM

As the trial progressed, White supremacy became an increasingly important "character" in the trial. Racism undeniably permeates every aspect of American life, and this trial, of course, is no different. The pervasiveness of racism, however, does not give us license to ignore or deny the equally life-steering roles of gender and class. As usual, however, America's obsession with race, particularly with Black and White relations, allowed far more than a fair share of the analysis of the O. J. Simpson trial to be race-based, *long before* the discovery of the tapes on which now retired Los Angeles Police Department detective Mark Fuhrman refers to Black people as "niggers" more than sixty times.

I agree that White folk, as a class, have not proven themselves worthy of the trust of African people. This case alone has revealed institutional racism in the form of Fuhrman. The entire LAPD was implicated by Fuhrman's hatefulness because, as an institution, it created a climate in which Fuhrman could repeatedly get away with planting evidence, beating suspects, and harassing citizens, and it condoned a climate in which this same rogue cop could feel cocky enough to document his abuses by verbally recording them for a decade. Indeed, it is very easy for us to believe that if Fuhrman did not plant evidence, he probably exaggerated it. And if the LAPD did not conspire to frame Simpson, it at least polluted the evidence, making it more difficult for outsiders to ferret out the truth.

Nevertheless, I have grown weary of hearing the charges that O. J. Simpson was being targeted because he is Black, and that his alleged persecution was yet another in the line of recent racist attacks on famous Black males, such as Mike Tyson, Michael Jackson, Clarence Thomas, and Ben Chavis. It was no surprise to hear such defenses of O. J. from Black men. They obviously felt the need to protect fellow Black men, regardless of what they do or are accused of doing. And although it was no surprise to hear Black women blindly defending Black men accused of heinous misogynist violence, it was no less painful to my ears and to my soul.

Nonanalytical, allegiance-rich arguments are known as nationalist arguments. Makers of such arguments refuse to entertain even the *possibility* that the above-named brothers may have indeed committed the evil of which they are accused because the "nation" must appear unified and we must "protect" each other no matter the cost. Besides, the argument goes, White people cannot be trusted.

After Fuhrman was exposed as a racist liar, White supremacy, for the first time, legitimately took center stage during the case, and naturally Black nationalist arguments gained more credence. But the truth is that nationalists do not need Fuhrmanesque characters in order to believe that a Black suspect should go free; the accused's Blackness and the system's Whiteness, within the context of racist America, are enough. I must admit that I somewhat identify with this last sentiment. There is a part of me that feels that the White community could spare one White woman, and that O. J. should not go to prison, whether he did it or not, as payback for all the bodies, minds, and souls that Black folk continue to lose to racism every day in this hateful society.

But despite the long history of White supremacy in this country, the well-documented proof that Black males are disproportionately incarcerated, and a vengeful sentiment that periodically emerges in everyday African people like me, I usually return to my sense of fairness. I also return to my desire to see women's lives valued as much as men's, a desire afforded little room for expression within a nationalist politic.

Nationalism seeks to put the race or "nation" above individual preservation and sound reasoning. (White people have perfected this into what is modernly known as "White supremacy," or racism.) The thought of O. J.'s guilt is not entertained by most Africans because he is a fellow member of the Black "nation." Nationalist arguments such as these are narrow and unproductive for Black folk and anyone else who employs them. Such arguments do not exalt the Black nation, but exalt a very small group within that nation—mainly middle-class male persons who are perceived to be heterosexual. In other words, nationalism, as it now exists in Black communities, exalts a Black version of the patriarchal capitalist structure under which we presently live.

Nationalist dispositions are especially harmful to Black women. They create a space in which Black men can be abusive and controlling of Black women and children without their authority to do so ever being questioned; this is what patriarchy means. Consider the fact that, save for Michael Jackson, each of the above mentioned African men is accused of a violent physical or spiritual assault of a woman: sexual harassment, rape, and murder preceded by battering. Consider even further that three out of these five famous cases involved *Black* women. Would assaults by Black men in a world run by Black men somehow be less painful? For the one in three of you readers who is an incest survivor, for the many of you who are rape survivors, and for the one in four who is a survivor of misogynist partner abuse, you know the answer.

Patriarchy and misogyny continue to exist in all segments of American society, as evidenced by the fact that misogynist violence is found in all races, occupations, income levels, and ages. A nationalist disposition that does not question the underlying patriarchal assumptions of the Black male members of our "nation" is particularly destructive for African women and undermines the *entire* Black nation. Consequently, this trial is not just about seeking justice for one White woman, but about insuring justice for Black folk who are not male, not perceived to be heterosexual, or not middle-class; that is, for most of us.

We, Black women, must begin to employ a sort of gender-analysis affirmative action by *first* consciously assessing our lives through a gender analysis, and *then* by assessing it through a race analysis. Don't worry about the race analysis getting lost. It will not subside, because the popular culture and the status quo, both Black and White, insist that race dominate all public discourse on difference. We will not survive if we continue to place one element of our essence, namely, race, far above our desire to fight for our dignity as women, especially within the African community. If both elements do not thrive, neither will we.

THE VERDICT

On October 3, 1995, Orenthal James Simpson received a verdict of "not guilty." As previously stated, I believe O. J. is guilty and should be punished accordingly. However, the prosecution was required to prove "beyond a reasonable doubt" that O. J. committed the murders. The defense did an excellent job of raising doubt in the form of Fuhrman and the evidence he came in contact with, in the form of untrustworthy evidence in general, in the form of questionable police conduct and medical examiner procedures, and in the form of upsetting the time period that was allegedly available for O. J. Simpson to commit the murders. In short, the prosecution did not prove its case beyond a reasonable doubt, and O. J. obtained his "not guilty" verdict fairly, that is, pursuant to the rules. Whether or not justice has been served, however, is questionable, even doubtful.

Class and race are obviously very important in this saga. But I want to stress that it was a misogynist and indifferent culture that allowed O. J. to batter Nicole for half of her life. And it was the shallowness of this profit-driven culture that allowed O. J. to remain popular, unscathed, and continually employed by two multinational corporations despite the initially well publicized 1989 beating of Nicole and other reported incidents of his misogynist violence.

This culture rewards men who deny women the right to their physical, spiritual, and economic safety, while employers, family, friends, and neighbors continually pass up opportunities to intervene. In the end, misogyny teamed up with White supremacy to legally acquit O. J. Simpson and to remind us that while O. J.'s trial is over, the battle to end misogynist violence has been powerfully jump-started.

Questions and Suggested Readings for Part 5

1. Is the concept of "spirit-murder" meaningful? Does it prove too much? Isn't it true that everyone experiences a certain amount of dignitary harm? Why should the law privilege certain kinds of dignitary harm (e.g., those occasioned by racism) over others (e.g., those occasioned by ageism or homophobia)?

2. To curb the abuse of women, Jenny Rivera argues that the Latino community and the police need to be reeducated. Is this something that needs to be implemented in other communities as well? If so, is it feasible? What type of barriers must be overcome to educate these communities about the abuse of women and the legal system?

3. Should the criminal justice system recognize the "cultural defense" as an aspect of mitigating criminal punishment? How has it currently been used? Should it be allowed but only in a limited context?

4. What advice would you give to a prosecutor who is attempting to discredit the credibility of a witness like Rosa Lopez? Does the advice differ if you are advising a black prosecutor like Christopher Darden, or a Latina female prosecutor, or a white female like Marcia Clark?

5. What does it mean to say that race, class, and gender are "socially constructed"? Is this true? Doesn't each of these categories have a material reality? How does Crystal Weston argue that society fails to acknowledge the gender and class issues involved in the Simpson case? She maintains that gender is more important than race. How does this square with Wing's notion of multiplicity discussed in part 1 or

Judy Scales-Trent's notion of strict scrutiny plus in part 6? Is "anti-woman violence" a better name than domestic violence? Is the distinction substantive in nature?

For further reading, see Sharon Allard, *Rethinking Battered Woman Syndrome: A Black Feminist Perspective*, 1 UCLA Women's L.J. 191 (1991); Regina Austin, *"The Black Community," Its Lawbreakers, and a Politics of Identification*, 65 S. Cal. L. Rev. 1769 (1992); Kevin Brown, *The Social Construction of a Rape Victim: Stories of African-American Males about the Rape of Desiree Washington*, 1992 U. Ill. L. Rev. 997; Kristen Bumiller, *Rape as a Legal Symbol: An Essay on Sexual Violence and Racism*, 42 U. Miami L. Rev. 75 (1987); Christy Chandler, *Race, Gender, and the Peremptory Challenge: A Postmodern Feminist Approach*, 7 Yale J.L. & Feminism 173 (1995); Dwight Greene, *Abusive Prosecutors: Gender, Race and Class Discretion and the Prosecution of Drug-Addicted Mothers*, 39 Buff. L. Rev. 737 (1991); Lani Guinier, *Violence, Intimidation and Harm: The Attitudes That Perpetuate Abuse of Women*, 25 U. Tol. L. Rev. 875 (1994); Paula Johnson, *At the Intersection of Injustice: Experiences of African American Women in Crime and Sentencing*, 4 Am. U. J. Gender & L. 1 (1995); Theresa Martinez, *Embracing the Outlaws: Deviance at the Intersection of Race, Class, and Gender*, 1994 Utah L. Rev. 193; Margo Nightingale, *Judicial Attitudes and Differential Treatment: Native Women in Sexual Assault Cases*, 23 Ottawa L. Rev. 71 (1991); Barbara Omolade, *Black Women, Black Men, and Tawana Brawley—The Shared Condition*, 12 Harv. Women's L.J. 11 (1989); Dorothy Roberts, *Crime, Race, and Reproduction*, 67 Tul. L. Rev. 1945 (1993); Dorothy Roberts, *Deviance, Resistance, and Love*, 1994 Utah L. Rev. 179; Adrien Wing & Sylke Merchan, *Rape, Ethnicity, and Culture: Spirit Injury from Bosnia to Black America*, 25 Colum. J. Hum. Rts. 1 (1993); Jennifer Wriggins, *Rape, Racism, and the Law*, 6 Harv. Women's L.J. 103 (1983).

6 | On Working

Issues of employment and discrimination law and their failures to deal with the plight of women of color are the focus of part 6. Regina Austin's provocative essay *Sapphire Bound!* addresses the termination of a black unwed mother. In *Chambers v. Omaha Girls Club,* the court held that the club did not violate Title VII of the Civil Rights Act when it terminated Crystal Chambers for violating its "negative role model" rule forbidding unwed motherhood for counselors. Austin analyzes the stereotype of the black woman as a tough and domineering "Sapphire," and calls for the black community to embrace Sapphire, in this case manifested as Chamber as she contests her termination. The author points out the irony of firing an adult female single parent and thereby reducing her to the economic condition that would face any of the black girls she counsels if they became pregnant. In Austin's view, Chambers should be seen as a role model for single parenthood. Her comments about role modeling are particularly interesting since she was the visiting professor at Harvard Law School when Derrick Bell went on leave to protest the lack of black female role model colleagues. His protest and comments about role modeling are addressed in part 2.

Paulette M. Caldwell provides an influential essay entitled *A Hair Piece: Perspectives on the Intersection of Race and Gender.* She analyzes *Rogers v. American Airlines,* a case in which the court upheld the right of the employer to prohibit the wearing of braids in the workplace. The legal analysis of the case is interwoven with powerful narratives of Caldwell's own experiences as a law professor who wears braids, "perversely visible and conveniently invisible." She points out the inability of the law to incorporate a dual race-gender critique to uphold Rogers's right to wear her hair as she chooses. Yet the employer did not have the obligation to provide a connection to work performance or business need.

In *Black Women and the Constitution: Finding Our Place, Asserting Our Rights,*

Judy Scales-Trent calls for a new standard of legal review for Fourteenth Amendment equal protection clause cases—strict scrutiny plus. Traditionally, the presence of a race stigma entitles all blacks to a strict scrutiny review of a state regulation, which will be sustained only if it meets a compelling state interest. Gender-based regulations invoke an intermediate standard of review. Since black women are subject to both race and gender discrimination, they should receive the benefit of a combination of the two standards—strict scrutiny plus. Practically speaking, the court could invoke the new standard by lessening the intent requirement for a black female plaintiff. Scales-Trent realizes that the current courts are unlikely to accept her approach.

Dorothy E. Roberts's essay *The Value of Black Mothers' Work* returns to the welfare debate issues raised in part 3 by Nathalie Augustin. Instead of Learnfare, this time we delve into workfare programs. Roberts tackles the question of why it is not acceptable to the white power structure for black mothers of young children to stay at home taking care of them. Despite maternalist legislation that originally supported the notion of mothers staying at home, black women have never been part of the mothers intended for such protection. Black women have always had to work inside and outside the home. Black motherhood has been devalued since slavery and black mothers are currently deemed inherently unfit parents, transmitters of transgenerational pathology to worthless children. Workfare's harm lies in the failure to couple it with day care, housing, education, health care, and guaranteed income. The author calls for welfare reforms that will support single black mothers in their struggle to raise children "against terrifying odds."

In *Structures of Subordination: Women of Color at the Intersection of Title VII and the NLRA. Not!* Elizabeth M. Iglesias introduces labor law into the discussion of employment remedies. She examines the procedures for collective organization in labor unions and the procedural structures available for enforcing Title VII of the Civil Rights Act. At first reading, Title VII and the National Labor Relations Act (NLRA) appear to provide women of color with "viable avenues for obtaining recourse and effecting change in the workplace." In actuality, legal interpretations have created structural violence against women of color and in fact negated their rights. They are forced to pursue either their class interests as union members or their race/gender interest under Title VII.

35 Sapphire Bound!

Regina Austin

"WRITE-OUS" RESISTANCE

I grew up thinking that "Sapphire" was merely a character on the *Amos 'n' Andy* program, a figment of a white man's racist/sexist comic imagination.[1] Little did I suspect that Sapphire was a more generally employed appellation for the stereotypical black bitch—tough, domineering, emasculating, strident, and shrill.[2] Sapphire is the sort of person you look at and wonder how she can possibly stand herself. All she does is complain. Why doesn't that woman shut up?

Black bitch hunts are alive and well in the territory where minority female law faculty labor. There are so many things to get riled about that keeping quiet is impossible. We really cannot function effectively without coming to terms with Sapphire. Should we renounce her, rehabilitate her, or embrace her and proclaim her our own?

I have given some thought to the tenets that a black feminist or "womanist"[3] legal jurisprudence might pursue or embrace. Other approaches are imaginable, and I hope that this essay will encourage or provoke their articulation. "[M]isty humanism" and "simplistic assertions of a distinguishable . . . cultural and discursive practice" are not adequate.[4] Begging won't get it either: I am not sappy and do not care whether white men love me.

The remedies we contemplate must go beyond intangibles. We must consider employing the law to create and sustain institutions and organizations that will belong to black women long after any movement has become quiescent and any agitation has died. Full utilization of the economic, political, and social resources that black women represent cannot depend on the demand of a society insincerely committed to an ethic of integration and equal opportunity.

A SAPPHIRE NAMED CRYSTAL

The tasks of articulating and advancing distinctive minority feminist jurisprudential stances will become easier as those of us interested in the status of minority women begin to analyze concrete cases and legal problems. To substantiate my point that a black feminist perspective can and must be made manifest, I have attempted to apply the rough, tentative thesis I advance above to the examination of a particular decision, *Chambers v. Omaha Girls Club.*[5]

The plaintiff, Crystal Chambers, was employed by the defendant Girls Club of Omaha (the club) as an arts and crafts instructor at a facility where approximately 90 percent of the program participants were black.[6] Two years later, Chambers, an unmarried black woman in her early twenties, was discharged from her job when she became pregnant.[7] Her dismissal was justified by the club's so-called negative role model rule, which provided for the immediate discharge of staff guilty of "[n]egative role modeling for Girls Club Members," including "such things as single parent pregnancies."[8]

In her lawsuit, Crystal Chambers attacked the role model rule on several grounds. In her Title VII claims, for example, she maintained that the rule would have a disparate impact on black women because of their significantly higher fertility rate.[9] She further asserted that her discharge constituted per se sex discrimination barred by the Pregnancy Discrimination Act of 1978.[10] Although the soundness of these arguments was acknowledged,[11] they were effectively countered by the business necessity[12] and the bona fide occupational qualification defenses.[13]

In the opinion of the district court, the club "established that it honestly believed that to permit single pregnant staff members to work with the girls would convey the impression that the Girls Club condoned pregnancy for the girls in the age group it serves."[14] Furthermore, "[w]hile a single pregnant working woman may, indeed, provide a good example of hard work and independence, the same person may be a negative role model with respect to the Girls Club objective of diminishing the number of teenage pregnancies."[15]

As painted by the court, there were numerous indications that the operative animus behind the role model rule was paternalistic, not racist or sexist. The North Omaha facility was "purposefully located to better serve a primarily black population."[16] Although the club's principal administrators were white,[17] the girls served were black,[18] the staff was black,[19] and Crystal Chambers's replacements were black.[20]

For those who have no understanding of the historical oppression of black women and no appreciation of the diversity of their contemporary cultural practices, the outcome of the *Chambers* case might have a certain policy appeal, one born of sympathy for poor black youngsters and desperation about stemming the "epidemic" of teenage pregnancy that plagues them.[21]

But for better-informed, more critical evaluators, the opinions are profoundly disturbing. Firing a young, unmarried, pregnant black worker in the name of protecting other young black females from the limited options associated with early and unwed motherhood is ironic, to say the least. The club managed to replicate the very economic hardships and social biases that, according to the district court, made the role model rule necessary in the first place.[22] Crystal Chambers was not much older than some of the club members, and her financial and social status after being fired was probably not that much different from what the members would face if they became pregnant at an early age, without the benefit of a job or the assistance of a fully employed helpmate. On the other hand, she was in many respects better off than many teen mothers. She was in her early twenties and had a decent job. Chambers's condition became problematic *because* of the enforcement of the role model rule.

Judged by the values and behavior that are said to be indigenous to low-income, black communities of the sort from which the club members came, sacking pregnant unmarried Crystal Chambers was not a "womanly" move. It was cold. Although disapproving of teenage pregnancy, black culture in general does not support abandoning the mothers or stigmatizing their offspring. Allowing for cultural heterogeneity, I admit that it is entirely possible that the black people of Omaha approved of the club's actions. By and large, however, excluding young mothers and their children from good standing in the community would not strike most black women as fair, feasible, or feminine.

No doubt, unmarried, pregnant Crystal was thought to be a problem because she functioned as an icon, a reminder of a powerful culture from which the club members had to be rescued. The club was supposed to be a wholesome haven where young black girls would be introduced to an alternative array of positive life choices. Crystal Chambers tainted the environment by introducing into it the messy, corrupting cultural orientations that were the target of the club's "repress and replace" mission.

There is a widespread belief that poor black women who raise children alone in socially and economically isolated enclaves encourage teenage pregnancy by example, subsidize it through informal friendship and extended family networks, and justify it by prizing motherhood, devaluing marriage, and condoning welfare dependency.[23] Operating on similar assumptions, the club set about exposing (literally, it seems) its young members to counterimages that would act as antidotes to the messages they absorbed at home.

Although Crystal Chambers's firing was publicly justified on the ground that she would have an adverse impact on the young club members, it is likely that the club in part sacked her because she resisted its effort to model *her* in conformity with white and middle-class morality. In its struggles against the culture of the girls' mothers, Crystal Chambers, employee and arts and crafts instructor, was supposed to be on the club's side. But like a treasonous recruit, Crystal turned up unmarried and pregnant. As such, she embodied the enemy. If the club could not succeed in shaping and restraining the workers whose economic welfare it controlled, how could it expect to win over the young members and supplant their mothers' cultural legacy?

Aside from the occasional piece that accuses black adolescents of absolute perversity,[24] news accounts and academic literature generally portray black teens who are pregnant or already parents as pursuing private, ad hoc solutions to pervasive systemic economic and political powerlessness. Teenage pregnancy is the product of the complex interaction of not only culture and individual adjustment, but also material conditions that present black teens with formidable obstacles to survival and success. Blame for black teenage pregnancy must be shared by an educational system that fails to provide black youngsters with either the desire or the chance to attend college, a labor market that denies them employment that will supply the economic indicia of adulthood, and a health care system that does not deliver adequate birth control, abortion, or family planning services.

Statistically speaking, teenage pregnancy is associated with a litany of economic and social disadvantages and adverse physical and psychological consequences for both mothers and children.[25] Pregnancy and motherhood are problematic for black teenagers and young adults in part because "[y]ounger mothers tend to have less education, less work experience, and thus fewer financial resources."[26] Their economic status is weakened by the difficulty they encounter in securing child care and child support. Black babies are dying at an alarming rate, and those born to adolescent mothers may be slightly more vulnerable.[27]

But then again, things could be worse. Being a mother is certainly better than committing suicide or getting hooked on drugs.[28] The young women often rise to the demands of the role of mother.[29] The responsibilities of motherhood, of having someone to care for and someone who cares for them, have a positive effect on them in terms of their schooling and commitment to the workforce. Young men are sometimes favorably affected as well. They provide whatever economic assistance they can.[30] Those who are gainfully employed take on the role of father and supporter.[31]

In too many cases, the odds are against poor black adolescents, and the outcome of their sexual behavior is not in doubt. The hardships will be more than they can overcome. To a certain extent, the adversity that they encounter is preordained because they and their parents do not control the material, social, and political resources that make for meaningful choice. Yet these consequences are also the product of shared understandings and practices knowingly and voluntarily engaged in. The teenagers' cultures function in a way that makes their ultimate oppression and subordination seem consensual.[32]

While some of their goals might be resistant and potentially liberating, the practices by which poor black teenagers pursue them are limited. Restricted to exploiting the factors at hand—the welfare system, the underground economy, their parents, their children, and each other—poor black teenagers become unintentional and effective accomplices of the forces that would confine them to marginal existences.

On a personal or micro level, poor black female adolescents need help in separating what it is that they want in the way of material and emotional security and familial and communal obligation from the means they presently employ to achieve them.[33] They need to confront the disparity between what they hope to achieve and the consequences that their cultural practices, in conjunction with their material conditions and the dominant ideology, produce.

On a societal or macro level, those interested in the welfare of poor black female adolescents should develop mechanisms that expand their opportunities for achieving what they want, which will no doubt change as their material circumstances improve. In the *Chambers* case in particular, the courts should have been more concerned about chastising employers like the club for restricting the employment opportunities of young unmarried black mothers than with reinforcing the club's message that single pregnancies and parenthood are not appropriate modes of conduct for young black women. The courts ignored the disparity between the club's hopes for its members and the structural impediments to their achievement. Furthermore, the courts compounded the obstacles for the plaintiff and others by failing to relate the club's position to those impediments, and by passing up an opportunity to condemn systemic racial, sexual, and economic injustice on behalf of young unmarried black mothers.

The motherhood of unmarried adult black women is being treated as if it were a social problem inextricably linked with, if not causally responsible for, teenage pregnancy. Both the adolescents and the adults have in common the degeneracy of engaging in intercourse that produces babies that other people think they should not have. But beyond their shared profligate sexuality, it is not entirely clear what connects single adult mothers and pregnant women with the conduct of their teenage counterparts. The concern may be that unmarried adult pregnancies and motherhood prompt teens to believe that sex before marriage is morally acceptable.

In any event, the condemnation of black unwed motherhood is so deeply embedded in mainstream thought that its invocation in connection with teenage pregnancy may be considered uncontroversial. The accusation of negative role modeling on the part of black single mothers represents an extension of long-standing indictments that are the product of the unique variants of patriarchy that apply to black women alone.

At bottom, unmarried black women workers who have babies are being accused of carrying on like modern-day Jezebels when they should be acting like good revisionist Mammies. Though not totally divorced from reality, Jezebel and Mammy were largely ideological constructs that supported slavery. Each pertained to black female slaves' intertwined roles as sexual beings and workers. Each justified the economic and sexual exploitation of black female slaves by reference to their character traits, rather than to the purposes of the masters. Jezebel was the wanton, libidinous black woman whose easy ways excused white men's abuse of their slaves as sexual "partners" and bearers of mulatto offspring.[34] Jezebel was both "free of the social constraints that surrounded the sexuality of white women," to whom she represented a threat, and "isolated from the men of her own community."[35]

In contrast, Mammy was "asexual," "maternal," and "deeply religious."[36] Her principal tasks were caring for the master's children and running the household.[37] Mammy was "the perfect slave—a loyal, faithful, contented, efficient, conscientious member of the family who always knew her place; and she gave the slaves a white-approved standard of black behavior."[38] She was "the personification of the ideal slave, and the ideal woman, . . . an ideal symbol of the patriarchal tradition. She was not just a product of the 'cultural uplift' theory [which touted slavery as a means of civilizing blacks], but she was *also* a product of the forces that in the South raised motherhood to sainthood."[39]

Role models are supposed to forgo the vices of Jezebel and exhibit the many virtues of Mammy. When Crystal Chambers refused to subordinate her interest in motherhood to the supposed welfare of the club girls, she essentially rejected the club's attempt to impose on her the "positive" stereotype of the black female as a repressed, self-sacrificing, nurturing woman whose heart extends to other people's children because she cannot (or should not) have kids of her own. Instead, like a Jezebel, Crystal Chambers "flaunted" her sexuality and reproductive capacity, but, unlike her counterpart in slavery, she did so in furtherance of her own ends, in defiance of her white employers, and in disregard of a rule that forbade her from connecting with a man outside the marriage relationship.

Crystal Chambers was supposed to expose the young club members, the beneficiaries of white benevolence, to images congruent with traditional notions of patriarchy that were not entirely consistent with the norms of the black community. She was supposed to be an accomplice in regulating the sexuality of other young black females, in much the same way that she was expected to tolerate the regulation of her own. The courts would have us believe that the club acted for the good of the girls who would miss out on a host of opportunities if they became teen mothers. Yet the distinction between paternalism and oppression is hardly crisper now than it was during slavery.

Crystal Chambers's experience is emblematic of the political significance of the professional "black role model" (including many of us lawyers and law professors) in this, the post-civil rights, post-black power era. Our attention is constantly being directed to some black person who is, should, or wants to be a role model for others. Many of these role models are black people who have achieved stature and power in the white world because they supposedly represent the interests of the entire black community. Such role models gain capital (literally and figuratively) to the extent that they project an assimilated persona that is as unthreatening to white people as it is (supposed to be) intriguing to our young. Because the emphasis on role modeling suggests that motivation and aspirations are the cure for the problems of poor minority people, those who accept the appellation "role model" help contain demands from below for further structural changes and thereby assist in the management of other blacks. Insofar as doing more for the poor is concerned, the service role models perform is regrettably distinguishable from mentoring or power brokering; the role models really do not have very much clout to wield on behalf of other blacks, racial and sexual discrimination and exploitation being what they are.

There are conceptions of "role modeling" that are not quite so alien to the political and cultural heritage of African American women.[40] As far as I am concerned, Crystal Chambers became more nearly a role model when she fought back, when she became a Sapphire. Her single motherhood represented an alternative social form that one might choose deliberately, rationally, and proudly. Refusing to go along with the program, she joined the host of nonelite black women who every day mount local, small-scale resistance grounded in indigenous cultural values, values whose real political potential is often hidden even from those whose lives they govern.

NOTES

1. New Dictionary of American Slang 368 (R. Chapman ed., 1986). *Amos 'n' Andy* originated as a radio comedy program about two black males. B. Andrews & A. Juilliard, Holy Mackerel! The Amos 'n' Andy Story 15–16 (1986). It was first broadcast in 1928, and the characters were played by the program's white originators. *Id. Amos 'n' Andy* came to CBS television in 1951, with a cast of carefully chosen black actors. *Id.* at 60–61, 45–59. Various black civil rights organizations condemned the television version as "insulting to blacks" and as portraying blacks "in a stereotyped and derogatory manner." The sponsor withdrew from the show, and it was dropped by the network in 1953. *Id.* at 61, 101. It lived on in syndication until 1966. *Id.* at 118, 121–22.

2. b. hooks, Ain't I a Woman? Black Women and Feminism 85–86 (1981); Scott, *Debunking Sapphire: Toward a Non-Racist and Non-Sexist Social Science, in* All the Women Are White, All the Blacks Are Men, but Some of Us Are Brave 85 (G. Hull et al. eds., 1982).

3. A. Walker, In Search of Our Mothers' Gardens xi–xii (1983).

4. H. Baker, Workings of the Spirit: The Poetics of Afro-American Women's Writing (forthcoming).

5. 629 F. Supp. 925 (D. Neb. 1986), *aff'd,* 834 F.2d 697 (8th Cir. 1987), *reh'g denied,* 840 F.2d 583 (1988).

6. *Id.* at 928.

7. *Id.* at 929.

8. 834 F.2d at 699 n.2.

9. 629 F. Supp. at 949 & n.45.

10. *Id.* at 946–47.

11. *Id.* at 947, 949.

12. 834 F.2d at 701–03. The burden of persuasion with regard to this defense is now clearly on the Title VII claimant. Wards Cove Packing Co. v. Antonio, 57 U.S.L.W. 4583 (June 5, 1989). The *Wards Cove* decision was overruled by the Civil Rights Act of 1991.

13. 834 F.2d at 703–05.

14. *Id.* at 950.

15. *Id.* at 951.

16. *Id.* at 934.

17. *Id.* at 945 n.40.

18. *Id.* at 928.

19. *Id.*

20. *Id.* at 934.

21. The trial court asserted, apparently based on the testimony, that "the number of teenage pregnancies among blacks is presently much higher than among whites." 629 F. Supp. at 928. It appears that in Douglas County, Nebraska, in 1981, "the fertility rate of black teenagers [was] approximately 2 1/2 times greater than that for whites." *Id.* at 949 n.45. Blacks, however, comprised only 12.8 percent of the population. *Id.*

Although the court's statement may have been true for Douglas County, it does not reflect the national picture. Marian Wright Edelman puts the "epidemic" in perspective:

> Contrary to popular perception, the majority of teen parents (342,283 of 499,038 in 1983) are white. Poor and minority teens, however, have a disproportionate share of teen births and are disproportionately affected by the social and economic consequences of early parenthood. A black teen is five times as likely as a white teen to become an unwed parent.

M. Edelman, Families in Peril: An Agenda for Social Change 57 (1987).

22. 629 F. Supp. at 950.

23. The prime exegesis of this perspective is C. Murray, Losing Ground: American Social Policy, 1950–1980 (1984).

24. *See* Read, *For Poor Teen-agers, Pregnancies Become New Rite of Passage,* Wall St. J., Mar. 17, 1988, § 1, at 1.

25. *See generally* National Research Council Panel on Adolescent Pregnancy and Childbearing, Risking the Future 123–39 (1987).

26. W. Wilson, The Truly Disadvantaged: The Inner City, the Underclass, and Public Policy 70 (1987).

27. *See* Edelman, *supra* note 21, at 53. *But see* Kleinman & Kessel, *Racial Differences in Low Birth Weight: Trends and Risk Factors,* 317 New Eng. J. Med. 749, 752–53 (1987) (the adverse impact of black adolescent childbearing on overall statistics has been *overemphasized*).

28. D. Frank, Deep Blue Funk and Other Stories: Portraits of Teenage Parents 11, 44 (1983); Diamant, *Teenage Pregnancy and the Black Family,* Boston Globe, May 18, 1986, Magazine, at 19, 47.

29. Frank, *supra* note 28, at 61–82.

30. Anderson, *Sex Codes and Family Life among Poor Inner-City Youths,* Annals, Jan. 1989, at 67.

31. *Id.* at 67, 71–73.

32. *See* Willis, *Cultural Production and Theories of Reproduction, in* Race, Class and Education 107 (L. Barton & S. Walker eds., 1983); Giroux, *Theories of Reproduction and Resistance in the New Sociology of Education: A Critical Analysis,* 53 Harv. Educ. Rev. 257 (1983).

33. Thompson, *Search for Tomorrow: On Feminism and the Reconstruction of Teen Romance, in* Pleasure and Danger: Exploring Female Sexuality 350, 376–78 (C. Vance ed., 1984).

34. D. White, "Ain't I a Woman": Female Slaves in the Plantation South 46, 61 (1985).

35. E. Fox-Genovese, Within the Plantation Household: Black and White Women of the Old South 292 (1988).

36. White, *supra* note 34, at 46.

37. E. Genovese, Roll, Jordan, Roll: The World the Slaves Made 353–56 (1972).

38. *Id.* at 356.

39. White, *supra* note 34, at 58 (emphasis in original).

40. *See* Gilkes, *Successful Rebellious Professionals: The Black Woman's Professional Identity and Community Commitment,* 6 Psychol. Women Q. 289 (1982).

36

A Hair Piece: Perspectives on the Intersection of Race and Gender

Paulette M. Caldwell

I want to know my hair again, to own it, to delight in it again, to recall my earliest mirrored reflection when there was no beginning and I first knew that the person who laughed at me and cried with me and stuck out her tongue at me was me. I want to know my hair again, the way I knew it before I knew that my hair is me, before I lost the right to me, before I knew that the burden of beauty—or lack of it—for an entire race of people could be tied up with my hair and me.

I want to know my hair again, the way I knew it before I knew Sambo and Dick, Buckwheat and Jane, Prissy and Miz Scarlett. Before I knew that my hair could be wrong—the wrong color, the wrong texture, the wrong amount of curl or straight. Before hot combs and thick grease and smelly-burning lye, all guaranteed to transform me, to silken the coarse, resistant wool that represents me. I want to know once more the time before I denatured, denuded, denigrated, and denied my hair and me, before I knew enough to worry about edges and kitchens and burrows and knots, when I was still a friend of water—the rain's dancing drops of water, a swimming hole's splashing water, a hot, muggy day's misty invisible water, my own salty, sweaty, perspiring water.

When will I cherish my hair again, the way my grandmother cherished it, when fascinated by its beauty, with hands carrying centuries-old secrets of adornment and craftswomanship, she plaited it, twisted it, cornrowed it, finger-curled it, olive-oiled it, on the growing moon cut and shaped it, and wove it like fine strands of gold inlaid with semiprecious stones, coral and ivory, telling with my hair a lost-found story of the people she carried inside her?

Mostly, I want to love my hair the way I loved hers, when as granddaughter among grandsons I stood on a chair in her room—her kitchen-bed-living-dining room—and she let me know her hair, when I combed and patted it from the crown of her head to the place where her neck folded into her shoulders, caressing steel-

gray strands that framed her forehead before falling into the soft, white, cottony temples at the border of her cheekbones.

Cotton. Cotton curled up in soft, fuzzy puffballs around her face. Cotton pulled out and stretched on top of her head into Sunday pompadours. Cotton, like the cotton blooming in August in her tiny cotton field. Cotton, like the cotton that filled the other room in her house—the cotton room—the storehouse for September's harvest, a cradle to shield her pickings from wind and rain, to await baling and ginning and cashing in. Cotton, which along with a cow, a pig, and a coop of chickens, allowed her to eke out a husband-dead, children-gone independence in some desolate place, trapped in the bowels of segregation. Here, unheard, unseen, free, she and her beauty and her hair could not be a threat to anyone.

ON BEING THE SUBJECT OF A LAW SCHOOL HYPOTHETICAL

The case of *Rogers v. American Airlines*[1] upheld the right of employers to prohibit the wearing of braided hairstyles in the workplace. The plaintiff, a black woman, argued that American Airlines' policy discriminated against her specifically as a black woman. In effect, she based her claim on the interactive effects of racial and gender discrimination. The court chose, however, to base its decision principally on distinctions between biological and cultural conceptions of race. More important, it treated the plaintiff's claims of race and gender discrimination in the alternative and independent of each other, thus denying any interactive relationship between the two.

Although *Rogers* is the only reported decision that upholds the categorical exclusion of braided hairstyles, the prohibition of such styles in the workforce is both widespread and long-standing. I discovered *Rogers* while reading a newspaper article describing the actual or threatened firing of several black women in metropolitan Washington, D.C., solely for wearing braided hairstyles. The article referred to *Rogers* but actually focused on the case of Cheryl Tatum, who was fired from her job as a restaurant cashier in a Hyatt Hotel under a company policy that prohibited "extreme and unusual hairstyles."

The newspaper description of the Hyatt's grooming policy conjured up an image of a ludicrous and outlandishly coiffed Cheryl Tatum, one clearly bent on exceeding the bounds of workplace taste and discipline. But the picture that accompanied the article revealed a young, attractive black woman whose hair fell neatly to her shoulders in an all-American, common, everyday pageboy style, distinguished only by the presence of tiny braids in lieu of single strands of hair.

Whether motivated by politics, ethnic pride, health, or vanity, I was outraged by the idea that an employer could regulate or force me to explain something as personal and private as the way I groom my hair.

My anger eventually subsided, and I thought little more about *Rogers* until a student in my course in Employment Discrimination Law asked me after class to explain the decision. I promised to take up the case when we arrived at that point in the semester when the issues raised by *Rogers* fit most naturally in the development of antidiscrimination law.

Several weeks passed, and the student asked about *Rogers* again and again (always privately, after class), yet I always put off answering her until some point later in the semester. After all, hair is such a little thing. Finally, in a class discussion on a completely unrelated topic, the persistent one's comments wandered into the forbidden area of braided-hair cases. As soon as the student realized she had publicly introduced the subject of braided hair, she stopped in midsentence and covered her mouth in embarrassment, as if she had spoken out of turn. I was finally forced to confront what the student had obviously sensed in her embarrassment.

I had avoided private and public discussions about braided hair not because the student had asked her questions at the wrong point in the semester. Nor had I avoided the subject because cases involving employer-mandated hair and grooming standards do not illustrate as well as other cases the presence of deeply ingrained myths, negative images, and stereotypes that operate to define the social and economic position of blacks and women. I had carefully evaded the subject of a black woman's hair because I appeared at each class meeting wearing a neatly braided pageboy, and I resented being the unwitting object of one in thousands of law school hypotheticals.

WHY WOULD ANYONE WANT TO WEAR THEIR HAIR THAT WAY?

In discussing braided hairstyles, I was not prepared to adopt an abstract, dispassionate, objective stance on an issue that so obviously affected me personally; nor was I prepared to suffer publicly, through intense and passionate advocacy, the pain and outrage that I experience each time a black woman is dismissed, belittled, and ignored simply because she challenges our objectification. Should I be put to the task of choosing a logical, credible, "legitimate," legally sympathetic justification out of the many reasons that may have motivated me and other black women to braid our own hair? Perhaps we do so out of concern for the health of our hair, which many of us risk losing permanently after years of chemical straighteners; or perhaps because we fear that the entry of chemical toxins into our bloodstreams through our scalps will damage our unborn or breast-feeding children. Some of us choose the positive expression of ethnic pride not only for ourselves but also for our children, many of whom learn, despite all our teachings to the contrary, to reject association with black people and black culture in search of a keener nose or bluer eye. Many of us wear braids in the exercise of private, personal prerogatives taken for granted by women who are not black.

The persistent student's embarrassed questioning and my obfuscation spoke of a woman-centered silence: she, a white woman, had asked me, a black woman, to justify my hair.[2] She compelled me to account for the presence of legal justifications for my simultaneously "perverse visibility and convenient invisibility."[3] She forced me and the rest of the class to acknowledge the souls of women who live by the circumscriptions of competing beliefs about white and black womanhood and in the interstices of racism and sexism.

Our silence broken, the class moved beyond hierarchy to a place of honest collaboration. Turning to *Rogers,* we explored the question of our ability to comprehend through the medium of experience the way a black woman's hair is related to the perpetuation of social, political, and economic domination of subordinated racial and gender groups; we asked why issues of experience, culture, and identity are not the subject of explicit legal reasoning.

TO CHOOSE MYSELF: INTERLOCKING FIGURATIONS IN THE CONSTRUCTION OF RACE AND GENDER

SUNDAY. *School is out, my exams are graded, and I have unbraided my hair a few days before my appointment at the beauty parlor to have it braided again. After a year in braids, my hair is healthy again: long and thick and cottony soft. I decide not to french roll it or twist it or pull it into a ponytail or bun or cover it with a scarf. Instead, I comb it out and leave it natural, in a full and big "Angela Davis" Afro style. I feel full and big and regal. I walk the three blocks from my apartment to the subway. I see a white male colleague walking in the opposite direction and I wave to him from across the street. He stops, squints his eyes against the glare of the sun, and stares, trying to figure out who has greeted him. He recognizes me and starts to cross over to my side of the street. I keep walking, fearing the possibility of his curiosity and needing to be relieved of the strain of explanation.*

MONDAY. *My hair is still unbraided, but I blow it out with a hair dryer and pull it back into a ponytail tied at the nape of my neck before I go to the law school. I enter the building and run into four white female colleagues on their way out to a white female lunch. Before I can say hello, one of them blurts out, "It is weird!" Another drowns out the first: "You look so young, like a teenager!" The third invites me to join them for lunch while the fourth stands silently, observing my hair. I mumble some excuse about lunch and interject, almost apologetically, that I plan to get my hair braided again the next day. When I arrive at my office suite and run into the white male I had greeted on Sunday, I realize immediately that he has told the bunch on the way to lunch about our encounter the day before. He mutters something about how different I look today, then asks me whether the day before I had been on my way to a ceremony. He and the others are generally nice colleagues, so I half-smile, but say nothing in response. I feel a lot less full and big and regal.*

TUESDAY. *I walk to the garage under my apartment building again wearing a big, full "Angela Davis" Afro. Another white male colleague passes me by, not recognizing me. I greet him and he smiles broadly, saying that he has never seen me look more beautiful. I smile back, continue the chitchat for a moment more, and try not to think about whether he is being disingenuous. I slowly get into my car, buckle up, relax, and turn on the radio. It will take me about forty-five minutes to drive uptown to the beauty parlor, park my car, and get something to eat before beginning the long hours of sitting and braiding. I feel good, knowing that the braider will be ecstatic when she sees the results of her healing handiwork. I keep my movements small, easy, and slow, relishing a rare, short morning of being free.*

My initial outrage notwithstanding, *Rogers* is an unremarkable decision. Courts generally protect employer-mandated hair and dress codes, and they often accord the greatest deference to codes that classify individuals on the basis of socially conditioned rather than biological differences.

But *Rogers* is regrettably unremarkable in an important respect. It rests on suppositions that are deeply embedded in American culture. *Rogers* proceeds from the premise that, although racism and sexism share much in common, they are nonetheless fundamentally unrelated phenomena—a proposition proved false by history and contemporary reality. Racism and sexism are interlocking, mutually reinforcing components of a system of dominance rooted in patriarchy. No significant and lasting progress in combating either can be made until this interdependence is acknowledged, and until the perspectives gained from considering their interaction are reflected in legal theory and public policy.

Among employment discrimination cases that involve black female plaintiffs, at least three categories emerge.

In one category, courts have considered whether black women may represent themselves or other race or gender discriminatees. Some cases deny black women the right to claim discrimination as a subgroup distinct from black men and white women.[4] Others deny black women the right to represent a class that includes white women in a suit based on sex discrimination, on the ground that race distinguishes them.[5] Still other cases prohibit black women from representing a class in a race discrimination suit that includes black men, on the ground of gender differences.[6] These cases demonstrate the failure of courts to account for race-sex intersection, and are premised on the assumption that discrimination is based on either race or gender, but never both.

A second category of cases concerns the interaction of race and gender in determining the limits of an employer's ability to condition work on reproductive and marital choices associated with black women.[7] Several courts have upheld the firing of black women for becoming pregnant while unmarried if their work involves association with children—especially black teenage girls. These decisions rest on entrenched fears of and distorted images about black female sexuality, stigmatize single black mothers (and by extension their children), and reinforce "culture of poverty" notions that blame poverty on poor people themselves. They also reinforce the notion that the problems of black families are attributable to the deviant and dominant roles of black women and the idea that racial progress depends on black female subordination.

A third category concerns black women's physical images. These cases involve a variety of mechanisms to exclude black women from jobs that involve contact with the public—a tendency particularly evident in traditionally female jobs in which employers place a premium on female attractiveness—including a subtle, and often not so subtle, emphasis on female sexuality. The latter two categories sometimes involve, in addition to the intersection of race and gender, questions that concern the interaction of race, gender, and culture.

The failure to consider the implications of race-sex interaction is only partially explained, if at all, by the historical or contemporary development of separate political movements against racism and sexism. Rather, this failure arises from the inability of political activists, policy makers, and legal theorists to grapple with the existence and political functions of the complex myths, negative images, and stereotypes regarding black womanhood. These stereotypes, and the culture of prejudice that sustains them, exist to define the social position of black women as subordinate on the basis of gender to all men, regardless of color, and on the basis of race to all other women. These negative images also are indispensable to the maintenance of an interlocking system of oppression based on race and gender that operates to the detriment of all women and all blacks. Stereotypical notions about white women and black men are developed not only when they are compared to white men, but also when they are set apart from black women.

THE *ROGERS* OPINION

The court gave three principal reasons for dismissing the plaintiff's claim. First, in considering the sex discrimination aspects of the claim, the court disagreed with the plaintiff's argument that, in effect, the application of the company's grooming policy to exclude the category of braided hairstyles from the workplace reached only women. Rather, the court stressed that American's policy was evenhanded and applied to men and women alike.[8] Second, the court emphasized that American's grooming policy did not regulate or classify employees on the basis of an immutable gender characteristic.[9] Finally, American's policy did not bear on the exercise of a fundamental right.[10] The plaintiff's racial discrimination claim was analyzed separately but dismissed on the same grounds: neutral application of American's antibraid policy to all races and absence of any impact of the policy on an immutable racial characteristic or of any effect on the exercise of a fundamental right.

The court's treatment of culture and cultural associations in the racial context bears close examination. It carefully distinguished between the phenotypic and cultural aspects of race. First, it rejected the plaintiff's analogy between all-braided and Afro, or "natural" hairstyles. Stopping short of concluding that Afro hairstyles might be protected under all circumstances, the court held that "an all-braided hairstyle is a different matter. It is not the product of natural hair growth but of artifice."[11] Second, in response to the plaintiff's argument that, like Afro hairstyles, braids reflected her choice for ethnic and cultural identification, the court again distinguished between the immutable aspects of race and characteristics that are "socioculturally associated with a particular race or nationality."[12] However, given the variability of so-called immutable racial characteristics such as skin color and hair texture, it is difficult to understand racism as other than a complex of historical, sociocultural associations with race.

In support of its view that the plaintiff had failed to establish a factual basis for her claim that American's policy had a disparate impact on black women, thus destroying any basis for the purported neutral application of the policy, the court pointed to American's assertion that the plaintiff had adopted the prohibited hairstyle only shortly after it had been "popularized" by Bo Derek, a white actress, in the film *10*.[13] Notwithstanding the factual inaccuracy of American's claim, and notwithstanding the implication that there is no relationship between braided hair and the culture of black women, the court assumed that black and white women are equally motivated (i.e., by the movies) to adopt braided hairstyles.

Wherever they exist in the world, black women braid their hair. They have done so in the United States for more than four centuries. African in origin, the practice of braiding is as American—black American—as sweet potato pie. A braided hairstyle was first worn in a nationally televised media event in the United States—and in that sense "popularized"—by a black actress, Cicely Tyson, nearly a decade before the movie *10*. More important, Cicely Tyson's choice to popularize (i.e., to "go public" with) braids, like her choice of acting roles, was a political act made on her own behalf and on behalf of all black women.[14]

The very use of the term "popularized" to describe Bo Derek's wearing of braids—in the sense of rendering suitable to the majority—specifically subordinates and makes invisible all the black women who for centuries have worn braids in places where they and their hair were not overt threats to the American aesthetic. The great majority of such women worked exclusively in jobs where their racial subordination was clear. They were never permitted in any affirmative sense of the word any choice so closely related to personal dignity as the choice—or a range of choices—regarding the grooming of their hair. By virtue of their subordination—their clearly defined place in the society—their choices were simply ignored.

The court's reference to Bo Derek presents us with two conflicting images, both of which subordinate black women and black culture. On the one hand, braids are separated from black culture and, by implication, are said to arise from whites. Not only do blacks contribute nothing to the nation's or the world's culture, they copy the fads of whites. On the other hand, whites make fads of black culture, which, by virtue of their popularization, become—like all "pop"—disposable, vulgar, and without lasting value. Braided hairstyles are thus trivialized and protests over them made ludicrous.

To narrow the concept of race further—and, therefore, racism and the scope of legal protection against it—the *Rogers* court likened the plaintiff's claim to ethnic identity in the wearing of braids to identity claims based on the use of languages other than English. The court sought refuge in *Garcia v. Gloor*, a decision that upheld the general right of employers to prohibit the speaking of any language other than English in the workplace without requiring employers to articulate a business justification for the prohibition.[15] By excising the cultural component of racial or ethnic identity, the court reinforces the view of a homogeneous, unicultural society, and pits blacks and other groups against each other in a battle over minimal deviations from cultural norms. Black women cannot wear their hair in braids because Hispanics cannot speak Spanish at work. The court cedes to private employers the power of family patriarchs to enforce a numbing sameness, based exclusively on the employers' whim, without the obligation to provide a connection to work performance or business need, and thus deprives employees of the right to be judged on ability rather than on image or sound.

HEALING THE SHAME

Eliminating the behavioral consequences of certain stereotypes is a core function of antidiscrimination law. This function can never be adequately performed as long as courts and legal theorists create narrow, inflexible definitions of harm and categories of protection that fail to reflect the actual experience of discrimination. Considering the interactive relationship between racism and sexism from the experiential stand-point and knowledge base of black women can lead to the development of legal theories grounded in reality, and to the consideration by all women of the extent to which racism limits their choices as women and by black and other men of color of the extent to which sexism defines their experiences as men of subordinated races.

Creating a society that can be judged favorably by the way it treats the women of its darkest race need not be the work of black women alone, nor will black women be the exclusive or primary beneficiaries of such a society. Such work can be engaged in by all who are willing to take seriously the everyday acts engaged in by black women and others to resist racism and sexism and to use these acts as the basis to develop legal theories designed to end race and gender subordination.

NOTES

1. 527 F. Supp. 229 (S.D.N.Y. 1981).

2. I know that the student intended no harm toward me. She, too, was disturbed by *Rogers.* She had come to law school later in life than many of her classmates and was already experiencing the prejudices of the labor market related to the intersection of gender and age. She seemed to sense that something in the underlying racism and sexism in *Rogers* would ultimately affect her in a personal way.

3. McKay, *Black Woman Professor—White University,* 6 Women's Stud. Int'l F. 143, 144 (1983).

4. *See, e.g.,* DeGraffenreid v. General Motors Assembly Div., 413 F. Supp. 142, 145 (E.D. Mo. 1976) (Title VII did not create a new subcategory of "black women" with standing independent of black males).

5. *See, e.g.,* Moore v. Hughes Helicopter, Inc., 708 F.2d 475, 480 (9th Cir. 1983) (certified class includes only black females, as plaintiff black female inadequately represents white females' interests).

6. *See, e.g.,* Payne v. Travenol, 673 F.2d 798, 810–12 (5th Cir. 1982) (interests of black

female plaintiffs substantially conflict with interests of black males, since females sought to prove that males were promoted at females' expense notwithstanding the court's finding of extensive racial discrimination).

7. *See* Chambers v. Girls Club of Omaha, 834 F.2d 697 (5th Cir. 1987).

8. *Rogers, supra* note 1, at 231.

9. *Id.*

10. *Id.*

11. *Id.* at 232.

12. *Id.*

13. *Id.*

14. Her work is political in the sense that she selects roles that celebrate the strength and dignity of black women and avoids roles that do not.

15. Garcia v. Gloor, 618 F.2d 264, 267–69 (5th Cir. 1980).

37 Black Women and the Constitution: Finding Our Place, Asserting Our Rights

Judy Scales-Trent

The economic, political, and social situation of black women in America is bad, and has been bad for a long time. Historically, they have borne both the disabilities of blacks and the disabilities that inhere in their status as women. The result is that black women are the lowest-paid group in America today when compared to white women, black men, or white men.

Despite, or perhaps because of, this dual disability and its negative effects on life opportunities for black women, the problems of black women often go unrecognized. By creating two separate categories for its major social problems—"the race problem" and "the women's issue"—society has ignored one of the groups that stand at the interstices of these two groups, black women in America.[1] The legal system has incorporated the same dichotomous system—"minorities" and "women"—into its way of analyzing problems.

This essay is a response to the dichotomous treatment of black women in the law. I will discuss how a new group, with a new status—black women—is formed by the combination of multiple statuses in society. I will also explore the question of how the group "black women" should be defined under the equal protection clause of the Constitution. Finally, I will address two implications of treating black women as a distinct group. First, should all subsets of blacks be treated in the same manner? The second question is concerned with other groups of women—Hispanic women or Asian women—and asks, Could they not make the same arguments as black women, and does this create problems in terms of the development of the equal protection clause or in terms of factionalizing American society?

BLACK WOMEN AS A DISCRETE GROUP

In a society that sees as powerful both whiteness and maleness, black women possess no characteristic associated with power. They are therefore treated by society in a manner that reflects a status different from, and lower than, both black men (who have the status ascribed to maleness) and white women (who enjoy the status ascribed to whiteness). Since black women share this disfavored status, they feel a need to come together for mutual protection. This "perceived need to band together in defense against domination or hostility" is one major source of cultural identity.[2] One example of how black women have asserted themselves as a group within the legal system is the litigation they have initiated under Title VII of the Civil Rights Act of 1964,[3] alleging employment discrimination.

Title VII of the Civil Rights Act of 1964 prohibits discrimination in employment based on race, sex, religion, national origin, or color.[4] When groups allege employment discrimination based on group status, often that discrimination is based on one characteristic, such as religion, sex, or race. However, employers who discriminate do not always do so in such neat categories. Just as widespread discrimination against black women as a class has always existed in American society, widespread employment discrimination against the class has existed as well. Since the enactment of Title VII, black women have gone to court claiming discrimination, as individuals and as a group, based on their distinct identity as black women. In 1980, the Fifth Circuit became the first court of appeals to rule on the issue of whether black women are protected as a discrete class under Title VII in *Jefferies v. Harris Cty. Community Action Association.*[5] The court held that they are so protected, noting that discrimination against black females can exist even in the absence of discrimination against black men or white women.[6]

Several courts have expressed concern as to how such claims would be proved and defended within the traditional evidentiary framework of Title VII. One district court noted that "the prospect of the creation of new classes of protected minorities, governed only by the mathematical principles of permutation and combination, clearly raises the prospect of opening the hackneyed Pandora's box."[7] Black women have sought to claim this distinct status, notwithstanding the Pandora's box concern, because it is often the only way they can prove that they have been victims of remediable harm.

Title VII and the equal protection clause of the Fourteenth amendment to the U.S. Constitution are similar in that both are used by disfavored groups to gain equal treatment by society. They are, however, also different. The major difference, for the purposes of this essay, between Title VII and the Constitution is that under Title VII, protected groups are always treated in the same manner. For example, a failure to hire claim raised by a group of women (sex discrimination) is assessed in the same way as one raised by a group of Mexican Americans (national origin discrimination). However, under the equal protection clause, the level of protection changes depending on which group is presenting the equal protection claim, and how much protection the court thinks is warranted based on that group's social and historical status. It is because of this difference between Title VII and the Constitution that a new analysis is required to situate the group "black women" within the equal protection clause, and to consider how this group should be treated by the courts.

THE EQUAL PROTECTION CLAUSE

THE FRAMEWORK FOR GROUP PROTECTION UNDER THE EQUAL PROTECTION CLAUSE

The groups possessing the clearest definition, and therefore the highest level of protection under the Constitution, are racial and ethnic minorities. "Legal restrictions which curtail the civil rights of a single racial group are immediately suspect."[8] Such laws are subject to strict scrutiny and will be sustained only if they serve a compelling state interest.[9] Thus, black Americans, both male and female, are entitled to the highest level of protection under the Constitution when confronted with state action that restricts them due to their race.

Women, along with several other groups,[10] come after racial and ethnic minorities in this hierarchy of protection. The Court has determined that a classification that has a negative effect on women is not "immediately suspect," although it is subject to a heightened standard of review. The government need only show that the classification is substantially related to an important government objective for it to be held constitutionally permissible under the equal protection clause.

The third category of groups are those that have been defined by the Court as not needing and therefore not entitled to any heightened level of scrutiny. The Court will defer to the legislative body in cases of classifications based on age,[11] out of state persons,[12] new residents in the state,[13] or the mentally retarded,[14] as long as the classification is "rationally related" to a legitimate state interest.

THE PROTECTION OF BLACK WOMEN AS A CLASS WITHIN THE FRAMEWORK OF THE EQUAL PROTECTION CLAUSE

There are three possible ways to protect black women within the equal protection framework. The first is to treat black women as a subset of blacks or of women, and to grant their claims the level of protection accorded that group under the current tripartite analysis of the Court. The second is to treat black women as a discrete group seeking protection under the Constitution, and to assess that group on its own merits to determine the level of protection it should be afforded. One might analyze the situation of black women in this society as that of a "discrete and insular" minority that is unable to enjoy the benefits of full citizenship, and thus entitled to strict scrutiny protection under the equal protection clause. Third, one might argue that since black women carry the burden of membership in the black group, which is already entitled to strict scrutiny protection, as well as membership in the disfavored female group, they should be entitled to *more* than strict scrutiny protection by the courts.

The Subset Theory

How are black women to be subclassified: in the black group or in the female group? This question is important because the level of protection granted black women will differ depending on whether they are placed in the black group or the female group. Yet the notion that the level of protection would change depending on which way they are classified is bizarre, since black women are always both black and female. As long as race is part of the group identity, any classification that limits their opportunities should be reviewed under the highest level of scrutiny.

The "Discrete and Insular Minority" Theory

The second possibility is to treat black women as a discrete group seeking protection under the Constitution and to assess the group on its own merits to determine the level of protection it should be afforded. In making this determination, the Court has traditionally looked at whether the group is defined by immutable characteristics,[15] whether there has been historical prejudice against the group,[16] and the extent to which the group is politically powerless.[17]

Both history and social science demonstrate that black women, a group defined by two immutable characteristics, have suffered over the centuries from prejudice based on their group characteristics. As a result, black women have suffered and continue to suffer from political powerlessness within our society. Therefore, black women clearly belong to a group which is entitled to be classified as "discrete and insular" for purposes of determining the level of scrutiny applicable to equal protection claims.

The "More Than Strict Scrutiny" Theory

The final possibility is that black women—who are burdened by the double stigma of race and sex—are entitled to more than even the "strict scrutiny" level of review accorded when there is a state action that harms based on race. If the race stigma alone is sufficient to trigger strict scrutiny review, the race stigma plus an additional stigma (sex) should entitle the group to an even higher level of scrutiny and protection by the Court.

How could a court provide more than a "strict scrutiny" level of review? It could ease the burden of proof in equal protection cases brought by black women by lessening the requirement for a showing of intent, for example. By so doing, a court would, in effect, be taking judicial notice of the double burdens carried by black women and the likelihood that their group identity continues to operate to their detriment.[18] Similarly, in an employment discrimination case, it could require a lesser showing of harm before requiring a state employer to engage in affirmative action for black women. There are many ways a court could recognize that "race plus another burden" should be protected at the level of "strict scrutiny plus more."[19] In analytical terms, such a step is a logical extension of the equal protection framework created by the Court. Realistically, however, it seems unlikely that the Court will break ground for a group that it barely acknowledges as a separate class. Nonetheless, it is a logical next step for a court brave enough to take it.

FURTHER QUESTIONS

What I have said thus far raises questions about the further direction of developments under the equal protection clause, questions I now turn to.

The first question concerns the theory that black women are a subset of the black group, and therefore qualify for the highest level of protection based on that status. If this theory applies, does it follow that other subsets of black groups, with secondary characteristics that do not warrant the highest level of protection (i.e., the aged, the retarded), merit the same consideration as black women?

The answer is yes. Subsets, such as the black aged and the black retarded, are in the same analytical position as black women for the purposes of the equal protection clause, and should be treated the same way.

A second issue is raised by the argument that black women can be considered a discrete group for purposes of the equal protection clause. If this is true, what about Asian women or Hispanic women? Where do these double categories stop? The concern is with the "slippery slope": What are we letting ourselves in for if we start down this path? Is there a limiting principle?

The simple response is that the equal protection clause has already been construed to be self-limiting. To the extent that other "dual" groups—Asian women, for example—could show a group identity and harm to the group based on that identity, it is hard to see why they should not be equally protected.

The Constitution was never intended to protect the rights of black Americans. Certainly, there was no intention of protecting black women. Only since the passage of the Fourteenth Amendment, with its statement that all citizens are entitled to equal protection of the laws, has the Constitution afforded such protection. Black women clearly have not been granted the "equal protection of the laws" in the past. It is only by demanding the highest level of scrutiny from the courts that they will receive such protection in the future.

NOTES

1. W. E. B. Du Bois alluded to this dual identity in recounting the following conversation: "Wait till the lady passes," said a Nashville white boy. "She's no lady; she's a nigger," answered another. W. E. B. Du Bois, Darkwater: Voices from Within the Veil 185 (1920).

2. Karst, *Paths to Belonging: The Constitution and Cultural Identity,* 64 N.C. L. Rev. 304 (1986).

3. 42 U.S.C. § 2000e.

4. *See* Civil Rights Act of 1964 § 703 as amended, 42 U.S.C. §§ 2000–2002 (1983).

5. 615 F.2d 1025 (5th Cir. 1980).

6. *Id.* at 1032.

7. DeGraffenreid v. General Motors Corp., 413 F. Supp. 142, 145. (E.D. Mo. 1976).

8. Korematsu v. United States, 323 U.S. 214, 216 (1944).

9. Graham v. Richardson, 403 U.S. 365 (1971); McLaughlin v. Florida, 379 U.S. 184, 192 (1964).

10. *See, e.g.,* Craig v. Boren, 429 U.S. 190, 197 (1976). *See also* Plyler v. Doe, 457 U.S. 202 (1982) (classification based on alienage).

11. Massachusetts Board of Retirement v. Murgia, 427 U.S. 307 (1976).

12. Metropolitan Life Ins. Co. v. Ward, 470 U.S. 869 (1985).

13. Williams v. Vermont, 472 U.S. 14 (1985)

14. City of Cleburne v. Cleburne Living Center, 473 U.S. 432 (1985).

15. *See, e.g.,* Frontiero v. Richardson, 411 U.S. 677 (1973).

16. *See, e.g.,* San Antonio v. Rodriguez, 411 U.S. 1, 28 (1973).

17. *See, e.g.,* Massachusetts Board of Retirement, 427 U.S. at 307, 313; Graham, 403 U.S. at 365, 372.

18. *Cf.* Bundy v. Jackson, 641 F.2d 934, 953 (D.C. Cir. 1981) (burden of proof eased in Title VII retaliation claim where plaintiff already proved underlying claims of sexual harassment).

19. Although I am convinced by the argument that the double burden carried by black women entitles them to more than strict scrutiny review, it is personally difficult to argue that black women should get more protection than black men under the equal protection clause. Black men are family, and it seems an unhappy splitting of the family to say that the women of that family are entitled to more than the men. The reality is, however, that black women are not creating factions within the black community but are responding to them. A legal analysis that recognizes the factions created by the larger society is only recognizing the historical and social realities that make certain remedies necessary.

38 | The Value of Black Mothers' Work

Dorothy E. Roberts

WHY MUST WELFARE MOTHERS WORK?

The common ground of contemporary welfare reform discourse is the belief that single mothers' dependence on government support is irresponsible and that these mothers should be required to get jobs. "Workfare" is a refrain of the general theme that blames the poor, because of their dependence mentality, deviant family structure, and other cultural depravities, for their poverty. Martha Minow reveals workfare's injustice by asking the unspoken question, "why should single mothers responsible for young children be expected to work outside the home?"[1] Why does society focus on welfare mothers' dependence on public assistance rather than on their children's dependence on them for care?

Minow correctly points out that the focus on welfare mothers' dependence rather than their valuable care reflects a radical departure from the original welfare policy toward mothers. During the late nineteenth century, women successfully lobbied for public relief for widowed mothers.[2] Women's organizations and their allies exploited the ideology of motherhood to attain mothers' pensions and other "maternalist" legislation. The logic that propelled maternalist welfare policy was precisely the opposite of that backing workfare: widowed mothers needed government aid so that they would not have to relinquish their maternal duties in the home in order to join the workforce.

The current workfare proposals, then, reflect an unprecedented depreciation of welfare mothers' contribution to society. The rhetoric of motherhood has lost all the persuasive force it wielded during the Progressive Era. The modern welfare state has increasingly degraded the work all mothers perform. It has abandoned the moral mother ideology and diminished the control of mothers over child care. As increasing numbers of women join the workforce, society decreasingly rewards mothers' socially productive labor in the home. An individual's entitlement to welfare benefits now depends on his or her relationship to the market. As unpaid caregivers with no connection to a male breadwinner, single mothers are considered undeserving clients of the welfare system.

This universal devaluation of mothers' work, however, does not explain entirely the revolution in welfare reform. When welfare reformers devise remedies for maternal irresponsibility, they have Black single mothers in mind. Although marital status does not determine economic well-being, there is a strong association between Black single motherhood and family poverty.[3] The image of the lazy Black welfare queen who breeds children to fatten her allowance shapes public attitudes about welfare policy.[4] Part of the reason that maternalist rhetoric can no longer justify public financial support is that the public views this support as benefiting primarily Black mothers.[5] Society particularly devalues Black mothers' work in the home because it sees these mothers as inherently unfit and their children as inherently useless.

THE VALUE OF BLACK MOTHERING

Maternalist rhetoric has no appeal in the case of Black welfare mothers because society sees no value in supporting their domestic service. The public views these mothers as less fit, less caring, and less hurt by separation from their children. First, workfare advocates fail to see the benefit in poor Black mothers' care for their young children. To the contrary, contemporary poverty rhetoric blames Black single mothers for perpetuating poverty by transmitting a deviant lifestyle to their children. Far from helping children, payments to Black single mothers merely encourage this transgenerational pathology.

The ideal Black mother figure, Mammy, selflessly nurtured *white* children (under her mistress's supervision).[6] In contrast, whites portrayed Black slave mothers as careless and unable to care properly for their *own* children. Modern social pundits from Daniel Patrick Moynihan to Charles Murray have held Black single mothers responsible for the disintegration of the Black family and the Black community's consequent despair.[7]

Second, workfare advocates fail to see the injury in requiring Black mothers to leave their young children. Welfare reform discourse gives little attention to the relationship between poor Black mothers and their children. The forced separation of Black mothers from their children began during slavery, when Black family members faced being auctioned off to different masters.[8] The disproportionate state disruption of Black families through the child welfare system reflects a continuing depreciation of the bond between Black mothers and their children.[9]

Finally, workfare advocates are not hindered by any disharmony in the idea of a Black working mother. The conception of motherhood confined to the home and opposed to wage labor never applied to Black women. Slave women's hard labor in the field defied the Victorian norm of female domesticity. Even after emancipation, political and economic conditions forced many Black mothers to earn a living outside the home.[10] American culture reveres no Black madonna; it upholds no popular image of a Black mother nurturing her child. Given this history, it is not surprising that policy makers do not think twice about requiring welfare mothers to leave their young children in order to go to work.[11]

THE VALUE OF BLACK CHILDREN

The state often uses the pretext of helping children to justify regulating their mothers.[12] What is striking about recent welfare proposals is that they do not even claim the traditional justification of promoting children's welfare. Indeed, they mandate or encourage practices traditionally regarded as harmful to children, such as mothers working outside the home and abortion. Welfare reformers cannot demonstrate that it is better for poor children to make their mothers work. Their mothers' employment may actually reduce the amount of money available for their needs and jeopardize their health care; it may deprive them of their only protection against a myriad of environmental hazards. Thus, it is not mothers' wage labor itself that is harmful to children; rather, workfare's harm lies in its failure to provide meaningful support for working mothers, such as day care, jobs, housing, health care, education, and a guaranteed income.

Underlying the consensus that welfare mothers should work is often the conviction that their children are socially worthless, lacking any potential to contribute to society. Welfare reform rhetoric assumes that these children will grow up to be poor and, consequently, burdens to society. The proposals dismiss any possible reason to nurture, inspire, or love these children. Minow asks at the end of her essay, "why not consider paying mothers of especially young children to care for their children?"[13] In addition to the historic resistance to compensating mothers' work, society's response is, "because these children are not worth it."

The reason for society's bleak assessment is not only the belief that Black mothers are likely to corrupt their children, but also the belief that Black children are predisposed to corruption.[14] Blaming single mothers for "nurturing a next generation of pathology" stigmatizes not only mothers but their children as well. The powerful Western image of childhood innocence does not seem to benefit Black children. Black children are born guilty. They are potential menaces—criminals, crackheads, and welfare mothers waiting to happen. Newspaper stories about "crack babies" warn of a horde of Black children, irreparably damaged by their mothers' prenatal drug use, who are about to descend on inner-city kindergartens. These stories present drugs, poverty, and race as fungible marks that inevitably doom Black children to a worthless future.

Serious talk about alternatives to current welfare reform proposals must center on society's dismissal of poor Black families' relationships and futures. Perhaps recognizing workfare's particular devaluation of Black mothers' work will lead some to reject these proposals and to search for ways of supporting poor single mothers' struggle to raise their children against terrifying odds. Perhaps recognizing the sheer dissonance of the hope that majority America will treasure poor Black children will lead others to work more strenuously toward "an economic game plan for poor black communities." [15]

NOTES

1. Martha Minow, *The Welfare of Single Mothers and Their Children,* 26 Conn. L. Rev. 817 (1994).

2. *See generally* Theda Skocpol, Protecting Soldiers and Mothers: The Political Origins of Social Policy in the United States 373–74 (1992); Linda Gordon, Pitied but Not Entitled: Single Mothers and the History of Welfare (1994).

3. From 1959 to 1987, the proportion of poor Black families maintained by women rose from 46 percent to 74 percent, compared to an increase from 20 percent to 42 percent of poor white families. Audrey Rowe, *The Feminization of Poverty: An Issue for the 90's,* 4 Yale J.L. & Feminism 73, 74 (1991) (citing U.S. Bureau of the Census, Current Population Rep., Ser. P-60, No. 163, Poverty in the United States: 1987, at 156 (1989)). *See also* Barbara Omolade, *The Unbroken Circle: A Historical and Contemporary Study of Black Single Mothers and Their Families,* 3 Wis. Women's L.J. 239 (1987) (describing the origins of Black single motherhood).

4. *See* Patricia Hill Collins, Black Feminist Thought: Knowledge, Consciousness, and the Politics of Empowerment 77 (1991) (describing the stereotypical image of Black welfare mothers).

5. The maternalist welfare legislation of the Progressive Era benefited white mothers almost exclusively. *See* Skocpol, *supra* note 2, at 471 (noting that only 3 percent of beneficiaries of mothers' pensions were Black).

6. *See* Elizabeth Fox-Genovese, Within the Plantation Household: Black and White Women of the Old South 292 (1988).

7. *See* Charles Murray, Losing Ground: American Social Policy, 1950–1980, at 154–66 (1984) (claiming that welfare induces Black women to refrain from marriage and to have babies); Office of Planning and Policy Research, U.S. Dep't of Labor, The Negro Family: The Case for National Action (1965).

8. *See* Anita Allen, *Surrogacy, Slavery, and the Ownership of Life,* 13 Harv. J.L. & Pub. Pol'y 139, 140–44 (1990) (noting that slave mothers had no legal claim to their children).

9. *See* Carol B. Stack, *Cultural Perspectives on Child Welfare,* 12 N.Y.U. Rev. L. & Soc. Change 539 (1983–84) (arguing that the misunderstanding of Black family patterns contributes to the disproportionate number of Black children placed in foster care). On the child welfare system's disproportionate removal of Black children, see generally Andrew Billingsley & Jeanne M. Giovannoni, Children of the Storm: Black Children and American Child Welfare (1972) (tracing the history of Black children in the American child welfare system); Sylvia S. Gray & Lynn M. Nybell, *Issues in African-American Family Preservation,* 69 Child Welfare 518 (1990) (discussing the cultural context in which the child welfare system operates).

10. *See generally* Jacqueline Jones, Labor of Love, Labor of Sorrow: Black Women, Work, and the Family from Slavery to the Present (1985). There was a dramatic racial disparity among married women who worked at the turn of the century. In 1900, 26 percent of married nonwhite American women were in the labor force, compared to only 3.2 percent of married

white women. Claudia Goldin, Understanding the Gender Gap: An Economic History of American Women 17 (1990) (Table 2.1).

11. The oppressive aspects of workfare proposals thus complicate white feminists' view of work as a liberating force for women. *See* Dorothy E. Roberts, *Racism and Patriarchy in the Meaning of Motherhood,* 1 Am. U. J. Gender & L. 1, 20–22 (1993) (noting that the experience of Black working mothers complicates the feminist response to domesticity). Black mothers historically experienced work outside the home as an aspect of racial subordination and economic exploitation.

12. *See* Dorothy E. Roberts, *Punishing Drug Addicts,* chapter 17 in this volume. *See generally* Dorothy E. Roberts, *Motherhood and Crime,* 79 Iowa L. Rev. 95, 109–15 (1993) (discussing the punishment of mothers who fail to protect their children from abuse).

13. *Id. See also* Carol Delaney, *Welfare Shouldn't Be Tied to Work,* N.Y. Times, Dec. 10, 1993, at A34 ("Why couldn't welfare be considered payment for the valuable job that many of these women do?").

14. Daniel Goleman, *New Storm Brews on Whether Crime Has Roots in Genes,* N.Y. Times, Sept. 15, 1992, at C1. *See also* Lynne Duke, *Controversy Flares over Crime, Heredity,* Wash. Post, Aug. 19, 1992, at A4 (discussing controversy over the government's biological research on crime).

15. *See* Regina Austin, *Left at the Post: One Take on Blacks and Postmodernism,* 26 Law & Soc. Rev. 751, 753 (1992).

39 Structures of Subordination: Women of Color at the Intersection of Title VII and the NLRA. Not!

Elizabeth M. Iglesias

LAW AS STRUCTURAL VIOLENCE

This essay explores the relationship between law and the social reality of subordination through the concept of "structural violence," a term I draw from liberation theology.[1] The critique implicit in the concept of structural violence entails a commitment to structural justice, defined here as a commitment to the evolution of institutional arrangements in which relations of domination can be effectively transformed through the agency of those whom the society subordinates.

I invoke the concept of structural violence to examine how legal interpretation constructs institutional power and how the organization of institutional power obstructs our liberation from the relations of oppression that are constituted through the socially constructed categories of race and gender. Focusing specifically on the workplace, I examine the procedures for collective organization in labor unions and the procedural structures available for enforcing Title VII.

At a superficial level, both the National Labor Relations Act (NLRA) and Title VII appear to provide women of color with viable avenues for obtaining recourse and effecting change in the workplace. The empathetic interpretation of particular legal issues in particular cases by particular judges also appears, at times, to have produced progressive results for women of color. Nevertheless, these avenues of agency and recourse are more apparent than real. Their limitations are often obscured because legal interpretation is practiced in and operates through a strategic fragmentation of doctrinal and institutional domains.

The politics of interpretative fragmentation results in and is based on the absence of women of color as a compelling reference point in the elaboration of boundaries and intersections between the different legal regimes that converge on the American workplace. The purpose of this essay is to foreground the woman of color and to bring this reference point to bear in a sustained critique of the cumulative and interactive impact the politics of interpretative fragmentation has had in regulating our agency and constructing our identities.

To define my project in this way is to invite assault on numerous fronts. The most immediate source of potential misunderstanding is the implicit assertion that women of color constitute a distinct political subject and represent a meaningful perspective from which existing legal regimes may be examined and judged.[2] Admittedly, the woman of color is a historically contingent,[3] culturally embedded, and politically contested subjectivity. Nevertheless, women of color represent the potential universality of a shared political identity, not because we constitute a homogeneous group, but because, as a political construct, we represent a shared context of struggle based on our individual experiences at the intersection of multiple practices of oppression and identity formation.

The institutional arrangements established by law present a reality in which a woman of color finds no home for herself as an integrated whole; to participate in the community she must sacrifice some significant aspect of herself.[4] My purpose is to illustrate how this is done at the boundaries of Title VII and the NLRA and, furthermore, to suggest how we might remedy this by reconstructing the processes of collective identity formation and the redistribution of institutional power.[5]

THE DUTY OF FAIR REPRESENTATION AT THE INTERSECTION OF TITLE VII AND THE NLRA

DEFINING THE CONTEXT: *STEELE V. LOUISVILLE AND N.R.R.*

The duty of fair representation (DFR) was first imposed on labor unions in the case of *Steele v. Louisville and N.R.R.*[6] Although purporting to act "as representative of the entire craft of firemen," the Brotherhood in Steele amended its collective bargaining agreement with the railroads to exclude all black firemen from employment. The black firemen brought suit, seeking an injunction prohibiting the union from representing blacks so long as it continued to exclude racial minorities. The Supreme Court held that unions had a statutory duty to represent fairly the interests of all workers in any appropriate bargaining unit they purported to represent.

Thus, the DFR first appeared as an obligation imposed on unions in exchange for the power to determine the working conditions of minority workers who were excluded from membership and who were legally prohibited from establishing their own competing organizations. The purpose of imposing the duty was to avoid the constitutional and practical problems that might be generated if a union were permitted to discriminate against a group it purported to represent. Since *Steele*, the duty of fair representation has been the subject of extensive judicial elaboration and legal scholarship.[7]

Rather than focusing initially on the legal standards that govern judicial review of majoritarian decisions under the DFR, I look at the institutional structures that have been created through the invocation of the DFR in a variety of different contexts where Title VII and the NLRA intersect. In each of these contexts, the decisions established boundaries between Title VII and the NLRA and invoked the fact of the DFR—that is, they invoked its existence as an alternative avenue of recourse. Crossing these domains is an important first step toward understanding the significance of this duty for women of color.

CHANNELING AGENCY AND ALLOCATING INSTITUTIONAL POWER: TOWARD A FIRST UNDERSTANDING OF STRUCTURAL VIOLENCE

This section explores two series of cases: one that ordered the integration of racially segregated unions and another that established the conditions under which minority workers will be legally protected from retaliation for opposing race discrimination in the workplace. The purpose of my analysis is to illustrate the cumulative impact of these decisions in the construction, or, more precisely, the deconstruction of the opportunities for collective alliance among and the exercise of transformative agency by women of color who inhabit the institutional arrangements that are constructed through these decisions.

The Duty of Fair Representation in the Integration of Segregated Union Locals

Almost thirty years ago, federal courts throughout the South invoked Title VII to compel the integration of racially segregated unions in the longshoring industry. In all the cases, the mergers were vehemently opposed, not only by white, but also by black and Latino union officials, and by a majority of the black and Latino workers these officials represented.[8]

In *EEOC v. Int'l Longshoremen's Ass'n,*[9] black union representatives were particularly explicit about the impact the merger would have on the interests of black longshoremen and the black community in general. Testifying before the trial court, they asserted that

> [T]he Negroes, by having their own unions and their own union officials, have been able to better themselves by being able to hold high positions in their locals, and have been recognized in the community as a separate, powerful voice for the Negro communities, and has attained for them and the Negro people of the community, a standing which they could not have otherwise attained.[10]

The court dismissed their objections. Merger was ordered, in part, on the theory that under the DFR the white majority representatives would owe black workers a duty to eliminate race discrimination if the segregated unions were merged and that the black workers were unlikely to make substantial progress at the bargaining table without it. Rather than merging the locals in the hopes that black workers would benefit from white representation subject to the DFR, the courts might have focused on developing legal doctrines that would make Title VII a more effective remedy against discrimination both at the bargaining table and in the employment decisions that were not then being channeled through the collective bargaining process.

The Duty of Fair Representation and Section 7 Rights of Concerted Activity

Like the integration cases, *Emporium Capwell Co. v. Western Addition Community Organization*[11] was concerned both with the appropriate relationship between Title VII and the NLRA and with the relative priority of individual and collective rights. However, the only similarity in the resolution of these cases was the way the DFR was invoked to legitimate the submergence and demobilization of minorities within a broader collectivity controlled by a white majority.

Doctrinally, *Emporium Capwell* turned on resolving the relationship between a union's status as exclusive bargaining representative under Section 9(a) of the NLRA[12] and the employees' right to engage in concerted activity under the protection of Section 7 of Title VII.[13] The case arose as a result of the employer's retaliatory discharge of two black workers who were involved in organizing a picket and a community boycott to protest the employer's racially discriminatory employment practices. When the workers were discharged, a community civil rights organization brought suit against the employer under Section 8(a)(1) of the NLRA.[14]

The National Labor Relations Board concluded that the employees' protest activities, though concerted, were not protected by Section 7 because they amounted to "nothing short of a demand that the [company] bargain with the picketing employees for the entire group of minority employees."[15] According to the board, a demand for separate bargaining would undermine the union's status as exclusive representative under Section 9(a).

The D.C. Circuit reversed. Recognizing that the policies of the two statutes might conflict at the intersector, the court concluded that the national policy of eliminating race discrimination took precedence over the NLRA's policy of promoting "orderly collective bargaining."

The Supreme Court purportedly agreed that the NLRA and Title VII should be interpreted as elements of a unified national labor policy and that eliminating racial discrimination is a highest priority of that "unified" policy.[16] The Court also recognized that Section 7 protection would give the black workers access to the enforcement procedures of the NLRB, which the Court reluctantly acknowledged might be instrumentally superior to the procedures established for enforcing Title VII.[17] Nevertheless, the Court refused to afford Section 7 protection to racial subgroups engaged in concerted activities in support of their demands for nondiscriminatory employment policies.

In so holding, the Court effectively ensured that the substantive rights created under one legal regime would not be enforced through the procedural mechanisms of the other, or, more precisely, that Title VII substantive rights would not be enforced through NLRA procedures, which include Section 7 protection for concerted action.

By fragmenting Title VII and the NLRA into separate doctrinal domains, *Empo-*

rium Capwell limited the extent to which the whole power of the state could be used to eliminate race and gender subordination in the workplace.[18] It also created an interpretative context in which the inconsistent and biased treatment of crucial conceptual structures, like the relationship between individual and collective rights, would remain hidden. From this perspective, legal interpretation produces structural violence against women of color because the fragmentation of these regimes obscures the extent to which the same interests and identities that are negated in the interpretation of one regime are also negated in the interpretation of the other.

A comparison of *Emporium Capwell* and the union integration cases provides a good illustration. In the union integration cases, black and Latino workers were denied the authority to maintain an independent collective identity as a result of the courts' judgment that collective rights and majority interests must give way to the individual's Title VII rights. The segregated locals were merged on the theory that the separate locals violated Title VII if only one individual could show that the arrangement tended to deprive him of equal employment opportunities. The merger caused black and Latino workers to lose an important institution through which they had been able to advance their collective interests, both in the workplace and in the local community.[19]

Like the integration cases, *Emporium Capwell* also denied minorities an independent collective identity. After fragmenting Title VII and the NLRA into separate regimes, the Court reviewed the policies and precedents established under the NLRA and concluded that the black workers were not entitled to Section 7 protection. This time, however, the suppression of minority collective agency was effected on the theory that the Title VII rights the black workers were attempting to enforce through their collective action were individual rights that must give way to the majority's collective rights.

Both *Emporium Capwell* and the union integration cases mediate the individual/collective rights conflict through a vision of group identity that is formally color-blind and gender-neutral. Both cases also invoke the duty of fair representation and contemplate a potential Title VII action against the employer or the union. In doing so, the courts create an impression that minority workers in majority unions have recourse. Since minority workers have alternatives other than disruptive protesting or separate bargaining, the court could in each case focus entirely on the costs of separate bargaining or concerted action by racial minorities. The practical consequence of this approach is to imprison minorities in institutional arrangements in which they can hold no effective power. The structure of institutional power that is maintained, at one end, by *Emporium Capwell* and, at the other, by the union integration cases constitutes racial minorities as a demobilized subset submerged in the majoritarian institutions it constructs and consolidates.

For women of color, the practical disempowerment effected by this structure is exponentially multiplied. Situated at the intersection of multiple socially constructed categories, women of color are constituted as members of various groups, whose most common characteristic, from our perspective, is that we are most often numerical minorities. Equally important, ostensibly gender- and/or color-blind collectives operate to deconstruct women of color, both as individuals and as a collective political identity. The move toward deconstruction is explicit in the priority given individual rights in the union integration cases and implicit in *Emporium Capwell's* refusal to recognize the collective nature of the black workers' claims and protests.

The way the courts negotiate the relationship between Title VII and the NLRA produces structural violence. By fragmenting these two regimes, the courts maintain an interpretative context that accords inconsistent priority to individual and collective rights and hides the practical consequences from view. However, the fragmentation of Title VII and the NLRA does more than simply provide a context in which individual and collective rights can be blindly manipulated. These fragmented domains are also the context in which the relationship between these two regimes is interpretatively manipulated to produce a legal structure in which our political identities and collective agency are systematically negated.

In *King v. Illinois Bell Telephone Co.*,[20] the relationship between Title VII and the NLRA was once again examined, this time in the context of a Section 704(a) claim.[21] About a year after King was hired, a group of black employees presented the company's representatives with a list of grievances alleging numerous instances of race discrimination and communicated their refusal to work until the grievances were resolved. When they were suspended from work, they formed a picket line outside the company's corporate headquarters in Chicago during working hours.

King was the group's spokesperson at a meeting with company officers. A few days later, King and the other demonstrators were discharged. About a month later, the company rehired a number of the suspended employees. King was not rehired.

While the company claimed that King was a poor worker with a poor attitude, King claimed that the company's refusal to rehire him was both racially motivated and retaliatory. King claimed that participation in the work stoppage and picketing activities was protected by Section 704(a). The company, on the other hand, argued that the strikes were not protected under Section 704(a) because they were conducted by union members during working hours in violation of a no-strike clause contained in the union's collective bargaining agreement with the company. In resolving the dispute, the court found it necessary not only to construe Title VII, but also to examine the policies embodied in the NLRA, since "strikes are an integral part of our labor laws."[22] Reviewing the Supreme Court's decision in *Emporium Capwell*, the *King* court noted that *Emporium Capwell* had expressly declined to decide whether the discharged employees were protected by the opposition conduct clause of section 704(a) of Title VII. Nevertheless, after quoting the Court for the proposition that Title VII rights "cannot be pursued at the expense of the orderly collective-bargaining process contemplated by the NLRA ... [whether they are thought to depend upon Title VII or have an independent source in NLRA]," the *King* court concluded that it was "reasonable to infer that the Court would reject the argument that an employee's Section 704(a) right to oppose employment discrimination encompasses the use of work stoppages which are prohibited by the terms of a collective bargaining agreement."[23]

The evolution of doctrine from *Emporium Capwell* to *King* is as significant as it was predictable.[24] If *King* represents the ultimate resolution of the issue left undecided in *Emporium Capwell,* namely, the degree to which Section 704(a) protects concerted activity that is unprotected under the NLRA, then the relationship between Title VII and the NLRA is not, after all, distinct and discontinuous. While *Emporium Capwell* ensures that the rights and privileges established by the NLRA will not be expanded to accommodate the antidiscrimination policies of Title VII, *King* means that the rights established under Title VII will be contracted to accommodate the policies and objectives of the NLRA. As a result, the antidiscrimination mandate of Title VII is subordinated to the policies of the NLRA in both regimes.

Consider the impact of this structure on a woman of color who inhabits a workplace regulated by these intersecting regimes.[25] She is at the intersection of a network of institutional arrangements that fragment her individual identity and diffuse her political identity. Each regime offers an alternative set of incentives and opportunities that conflict with each other but converge on her in a manner that ignores the integrity of her reality as an individual situated at the intersection of the multiple practices of race-, gender-, and class-based oppression.

Collective action through unions is the recognized vehicle through which working people protect and promote their interests. Yet, given the union integration cases, the woman of color cannot realistically hope to establish a union in which she would be a majority member.[26] Supporting unionization as a minority/woman may further her class interests, but perhaps at the expense of her race/gender interests.[27] If the workplace is unionized, the woman of color may lose the legal protection her oppositional agency might otherwise receive under Title VII. On the other hand, resisting unionization may further her race/gender interests, but perhaps at the expense of her class interests.[28] That Title VII and the NLRA were not created for her is best evidenced by the fact that she neither exists for them except as a fragment of who she is, nor can she, through them, affirm her interests as an integrated whole.

STRUCTURAL CLOSURE: THE DUTY OF FAIR REPRESENTATION AS LEGAL FICTION

I have argued that the fragmentation of Title VII and the NLRA provides an interpretative context in which the distinct interests and collective identity of women of color are systematically suppressed through inconsistent interpretations of the relationship between the policies and procedures of Title VII and the NLRA. Cumulatively, these interpretations constitute women of color as submerged minorities in an institutional structure that affords them no legal avenue of effective self-determination. In these cases, the DFR functions as a legitimating image—as the conceptual cement that holds together a series of arrangements that deprive women of color of an institutionally recognized collective identity. To support the weight of this institutional structure of suppressed agency and compulsory submergence, the substantive standards of the DFR and Title VII would have to be rigorous. These substantive standards are in fact inadequate to counteract the structural disempowerment erected on the basis of the duty of fair representation. Thus, structural violence reaches closure in the interpretative illusion of a duty without substance.

The key case defining the substantive elements of the DFR is *Vaca v. Sipes*.[29] There the Court held that the DFR is breached "only when a union's conduct toward a member of the collective bargaining unit is arbitrary, discriminatory or in bad faith." This standard has prevented the DFR from being an effective vehicle for challenging majoritarian decisions that negatively affect the interests of racial minorities and women of any race. *NAACP v. Detroit Police Officers Association*[30] *(DPOA [I]* and *DPOA [II])* and *Seep v. Commercial Motor Freight, Inc.*[31] are illustrative.

In *DPOA [II]*, the Sixth Circuit reversed a lower court decision holding that the police officers' union had violated its DFR by failing to oppose the massive layoff of recently hired black police officers. Most of these officers were hired pursuant to an affirmative action program adopted as a result of a judicial determination that the city had discriminated against blacks. The layoffs were made pursuant to the collective bargaining agreement between the city and the DPOA, which required that the layoffs be based strictly on reverse seniority, the last hired being the first fired. Of the approximately 1,100 laid-off police officers, approximately 75 percent were black. Thus, the effect of the layoffs was to wipe out most of the affirmative action recruiting that had increased minority representation on the Detroit police force.

The lower court found a breach of the DFR based on the DPOA's complete failure to take any action to preserve the jobs of the black officers. On appeal, the Sixth Circuit reversed.[32] Citing *Vaca*, the court found no basis for holding the union liable for its failure to resist the layoffs of the black officers. The union's mere failure to bargain forcefully does not by itself constitute bad faith or discrimination.[33] In characterizing the lower court's opinion, the Sixth Circuit *completely and inexplicably ignored* the extent to which that holding was based explicitly on the lower court's findings that the all-white union leadership was affirmatively hostile toward the interests of the black police officers and intentionally and discriminatorily refused to act on their behalf in the same way they acted on behalf of white police officers when the latter were threatened with similar layoffs.

The question is whether the *Vaca* standards for breach of the DFR simply confer too much discretion on unions to discriminate and on courts to "wash their hands" in the name of preserving "the integrity and autonomy" of unions' internal decision-making processes. These standards have not only permitted all-white union leaderships, like the DPOA's, to discriminate with impunity against racial minorities of both genders, but have also insulated all-male union leaderships from liability to the female workers on whose behalf they have failed to act.

In *Seep v. Commercial Motor Freight, Inc.*, female clerical employees brought suit challenging a number of actions and inactions by their union under Title VII and the DFR. According to the court, the union's decision to permit workers in the other all-male units to cross the female workers' picket line was not discriminatory under *Vaca* because those units "represented the overwhelming majority of the local's membership at Commercial."[34] Thus, *"it was the size of the unit rather than the gender of its members which influenced the union's decision.* Such action was within the permissible scope of the union's discretion."[35]

The court's reasoning in *Seep* is particularly disturbing. Like *DPOA II*, it suggests that decisions benefiting white/male majorities at the expense of nonwhite/female subgroups are presumptively within the scope of the union's statutory duty toward the minority under both the NLRA and Title VII.[36] If the DFR is presumptively satisfied by decisions promoting the interests of the numerical majority and Title VII is presumptively satisfied in the absence of a breach of the DFR, then it is difficult to see how this duty can really protect the interests of subordinated social groups, at least in cases like *Seep* where the subordinated group is a numerical minority.

The application of *Vaca* standards in *DPOA* and *Seep* raises serious doubts about the extent to which minority interests will be adequately protected in a system of exclusive representation by majority rule that denies subordinated subgroups the power of self-representation in exchange for the promise of a judicially enforced duty of fair representation. In these cases, the courts refused to impose on unions an affirmative duty to combat discrimination; yet the union's affirmative duty to combat discrimination is the *assumption* that underlies a whole series of cases that systematically suppress minority agency. This assumption was invoked expressly in the union integration cases and implicitly in *Emporium Capwell*. If, as it now appears, the duty of fair representation does not require unions to act forcefully and affirmatively to protect minority interests in eliminating discrimination, then the legitimacy of the restrictions imposed on our agency and our authority of self-representation must be seriously reconsidered.

Equally important, the *DPOA* cases give reason to pause at another level. If courts can ignore the many institutional contexts in which minority agency has been restricted on the theory that majority representatives have an affirmative duty to combat discrimination and instead declare that the majority has no such obligation, then judicial review is a wholly unreliable alternative to the power and authority of self-representation. Minorities are well justified in rejecting the offer of "fair representation" and demanding, instead, the legal authority of self-representation, particularly when the courts' vision of the requirements of fair representation differs so markedly from the vision of the unrepresented.

TRANSFORMING THE STRUCTURAL VIOLENCE OF LAW

STRUCTURAL VIOLENCE: CAUSES AND CURES?

The institutional arrangements developed through the interpretation of the boundaries between Title VII and the NLRA constitute a structure that suppresses the agency, restricts the institutional authority, and ignores the collective identity of women of color. If the cases I have discussed are viewed individually, there may be legitimate reasons for defending any one of them. But when one considers their cumulative impact surely something is wrong. The impact of these otherwise inconsistent cases is the systematic suppression of minority agency and the elimination of any effective recourse against the consequences of institutional powerlessness.

What holds these cases together is the complete and total absence of the woman of color as a legitimate agent or remedial reference point and the structure of power-lessness that is thereby established and maintained. It is as though our interests do not matter because we simply do not exist. To the extent we attempt to locate ourselves in these cases, we find ourselves situated in a network of interpretative practices that appear committed to restricting our institutional authority,[37] suppressing our agency,[38] and denying us a distinct identity as individuals or as a group.[39]

This consistent and systematic suppression of women of color through the interpretative practices that construct these various doctrinal domains and institutional arrangements raises one of the most fundamental questions in recent political theory.[40] The question raised by "the ironic situation [of contemporary welfare corporate societies] in which power is widely dispersed and diffused, yet social relations are tightly defined by domination and oppression"[41] is, "why is this general pattern [of unequal distribution of high-level positions across women and men] reproduced even in the face of conscious efforts to change it?" The question is particularly compelling when we consider that adjudication occurs in many different courts, presided over by many different judges, who have many different ideologies and adjudicate ostensibly unrelated issues in distinct doctrinal domains.[42] How can it be that this system of decentralized power nevertheless operates to maintain a systematic, cumulative, and interactive suppression of women of color as legitimate actors in workplaces?

Structural Violence and the Illusion of Objectivity

To overcome structural violence against women of color (and indeed against any other political identity that has been systematically suppressed in the practice of legal interpretation), we must first learn to recognize it when we don't see it. This task is made all the more difficult by the fact that structures of violence are constructed on the absence of the suppressed interests and identities. The absence of women of color does not, however, occur in a vacuum. On the contrary, the refusal to accord us a legally operative identity or to preserve our agency within the institutional arrangements under review is bounded on all sides by the illusion of objectivity, the illusion that individuals can escape the "constitutive group relations" in which they are embedded. Both the fragmentation of Title VII and the NLRA and the repeated assertion that the DFR is an adequate substitute for self-representation are expressions of this illusion.

The illusion of objectivity that is invoked in legal discourse and institutionalized in some representational structures was shattered by the legal realists.[43] Their insights triggered a crisis of legitimacy from which we have yet to recover, for if legal doctrine is truly indeterminate, then we can never be sure that judicial decisions turn on anything more "objective" than the judge's fabled breakfast or, even more alarming, his prejudices and stereotypes and the limited perspectives of his contingent life experiences.

The illusion of objectivity does not, however, explain why judges, agencies, and arbitrators with different ideological agendas operating in different doctrinal domains and reviewing different institutional arrangements nevertheless produce decisions that operate systematically and cumulatively across these domains to suppress the identity and agency of women of color. Because discursive domains are so fragmented, adjudication may be seen as a vehicle for the blind reproduction of subordination, but the opportunity does not explain the actuality. This actuality is best explained by what I call "the unitary consciousness of law," that is, the fact that legal doctrine is an inherited artifact that articulates the perspectives, assumptions, and normative commitments of the group that has controlled the interpretative practices through which legal doctrine is articulated. To the extent interpretative authority has been concentrated in one social group, law (read now as the legal doctrine and the repertoire of permissible interpretative moves already developed) is not objective; it is affirmatively subjective, an expression of the subjectivity of the group in whom interpretative authority has been concentrated.

The structural violence of law against women of color is perpetuated because an inherited consciousness that devalues and suppresses the self-identity of the woman of color, as much in her presence as, more commonly, in her absence, is embedded in legal doctrines and interpretative norms. The unanswered question is whether the redistribution of interpretative power can transform the subjectivity of the unitary consciousness we have inherited into the objectivity of a multiple consciousness, whose substance we have yet to fully comprehend.

Toward Self-Representational Structures

The structure of representational authority that is maintained by the fragmentation of Title VII and the NLRA and legitimated through the invocation of the DFR is based ultimately on the strategically manipulated illusion that the distribution of institutional power among the various socially constructed race/gender groups is irrelevant to an "objective" resolution of conflicting claims. This illusion tells us that the common good can be objectively determined despite the concentration of effective power in one of these groups (namely, and almost uniformly, white men). By way of contrast, I want to briefly explore three alternative models of representational authority that would much more readily establish the conditions for objectively identifying the common good.

The first model, proposed by Eileen Silverstein, establishes a procedure for the certification of interest groups within an exclusive bargaining unit.[44] In Silverstein's system, workers with common interests affected by a union's collective bargaining agenda can form interest groups, which the union is required to deal with in good faith. After they are certified as interest groups,[45] the groups possess a limited right to veto collective bargaining decisions made by the majority. A veto by the majority vote of any certified interest group constitutes a binding rejection of the proposed collective bargaining agreement and forces the union to reopen negotiations with management. Once a second agreement is reached between the union and management, interest groups have only a limited veto subject to a super-majority override. The novel feature of Silverstein's proposal is that it attempts to achieve fair representation through the construction of a procedural mechanism that permits the redistribution of institutional power among self-identified subgroups within the union, rather than through some judicially enforceable standard of fairness.

A second possible model for achieving the redistribution of institutional power draws on the work of Lani Guinier. In two remarkable articles,[46] Guinier launches a compelling critique of the assumptions underlying the purported legitimacy of majority rule[47] and persuasively defends a series of proposals for resolving the problem of unfair and nonresponsive political representation through a system of proportionate interest representation.[48] This model for achieving fair representation through cumulative voting could be used in the election of union officials to redistribute institutional power within unions.

The third and perhaps most radical model follows George Schatzki's proposal to abolish exclusive representation altogether, to eliminate the NLRB determination of "appropriate bargaining units," and to establish a system of self-determined representation.[49]

Despite their differences, all three models share one common feature. They all strive to resolve the problem of fair representation by facilitating the formation of self-identified collectivities and by creating structural arrangements through which institutional power may be more effectively and equally distributed among these various self-determined groupings. Their approach is entirely different from and infinitely more promising than the search for substantive standards and the dead-end debate that DFR jurisprudence has spawned.

TOWARD A GENUINE SOLIDARITY BEYOND THE INDIVIDUAL AND COLLECTIVE RIGHTS CONFLICT

The institutional suppression of minority agency and denial of collective political identity that were effected through the interpretative manipulation of the relative priority of individual and collective rights in the union integration cases and *Emporium Capwell* are profoundly disturbing because they suggest that women of color are situated in a Catch-22. Located at the intersection of multiple practices of subordination and competing political communities, women of color are as much oppressed by collectivist regimes, which proceed through the external imposition of a group identity, as by individualist regimes, which restrict the opportunity for collective alliances and ignore the material reality of our group interests. Despite the competing claims made for and against these alternative regimes, the social reality of women of color negates this dichotomy because this dichotomy negates our reality. While the experience of multiple consciousness teaches us the interdependence of individual and collective identities and the importance of both individual autonomy and group solidarity to our liberation, interpretative practices at the intersection of

Title VII and the NLRA affirm each—only at the expense of the other. For women of color, liberation will require a reconstructed relationship between the individual and collective, both as this relationship is ideologically conceptualized and as it is institutionally constituted.

My analysis is driven by a recognition that individuals are in fact embedded in constitutive group relations, that these relations can be as negative and life destroying as they are positive and community building, and that the preservation of a space for the formation and expression of individual identity is crucial to our ability to mediate and ultimately transcend the constitutive relations that otherwise imprison our agency. By authorizing the formation of more fluid yet institutionally effective alliances among individuals whose social reality may call them to organize across multiple political identities, legal regimes like Silverstein's interest group certification, Guinier's system of proportionate representation, and Schatzki's system of separate representation create the institutional context for self-determination and transformative political alliances. They empower individuals to negotiate for themselves the way the competing claims of their different political identities should be resolved on specific issues of concern in the workplace.

Equally important, the future vitality of the American labor movement depends on our ability to design a new representational structure that preserves the efficacy of collective action while simultaneously promoting internal democracy, equality, and the development of alternative bases of collective power.[50] While the system of exclusive representation based on majority rule is an arrangement through which working people have secured significant benefits, further concentration of union authority is only one possible model for the future.

Multiple bargaining among institutionally empowered self-determined groups is a different and more promising trajectory for minorities, for local communities whose interests have not been adequately represented by unions, and for the evolution of a genuine economic democracy. This new representational structure would need to effect the redistribution and decentralization of institutional power across race/gender subgroups in ways that increase the incentives and opportunities for the inter-movement linkages that scholars like William Gould and Herbert Hill[51] and, more recently, Karl Klare[52] and James Gray Pope[53] have so rightly advocated. Jurisprudentially, this new structure would be grounded in a reunification of Title VII and the NLRA. While the current system of exclusive representation is based on the fragmentation of these regimes (and the strategic subordination of Title VII), a structure of multiple representation would be grounded in a genuinely unified labor policy committed to the ultimate priority of Title VII on the understanding that solidarity presupposes political equality.

Legal theory is relevant to social transformation. To be relevant as a liberation practice, legal theory must help us understand the ways the symbolic/analytical structure of law as a system of meanings—of practical reason and reasoned justification—participates in maintaining the material structures of power. Rather than debating what law is, we need to demonstrate how it works now and how it might be made to work differently. Rather than deep theory, we need practical knowledge.

It is fair to say, at a minimum, that the relationship between Title VII and the NLRA as it has been analytically interpreted and institutionally enforced has played a significant role in maintaining the current structure of race and gender subordination in the American labor force. The jurisprudential and institutional unification of these regimes would be a significant step forward.

NOTES

1. *See, e.g.,* Dominique Barbe, Grace and Power: Base Communities and Nonviolence in Brazil 70–77 (1987).

2. Chandra Mohanty, *Cartographies of Struggle, in* Third World Women and the Politics of Feminism 5–7 (Chandra Mohanty et al. eds., 1991).

3. As Chandra Mohanty notes, "few studies have focused on women workers as subjects— as agents who make choices, have a critical perspective on their own situations, and think and organize collectively against their oppressors." *Id.* at 29.

4. For example, a black woman joins the black liberation movement at the expense of her interests as a woman. Deborah King, *Multiple Jeopardy, Multiple Consciousness: The Context of a Black Feminist Ideology,* 14 Signs 42 (1988). The women's liberation movement neglects her interests as a black. *Id. See also* bell hooks, Feminist Theory: From Margin to Center (1984). And the labor movement's struggle against exploitation in the workplace has often been affirmatively hostile to her interests as both.

5. *See, e.g.,* Lani Guinier, *The Triumph of Tokenism: The Voting Rights Act and the Theory of Black Electoral Success,* 89 Mich. L. Rev. 1077 (1991) [hereinafter Guinier, *Triumph of Tokenism*]; Lani Guinier, *No Two Seats: The Elusive Quest for Political Equality,* 77 Va. L. Rev. 1413 (1991) [hereinafter Guinier, *No Two Seats*]; Eileen Silverstein, *Union Decisions on Collective Bargaining Goals: A Proposal for Interest Group Participation,* 77 Mich. L. Rev. 1485 (1979); George Schatzki, *Majority Rule, Exclusive Representation, and the Interests of Individual Workers: Should Exclusivity Be Abolished?,* 123 U. Pa. L. Rev. 897 (1975).

6. 323 U.S. 192 (1944). *See also* Ford Motor Co. v. Huffman, 345 U.S. 330 (1953) (applying the DFR under the NLRA).

7. *See, e.g.,* Ross E. Cheit, *Competing Models of Fair Representation: The Perfunctory Processing Cases,* 26 B.C. L. Rev. 1 (1982); Matthew W. Finkin, *The Limits of Majority Rule in Collective Bargaining,* 64 Minn L. Rev. 183 (1980); Mayer G. Freed et al., *Unions, Fairness, and the Conundrums of Collective Choice,* 56 S. Cal. L. Rev. 461 (1983).

8. *See* United States v. Int'l Longshoremen's Ass'n, 334 F. Supp. 976, 978 (S.D. Tex. 1971); *Bailey v. Ryan Stevedoring Co.,* 528 F.2d 551 (1976); *Williams,* 466 F. Supp. at 680.

9. 511 F.2d 273 (5th Cir. 1975) [hereinafter EEOC v. ILA], *aff'g* United States v. Int'l Longshoremen's Ass'n, 334 F. Supp. 976 (S.D. Tex. 1971).

10. *Int'l Longshoremen's Ass'n,* 334 F. Supp. at 978.

11. 420 U.S. 50 (1975).

12. Section 9(a) of the NLRA provides in part, "Representatives designated or selected for the purposes of collective bargaining by the majority of the employees in a unit appropriate for such purposes, shall be the exclusive representatives of all the employees in such unit for the purposes of collective bargaining in respect to rates of pay, wages, hours of employment, or other conditions of employment." 29 U.S.C. § 159(a) (1988).

13. Section 7 of the NLRA provides that

Employees shall have the right to self-organization, to form, join, or assist labor organizations, to bargain collectively through representatives of their own choosing, and to engage
in other concerted activities for the purpose of collective bargaining or other mutual aid or
protection, and shall also have the right to refrain from any or all of such activities except
to the extent that such right may be affected by an agreement requiring membership in a labor organization as a condition of employment as authorized in section 158(a)(3) of this
Title.

29 U.S.C. § 157 (1988).

14. Section 8(a)(1) of the NLRA states that "It shall be an unfair labor practice for an
employer—(1) to interfere with, restrain, or coerce employees in the exercise of the rights
guaranteed in Section 157 of this Title." 29 U.S.C. § 158(a)(1) (1988).

15. *Emporium,* 192 N.L.R.B. 173, 185.

16. *Emporium Capwell,* 420 U.S. at 66.

17. *Id.* at 72–73.

18. *See generally* Herbert Hill, *The National Labor Relations Act and the Emergence of
Civil Rights Law: A New Priority in Federal Labor Policy,* 11 Harv. C.R.-C.L. L. Rev. 299
(1976).

19. *Compare* Williams v. New Orleans S.S. Ass'n, 466 F. Supp. 662 (E.D. La. 1979)
(questioning whether this was an appropriate purpose for a labor union) *with* James Cone,
Black Theology and Black Power (1969) (discussing the decomposition of the ghetto for want
of community-creating institutions).

20. 476 F. Supp. 495 (N.D. Ill. 1978).

21. *Id.* at 501.

22. *King,* 476 F. Supp. at 500.

23. *Id.* at 501.

24. For an early prediction of the perverse impact of *Emporium Capwell,* see Note, *Title
VII and NLRA: Protection of Extra-Union Opposition to Employment Discrimination,* 72
Mich. L. Rev. 313, 325 (1973) (protection under Section 704(a) for employees in unionized
workplaces may be restricted after *Emporium*).

25. Clearly, not only women of color may find themselves suppressed and demobilized by
this structure. Rather than undermining my analysis, this fact provides all the more reason for
changing this structure along the lines I advocate below.

26. *But see* Allegheny General Hospital v. NLRB, 608 F.2d 965 (3d Cir. 1979).

27. *See, e.g.,* Rhonda M. Williams & Peggie R. Smith, *What "Else" Do Unions Do? Race
and Gender in Local 35,* Rev. Black Pol. Econ., Winter 1990, at 59.

28. *See, e.g.,* Union Labor Report Weekly Newsletter (BNA), Apr. 2, 1992, at 100–02.
According to the Bureau of Labor Statistics, union members received higher pay than non-
union workers both in 1990 (when median weekly pay was $509 and $390, respectively) and
in 1991 (when median weekly pay was $526 and $404, respectively). Unionized men received
median weekly earnings of $568 compared to unionized women, who received $467. Non-
union men and women received median weekly pay of $473 and $348, respectively. Black
union members received $461 median weekly pay. There was no breakdown by sex.

29. 386 U.S. 171 (1966).

30. 591 F. Supp. 1194 (1984) [hereinafter *DPOA [I]*], *rev'd* 821 F.2d 328 (6th Cir. 1987)
[hereinafter *DPOA [II]*].

31. 575 F. Supp. 1097 (1983).

32. *DPOA [II]*, 821 F.2d at 328.

33. *Id.*

34. *Id.* at 1105.

35. *Id.* at 1105 (italics added).

36. According to the court, the unions' conduct did not violate Title VII because "[t]his conclusion follows from holding that there was no breach of the duty of fair representation, since discriminatory conduct constitutes such a breach." *Seep,* 575 F. Supp. at 1105.

37. *See Payne v. Travenol Laboratories, Inc.,* 673 F.2d 798 (5th Cir. 1982).

38. *See Emporium Capwell,* 420 U.S. at 50; *King,* 476 F. Supp. At 495.

39. *See, e.g.,* ILA Baltimore, 460 F.2d at 497.

40. *See generally* Michel Foucault, Power/Knowledge: Selected Interviews and Other Writings, 1972–1977 (Colin Gordon ed., 1980).

41. Iris Marion Young, Justice and the Politics of Difference 32 (1990).

42. The problem is that while social control may be effectively disbursed across multiple decision-making roles, these institutional roles are occupied for the most part by the same people with the same values. Members of groups that deviate from these norms come to occupy positions of authority and power only to the extent they assimilate themselves to the governing values. *See* Richard Delgado, *Affirmative Action as a Majoritarian Device, or Do You Really Want to Be a Role Model?,* 89 Mich. L. Rev. 1222 (1991). Individuals who assimilate and later change their minds are quickly deposed or isolated by their peers. *Id.*

43. *See, e.g.,* Karl Llewelyn, Bramble Bush 74 (1960) (celebrating the decisional flexibility afforded by the possibility of reading precedents narrowly or broadly).

44. Silverstein, *supra* note 5.

45. Certification requests would, initially, be directed to the national leadership and would include three items: (1) the names of the group leaders; (2) the common economic interest defining the group; and (3) the common negotiation issues on which the interest group disagrees with the union leadership position. Within some specified time period, the national union leadership would have to decide whether to certify the interest group. If denied certification, the interest groups could petition the NLRB. If the union granted certification, the interest group members would be assured a voice in the formulation of contract demands. *Id.* at 1520–21.

46. Guinier, *No Two Seats, supra* note 5; Guinier, *Triumph of Tokenism, supra* note 5.

47. *See* Guinier, *No Two Seats, supra* note 5, at 1437–43.

48. *Id.* at 1458–82.

49. Schatzki, *supra* note 5, at 897–900.

50. *See generally* Building Bridges: The Emerging Grassroots Coalition of Labor and Community (J. Brecher & T. Costello eds., 1990).

51. *See generally* William Gould, Black Workers in White Unions 37–38 (1977); William B. Gould, *Labor Arbitration of Grievances Involving Racial Discrimination,* 118 U. Pa. L. Rev. 40 (1969). *See also* Hill, *supra* note 18.

52. Karl E. Klare, *The Quest for Industrial Democracy and the Struggle against Racism: Perspectives from Labor Law and Civil Rights Law,* 61 Or. L. Rev. 157 (1982).

53. James Gray Pope, *Labor-Community Coalitions and Boycotts: The Old Labor Law, the New Unionism, and the Living Constitution,* 69 Tex. L. Rev. 899 (1991).

Questions and Suggested Readings for Part 6

1. Judy Scales-Trent argues that black women experience a compounded discrimination because of their race and gender. Is her solution that black women be considered a separate class of plaintiffs practical? Does it lead to a dangerous and unmanageable slippery slope?

2. Why was Crystal Chambers's firing problematic? What is wrong with a school for teenage black girls adopting a policy that prohibits teachers from having babies out of wedlock? Does this type of policy discourage teenage pregnancy, and thus offer a positive message?

3. Is hair a meaningful metaphor for cultural hegemony? According to Regina Austin, the Rogers opinion reflects society's lack of understanding of the ethnic and cultural identity of black women. Is that a fair reading of the case? Why shouldn't employers be allowed to regulate "something as personal and private as the way" a woman of color grooms her hair? Are there business justifications for such regulations? Is it necessarily the case that racism is at work here?

4. Is there a solution to last hired/ first fired rules that end up gutting affirmative action programs?

5. Can law be objective? How can we transform the subjectivity of unitary consciousness into the objectivity of multiple consciousness? Why is this objective? Do you agree with the author's three alternate models of representational authority? How do Lani Guinier's voting rights ideas on proportional representation translate in the labor union context? (See Lani Guinier, The Tyranny of the Majority: Fundamental Fairness in Representative Democracy [1994]). In what other ways might the

tension between the collective and the individual be reconstituted to assist women of color in the workplace?

For further reading, see Susan Bisom-Rapp, *Contextualizing the Debate: How Feminist and Critical Race Scholarship Can Inform the Teaching of Employment Discrimination Law*, 44 J. Legal Educ. 366 (1994); Lisa Crooms, *Trying to Make It Real Compared to What? Black Women, Work and Welfare Reform, in* Women, Children and Poverty (Martha Fineman & Twila Perry eds., 1996); Maria Ontiveros, *The Myths of Market Forces, Mothers and Private Employment: The Parental Leave Veto,* 1 Cornell J.L. & Pub. Pol'y 25 (1992); Judy Scales-Trent, *Compound Discrimination: The Intersection of Race and Gender, in* Employment Discrimination: Law and Litigation (Merrick T. Rossein ed., 1994); Cathy Scarborough, *Contextualizing Black Women's Employment Experience,* 98 Yale L.J. 1457 (1989); Peggy Smith, *Separate Identities: Black Women, Work, and Title VII,* 14 Harv. Women's L.J. 21 (1991); Judith Winston, *Mirror, Mirror on the Wall: Title VII, Section 1981, and the Intersection of Race and Gender in the Civil Rights Act of 1990,* 79 Cal. L. Rev. 775 (1991).

7

Beyond Our Borders:
Global Issues

Critical Race Feminism has transcended the boundaries of domestic law. Just as most anthologies on race or gender issues focus on the United States to the exclusion of the majority of the world's people of color, most volumes on international themes omit the concerns of women of color. The few international readers dealing with women's issues often omit legal perspectives. Part 7 fills this gap, exploring issues of international and comparative law norms affecting women of color. CRF's narrative technique and analysis of multiple identities is combined with an assessment of patriarchy and racism, which may take the form of neocolonialism or imperialism as well.

Devon W. Carbado of the University of Iowa uses the narrative technique of Critical Race Theory to augment our understanding of motherhood discussed in part 3 and working discussed in part 6. He examines the sacrifices his Jamaican mother made raising nine children in Great Britain in *Motherhood and Work in Cultural Context: One Woman's Patriarchal Bargain*. His mother's multiple identities as foreigner, female, mother, and worker gave her a "freedom," in her own view, which the author suggests was really his father's—the freedom from child care and work inside the home, consequences of unstated patriarchal bargains that many women make, whether they be in Great Britain, the United States, or elsewhere.

Two articles explore the little understood practice of female genital surgery (FGS), which is sometimes called the more neutral term "circumcision," and sometimes the more inflammatory term "mutilation." Isabelle R. Gunning, who was introduced in part 3 wearing her black lesbian mother identities, now wears her identity of black female international law professor and human rights activist. In her seminal article *Arrogant Perception, World Traveling and Multicultural Feminism: The Case of Female Genital Surgeries*, she calls for feminists of all colors to engage in world traveling, in which we can learn to identify our interconnectedness while respecting

335

the independence of other peoples. Applying this theoretical construct to the culturally challenging practice of FGS, Gunning develops a three-pronged feminist methodology. Using this methodology, she critiques current international human rights norms that are intertwined in the universalism versus cultural relativism dichotomy, that is, the universalist notion that there is one right way, the Western way, of doing things, versus respect for diversity of cultural practices. She calls for a dialogue that would hopefully lead to a universal assessment to limit the practice of FGS.

Hope Lewis builds on Gunning's work in *Between* Irua *and "Female Genital Mutilation": Feminist Human Rights Discourse and the Cultural Divide.* Her essay focuses on the challenges facing African American feminists in dealing with FGS. Ineffective theoretical condemnations of FGS are just as bad as draconian, imperialist attempts to eradicate FGS. Lewis calls for African American feminists to adopt an integrated methodology that clarifies the context in which FGS occurs, develops pragmatic, action-oriented approaches to human rights law, and engages in coalition building.

The part changes continents again with Sharon K. Hom's chapter, *Female Infanticide in China: The Human Rights Specter and Thoughts toward (An)other Vision.* As a Chinese-American "other," Hom includes in her story the narratives of her father's youth in China and her own "return" there as an adult with her father and daughter. Hom calls for a reconceptualization of the ancient but continuing practice of female infanticide, which is built on the historical preference for boys. Recast as social femicide, it would be viewed as more than a crime practiced by individuals continuing archaic ways in light of China's one child population policy. Her vision is not abstract theorizing, but involves the multiplicities of realities of Chinese men and women. The government, feminists, activists, scholars, and the public would all be involved in creating realities of justice that included women.

In *Spouse-Based Immigration Laws: The Legacy of Coverture,* Janet M. Calvo traces the various U.S. immigration law statutes and shows how they perpetuate the concept of coverture, the idea that a wife is under the legal control of her husband. Much like the customary law described in the final chapter by Wing and de Carvalho, coverture gave a husband total control over his wife and children. While current domestic law has ended this legal subordination, immigration law continues it by tying the alien spouse's status to her citizen husband. The net result is that predominantly poor women of color immigrants can be abused and abandoned by their husbands, and cannot invoke the limited U.S. legal remedies for fear of deportation. Assessing the tension between government fears of marital fraud and the need to empower immigrating women, Calvo calls for the foreign spouse to be able to achieve permanent status without her husband as long as she could prove the marriage was entered in good faith. The new legal exceptions benefiting abused spouses and children should be further eased to send the message that married women are not the property of their husbands.

Finally, Adrien Katherine Wing, an African American, and Eunice P. de Carvalho, an Angolan, collaborate on *Black South African Women: Toward Equal Rights.* Using the critical race feminist construct of analyzing multiple discriminations, the authors explore how black women suffered under apartheid as all blacks did, but under the black patriarchy of customary law as well. Looking at the 1993 Interim Constitution, Wing and de Carvalho find it an improvement on the past, but not sufficient to remedy the centuries of multiple oppressions. They call for the involvement of more black women as parliamentarians and activists in the permanent constitution-making process, and the creation of new constitutional norms that will empower black women.

40

Motherhood and Work in Cultural Context: One Woman's Patriarchal Bargain

Devon W. Carbado

> Of course, your mother is not only that woman whose womb
> formed and released you. . . . But naming your own mother (or her
> equivalent) enables people to place you precisely within the
> universal web of your life, in each of its dimensions: cultural,
> spiritual, personal, and historical.
>
> —Paula Gunn Allen, *Who Is Your Mother?*

As I write this, my wife and I are expecting a child. We already know that it's a girl. We've named her Nyala. She will be our second daughter. Asmara, who has just turned eight, is our first.

I am writing about my mother because I am a father and because fathers need to learn how to "mother" (or more properly, how not to father). I am still learning. My mother's life bears out some of what is subordinating about motherhood—the extent to which it is socially constructed so that primary parenting is gendered—and some of what is privileging about fatherhood—the extent to which men (knowingly or unknowingly) benefit from the patriarchal allocation of family responsibilities. My mother's subordination was culturally specific—West Indian. Black West Indian. But I think her experiences with intra- and extra-household work as she negotiated "her" parental and family responsibilities are not unlike the experiences of many women in the United States. I think they will have cross-cultural resonance.

ON THE CONSTRUCTION OF MOTHERHOOD

My mother "mothered." That is to say, she not only physically bore us, she sustained us—spiritually, emotionally, and (along with my father) economically. She was our primary parent.[1]

(My father had an invisible presence. Emotionally, he was disconnected from us.)

But you're probably thinking that my construction of "mothering" acquiesces in

339

the image of women as nurturers and emotional givers. True. However, some cultural feminists such as Carol Gilligan maintain that the image of women as "givers" and "nurturers" is real and results from women's tendency to view the world through relationships and through an existential sense of connection.[2]

Significantly, Gilligan and many other cultural feminists do not base their "connection thesis" (that "[w]omen are actually or potentially materially connected to other human life [in a way that men are not]")[3] on notions of biological essentialism.[4] Rather, their argument is that "women are more 'connected' to life than men because it is women who are the primary caretakers of young children."[5]

Gilligan's attribution of "care," "responsibility," and "nurturing" to women certainly applies to my mother. She was more connected to us than my father was and more responsible for our day-to-day existence. She knew what was happening at school, what we liked to read, how we liked our hair cut.

And we *knew* her.

But my interaction with my parents need not have been gendered that way. My father could have been our primary parent. He could have been the "emotional giver," the "nurturer." He could have "mothered." That is why "mothered" is in quotes—to convey the idea that there is no a priori reason, or biological basis, for the gendered construction of the characteristics I ascribe to my mother. My father could have exhibited an "ethic of care."

The question then becomes, why didn't he and why don't many other men? It is here that I think Gilligan's analysis is truncated. While she is careful to point out the difference between *the male* moral imperative and *the female* moral imperative, and how this difference is manifested in family life,[6] she does not answer the more fundamental question about the gendered allocation of family responsibilities: "why do women, rather than men, raise, nurture, and cook for children? What is the cause of this difference?"[7] If my essay had begun with the statement, "My father 'fathered,' " the subsequent explanation would not have been that he emotionally and spiritually sustained us.

To be sure, there were external factors operating on our family life that contributed to my father's invisibility. It wasn't simply a matter of him not wanting to connect with us. He was a factory worker. He worked nights. He slept in the day. The extent to which he could interact with us was necessarily circumscribed.

And yet I don't think issues of class or socioeconomic status explain completely the patriarchal aspects of my family life, the extent to which my mother was responsible for family-related work. Patriarchy operates across class boundaries. The allocation of work within our family would not have been terribly different if we had been upper- or middle-class. Jamaican cultural norms with respect to domesticity are gender-, but not class-, determinative: Women, and not men, "raise" children. My mother raised us.

ON MOTHER AND FEMINISM (THE *F* WORD)

There were nine of us to raise—five boys, four girls. One through six were born in Jamaica; seven, eight, and nine were born in Birmingham, England. I was number eight. West Indians are famous for having lots of kids.

The house in which I grew up was at 15 Railway Side, a two-story, semidetached house in Smethwick, Birmingham, that has since been condemned. It was a large enough house, I suppose, affording nothing more or less than any other house on our street; there were a bathroom, a kitchen, a den downstairs, and three rooms upstairs where we all slept.

Attached to the side of the kitchen was an "outhouse," the functional equivalent of a basement. Kim, our dog, spent most of his time there digging the chalk out of the side of the walls; my mother did "her" laundry there every Saturday morning; my father used it principally as an entrance to the backyard; my brothers and I went fishing there—for cod from my mother's stainless steel washing bowls. Carbolic soap was our bait. The soaking clothes (placed there one or two days, as a sort of prewash, before my mother scrubbed them) made our waves.

We all loved Railway Side: my siblings and I because we could watch the trains go by from our living room, experiencing an earthquake-like jitter each time; my father because it had a fairly large yard in which he could store all his electrical paraphernalia; my mother because it symbolized her hard work. Because she owned it. She made a point of always telling us that "non-a my kids kyan sey dat dem grow-up inna council [government] property. A werk too hard fi dat."[8]

I think before I ever understood what feminism means or what it might mean, I knew that women were as capable as and often more capable than men because of my mother and *her* work. My mother never knew how to spell the word "lazy." That's what she used to tell us. It wasn't in her vocabulary. "Work," however, was. She would always say there is dignity in work; that it teaches us humility; that it is its own good; that it emancipates us. I never doubted any of this. Mother's aphorisms were the stuff we were made of. We grew up on them.

"Sometime yuh have to leave de nest to fine de worm." That was the aphorism my mother invoked to explain her decision to immigrate to England in 1961, initially without my father. The "motherland" offered economic opportunities, new options for social and self-definition, the possibility of college after kids.[9] Still, my mother's "passage" to England by herself, as a woman, was not the norm. As a general matter, men went first and subsequently "sent" for their families.[10] My mother had decided, however, that notwithstanding my father's apprehensions about Britain, she had to "beat the ban on immigration." With the steady flow of "coloureds" to Britain after World War II,[11] British politicians, in response to strong public pressure, began discussing the need to restrict immigration.[12] The following was the prevailing political sentiment:

We cannot overwhelm ourselves with large numbers of people who, however worthy, *are alien, have alien cultures, different temperaments, totally different backgrounds and habits and different ways of life.* If we allow them to come in at a rate faster than we can absorb them, we will create a growing fear in the minds of *our own people* who, rightly or wrongly, say that before the end of the century there will be large minorities of *alien people* in various parts of the country, and they fear that the British way of life will change. That fear exists in the minds of many people and, for this reason, entry must be regulated.[13]

The battle cry to "keep Britain white" was answered in 1962 with the passage of the Commonwealth Immigrant's Act. The act officially ended Britain's open-door immigration policy with respect to "Her Majesty's subjects." Though not racially discriminatory on its face, the act had a racially discriminatory effect. It called for "special entry" regulations for all Commonwealth and colonial immigrants with two notable exceptions—the Irish (mostly white) and citizens of the Commonwealth holding passports issued by the British government (again, mostly white).[14]

Had my mother entered England after 1962, she would have had to qualify for one of three types of vouchers issued by the Ministry of Labour: (1) voucher A, issued to persons who are coming to England for a specific job; (2) voucher B, issued to persons with "training skills," or educational qualifications likely to be useful in Britain; or (3) voucher C, issued to all other persons.[15]

My mother would not have been issued a class A voucher; she had no specific job in England. Nor would the Ministry of Labour have issued her a class B voucher; she was not a doctor, a nurse, a teacher, a dentist, or a lawyer. With respect to obtaining a class C voucher, she would have had to compete with almost every other West Indian who was attempting to immigrate to Britain, since most of them also would have been unlikely candidates for class A or class B vouchers.[16]

Yet my father's hesitance was understandable. Racism was very real in England. People wrote home about the riots in Birmingham, London, and Nottingham, about police brutality,[17] about employment discrimination,[18] about how difficult it was to get housing.[19]

And there was a gendered component to British racism. Black men and black women experienced British racism differently.[20] My mother never experienced police abuse. Mostly, that was a problem for West Indian men. But she did experience housing and employment discrimination.

As I have stated, my mother never wanted us to grow up in government housing. She intended for such housing to be temporary. As it turned out, (decent) government housing was not available to my mother when she arrived in Britain, notwithstanding her very limited economic resources. The problem for my mother and many other West Indians was that the public housing sector was locally based and oriented toward "its own people"[21] and "Good families, i.e., quiet, clean, regular-earning families *with not too many children.*"[22] Apparently, West Indian families did not "fit" this profile.

In the private sector, only East Indians were willing to rent my mother a room. It would not be uncommon to see advertisements in the papers that read: "Room for rent. Outdoor bathroom. No kitchen. Preferably white." There was no legislation prohibiting private housing discrimination.[23] The fact that there was a housing shortage throughout Britain compounded the problem.[24]

In the employment context, my mother's opportunities were circumscribed by her race and gender. Although my mother could do basic bookkeeping and knew a little shorthand, she could not get a secretarial job or a job as an administrative assistant. Those were reserved for white women. My mother's options were twofold: she could work as a cook or a domestic. Significantly, neither of these jobs involved public contact.[25] According to my mother, "dem [white people] doe waunt black people wey [white] people can see dem. Dem jus waunt we fi cook dem food and clean dem house." My mother "chose" to work as a cook in a hospital.

But West Indian men weren't required to cook white people's food or clean white people's homes. They got the "better-paying" jobs—with British Railways, in the steel factories, and on the buses.

My mother doesn't think there was anything particularly courageous about her decision to go to England first (i.e., before my father). And I doubt that she would consider it an act of feminism. Generally speaking, "feminism" in Jamaican culture is a dirty word (just as it is in mainstream American culture).[26] Calling a Jamaican woman a feminist at once undermines her racial and cultural loyalty (since feminism is associated with white European and white American women)[27] and her identity as a woman (since feminism is associated with women who want to be "men").

Nor do I think many people would consider my mother a feminist, given her views about family life (the who-is-supposed-to-do-what issues). She believes that women "kyan du anyting dey waunt." But there is a proviso: "so long as dey does keep up de house, do de cookin', and tek care a de kids." My mother never tires of asking my wife, "What yuh cookin' fi Devon's and Asmara's dinna?"

Based on this gendered construction of family responsibility (that it attaches to women and not men), one could certainly argue that my mother is wittingly or unwittingly acquiescing in sexist, essentialist notions of manhood and womanhood, namely, that men don't do housework—women do. But my mother has to be looked at in *her own* social context, a Caribbean context. To understand my mother one would have to, borrowing a term from Isabelle Gunning, "World travel" and situate oneself squarely within *her* social reality.[28]

ON MOTHER IN CULTURAL CONTEXT AND THE PARTICULARIZATION OF PATRIARCHY

Women are perceived simultaneously as workers and mothers in Jamaican culture. They are patriarchally suited for both.[29] Thus, even to the extent that a woman works outside the home, she is still expected to perform all the duties inside the home. This my mother did as a matter of course. If she considered this a burden, we wouldn't have known. If she considered this oppressive, we wouldn't have known.

She never complained. Seemingly, she was being a mother and a wife in the only way she knew how. She lived to work for her family. My mother is now sixty-nine, and one of the few things she regrets about growing old is that "A doe have de strent fi help unu [you all] no more."

My mother grew up understanding that her social context imposed real limitations on her ability to transcend the gendered expectations of how she would live her life. She knew that her social existence would have to be organized around a socially constructed, *existential given*: that housework and child rearing were "her" responsibilities. Her mother wanted her to be a schoolteacher because that wouldn't interfere with her ability to be a housewife and mother. Her father wanted her to be a "good" housewife, which, in his mind, prevented her from being much of anything else. These expectations were not simply the private, familial expectations having to do with what-we-want-our-kids-to-be-when-they-grow-up; they were public expectations as well, socially and culturally informed and intimately bound up with family life and relationships. Fighting these expectations required one to fight with one's self, one's cultural identity, as much (or more so) than it required one to fight with one's family and society as a whole.

And my mother did fight. Her way of fighting was to demonstrate that women could perform all that was required of them in the home and still pursue opportunities outside the home. In this sense, she was engaged in micro-aggressive politics, undertaking to transform the very personal and private aspects of her social life. Somewhere along the line, though, I think my mother normalized her fight, so that it was no longer a fight as such and became instead a way of life for her. She invested her identity in it.

My mother would always praise my father for never trying to "rule" or "dominate" her. "A spen money as A see fit," she always used to say (and still does). "If A waunt to go out anywey, George does drop me off and pick me up. I am a free woman."

My mother's statements concerning my father are certainly true. He did "permit" her to live her life as she saw fit. He never insisted, for example, that my mother cook. And my sense was that if *she had given up* the responsibility of cooking, my father would simply have assumed it. I honestly don't think my mother wore so many hats because she thought my father would have been angered if she decided not to. Still, my father probably harbored an expectation that my mother would cook. Jamaican cultural and social norms required him to. It was probably one of his many silent, culturally informed expectations of my mother.

Presumably, my mother knew my father had unarticulated expectations about family life and responsibilities. She must have known. Every Jamaican grows up knowing who is "supposed" to do the cooking and who is "supposed" to take care of the kids. Our culture is noisy about issues of family life.

Indeed, I think, in part, it is precisely because my mother knew about my father's expectations, and because of other patriarchal expectations of Jamaican women, that she juggled so many roles and responsibilities. Doing extra- and intra-household work was her way of negotiating her conception of what women could do with what Jamaican cultural conceptions required women to do: housework and child rearing. This negotiation gained her a certain amount of autonomy outside the home. It was not a cost-free negotiation, however. It resulted in her having a greater stake in the patriarchal aspects of her life than my father: whatever she chose to do outside the home could not interfere with what she (felt she) had do inside the home. Yet she considered herself free!

I remember when I was about twelve, my mother asked my brothers and me whether we were troubled by the fact that she worked so hard and whether we would be happier if, like my aunt, who lived just down the road from us, she became a homemaker. I remember the moment very well because it was the only time my mother looked to us, her three youngest ("the boys," as we were called), to affirm her decision to exist as a woman outside her role as mother. My brothers and I understood this. We knew that my mother's concerns were not simply about work; they were also about her sense of identity as a Jamaican woman, about having a public identity that transcended traditional motherhood, about composing her life.[30] Of course, we didn't think about the matter in precisely those terms. All we knew was that mother would always talk about how maddening it would be for her to stay home *every day,* and that she couldn't understand how my aunt spent "my uncle's" money so freely: "how she spen Ustas' money when she doe mek none, a jus doe know." My mother, like many other people, has a very narrow conception of what constituted income-producing work and it didn't include what my aunt was doing at home with her kids. That kind of work could never "buy" her freedom. We knew that my mother could not survive the life of a housewife. Her question was disingenuous, but she needed to ask it and she needed us to answer it.

"No, we don't mind that you work so much, and we don't want you to stay home like Aunt Tancy."

We spent the rest of our adolescence proving to mother that we meant those words, that we were prepared to live by them. Rather than allocate some of "her" family responsibilities to my father (which, presumably, would have reflected badly on her motherhood), my mother involved us in her housework rituals. In this way, she retained the responsibility for homemaking.

Work became an essential part of our lives. Each evening, my mother dished out our chores after grace with dinner.

"Devon, A season de meat fi tomorrow dinna. Put it in de oven at half-pass-five. Let it cook fi a-houa-an-a-half. Den, cova it up and turn off de oven. Colin, bring unu clothes from upstairs and put dem fi soak so a can wash dem. Lenny, sweep wey de mess dat Kim mek in de outhouse. A kya bare fi see dat mess when a-doing mi washin'."

We performed our chores religiously (most of the time). And when we were not doing chores, we spent our time "sensibly." At thirteen, I could make a decent pot of curry and my fourteen-year-old brother could bake an apple pie from scratch.

ON FATHER AND PATRIARCHY

I don't think I fully understood how my father was implicated in my mother's assertion that she is "a free woman" until I started reading bell hooks. According to hooks, black male sexism is not limited to explicit attempts to discriminate against women.[31] It includes "romantic visions of black men lifting black women to pedestals," protecting the "femininity" of black women, maintaining social inequality of black women,[32] and failing to unburden the family responsibilities of black women.[33]

I see my father's failure to unburden "my mother's" family responsibilities as patriarchy—passive or unconscious patriarchy.[34] hooks does not use either of these terms, but I think this is what she has in mind when she tells the story of Ida B. Wells, whose husband supported her work outside the home as a political activist but did not relieve Wells of the family responsibilities that had been assigned to her as a woman; on various occasions Wells appeared at public engagements with her small children.[35]

The patriarchy is passive in the sense that women who experience it are not told, for example, that they cannot perform work outside the home. In other words, there is no obvious resistance to the woman's decision to do extra-household work. Indeed, such work might even be encouraged. It is (or *can be*) unconscious in the sense that "the man of the house" does not necessarily actively erect barriers to prevent women from (or make it difficult for women to) work outside the home. The barriers (e.g., child care responsibilities and homemaking more generally) exist because men unconsciously acquiesce in the "natural" female-gendered allocation of family responsibilities.[36] They do little to challenge them. They accept them as the "what is" of family life, necessarily incidental to motherhood.

Unconscious patriarchy definitely applies to my father. His conduct in the context of our family life and vis-à-vis my mother was never overtly sexist. He *never* told my mother what to do. He *never* made any demands. But he needn't have done either; whatever his burdens were, they did not include the day-to-day responsibilities of childcare and housework.[37] My mother (with our help) made sure of it. My father "didn't have to" tell my mother what to do.

Because my father was not responsible for our day-to-day existence, I never really got to know him—beyond knowing who he was. I have no childhood memories of real intimacy with him. On those rare evenings he was home, he avoided us and we avoided him. (I tell myself that his avoidance came first.) I got better and better at avoiding him as I got older. I spoke to him only when it was necessary: "Daddy, *mommy said to ask you* for some lunch money," or "Daddy, *mommy said to tell you* to pick her up at six o'clock." I spoke to my father with the authority of mother behind me. My brothers did the same. Mostly my father spoke to us when we needed to be disciplined: "Colin, how much time A must tell yuh not to trouble mi speakers," or "Lenny, turn off dat television and go to yuh bed," or "Devon, tek-up a book an' read and leave dat dog alone." I wish I could say that, despite our avoidance of each other and our functional conversation, I knew that my father was *as* concerned about our well-being as my mother was.

But as I have already said, and want to say more directly here, our family life did not exist in an economic, cultural, or social vacuum. We were working class. And we were West Indians in Britain. These "externalities" acted on all of us, including my father. In a sense, he was being a father in the only way he knew how—as a financial provider. That was his socially constructed, *existential given.* There was no cultural precedent for him to be actively involved in parenting, or for him to cook,[38] or for him to do housework. Every Jamaican grows up knowing what men, as a general matter, don't do.

And maybe my father knew that there was a certain amount of power inherent in housework and child rearing (the ability to define the character of the home and shape the development of life) and that my mother had invested her identity in both. Maybe my father "fathered" so that my mother could "mother."

Still, my father was a beneficiary of my mother's double-work. (We all were.) And the issue of agency (the extent to which he was individually responsible for the allocation of work in our family and the question of whether he could have transcended West Indian cultural norms) is, on some level, not important. The reality is that my mother was burdened with housework and child care responsibilities because she is a woman and because family responsibilities are gendered. While my father is not completely to blame for this (there was a cultural/functional dimension to the patriarchal aspects of our family life that all of us, including my mother, internalized and re-created), he is culpable. Unlike my mother, he rarely came home to work.

If you were to ask my mother what she regrets about her life, she would probably say, "Not a ting. A lived my life de wey *a* wanted to." But I think my mother knows she made a patriarchal bargain. Her "freedom" required it. Though I doubt my mother would openly admit it, her "freedom," in the context of our family life, was really my father's.

NOTES

1. For a discussion of how motherhood has been constructed so that women bear the brunt of child-rearing responsibilities, see Nancy Chodorow, *Mothering, Male Dominance, and Capitalism, in* Capitalist Patriarchy and the Case for Socialist Feminism (Z. Eisenstein ed., 1979) ("women's mothering is that pivotal structural feature of our sex-gender system—of the social organization of gender, ideology about women, and the psychodynamic of sexual inequality—that links it most significantly with our mode of production."). For a discussion of how motherhood has been configured to subordinate black women, see Dorothy Roberts, *Racism and Patriarchy in the Meaning of Motherhood* 1 Am. U.J. Gender & L. 1 (1993) (asserting that motherhood is constructed with both race and gender in mind: "the image of the Black mother has always diverged from, and often contradicted, the image of the white mother."). Roberts's point, with which I agree, is that whiteness is normalized in the construction of motherhood, and to the extent that a Black woman "diverges from" or "contradicts" the white, middle-class, heterosexual, married woman, she is perceived as deviant. *See also* Nathalie A. Augustin, *Learnfare and Black Motherhood: The Social Construction of Deviance,* chapter 19 in this volume (discussing the degree to which Black mothers are considered deviant in the context of Learnfare).

2. *See generally* Carol Gilligan, In a Different Voice (1982). According to Gilligan, "women's description of identity is . . . judged by a standard of responsibility and care." *Id.* at 160. *See also* Marilyn French, Beyond Power 482–83 (1985). Not all feminists agree with Gilligan's "different voice" thesis. *See, e.g.,* Catharine A. MacKinnon, *Difference and Dominance: On Sex Discrimination, in* Feminism Unmodified: Discourses on Life and Law 33–34 (critiquing Gilligan); Katha Pollitt, *Marooned on Gilligan's Island: Are Women Morally Superior to Men?,* The Nation, Dec. 28, 1992, at 799 ("In the arts, we hear a lot about what women's 'real' subjects, methods and materials ought to be. Painting is male. Rhyme is male. Plot is male. Perhaps, say Lacanian feminists, even logic and language are male. What is female? Nature. Blood. Milk. Communal gatherings. The moon. Quilts."). For a discussion of the various strands of feminism, see Cass R. Sunstein, *Feminism and Legal Theory,* 101 Harv. L. Rev. 826–28 (1988) (reviewing MacKinnon, Feminism Unmodified, *supra*). In addition to Gilligan's "different voice thesis," Sunstein identifies two other brands of feminism: "difference" feminism, according to which "women should be permitted to compete on equal terms with men," and "dominance" feminism, which argues that gender inequality results from the "social subordination of women." (*cited in* Daniel R. Ortiz, *Feminism and the Family,* 18 Harv. J.L. & Pub. Pol'y 523 (1995). *See also* Patricia Cain, *Feminist Jurisprudence: Grounding the Theories,* 4 Berkeley Women's L.J. 191 (1990) (discussing the historical development of feminist theory). For examples of black feminist thought, see bell hooks, Yearnings (1990); Michele Wallace, Black Macho and the Myth of the Super Woman (1978); and Patricia Hill Collins, Black Feminist Thought: Knowledge, Consciousness, and the Politics of Empowerment (1990).

3. Robin West, *Jurisprudence on Gender,* 55 U. Chi. L. Rev. 1, 14 (1988).

4. *But see* Nel Noddings, Caring 128 (1984) (maintaining that biology does play a role in shaping the identities of men and women). The extent to which biology explains the difference between the sexes (the "nature" *vs.* "nurture" debate) is contested inside and outside the context of feminist theory. *Compare* Richard Dawkins, The Selfish Gene 152–76 (1976) (arguing that biology determines behavior) *with* Herma H. Kay, *Perspectives on Sociobiology, Feminism, and the Law, in* Theoretical Perspectives on Sexual Difference 74, 75 (Deborah L. Rhode ed., 1990) (maintaining that arguments about gender based on biological determinism legitimize the subordination of women).

5. West, *supra* note 3, at 16.

6. According to Gilligan, "[t]he moral imperative . . . for women is an injunction to care, a responsibility to discern and alleviate the 'real and recognizable trouble' of this world. For men, the moral imperative appears rather as an injunction to respect the rights of others and thus to protect from interference the rights to life and self-fulfillment." Gilligan, *supra* note 2, at 100.

7. *Id.*

8. I have chosen not to translate my mother's patois into (standard) English. Patois is my mother's language. It is a part of her identity. My mother never speaks (standard) English to us.

9. My mother started college when she was forty-six, after having the nine of us. She earned a Management Certificate in catering from Birmingham's College of Food and Domestic Arts in 1976.

10. Aubrey W. Bonnett, *The New Female West Indian Immigrant Dilemma of Coping in the Host Society, in* In Search of a Better Life: Perspectives on Migration from the Caribbean 140 (Ransford M. Palmer ed., 1990).

11. For a discussion of West Indian immigration to Britain after the Second World War, see James Walvin, Passage to Britain 182–98 (1984). *See also* Ceri K. Peach, West Indian Migration to Britain (1968).

12. *See* Gary P. Freeman, Immigrant Labor and Racial Conflict in Industrial Societies 261–62 (1979). *See also* Frank Reeves, British Racial Discourse 94 (1983) ("The novel circumstances of black migration were dealt with by both Conservative and Labour Parties in accordance with their respective longstanding ideological tradition, tempered . . . by their recognition and fear of the electorate's apparent hostility towards black people.").

13. Robert Miles & Annie Phizacklea, White Man's Country: Racism in British Politics 63 (1984) (emphasis added) (quoting John Hall). For another discussion of how British politicians responded to West Indian immigration, see generally Stephan David, Immigration and Race Relations (1970).

14. Richard T. Schaefer, The Extent and Content of Racial Prejudice in Great Britain 31 (1976). The act was unable to "keep out" Kenyans of Indian ancestry, whose British passports were issued by the British High Commission. Enoch Powell, a very influential member of Parliament, referred to the Kenyans as a "loophole" in the act. Miles & Phizacklea, *supra* note 13, at 59.

15. *See* Schaefer, *supra* note 14.

16. *See* Sheila Patterson, Immigration and Race Relations in Britain, 1960–1967, at 142–43 (1969) (discussing the "voucher system" and the extent to which it affected immigration of people of color from the Commonwealth). No class C vouchers were issued after 1965. *Id.*

17. *See, e.g.,* John R. Lambert, Crime Police and Race Relations (1970); Martin Adeney, *Police Accused of Violence against Blacks,* Guardian, Sept. 25, 1971, at 5.

18. *See, e.g.,* Robert Hepple, Race, Jobs, and Law in Britain (1968).

19. *See generally* Patricia Salter et al., *Race Relations in Public Housing,* 7 J. Soc. Issues (1951). In 1965 Parliament passed the Race Relations Act, which, among other things, prohibited discrimination in "places of public resort." Patterson, *supra* note 16, at 87.

20. In the United States, Critical Race Theory scholars have began to critique the degree to which antiracist politics uses men's experiences as a starting point to address discrimination against Black people. *See, e.g.,* Kimberlé Crenshaw, *Demarginalizing the Intersection of Race and Sex: A Black Feminist Critique of Antidiscrimination Doctrine, Feminist Theory and Antiracist Politics,* 1989 U. Chi. Legal F. 139; Judy Scales-Trent, *Black Women and the Constitution: Finding Our Place, Asserting Our Rights,* 24 Harv. C.R.-C.L. L. Rev. 9 (1989) (also chapter 37 in this volume).

21. There were several devices used to ensure local preference, but perhaps the most common were residential qualifications of varying lengths. For a discussion of the effects of residential qualifications on certain immigrant groups, see The Housing of Commonwealth Immigrants, London, N.C.C.I. 9–10 (1967).

22. Patterson, *supra* note 16, at 211. In the application process, my mother was required to inform the housing authorities of my father's intention to immigrate (as an unskilled laborer) with the rest of the family (my six siblings who were born in Jamaica).

23. One of the criticisms leveled at the Race Act was that it did not cover housing discrimination. *See* Patterson, *supra* note 16, at 86.

24. *Id.* at 207.

25. *Id.* at 136 (observing that West Indians were "greatly underrepresented as clerical workers" and in sales jobs and "over-concentrated in laboring jobs.").

26. *See, e.g.,* Leslie Bender, *A Lawyer's Primer on Feminist Theory and Tort,* 38 J. Legal

Educ. 3 (1988) ("Feminism is a dirty word. . . . Feminists are portrayed as bra-burners, men haters, sexist, and castrators. . . . No wonder many women . . . struggle to distance themselves from the opprobrium appended to the label. 'I am not a feminist; I'm safe; I'm ok,' is the message they seek to convey."); Louise Bernikow, *Let's Hear It for the "F" Word*, Newsday, June 18, 1993, at 62 ("It's a touchy word, 'feminist.' But [Ruth Bader Ginsburg] is an unabashed feminist. For every Ginsburg, there are many women who harbor feminism in their hearts but dare not speak its name.").

27. Several black American feminists have critiqued the extent to which feminism in the United States has been a movement mostly concerned with white women's issues. *See, e.g.,* Crenshaw, *supra* note 20; Angela Harris, *Race and Essentialism in Feminist Legal Theory*, 42 Stan. L. Rev. 581 (1990) (also chapter 1 in this volume); Alice Walker, In Search of Our Mothers' Gardens (1983) (preferring to use "womanist" rather than "feminist"); Deborah E. King, *Multiple Jeopardy, Multiple Consciousness: The Context of a Black Feminist Ideology*, 14 Signs 265 (1988); Audre Lorde, *Age, Race, Class and Sex: Women Redefining Difference*, *in* Sister Outsider 114 (1984).

28. *See generally* Isabelle R. Gunning, *Arrogant Perception, World Traveling and Multicultural Feminism: The Case of Female Genital Surgeries*, 23 Colum. Hum. Rts. L. Rev. 189 (1991–92) (also chapter 41 in this volume) (arguing that, to avoid cultural and political imperialism, Western feminists, as outsiders, should "world travel" before formulating policy initiatives to address female genital surgeries).

29. *See* Marlee Kline, *Race, Racism, and Feminist Legal Theory*, 12 Harv. Women's L.J. 115 (1989) (discussing the extent to which the "traditional expectation of stay-at-home mother-hood" does not apply to black American women because there is a presumption that black mothers do work outside the home). *See also* Angela Davis, Women, Race and Class (1981).

30. Mary Catherine Baterson, Composing Life (1990) (using the lives of five women to discuss how life is composed through work).

31. bell hooks, Ain't I a Woman? Black Women and Feminism 89 (1981).

32. *Id.* at 91.

33. *Id.* at 90–91.

34. I use "unconscious" with respect to patriarchy here in the same way Charles Lawrence uses "unconscious" with respect to racism. *See* Charles Lawrence, *The Id, the Ego, and Equal Protection: Reckoning with Unconscious Racism*, 39 Stan. L. Rev. 317 (1987) (arguing that the Supreme Court's focus on intent in the context of Fourteenth Amendment jurisprudence is inadequate to combat racism that is not explicit or manifest but latent and implicit—a part of our cultural norm).

35. hooks, *supra* note 31, at 90. hooks's reading of Wells's appearance in public with her children might well say something about our expectations for political discourse—that they don't include children.

36. My use of "unconscious" in this context is not meant to suggest that men don't actively engage in sexist conduct that limits women's ability to work outside the home. "Unconscious" here is intended to apply to men whose conduct functions to subordinate women but who would say either that their conduct is not the result of any antiwoman animus and that they do not believe in inequality between the sexes or that they are not intentionally conducting themselves to subordinate women in the context of family life. *See generally* Lawrence, *supra* note 34 (discussing racism as an unconscious internalization process, which is not necessarily related to racial animus, but which has the effect of subordinating minorities).

37. *See* Joan Williams, *Selfless Women and the Republic of Choice*, 66 N.Y.U. L. Rev. 1559,

1599 (arguing that wives "do seventy-nine percent of the housework" and that "husbands of employed wives barely contribute enough domestic labor to make up for the additional work their presence in the household creates."). *See also* Heidi Hartmen, *The Family as the Locus of Gender, Class and Political Struggle: The Example of Housework*, 6 Signs 366–94 (1980) (observing that the presence of men in the home actually creates more work for women).

38. I make a distinction here between cooking as a part of one's family responsibility and cooking more generally. I would imagine that most West Indian men *can* cook and that many *do* in fact cook. I suspect, though, that few would consider cooking a part of their parental or family responsibility, West Indian cultural norms being what they are. *See* Chodorow, *supra* note 1, at 86 (observing that "all societies do have a sexual division of labor. These include women's involvement in routine daily cooking for their immediate families (*festive cooking, by contrast, is often done by men*)") (emphasis added).

41

Arrogant Perception, World Traveling, and Multicultural Feminism: The Case of Female Genital Surgeries

Isabelle R. Gunning

In the spring of 1990, I reencountered a practice that for many years I had found distressing, female genital surgeries.[1] In their essence, the surgeries involve the cutting or burning away of the female sexual organ, the clitoris, as well as the removal, in whole or part, of the other external female genitalia. As I started my research, I continued to feel anger and revulsion at the practice and a strong desire to see it eradicated as quickly as possible. In thinking about eradicating the practice, I confronted two major problems: (1) what right did I, a Western feminist, have to criticize as right or wrong the practices of an entirely different culture? and (2) should and can law, with its attribution of right and wrong, exoneration and punishment, be used to eradicate a cultural practice?

This chapter will use the culturally challenging practice of genital surgeries as a way to explain and analyze my proposed method for understanding culturally challenging practices. In addition, the piece argues that the law, specifically human rights law, can be used in the eradication of such practices but, I argue, the development of such laws must be the result of a multicultural dialogue and consensus.

FEMALE GENITAL SURGERIES

Genital surgeries encompass a range of operations performed on the female genitalia. There are generally three types of operations: (1) pharaonic or infibulation, (2) intermediate, and (3) sunna.[2] The pharaonic type is the oldest, most prevalent, and most drastic of the operations. In both its classical and modernized forms it involves the removal of the entire clitoris along with the labia minora and labia majora. The intermediate and sunna forms are less radical procedures that allow more of the genitalia to remain intact. The practice of female genital surgeries is explained in various ways: ensuring the virginity of a woman before marriage and inducing chastity for divorced women or married women whose husbands are away;[3] birth control;[4] initiation into and celebration of womanhood;[5] hygienic reasons;[6] and religious requirements.[7]

Concerns about and objections to genital surgeries have been raised on a number of grounds, many of which are health-related. At the time of the surgery children suffer "complications [like] hemorrhage, infections, septicemia, retention of urine or shock," and deaths have occurred.[8] In addition, as a result of the surgery, intercourse and childbirth can be both painful and difficult, either or both requiring some tearing or cutting of the infibulated tissue.[9]

Concerns have also been raised on sexual health grounds, and one might intuitively presume that female genital surgeries, especially the more severe forms that involve removal of the clitoris, would rob a woman of all sexual sensation and pleasure.[10] Critiques of the practice have also addressed the broader sociological role it plays in the subordination of women—that the physical (and concomitant psychological) attack on female sexuality serves as part and parcel of a patriarchal plan of control over women's reproductive and productive powers.

THE WORLD-TRAVELING METHOD OF UNDERSTANDING

Culturally challenging patriarchal practices like genital surgeries require a complex vision of independence[11] and connectedness. The distance that arrogance creates must be bridged, but the interconnectedness built must be complex and must preserve independence.

ARROGANT PERCEPTION AND DISTANCE

The negative impact of universalism or ethnocentrism in the analysis of culturally challenging practices has been characterized (in a different context) by one feminist scholar as "arrogant perception."[12] For the arrogant perceiver there is distance between oneself and the other that makes her different. The distance, while it emphasizes dissimilarity, is not devoid of similarity. Feminist scholars who have focused on the dependent hierarchical relationship between men and women have concentrated on extending the distance in an effort to break the dependence and "defectiveness" of the "other": a loving eye is required to replace the arrogant perception so as to preserve and accentuate the independence of the "other."[13] While it is appropriate to understand and respect the separateness of the "other" by rejecting arrogant perception, there is a pitfall of too much independence. If "I" and the "other" are totally independent, there is no basis for shared values or perspectives.

WORLD-TRAVELING AND INTERCONNECTEDNESS

One feminist scholar has described a method by which feminists of various colors can learn to identify their interconnectedness even as they respect independence:

world-traveling.[14] "Worlds" are any social situation, ranging from "an incomplete visionary utopia" to a subculture or community within a larger dominant community to a "traditional construction of life."[15] "Traveling" is the shift from being one person in one world to a different person in another world. But the "difference" is part of a coherent whole; one does not act or pose as someone else.

WORLD-TRAVELING MODIFIED TO METHODOLOGY

The recognition of both independence and interconnectedness is essential for cross-cultural understanding. I suggest a three-pronged approach to creating that recognition. In order to understand the independence of the "other" one needs to be clear about one's own boundaries. This requires understanding oneself in one's own historical context, with an emphasis on the overlaps, influences, and conditions one is observing in the "other." Recognizing interconnectedness requires two additional approaches. The first is to understand one's historical relationship to the "other" and to approach that understanding from the "other's" perspective, that is, to see the self as the "other" might see you. Second, one must see the "other" in her own cultural context as she sees herself.

THE WORLD-TRAVELING METHOD AND GENITAL SURGERIES

SEEING ONESELF IN HISTORICAL CONTEXT

The most interesting aspect of seeing oneself (meaning a Westerner) in historical context is exploring a fact that is often omitted, if not actually denied: that genital surgeries have been performed in Western countries as well. Ben Barker-Benfield's article *Sexual Surgery in Late Nineteenth Century America* is fascinating because he places genital surgeries—both clitoridectomies and female castration—firmly within their historical and social contexts.[16] Two important points emerge from an examination of genital female surgeries in our own historical context. The first is the recognition that the practice of reconstructing female genitalia through surgery is a universal one and crosses cultural boundaries. It is a part of our own history. The second is that, although the specific American version of genital surgeries has largely been discontinued, the attitudes and assumptions about gender roles that provide the justification for female genital surgeries remain largely in place in our contemporary Western culture.

SEEING YOURSELF AS THE "OTHER" SEES YOU

In an examination of how Westerners are perceived by women in Third World nations, the two most important issues are imperialism and racism. In addition to understanding the new relationship between Western and non-Western cultures and appreciating that the non-Western perspective on Western cultures is almost always influenced by prior negative racial and colonial policies, one must take the micro view and see oneself as the other sees one.

Seeing yourself as the other sees you involves appreciating the fact that just as a Westerner may view the surgeries as a cultural challenge, the street runs two ways: non-Westerners too can view Western practices as culturally challenging.

SEEING THE "OTHER" IN HER OWN CONTEXT

In taking a fresh look at one's own cultural norms and assumptions, one could explore any number of cultural practices. The practice that seems especially relevant in a discussion of genital surgeries is the practice of cosmetic surgeries, particularly breast augmentation.[17] How bizarre and barbaric must a practice like implanting polyurethane-covered silicone into one's breasts be perceived by one not accustomed to the practice. The easy part of understanding female genital surgeries in their own organic social environment, for the Western feminist, is understanding them as part of a complex system of male domination of women. Not unlike Western societies, women in cultures where genital surgeries are performed find that "their social status and economic security [derive] from their roles as wives and mothers."[18] Aside from the bad (often "economic") consequences that will likely befall one if one remains uncircumcised, one would *be* essentially bad or unclean.[19]

"The most difficult part in understanding female genital surgeries as an outsider is comprehending how women within the cultures can support such procedures. Clearly there are a lot of coercive pressures. . . . But there are also positive ways of viewing the procedure that cause many women to embrace it. . . . It is important to point out that within many of the cultures that continue to perform female genital operations, like the Sudan, the surgeries, although performed largely on young girls, constitute a central part of a celebration of womanhood. The surgeries are performed by women, largely midwives[20] and are a part of the creation of a special and exclusive 'women's space.'[21] A young girl often has the surgery performed along with other youngsters, her sisters, or other girls in the area of the same age group.[22] She is never alone during the ceremony. Whatever pain is endured by the girl has to mingle with the joy of being like the other women, becoming clean, and experiencing "the most important day of a girl's life."[23] In this context, supporting the surgeries can be viewed as rational and empowering.

When one sees that "other" within her own context, one sees women making a number of choices within the context of their complex social fabric. Different women struggle for their own vision of what is best and possible, both within and against the constraints of their culture. The question then is, can the law respect and accommodate the complexity of these issues and the required multicultural dialogue and remain an effective tool for change?

WORLD TRAVELING AND THE USE OF LAW

INTERNATIONAL HUMAN RIGHTS AND FEMALE GENITAL SURGERIES

There are no international treaties that directly address the issue of female genital surgeries. However, several human rights norms have been suggested as the basis for a law that might currently outlaw the practice. This section will review the strengths and weaknesses of the arguments.

Because the surgeries are performed on young girls, human rights norms that protect the rights of children are often cited as a basis for arguing that the surgeries constitute a human rights violation. Principle 2 of the Declaration of the Rights of the Child, adopted by the United Nations General Assembly in 1959, states,

> [T]he child shall enjoy special protection, and shall be given opportunities and fa-
> cilities, by law and other means, to enable him to develop physically, mentally, morally,
> spiritually and socially in a healthy and normal manner and in condition of freedom
> and dignity.[24]

Even though young girls, ridiculed by their friends for being uncircumcised, may want to be circumcised and even pressure their mothers to have some operation done,[25] one can still argue that a child is too immature to knowingly consent.[26] On the other hand, it is clear that many parents, entrusted with their children's care, could easily interpret the language in the Declaration of the Rights of the Child as supporting the surgeries. They could argue that by circumcising their daughters they are enabling them to "develop physically, mentally, morally, spiritually and socially in a healthy and normal manner" in accordance with the dictates of their culture.[27] The singular focus of this approach on the physical harm, while compelling, raises issues exposed by the world-traveling analysis: culturally challenging issues are complex and organic, not one-dimensional.

How might African women (the "other") perceive the presentation of the children's rights argument? One reasonable suggestion has been made that African women (in particular) are likely to feel that they are being called "incompetent and abusive mothers."[28] Such a perception impedes the multicultural dialogue that is necessary to address this issue.

A second human rights argument against the practice has been described as the right to sexual and corporeal integrity.[29] Article 3 of the Universal Declaration of Human Rights states, "everyone has the right to liberty and the security of person."[30] However, this argument is not supported by the language of the treaties. The rhetoric of the human rights treaties regarding security of one's person on which the right rests is quite broad. In some of the treaties that give any elaboration of what "security" might mean, the language refers to prohibiting arbitrary detention and arrest, that is, physical seizure as opposed to invasion.

Two other unsuccessful arguments rest on the international prohibitions against torture and slavery. The prohibition against torture is most clearly enunciated in the

Convention against Torture and Other Cruel, Inhuman or Degrading Treatment or Punishment.[31] The slavery argument rests on the international norm against slavery.[32]

The final and most popular human rights objection to the surgery is that it violates the right to health. Article 15 of the Universal Declaration provides that "[e]veryone has the right to a standard of living adequate for the health and well-being of himself." One major drawback of focusing on health is that proponents could avoid the hard problems of changing cultural norms and focus very narrowly on health issues. The result would be that the surgeries would be done in hospitals by trained doctors, not eliminated.

Even if one could choose the "right" human rights norm, given the world-traveling analysis's concern with cultural complexity,[33] would it be appropriate to use the human rights system to outlaw or even criticize a specific culture's norm? Again one must confront the issues of whether human rights law is representative of multicultural or shared values and whether the punitive aspects of the system as a legal system preserve multicultural respect.

WEAKNESSES AS STRENGTHS IN HUMAN RIGHTS LAW

There are two ways of reformulating the problem of preserving respect for different cultures in the human rights law context. The first is the argument that the way the human rights system has preserved mutual cultural respect has been to avoid criticizing cultural activity. The second is that the human rights system has never avoided the imposition of one set of cultural values, that is, Western values, and that it is inappropriate to think it ever could.

If human rights law does affect cultural activity and impose values, should it continue to criticize any single "other" culture or retreat from doing even as much as it currently does? From the perspective of cultural relativity, since all cultures are equally valid and to be respected, it would seem that retreat is in order.[34] The relativism perspective is one that has enjoyed renewed popularity this century because it provides a pointed criticism of Western colonialism.[35]

Relativism questions the universality of the existing human rights norms. The current human rights doctrine is only one cultural way, the Western way, of ensuring and preserving what all cultures value: human dignity. The existing human rights approach centers on the individual's rights; it does not address the more communal nature of many, especially African, cultures.

For human rights proponents there are two major responses to the relativism critique. One, universalism, simply contradicts the notion that there can be no universal norms that transcend all cultures.[36] The other, the positivist view, states that as long as diverse nations sign and ratify human rights treaties they have willingly consented to be governed by the enumerated standards and cannot exempt themselves whenever it suits them.[37]

The world-traveling methodology suggests that there is not an "either/or" proposition. One is not stuck between choosing "universal standards" and "everything is relative." It is not that there are "universals" out there waiting to be discovered. But through dialogue, shared values can become universal and be safeguarded. The process by which these universal standards are created is important. A dialogue, with a tone that incorporates world-traveling concerns and respects cultural diversity, is essential. From that dialogue a consensus may be reached; and we must understand that as people and cultures interact they do change and learn from each other.

Even if an international treaty banning the practice can be realized, it may be wise not to pressure or embarrass national governments to pass laws at the domestic level. We may want more open health or educational efforts that allow African feminists and women to continue the process of change within their own cultures.

The process of creating shared values could (hopefully) lead to a firmer and more widely held norm against the practice. In this situation one could imagine that the use of law in its traditional form with punitive and coercive measures would be appropriately invoked. In this scenario, punishment of individuals for violating shared norms would be apt when punishment of cultures for violating external norms was not.

The difficult question regarding my preferred scenario, where the process of dialogue leads to a firmer and more broadly shared value against the surgery, is, when do we know we have such a shared norm against the surgery that punishment and coercion can be used? There is no easy, abstract answer to the question. In practical terms, we will know "after the fact." Only after nations have introduced or reintroduced domestic legislation, and their citizenry largely abide by and welcome it, can we be more assured that the norm is shared.

Culturally challenging practices like female genital surgeries represent crucial areas of multicultural dialogue for feminists applying international human rights law to the specific concerns of women. Improvement in the quality of women's lives and in their status in all the world's cultures must be coordinated with respect for the diverse views among women on how these goals will be achieved. My three-pronged analysis, (1) seeing oneself in historical context; (2) seeing oneself as the "other" might see you; and (3) seeing the "other" within her own complex cultural context, is designed to aid in the process of respecting independence and interconnectedness.

NOTES

1. The range of excisive operations performed on the female genitalia described *infra* are characterized either as "female circumcision" or "genital mutilation." I use the term "genital surgeries" in an effort to strike a neutral tone.

2. Asma El Dareer, Woman, Why Do You Weep: Circumcision and Its Consequences 1–5 (1982).

3. L. F. Lowenstein, *Attitudes and Attitude Difference to Female Genital Mutilation in the Sudan: Is There a Change on the Horizon*, 12 Soc. Sci. & Med. 417 (1978) (citing anthropological studies involving surveys/interviews with primarily Sudanese people).

4. *Id.*

5. *Id.;* Ellen Gruenbaum, *Reproductive Ritual and Social Reproduction: Female Circumcision and the Subordination of Women in Sudan, in* Economy and Class in Sudan 310 (Norman O'Neil & Jay O'Brien eds., 1988).

6. Traditional Practices Affecting the Health of Women and Children: Female Circumcision, Childhood Marriage, Nutritional Taboos, Etc., World Health Organization/Eastern Mediterranean Regional Office, Technical Publication No. 2, Reprint of a Seminar, Khartoum, 10–15 February, 1979 at 44 (presentation by Dr. A. H. Taba).

7. *Id.*

8. Gruenbaum, *supra* note 5, at 311.

9. *Id.*

10. *See* G. Zwang, Female Sexual Mutilations, Techniques and Results (1979), *cited in* Hanny Lightfoot-Klein, Prisoners of Ritual: An Odyssey into Female Genital Circumcision in Africa 81 (1989). Raqiya H. D. Abdalla, Sisters in Affliction: Circumcision and Infibulation of Women in Africa 26 (1982). Both report frigidity in circumcised women.

11. I use the term "independence" to suggest enough distance between oneself and the "other" so that the "other" is recognized as engaged in and entitled to the same process of self-definition as oneself.

12. Marilyn Frye, *In and Out of Harm's Way, in* The Politics of Reality: Essays in Feminist Theory 52–83 (1983).

13. *Id.* at 75.

14. Maria Lugones, *Playfulness, World-Traveling and Loving Perception,* 2 Hypatia 3 (1987).

15. *Id.* at 9–10.

16. Ben Barker-Benfield, *Sexual Surgery in Late Nineteenth Century America,* 5 Int'l J. Health Services 279 (1975).

17. *See, e.g.,* Ruth Rosen, *Draw the Line at the Knife,* L.A. Times, Nov. 17, 1991, at M5 (comparing breast implants with footbinding, dowry deaths, and clitoridectomies).

18. Gruenbaum, *supra* note 5, at 311.

19. Lightfoot-Klein, *supra* note 10, at 161.

20. Gruenbaum, *supra* note 5, at 310.

21. *Id.* at 313.

22. Lightfoot-Klein, *supra* note 10, at 73, 141.

23. *Id.* at 72–73.

24. Declaration of the Rights of the Child adopted 20 November 1959; G.A. Res 1386 (XIV) U.N. Doc. A/4354 (1959). These sentiments are underscored in the Draft Convention on the Rights of the Child, which was adopted by the U.N. Open-Ended Working Group on the Question of a Convention on the Rights of the Child: 1979–1988.

25. *See* Kay Boulware-Miller, *Female Circumcision: Challenges to the Practice as a Human Rights Violation,* 8 Harv. Women's L.J. 155, 167 (1985).

26. Allison Slack, *Female Circumcision: A Critical Appraisal,* 10 Hum. Rts. Q. 437, 469–70 (1988).

27. *See* Boulware-Miller, *supra* note 25, at 166–67. Here, Bouleware-Miller discusses two problems with the children's rights approach: (1) it ignores the parents' desires and ideas of child-rearing, and (2) it focuses on physical harm to the exclusion of issues of social acceptance.

28. *Id.* at 166.

29. *Id.* at 169.

30. Universal Declaration of Human Rights, G.A. Res. 217A (III) U.N. Doc. A/1810, at 71 (1948), Article 2.

31. U.N. Doc A/39/708 (1984).

32. Slavery Convention, concluded Sept. 25, 1926, 46 Stat. 2183, T.S. No. 778, 60 L.N.T.S. 253 (entered into force Mar. 9, 1927).

33. In addition to the concerns raised by the world-traveling analysis, there is also the issue of self-determination guaranteed by several human rights treaties.

34. Ruth Benedict, Patterns of Culture 45–46 (1934).

35. Katherine Brennan, *The Influence of Cultural Relativism on International Human Rights Law, Female Circumcision as a Case Study,* 7 Law & Ineq. J. 367, 370 (1989).

36. *Id.* at 371–72.

37. *Id.* at 372–73.

42

Between *Irua* and
"Female Genital Mutilation":
Feminist Human Rights Discourse
and the Cultural Divide

Hope Lewis

AT THE INTERSECTION OF "WESTERN" AND "AFRICAN": THE CHALLENGE FOR AFRICAN AMERICAN FEMINISTS

The work of African American "womanist"[1] Alice Walker, more than that of any other African American feminist, has increased the scope and urgency of the international campaign to educate and organize against female genital surgeries (FGS). The widespread publicity surrounding the publication of *Possessing the Secret of Joy*,[2] Walker's fictional account of the impact of traditional female genital surgeries on one African woman and her family, followed by the documentary and companion book *Warrior Marks*, has made the issue of FGS more accessible to a Western audience.

Walker expresses unequivocal opposition to the continued practice of FGS. Her objections generally reflect some Western feminist apprehensions: humanitarian concern for the physical effects of FGS and identification of FGS as a form of patriarchal control rather than legitimate cultural expression. In addition, Walker expresses a heightened sense of special responsibility and "duty" that arises from her status as an educated African American woman. Her connection to African women who undergo FGS is perceived to stem from her status as a woman who herself has suffered "a patriarchal wound,"[3] and as a black woman who shares cultural influences with women in Africa.

Initially, some activists perceived Walker, an African American feminist, as an ideal ambassador to bridge the cultural divide between white Western feminists and African feminists.[4] Following the success of her novel, Walker produced the documentary and companion book, *Warrior Marks*, with feminist filmmaker Pratibha Parmar. Some observers applauded the film's sensitive presentation of FGS through dance as informative and moving. Others, in contrast, felt that the film drew too direct an analogy between FGS and Walker's own "patriarchal wound"[5] and charged that it insensitively and inaccurately portrayed the older women who perform FGS as uniformly cruel and inept.[6]

These responses illuminate the complexities underlying the larger human rights debate between universalists and cultural relativists. They also illustrate the danger of making uncritical assumptions about one's ideology based solely on (one's) race or gender. Although some Africans appreciate and praise Walker's participation in the campaign against FGS,[7] others find aspects of her work to be imperialist or underinformed.[8] Some African Americans have expressed discomfort at the critique of African practices by "one of our own" as disloyal or inappropriate, given the negative images of Africa that already pervade the Western media.[9]

The expected diplomatic resolution between African and Western feminists may yet occur, but Walker's efforts and the corresponding reactions reveal another complex layer of conflicts and opportunities for cross-cultural feminism. As these responses indicate, gender and racial connections alone will not resolve tensions between groups of feminists.

The practice of FGS raises a number of concerns in African American social and political discourse on African traditional practices as well.[10] Ironically, the "status of African women" and "women in development" are now popular focal points of Western political science discourse.[11] Although much of this literature identifies the significant socioeconomic barriers to improving the status of African women, some of it nevertheless tends to adopt an imperialist tone or to exclude the voices of African women entirely.

At the other extreme, African American feminists often experience great difficulty in reconciling themselves to a strict cultural relativist view of FGS. Rather than remain silent or unengaged, it seems to some African American feminists more appropriate that they work with Africans and other peoples of the African diaspora to reclaim, place in context, and critically analyze those human rights issues that carry extra baggage with regard to race, ethnicity, or gender.[12] Still, the troubling question for African American feminists—and Western feminists in general—remains how to avoid inappropriate criticism, intentional or not.

The two leading human rights articles by African American feminists on FGS discuss the personal ambivalence of the authors as Western women of color writing about human rights-based approaches to FGS.[13] Kay Boulware-Miller, one of the first Western feminists to analyze FGS in the context of human rights scholarship, describes her concern:

> My initial response to this issue was ambivalent and confused. As a woman, I felt rage that the practice helped solidify and preserve society by the violation of female bodies; as a Black, I felt a perverse pride that an African tradition had managed to hold its own amid invasive values of beauty, morality, and self-worth; and as mother of a little girl at the age of most who are circumcised, I felt threatened by a vividly-imagined, but never-to-be-known loss.[14]

Isabelle Gunning's more recent and comprehensive article recounts even more extensively and compellingly her uncertainty about the appropriate response to the human rights implications of FGS.

Gunning's and Boulware-Miller's personal reflections indicate that these feminists consider themselves physically, culturally, or emotionally "related" to African women and children. That sense of connectedness legitimizes their desire to eradicate FGS.

African American feminists have experienced the impact of structural sexism, racism, and classism in their own cultures. As African American women raised in cultures suffering the adverse effects of those forces, both Boulware-Miller and Gunning recognize the importance of the preservation of cultural traditions and feel initial distrust of "outsiders" who would challenge those traditions for ulterior or even altruistic motives.[15] African American feminists recognize and understand the choice of some African women to defend the practice of FGS or to reject the manner in which some non-Africans have shaped the discourse of the eradication campaigns. Their belief in cultural self-determination leads them to resist prescribing solutions for others who do not want their help. At the same time, many African American feminists—as illustrated by Gunning and Boulware-Miller—also feel a special sense of frustration that the continued practice of FGS puts millions of their "sisters" at psychological and physical risk.

Do these concerns leave any room for respectful cross-cultural engagement among African and African diaspora feminists on the issue of FGS? While the debates over cultural relativism and cultural imperialism continue, female genital surgeries are practiced on millions of black children and women, leading to illness or even death. What, then, should be the response of black feminists to this form of human rights violation?

African American and other black feminists encounter a variety of international, regional, and domestic human rights approaches to FGS from which to choose. Two of these approaches are discussed below.

CROSS-CULTURAL CONSENSUS BUILDING

Cross cultural consensus building, most closely identified with Gunning, relies on international human rights fora as a space for the creation of consensual human rights norms prior to the use of domestic sanctions such as criminalization.[16] Because the priority is on consensus building, the relatively weak enforcement mechanisms under the international human rights system are viewed as "strengths."[17] This approach emphasizes a slow, grassroots process of health education and norm creation that is intended to lead to gradual abandonment of the practices. It prioritizes collective context and consensus over state control in preventing individual harm.

INTEGRATED APPROACHES

Integrated approaches combine domestic legal and nonlegal approaches, international standard setting, and technical assistance and monitoring with grassroots health and education campaigns in order to eradicate FGS. This mixture of techniques, rather than universalist condemnation and "enlightenment" or exclusionary rejection of Western influence, appears to be the most promising basis for cross-cultural Western and African feminist activism on FGS.

Feminists from both Africa and the West have argued that the adoption and widespread ratification of the Convention on the Elimination of All Forms of Discrimination against Women (CEDAW) is the most promising UN-based effort that focuses specifically on gender-based violations of human rights.[18] CEDAW broadly defines "discrimination against women"[19] and specifically requires states that are parties to the convention to take action to address traditional practices that are harmful to women.[20] The committee responsible for CEDAW's implementation has issued specific recommendations to state parties on their responsibility to address violence against women in general and FGS in particular.[21]

The Committee on the Elimination of All Forms of Discrimination against Women has issued recommendation 14, which says state parties should take an integrated approach to eradicating FGS that would include collecting and disseminating information, supporting national and local women's organizations, funding educational programs, integrating FGS into national health policies, inviting assistance from international bodies, and reporting on progress.

The integrated approach of CEDAW includes a number of elements that take account of the concerns of both Western and African feminists discussed above. It establishes an international context of concern and focus, but prioritizes African feminist activism. It recognizes that African women in practicing regions are themselves taking action to identify and combat practices that are harmful to them, but that such action needs the support and encouragement of their local governments. The recommendation also states that the measures must be consistent with the nature of the practices ("appropriate") as well as effective.[22]

Although it seems promising, the approach taken by the committee's recommendation is not without significant limitations. First, because of the weakness and complexity of enforcement mechanisms under UN human rights systems, recommendation 14 could effectively be irrelevant to the daily lives of grassroots African women.[23] Moreover, despite having been widely ratified, CEDAW is also the subject of the largest number of substantive reservations of any of the major human rights treaties.[24]

CEDAW also shares the weakness of all other human rights instruments—its enforcement depends on the political will of the state parties to the convention. Furthermore, by creating room for non-African dialogue with African women by recommending that state parties invite assistance from UN organizations, the recommendation seems to assume that the assistance and advice of international organizations generally will be benevolent.

Finally, the recommendation fails to address the need for data collection, education, and organizing activities to reflect important aspects of the lives of African women other than FGS. This poses the most serious area of conflict, yet the greatest opportunity, with respect to cross-cultural work on FGS. It is relatively easy to argue that educational and economic opportunity for women will aid in the eradication of FGS. The integrated approaches, however, fail to consider fundamental questions of domestic and international economic and political restructuring that also may be relevant to FGS.[25]

SOLIDARITY AND SUBJECTIVITY

This essay does not propose a resolution of the tensions and conflicts over approaches to FGS. Rather, it suggests three important components of restructuring cross-cultural engagement on the eradication of FGS: first, the clarification of the contexts in which FGS occurs; second, the need for pragmatic, action-oriented approaches to human rights law that take account of context; and third, the need to build fluid coalitions within and beyond existing human rights institutions and structures that better meet the needs and goals of black women. It is time to ask different questions than those that have been at the center of most feminist discourse on this subject.

IMAGE AND CONTEXT

African American feminists who also have experienced the damaging impact of negative stereotyping could insist on the prioritization of information that would clarify these incorrect images. For example, they could support the work of African women, trained in modern medicine and possessing direct knowledge of traditional practices, in helping both Westerners and Africans separate myth from fact.[26] They could ask whether and how African American feminist scholars could assist in the process of norm creation and clarification.[27]

TIME FOR ACTION

How could black feminists actively address the responsibility they feel for the well-being of others while avoiding the pitfalls of cultural imperialism and discrimination against ethnic groups whose traditions are unfamiliar? It is not possible to achieve both goals completely. Nevertheless, many black feminists, including Boulware-Miller and Gunning, share the intuition that the importance of the problem obligates them to choose respectful engagement rather than respectful isolation.

Domestic Legislation in the West

Black feminists must address the fact that FGS is a human rights issue in the West.[28] Some Western feminists, for example, advocate the introduction of domestic legislation that criminalizes the practice of FGS among immigrant communities in the West.[29] The United Kingdom passed the Prohibition of Female Circumcision Act of 1985, which makes the practice illegal under most circumstances.[30] In France, the practice of FGS has been officially interpreted to violate existing penal provisions against child abuse.[31] France is the only Western country that has prosecuted and imprisoned those who perform or pay for FGS.[32]

A bill that would outlaw FGS in the United States has been introduced in the U.S. Congress.[33] It would criminalize FGS and impose fines or imprisonment for violations, but also would require that immigrants from practicing regions be informed that FGS is illegal in the United States.[34]

Should black feminist activism on this issue take the form of calls for aggressive enforcement of criminal sanctions or against efforts to legalize the practice in the West?[35] Should it instead expose and critique the racism and sexism involved in the implementation or enactment of such domestic laws?[36] How should African American feminists address the question of the "medicalization" of FGS in the West? What sanctions should be imposed on formally licensed health professionals who profit from the continuation of the practice?[37] Do any of the proposed legislative efforts reflect a serious commitment by the state and the international community to place political and economic priority on the general health and well-being of black women and girls?

Aid Conditionality

Some activists have urged that U.S. foreign assistance law explicitly condition aid on the degree to which recipient countries engage in efforts to eradicate FGS.[38] The use of aid conditionality raises troubling and important questions. Should African American feminists support proposals to condition aid on a government's FGS policies, potentially cutting the already grossly inadequate international aid to Africa? If so, should conditionality turn on the criminalization of FGS or on whether governments adopt policies that reflect a good-faith "integrated" approach? If not, should aid be better targeted to the women's groups who are working on grassroots campaigns to eradicate the poverty, illiteracy, and lack of health care under which the practice of FGS can flourish?

Gender Asylum

The efforts of Lydia Oluloro, a Nigerian citizen, to seek asylum in the United States received significant media attention.[39] Oluloro requested asylum based on her fear that her two daughters would be forcibly subjected to FGS if they returned with her to Nigeria. Her deportation was suspended on humanitarian grounds because it would result in "extreme hardship."[40]

In light of the outrage expressed in the West over the practice of FGS, African American feminists could ask why there has only recently been progress in efforts to make fear of or opposition to FGS a basis of gender asylum.[41] What guidelines should black feminists in the West support in regard to the development of gender asylum policies in fulfillment of international human rights obligations?

An ineffective theoretical condemnation of FGS may be just as objectionable as a draconian, imperialist attempt to coerce the eradication of FGS. The engagement in active conflict on these issues at least removes FGS from the realm of a theoretical debate over whether Westerners should ignore an exotic cultural practice and forces us to confront the question of how human rights law and policy should impact the lives of women on a day-to-day basis.

For black feminists and other concerned people in the West, developing a deeper understanding of context creates greater responsibility for the protection of human rights, not an abdication of responsibility.

BUILDING (FLUID) COALITIONS

Finally, black feminists must strengthen and expand the coalitions and networks they have built to express cross-cultural solidarity. A multidirectional discourse creates opportunities for both solidarity and conflict. Efforts at cross-cultural cooperation and coalition building within and outside existing domestic and international legal structures already have begun. Women have made use of existing human rights institutions at official and nongovernmental fora to create new spaces for dialogue. Perhaps within these spaces new questions and pragmatic approaches will reshape old debates among Western women, African women, and those in between.

NOTES

The title of this essay refers to the varying terms used to describe female genital surgery. *Irua* is the Kikuyu word for traditional initiation ceremonies associated with the clitoridectomy of girls and the circumcision of boys within that Kenyan ethnic group.

1. Alice Walker defines a "womanist" as a "black feminist or feminist of color." Alice Walker, In Search of Our Mothers' Gardens xi (1983).

2. Alice Walker, Possessing the Secret of Joy (1982).

3. In the film and accompanying book, Walker describes having been blinded in childhood by her brother's toy gun. She describes her wound as "patriarchal" because her parents gave the toy weapon to her brother as the result of cultural influences that encourage boys to be violent. Alice Walker & Pratibha Parmar, Warrior Marks: Female Genital Mutilation and the Sexual Blinding of Women 15–19 (1993).

4. See Judith Seddon's discussion of her discomfort at writing an article on FGS as a white Western woman. Judith Seddon, *Possible or Impossible? A Tale of Two Worlds in One Country,* 5 Yale J.L. & Feminism 265, 268 (1993). *See also* Alison T. Slack, *Female Circumcision: A Critical Appraisal,* 10 Hum. Rts. Q. 437 (1988).

5. In the film and book, Walker discusses her belief that her patriarchal wound resulted because her brother deliberately aimed the gun at her. She expresses her anger and confusion at her family's subsequent references to the incident as "the accident." *See* Walker & Parmar, *supra* note 3, at 15–19.

6. Seble Dawit & Salem Mekuria, *The West Just Doesn't Get It,* N.Y. Times, Dec. 7, 1993,

at A27. A recent panel of African scholars in the United States criticized Walker's novel and nonfiction work as reflecting a Western imperialist view of African women. Leslye Obiora et al., Inventions of Africa, Black Women in the Academy: Defending Our Name, 1894–1994, Panel Held at the Massachusetts Institute of Technology (Feb. 13–15, 1994).

7. A number of African anti-FGS activists cooperated in the making of *Warrior Marks*. *See* Walker & Parmar, *supra* note 3.

8. *See* Dawit & Mekuria, *supra* note 6.

9. For discussions of these negative images, see Blaine Harden, Africa: Dispatches from a Fragile Continent 14–17 (1990); Makau wa Mutua, *One Dimensional Pessimism: A 'Black-american' Rejection of Africa*, 2 Reconstruction 55 (1992); Hope Lewis, *Images of Africa*, 2 Reconstruction 153 (1994).

10. My own involvement in cross-cultural discussions about FGS as a source of international concern began when I had the opportunity to research women's human rights issues through the Women's Law and Public Policy Program sponsored by the Revson Foundation. I did so as a member of the staff of TransAfrica Forum, an African American research and educational organization that takes a Pan-african approach to U.S. foreign policy. The project was to expand the organization's work on cross-cultural human rights issues affecting black women. These issues often included violations of the economic, social, or cultural rights of black women, including the right to health. Female genital surgery was one of the more controversial topics in discussions among the African, African American, and African Caribbean people who worked with TransAfrica Forum. None of the opinions expressed in this article necessarily reflect the policy of TransAfrica Forum or of TransAfrica.

11. The most significant early work in the "women in development" movement was Ester Boserup, Woman's Role in Economic Development (1970).

12. There are also strong criticisms of the prevalent view that human rights discourse is a construct solely of Western liberalism. *See* Francis M. Deng, *A Cultural Approach to Human Rights among the Dinka, in* Human Rights in Africa: Cross Cultural Perspectives 261 (1990); Lakshman Marasinghe, *Traditional Conceptions of Human Rights in Africa, in* Human Rights and Development in Africa 32–45 (Claude E. Welch, Jr., & Ronald I. Meltzer eds., 1984). For a critique of Western liberal approaches to human rights, see Adamantia Pollis & Peter Schwab, *Human Rights: A Western Construct with Limited Applicability, in* Human Rights: Cultural and Ideological Perspectives 1 (1979).

13. Kay Boulware-Miller, *Female Circumcision: Challenges to the Practice as a Human Rights Violation*, 8 Harv. Women's L.J. 155, 170 n.89 (1985); Isabelle R. Gunning, *Arrogant Perception, World Traveling, and Multicultural Feminism: The Case of Female Genital Surgeries*, 23 Colum. Hum. Rts. L. Rev. 189, 193 n.15 (1991–92) (also chapter 41 in this volume).

14. Boulware-Miller, *supra* note 13, at 176 n.121.

15. *Id.*

16. *Id.* at 163. *See also* Gunning, *supra* note 13, at 241.

17. Gunning, *supra* note 13, at 241.

18. Marsha Freemen, *Women, Development and Justice: Using the International Commission on Women's Rights, in* Ours by Right 93 (Joanna Keer ed., 1993).

19. Article 1 broadly defines "discrimination against women" to mean "any discrimination, exclusion or restriction made on the basis of sex, which has the effect or purpose of impairing or nullifying the recognition, enjoyment or exercise by women, irrespective of their marital status, on a basis of equality of men and women, of human rights and fundamental freedoms

in the political, economic, social, cultural, civil or any other field." Convention on the Elimination of All Forms of Discrimination against Women, art. 1, pt. 1, 1249 U.N.T.S. 14 [hereinafter CEDAW].

20. Article 5 provides that state parties shall take all appropriate measures "(a) To modify the social and cultural patterns of conduct of men and women, with a view to achieving the elimination of prejudices and customary and all other practices which are based on the idea of the inferiority or the superiority of either of the sexes or on stereotyped roles for men and women." *Id.* at art. 5, pt. 1.

21. *See Report of the Committee on the Elimination of Discrimination against Women, General Recommendation No. 19; Violence against Women,* U.N. GAOR, 47th Sess., U.N. Doc. A/47/38 (1992); *Report of the Committee on the Elimination of Discrimination against Women, General Recommendation No. 14; Female Circumcision,* U.N. GAOR, 45th Sess., U.N. Doc. A/45/38 (1990).

22. *Report of the Committee on the Elimination of Discrimination against Women, General Recommendation No. 14, supra* note 21.

23. *See* Gunning, *supra* note 13, at 236–38. The committee has been praised for its members' professionalism and for its active approach to following up on reporting and other requirements under CEDAW. There is currently no mechanism, however, for raising individual complaints under CEDAW. *See* Andrew Byrnes, *The 'Other' Human Rights Treaty Body: The Work of the Committee on the Elimination of Discrimination against Women,* 14 Yale J. Int'l L. 1 (1989).

24. These limitations are part of the broader problem with CEDAW: implementation. The convention has been widely ratified by many countries, including those in which FGS is practiced. Nahid Toubia, Female Genital Mutilation: A Call for Global Action 45 (1993). Anna Funder notes, however, that at least forty-one of the state parties have made substantive reservations to CEDAW, particularly with respect to settlement of disputes "over the interpretation or application of the Convention." Anna Funder, *De Minimis Nor Curat Lex: The Clitoris, Culture and the Law,* 3 Transnat'l L. & Contemp. Probs. 417, 422 (1993). *See also* Belinda Clark, *The Vienna Convention Reservations Regime and the Convention on Discrimination against Women,* 85 Am. J. Int'l L. 281 (1991).

25. Boulware-Miller notes that FGS died out in Eritrea during the Eritrean People's Liberation Front's civil war with the Ethiopian government. Boulware-Miller, *supra* note 13, at 168 n.77. Ethiopian girls were said to join the rebel initiative in an effort to avoid FGS. She notes that the practice did not return "[e]ven in the parts from which the army retreated." *Id.*

26. The publicity generated by Walker's efforts has created space for African activists to speak in Western fora. Efua Dorkenoo, the head of Forward, participated in a recent tour of U.S. organizations and testified before Congress on proposed anti-FGS legislation. *All Things Considered: Activists Denounce Female Genital Mutilation* (National Public Radio, Mar. 23, 1994).

27. Although a great deal of work remains to be done in breaking down cross-cultural barriers between African American feminists and African feminists, there have been and continue to be significant efforts to cross the cultural divide. *See, e.g.,* Peggy Antrobus, *An International Perspective on Self-Help,* Vital Signs, Oct./Nov./Dec. 1994, at 24 (*Vital Signs* is published by the National Black Women's Health Project).

28. Efforts at domestic legislation have not always been intended to eradicate FGS. Recently, African women activists in the United Kingdom organized to protest the introduction of

legislation by a Kenyan-born female member of the London's Brent Council to legalize FGS. Helen Pitt, *A Knife in Any Language,* Guardian (U.K.), Mar. 3, 1993, at 9.

29. Sweden was one of the first Western countries to adopt domestic legislation in 1982. Nahid Toubia, *Female Circumcision as a Public Health Issue,* 331 New Eng. J. Med. 712, 715 (1994).

30. The act allows FGS to be performed when it is "necessary for the physical or mental health of the person on whom it is performed," but no criteria for determining necessity have been established. Toubia, *supra* note 19, at 46. Toubia also notes, "[I]n the United Kingdom, anti-FGM legislation is supplemented by the Children's Act of 1989, which provides for investigation of suspected violations of the FGM prohibition, as well as removal of a child from her home in extreme cases where there is no better way to protect the child. The Children's Act also enables the courts to prohibit parents from removing their child from the country to have the operation performed elsewhere." *Id.*

31. Although France has not enacted specific legislation on FGS, it considers the practice a criminal offense under Article 312–3 of the French Penal Code. Efua Dorkenoo & Scilla Elworthy, Female Genital Mutilation: Proposals for Change 11 (3d ed. 1992).

32. *Id.*

33. H.R. 3247, 103d Cong., 1st Sess. (1993). The bill was introduced October 7, 1993, by Representatives Patricia Schroeder and Barbara Rose Collins. Patricia Schroeder, *Female Genital Mutilation: A Form of Child Abuse,* 331 New Eng. J. Med. 739, 739–40 (1994); Mary Ann James, *Recent Developments: Federal Prohibition of Mutilation: The Female Genital Mutilation Act of 1993, H.R. 3247,* 9 Berkeley Women's L.J. 206 (1994).

34. *See* Barbara Reynolds, *The Move to Outlaw Female Genital Mutilation,* Ms., July-Aug. 1994, at 92.

35. Pitt, *supra* note 28.

36. Rone Tempest, *Ancient Traditions v. the Law,* L.A. Times, Feb. 18, 1993, at A1.

37. Although the surgeries might be performed under more antiseptic conditions and with the use of anesthesia, they still have severe short-term and long-term consequences. The motivation of economic gain supports the view that the practice in professional contexts could be a state-licensed violation of human rights.

38. A. M. Rosenthal, *Female Genital Torture I,* N.Y. Times, Dec. 29, 1992, at A15; A. M. Rosenthal, *Female Genital Torture II,* N.Y. Times, Nov. 12, 1993, at A33.

39. *See, e.g.,* Timothy Egan, *An Ancient Ritual and a Mother's Asylum Plea,* N.Y. Times, Mar. 4, 1994, at A25; *Nigerian Says Daughters Face Mutilation if Deported* (CNN television broadcast, Mar. 23, 1994). *See also* Elsa Wash, *Three-Way Intercontinental Custody Battle Rages over Seven-Year-Old Girl,* Wash. Post, Jan. 18, 1987, at D1.

40. *See* Jill Lawrence, *Gender Persecution New Reason for Asylum,* L.A. Times, Mar. 27, 1994, at A14; Sally Jacobs, *Persecution Based on Sex is Viewed as a Cause for Asylum,* Boston Globe, Apr. 8, 1994 at 1; Dimitra Kessenides, *Finding the Right Strategy to Stop a Deportation,* Am. Law, June 1994, at 35. The basis of Oluloro's claim was strongly objected to by some Nigerians living in the United States. *See, e.g.* Zuhair M. Kazaure, *Forced Circumcision is Alien to Nigeria,* N.Y. Times, Apr. 9, 1994, at 20; Uche Okoronkwo II, *Barbaric Ritual?,* Time, Apr. 11, 1994, at 10 (letter to editor).

41. The French government initially denied the asylum request of Aminata Diop on the grounds that this would open the floodgates to African women refugees. "On appeal, the French Commission for Appeals of Refugees recognized that the threat of practice of genital

mutilation is a form of persecution and that Diop consequently fell within the definition of 'refugee' set out in the Geneva Convention." Valerie Oosterveld, *Refugee Status for Female Circumcision Fugitives: Building a Canadian Precedent,* 51 U. Toronto Fac. L. Rev. 277, 279 (1993).

43 | Female Infanticide in China: The Human Rights Specter and Thoughts toward (An)other Vision

Sharon K. Hom

A recurring story that my father tells is about the silent death of a girl infant from his village during the Second World War. Fleeing with a group of peasant families, my father took refuge under a bridge, huddled in the night. He was young, only a teenager, and it was so very long ago, but he remembers a family: a mother with an infant tied to her back and holding two small boys by the hands. The baby started to make crying sounds, perhaps sensing approaching danger, the sounds of war and death coming closer and closer in the darkness. The father of the family wrenched the baby from the mother's back and quickly submerged her in the waters, silencing any sounds that might endanger the survival of the group. My father, who takes pride in being tough, in being hard on his children, in order to survive at all costs, always pauses at the end of this story, and there is a moment when the past death of that nameless infant fills our silence and demands a response.

As I reflect on the literature on women in China and the inextricably connected literature on Chinese family and population policy, in an effort to understand something about the lives of women and the role that domestic and international law might play, I am haunted by that small infant's death.

Although female infanticide in China is arguably not a general norm of social practice but rather an extreme, persistent form of abuse and devaluation of female life, as a crime of gender it suggests disturbing insights into ideological, structural, and political factors that contribute to maintaining the inferior status of Chinese women. By underscoring the life and death consequences of ideology and contingent constructions of social life (e.g., law, government policy, or family), female infanticide provides a radical lens through which broader questions of social justice and gender-based oppression can be analyzed.

FEMALE INFANTICIDE: SPHERES OF VIOLENCE AND GHOSTS AT THE WELL

OVERVIEW: FEMALE INFANTICIDE IN CHINA

Defined narrowly, infanticide is the deliberate killing of a child in its infancy; it includes death through neglect.[1] It "has been practiced on every continent and by people on every level of cultural complexity. Rather than being the exception, it has been the rule."[2] Although not viewed as cruel or violent by the societies that practiced it in the past, infanticide is now considered a crime by national governments all over the world.[3] Because there are very few cases of preferential male infanticide, as a universal social practice, female infanticide is a reflection of the deadly consequences of the cross-cultural domination of patriarchal values and culture.

Although female infanticide[4] in China is arguably a crime within the existing legal framework of domestic civil and criminal law, and is clearly officially condemned by Chinese leaders, the tendency to narrowly define female infanticide in isolation from the broader question of gender inequality and violence against women limits the analysis of the problem and the possible responses. Chinese literature and official rhetoric and the Western analysis of the problem focus on the persistence of feudal thought and practices and reflect a tendency to characterize female infanticide as the "unfortunate consequence" of Chinese population control and modernization policies. This narrow definition and its resulting explanations, however, need to be reexamined. How the problem is conceptualized filters our capacity to imagine solutions and alternative visions that might inform these approaches.

RECONCEPTUALIZING FEMALE INFANTICIDE AS SOCIAL FEMICIDE

The killing of girl infants is a form of violence against the infant herself, the mother, and all women in the society in which the practice occurs. Female infanticide is no less than a gender-based discriminatory judgment about who will survive. At the familial and societal level at which the mother is subjected to enormous pressure to bear a son or face the consequences of abuse and humiliation, female infanticide is a form of policing and terrorist practice of control over women to keep them in their prescribed reproductive role as the bearers of sons.

At the same time, it is important to clarify the actors involved and not leave my proposed reconceptualization adrift in a sea of unmediated social forces or faceless individuals, institutions, or ideologies. If female infanticide is viewed narrowly as the killing of female infants, the guilty responsible parties appear to be the mother herself, or the father, relatives, midwives, or medical workers who might get involved. An appropriate "solution" to this privatized conception of the problem would be to criminalize this behavior and to focus on education, deterrence, and punishment of individuals. This "solution" in fact describes the Chinese government's approach.

Although legal prohibitions and protections are clearly significant in terms of building norms and contributing to a climate of equality for girls and women, the isolated privatized criminalization of the practice is not enough to eradicate the problem or its underlying ideological and structural causes. If viewed as a form of social femicide[5] that occurs as a result of the existence of spheres of violence against women, female infanticide would be viewed as more than a crime committed by individuals. Within a "spheres of violence conceptualization," female infanticide, the forced abortion of fetuses against the consent of pregnant women, the abortion of supernumerary children, the abuse of wives who "fail" to bear sons, suicides by despondent women, and malnutrition of female versus male children are all forms of the devaluation of female life.

All these forms of abuse against females are in fact inevitable and foreseeable gender-based consequences of official Chinese policies adopted in the context of the existing structural, ideological, and cultural realities. Government leaders cannot simply point to a formal system of law and policy to avoid responsibility for promulgating policies that have deadly gender-based consequences, and for failing to adequately plan for the inevitable resistance and reaction of the Chinese people.

As social femicide, these cultural practices and abuses implicate government policy makers and leaders at the institutional and ideological level, and raise questions about the locus of responsibility for the impact of these policy decisions. Reconceptualization of the problems as social femicide urges the framing of a more appropriate social response.

INTERNATIONAL AND DOMESTIC NORMS: DISCOURSES OF UNIVERSALITY AND FALSE GENDER NEUTRALITY

Although China's signing of the UN Convention on the Elimination of All Forms of Discrimination against Women (CEAFDAW)[6] may be a positive indication of its continued doctrinal commitment to a formal domestic policy of equality for women, and perhaps acceptance by the Chinese government that gender equality is not just a question of domestic policy but is subject to commitments made under international law,[7] the implementation presents a continuing challenge to women's/human rights activists. In its two country reports submitted to date for review by CEAFDAW, China has pointed to the body of domestic law that has been promulgated to address and protect the status of women. These include the 1982 Constitution;[8] the marriage law (1980);[9] and particular provisions of the criminal[10] and civil law.[11]

Despite the self-reported claims by China of formal compliance with the requirements of the Convention, a number of problems remain. First, although the Chinese legal system reflects a high degree of formal equality for women, the qualification of all rights in China by the 1982 Constitution[12] underscores the contingency of any rights and the subordination of rights to their usefulness to the state, the society, and the collective as determined by the party. The exercise of these rights is entirely contingent on the party's definition of women's "real" needs and interests.[13]

Second, there is a gap between the formal guarantees and their actual impact on the lives of Chinese women, between the government's stated policy of equality and the reality of women's rights and status in China. Some factors that have been suggested as contributing to this gap between constitutional legal guarantees and social reality are the absence of an effective enforcement mechanism, the absence of an independent judiciary, and the absence of a rights consciousness. However, as the recent democracy movements demonstrate, the demand for rights is not foreign to Chinese citizens.

BEYOND HUMAN RIGHTS: THOUGHTS TOWARD AN(OTHER) VISION

Chinese scholars, feminists, activists, and government officials and policy makers face the difficult task of moving China into the twenty-first century with a vision of justice that is inclusive of the rights of all members of its society, including women. A proposal for a feminist re-envisioning of rights in the Chinese context is beyond the scope and goal of this essay; it also may not be the political or ideological task of any individual scholar, Chinese, American, woman or man, or the perspective of any juxtaposition of these or other positive categories of experience. The goal of a feminist alternative framework should not be grand abstract theory building, but the weaving and living out of a vision shaped by the promises and contradictions inherent in the constraints of the present and the past, and the multiplicity of realities and aspirations of Chinese women and men. It might be a vision that recognizes the power and significance of law but would de-center law clothed in its Western rights-based hegemony as the exclusive social construction that will contribute to social transformation.

I begin thinking about the future by remembering a past journey. In 1987, I returned to my village in Guangzhou with my parents and my little boy. After forty years away from his home village, the hardest decision for my father was to return, but we made our way on the modern express train from Hong Kong, onto two ferry crossings, and along a dusty rural road. And there at the end of a cloud of dust of our approaching noisy van was a throng of several hundred people, all my relatives, all Homs (yes, a patrilocal village). We paid respects before the shrine of my great-grandfather, my ancestors, three generations of us: father, daughter, and grandson. With no running water or sewage system, the villagers still cleaned out the old stone well every spring. They still grew fish for market in the pond over which the village outhouse was situated. My cousin, one baby boy tied to her back, while two smaller children (a boy and a girl) ran around her legs, pointed to a huge mountain of grain that she had just harvested. My father said that nothing had changed except for the paved road into the village. I begin thinking about the future by remembering the unknown lives of millions of people who will never travel beyond these mountains, beyond that paved road.

What might Chinese society look like if the current male-dominated hierarchies of power and hegemonic narratives about women's realities were de-centered? What are strategies for rethinking existing "relations of ruling" and their attendant private and public violence? In locating the sites of resistance, we must recognize that resistance not only is present in organized movements, but "inheres in the very gaps, fissures, and silences of hegemonic narratives. Resistance is encoded in the practices of remembering, and of writing. Agency is thus figured in the minute, day-to-day practices and struggles of Third World women." [14] One way women can exercise this agency is to resort to the "ordered use of the power to disbelieve," [15] to reject the definitions by the powerful of their/our realities, even in the midst of poverty, exploitation, or oppression. What if more and more Chinese women and men exercised their "power to disbelieve" the reified truths presented by the current patriarchs?

I frame these questions suggesting the centrality of alternative vision(s), values, and decision-making frameworks. The "intentionally provisional" framework suggested by this discussion is premised on a central recognition of Chinese women (and men) as human agents within (an)other vision of women as not only victims of the violence that pervades their/our lives, but also as already possessing the power to transform their/our lives and societies. This tentative framework is grounded in awareness of the powerful historical legacy [16] and glimpses of the daily and numerous ways Chinese men and women are already exercising this inherent power to disbelieve and to live, to construct alternative visions and realities in the face of an apparently hegemonic reality of power and control over every aspect of social life.

At a recent conference on women in China, Chinese women academics, researchers, and writers from China shared their work on sex education, population policy, Chinese rural women, Chinese families, literature, and perspectives on feminism with Western feminist scholars and activists. [17] In a panel on multiple perspectives on feminism, several Chinese women who had completed postgraduate studies in the United States powerfully shared their deep sense of despair and their awareness that they had become inhabitants of the borderlands between cultures, the forever "outsider" perspective. They/I went "home," but discovered it was no longer a place they/I could "fit in." Yet it is precisely from these borderlands, the margins, as it were, that it may be possible to develop a "consciousness of the borderlands," [18] a plural consciousness necessitated by the internationalization of many of the issues affecting our lives in our different cultures. It is this outsider consciousness, the view from the borderlands, that may provide the images, the experiences that might shape (an)other vision(s) that will uproot dualistic consciousness and open the door to cross-cultural strategies. "It is only by understanding the contradictions inherent in women's location within various structures that effective political action and challenges can be devised." [19]

By engaging in the discursive arena(s) of feminism(s), I am also mindful of Rey Chow's critical reminder to non-Western but Westernized women to ask themselves/ourselves, "How do I speak? In what capacity and with whose proxy?" [20] I speak from the borderlands: an American by citizenship; a British colonial subject by birth; a Chinese-American by culture. I speak not on behalf of my Chinese comrades in

China and here in this country. I do speak to encourage them/us to continue to exercise our "power to disbelieve." I imagine more Chinese women standing up and singing powerfully their own words and music. I imagine Chinese women in rural villages choosing to fight for the life of the girl-child born, in loving their daughters, an honoring and claiming of themselves.[21] I imagine Chinese women writing women's scripts that will change the languages of power forever.

What vision(s) can guide our efforts? What might the world of the twenty-first century be like? What kind of country might China develop to be? What might our lives be like? Women have been conditioned in different societies to view themselves/ourselves as "the other." What might a vision of the future look like if the perspective of this marginalized "other" were included, if the vision not only began from the primacy and centrality of (an)other, but included the recognition of multiplicities of many possible subject "others"?

I would also envision a country where "human" rights unquestionably included the rights of women, perhaps a country in which the Convention on the Elimination of All Forms of Discrimination against Women is also taught in every school and where the vision and principles of the convention shape the public and private domains of power and justice. It might be a country where "people," "citizens," and "individual" included women beyond linguistic gender-neutrality, a country in which a vision of equality and justice was present in the hearts and lives of every man, woman, and child. It might be a country where the convention and all such formal "rights" documents were superfluous anachronisms of a more primitive time. It might be a country where the birth of a female child as well as a male child will be welcomed with tears of joy and pride. It might be a country where all the adults, men and women, share equally the responsibility and gifts of raising these precious charges. It is a country that may not exist anywhere in the world yet. Or it may already exist. We may only have to recognize it in ourselves and in others. We may only have to continue to exercise our individual and collective power to disbelieve the inevitability of existing "truths" and to call on ourselves to honor and bear witness with our lives to the vision(s) we want to believe.

NOTES

1. Laila Williamson, *Infanticide: An Anthropological Analysis, in* Infanticide and the Value of Life 62–63 (Marvin Kohl ed., 1978).

2. *Id.* at 61. Williamson points out that infanticide has satisfied important familial, economic, and societal needs. In Imperial China, Japan, and Europe, it has been practiced as a method of controlling population growth and avoiding starvation and social disruption.

3. *Id.* at 72.

4. I use the term to mean the induced death (euthanasia) of infants by suffocation, drowning, abandonment, exposure, or other methods. In China, reported methods also include crushing the infant's skull with forceps as it emerges during birth or injecting formaldehyde into the soft spot of the head. Maria Hsia Chang, *Women, in* Human Rights in the People's Republic of China 260 (Yuan-li Wu et al. eds., 1988).

5. I use the term "social femicide" to suggest the implication of the role of an existing social order in practices that result in death and devaluation of female lives. For an international example of attention to the problem of the impact of social practices on women, see *Report of the Working Group on Traditional Practices Affecting the Health of Women and Children,* Working Group on Slavery of the Sub-Commission on Prevention of Discrimination and Protection of Minorities, U.N. Doc. E/CN.4/1986/42 (1986). The Working Group on Slavery of the Sub-Commission on Prevention of Discrimination and Protection of Minorities of the U.N. Commission on Human Rights identified various traditional practices that have an adverse impact on the health of women. These practices include female circumcision, traditional birth practices, and preferential treatment for male children. In selecting these practices as priority problems, the working group considered the extent of the phenomenon, the mortality and morbidity rate, and other factors. The working group's report suggests a clear link between preferential treatment of boys and the excess morbidity and mortality among girls. It estimated that about one million female children per year die as the result of neglect. As one of the consequences of son preference, female infanticide reflects the deadly impact for female children of the value systems and "preferences" of patriarchal societies, and thus is a form of social femicide.

6. U.N. Convention on the Elimination of All Forms of Discrimination against Women (CEAFDAW), opened for signature, Dec. 18, 1979, 34 U.N. GAOR Supp. No. 46 at 193, U.N. Doc. A/34/36 (1979).

7. Paul D. McKenzie, *China and the Women's Convention: Prospects for the Implementation of an International Norm,* 7 China L. Rep. 23 (1991). Since China's admission to the United Nations in 1979, it has ratified international treaties; used international standards to criticize other governments; and participated in UN human rights decisions to investigate human rights in other countries, including Afghanistan (1984) and Chile (1985). Roberta Cohen, *People's Republic of China, The Human Rights Exception,* 9 Hum. Rts. Q. 448, 536–37 (1987).

8. The 1982 Constitution protects freedom of marriage and the duty of children and parents to support each other, Chin. Const. (1982) ch. II, art. 49; and sets forth the duty to practice family planning, Chin. Const. (1982) ch. I, art. 2.

9. Although it is titled the "marriage law," the scope of the law is broader and also addresses the regulation of the family. This law contains a marriage system based on free choice of partners, monogamy, and equality between the sexes.

10. Articles 179 through 184 set forth offenses against marriage and the family, for example, interference with the family, bigamy, spousal and child abuse, and child abduction. Rape (Article 139) is punishable by the death penalty. Prison terms of two to fourteen years may be imposed for a range of crimes against the family and marriage.

11. The General Principles of Civil Law of the People's Republic of China (1986) provide for civil rights and equality within the family.

12. For example, the preamble of the 1982 Chinese Constitution sets forth the guiding ideology, the Four Fundamental Principles: adherence to the socialist road; loyalty to the party; following through with the dictatorship of the proletariat; and adherence to Marxist/Leninist and Mao Zedong thought. Chin. Const. (1982) pmbl.

13. Chang, *supra* note 4, at 250–51.

14. Chandra T. Mohanty, *Cartographies of Struggle: Third World Women and the Politics of Feminism, in* Third World Women and the Politics of Feminism 38 (Chandra T. Mohanty et al. eds., 1991).

15. bell hooks, Feminist Theory: From Margin to Center 90 (1984) (citing Elizabeth Janeways, Powers of the Weak (1981)).

16. Chinese women have a long history of participation in rebellions and revolutionary struggle in China dating back to premodern China. There were secret all-women societies, such as the White Lotus sect in the 1790s, all-women associations in the 1660s, women's units in the Boxer Rebellion of 1900, and outstanding women leaders and revolutionaries like Jiu Jin (1875–1907), who shocked and inspired a generation with her courage and personal life choices, including a life of fighting for national and women's liberation until her execution for plotting to overthrow the government. Jiu Jin urged her female compatriots to "hurry, hurry, women, save yourselves." Kumari Jayawardena, Feminism and Nationalism in the Third World 180 (1986).

17. *See* Engendering China: Women, Culture and the State Conference, held February 7–9, 1992 at Harvard University and Wellesley College.

18. I borrow the phrase from Chandra Mohanty's discussion of what Gloria Anzaldúa calls a "mestiza consciousness," "a consciousness born of the historical collusion of Anglo and Mexican cultures and frames of reference." Mohanty, *supra* note 15, at 36.

19. Chandra T. Mohanty, *Under Western Eyes: Feminist Scholarship and Colonial Discourse, in* Third World Women, *supra* note 14, at 66.

20. Rey Chow, *Violence in the Other Country: China as Crisis, Spectacle, and Woman, in* Third World Women, *supra* note 15, at 95.

21. *See Heart of the Dragon Mediating* (PBS television broadcast (1987)), depicting a young woman who demanded a divorce because she was convinced her husband wanted to murder their infant girl baby. After mediation among their respective work units, the couple, and their two families, the couple agreed to reunite and everyone agreed to honor and help raise the baby girl.

44 | Spouse-Based Immigration Laws: The Legacy of Coverture

Janet M. Calvo

A woman from the Philippines was abused by her U.S. citizen spouse. He threatened to have immigration authorities deport her to the Philippines if she tried to leave him. She stayed. He later cut her all over her back, head, and hands with a meat cleaver. A U.S. citizen never filed a petition for his Ecuadorian wife even though he had been married to her for three years and she was pregnant. She therefore could not gain legal status.[1]

A Dominican woman fled from her U.S. citizen husband's violent assaults only after being hospitalized for the fifth time as a result of his beatings. Her husband bashed her head against the wall and threatened to kill her if she told her doctor what happened. She had been afraid to leave him because he controlled her immigration status.[2]

A Chinese woman married an American citizen. Within a month of her arrival in the United States, her husband threatened her with a gun and subjected her to repeated physical abuse. She did not initially leave because she feared deportation and physical reprisal, and could not speak enough English to gain information about her legal rights. After being repeatedly threatened with a gun, however, she sought help from a battered woman's shelter in New York. Later, during divorce proceedings, she discovered that her citizen husband had previously married two other alien wives, who both had been deported.[3]

These situations are a few of many that illustrate the consequences of the legacies of coverture in the immigration law. The notion of coverture, that a wife is subordinate to her husband and under his control, was incorporated into the early immigration laws and strengthened by the 1986 Immigration Marriage Fraud Amendments.[4] It was ameliorated but not removed by changes made in the law in 1990 and 1994. This article discusses the history and impact of spousal domination in the immigration law.

THE COMMON LAW DOCTRINE OF COVERTURE
AND THE DOMESTIC LAW'S RESPONSE

Under the doctrine of coverture, a wife could not make a contract with her husband or with others. She could not engage in litigation. She could not sue or be sued without joining her husband. She could not sue her husband at all. She could not make a will. The personal property that a woman owned before marriage and that she acquired during the marriage became her husband's property. A husband had the use of his wife's real property during the marriage. If the marriage produced a child, the husband was entitled to the rents and profits of the wife's property during the husband's life.[5] The husband was the sole guardian of the couple's children.[6]

The coverture doctrine thus did two things. First, it established the notion of spousal domination and control. A married couple were not viewed as two coequal parties. Rather, one spouse was legally given absolute power over the other. Second, the coverture doctrine gave all the power to the male spouse.

A husband's total control over his wife's livelihood, home, and children created a coercive situation that was reflected in a subsidiary doctrine, the right of "chastisement." This kind of control over activity, livelihood, and children established by coverture carried with it the power to enforce that control. The American courts reflected ambivalence on this issue: some courts upheld a husband's right to use force and others rejected it.

It is, however, undisputed that the American common law failed to protect wives from injury by their husbands. A wife could not sue her husband in tort for injuries caused by him. She had no resources with which to escape her husband's abuse, as all her property was under his control.

THE INCORPORATION AND PERPETUATION OF COVERTURE
IN IMMIGRATION LAW

The premises underlying the coverture doctrine were incorporated into the initial laws controlling immigration status passed in the late nineteenth and early twentieth centuries. From the inception, immigration laws incorporated and enforced the notion of spousal domination and gave the control and power to the male spouse. Male citizens and resident aliens were given the right to control the immigration status of their alien wives. Before any immigration benefit could attach to an immigrant wife, her husband had to petition for her or she had to accompany him.[7] These restrictions incorporated the assumptions of coverture, that a wife was under the control and authority of her husband and subservient to him.

In an attempt to address different treatment of the sexes, the Immigration and Nationality Act of 1952 changed the word "wife" to the word "spouse." However, it continued the basic notion of coverture, total control over the immigrant status of one spouse by the other spouse.[8] The 1965 act changed the immigration system from one that promoted the immigration of certain racial or ethnic groups to one that was based on family relationships and the unfulfilled labor needs of U.S. business.[9] Under the 1965 act, spouse-based immigration was a substantial part of immigration based on family relationship. "Immediate relatives" of U.S. citizens were allowed to immigrate without regard to any numerical quotas.[10] The definition of "immediate relative" included the spouse of a U.S. citizen.[11] Numerical quotas were imposed on other immigrants.[12] These quotas were distributed according to a preference system that also favored family relationships.[13] The second preference included the spouses of legal permanent residents.[14] However, the alien spouse could not gain legal immigration status unless the citizen or resident spouse filed a petition, which he could withdraw.

Even though the 1965 law favored immigration based on family relationships, in which spouse-based immigration played a large part, Congress did not confront the historical sexism of marriage-based immigration. To the contrary, the 1965 act continued the spousal control underlying coverture's discrimination against women.

In 1986, Congress enacted the Immigration Marriage Fraud Amendments of 1986.[15] This law substantially added to the control of a citizen or resident spouse over his alien spouse's immigration status. The alien spouse's legal status was made conditional. The law allowed the citizen or resident's actions to affect whether his spouse continued to maintain legal status after it was initially obtained. Loss of legal immigration status establishes the basis for deportation.[16] Under this law the legal permanent resident spouse could lose her legal status unless her spouse cooperated in petitioning for continuation of her legal status.

As a result of the 1986 Marriage Fraud Amendments, the citizen or resident spouse had enormous power over the alien spouse. He controlled whether she and her children could stay, live, and work in the United States. He could make his spouse and her children illegal aliens by refusing to initially file a petition for her, by refusing to file a petition to continue her legal status, or by refusing to appear at an interview.

The 1986 act contained two very limited discretionary waivers that somewhat ameliorated the strictures of this power. Under the 1986 law, an alien spouse could request that the attorney general transform her conditional status into permanent status, even if her spouse would not cooperate in the joint petition and interview requirements, if she could satisfy the criteria for an extreme hardship waiver or a good faith, good cause waiver.[17] However, restrictive INS interpretations made it very difficult for abused spouses to qualify for the waiver.

While the Immigration Act of 1990[18] substantially revised the legal immigration system,[19] it basically maintained family-based immigration and the role of spouse-based immigration in that system. Under the 1990 law, immediate relatives, including the spouses of U.S. citizens, may become permanent residents without regard to numerical quotas.[20] The spouses of permanent residents are part of a group that receives preference in the distribution of worldwide numerical quotas.[21] While spouse-based immigration is thus favored, the 1990 law continued the coverture-based control first incorporated into the 1917 and 1924 acts. Under the 1990 law, an alien spouse could still become a legal resident only if her citizen or permanent resident spouse filed a petition for her to become a resident.[22] The citizen or resident spouse could still withdraw the petition at will and was the only one who could appeal a denial of the petition.[23] The basic conditional resident system for spouses established in 1986 continued. The alien had to have the cooperation of her citizen or resident spouse to continue in a legal status after a two-year period.[24]

However, in 1990 Congress modified the opportunity for the alien spouse to request a waiver of the citizen or resident spouse's cooperation. An additional waiver based on the abuse of the conditional resident or her child by the citizen or resident spouse was created.[25] However, all waivers are subject to the exercise of the attorney general's discretion; that is, the alien may qualify for the waiver and still be denied.[26] These statutory waivers, while an improvement over the 1986 provisions, are still very limited and do not remove spousal domination from the law.

In 1994, the Violence against Women Act was passed as part of the Violent Crime Control and Law Enforcement Act.[27] Changes were made in the immigration law that diminished, but did not eliminate, the control of abusive citizen or resident spouses.

The Violence against Women Act amended provisions of the immigration law that applied to petitions to classify aliens as relatives eligible to apply for permanent resident status, suspension of deportation, and the evidence necessary to make these applications.[28] Under these amendments, certain alien spouses who were abused or whose children were abused by the alien's citizen or resident spouse can file the petition necessary to initiate their applications for legal status without the abusive spouse's cooperation.[29] However, in addition to proving the abuse, these aliens must demonstrate several additional factors. The most difficult and burdensome requirement is that they must demonstrate, in addition to the abuse, that their deportation would result in extreme hardship to themselves or their children. These alien spouses must further show that they are persons of good moral character and entered into their marriages in good faith; they are currently residing in the United States and at some time resided with the abusive U.S. citizen or legal permanent resident in the United States, the abuse of the spouse or spouse's child happened sometime during the marriage; and they are otherwise eligible for immediate relative or preference classification.

The suspension of deportation law was also amended by the addition of a new category of aliens eligible to suspend deportation and change their status to legal permanent residence. Aliens who were battered or subjected to extreme cruelty by U.S. citizen or legal permanent resident spouses and aliens who are the parents of children who were battered or subjected to extreme cruelty by the U.S. citizen or legal permanent resident parents are included.[30] The alien must meet the criteria in addition to demonstrating that she fits into a recognized group of abused. A suspension applicant alien must also show that deportation would result in extreme hardship to herself or her child. She must further show that she has been physically present in the United States for a continuous period of at least three years; the abuse took place in the United States; she is currently a person of good moral character and has been for the three-year period preceding her application; she is a deportable alien, but not deportable on certain serious grounds.[31]

After the passage of these amendments, the citizen or resident spouse still maintains control over the alien spouse's immigration status, but with some limited exceptions. If the alien spouse can demonstrate that she or her child was abused and she meets the extreme hardship and additional criteria, she may be able to pursue her legal status independently. However, this approach, while being of assistance to some individuals, does not break the control of spousal domination even when a spouse is engaged in battering or extreme cruelty. The principle of coverture and the right to chastise that flows from it have not been fully rejected.

IMPACT OF SPOUSE-BASED IMMIGRATION LAWS

This kind of spousal control in the immigration laws is analogous to the power over married women's livelihood, home, and children imposed by coverture. Alien spouses of both sexes are theoretically subject to the law's spousal domination. However, the law has the greatest adverse impact on women immigrants. This is true for three reasons. First, the immigrants gaining status as spouses have been predominantly female. Second, wives have legally and socially been the historical target of subordination in marriage. Third, spouse abuse in the United States is pervasive and the majority of victims of spouse abuse are women. Furthermore, because women are most frequently the primary caretakers of children, and wife abuse is associated with child abuse, the spouse-based immigration laws harm the alien and citizen children of alien spouses.

Since wife abuse is so pervasive in the United States, it is not surprising that alien wives are abused by their citizen and resident husbands, as the individual situations discussed in the introduction illustrate. Surveys of alien women have also found that they suffer substantial abuse. For example, a survey of alien women in San Francisco found that 24 percent of the Latina and 20 percent of the Filipina study participants had experienced domestic violence, and that for 42 percent of the Latinas and 20 percent of the Filipinas their dependence on their husbands for legal status was a major problem.[32] Another survey reported that 60 percent of the surveyed Korean immigrant women had been abused by their spouses.[33]

Furthermore, the social situation of many immigrant women makes them particularly vulnerable to domination and abuse by a spouse. A recent immigrant is frequently very socially dependent on her citizen or resident spouse. Often she has left behind the family and friends that could provide her other support. She is unlikely to be familiar with the culture, the legal system, her legal rights, social service agencies, or medical care services.

CHANGES NEEDED TO REMOVE THE LEGACIES OF COVERTURE

Changes are needed in the current immigration law to finally exorcise the legacies of chastisement and coverture. While seeming neutral, the law in reality perpetuates discrimination against women. Factually, the majority of alien spouses are women. Socially, in good part because of laws that made subordination of wives the cultural norm, it is husbands and not wives who subject their spouses to domination and abuse. Sexual equality cannot be achieved by a law that purports to be neutral, but in reality perpetuates the premises of past sex discrimination and disproportionately impacts on women. Sexual equality can be achieved when the law confronts and rejects the premises of its historical sex discrimination and gives women the ability to live equally with men in a society that still has remnants of that discrimination. Sexual equality is not the freedom to be treated without regard to sex. It is the freedom from subordination because of sex.[34]

Congressional response to the harm to women perpetuated by the immigration law need not be sex-specific, that is, give benefits to women over men. The law can be sex-neutral, but take into account the impact of and basis for its historical sex discrimination. Instead of allowing both men and women to be subject to spousal control, the law should reject the notion of spousal domination.

A simple solution to the spousal domination in the conditional residency scheme would be to allow an alien spouse to petition to achieve and keep permanent resident status without the citizen or resident spouse's cooperation. This solution, however, may not be politically realistic because of administrative and legislative concern about preventing marriage fraud. Requiring alien spouses to demonstrate that they married in good faith and not solely for immigration purposes should be sufficient to meet fraud concerns. The existence of a child of the marriage should remove any doubts about the good faith nature of the marriage. Most important, citizens or residents should not use control over immigration status to entrap their alien spouses in abusive relationships. Aliens who demonstrate that they or their children have been abused by their spouses should be able to apply for and maintain legal status without demonstrating criteria in addition to proving the abuse. These changes would send the message that a married woman is not the possession of her husband and spouse abuse will not be sanctioned in this society.

NOTES

1. National Coalition against Domestic Violence (May 17, 1989).

2. Walt, *Immigrant Abuse: Nowhere to Hide,* Newsday (New York), Dec. 2, 1990, at 8.

3. *Hearings on Legal Immigration Reform before the Subcomm. on Immigration, Refugees and International Law of the House Comm. on the Judiciary,* 101st Cong., 1st Sess. 667 (1989).

4. Immigration Marriage Fraud Amendments of 1986, Pub. L. No. 99–639, 100 Stat. 3537 (codified as amended in scattered sections of 8 U.S.C.).

5. H. Clark, The Law of Domestic Relations in the U.S. § 8.1, at 500 (2d ed. 1987).

6. B. Babcock et al., Sex Discrimination and the Law 561 (1975).

7. *See, e.g.,* Act of May 26, 1924, Pub. L. No. 139, § 4(a), 43 Stat. 155.

8. Immigration and Nationality Act of 1952, Pub. L. No. 414, 66 Stat. 166.

9. Act of October 3, 1965, Pub. L. No. 236, 79 Stat. 911.

10. 8 U.S.C. §§ 1151(a)-(b) (1988).

11. 8 U.S.C. § 1151(b) (1988).

12. 8 U.S.C. §§ 1151(a), 1153(a) (1988).

13. 8 U.S.C. § 1153(a) (1988).

14. 8 U.S.C. § 1153(a)(2) (1988).

15. Pub. L. No. 99–639, 100 Stat. 3537 (codified as amended in scattered sections of 8 U.S.C.).

16. 8 U.S.C.A. § 1251(a)(1)(D) (West Supp. 1991).

17. 8 U.S.C. § 1186a(c)(4)(1988).

18. Pub. L. No. 101–649, 104 Stat. 4978 (codified as amended in scattered sections of 8 U.S.C.).

19. The law expanded employment-based immigration and added a category designated "diversity" to allow the immigration of aliens from recently low admission countries. Among other changes, it modified grounds for exclusion and deportation. T. Aleinkoff & D. Martin, Immigration Process and Policy 61 (1991).

20. 8 U.S.C.A. §§ 1151(a)-(b) (West Supp. 1991).

21. 8 U.S.C.A. § 1153(a)(2)(A) (West Supp. 1991).

22. 8 U.S.C.A. § 1154(a) (West Supp. 1991).

23. 8 C.F.R. §§ 204.1(a)(4), 205.1(a)(1) (1991).

24. 8 U.S.C.A. § 1186a (West Supp. 1991).

25. 8 U.S.C.A. §§ 1186a(c)(4)(B), (C) (West Supp. 1991).

26. 8 U.S.C.A. § 1186a(c)(4) (West Supp. 1991).

27. Violent Crime Control and Law Enforcement Act of 1994, Pub. L. No 103–322, 108 Stat. 1796.

28. The amendments stated that any relevant credible evidence must be considered in determinations of any applications filed by the abused, including petitions for classification as immediate relatives of preference, applications for suspension, and waivers of petition requirement to remove conditional resident status. The attorney general can determine what evidence is credible and its weight.

29. Alien children abused by their citizen or resident parents can also file petitions.

30. Also included are aliens who were battered or subjected to extreme cruelty by U.S. citizen or legal permanent resident parents.

31. Marriage fraud, criminal offenses, falsification of documents, or security and related grounds.

32. C. Hogeland & R. Rosen, Dreams Lost, Dreams Found: Undocumented Women in the Land of Opportunity 15 (1990).

33. Ramirez, *Violence at Home Grips Alien Women,* S.F. Examiner, Mar. 10, 1991, at A20; *see also* Lin, *Is INS Hindering Abused Wives?,* Newsday (New York), July 8, 1991, at 21 (reporting on the large percentage of battered immigrant women with citizen or resident spouses serviced by the Asian Women's Shelter in New York City).

34. Scales, *The Emergence of a Feminist Jurisprudence: An Essay,* 95 Yale L.J. 1373, 1395 (1986); *see also* Schneider, *The Dialectic of Rights and Politics: Perspectives from the Women's Movement,* 61 N.Y.U. L. Rev. 589 at 629, 645 (1986) (stating that equality requires social reconstruction of gender roles and freedom from sexual subordination and violence).

45 | Black South African Women: Toward Equal Rights

Adrien Katherine Wing and Eunice P. de Carvalho

South Africa needs a vision of equality that gives particularized attention to the needs of black women,[1] who have endured unequal treatment because of their race and gender. Black women are in the unique position of being the least equal of all groups in South Africa. They have been oppressed by whites on the basis of race, and they have been oppressed by men, both white and black, on the basis of gender.

On becoming the first democratically elected president of South Africa, Nelson Mandela called for the creation of a nonsexist as well as nonracist South Africa. His campaign for gender equality will have to struggle against well-developed social forces in South Africa. For example, tribal leaders have historically opposed equal rights for women. Indeed, men's attitudes are often more important than written constitutions and legal instruments in determining the advancements of women. Constitutional, statutory, and other legal changes without corresponding modifications in attitude will not dramatically improve the situation of black women.

This chapter focuses on the struggle of black South African women in overcoming the dual legacy of racism and sexism. It focuses on four social arenas—employment, education, rape and domestic violence, and health care—that have a significant impact on the lives of these women. Because the oppression of black women in South Africa has persisted in the twentieth century as a result of apartheid and customary law, it has become entrenched in the experiences of daily life in these four arenas.

THE LEGACY OF DISCRIMINATION AGAINST BLACK WOMEN

Black women in pre-1993 South Africa lived under a dual burden of discrimination: apartheid and sexism. This discrimination was promoted through state-sponsored legal instruments, as embodied in the system of law known as apartheid, as well as in tribal systems of law known as "customary law."

An understanding of how apartheid oppressed blacks provides part of the background necessary for an appreciation of the oppression of black women. Apartheid imposed on South African blacks a badge of inferiority in all areas of life, including housing, land ownership, education, health care, employment, judicial administration, freedom of speech, freedom of association, public accommodations, and marriage. State-sponsored discrimination retarded the progress of black women by impeding the progress of blacks as a whole.

CUSTOMARY LAW

In addition to apartheid, black women were subjected to black male domination under customary law, which affected marriage, guardianship, succession, contractual power, and property rights. These laws are still in effect, but we refer here to the apartheid era. Customary law is defined in the Law of Evidence Amendment Act of 1988 as "the Black law or customs as applied by the Black tribes in the Republic or in territories which formerly formed part of the Republic."[2] Customary law viewed women as perpetual minors and lifelong wards of their fathers, husbands, brothers, or sons. Women could not engage in contracts of any kind, acquire property, inherit, or marry without the permission of a guardian, who was usually a male relative.[3] After a woman obtained permission to marry, her future husband validated the marriage through *lobolo,* the payment of money or property to the father of the bride.[4]

Under customary law, all of a woman's assets became the sole property of her husband after marriage.[5] The male head of the family had sole control over the family's assets, which were supposed to be used for the common good of the family. A woman could not inherit her husband's estate, which included any property that she may have brought to the marriage. The husband's estate was passed down to his firstborn son, who then became the head of the family.

Under customary law, polygamy is legal, but civil South African law recognizes only monogamous marriages.[6] Thus, a black man could marry several women under customary law, but only one under civil law. Prior to 1988, if a customary wife was abandoned, she and her children had no legal rights, while a civil law wife had enforceable legal rights. Since 1988, no man in a customary marriage can contract a civil marriage with another woman.[7] Since the amendment in the law was not retroactive, those customary wives married prior to 1988 remain unaffected by the new law.

The system's subjugation of women under customary law reinforced the way black men viewed black women. Women were subject to the will of men because they needed their husbands' permission to work and their fathers' permission to marry.

THE FOUR ARENAS

The interaction of apartheid and customary law had a dramatic effect in subjugating black South African women. This is clearly evident in the four social arenas of employment, education, rape and domestic violence, and health care.

Employment

Apartheid's formal restrictions impeded the entry of black women into the workplace. Traditionally, black women in South Africa worked predominantly in the agricultural and service areas, holding the least-skilled, lowest-paid, and most insecure jobs. Within the industrial sector, black women constituted the majority of low-level laborers, while white women had better access to clerical and administrative positions.[8] Many black women also worked in the unpaid labor force, performing jobs like cooking, cleaning, child rearing, and subsistence agriculture.

Several independent components of the pre-1993 regime acted to block the movement of black women into higher-skilled, higher-wage sectors of the economy. First, the availability of education for black women was restricted under apartheid. Second, pass laws legally kept black women out of urban areas and denied them access to the skills and opportunities that they needed to become participants in an organized labor force.

Third, many of the jobs traditionally held by black women during apartheid were not protected by fair labor standards. The estimated one million black women who worked as domestic servants were not protected by legislation stipulating minimum wages, maximum hours, maternity benefits, paid sick leave, disability insurance, or any kind of job security.[9]

Fourth, geographic restrictions posed burdensome working conditions on domestic servants and other black workers in predominantly white areas. Under apartheid, it was against the law for a domestic worker to have her husband or children live with her, and those who broke the law were subjected to large fines. Similarly, the burden of commuting a long distance from home had a detrimental effect on black South African home life and discouraged some women from entering the workforce. Fifth, black women were unprotected from harassment in the workplace, where sexual harassment was a common problem.[10]

Education

Under apartheid, South Africa created segregated educational systems designed to prepare or limit each racial group for perceived economic niches. Black men and women were educated under the system of "Bantu education," which was based on the Black Education Act.[11] Under this law, the education of black children was designed to relegate them to menial labor roles. The act excluded from the curriculum the classes necessary to prepare these children for higher education and for higher-skilled careers.

The patriarchal nature of both black and white South African culture was reflected in the educational system, and as a result, all South African women suffered. Patriarchy compounded Bantu education in several ways. First, sexism was reflected in the norms created by society, such as the different expectations that parents had for their sons and daughters. Since education was not free for black South Africans under apartheid, black parents were forced to withdraw their children from school at an early age. In light of the economic incentives to educate sons over daughters, black families placed more emphasis on educating male children. As a result, girls were the first to leave school to help their families.

A second obstacle was the lack of access to education, particularly for rural women. Large numbers of black women lived in bantustans due to the "forced removal" policy of the National Party. The government passed influx control and pass laws that prevented women from lawfully residing in the cities and urban areas. The system of influx control made it virtually illegal for women and children to live away from the bantustans [12] and therefore to reside where educational opportunities may have been more abundant. A third obstacle was the high dropout rate due to the lack of reproductive freedom. Lack of access to birth control and abortion traditionally resulted in extremely high rates of pregnancy, which in turn correlated to high dropout rates for black girls. [13]

Rape and Domestic Violence

Black South African women have historically been subjected to a great deal of physical abuse, primarily as a result of rape and domestic violence. South Africa's culture of violence has led many men and women to accept domestic violence as a fact of life. [14] Women who are victims of domestic violence find it extremely difficult to obtain any assistance from doctors, counselors, psychiatrists, or the police. Since the authorities generally question the credibility of black women, those who are victims of abuse have little legal recourse. The operation of the legal system often forces women to endure brutal cross-examinations and insinuations of promiscuity. Furthermore, the legal definition of rape excludes spousal rape. [15]

Health Care

Under apartheid, black South African families suffered from malnutrition and often received inadequate health care. The Group Areas Act of 1950 and the pass laws resulted in the removal of millions of people to homelands with inadequate public health infrastructures and poor living conditions. The homelands lacked clean water and waste disposal systems, resulting in the availability of only polluted water for personal consumption, especially in areas with high population densities. All these factors contributed to increased incidences of tuberculosis, cholera, gastroenteritis, and typhoid. [16]

The migrant labor system also had a tremendous impact on the lives of rural blacks. When men returned from the work centers, they brought with them tuberculosis and venereal diseases, which quickly became endemic to the countryside because of the lack of adequate nutrition.

In addition to the overall scarcity of health services for black South Africans, access to reproductive health care under apartheid was limited. Abortion was illegal in South Africa, except in very limited situations, such as when the life of the mother was threatened or the pregnancy was a result of rape or incest.[17] Due to legal restrictions on abortion, many women resorted to illegal abortions.

THE INTERIM CONSTITUTION

As South Africa enters a new era of empowerment for blacks with its first universally elected parliament, it must embark on a campaign to achieve equality for black women. The Interim Constitution of 1993 is potentially a significant step toward that end. It guarantees equal protection under the law to all people[18] and prohibits discrimination on the basis of gender.[19] Importantly, the Interim Constitution permits the introduction of affirmative action programs to benefit black women as well as others discriminated against under apartheid.[20] The Interim Constitution will stay in effect until 1999, when a Permanent Constitution will go into effect. Despite the promise of a new legal order, the Interim Constitution will face difficulties in achieving equality for black women. The roots of these problems are evident in the initial failure of the drafters to seek the input of black women. Additionally, five years is perhaps too brief a period in a 350-year history of discrimination to expect much fundamental change to occur.

THE INTERIM CONSTITUTION AND TRADITIONAL OPPRESSION

Although formal equality is required under the Interim Constitution, this does not guarantee that black women will gain substantive equality. Affirmative action programs are needed to overcome existing discrimination against black women. One area of particular concern is employment. Without employment, black women will not be able to gain economic independence, and will be less able to gain access to education and health care. Another area that requires particular attention is education. Without education, black women will not be able to compete for jobs, participate effectively in the political process, or alter the course of their lives. Likewise, attention must be devoted to improving the access of black women to health care. Government agencies must intervene to prevent sexual and physical violence against women, which may prevent black women from benefiting from education or employment.

The government has formulated a Reconstruction and Development Plan (RDP) to guide its efforts in transforming South African society in the next few years. This plan integrates "growth, development, reconstruction, and redistribution into a unified program."[21] In the RDP, the government has promised to focus some programs, which may or may not involve affirmative action, on black women. As affirmative action programs are not mandated by the Interim Constitution but are merely discretionary, these programs may never materialize.

A CRITIQUE OF THE INTERIM CONSTITUTION

Black women will not be fully emancipated by a reform of South African law unless such reform is followed by the abolition of patriarchal norms, the spread of education, the absorption of women into remunerative occupations outside the home, and participation by women in the work of the government. The Interim Constitution fails to accommodate the intersectionality of race and gender or to attack oppression of black women within the private sphere. Although there have been some successes, where black women have achieved high office in political life, these fundamental discrepancies threaten to make the Interim Constitution ineffective in addressing the special disadvantages of black women.

Successes of Women in the Public Sphere

Some positive changes have already begun to occur in the political arena. Approximately 25 percent of the members of the new four-hundred-seat National Assembly are women, and women also hold seats in all nine of the provincial legislatures. President Nelson Mandela has now appointed three black women to his cabinet. Three deputy cabinet ministers are also black women. Frene Noshir Ginwala, the speaker of parliament, is the first woman and nonwhite ever to be named to this position. Further, two of nine judges on the new Constitutional Court are women.

Customary Law Problems

The present status of customary law under the Interim Constitution is unclear. Chapters 3 (Bill of Rights) and 11 (Traditional Authorities) both acknowledge the role of customary law. While the Interim Constitution binds all three branches of government, it does not necessarily bind traditional leaders exercising customary law powers. A provision that would have insulated customary law from constitutional scrutiny was deleted at the last minute, but a provision that would have subjected customary law to the provisions of the Bill of Rights was also not adopted. By implicitly recognizing customary law while simultaneously calling for gender equality, the Interim Constitution sets up an apparent confrontation between different cultures.[22] The government will not be successful in improving the plight of black women if it does not resolve the seeming conflict between the equal protection clause and customary law.

An Intersectionality Critique

In the South African context, black women suffer discrimination both as blacks and as women. Therefore, a legal system that demands that black women establish their legal claims as one or the other will fail to address the special problems generated by the intersection of race and gender.

The intersection of race and gender justifies calls for the creation of a separate constitutional status for black women. This is especially important, given that the interests of black and white women diverge considerably. Black women cannot expect that measures designed to benefit women will directly enhance their condition, since the measures may in practice favor white women, whose social and economic position makes them better situated to take advantage of the measures.

A Public and Private Split?

The Interim Constitution fails to provide remedies for discrimination in the private sphere. Although much discrimination against black women by the state exists, most discrimination takes place in the private sphere. This is particularly true with regard to sexual and domestic violence.

Class: A New Problem?

An additional factor that needs to be further analyzed is the impact of class on the status of black women. Under apartheid, most black men and women were confined to the lower classes, though a small number of middle-class blacks existed.[23] Under the new government, the black middle and upper classes should grow as more blacks become civil servants or take advantage of business opportunities. Expanded education will also add to the ranks of black elites. The experiences of many other African nations suggest that black women may remain disproportionately poor because of custom, lack of education, and the undervaluing of women's work. Thus, the government must create programs specifically targeted at removing class gaps. Special programs aimed at enhancing the skills of uneducated black women would help.

LOOKING TO THE FUTURE: THE WOMEN'S CHARTER

While the Interim Constitution potentially provides for equal protection and affirmative action for black women, there are significant concerns among black women as to whether these measures will ever be fully realized. In response to the initial exclusion of women from the Convention for a Democratic South Africa (CODESA) constitution-making process, a racially integrated group of women formed a political lobby group, the Women's National Coalition (WNC), to represent the collective demands of South African women. In meeting, these women realized that they had certain common plights, despite their differing party affiliations.

After much discussion on the Interim Constitution's prospects for furthering women's interests, the WNC produced a Women's Charter in 1994 as a collective response to the perceived deficiencies in the Interim Constitution. The document reflected a consensus of a majority of the women involved. Black women had a central role in the development process and constituted a plurality of participants in the process.

The Women's Charter constitutes an important proposal to the drafters of the Permanent Constitution on how to affirm women's rights more effectively. It calls for the principle of equality to be implemented at all levels of government legislation and policy. Specific legislation is sought to ensure social, economic, political, and legal equality for all South African women. The Women's Charter also focuses on how women can enforce their rights to equality.

The joint purposes of the Women's Charter are to build momentum for a long-term lobbying campaign to ensure that the Permanent Constitution reflects the needs of women, and to provide the government with guidelines for interpreting and implementing the new constitutional order. The Women's Charter is an educational tool for the people of South Africa because it expressly sets out the requirements for South Africa to become a nonsexist and nonracist society.

Black women have suffered multiple disadvantages precisely because of both their sex and race. To a limited extent, the Interim Constitution of 1993 addresses that oppression. Nevertheless, black women are not sufficiently empowered by the new constitutional order, nor did they have any substantial input in its creation.

It is up to black South African women, now taking at least part of their rightful place in the Constitutional Assembly, to decide what provisions of the Interim Constitution should be carried over into the Permanent Constitution. The Women's Charter provides a preliminary blueprint of the other rights that the women of South Africa believe should be included in the Permanent Constitution. Black South African women should not have to rely on unpredictable judicial and legislative interpretations of the framers' intent of their rights. Clarity and simplicity should govern, so that even illiterate black women may understand their basic rights. Nevertheless, if progress is made, it is likely to be gradual, messy, fitful, and slow.[24] South African women will want to strive to avoid the plaintive lament of Derrick Bell's fictional heroine Geneva Crenshaw: "We have attained all the rights we sought in law and gained none of the resources we need in life, like the crusaders of old, we sought the Holy Grail of Equal Opportunity, and having gained it in court decisions and civil rights statutes, find it transformed into one more weapon the society can use to perpetuate the sexual status quo."[25]

NOTES

1. This chapter discusses the status of black African women. We leave to others the task of documenting the compelling stories of colored, white, and Asian women. Thus we are not using the term "black" in the anti-apartheid activist sense of including all nonwhites in the term. An article that would attempt to discuss the situation of all South African women would mask the important differences in the level of discrimination confronted by black South African women as opposed to other South African women.

2. L. H. Hoffman & D. Zeffertt, The South African Law of Evidence 428 (4th ed. 1988).

3. *See* H. J. Simons, African Women: Their Legal Status in South Africa (1968); Thanda-

bantu Nhlapo, *Women's Rights and the Family in Traditional and Customary Law, in* Putting Women on the Agenda 111 (Susan Bazilli ed., 1991); Penelope Andrews, *Spectators at the Revolution: Gender Equality and Customary Law in a Post-Apartheid South Africa,* 7 Law & Anthropology (1994).

4. J. C. Bekker, Seymour's Customary Law in Southern Africa 150 (1989).

5. Kshama Sharma, Women in Africa 25 (1989).

6. *See* T. W. Bennett, *The Equality Clause and Customary Law,* 10 S. Afr. J. Hum. Rts. 122, 124 (1994).

7. Marriage Act of 1988, Section 1, Act 3, amending Section 22 of the Black Administration Act, *cited in* Bennett, *supra* note 6, at 457. *See also* Bekker, *supra* note 4, at 253–54.

8. Cherryl Walker, Women and Resistance in South Africa 5 (1991).

9. Tom Cohen, *Apartheid Lingering for Domestic Workers,* Chi. Trib., Dec. 27, 1992, at C12. *See also* Jacklyn Cock, *Trapped Workers: The Case of Domestic Servants in South Africa, in* Patriarchy and Class: African Women in the Home and the Workforce 206, 206–19 (Sharon B. Stichter & Jane L. Parpart eds., 1988); Jacklyn Cock, Maids and Madams: A Study in the Politics of Exploitation (1980).

10. Fatima Meer et al., Black Woman Worker 157 (1990).

11. Black Education Act, No. 47 (1953) (S. Afr.). This statute has been superseded by the New Education and Training Act, No. 90 (1979) (S. Afr.).

12. *See* Francis Wilson, Migrant Labour in South Africa (1972); L. Clarke & J. Ngobese, Women without Men (1975); South Africa, a Land Divided (E. Wait ed., 1982).

13. Hilda Bernstein, For Their Triumphs and for Their Tears: Women in Apartheid South Africa 77 (1985).

14. Robert Shepard, *Working to Fix a Violent Culture,* Chi. Trib., Aug. 28, 1994, at 1.

15. South African Law Commission, Women and Sexual Offenses in South Africa 2–3 (1985).

16. Cedric De Beer, The South African Disease: Apartheid Health and Health Services 54 (1984).

17. Bernstein, *supra* note 13, at 51.

18. S. Afr. Const. ch. III, § 8(1) states, "Every person shall have the right to equality before the law and to equal protection of the law."

19. The chapter goes on to state, "No person shall be unfairly discriminated against, directly or indirectly, and, without derogating from the generality of this provision, on one or more of the following grounds in particular: race, gender, sex, ethnic or social origin, colour, sexual orientation, age, disability, religion, conscience, belief, culture or language."

20. Chapter III, § 8 states, "[The Equal Protection Clause] shall not preclude measures designated to achieve the adequate protection and advancement of persons or groups or categories of persons disadvantaged by unfair discrimination, in order to enable their full and equal enjoyment of all rights and freedoms."

21. Anne Shepherd, *The Task Ahead,* Afr. Rep., July-Aug. 1994, at 38.

22. *See* South Africa: The Countdown to Elections, S. Afr. Project (Lawyer's Committee for Civil Rights, Washington, D.C.), Feb. 14, 1994, at 6.

23. *See* Frank James, *The Black Middle Class,* Ebony, Aug. 1994, at 92–93.

24. *See* Larry Diamond, *Beyond Autocracy: Prospects for Democracy in Africa, in* Beyond Autocracy in Africa 24 (Carter Center, 1989).

25. Derrick Bell, *The Elusive Quest for Racial Justice: The Chronicle of the Constitutional Contradiction, in* The State of Black America 9 (Janet Dewart ed., 1991).

Questions and Suggested Readings for Part 7

1. Devon Carbado uses the terms *unconscious patriarchy* and *passive patriarchy* to describe his father's conduct in the context of their family life. Does it make sense to think of patriarchy in those terms? Can either of these terms function as political apologia for patriarchy?

2. Why are girls and women not valued as highly as men in many countries? What role does patriarchy play? What role does government play in the treatment of women in various countries? Compare the various articles on Africa, China, and the United States. Even though domestic laws and international treaties exist that advocate the equal treatment of women, what is the actual status of women? What do you suggest can be done to rethink the private and public violence against women worldwide? Should the corporate sector play a role in improving women's lives and status? What about the role of nongovernmental organizations?

3. Can Critical Race feminists criticize practices in other countries without falling into the traps of cultural relativism and cultural imperialism? Aren't some societal practices just wrong? Which ones, if any?

4. Explain Isabelle Gunning's three-pronged method of world traveling. Is this world traveling idea simply cultural relativism in disguise? How does the world traveler view FGS? How would such a traveler view bride burning in India, bride price in Africa, veiling in the Middle East, prostitution in Thailand, female infanticide in China, arranged marriages, polygamy, anorexia and bulimia, breast implants, and so forth?

5. How does societal pressure to bear a son affect women in society? Why does Sharon Hom prefer to reconceptualize infanticide as "social femicide"? Explain the "spheres of violence conceptualization." Would the killing of female infants be considered a "crime"? Does criminalizing such behavior eradicate the problem? What more would need to be done? What is Hom's other vision?

For further reading, see Sharon Hom, *Law, Ideology and Patriarchy in the People's Republic of China: Feminist Observations of an Ethnic Spectator,* 4 Int'l Rev. Comp. Pub. Pol'y 173 (1992); Sharon Hom & Robin Malloy, *China's Market Economy: A Semiosis of Cross Boundary Discourse between Law and Economics and Feminist Jurisprudence,* 45 Syracuse L. Rev. 101 (1995); Antoinette Lopez, *Two Legal Constructs of Motherhood: Protective Legislation in Mexico and the United States,* 1 S. Cal. Rev. L. & Women's Stud. 239 (1991); Jenny Rivera, *Puerto Rico's Domestic Violence Prevention and Intervention Law and the United States Violence against Women Act of 1994: The Limitations of Legislative Responses,* Colum. J. Gender & L. (1995); Celina Romany, *Women as Aliens: A Feminist Critique of the Public/Private Distinction in International Human Rights Law,* 6 Harv. Hum. Rts. J. 87 (1993); J. Clay Smith, *United States Foreign Policy and Goler Teal Butcher,* 37 How. L.J. (1994); Adrien Wing, *Custom, Religion, and Rights: The Future Legal Status of Palestinian Women,* 35 Harv. Int'l L.J. 149 (1994); Adrien Wing & Shobhana Kasturi, *The Palestinian Women's Charter: Beyond the Basic Law,* Third World Legal Stud. (1995); Adrien Wing & Sylke Merchan, *Rape, Ethnicity, and Culture: Spirit Injury from Bosnia to Black America,* 25 Colum. J. Hum. Rts. 1 (1993); Margaret Woo, *Biology and Equality: Challenge for Feminism in the Liberal and Socialist State,* 42 Emory L.J. 143 (1993); Women's Rights, Human Rights: International Feminist Perspectives (Julie Stone Peters & Andrea Wolper eds., 1995).

Bibliography

There were many fine articles that could not be included in this volume that could be generally categorized as Critical Race Feminism. Additionally, there are many publications that deal with race and/or gender discrimination. A selection of these articles is listed here. There is one bibliography, entitled Women of Color in Legal Academia: A Biographic and Bibliographic Guide, 16 Harv. Women's L.J. 1 (1993).

Allard, Sharon. *Rethinking Battered Woman Syndrome: A Black Feminist Perspective,* 1 UCLA Women's L.J. 191 (1991).

Allen, Anita. Uneasy Access: Privacy for Women in a Free Society (1988), ch. 3 *reprinted in* Revisioning the Political: Feminist Reconstructions of Traditional Concepts in Western Political Theory (N. Hirschman ed., 1994), *and* ch. 4 *reprinted in* Nagging Questions (D. Bushnell ed., 1995).

———. *Affirmative Action, in* Encyclopedia of African American History and Culture (Mac-Millan 1995).

———. *Comment on Angela Davis' Surrogates and Outcast Mothers: Racism and Reproductive Ethics, in* "It Just Ain't Fair": The Ethics of Health Care for African Americans (Annette Dula & Sara Goering eds., 1994).

———. *Constitutional Privacy, in* Blackwell's A Companion to Jurisprudence and Legal Philosophy (D. O. Patterson ed., 1996).

———. *Legal Aspects of Abortion, in* Encyclopedia of Bioethics (2d ed. 1994).

———. *Legal Rights for Poor Blacks, in* The Underclass Question (W. Lawson ed., 1992).

———. *Moral Multiculturalism, Childbearing, and AIDS, in* HIV, AIDS, and Childbearing: Public Policy, Private Lives (R. Faden & N. Kass eds., 1994).

———. *Privacy in Health Care, in* Encyclopedia of Bioethics (2d ed. 1994).

———. *Assessing the Proposed Equal Protection Fix for Abortion Law: Reflections on Citizenship, Gender and the Constitution,* 18 Harv. J.L. & Pub. Pol'y 419 (1995).

———. *Autonomy's Magic Wand: Abortion Law and Constitutional Interpretation,* 72 B.U. L. Rev. 633 (1992).

———. *The Black Surrogate Mother*, 8 Harv. BlackLetter J. 17 (1991).

———. *Discrimination, Jobs and Politics*, 6 J.L. & Com. 227 (1986).

———. *Do Children Have a Right to a Certain Identity?*, 15 Rechtstheorie 109 (1993), reprinted in Children's Rights Revisioned: Philosophical Readings (R. Ladd ed., 1994).

———. *Equality and Private Choice*, 13 Nova L. Rev. 625 (1989).

———. *On Being a Role Model*, 6 Berkeley Women's L.J. 46 (1990–91), *reprinted in* Black Women in the Academy: Defending Our Name, 1894–1994: Papers from the Conference (R. Kilson ed., 1995), *and in* Multiculturalism: A Critical Reader (D. T. Goldberg ed., 1994).

———. *Privacy, Surrogacy and the Baby M Case*, 76 Geo. L.J. 1759 (1988), *reprinted in* Feminist Legal Theory: Applications (Kelly D. Weisberg ed., 1993).

———. *Reading Afrocentric History*, 9 Law & Ineq. J. 407 (1991).

———. *Response to Elizabeth Bartholet's Where Do Black Children Belong*, 1 Reconstruction 46 (1992).

———. *Surrogacy, Slavery, and Ownership of Life*, 13 Harv. J.L. & Pub. Pol'y 139 (1990).

———. *Taking Liberties: Privacy, Private Choice and Social Contract Theory*, 56 U. Cin. L. Rev. 401 (1987).

———. *Tribe's Judicious Feminism*, 44 Stan. L. Rev. 179 (1991).

Allen, Anita, & Erin Mack. *How Privacy Got Its Gender*, 10 N. Ill. U. L. Rev. 441 (1991).

Allen, Anita, et al. Privacy: Cases and Materials (1992).

Armstrong, Margalynne J. *African Americans and Property Ownership: Creating Our Own Meanings, Redefining Our Relationships*, 1 Afr. Am. L. & Pol'y Rep. 79 (1994).

———. *Meditations on Being Good*, 6 Berkeley Women's L.J. 43 (1990–91).

———. *Protecting Privilege: Race, Residence and Rodney King*, 12 Law & Ineq. J. 351 (1994).

Ashe, Marie. *"Bad Mothers," "Good Lawyers," and "Legal Ethics,"* 81 Geo. L.J. 2533 (1993).

Atwell, Barbara. *A Lost Generation: The Battle for the Private Enforcement of the Adoption Assistance and Child Welfare Act of 1980*, 60 U. Cin. L. Rev. 593 (1992).

———. *Surrogacy and Adoption: A Case of Incompatibility*, 20 Colum. Hum. Rts. L. Rev. 1 (1988).

Austin, Regina. *Employer Abuse of Low Status Workers: The Possibility of Uncommon Relief from the Common Law, with Sharon Dietrich, in* The Politics of Law (David Kairys ed., rev. ed. 1990).

———. *Beyond Black Demons and White Devils: Antiblack Conspiracy Theorizing and the Black Public Sphere*, 22 Fla. St. L. Rev. 1021 (1995).

———. *Black, Brown, Poor and Poisoned: Minority Grassroots Environmentalism and the Quest for Eco-Justice*, 1 Kan. J.L. & Pub. Pol'y 69 (1991).

———. *"The Black Community," Its Lawbreakers, and a Politics of Identification*, 65 S. Cal. L. Rev. 1769 (1992).

———. *Black Women, Sisterhood, and the Difference/Deviance Divide*, 26 New Eng. L. Rev. 877 (1992).

———. *Commentary: Concerns of Our Own*, 24 Rutgers L.J. 731 (1993).

———. *An Honest Living: Street Vendors, Municipal Regulation, and the Black Public Sphere*, 103 Yale L.J. 2119 (1994).

———. *Left at the Post: One Take on Blacks and Postmodernism*, 26 Law & Soc'y Rev. 751 (1992).

———. *A Nation of Thieves: Securing Black People's Rights to Shop and to Sell in White America,* 1994 Utah L. Rev. 147.

———. *Resistance Tactics for Tokens,* 3 Harv. BlackLetter J. 52 (1986).

———. *Sapphire Bound!,* 1989 Wis. L. Rev. 539.

———. *"Write On, Brother" and the Revolution Next Time: Justice Marshall's Challenge to Black Scholars,* 6 Harv. BlackLetter J. 79 (1989).

———. Comment, *The Problem of the Legitimacy of the Welfare State,* 130 U. Pa. L. Rev. 1510 (1982).

Azar, Sandra, & Corina Benjet. *A Cognitive Perspective on Ethnicity, Race and Termination of Parental Rights,* 18 Law & Hum. Behav. 249 (1994).

Banks, Taunya Lovell. *Discretionary Justice and the Black Offender, in* Blacks and Criminal Justice (Jimmy Bell & Charles E. Owens eds., 1977).

———. *Reproduction and Parenting, in* AIDS Law Today: A New Guide for the Public (Scott Burris et al. eds., 1993).

———. *The Right to Medical Treatment, in* AIDS and the Law 175 (Harlon L. Dalton et al. eds., 1987).

———. *AIDS and the Right to Health Care,* 4 Issues L. & Med. 151 (1988).

———. *The Americans with Disabilities Act and the Reproductive Rights of HIV-Infected Women,* 3 Tex. J. Women & L. 57 (1994).

———. *Discretionary Decision-Making in the Criminal Justice System: Some Alternatives,* 5 Black L.J. 20 (1977).

———. *Gender Bias in the Classroom,* 38 J. Legal Educ. 137 (1988).

———. *Gender Bias in the Classroom,* 14 S. Ill. L.J. 527 (1990).

———. *Rethinking* Novotny *in Light of* United Brotherhood of Carpenters and Joiners v. Scott: *The Scope and Constitutionally Permissible Periphery of Section 1985(3),* 27 How. L.J. 1497 (1984).

———. *Toilets as Feminist Issue,* 6 Berkeley Women's L.J. 263 (1990–91).

———. *Two Stories: Reflections of One Black Woman Law Professor,* 6 Berkeley Women's L.J. 46 (1990–91).

———. *Women and AIDS: Racism, Sexism and Classism,* 17 N.Y.U. Rev. L. & Soc. Change 351 (1989).

Barnes, Robin. *Black Women Law Professors and Critical Self-Consciousness: A Tribute to Professor Denise Carty-Bennia,* 6 Berkeley Women's L.J. 57 (1990–91).

———. *Race Consciousness: The Thematic Content of Racial Distinctiveness in Critical Race Scholarship,* 103 Harv. L. Rev. 1864 (1990).

———. *Standing Guard for the P.C. Militia, or Fighting Hatred and Indifference: Some Thoughts on Expressive Hate-Conduct and Political Correctness,* 1992 U. Ill. L. Rev. 979.

Bell, Derrick A. And We Are Not Saved: The Elusive Quest for Racial Justice (1987).

———. Confronting Authority: Reflections of an Ardent Protestor (1994).

———. Faces at the Bottom of the Well: The Permanence of Racism (1992).

———. Race, Racism and American Law (3d ed. 1992).

Bisom-Rapp, Susan. *Contextualizing the Debate: How Feminist and Critical Race Scholarship Can Inform the Teaching of Employment Discrimination Law,* 44 J. Legal Educ. 366 (1994).

———. *Of Motives and Maleness: A Critical View of Mixed Motive Doctrine in Title VII Sex Discrimination Suits,* 1995 Utah L. Rev.

Brown, Kevin. *The Social Construction of a Rape Victim: Stories of African-American Males about the Rape of Desiree Washington,* 1992 U. Ill. L. Rev. 997.

Brown-Scott, Wendy. *The Communitarian State: Lawlessness or Law Reform for African Americans,* 107 Harv. L. Rev. 1209 (1994).

Bullock, Alice. *A Dean's Role in Supporting Recruitment of Minority Faculty,* 10 St. Louis U. Pub. L. Rev. 347 (1991).

Bumiller, Kristen. *Rape as a Legal Symbol: An Essay on Sexual Violence and Racism,* 42 U. Miami L. Rev. 75 (1987).

Burnham, Margaret A. *The Supreme Court Appointment Process and the Politics of Race and Sex, in* Race-ing Justice, En-gendering Power: Essays on Anita Hill, Clarence Thomas and the Construction of Social Reality 290 (Toni Morrison ed., 1992).

Caldwell, Paulette. *A Hair Piece: Perspectives on the Intersection of Race and Gender,* 1991 Duke L.J. 365.

———. *Reaffirming the Disproportionate Effects Standard of Liability in Title VII Litigation,* 46 U. Pitt. L. Rev. 555 (1985).

Calvo, Janet. *Spouse-Based Immigration Laws: The Legacy of Coverture,* 28 San Diego L. Rev. 593 (1991).

Chamallas, Martha. *Jean Jew's Case: Resisting Sexual Harassment in the Academy,* 6 Yale J.L. & Feminism 71 (1994).

Chandler, Christy. *Race, Gender, and the Peremptory Challenge: A Postmodern Feminist Approach,* 7 Yale J.L. & Feminism 173 (1995).

Chang, Robert. *Toward an Asian American Legal Scholarship: Critical Race Theory, Post-Structuralism, and Narrative Space,* 81 Cal. L. Rev. 1241 (1993).

Cho, Sumi. *Korean Americans vs. African Americans: Conflict and Construction, in* Reading Rodney King, Reading Urban Uprising 1996 (Robert Gooding-Williams ed., 1993), *reprinted in* Race, Class, and Gender: An Anthology 461 (Margaret L. Anderson & Patricia Hill Collins eds., 2d ed. 1994).

Chon, Margaret. *On the Need for Asian American Narratives in Law: Ethnic Specimens, Native Informants, Storytelling and Silences,* 3 UCLA Asian Pac. L.J. (1995).

Colker, Ruth. *Anti-Subordination Above All: Sex, Race and Equal Protection,* 61 N.Y.U. L. Rev. 1003 (1986).

———. *An Equal Protection Analysis of United States Reproductive Health Policy: Gender, Race, Age, and Class,* 1991 Duke L.J. 324.

Crane, Linda. *Colorizing the Law School Experience,* 1991 Wis. L. Rev. 1427.

Crenshaw, Kimberlé. *Beyond Racism and Misogyny: Black Feminism and 2 Live Crew, in* Words That Wound: Critical Race Theory, Assaultive Speech and the First Amendment 111 (Mari J. Matsuda et al., 1993).

———. *Whose Story Is It, Anyway? Feminist and Antiracist Appropriations of Anita Hill, in* Race-ing Justice, En-gendering Power: Essays on Anita Hill, Clarence Thomas and the Construction of Social Reality 402 (Toni Morrison ed., 1992).

———. *Demarginalizing the Intersection of Race and Sex: A Black Feminist Critique of Antidiscrimination Doctrine, Feminist Theory and Antiracist Politics,* 1989 U. Chi. Legal F. 139.

———. *Foreword: Toward a Race-Conscious Pedagogy in Legal Education,* 11 Nat'l Black L.J. 1 (1989).

———. *Mapping the Margins: Identity Politics, Intersectionality and Violence against Women of Color,* 43 Stan. L. Rev. 1241 (1991).

———. *Panel Presentation on Cultural Battery,* 25 U. Tol. L. Rev. 891 (1994).

———. *Race, Gender and Sexual Harassment,* 65 S. Cal. L. Rev. 1467 (1992).

———. *Race, Reform, and Retrenchment: Transformation and Legitimation in Antidiscrimination Law,* 101 Harv. L. Rev. 1331 (1988).

———. *Reel Time/Real Justice,* 70 Denv. U. L. Rev. 283 (1993)(with Gary Peller).

———. *Stranger Than Fiction,* 15 Cal. L. Rev. 63 (1995).

Crenshaw, Kimberlé, Neil Gotanda, Gary Peller, & Kendall Thomas, eds. Critical Race Theory: The Key Writings That Formed the Movement (1996).

Crooms, Lisa A. *Tryin' to Make It Real Compared to What? Black Women, Work and Welfare Reform, in* Women, Children and Poverty (Martha Fineman & Twila Perry eds., 1996).

———. *Don't Believe the Hype: Black Women, Patriarchy, and the New Welfarism, in* 38 How. L.J. 611 (1995).

Dark, Okainer. *Cosmic Consciousness: Teaching on the Frontiers,* 38 Loy. L. Rev. 101 (1992).

Davis, Adrienne. *Foreword—Symposium: Surrogacy Legislation in California,* 28 U.S.F. L. Rev. (1994).

Davis, Adrienne, & Stephanie Wildman. *The Legacy of Doubt: Treatment of Race and Sex in the Hill-Thomas Hearings,* 65 S. Cal. L. Rev. 1367 (1992).

Davis, Deirdre Elizabeth. *The Harm That Has No Name: Street Harassment, Embodiment, and African American Women,* 4 UCLA Women's L.J. 133 (1994).

Davis, Peggy. *Contextual Legal Criticism: A Demonstration Exploring Hierarchy and "Feminine" Style,* 66 N.Y.U. L. Rev. 1635 (1991).

———. *Neglected Stories and the Lawfulness of* Roe v. Wade, 20 Harv. C.R.-C.L. L. Rev. 299 (1993).

Delgado, Richard, ed. Critical Race Theory: The Cutting Edge (1995).

Duclos, Nitya. *Lessons of Difference: Feminist Theory on Cultural Diversity,* 38 Buff. L. Rev. 325 (1990).

Ellis, Judy Trent. *Sexual Harassment and Race: A Legal Analysis of Discrimination,* 8 J. Legis. 30 (1981).

Evans, Monica. *Stealing Away: Black Women, Outlaw Culture, and the Rhetoric of Rights,* 28 Harv. C.R.-C.L. L. Rev. 263 (1993).

Fineman, Martha L. *Images of Mothers in Poverty Discourses,* 1991 Duke L.J. 274.

Freedman, Estelle B. *The Manipulation of History at the Clarence Thomas Hearings,* 65 S. Cal. L. Rev. 1361 (1992).

Gilmore, Angela. *It Is Better to Speak,* 6 Berkeley Women's L.J. 74 (1990–91).

———. *They're Just Funny That Way: Lesbians, Gay Men and African-American Community as Viewed through the Privacy Prism,* 38 How. L.J. 231 (1994).

Gomez, Laura E. Misconceiving Mothers: Lawmakers, Prosecutors and the Politics of Prenatal Drug Exposure (1996).

Greene, Dwight. *Abusive Prosecutors: Gender, Race and Class Discretion and the Prosecution of Drug-Addicted Mothers,* 39 Buff. L. Rev. 737 (1991).

Greene, Linda S. *Civil Rights at the Millennium: A Response to Bell's Call for Racial Realism,* 24 Conn. L. Rev. 499 (1992).

———. *Equal Employment Opportunity Law Twenty Years after the Civil Rights Act of 1964,* 28 Suffolk U. L. Rev. 593 (1984).

———. *Feminism, Law and Social Change: Some Reflections on Unrealized Possibilities,* 87 Nw. U. L. Rev. 1260 (1993).

———. *Gender, Law and Social Change: Symposium,* 87 Nw. U. L. Rev. 1260 (1992).

———. *Multiculturalism as Metaphor*, 41 DePaul L. Rev. 1173 (1992).

———. *The NCAA Rules of the Games: Academic Integrity . . . ?*, 28 St. Louis U. L.J. 101 (1984).

———. *Race in the Twenty-First Century: Equality through Law?*, 64 Tul. L. Rev. 1515 (1990).

———. *Serving the Community: Aspiration and Abyss for the Law Professor of Color*, 10 St. Louis U. Pub. L. Rev. 297 (1991).

———. *A Short Commentary on the Chronicles*, 3 Harv. BlackLetter J. 60 (1986).

———. *Title VII Class Actions: Standing at Its Edge?*, 58 U. Det. J. Urb. L. 645 (1981).

———. *Tokens, Role Models and Pedagogical Politics: Lamentations of an African-American Female Law Professor*, 6 Berkeley Women's L.J. 81 (1991).

Grider, Katrina. *Hair Salons and Racial Stereotypes: The Impermissible Use of Racially Discriminatory Pricing Schemes*, 12 Harv. Women's L.J. 1989 (1983).

Grillo, Trina. *Sexism, Racism, and the Analogy Problem in Feminist Thought, in* Racism in the Lives of Women (Jeanne Adleman & Gloria M. Enguidanos-Clark eds., 1995).

———. *Anti-Essentialism and Intersectionality: Tools to Dismantle the Master's House*, 10 Berkeley Women's L.J. 11 (1995).

———. *The Mediation Alternative: Process Dangers for Women*, 100 Yale L.J. 1545 (1991).

Grillo, Trina, & Stephanie Wildman. *Obscuring the Importance of Race: The Implication of Making Comparisons between Racism and Sexism (or Other Isms)*, 1991 Duke L.J. 397.

Guerra, Sandra. *Voting Rights and the Constitution: The Disenfranchisement of the Non-English Speaking Citizen*, 97 Yale L.J. 1419 (1988).

Guinier, Lani. Tyranny of the Majority: Fundamental Fairness In Representative Democracy (1994).

———. *Becoming Gentlemen: Women's Experiences at One Ivy League Law School*, 143 U. Pa. L. Rev. 1 (1994).

———. *(E)racing Democracy: The Voting Rights Cases*, 108 Harv. L. Rev. 109 (1994).

———. *Groups, Representations, and Race-Conscious Districting: A Case of the Emperor's Clothes*, 71 Tex. L. Rev. 1589 (1993).

———. *Keeping the Faith: Black Voters in the Post-Reagan Era*, 24 Harv. C.R.-C.L. L. Rev. 393 (1989).

———. *Keynote Address, Violence, Intimidation and Harm: The Attitudes That Perpetuate Abuse of Women*, 25 U. Tol. L. Rev. 875 (1994).

———. *No Two Seats: The Elusive Quest for Political Equality*, 77 Va. L. Rev. 1413 (1991).

———. *Of Gentlemen and Role Models*, 6 Berkeley Women's L.J. 93 (1990–91).

———. *The Representation of Minority Interests: The Question of Single-Member Districts*, 14 Cardozo L. Rev. 1135 (1993).

Gunning, Isabelle R. *Arrogant Perception, World Traveling and Multicultural Feminism: The Case of Female Genital Surgeries*, 23 Colum. Hum. Rts. L. Rev. 189 (1991–92).

———. *Intersection of Race, Gender and Sexual Orientation: Stories from the Margin*, S. Cal. Women's L. Rev. (1995).

———. *A Story from Home: On Being a Black Lesbian Mother*, USC Rev. L. & Women's Studies (1996).

Harris, Angela. *The Jurisprudence of Reconstruction*, 82 Cal. L. Rev. 741 (1994).

———. *The Jurisprudence of Victimhood*, 1991 Sup. Ct. Rev. 77.

———. *Race and Essentialism in Feminist Legal Theory*, 42 Stan. L. Rev. 581 (1990).

———. *Women of Color in Legal Education: Representing La Mestiza*, 6 Berkeley Women's L.J. 107 (1990–91).

Harris, Cheryl. *Law Professors of Color and the Academy: Of Poets and Kings*, 68 Chi.-Kent L. Rev. 331 (1992).

———. *Whiteness as Property*, 106 Harv. L. Rev. 1707 (1993).

Herbert, Jacinth. *"Otherness" and the Black Woman*, 3 Can. J. Women & L. 269 (1989).

Hernandez Truyol, Berta Esperanza. *Building Bridges—Latinas and Latinos at the Crossroads: Realities, Rhetoric, and Replacement*, 25 Colum. Hum. Rts. L. Rev. 369 (1994).

———. *Women's Rights as Human Rights—Rules, Realities and the Role of Culture*, 21 Brooklyn J. Int'l L. 605 (1996).

Hill, Anita. *Sexual Harassment: The Nature of the Beast*, 65 S. Cal. L. Rev. 1445 (1992).

———. *A Tribute to Thurgood Marshall: A Man Who Broke with Tradition on Issues of Race and Gender*, 47 Okla. L. Rev. 127 (1994).

Hill, Anita, & Emma Coleman Jordan, eds. Race, Gender and Power in America: The Legacy of the Hill-Thomas Hearings (1995).

Hom, Sharon K. *Female Infanticide in China: The Human Rights Specter and Thoughts toward (An)other Vision*, 23 Colum. Hum. Rts. L. Rev. 249 (1992).

———. *Four A.M. Thoughts on Teaching and Learning Contracts: An Open Letter to Pat Williams*, 2 Colum. J. Gender & L. 145 (1992).

———. *Law, Ideology and Patriarchy in the People's Republic of China: Feminist Observations of an Ethnic Spectator*, 4 Int'l Rev. Comp. Pub. Pol'y 173 (1992).

Hom, Sharon K., and Robin Paul Malloy. *China's Market Economy: A Semiosis of Cross Boundary Discourse between Law and Economics and Feminist Jurisprudence*, 45 Syracuse L. Rev. 101 (1995).

Horsburgh, Beverly. *Jewish Women, Black Women: Guarding against the Oppression of Surrogacy*, 8 Berkeley Women's L.J. 29 (1993).

Hylton, Maria. *Parental Leaves and Poor Women: Paying the Price for Time Off*, 52 U. Pitt. L. Rev. 475 (1991).

Iglesias, Elizabeth. *Structures of Subordination: Women of Color at the Intersection of Title VII and the NLRA. Not!* 28 Harv. C.R.-C.L. L. Rev. 395 (1993).

Ikemoto, Lisa. *Race under Construction: The Master Narrative of White Supremacy in the Media Representation of African American/Korean American Conflict, in* Feminism, Media and Law (Martha L. Fineman & M. McCluskey eds., 1996).

———. *The Code of Perfect Pregnancy: At the Intersection of the Ideology of Motherhood, the Practice of Defaulting to Science, and the Interventionist Mindset of Law*, 53 Ohio St. L.J. 1205 (1992).

———. *Destabilizing Thoughts on Surrogacy Legislation*, 28 U.S.F. L. Rev. 633 (1994).

———. *Furthering the Inquiry: Race, Class, and Culture in the Forced Medical Treatment of Pregnant Women*, 59 Tenn. L. Rev. 487 (1992).

———. *Providing Protection for Collaborative, Noncoital Reproduction: Surrogate Motherhood and Other New Procreative Technologies, and the Right of Intimate Association*, 40 Rutgers L. Rev. 1273 (1988).

———. *Traces of the Master Narrative in the Story of African American-Korean American Conflict: How We Constructed "Los Angeles,"* 66 S. Cal. L. Rev. 1581 (1993).

Inness, Julie. *Going to the Bottom*, 9 Berkeley Women's L.J. 162 (1994).

Johnson, Alex M. *The New Voice of Color*, 100 Yale L.J. 2007 (1991).

Johnson, Paula. *At the Intersection of Injustice: Experiences of African American Women in Crime and Sentencing,* 4 Am. U. J. Gender & L. 1 (1995).

Jordan, Emma Coleman. *The Future of the Fifteenth Amendment,* 28 How. L.J. 3 (1985).

———. *The Gender Paradox in Civil Rights Theory,* Berkeley Women's L. J. (1995).

———. *Images of Black Women in the Legal Academy: An Introduction,* 6 Berkeley Women's L.J. 1 (1991).

———. *Nepenthe,* 6 Berkeley Women's L.J. 113 (1991).

———. *Race, Gender and Social Class in the Thomas Sexual Harassment Hearings: The Hidden Fault Lines in Political Discourse,* 15 Harv. Women's L.J. 1 (1992).

———. *Race in The Market Domain: The Call of Economic Justice,* 29 Ind. L. Rev. (1995).

———. *Race in the Market Place: The Role of Government in Adjusting for Persistent Economic Inequality,* 28 Suffolk U. L. Rev. (1995).

———. *Taking Voting Rights Seriously: Rediscovering the Fifteenth Amendment,* 64 Neb. L. Rev. 389 (1985).

Kennedy, Duncan. *A Cultural Pluralist Case for Affirmative Action in Legal Academia,* 1990 Duke L.J. 705.

King, Pat. *Should Mom Be Constrained in the Best Interests of the Fetus,* 13 Nova L. Rev. 393 (1989).

Kline, Marlee. *Race, Racism, and Feminist Legal Theory,* 12 Harv. Women's L.J. 115 (1989).

Lewis, Hope. *Between* Irua *and "Female Genital Mutilation": Feminist Human Rights Discourse and the Cultural Divide,* 8 Harv. Hum. Rts. J. (1995).

Lopez, Antoinette. *Two Legal Constructs of Motherhood: Protective Legislation in Mexico and the United States,* 1 S. Cal. Rev. L. & Women's Stud. 239 (1991).

Macklin, Audrey. *Foreign Domestic Worker: Surrogate Housewife or Mail Order Servant?,* 37 McGill L.J. 681 (1992).

Martinez, Theresa. *Embracing the Outlaws: Deviance at the Intersection of Race, Class, and Gender,* 1994 Utah L. Rev. 193.

Matsuda, Mari. *Looking to the Bottom: Critical Legal Studies and Reparations,* 22 Harv. C.R.-C.L. L. Rev. 323 (1987).

———. *The Voices of America: Accent, Antidiscrimination Law, and a Jurisprudence for the Last Reconstruction,* 100 Yale L.J. 1329 (1991).

———. *When the First Quail Calls: Multiple Consciousness as Jurisprudential Method,* 14 Women's Rts. L. Rep. 297 (1992).

Montoya, Margaret. *Máscaras, Trenzas y Greñas: Un/masking the Self While Un/braiding Latina Stories and Legal Discourse,* 15 Chicano-Latino L. Rev. 1 (1994).

Moran, Beverly. *Quantum Leap: A Black Woman Uses Legal Education to Obtain Her Honorary White Pass,* 6 Berkeley Women's L.J. 118 (1990–91).

Moran, Rachel. *Introduction, in* Perspectives on Diversity (1996).

———. *Getting a Foot in the Door: Hispanics and the Push for Equal Educational Opportunity in Denver,* 2 Kan. J.L. & Pub. Pol'y 35 (1992).

———. *Knocking on the Schoolhouse Door and Wondering What's Inside,* 4 Berkeley Women's L.J. 3259 (1989).

Morgan, Denise. *Role Models: Who Needs Them Anyway,* 6 Berkeley Women's L.J. 122 (1990–91).

Neal, Odeana Rae. *The Making of a Law Teacher,* 6 Berkeley Women's L.J. 128 (1990–91).

Nightingale, Margo. *Judicial Attitudes and Differential Treatment: Native Women in Sexual Assault Cases,* 23 Ottawa L. Rev. 71 (1991).

Omolade, Barbara. *Black Women, Black Men, and Tawana Brawley: The Shared Condition,* 12 Harv. Women's L.J. 11 (1989).

———. *The Unbroken Circle: A Historical and Contemporary Study of Black Single Mothers and Their Families,* 3 Wis. Women's L.J. 239 (1981).

Ontiveros, Maria Linda. *The Myths of Market Forces, Mothers and Private Employment: The Parental Leave Veto,* 1 Cornell J.L. & Pub. Pol'y 25 (1992).

———. *Rosa Lopez, Christopher Darden, and Me,* 6 Hastings Women's L.J. 135 (1995).

———. *Three Perspectives on Workplace Harassment of Women of Color,* 23 Golden Gate U. L. Rev. 817 (1993).

———. *To Help Those Most in Need: Undocumented Workers' Rights and Remedies under Title VII,* 20 N.Y.U. Rev. L. & Soc. Change 607 (1993).

Overton, Spencer. *The Threat Diversity Poses to African Americans: A Black Nationalist Critique of Outsider Ideology,* 37 How. L.J. 465 (1994).

Pacheco, Yvonne Cherena. *Latino Surnames: Formal and Informal Forces in the U.S. Affecting the Retention and Use of the Maternal Surname,* 18 T. Marshall L. Rev. 1 (1992).

Perry, Twila. *Alimony: Race, Privilege and Dependency in the Search for Theory,* 82 Geo. L.J. 2481 (1994).

———. *Race and Child Placement: The Best Interests Test and the Cost of Discretion,* 29 J. Fam. L. 51 (1990).

Pinder, Wilma. *When Will Black Women Lawyers Slay the Two Headed Dragon: Racism and Gender Bias?,* 20 Pepp. L. Rev. 1053 (1993).

Porras, Ileana. *On Terrorism: Reflections on Violence and the Outlaw,* 1994 Utah L. Rev. 119.

Post, Deborah Waire. *Critical Thoughts about Race, Exclusion, Oppression and Tenure,* 15 Pace L. Rev. 69 (1994).

———. *Race, Riots and the Rule of Law,* 70 Denv. U. L. Rev. 237 (1993).

———. *Reflections on Identity, Diversity, and Morality,* 6 Berkeley Women's L.J. 136 (1990–91).

Randall, Vernellia. *Racist Health Care: Reforming an Unjust Health Care System to Meet the Need of African Americans,* 3 Health Matrix 127 (1993).

Reuben-Cook, Wilhelmina M. *Communicating the Unspeakable and Seeing the Invisible,* 6 Berkeley Women's L.J. 167 (1990–91).

Rivera, Jenny. *Domestic Violence against Latinas by Latino Males: An Analysis of Race, National Origin, and Gender Differentials,* 14 B.C. Third World L.J. 231 (1994).

———. *Puerto Rico's Domestic Violence Prevention and Intervention Law and the United States Violence against Women Act of 1994: The Limitations of Legislative Responses,* 5 Colum. J. Gender & L. 78 (1995).

Roberts, Dorothy E. *Racism and Patriarchy in the Meaning of Motherhood, in* Feminist Legal Theory (Frances E. Olsen ed., 1994).

———. *Racism and Patriarchy in the Meaning of Motherhood, in* Mothers in Law: Feminist Theory and the Legal Regulation of Motherhood 224 (Martha L. Fineman & Isabel Karpin eds., 1995).

———. *Reconstructing the Patient: Starting with Women of Color, in* Feminism and Bioethics: Beyond Reproduction (Susan M. Wolf ed., 1995).

———. *Crime, Race and Reproduction,* 67 Tul. L. Rev. 1945 (1993).

———. *Deviance, Resistance, and Love,* 1994 Utah L. Rev. 179.

———. *Foreword: The Meaning of Gender Equality in Criminal Law, Symposium on Women and Criminal Law,* 85 J. Crim. L. & Criminology 1 (1994).

———. *The Future of Reproductive Choice for Poor Women and Women of Color,* 12 Women's Rts. L. Rep. 59 (1990), *reprinted in* 14 Women's Rts. L. Rep. 305 (20th anniversary ed. 1992).

———. *The Genetic Tie,* 62 U. Chi. L. Rev. 209 (1995).

———. *Irrationality and Sacrifice in the Welfare Reform Consensus,* 81 Va. L. Rev. 2607 (1995).

———. *Motherhood and Crime,* 79 Iowa L. Rev. 95 (1993).

———. *Motherhood and Crime,* 42 Soc. Text 99 (1994).

———. *The Only Good Poor Woman: Unconstitutional Conditions and Welfare,* 72 Denv. U. L. Rev. 931 (1995).

———. *Punishing Drug Addicts Who Have Babies: Women of Color, Equality, and the Right of Privacy,* 104 Harv. L. Rev. 1419 (1991), *reprinted in* Fifty Years War: A Half Century of Abortion Politics 1950 (R. Solinger ed., 1996).

———. *Race, Gender, and the Value of Mothers' Work,* 2 Soc. Pol'y (1995).

———. *Racism and Patriarchy in the Meaning of Motherhood,* 1 Am. U. J. Gender & L. 1 (1993).

———. *Rape, Violence and Women's Autonomy, American Bar Association Symposium, Is the Law Male?,* 69 Chi.-Kent L. Rev. 359 (1993).

———. *Rust v. Sullivan and the Control of Knowledge,* 61 Geo. Wash. L. Rev. 587 (1993).

———. *Sandra Day O'Connor, Conservative Discourse, and Reproductive Freedom,* 13 Women's Rts. L. Rep. 95 (1991).

———. *The Value of Black Mothers' Work,* 26 Conn. L. Rev. 871 (1994).

Roberts, Dorothy E., et al. A First Amendment Anthology (1994).

Romany, Celina. *Killing the Angel in the House: Digging for the Political Vortex of Male Violence against Women, in* The Public Nature of Private Violence (Martha L. Fineman ed., 1994).

———. *State Responsibility Goes "Private": A Feminist Critique of the Public/Private Distinction in Women's International Human Rights Law, in* Human Rights of Women (R. Cook ed., 1994).

———. *On Surrounding Privilege: Diversity in a Feminist Redefinition of Human Rights Law (from Vienna to Beijing), in* Basic Needs to Basic Rights (1994).

———. *Ain't I a Feminist?,* 4 Yale J.L. & Feminism 23 (1991).

———. *Hacia una Critica Feminista del Derecho Internacional en Materia de Derechos Humanos,* FEM (Mexico, 1993).

———. *Women as Aliens: A Feminist Critique of the Public/Private Distinction in International Human Rights Law,* 6 Harv. Hum. Rts. J. 87 (1993).

Russell, Jennifer. *On Being a Gorilla in Your Midst, or The Life of One Blackwoman in the Legal Academy,* 28 Harv. C.R.-C.L. L. Rev. 259 (1993).

Scales-Trent, Judy. Notes of a White Black Woman: Race, Color, Community (1995).

———. *Compound Discrimination: The Intersection of Race and Gender, in* Employment Discrimination: Law and Litigation (Merrick T. Rossein ed., 1994).

———. *The Law as an Instrument of Oppression and the Culture of Resistance, in* 1 Black Women in America: An Historical Encyclopedia 701 (D.C. Hine ed., 1993).

———. *Black Women and the Constitution: Finding Our Place, Asserting Our Rights,* 24 Harv. C.R.-C.L. L. Rev. 9 (1989).

———. *Commonalities: On Being Black and White, Different and the Same,* 2 Yale J.L. & Feminism 290 (1990).

———. *Sameness and Difference in the Law School Classroom: Working at the Crossroads*, 4 Yale J.L. & Feminism 421 (1992).

———. *Using Literature in Law School: The Importance of Reading and Telling Stories*, 7 Berkeley Women's L.J. 90 (1992).

———. *Women in the Lawyering Process: The Complications of Categories*, 35 N.Y.U. L. Rev. 337 (1990).

———. *Women of Color and Health: Issues of Gender, Community and Power*, 43 Stan. L. Rev. 1357 (1991).

Scarborough, Cathy. *Conceptualizing Black Women's Employment Experience*, 98 Yale L.J. 1457 (1989).

Shoben, Elaine. *Compound Discrimination: The Intersection of Race and Sex in Employment Discrimination*, 55 N.Y.U. L. Rev. 793 (1980).

Smith, J. Clay, Jr. *United States Foreign Policy and Goler Teal Butcher*, 37 How. L.J. 139 (1994).

Smith, Pam. *We Are Not Sisters: African-American Women and the Freedom to Associate and Disassociate*, 66 Tul. L. Rev. 1467 (1992).

Smith, Peggy. *Separate Identities: Black Women, Work, and Title VII*, 14 Harv. Women's L.J. 21 (1991).

Squires, Madelyn. *Discovering Our Connections: Reflections on Race, Gender and the Other Tales of Difference*, 23 Golden Gate U. L. Rev. 795 (1993).

———. *Tribute: A Tribute to Goler Butcher and Her Legacy to Howard University Law Students*, 37 How. L.J. 231 (1994).

Tarpley, Joan R. *Grounded Feminist Theory: And I Sprang Full Grown from My Father's Head or Was It Really from My Mother's*, 24 U. Tol. L. Rev. 583 (1993).

Taylor, Kim. *Invisible Woman: Reflections on the Clarence Thomas Confirmation Hearing*, 45 Stan. L. Rev. 443 (1993).

Verdun, Vincene. *If the Shoe Fits Wear It: An Analysis of Reparations to African Americans*, 67 Tul. L. Rev. 597 (1993).

Weston, Crystal H. *Orenthal James Simpson*, 6 Hastings L.J. 223 (1995).

Wildman, Stephanie. *Privilege Revealed: How Invisible Preference Undermines America* (1996).

———. *Integration in the 1980s: The Dream of Diversity and the Cycle of Exclusion*, 64 Tul. L. Rev. 1625 (1990).

Williams, Joan. *Dissolving the Sameness/Difference Debate: A Post Modern Path beyond Essentialism in Feminist and Critical Race Theory*, 1991 Duke L.J. 296.

Williams, Patricia J. The Alchemy of Race and Rights (1991).

———. The Rooster's Egg: On the Persistence of Prejudice (1995).

———. *In Search of Pharaoh's Daughter, in* Women and the Bible (1994).

———. *A Rare Case of Muleheadedness and Men, or How to Try an Unruly Black Witch, with Excerpts from the Heretical Testimony of Four Women, Known to Be Hysterics, Speaking in Their Own Voices, as Translated for This Publication by Brothers Hatch, Simpson, DiConcini and Specter, in* Race-ing Justice, En-gendering Power 159 (Toni Morrison ed., 1992).

———. *Re-Ordering Western Civ: The Socioeconomic Status of Women of Color, in* Theorizing Black Feminisms: The Visionary Pragmatism of Black Women (1993).

———. *Alchemical Notes: Reconstructing Ideals from Deconstructed Rights*, 22 Harv. C.R.-C.L. L. Rev. 401 (1987).

———. *Fetal Fictions: An Exploration of Property Archetypes in Racial and Gendered Contexts,* 42 U. Fla. L. Rev. 81 (1990).

———. *The Obliging Shell: An Informal Essay on Formal Equal Opportunity,* 87 Mich. L. Rev. 2128 (1989).

———. *On Being the Object of Property,* 14 Signs 5 (1988).

———. *Spare Parts, Family Values, Old Children, Cheap,* 28 New Eng. L. Rev. 913 (1994).

———. *Spirit-Murdering the Messenger: The Discourse of Fingerpointing as the Law's Response to Racism,* 42 U. Miami L. Rev. 127 (1987).

Williams, Phoebe. *A Black Woman's Voice: The Story of Mabel Raimey,* 74 Marq. L. Rev. 375 (1991).

Wing, Adrien K. *Brief Reflections toward a Multiplicative Theory and Praxis of Being,* 6 Berkeley Women's L.J. 181 (1990–91).

———. *Communitarianism v. Individualism: Constitutionalism in Namibia and South Africa,* 11 Wis. Int'l L.J. 295 (1993).

———. *Custom, Religion and Rights: The Future Legal Status of Palestinian Women,* 35 Harv. Int'l L.J. 149 (1994).

———. *Democracy, Constitutionalism and the Future State of Palestine: With a Case Study of Women's Rights* (PASSIA Institute, Jerusalem 1994).

Wing, Adrien K., & Eunice de Carvalho. *Black South African Women: Toward Equal Rights,* 8 Harv. Hum. Rts. J. 57 (1995).

Wing, Adrien, & Shobhana Kasturi. *The Palestinian Women's Charter: Beyond the Basic Law,* Third World Legal Stud. (1995).

Wing, Adrien, & W. H. Knight. *Weep Not Little Ones: An Essay to Our Children about Affirmative Action, in* African Americans and the Living Constitution 208 (J. Hope Franklin & Genna Rae McNeil eds., 1995).

Wing, Adrien, & Sylke Merchan. *Rape, Ethnicity and Culture, in* Critical Race Theory Reader: The Cutting Edge (Richard Delgado ed., 1995).

———. *Rape, Ethnicity and Culture: Spirit Injury from Bosnia to Black America,* 25 Colum. J. Hum. Rts. 1 (1993).

Winston, Judith. *An Antidiscrimination Legal Construct That Disadvantages Working Women of Color,* 24 Clearinghouse Rev. 403 (1991).

———. *Mirror, Mirror on the Wall: Title VII, Section 1981, and the Intersection of Race and Gender in the Civil Rights Act of 1990,* 79 Cal. L. Rev. 775 (1991).

Woo, Margaret. *Biology and Equality: Challenge for Feminism in the Liberal and Socialist State,* 42 Emory L.J. 143 (1993).

Wriggins, Jennifer. *Rape, Racism and the Law,* 6 Harv. Women's L.J. 103 (1983).

Yarborough, Marilyn. *Disparate Impact, Disparate Treatment, and the Displaced Homemaker,* 49 Law & Contemp. Probs. 107 (1986).

Zack, Naomi. Race and Mixed Race (1993).

Contributors

ANITA L. ALLEN, a professor at Georgetown Law School, teaches courses in Jurisprudence, Privacy in American Law, and Torts. She earned a B.A. and M.A. from New College, a Ph.D. from the University of Michigan, and a J.D. from Harvard Law School. She was an associate attorney for Cravath, Swaine and Moore in New York before beginning her law teaching career at the University of Pittsburgh Law School. She has also been a visiting professor at Harvard Law School. Allen's publications, which focus on privacy issues and gender, include two books, *Uneasy Access: Privacy for Women in a Free Society,* and *Privacy: Cases and Materials.* She sits on the board of directors of Planned Parenthood of Metropolitan Washington and serves on the Committee on Legal and Ethical Issues Relating to Women in Clinical Studies for the National Academy of Sciences. She has appeared on *ABC Nightline, Face the Nation,* and a number of other television and radio programs.

MARGALYNNE J. ARMSTRONG, an associate professor at Santa Clara Law School, teaches courses in Comparative Law, Property, Race and the Law, and Remedies. She earned a B.A. from Earlham College and a J.D. from the Boalt Hall School of Law at the University of California at Berkeley, where she was associate editor for the *Ecology Law Quarterly.* Upon graduation, she served as a staff attorney for the Legal Aid Society of Alameda County in Hayward, California. She has been a visiting professor at the University of California at Berkeley.

NATHALIE A. AUGUSTIN is a law clerk to the Honorable Sterling Johnson, Jr., U.S. district judge for the Eastern District of New York. She received her B.A. from Columbia College and her law degree from Harvard, where she was editor in chief of the *Harvard BlackLetter Law Journal.*

REGINA AUSTIN, a professor of law at the University of Pennsylvania Law School, teaches courses in Insurance, Products Liability, and Torts. She received her B.A. from the University of Rochester and her J.D. from the University of Pennsylvania, where she graduated *cum laude* and was a member of the Order of the Coif. Upon graduating she served as a law clerk for Judge Edmund B. Spaeth on the Superior Court of Pennsylvania. She then worked in private practice until she began teaching at the University of Pennsylvania in 1977. She has served as a visiting professor at Harvard and Stanford Law Schools.

TAUNYA LOVELL BANKS, the Jacob A. France Professor of Equality Jurisprudence at the University of Maryland School of Law, teaches courses in Civil Rights, Constitutional Law, Health Care Law, and Torts. She earned a B.A. from Syracuse and a J.D. from Howard, where she served on the *Howard Law Review* editorial board. She has previously taught at Texas Southern University Law School and the University of Tulsa Law School. She was a visiting professor at Washburn University School of Law and the University of Hawaii Law School. She currently serves on the executive committee of the American Association of Law Schools.

SHERRI L. BURR, a professor of law at the University of New Mexico School of Law, teaches courses in Intellectual Property, Art Law, International Law, Property, and Wills and Trusts. She received her A.B. degree from Mount Holyoke, her M.P.A from Princeton, and her J.D. degree from Yale, where she was an editor of the *Yale Journal of International Law* and the *Yale Journal of World Public Order*. After graduation, Burr clerked for the Honorable Thomas Tang, U.S. circuit judge for the Ninth Circuit Court of Appeals. She is currently a member of the executive council of the International Law Association, American Branch.

PAULETTE M. CALDWELL, a professor at New York University Law School, teaches courses in Civil Rights, Nonprofit Corporations, Property and Real Estate Transactions. She earned a B.A. and J.D. *cum laude* from Howard, where she was managing editor of the *Howard Law Journal*. She entered private practice as an attorney at Patterson, Belknap, Webb and Tyler in New York City and served as assistant counsel at the Ford Foundation before returning to private practice. She began teaching in 1979 at New York University.

JANET M. CALVO is an associate professor at City University of New York Law School at Queens. She teaches courses in Civil Clinic, Civil Procedure, Immigration and Nationality Law, and Legal Approaches to Social Problems. She earned a B.A from William Smith College and a J.D. from New York University. After graduating, she served as an attorney for the Legal Aid Society in New York. She taught at New York University prior to her position at CUNY. Some of Calvo's civic activities include serving on the National Steering Committee on Battered Immigrant Women, as well as the board of directors for the Center for Social Welfare Policy and Law.

DEVON W. CARBADO is a visiting assistant professor at the University of Iowa College of Law. He received his B.A. from the University of California at Los Angeles and his J.D. *cum laude* from Harvard, where he was editor in chief of the *Harvard BlackLetter Law Journal*. He also worked at the Los Angeles law firm of Latham and Watkins.

SUMI K. CHO is an assistant professor at DePaul Law School. She received a B.A. and a Ph.D. from the University of California at Berkeley, and a J.D. from the Boalt School of Law at the University of California at Berkeley. She was an assistant professor at the University of Oregon in political science and ethnic studies and a visiting assistant professor at the University of Iowa Law School.

KATHLEEN NEAL CLEAVER, on leave as an assistant professor at Emory Law School, is a visiting scholar at Harvard University's W. E. B. DuBois Institute. She taught classes in Torts, Professional Responsibility, and Legal History at Emory. Professor Cleaver received her B.A. and J.D. from Yale. Upon graduation, she entered private practice with Cravath, Swaine and Moore in New York City. In 1991 Cleaver clerked for Judge A. Leon Higginbotham of the U.S. Third Circuit Court of Appeals. Cleaver's forthcoming memoir is entitled, "Memories of Love and War." She has also lectured extensively at colleges as well as on radio and television programs on issues concerning the black power movement.

ADRIENNE D. DAVIS is an associate professor at American University Washington College of Law, where she teaches courses in Property, Contracts, Critical Race Theory, Slavery, and the Human Body as a Legal Metaphor. She received her B.A. and J.D. from Yale, where she served as executive committee editor for the *Yale Law Journal*. She has also taught at the University of San Francisco School of Law. She clerked for Judge A. Leon Higginbotham of the U.S. Third Circuit Court of Appeals.

DEIRDRE E. DAVIS earned her B.A. from Wesleyan University and a J.D. from the Boalt Hall School of Law at the University of California at Berkeley. She served as editor in chief for the *Berkeley Women's Law Journal*. Upon graduating, she entered private practice as a litigation associate with LeBoeuf, Lamb, Greene and MacRae in New York.

EUNICE P. DE CARVALHO, a native of Angola, received her B.A. from Northwestern University and her J.D. from the University of Iowa. After graduation, she entered and is currently in private practice in Minneapolis, with the Faegre and Benson law firm.

ANGELA D. GILMORE, an associate professor at Nova Southeastern University Law Center, teaches courses in Property, Professional Responsibility, and Antidiscrimination Law. She earned a B.A. from Houghton College and a J.D. *cum laude* from the University of Pittsburgh School of Law, where she was senior editor for the *Journal of Law and Commerce*. After graduating, she entered private practice as a corporate associate with Weinburg and Green in Baltimore. She was also a visiting assistant professor at the University of Iowa College of Law.

LINDA S. GREENE is a professor of law who teaches Constitutional Law at the University of Wisconsin Law School. She received an A.B. from California State University and is a graduate of the Boalt Hall School of Law at the University of California at Berkeley. She began her career as an attorney with the NAACP Legal Defense and Education Fund, and she began her teaching career at Temple University. She was a tenured associate professor at the University of Oregon Law School and a visiting professor at Harvard University Law School and Georgetown University Law Center. She taught part-time at Georgetown while serving as counsel to the U.S. Senate Judiciary Committee from 1986 to 1989, and thereafter returned to full-time teaching at Wisconsin. Greene was the chair of the 1990 Wisconsin Critical Race Theory Conference, the chair of the AALS Section on Minority Groups, and the founder and president of the Midwestern People of Color Legal Scholarship Conference, which is the model for several regional conferences that focus on the enhancement of scholarship and teaching. She is the president of the Society of American Law Teachers and is also a political and legal analyst for Wisconsin Public Television.

TRINA GRILLO, was a professor at the University of San Francisco School of Law, teaching courses in Constitutional Law, Mediation, and Torts. She received an A.B. from the University of California at Berkeley and a J.D. *summa cum laude* and Order of the Coif from the University of Minnesota, where she served as a note editor for the *Minnesota Law Review*. Upon graduation, Grillo served as a clerk for the U.S. District Court in Madison, Wisconsin. She practiced with Altshuler and Berzon in San Francisco and served as an attorney and mediator in Oakland before she began teaching at San Francisco.

LANI GUINIER, a professor at the University of Pennsylvania Law School, teaches courses in Criminal Process, Law and Political Process, Professional Responsibility, Critical Perspectives on the Law: Issues of Race and Gender, and Public Interest Lawyering. She received her B.A. from Radcliffe College and her J.D. from Yale. Upon graduating, she clerked for Judge Damon J. Keith of the U.S. Sixth Circuit Court of Appeals. She served as special assistant to the assistant attorney general in the U.S. Department of Justice, Civil Rights Division, and worked as assistant counsel to the NAACP Legal Defense Fund in New York City before she began teaching. She is the author of *Tyranny of the Majority*. Guinier has also received honorary degrees from the University of Pennsylvania, Northeastern University School of Law, and Hunter College.

ISABELLE R. GUNNING, a professor at the Southwestern University School of Law, teaches courses on International Human Rights, Women and the Law, Immigration Law, Evidence, and Lawyering Skills. She received her B.A. and J.D. from Yale.

ANGELA P. HARRIS, a professor at the University of California at Berkeley, Boalt Hall School of Law, teaches courses in American Legal Theory, Civil Rights, and Criminal Law. She earned a B.A. from the University of Michigan and an M.A. and J.D. from the University of Chicago, where she wrote for the *University of Chicago Law Review*. She served as a clerk for Judge Joel L. Flaum on the U.S. Court of Appeals for the Seventh Circuit and entered private practice as an associate at Morrison and Foerster in San Francisco. Harris has also served as a visiting assistant professor at Stanford School of Law.

CHERYL I. HARRIS, an assistant professor at Chicago-Kent Law School, teaches courses in Constitutional Law, Justice and the Legal System, and Race-Conscious Remedies. She earned a B.A. from Wellesley College and a J.D. from Northwestern Law School. After graduating, she entered private practice in Chicago with a firm specializing in criminal defense and appellate practice. She served as senior attorney for the city of Chicago during the administration of the late mayor Harold Washington. Later she became the first assistant general attorney for the Chicago Park District. Her civic activities include serving as national cochair for the National Conference of Black Lawyers, through which she has led and participated in a number of international delegations and panels on human rights and comparative constitutional law. She is currently a visiting professor at UCLA Law School. Among her publications is *Whiteness as Property* in the *Harvard Law Review*.

ANITA F. HILL has been a professor at the University of Oklahoma Law School since 1986; previously, she was an assistant professor at Oral Roberts University. She teaches courses in Civil Rights, Commercial Law, and Contracts. She received a B.S. from Oklahoma State University and a J.D. from Yale. After graduation, she entered private practice with the firm of Wald, Harkrader and Ross in Washington, D.C. She served as special counsel to the assistant secretary in the Department of Education in the Civil Rights Office and worked as special assistant to the chairman of the Equal Employment Opportunity Commission. She is coeditor with Emma Coleman Jordan of *Race, Gender, and Power in America*. She is a member of the board of directors of the National Women's Law Center and the executive committee of the Council on Legal Education Opportunity.

SHARON K. HOM, a professor of law at CUNY School of Law, teaches Contracts, Feminist Jurisprudence, and seminars in the international program. She received her B.A. from Sarah Lawrence College and her J.D. from New York University School of Law where she was also a Root-Tilden Scholar. From 1986 to 1988 she was a Fulbright scholar in residence at the China University of Politics and Law. She has also been a visiting professor at the Benjamin N. Cardozo School of Law at Yeshiva University, and since 1990 she has served on the faculty and codirected the China Center for American Law Study in the People's Republic of China. Hom sits on the Committee for Legal Education Exchange with China (CLEEC), the advisory board of Human Rights Watch/Asia, and the Second Circuit Task Force on Gender, Racial and Ethnic Fairness in the Courts. Her book publications include *American Legal Education Methodology in China: Notes and Resources, English-Chinese Lexicon on Women and Law (Yinghan funu yu falu cihuishiyi)*, coedited with Xin Chunying, and *Contracting Law*, coedited with Amy Kastely and Deborah Waire Post.

ELIZABETH M. IGLESIAS, an associate professor at the University of Miami Law School, teaches courses in Criminal Procedure, Individual Employment Relations, and International Economic Law. She received a B.A. from the University of Michigan and a J.D. from Yale. Upon graduating, she entered private practice with the firm of Skadden, Arps, Slate, Meagher and Flom in Boston. She also worked as an attorney for Miller, Linfield, Paddock and Stone in Detroit and has been a visiting professor at Rutgers University.

LISA C. IKEMOTO, a professor at Loyola Law School in Los Angeles, teaches courses in Property, Family Law, and Bioethics. She received her B.A. from the University of California at Los Angeles, her J.D. from the University of California, Davis, School of Law, and an L.L.M. from Columbia University School of Law. She is on the board of governors of the Society of American Law Teachers and the board of directors of the California Women's Law Center.

EMMA COLEMAN JORDAN, a professor at Georgetown Law Center, teaches courses in Commercial Law, Federal Regulation of Financial Institutions, Consumer Financial Services, and Torts. She earned a B.A. from the University of California at San Francisco and a J.D. with honors from Howard, where she served as editor in chief of the *Howard Law Journal*. She also served as a White House Fellow. She has taught at Santa Clara Law School and the University of California at Davis. She has served as president of the American Association of Law Schools and the Society of American Law Teachers, and was a member of the board of trustees of the Law School Admissions Council. Jordan was part of the legal team that represented Anita Hill during the Clarence Thomas Supreme Court confirmation hearings. She is coeditor with Hill of *Race, Gender, and Power in America*.

HOPE LEWIS, an associate professor at the Northeastern University School of Law, teaches courses in International Human Rights, Securities Regulation, Corporations, and Nonprofits. She holds her A.B. and J.D. from Harvard. She has worked with the TransAfrica Forum and served as an attorney advisor at the U.S. Securities and Exchange Commission.

MARGARET E. MONTOYA, an associate professor at the University of New Mexico Law School, teaches courses in Clinical Law, Employment Law, Legal Research and Writing, and Critical Race Feminism. She earned an A.B. from San Diego State and a J.D. from Harvard. After graduating, she served as assistant to the president at Potsdam College and worked as associate university counsel at the University of New Mexico. She is involved in many civic activities, including serving on the board of governors of the Society of American Law Teachers. She has also been named to the National Advisory Organization for the NAFTA labor side-agreement.

RACHEL F. MORAN, a professor at the University of California at Berkeley, Boalt Hall School of Law, teaches Torts, Bilingualism and the Law, Criminal Procedure, and Education and the Law. She received her A.B. from Stanford and her J.D. from Yale, where she was an editor of the *Yale Law Journal*. She clerked for the Honorable Wilfred Feinberg, chief judge of the U.S. Court of Appeals, Second Circuit. Prior to her teaching career, she was an associate at Heller, Ehrman, et al. in San Francisco. In 1995 she won a distinguished teaching award at Berkeley, and she has been a visiting professor at UCLA and Stanford Law Schools. She is currently writing a book on interracial intimacy.

MARIA L. ONTIVEROS, an associate professor at Golden Gate University School of Law, teaches courses in Employment Discrimination, Evidence, and Labor Law. She earned an A.B. at the University of California, Berkeley, a J.D. from Harvard, where she graduated *cum laude*, a Master's in Industrial and Labor Relations from Cornell University, and a J.S.D. from Stanford Law School. Before entering teaching, Ontiveros practiced in the field of labor and employment law for five years. Her civic activities include serving on the board of directors and executive committee for the ACLU of Northern California, the board of directors for the national ACLU, and the National Advisory Committee for the North American Agreement on Labor Cooperation.

JENNY RIVERA, an assistant professor at Suffolk University Law School, teaches Property Law, Administrative Law, and State and Local Government Law. She earned an A.B. from Princeton, a J.D. from New York University, and an L.L.M. from Columbia. At New York University, she was an articles editor on the *Annual Survey of American Law*. Rivera previously worked as a staff attorney for the Homeless Family Rights Project of the Legal Aid Society in New York and as associate counsel for the Puerto Rican Legal Defense and Education Fund. Rivera served as an administrative law judge of the New York State Division on Human Rights, prior to teaching, and was a clerk for Judge Sonia Sotomayor of the U.S. District Court, Southern District of New York.

DOROTHY E. ROBERTS, a professor at Rutgers University School of Law-Newark, teaches courses on Criminal Law, Family Law, and Civil Liberties. She received her B.A. from Yale and her J.D. from Harvard. She is coeditor of *A First Amendment Anthology* and is currently writing a book tentatively entitled *Race, Reproduction and the Meaning of Liberty,* which she began during a fellowship at Harvard University's Program in Ethics and the Professions. She has also been a visiting professor at the University of Pennsylvania and has served as consultant for the Center for Women's Policy Studies in Washington, D.C.

CELINA ROMANY is a professor at City University of New York Law School, where she was codirector of the International Women's Human Rights Program. She teaches in the areas of International Human Rights, Jurisprudence, Feminist Jurisprudence, Employment Law, and Civil Rights. She sits on the board of directors of several public interest organizations, including the Center for Constitutional Rights, the Women's Advisory Board of Human Rights Watch, and the Puerto Rican Legal Defense and Education Fund, where she is the cochair of the advisory board of its Latina Rights Initiative. Romany is also an artist whose first solo exhibit will take place at Puerto Rico's Museum of Art and History. She has been a visiting professor at Inter-American University and the University of Puerto Rico Schools of Law. She will be visiting at the University of Pennsylvania Law School.

JENNIFER M. RUSSELL was formerly an assistant professor at Case Western Reserve University School of Law, where she taught courses in Administrative Law, Civil Procedure, Contracts, and Feminist Jurisprudence. She earned a B.A. from Queens College and a J.D. from New York University. After graduation, she worked as a staff attorney for the Securities and Exchange Commission in New York. She entered private practice as an associate attorney with Sills, Cummis, Zuckerman, Radin, Tischman, Epstein and Gross. She is at present a research scholar at the UCLA Center for the Study of Women.

JUDY SCALES-TRENT, a professor at the State University of New York at Buffalo Law School, teaches courses in Law and Literature, Constitutional Law, Employment Discrimination Law, and Legal and Policy Issues Affecting Women of Color. She received her B.A. from Oberlin College, her M.A. from Middlebury College, and her J.D. from Northwestern University School of Law. After graduation she served as an attorney for the Equal Employment Opportunity Commission. Her publications include *Notes of a White Black Woman: Race, Color, Community.*

KIM A. TAYLOR-THOMPSON is an associate professor at the Stanford Law School, where she teaches Criminal Law. She received her A.B. from Brown University and her J.D. from Yale. After graduation she worked for the Crowell and Moring law firm in Washington, D.C. Prior to her teaching career, she was director of the Public Defender Service for the District of Columbia. She serves on the board of directors of the Center for Excellence in Non-Profits and was a member of the ABA Ethics and Professional Responsibility Committee.

CRYSTAL H. WESTON is Thurgood Marshall Civil Rights Fellow at the Lawyers Committee for Civil Rights of the San Francisco Bay area. She received her B.A. from City College of New York and her J.D. from Northeastern University School of Law. She is a member of Bay Area Lawyers for Individual Freedom, the National Gay and Lesbian Task Force, and the Umoja Strategy Group.

STEPHANIE M. WILDMAN, a professor at the University of San Francisco School of Law, teaches courses in Torts and Feminist Theory and Law. She received an A.B. and a J.D. from Stanford. She clerked for the Honorable Charles M. Merrill on the U.S. Ninth Circuit Court of Appeals. She has also been a visiting professor at the University of California at Hastings, Stanford, and Santa Clara. Wildman served on the Northern District Judicial Appointments Committee for Senator Barbara Boxer and is a president-elect of the Society of American Law Teachers. She has written *Privilege Revealed: How Invisible Preference Undermines America* (with contributions by Margalynne J. Armstrong, Adrienne D. Davis, and Trina Grillo).

PATRICIA J. WILLIAMS, a professor at Columbia University Law School, teaches courses in Commercial Law, Contracts, and Jurisprudence. She earned a B.A. from Wellesley College and a J.D. from Harvard, where she was an articles editor for the *Black Law Journal* and the *Harvard Civil Rights-Civil Liberties Law Review*. She served as the deputy city attorney for Los Angeles after graduating. She has also worked as a staff attorney for the Western Center on Law and Poverty in Los Angeles. She has previously taught at Golden Gate University, the City University of New York Law School at Queens College, and the University of Wisconsin. She was a visiting professor at Stanford as well. Her publications include the award-winning *Alchemy of Race and Rights* and *The Rooster's Egg*. Her civic activities include sitting on the board of governors for the Society of American Law Teachers, the national editorial board of *Signs, the Journal of Women in Culture and Society*, and the board of scholars of *Ms.* magazine.

CHRISTINE A. WILLIS holds a B.S. in Criminal Justice from Central Missouri State University. She will receive her J.D. from the University of Iowa College of Law in 1997.

ADRIEN KATHERINE WING, a professor of law at the University of Iowa College of Law, teaches courses in Constitutional Law, Race, Racism and American Law, Comparative Law, and Comparative Constitutional Law. She received her A.B. from Princeton University, an M.A. from the University of California at Los Angeles, and a J.D. from Stanford, where she served as an editor of the *Stanford Journal of International Law*. Upon graduation, she worked for Curtis, Mallet-Prevost, Colt, and Mosle, and then Rabinowitz, Boudin et al. in New York. Some of her civic activities include serving on the board of visitors for the Stanford Law School, the board of directors for the Iowa Peace Institute, the executive council of the American Society of International Law, and the board of the National Conference of Black Lawyers. She was a candidate for the Princeton board of trustees in 1995.

Permissions

Grateful acknowledgment is made to the following for giving us permission to quote from copyrighted material:

BERKELEY WOMEN'S LAW JOURNAL

Anita L. Allen, *On Being a Role Model.* ©1991 by Berkeley Women's Law Journal. Reprinted from Berkeley Women's Law Journal 6, no. 1:22–42.

Margalynne J. Armstrong, *Meditations on Being Good.* ©1991 by Berkeley Women's Law Journal. Reprinted from Berkeley Women's Law Journal 6, no. 1:43–45, by permission.

Taunya Lovell Banks, *Two Life Stories.* ©1991 by Berkeley Women's Law Journal. Reprinted from Berkeley Women's Law Journal 6, no. 1:46–56, by permission.

Angela D. Gilmore, *It Is Better to Speak.* ©1991 by Berkeley Women's Law Journal. Reprinted from Berkeley Women's Law Journal 6, no. 1:74–80, by permission.

Linda S. Greene, *Tokens, Role Models.* ©1991 by Berkeley Women's Law Journal. Reprinted from Berkeley Women's Law Journal 6, no. 1:81–92, by permission.

Lani Guinier, *Of Gentlemen and Role Models.* ©1991 by Berkeley Women's Law Journal. Reprinted from Berkeley Women's Law Journal 6 no. 1:93–106, by permission.

Adrien Katherine Wing, *Brief Reflections toward a Multiplicative Theory.* ©1991 by Berkeley Women's Law Journal. Reprinted from Berkeley Women's Law Journal 6 no. 1:181–201, by permission.

BOSTON COLLEGE THIRD WORLD LAW JOURNAL

Jenny Rivera. *Domestic Violence against Latinas by Latino Males: An Analysis of Race, National Origin and Gender Differentials.* Originally published at 14 B.C. Third World L.J. 231 (1994). Reprinted by permission of the Boston College Third World Law Journal.

CHICAGO-KENT LAW REVIEW

Cheryl I. Harris, *Law Professors of Color and the Academy.* First appeared in 68 Chi. Kent L. Rev. 331 (1992). Copyright 1993. Reprinted by special permission of Chicago-Kent College of Law, Illinois Institute of Technology.

COLUMBIA HUMAN RIGHTS LAW REVIEW

Isabelle R. Gunning, *Arrogant Perception.* Originally appeared in the Columbia Human Rights Law Review.

Sharon K. Hom, *Female Infanticide in China.* Originally appeared in the Columbia Human Rights Law Review.

CONNECTICUT LAW REVIEW

Dorothy E. Roberts, *The Value of Black Mother's Work.* Reprinted from 26 Connecticut Law Review 871 (1994).

DUKE LAW JOURNAL

Paulette Caldwell. *A Hair Piece: Perspectives on the Intersection of Race and Gender.* This article was published originally at 1991 Duke L.J. 365 and this version is reprinted by permission of the Duke Law Journal.

Trina Grillo and Stephanie M. Wildman. *Obscuring the Importance of Race: The Implication of Making Comparisons between Racism & Sexism (Or Other -Isms).* This article was published originally at 1991 Duke L.J. 397 and this version is reprinted by permission of the Duke Law Journal.

GOLDEN GATE UNIVERSITY LAW REVIEW

Maria L. Ontiveros. *Three Perspectives on Workplace Harassment of Women of Color.* First published at 23 Golden Gate U. L. Rev. 817 (1993). Reprinted by permission of the Golden Gate University Law Review.

HARVARD CIVIL RIGHTS-CIVIL LIBERTIES LAW REVIEW

Elizabeth M. Iglesias, *Structures of Subordination.* Permission granted by the Harvard Civil Rights-Civil Liberties Law Review. ©(1993) by the President and Fellows of Harvard College.

Jennifer M. Russell, *On Being a Gorilla in Your Midst.* Permission granted by the Harvard

Civil Rights-Civil Liberties Law Review. ©(1993) by the President and Fellows of Harvard College.

Judy Scales-Trent, *Black Women and the Constitution*. Permission granted by the Harvard Civil Rights-Civil Liberties Law Review. ©(1989) by the President and Fellows of Harvard College.

HARVARD HUMAN RIGHTS JOURNAL

Hope Lewis, *Between Irua*. © 1995. Permission granted by the President and Fellows of Harvard College.

Adrien Katherine Wing and Eunice P. de Carvalho, *Black South African Women*. © 1995. Permission granted by the President and Fellows of Harvard College.

HARVARD LAW REVIEW

Dorothy E. Roberts, *Punishing Drug Addicts*. Copyright © 1991 by the Harvard Law Review Association.

HARVARD WOMEN'S LAW JOURNAL

Emma Coleman Jordan, *Race, Gender, and Social Class*. Permission granted by the Harvard Women's Law Journal. © 1992 by the President and Fellows of Harvard College.

Margaret E. Montoya, *Máscaras, Trenzas, y Greñas*. Permission granted by the Harvard Women's Law Journal. Vol. 17 © 1994 by the President and Fellows of Harvard College.

HASTINGS WOMEN'S LAW JOURNAL

Maria L. Ontiveros, *Rosa Lopez, Christopher Darden, and Me*. © 1995 by University of California, Hastings College of the Law. Reprinted from *Hastings Women's Law Journal*, Vol. 6, No. 2, by permission.

Crystal H. Weston, *Orenthal James Simpson*. © 1995 by University of California, Hastings College of the Law. Reprinted from *Hastings Women's Law Journal*, Vol. 6, No. 2, by permission.

NEW ENGLAND SCHOOL OF LAW

Regina Austin, *Black Women, Sisterhood*. Copyright © 1992 New England School of Law. All Rights reserved. Reprinted by permission.

Patricia J. Williams, *Spare Parts, Family Values*. Copyright © 1994 New England School of Law. All Rights reserved. Reprinted by permission.

OKLAHOMA LAW REVIEW

Anita F. Hill. *A Tribute to Thurgood Marshall: A Man Who Broke with Tradition on Issues of Race and Gender.* This article was first published at 47 Okla. L. Rev. 127 (1994) and is reprinted by permission of the author and the Oklahoma Law Review.

SAN DIEGO LAW REVIEW

Janet M. Calvo, *Spouse-Based Immigration Laws.* Copyright 1991 San Diego Law Review Association. Reprinted with the permission of the *San Diego Law Review.*

S. CALIFORNIA LAW REVIEW

Adrienne D. Davis and Stephanie M. Wildman, *The Legacy of Doubt.* Originally published at 65 S. Cal. L. Rev. 1367–91 (1992). Reprinted with the permission of the *Southern California Law Review.*

STANFORD LAW REVIEW

Angela P. Harris, *Race and Essentialism.* © 1990 by the Board of Trustees of the Leland Stanford Junior University. 42 Stan. L. Rev. 581 (1990).
Kim A. Taylor, *Invisible Woman.* © 1993 by the Board of Trustees of the Leland Stanford Junior University. 45 Stan. L. Rev. 443 (1993).

TENNESSEE LAW REVIEW

Lisa C. Ikemoto, *Furthering the Inquiry.* This article was published originally at 59 Tenn. L. Rev. 487 (1992) and this version is reprinted by permission of the author and the Tennessee Law Review Association, Inc., College of Law—Dunford Hall, 915 Volunteer Boulevard, Knoxville, TN 37996–4070.

UCLA WOMEN'S LAW JOURNAL

Deirdre E. Davis, *The Harm That Has No Name.* Originally published in 4 UCLA Women's Law Journal 133. Copyright 1994, The Regents of the University of California. All rights reserved.

UNIVERSITY OF MIAMI LAW REVIEW

Patricia J. Williams, *Spirit-Murdering the Messenger.* Reprinted from the *University of Miami Law Review,* 42 U. Miami L. Rev. 127 (1987), which holds copyright on this article.

USC REVIEW OF LAW & WOMEN'S STUDIES

Isabelle R. Gunning. *A Story from Home: On Being a Black Lesbian Mother.* Copyright permission was received from the USC Review of Law & Women's Studies.

WISCONSIN LAW REVIEW

Regina Austin, *Sapphire Bound.* Copyright 1989 by the Board of Regents of the University of Wisconsin System. Reprinted by permission of the Wisconsin Law Review.

YALE JOURNAL OF LAW AND FEMINISM

Celina Romany, *Ain't I a Feminist?* Reprinted by permission of the Yale Journal of Law and Feminism. From *The Yale Journal of Law and Feminism,* Vol. 4, No. 1, pp. 23–33.

Index

abortion rights, 128
acculturation, 60
Achebe, Chinua, 101, 105
activism, 86
adoption, 151–59
affirmative action, 83, 104, 112, 116, 185, 210;
    in South Africa, 391–92
Africa, 101
African American Women in Defense of Our-
    selves, 170
Aid to Families with Dependent Children
    (AFDC), 144–48
"Ain't I a Woman," 7
alcohol consumption, 129
alienation, 70, 74
Allen, Paula Gunn, 339
Ameri-I-Can, 249
Amos 'n' Andy, 289
analogies, 44–50; as a benefit, 49–50; and discrim-
    ination, 45, 46, 49; negative aspects, 45–46; as
    protection, 47
analogizing, 8
Anthills of the Savannah, 101
anti-discrimination, 130–32, 304, 323
anti-essentialism, 7
anti-subordination, 131–32, 139
apartheid, 88, 388–91, 393
aphorisms, 341
appearance, 58
archipelago of upward mobility, 114–15
arrogant perception, 353
asexuality, 73
Asian American women, 203–13

assimilation, 70, 90, 98
authenticity, 77, 113

babies, 127, 151–58
Baby M case, 157
Baker, Ella, 36
Bantu education, 389–90
Barker-Benfield, Ben, 354
Barry, Marion, 172
Bartholet, Elizabeth, 153
beauty standards, 15
Bell, Derrick, 69, 81, 103, 394
bilingual, 58; and education, 116; and law en-
    forcement, 261–63; in law school, 108
biological essentialism, 340
Black Madonna, 314
black male, xiii–xv; and family, xv, 247
Black Panther Party, 37–38
Black sisterhood, 238–42
Borges, Jorge Luis, 117
Boulware-Miller, Kay, 362–63, 365
Bowman, Cynthia Grant, 192
Bradwell, 119
breast augmentation, 355
Britain, 341–43
Brotherhood in Steele, 318
Brown, Jim, 249
Brown v. Board of Education, 157
Bumpurs, Eleanor, 230–32, 234
Bush, George, 176, 179

cancer, 44
Carby, Hazel, 196

Carter, Stephen, 121
categorization, 11; in employment discrimination, 301; and legal academy, 99
Catholicism, 59, 260
cesarean surgery, 137, 141–42
Chambers, Crystal, 290–95
Chambers v. Omaha Girls Club, 290, 294
Chicago-Kent Law School, 103
children, 127; exposure to drugs, 127–34; and Jamaican culture, 344–45; and welfare, 314–15
China, 372–77
Chodorow, Nancy, 21
Chow, Rey, 376
Civil Rights Act of 1964, 35, 307
Civil Rights Legislation, 35, 91, 307
Civil Rights Movement, 8, 35–40, 157
Civil War, 37, 255
Clark, Ruby, 238–41
Clark v. ABC, 238–41
class, 273–74; and O. J. Simpson trial, 278, 280–81
Cleaver, Eldridge, 37
coalition building, 46, 125, 141–42
cocaine (crack), 127, 129–30, 132, 134; and babies, 314
Cochran, Johnnie, 279
Cohen, Albert, 245
collateral impeachment, 273–75
collective bargaining, 324, 327–28
collective rights, 317–30
colonialism, 37–38, 101, 355, 357
colorblindness, 14–15, 180; in education, 75; impossibility of, 153–57
coming out, 160–61
Commonwealth Immigration Act, 342
communicative discourse, 76, 78
connection thesis, 340
constitutional issues, 132–33
constitutionality, 128
controlled substance, 127
Convention on the Elimination of All Forms of Discrimination Against Women, 364–65, 374, 377
Cooper, Anna Julia, 86
Court TV, 273
Cover, Robert, 19, 21
coverture, 380–85
crack addiction, 127, 129–30, 132, 134
criminality, 223, 243–50; and deviance, 237–42
Critical Legal Studies, 2–3, 6
Critical Race Feminism, 1–6
Critical Race Theory, 2–6
Critical White Studies, 2
Cross, George Lynn, 120
cross-cultural consensus, 363
cross-cultural resonance, 339
Cruse, Harold, 97

cult of true womanhood, 196
cultural defense, 170, 190, 263
cultural relativism, 171, 357; and genital surgery, 362–63; and Rosa Lopez, 273–75; in *Rogers* case, 302–4
culture conflict, 141
cummings, e. e., 27
customary law, 388–89

Darden, Christopher, 270–75
Davis, Angela, 39, 300
deconstructionism, 2
defamation, 238
Degraffenreid v. General Motors, 30
deportation law, 383–84
desegregation, 118–21
deviance, 237–42, 243–50, 255–58
discrete minority, 308–9
discrimination, 30, 130, 298–99; in Britain, 342–43; de facto, 2; employment, 301–4, 307; fear of, 108; group status, 307–8; poverty, 127–29, 301; sex, 45–46; sexuality, 52; in South Africa, 387–94; subtle harms, 46
disorganization theory, 245
disparate impact, 303
dissonance, 51–52, 142, 199
diversity, 86; among black women academics, 97; in legal academy, 112; vs. merit, 112
domestic violence, 259–65, 279, 390; in China, 373–74; and immigration law, 380–85; Latinas, 259–65; and O. J. Simpson, 279–81; in South Africa, 390–91
dominance theory, 12–16
dominant group, 46–48, 60; and group inferiority, 91–92
double oppression, 184–87, 262, 306–10
Douglass, Frederick, 155
Dred Scott, 119
drug addiction, 127; and motherhood, 127–34
DuBois, W. E. B., 40, 75; and dual consciousness, 103
duty of care, 138
duty of fair representation, 318–20, 323–28; and integration, 319–20

Economics of the Baby Shortage, 151
education: bilingual, 116; legal, 75; and welfare, 144–48
E.E.O.C. v. Int'l. Longshoremen's Association, 319
El Salvador, 269, 272–74
employment discrimination, 301
Emporium Capwell Co. v. Western Addition Community Organization, 320–23, 325, 328
England, 342; and racism, 341–43
Equal Protection Clause, 130, 306–10; and employment, 307–10

erotomania, 172
essentialism, 4, 7, 11–16, 21–22, 46, 48, 139; and analogies, 48; biological, 340; and standard story, 139
Estrich, Susan, 16
ethical template, 84–86
ethnocentrism, 353
eugenics, 156
exclusion, 90; vs. inclusion, 90, 92–93
exclusive representation, 328

faculty mascot, 76
fallibilistic approach, 23
female deviance, 237–42, 243–50
female gang members, 243–46, 249–50; in auxiliary gangs, 246; in co-ed gangs, 246
female gangs, 243–50
female genital surgeries, 352–58, 361–67; in Western world, 354–55, 361–67
female infanticide, 372–77
feminism, 11, 19, 39, 185, 340; African American, 290, 361–67; in China, 375–77; and Jamaican culture, 343
"Feminism Limited," 22
feminist consciousness, 21
feminist legal theory, 11, 19; for female delinquency, 245; as a liberation project, 19–25
feminist theory of subjectivity, 20
fetal abuse, 129–30
fetal rights, 130
fetus, 128, 137–38
Fineman, Martha, 147
Fisher, Ada Lois Sipuel, 118–21
formulaic approach, 137–38
fragmentation, 11, 13, 30; in interpretation, 317
Fraser, Nancy, 22
freedom, 36
freedom rides, 36
Freud, Sigmund, 172
Fuhrman, Mark, 270, 278, 281–82

Gaines ex rel Canada v. Missouri, 119
Gallagher, Janet, 141
gangs, 243–50; auxiliary gangs, 246; co-ed gangs, 246; and females: as gang members, 244–46, as girlfriends, 247, as mothers, 247–48, as relatives, 248–49; and fathers, 247–48; and patriarchy, 243
gang violence, 243
Garcia v. Gloor, 303
Gates, Henry Louis, 170
gender, 136–38; defined, 378; and equality, 118; and Equal Protection Clause, 308–10; neutrality, 75, 137; patriarchy, 138–39; and O. J. Simpson trial, 278–81
gender asylum, 366–67
gender essentialism, 11

genderization, 194
gender oppression, 21, 176, 372; and street harassment, 194
genetic characteristics, 152
genital surgeries, 352–58, 361–67; American version, 354; and breast augmentation, 355; and international law, 356–58, 364–67
"gentlemen," 73–78
Gerchas, Mary Ann, 274
Gilliam, Vincent, 272
Gilligan, Carol, 21, 340
Ginwala, Frene Noshir, 392
Gone With the Wind, 255–58
Gould, William, 329
grenudas, 58, 61
gringos, 58
Guinier, Lani, 1, 328–29
Gunning, Isabelle, 343, 363, 365

hair, 297–304
hairstyles, 297–304; afro, 300, 302; braided, 298–304
Hamer, Fannie Lou, 36
harassment: intraracial, 197–98; sexual, 39, 169–73, 175–79, 183–87, 389; street, 192–200; and workplace, 188–91, 203–13
Harvard Law School, 69, 81, 96, 103
health care, in South Africa, 390–91
hegemonic narratives, 376
hegemony, 88; in Chinese culture, 375–77
Helms, Jesse (Senator), 184
heterosexuality, 12, 52
hierarchy, 102; of protection, 308
Hill, Anita, 1, 165; and Thomas hearings, 169–73, 175–79, 183–87, 191
Hill, Herbert, 329
Hispanic Women's Demonstration Resource Centers Act, 250
home voice, 108
homophobia, 52, 126, 159; and the black community, 159–60; and oppression, 52
hooks, bell, 20, 45, 177, 197–98, 346
housework, 340–47
housing discrimination, 342–43
human rights, 356–58, 361–67; and law, 352, 374–77

Ice-T, 248
identity politics, 115–16
immigrant women, 189, 380–85
immigration, 341–42; and law, 380–85; and waivers, 382
Immigration Marriage Fraud Amendments, 380, 382
Immigration and Nationality Act, 381
infanticide, 372–77
inferiority, 84, 91–91; intellectual, 97

infibulation, 352
institutional logic, 103, 141
institutional racism, 263, 281
integration, of unions, 318–30
interest balancing, 137
interracial adoption, 153
intervention, 127; and adoption, 154–56
introspection, 111
invisibility, 23–25, 46, 48, 101, 183; and homosexuality, 51–52; and law school, 70, 103; and
  racism, 177–78; and street harassment, 194
I.Q. testing, 114
Ito, Lance (Judge), 272
ivory tower, 5

Jamaica, 341; and feminism, 343
Jamaican culture, 339–47
*Jeffries v. Harris Cty. Community Action Associa-
  tion,* 307
Jew, Dr. Jean, 208–12
Jew v. University of Iowa, 210–11
Jezebel, 196–97, 293–94
Jim Crow, 93, 120
judicial notice, 309
juris-generative operation, 19
jurisprudence of resistance, 102

Kanter, Rosabeth Moss, 90
Kassebaum, Nancy (Senator), 179
King v. Illinois Bell Telephone Co., 322–23
Kissling, Elizabeth, 192
Koch, Ed (Mayor), 231–32
Kornhauser, R. R., 245
Kramarae, Cheris, 192

Landes, Elizabeth, 126, 151–52, 154, 157
Latina/Latino culture, 57–61, 113–17, 188–89,
  259–65, 269–75
Latin poetry, 57
law school, 51–54; and alienation, 70, 73–78; and
  privacy, 93; use of narratives and women of
  color, 81–86, 89–90, 289
learnfare, 144–48; and motherhood, 147–48; and
  patriarchy, 144, 146–47
legal academy and women of color, 74–78, 81–
  86, 90–93, 96–99
legal action, 210–12; vs. nonlegal, 364–65
legal classifications, 30, 99, 101–5, 107–21
legal literalism, 232
Legal Realists, 326
legal story, 136–37
legislation, 32; and domestic violence, 261–63;
  and drug addiction, 127–34
lesbianism, 52; and black women, 51–54; and
  motherhood, 159–61
libel, 239
liberal theory and legalism, 53–54

liberation project, 22–23
liberation theology, 317
life skills management, 249
lobolo, 388
Lopez, Rosa, 269–75; and class, 273–74; and cultural differences, 272–75
Lorde, Audre, 9, 52–53
Love, Jean, 52
lynching, 16; as a metaphor, 171, 176–77

macho image, 260
MacKinnon, Catharine, 12, 21; and dominance
  theory, 12–16; and rape, 15–16; and sexuality,
  12, 15
male dominance, 12–14
mammie/y, 1, 293–94, 313
Mandela, Nelson, 387, 392
marginalization, 12, 39, 46, 178–79; in South Africa, 389–94
marriage, xiii; and immigration, 380–85
marriage fraud, 380, 382, 385
Marshall, Thurgood, 71, 118–21
Marxism, 6, 12–13; critiques, 21
mascara, 57, 61
mask, 9, 57, 59–61
maternity, 110
McCarthyism, 117
medical care, 136; and forced treatment, 136–42;
  and intervention, 136–42
mentor, 76–78, 96
Meredith March, 37
merit/meritocracy, 93, 112
Merton, Robert, 245
mestizaje, 61
Mexican American, 269
Mexicanos, 58
Mexican women, 189
micro-aggressive politics, 344
Miller, Walter, 245
Million Man March, xv
Mills, Kay, 36
Minow, Martha, 312, 314
miscegenation laws, 16
misogynist, 279; and violence, 279–84
Mitchell, Margaret, 255–56
model minority, 205, 209
Moore v. Hughes Helicopter, 30
"mothered," 339–40
motherhood, 125, 127–34, 136–42, 196; and
  adoption, 155; devaluation of, 312–15; and
  gangs, 247–48; and lesbianism, 159–61; and patriarchy, 343–44; single mothers, 290–93; and
  stereotypes, 140–41, 147; teenage mothers,
  290–93; and welfare, 312–14
Moynihan, Daniel Patrick (Senator), 313
multiple consciousness, 30, 54, 74–75, 198–200,
  327–28

multiple subordination, 197
multiplicative legal praxis, 32–33
multiplicity, 30–33, 60
murder, 257, 270
Murray, Charles, 313

N.A.A.C.P. v. Detroit Police Officers' Association,
    324–25
narratives, 3, 19–25, 102, 155; in China, 376;
    and Critical Race Theory, 69; Latin, 57; in legal
    education, 78
Nash, Diane, 36
National Association for the Advancement of Col-
    ored People (NAACP), 35, 119–20, 185
nationalism, 281–83
National Labor Relations Act, 317–30
Newton, Huey, 37
New York City, 229
Nicholson, Linda, 22
Nigeria, 141
nuance theory, 14–15
nurturer, 84–86

objectivity, 97; illusion of, 326–27
Oluluro, Lydia, 366
oppression, xv, 20–21, 24, 45–49, 177, 192, 198,
    237, 290, 292, 317–18; gender, 21, 176, 372;
    multiple forms, 11, 21, 31, 184; psychological,
    194–95; sexual, 21, 52, 198
other, 20, 24
outsider perspective, 69, 75–76, 376; and legal
    academy, 103–5

Parmar, Pratibha, 361
Parry, Benita, 23
patriarchal wound, 361–62
patriarchy, 3, 136, 138–39, 141–42, 159, 179,
    198, 246, 260, 263, 279, 283, 340, 390; and fa-
    thers, 346–47; passive, 346; racist, 240
Patterson, Orlando, 171
Pavelic, Bill, 271
Payne v. Travenol, 30
Perkins, Useni, 245
pharaonic surgery, 352
phenotypic, 302
Plessy v. Ferguson, 119–20
polychronic, 273
polygamy, 388
positivism, 357–58
Posner, Richard (Judge), 126, 151–52, 154, 156–
    57
postmodernism, 2, 19, 22–23
poverty, 129–30, 248; and motherhood, 313
pregnancy, 125, 141, 290
Pregnancy Discrimination Act of 1978, 290
prenatal care, 127, 132
prenatal drug use, 127–34

prima facie case of discrimination, 131
privacy doctrine, 133
privatization, 230
professional privacy, 92–93
progressive era, 312
prosecution of drug addicted mothers, 127–34
prostitution, 238–41, 244, 249
protectionism, 153

racial essentialism, 11
racial hierarchy, 131, 133, 139
racial identity, 169–71
racial imagery, 171–72
racism, 39–40, 45, 177–78, 192, 232, 281; in Brit-
    ain, 341–43; institutional, 263, 281; uncon-
    scious, 98
rape, 15–16, 230, 390; and gangs, 246; and street
    harassment, 193
rationality, 138; and equal protection, 308
reductionists, 21
reproductive choices, 128, 130, 133, 136, 142; in
    South Africa, 391
Rich, Adrienne, 11
Richardson, Gloria, 36
right of autonomy, 133–34
right of privacy, 128, 130, 133
Robinson, Jackie, 89
Robinson, Ruby Doris, 36
Rogers v. American Airlines, 298–303
role models, 53–54, 69, 75–78, 81–86, 96, 290–
    91, 293–94; role model argument, 81–86
Roth, Philip, 113

Salvadoran, 269, 272
Sapphire, 172, 289–90, 294
Scales-Trent, Judy, 49
Scarlett, 255–58
Schatzki, George, 328–29
scholarly dialogue, 97
Scott, Dred, 38
Seep v. Commercial Motor Freight, Inc., 324–25
segregation, 90, 119; of unions, 318–20
self-determination, 38
self-hate, 60; and racism, 232–33
Senate Judiciary Committee, 171, 178, 183–84
senators, 172, 177–79, 183–85
separate but equal doctrine, 119–20
sex discrimination, 45; in *Rogers* case, 301–2
sexism, 178–79
sex organs, 352
sexual abuse, 176
sexual harassment, 39, 165, 169–73, 175–79,
    183–91; and Asian Pacific women, 203–13
sexuality, 12, 15, 176, 353
sexual orientation, 52, 126, 159–61, 195
sexual predation, 171–72
sexual promiscuity, 239

sexual stereotypes, 171
sexual terrorism, 192–200
Sheffield, Carole, 193
silence, 136, 139, 299; and tokenism, 93
silencing, 53–54, 73–74, 77–78, 116, 141–42,
    192, 194
Silverstein, Eileen, 327–29
Simpson, Alan (Senator), 178
Simpson, Nicole Brown, 270, 274, 278–84
Simpson, O. J., 269–75, 278–84
Singapore Girl, 209
Sipuel (Ada Lois Sipuel Fisher), 118–21
sisterhood, 238, 241–42
slavery, 15, 29–30, 38, 128, 153, 171, 195–98,
    239, 293, 313
Smith, Barbara, 53
Smith, Susan, 255–58
social femicide, 373–74
socialism, 6
societal ordering, 49
South Africa, 387–94; and education, 389–90;
    and interim constitution, 391
Southern Christian Leadership Conference
    (SCLC), 35
Spanish, 57–61
Specter, Arlen (Senator), 178, 185–86
spirit injury, 28–30, 199
spirit murder, 28, 53, 199–200, 230, 234
Spivak, Gayatri, 23
spokesmodels, 76
spouse-based immigration, 382
standard legal story, 136–37
Steele v. Louisville & N.R.R., 318
stereotypes: of Asian women, 204–7, 209, 212–
    13; of black women, 83, 237, 289–91, 294,
    302; and Latina women, 260
strain theory, 245
street harassment, 192–200; and multiple con-
    sciousness, 198–99
streetwalkers, 241
strict scrutiny, 308–10
structural justice, 317
structural violence, 317–30
Student Non-Violent Coordinating Committee
    (SNCC), 37
subaltern voice, 23
subordination, 7, 20, 60, 131, 136, 138, 140–42,
    193–200, 270–75, 292, 301, 304, 317, 321,
    328; cultural, 339; multiple, 197; sexual, 353;
    of voices, 108–9; of wives, 385
subset theory, 309
subtle discrimination, 27–28
sunna, 352
superstition, 235
Supreme Court, 170, 175, 179, 183–84
"Suzy Wong," 206
Sweatt v. Painter, 119

symbols, 84–86, 89, 111; in Thomas-Hill hear-
    ings, 175–79
systematic exclusion, 131

Taney, Roger (Justice), 38
Tatum, Cheryl, 298
teenage pregnancy, 290–93
Thomas, Clarence (Justice), and confirmation
    hearings, 1, 165, 169–73, 175–79, 183, 187
Thrasher, Frederick, 244
Thurmond, Strom (Senator), 184
Title VII, 208, 211, 290, 307–8, 317–30
token/tokenism, 70, 89–93, 111
Tribe, Laurence, 133
truancy, 125, 145–46
Truth, Sojourner, 7
Tung, Rosalie, 206–8
Turner, Tina, 280
Tyson, Cicely, 303

underclass, 40
unions, 317–28
Unitary Consciousness of Law, 327
United States Senate, 184–86
universalism, 20–21; and genital surgery, 357–58,
    362; and pregnancy, 139
universal woman, 51
University of Iowa, 208–12
University of Oklahoma, 118–21
University of Pennsylvania, 206–8
unmodified feminism, 13, 16
upward mobility, 77

Vaca v. Sipes, 324–25
victimization, 16
victim status, 112
Vietnamese language, 233
Violence Against Women Act, 383
Voting Rights Act, 35
vouchers, 342

Walker, Alice, 361–62
Ward, Benjamin (Commissioner), 231–32
Warrior Marks, 361
welfare, 4, 125; and motherhood, 144–48, 312–
    15
welfare queen, 1, 146, 313
Wells, Ida B., 16, 346
West Indian culture, 339–47
white norm, 46, 48–49
white protectionism, 153
white solipsism, 11
white supremacy, 45–50, 177, 281–82, 284
white womanhood, 196
Williams, Karen Hastie, 121
Williams, Patricia, 177–78
Wing, Adrien, 199

Women's Liberation Movement, 37
Women's National Coalition, 393
workfare, 312–14
workplace harassment, 188–91
world travel, 343
world traveling method, 353–58; defined, 354;
  and genital surgery, 354

World War II, 372
writ of mandamus, 120

Yale Law School, 73–74, 185
Youth Gang Drug Prevention Program, 250

zone of dissonance, 199